Cognitive Psychology and Instruction
Fourth Edition

ROGER H. BRUNING
University of Nebraska–Lincoln

GREGORY J. SCHRAW
University of Nevada–Las Vegas

MONICA M. NORBY
University of Nebraska–Lincoln

ROYCE R. RONNING

PEARSON

Merrill
Prentice Hall

Upper Saddle River, New Jersey
Columbus, Ohio

Library of Congress Cataloging-in-Publication Data

Cognitive psychology and instruction / Roger H. Bruning ... [et al.].—4th ed.
  p. cm.
Rev. ed. of: Cognitive psychology and instruction / Roger H. Bruning,
Gregory J. Schraw, Royce R. Ronning. 3rd ed. c1999.
  ISBN 0-13-094794-6
  1. Learning. 2. Cognitive psychology. 3. Cognitive learning. 4. Instructional systems—Design.
  I. Bruning, Roger H.
  LB1060 .B786 2003
  370.15'23—dc21

2003009803

Vice President and Executive Publisher: Jeffery W. Johnston
Publisher: Kevin M. Davis
Editorial Assistant: Autumn Crisp
Production Editor: Mary Harlan
Project Coordinator: Penny Walker, *The GTS Companies*/York, PA Campus
Design Coordinator: Diane Lorenzo
Text Design and Illustrations: *The GTS Companies*/York, PA Campus
Cover Design: Ali Mohrman
Cover Image: SuperStock
Production Manager: Laura Messerly
Director of Marketing: Ann Castel Davis
Marketing Manager: Amy June
Marketing Coordinator: Tyra Poole

This book was set in Garamond Book by *The GTS Companies*/York, PA Campus. It was printed and bound by R. R. Donnelley & Sons Company. The cover was printed by Phoenix Color Corp.

Pearson Education Ltd.
Pearson Education Singapore Pte. Ltd.
Pearson Education Canada, Ltd.
Pearson Education—Japan

Pearson Education Australia Pty. Limited
Pearson Education North Asia Ltd.
Pearson Educación de Mexico, S.A. de C.V.
Pearson Education Malaysia Pte. Ltd.

10 9 8 7 6 5 4 3
ISBN: 0-13-094794-6

Preface

*C*ognitive Psychology and Instruction, Fourth Edition, is the latest revision of a text first published in 1990. This book, like the earlier editions, is aimed at giving educators a solid grounding in cognitive psychology and helping them tie the important findings of cognitive psychology to instruction. It is directed at those who are interested in understanding the principles of cognitive psychology and in applying them to instruction and curriculum design.

The original book had a simple two-part structure; the first part laid out the basic principles of cognitive psychology, and the second part concentrated on school-based applications of a cognitive approach. We subsequently added two new sections, one reflecting the growing emphasis on the importance of beliefs in cognition and a second describing new approaches to problem solving, critical thinking, and reflective thought. We have retained this four-part structure in the current edition but have substantially revised the book throughout and added a chapter on technology to reflect new developments in this important area.

Organization of This Edition

Cognitive Psychology and Instruction, Fourth Edition, begins with an introduction to cognitive psychology in chapter 1, which explains how cognitive psychology developed into its current position of dominance. Part I, "Information Processing Theory," describes key elements of a cognitive model in chapters 2 through 5. Chapter 2, "Sensory, Short-Term, and Working Memory," has been substantially revised and rewritten. It presents the modal memory model and describes the latest research and theory on sensory, short-term, and working memory. Chapter 3, "Long-Term Memory: Structures and Models," is devoted to long-term memory and identifies the key concepts that have guided cognitive research during the past quarter-century. Chapters 4 and 5, "Encoding Processes" and "Retrieval Processes," provide detailed accounts of how encoding and retrieval affect the nature and quality of cognitive processes.

Many models of cognition now incorporate variables related to learner beliefs, choices, and motivation. Such variables are of great interest to educators, and Part II, "Beliefs and Cognition," focuses on them. Chapter 6, "Beliefs About Self," examines motivational issues of special importance to educators, including Bandura's social cognitive theory, attribution theory, and issues of student autonomy and control.

Chapter 7, "Beliefs About Intelligence and Knowledge," shows how students' beliefs about their ability and the nature of knowledge are critical determinants of what they choose to do and what they achieve.

The three chapters in Part III, "Fostering Cognitive Growth," extend the basic cognitive model as they describe the nature and development of high-level cognitive processes in school settings. Chapter 8, "Problem Solving and Critical Thinking," translates research from these two vital areas into practical applications for teaching and learning. Chapter 9, "Classroom Contexts for Cognitive Growth," provides an integrated view of how educators can design environments based on cognitive principles that will stimulate cognitive growth, reflection, and self-regulation. Chapter 10, "Technological Contexts for Cognitive Growth," is an exciting new addition to our book. It links cognitive theory to technology use and highlights some of the most innovative ways that cognitively oriented educators are using technology to promote cognitive growth.

Part IV, "Cognition in the Classroom," presents research that shows how cognitive perspectives have profoundly affected our views of schooling. Three of the five chapters in this section focus on literacy. Chapter 11, "Learning to Read," and Chapter 12, "Reading to Learn," are detailed accounts of linguistic and cognitive processes in beginning and later reading. Chapter 13, "Writing," illustrates how cognitive analyses are applied to writing and writing instruction. Chapter 14, "Cognitive Approaches to Mathematics," and Chapter 15, "Cognitive Approaches to Science," show how cognitive theory has fundamentally altered the conceptions of learning and teaching in mathematics and science.

Philosophy of This Text

We do not believe that cognitive psychology is the only psychological viewpoint that can inform education. We remain strongly committed, however, to the belief that a cognitive perspective greatly enhances our ability to understand educational goals and processes. There are few educational decisions to which the cognitive issues of memory, thinking, problem solving, and motivation are not relevant. Also, in the years since the third edition was published, cognitive psychology has not remained static. We expect its evolution to continue into the foreseeable future.

Acknowledgments

Many individuals were involved in making this latest edition a reality. Kevin M. Davis, Publisher, served as editor for the second, third, and fourth editions. We are extremely grateful for his wise and extraordinarily patient guidance. We also wish to express appreciation to two past editors: Chris Jennison, who first encouraged our author group when we began this project years ago, and Robert Miller, then an acquisitions editor for Merrill, who provided us with much appreciated support and counsel. We are also grateful to a very capable group of reviewers of this edition: Catharine C. Knight, University of Akron; Jane B. Pemberton, University of North Texas; and Radhi H. Al-Mabuk, University of Northern Iowa. Their perceptiveness and suggestions led us to thoroughly reexamine the content of the book and prompted many positive changes. We also wish to acknowledge reviewers of previous editions: Robert L. Benefield, Louisiana State University, Shreveport; Michael L. Bloch, University of San Francisco; Martha Carr, University of Georgia; Linda D. Chrosniak, George Mason University; Wallace Hannum, University of North Carolina; Mary Lou Koran, University of Florida; Raymond W. Kulhavy, Arizona State University; Michael S. Meloth, University of Colorado; S. J. Samuels, The University of Minnesota; Robert Tennyson, University of Minnesota; Charles K. West, University of Illinois; and Karen Zabrucky, Georgia State University. We especially wish to thank Penny Walker for her very able service as Project Coordinator for this edition, our copyeditor Dana Polachowski, and Production Editor Mary Harlan. We have come away from our interactions with them with great admiration for their professional skills and dedication and with gratitude for their assistance in improving this text. Finally, we offer our sincere appreciation to Mary Bodvarsson for her reactions to chapter 10 and her capable help with the test bank for this edition.

We again dedicate this edition to Royce R. Ronning, whose personal qualities, scholarly excellence, and leadership continue to energize our efforts, and to his wife, Ruth, who has supported our efforts with characteristic warmth and generosity of spirit. We are deeply grateful to both Royce and Ruth and are inspired by their examples.

Roger Bruning
Gregory Schraw
Monica Norby

Brief Contents

Contents

Chapter 1

Introduction to Cognitive Psychology

A Brief History ■ *Cognitive Themes for Education* ■ *Summary* ■
Suggested Readings ■

THIS BOOK IS ABOUT COGNITIVE PSYCHOLOGY and its implications for education. Cognitive psychology is a theoretical perspective that focuses on understanding human perception, thought, and memory. It portrays learners as active processors of information—a metaphor borrowed from the computer world—and assigns critical roles to the knowledge and perspective that students bring to their learning. What learners do to enrich information, in the view of cognitive psychology, determines the level of understanding they ultimately achieve.

The cognitive psychology we describe has risen over the past quarter-century to become the major force in American psychology. Powerful concepts have arisen within cognitive psychology, each with considerable explanatory value for education. Among these concepts are **schemata** (sing., schema), the idea that there are mental frameworks for comprehension; **levels of processing,** the notion that memory is a by-product of the kind of processing that information receives; and **constructive memory,** the view that knowledge is created by learners as they confront new situations. Now, as cognitive psychology evolves into a more mature form, it emphasizes social influences on cognitive development; connections among cognition and motivation, as well as between self-awareness and cognitive strategies; and the growth of subject matter expertise in such areas as mathematics and science. The major emphasis of this book is to describe and elaborate these concepts and themes of cognitive psychology and relate them to education.

A Brief History

The Associationist Era

Each of us has his or her own view of the world, a "world hypothesis" (Pepper, 1942/1961), that guides our observations, actions, and understanding of our experience. Any theoretical perspective in psychology similarly rests on a particular view of the world; it counts some things as evidence but not others, organizes that evidence, and leads to hypotheses about what the evidence means and how it is interrelated.

Cognitive psychology is one such theoretical perspective; it makes the claim that the purpose of scientific psychology is to observe *behavior*—the observable responses of individuals—in order to make inferences about unobservable, underlying factors that can explain the actions we see. In cognitive psychology, observations are used to generate inferences about such factors as thought, language, meaning, and imagery. The field of cognitive psychology seeks to construct formal, systematic explanations about the nature and functions of our mental processes.

For much of the 20th century, however, the world of psychology in the United States was dominated by a theoretical perspective of an entirely different sort—*associationism* (Dellarosa, 1988). Learning, in this view, involves associating or linking a *stimulus* (e.g., a flashing light on a panel or an English word) with a *response* (e.g., a bar pressed by a lab animal or saying the foreign language equivalent of the English word). The general goal of this stimulus–response paradigm of psychology was the derivation of elementary laws of behavior and learning and their extension to more complex settings. Inferences about these laws were tied closely to observed behavior. Animals, as well as humans, were suitable objects of study; investigations of learning and memory in "lower organisms" were fueled by a faith that the laws of learning were universal and that work with laboratory animals could be extrapolated to humans. Especially during the period from 1920 to 1970, associationism was *the* American psychology; there was no real alternative in the United States (Glover & Ronning, 1987).

Among the clearest formulations of associationistic principles of learning were those made by Clark Hull (1934, 1952) and his colleague, Kenneth Spence (1936, 1956). Reasoning from the data of numerous experiments with laboratory animals, Hull and Spence derived equations based on hypothesized variables, such as strength of habits, drive, and inhibition, which enabled predictions to be made about behavior in laboratory settings. Elementary laws of learning captured in equations such as these could account for many phenomena, such as animals learning to make simple distinctions (e.g., choosing a circle instead of a square button when pressing the circular button was followed by a food pellet) or learning by **trial and error** (Hull, 1952).

The use of an associationistic theoretical framework was not limited only to those psychologists interested in animal learning, however. Especially in the United States, an associationistic paradigm also dominated the study of memory, thinking, and problem solving (Dellarosa, 1988). Most research in memory during this period focused on rote or nonmeaningful learning. Following a tradition begun by Hermann Ebbinghaus well before 1900, researchers studied subjects' memory for individual items, most commonly nonsense syllables (e.g., KAJ, WUV, and XJC) and individual words. Researchers assumed that understanding learning and memory for these simple materials would lead to principles that could explain complex learning and memory phenomena.

The preferred research methods were those of **serial list learning,** in which one item cues the next item in the list, and **paired associate learning,** in which a response must be linked with a stimulus. These methods allowed the development of associations to be most clearly predicted and studied. As this research was refined further, tables of norms were developed in which nonsense syllables and words were calibrated for their "meaningfulness"; that is, they were rated for the likelihood that they could elicit responses from learners. Knowing these characteristics of words and syllables permitted researchers to manipulate features of their materials with precision (see Noble, 1952, and Underwood & Schultz, 1960, for examples of these materials). Like the aims of Hull and Spence's work with animals, the goal was to develop basic principles from research using simple materials in highly controlled settings that would apply to such broader contexts as learning and recall of materials in school.

A fundamental difficulty, however, was that as experimental psychologists made finer and finer distinctions within the confines of laboratory research on animal **trial-and-error** learning and studies of human memory, their findings seemed to apply to more limited aspects of human functioning and to become less and less relevant for education. The search for general laws of learning that crossed all species and settings was failing. At the same time that experimental methodologies for studying learning and memory were becoming highly refined and experiments more valid internally (Campbell & Stanley, 1963), they were becoming less valid externally. That is, even though these studies had very sophisticated methodologies, their findings could not be easily generalized. As elucidated by experimental psychology in the United States, the laws of learning seemed to be described more properly as the "laws of animal learning," the "laws of animals learning to make choices in mazes," or the "laws of human rote memory" rather than as the universal learning principles associationists sought (but see Dempster & Corkill, 1999, for an argument for the relevance of associationist learning principles to a variety of domains, including school learning).

Near the end of the associationistic period, the so-called radical behaviorists, led by scientist-philosopher B. F. Skinner, made a strong impact on both psychology and education. Skinner's views were strongly environmental, in the tradition of the early behaviorist John B. Watson (see Watson, 1913). Learners were seen as coming to learning *tabula rasa*, subject to conditioning by their environment. Like Watson, Skinner rejected the idea that the purpose of psychology was to study consciousness; the goal of a scientific psychology, he asserted, was to predict and control behavior. What organisms do, Skinner contended, is largely a function of the environment in which they are placed and their learning histories (Skinner, 1938, 1953). By managing the antecedents and consequences for behavior, prediction and control can be achieved. Consequences for behavior are particularly critical, he argued. By providing positive consequences for behavior and by arranging the schedule by which these consequences were delivered, behavior could be controlled and shaped.

In his research, Skinner demonstrated that his laboratory animals indeed were exquisitely sensitive to manipulations of both antecedents and consequences of their actions. Skinner and his associates showed that animals' patterns of responding (e.g., of pressing a bar or pecking) were predictable from the ways consequences such as food or drink were delivered (see Ferster & Skinner, 1957). Skinner also demonstrated that by working backward from consequences to the behaviors that preceded them, very complex sequences or chains of behaviors could be developed.

By the mid-1960s, behaviorism as guided by Skinner's views had become such a potent force in American psychology that, in many settings, consciousness was discredited as a respectable topic for research and theory (Baars, 1986). Part of the reason for behaviorism's extraordinary influence was that Skinner and his students saw the potential utility of behavioral principles in human learning and began to apply them successfully in a variety of settings. Initial applications were in residential treatment facilities for persons with mental illness and mental retardation; standardizing learning environments and carefully specifying behavioral goals was shown to be very useful for treating a wide range of problems. Extensions of behavioral principles to education soon followed, appearing in such technologies as classroom management (e.g., Baer, Wolf, & Risley, 1968) and teaching machines (Holland & Skinner, 1961; Skinner, 1968). Teaching machines, Skinner contended, could provide the key elements of learning: frequent responding, progress in small steps, shaping, and positive reinforcement. By the early 1970s, as the cognitive movement was just beginning to emerge in American psychology, behavioral principles were being applied to a wide range of therapeutic and educational settings.

Education today continues to reflect behaviorism's influence. For instance, behavioral theory is readily recognizable in such familiar educational approaches as instructional objectives, task analysis, and the use of positive reinforcers. All evolved out of a behavioral philosophy of learning specifying that responses must be sequenced appropriately, made overtly, and rewarded. Many of these derivations from behavioral psychology have helped make education more effective, accountable, and humane. In special education settings, especially, behavioral principles have provided an effective set of technologies for teaching that simply did not exist before.

However, at just about the same time Skinner's behaviorism was becoming widely applied to education, the American psychological community was growing dissatisfied with the ability of strict stimulus/response psychologies to provide an adequate account of human thought and memory. For instance, the radical behaviorists' concentration on only observable activity was considered by many to be too limiting, even by those who saw careful observation as the *sine qua non* of any scientific enterprise (e.g., Bandura, 1969). Others decried what they believed to be behaviorism's mechanistic view of human beings as controlled by their environments. A few voiced fears that behavioral principles would be misused by those with totalitarian goals.

At the same time, many psychologists who were interested in mental processes were increasingly frustrated as they attempted to use associationist theoretical frameworks and behavioral concepts to describe the complexity of human memory, thinking, problem solving, decision making, and creativity. To try to explain this vast array of mental processes within a stimulus/response framework seemed neither to satisfy nor to contribute greatly to our understanding of human cognition. Even as researchers employed ever more sophisticated methodologies in their research, their explanatory system, associationism, seemed to have reached its limits in its ability to produce generalizable principles.

Adding to the growing perception of the narrowness of associationism were voices raised from outside psychology when some psychologists tried to explain language development from a behavioral perspective. For instance, Skinner's publication of *Verbal Behavior* in 1957 prompted immediate reactions from linguists and set off a heated debate about the adequacy of behavioral explanations of language development. In Skinner's judgment, language was acquired largely through processes of imitation, shaping, and reinforcement. Linguists disagreed strongly, citing developments in linguistic theory (e.g., Chomsky, 1957, 1965) and research showing qualitative differences in child and adult speech and less-than-theoretically-expected levels of imitation (see R. Brown, Cazden, & Bellugi, 1968; Ervin, 1964). The persuasiveness of their arguments had the effect of weakening behaviorism as a generally applicable theory of language development.

The Cognitive Era

No single event signaled an end to the associationistic era and the beginning of the cognitive revolution in American psychology. Early on, the cognitive revolution was a quiet one. Certainly, the time was right, as American psychologists were becoming increasingly frustrated with limitations in behavioral theory and methods. As mentioned, research by linguists on the nature of language development supplied evidence against the radical environmentalist perspective offered by the behaviorists. Another prominent factor was the emergence of computers, which provided both a credible metaphor for human information processing and a significant tool for modeling and exploring human cognitive processes.

Beyond these general trends, the work of many individuals clearly was pivotal in creating a cognitive revolution. For instance, some point to the publication of Ulrich Neisser's *Cognitive Psychology* in 1967, which provided early definition to the new area of cognitive psychology or, even earlier, to the work of Jerome Bruner (Bruner, Goodnow, & Austin, 1956) or David Ausubel (Ausubel, 1960; Ausubel & Youssef, 1963), which emphasized mental structures and organizational frameworks. Others would nominate G. A. Miller's frequently cited article "The Magical Number Seven, Plus-or-Minus Two: Some Limits on Our Capacity for Processing Information" (1956) or his founding, with Jerome Bruner, of the Center for Cognitive Studies at Harvard in 1960 (Baars, 1986). Many cite J. J. Jenkins's 1974 *American Psychologist* article in which the fundamental differences among the mass of rote learning research that he and others had done for a generation and their work within the new cognitive paradigm were contrasted. Still others would cite Marvin Minsky's 1975 "frames paper," which outlined the necessary features of a vision system that could recognize simple objects. This article highlighted the critical role of mental structures in human thinking and decision making, a theme echoed by others in the related concepts of **schemata** (Rumelhart, 1975) and **scripts** (Schank & Abelson, 1977).

Today, cognitive psychology is mainstream American psychology, and the cognitive perspective is no longer considered revolutionary. In education, however, its applications only now are being fully explored (see, e.g., Brandt, 2000; Bransford, Brown, & Cocking, 2000; Cowie & van der Aalsvoort, 2000; Das & Gindis, 1995; Jonassen & Land, 2000; Kirschner, 2002; Marshall, 1996). What we attempt to do in this text is present many of cognitive psychology's important concepts and points of view. We do this by organizing our thinking around several key themes in cognitive psychology that we see as most potent for educational practice.

Cognitive Themes for Education

Cognitive psychology now encompasses an enormous body of research on a wide range of topics (see Anderson, 2000; Sternberg, 1999b; Sternberg & Ben-Zeev, 2001). Not all of these have relevance for education, of course, and our strategy in this text is to organize the information we present around a few powerful themes. We hope that presenting these seven themes will help you judge cognitive psychology's relevance for teaching and learning.

1. *Learning is a constructive, not a receptive, process.* In the view of most cognitive psychologists, learning is a product of the interaction among what learners already know, the information they encounter, and what they do as they learn. Learning is not so much knowledge and skill acquisition as it is the *construction of meaning* by the learner (Prawat, 1996). Knowledge is created and re-created on the basis of previous learning, not simply acquired. What motivates learning is the "search for meaning."

The old adage "You get out of it only what you put into it" aptly describes a cognitive perspective. Some students approach learning in passive and "shallow" ways, either failing to engage fully or relying heavily on rote memorization. Both cognitive research and our experience as educators tell us that the resultant learning is likely to be both superficial and transitory. In contrast, other students' attempts at learning clearly are aimed at deeper understanding; they relate new information to what they already know, organize it, and regularly check their comprehension.

2. *Mental frameworks organize memory and guide thought.* Among the most potent concepts of cognitive psychology is the concept of schema. Schemata are mental frameworks we use to organize knowledge. They direct perception and attention, permit comprehension, and guide thinking. The concept of schema appeared at about the same time under different labels in the work of several theorists, including Minsky (1975), Rumelhart (1975), Schank and Abelson (1977), and Winograd (1975). Clever experimental demonstrations soon showed how powerfully these mental structures affected perception, learning, and memory.

Pichert and Anderson (1977), for example, asked individuals to read a passage describing a house from the perspective of either (1) a prospective home buyer or (2) a burglar. They hypothesized that these perspectives would activate different frameworks for comprehending the passage (activate different schemata) and result in different recall patterns. As predicted, their readers did recall significantly more information relevant to their own perspective (e.g., "home buyers" were more likely to recall a leaking roof, information important to a prospective home buyer) than information relevant to the other perspective (e.g., remembering three parked 10-speed bikes, a detail the "burglars" noticed).

Experiments like these shifted the attention of many researchers away from the abstract phenomenon of learning to *learners themselves*—to their prior knowledge and frames of reference, to the activities they undertook and the strategies they used as they learned, and to their role in creating new knowledge. Soon cognitive psychologists (e.g., R. C. Anderson & Pearson, 1984; A. L. Brown & Palincsar, 1982) were suggesting instructional approaches based on these ideas—methods encouraging students to describe what they already knew and how they felt about it, to link new information with old, to use analogies and metaphors as tools for understanding, and to create their own structures for organizing new information. As is shown later, concepts like these have had a significant impact on thinking about instruction in virtually every area of the curriculum.

3. *Extended practice is needed to develop cognitive skills.* The old adage "practice makes perfect" is equally as true for cognition as it is for physical skills. Although we typically think of cognitive psychology's emphasis on meaning and thought, the other side of cognition—automated processes—is equally important. Automated processes in attention, perception, memory, and problem solving allow us to perform complex cognitive tasks smoothly, quickly, and without undue attention to details. Because skilled readers' word recognition and understanding of language structures are rapid and automatic, for example, they can concentrate on the meaning of what they are reading.

Expertise depends on building repertoires of automated cognitive processes and, as is shown in coming chapters, there are really no shortcuts to acquiring them. In virtually any domain—from reading and quilting to baseball to beekeeping—developing the underlying automatic processes on which expertise depends can require literally thousands of hours of practice. Thus, in our upcoming chapters, we often stress the importance of repetition and practice in helping our students increase their cognitive capabilities.

4. *Development of self-awareness and self-regulation is critical to cognitive growth.* Cognitive psychology has consistently promoted the idea of a self-directed, strategic, reflective learner. This idea has been supported by a large body of research in **metacognition,** which generally refers to two dimensions of thinking: (1) the knowledge students have about their own thinking and (2) their ability to use this awareness to regulate their own cognitive processes. As students progress through their school years, they typically develop along both dimensions, becoming (1) *more aware* of their own abilities to remember, learn, and solve problems and (2) *more strategic* in their learning, better able to manage their own learning, thinking, and problem solving. For instance, younger students often have little sense of their own memory and thought processes and tend not to use such cognitive strategies as rehearsing or organizing information to help them remember. Older students, however, typically will try at least some strategies to assist them in comprehension and recall.

One of the most important educational implications of metacognitive research has been the growing awareness that knowledge and skill acquisition are only a part of cognitive growth. Although knowledge and skills are important, students' learning strategies and their ability to reflect on what they have learned—to think critically—may be even more important. Unless learners monitor and direct their cognitive processes, they are unlikely to be either effective learners or flexible, effective problem solvers (see, e.g., Boekaerts, Pintrich, & Zeidner, 2000). Students need to acquire not only knowledge but also "ways of knowing" and "thinking dispositions" (Tishman, Perkins, & Jay, 1995).

5. *Motivation and beliefs are integral to cognition.* Cognitive psychology's scope has expanded greatly as it has matured. Early cognitive research stressed memory, thinking, and problem-solving processes and their applications to instruction.

Newer conceptions of cognitive psychology include not only the "purely cognitive" variables of memory and thought but also learners' motivational and belief systems. How confident, for instance, are students in their ability to perform certain actions, and what outcomes do they believe will result if they are successful? How do they analyze their successful and unsuccessful performances? What kinds of goals do learners typically seek? What beliefs do they hold about the nature of knowledge, their own abilities, and their intelligence?

Research on such questions as these has shown the importance of learners' goals, beliefs, and strategies for motivating and regulating learning. For instance, theory and research focusing on such constructs as self-efficacy, outcome expectancy, and self-regulated learning (see Dweck, 2000; Pintrich & Schunk, 2002; Randi & Corno, 2000; Zimmerman, 1995, 2000) have shown that individuals constantly judge their own performances and relate them to desired outcomes. These judgments are an integral part of whether activities are attempted, completed, and repeated. Similarly, cognitive researchers have shown that the reasons individuals supply for their successes and failures—their attributions (Graham & Weiner, 1996; Weiner, 1995, 2000)—also have important consequences for learning, as do the kinds of goals they seek (Ames & Archer, 1988). Still other researchers have stressed beliefs that people hold about the nature of knowledge (e.g., Duell & Schommer-Aikins, 2001), intelligence (e.g., Dweck & Leggett, 1988), and literacy (e.g., Schraw & Bruning, 1996).

This growing area of research demonstrates that both cognitive and motivational variables need to be considered in accounting for student learning. Successful learning involves not only comprehending content but also learning to become an active, motivated, self-regulated, and reflective learner. Cognitive activity occurs within a framework of learners' goals, expectancies, and beliefs, all of which have important consequences for determining what students choose to do, how persistent they are, and how much success they enjoy.

6. *Social interaction is fundamental to cognitive development.* Cognitive psychology's evolution has led to another important understanding: the role of social interaction and discourse in cognitive development. Cognitive psychology has helped us see that, like other traits, "ways of thinking" and "ways of knowing" need to be nurtured in a supportive social context.

Educators traditionally have stressed individual study as the route to cognitive growth. Cognitive research, however, has shown that social-cognitive activities, such as well-managed cooperative learning and classroom discussions, stimulate learners to clarify, elaborate, reorganize, and reconceptualize information (e.g., Calfee, Dunlap, & Wat, 1994; Cowie & van der Aalsvoort, 2000). Peer interaction gives students the opportunity to encounter ideas and perceptions that differ from their own; new knowledge can be constructed out of these exchanges. Collaborative efforts seem to have particular potential for cognitive development, affording students the opportunity to observe others, express ideas, and get feedback. As they work on meaningful tasks with others, students begin to internalize modes of expression and reflection that lead to higher levels of cognitive activity (Das, 1995).

7. *Knowledge, strategies, and expertise are contextual.* Throughout its history, cognitive psychology's dominant metaphor has been the computer. The human being

is portrayed in this metaphor as an information processor in which information enters into the system, is processed and stored, and can be recalled. In short, the mind is machinelike.

From cognitive psychology's earliest beginnings, however, another worldview—*contextualism*—was strongly voiced. The contextualist perspective in cognitive psychology, which emphasizes history and situation (Gillespie, 1992), views the event as the root metaphor. Events are inherently situational, occurring in contexts that include other events and taking some or even much of their meaning from those contexts (Gauvain, 2001; Lave & Wenger, 1991; Rogoff, Bartlett, & Turkanis, 2001).

Contextualist views underlie many of the most fertile ideas of cognitive psychology. In early experimental demonstrations, for instance, Bransford and his colleagues (e.g., Bransford, Barclay, & Franks, 1972; Bransford & Franks, 1971) clearly showed that memory was strongly affected not only by the manipulations of the experiment but also by participants' knowledge of relations and events. Similarly, other work (Hyde & Jenkins, 1969; Jenkins, 1974; Tulving & Thompson, 1973) showed that memory was strongly influenced by the actions of learners as they attempted to encode information. Learning and memory are not, it seems, so much a product of machinelike input and output as they are something learners construct in a social context from their prior knowledge and intentions, and the strategies they use (e.g., see Gauvain, 2001).

Today, this viewpoint underlies a strong interest in cognitive strategy instruction and self-regulated learning (e.g., see Boekaerts et al., 2000). The goal is to help students manage their own learning. A general finding of research in this area is that successful strategy use and self-regulation require attention not only to the strategies themselves but also to metacognitive knowledge—especially conditional knowledge about how, when, and why to use particular strategies (Pressley & Schneider, 1997; Zimmerman, 2000). Effective strategy use and self-regulation, in short, are thoroughly contextual; they need to be used at the right time and place and to be grounded in learners' understanding of themselves as learners and their social worlds.

Our experience tells us that if we describe the concepts of cognitive psychology well and organize them thematically, you will see their considerable power for education. They not only can help you conceptualize your goals for education in cognitive terms but also should aid you in developing highly motivated and capable students.

The cognitive concepts and principles described in this book fit well with many of our beliefs as educators: our sense of students as whole human beings; our advocacy of active, not passive, learning; and our valuing of individual differences. We believe that you will find yourself drawn to this perspective; the "cognitive view" will begin to affect your thinking about your students and your beliefs about how they should be taught.

An Example

To help you get a better sense of the direction in which cognitive psychology will likely take you, think for a moment about one student—Kari, a 15-year-old girl in her first year at Southeast High School. It is midway through the fall semester, and, all in all, Kari has made a reasonably good transition from middle school to high school. Her grades are holding up fairly well, with one exception—a history class with the dreaded Mr. Bergstrom. But then, at this point, no one in the class has higher than a B anyway. Kari's immediate concern, however, is an assignment for Ms. Lawrence's Citizenship Issues class. Printed on a half-sheet of photocopied paper, the assignment reads:

> Produce a first draft of a two-page paper on the issue YOU consider to be the most critical issue facing American youth today. Please type your draft and double-space it. As we have done in the past, you need to make four copies. As usual, plan to read it in your small group and to get written comments from each member. This draft is due Friday, the 13th. Final drafts are due a week from Friday, the 20th. P. S. Papers with lines shorter than four inches in length are NOT acceptable. This means you, Bobby!

We next see Kari the following Thursday before school in the school computer lab. As she pulls the assignment from her notebook, she mulls over her choices: "Hmmm . . . a two-pager . . . problems facing youth. Let's see, what should I pick? Jobs? Stress and suicide? Drugs? AIDS? Gangs?"

"Jobs . . . much too dull," she thinks. "Stress and suicide? I've been reading about that, but writing about that would be so depressing. Drugs? Maybe . . . AIDS? It'd be good, but I'm not going to write about it for Lawrence. Gangs, well . . . maybe. Hey, there were articles about drugs in the paper last Sunday; I could go look at those." She smiles at Ms. Lawrence's instructions to Bobby.

Twenty minutes later, Kari has yet to type a word, but we see her visiting with her classmate and friend Hannah, who has come into the lab on a similar mission. They chat a bit, looking at a CNN.com article on Kari's computer and sharing some ideas about what Ms. Lawrence *really* wants. By the half-hour, however, Kari is typing busily, switching back and forth between the word processor and the CNN article, and occasionally looking into two books from the school library. Ten minutes before the hour ends, we see success: The printer is humming away, and a second page emerges—with six-inch lines, no less.

In many ways, Kari's assignment is a straightforward one, not much different from those given hundreds of thousands of times every day by teachers in schools across the United States and around the world. In each of them, a directive motivates a set of actions—the need to recall earlier events, make decisions, gather and use information, and create a product. Most are simple assignments, yet all are very rich from a cognitive perspective. For Kari to be successful (and we presume she will be), she needs to engage in and guide herself in cognitive operations as diverse as extracting meaning from written instructions; translating thoughts and her implicit knowledge about how school works into plans of action; searching for and organizing information; generating words and sentences from stored and newly acquired information; and, of course, just making the computer and printer work. When all of these dimensions are considered, the array of cognitive functions required seems almost so complex as to defy understanding.

 In Kari's sequence of activities, however, we can see certain basic elements. To succeed, she must understand at some basic level what the tasks requires her to do. She needs to draw on a body of knowledge in memory and guide her mental activities by directing her attention toward some things and away from others. She must make sense of the details she encounters and get information in and out of her memory. She must use language to express this information and, to finish the assignment successfully, monitor her progress and make appropriate decisions about whether the emerging document "solves the problem," that is, meets the assignment criteria.

We chose Kari as an example not because she is unique, but because the cognitive resources on which she draws and the actions she takes show many features of cognitive psychology. Her actions, though thoroughly familiar, illustrate key elements of human cognitive functioning: perception, attention, short- and long-term memory, associative processes, and problem solving and decision making. They represent motivated and self-directed cognitive activity in school, which is the most important social context supporting students' formal learning. At the same time, they raise the following important questions about our information-processing capabilities:

- How do learners focus their attention on certain elements in the world "out there" while ignoring others, and what are the limits of learners' capacities for "paying attention"?

- How do learners acquire information, make sense of it, store it in memory, and retrieve it? Then, once information is stored, how is it organized, what makes it more or less available when it is needed, and what role does it play in cognitive processes? In other words, why do we sometimes remember and sometimes forget?

- How does cognition change and develop? How are later cognitive, self-regulation, and motivational processes related to the early learning habits and predispositions of young children?

- What role do learners' goals play in cognition and how important are the beliefs that students hold about their capabilities and the nature of intelligence? How do students learn to become self-regulated and autonomous?

- How do learners use their cognitive processes in solving problems, and what kinds of social contexts, learning tasks, and educational practices are likely to foster reflective thought?

In the chapters that follow in Part I, "Information Processing Theory," we begin to examine these questions. Chapter 2, "Sensory, Short-Term, and Working Memory," provides a general model of information processing, describes what happens as we encounter new information, and relates features of sensory and working memory to education. Chapter 3, "Long-Term Memory: Structures and Models," focuses on a topic of concern to all educators—how information is organized and stored in memory. In the chapter, we examine the research and theory on the nature and organization of long-term memory and relate key findings to education. Chapter 4, "Encoding Processes," expands our discussion of memory. It describes how the activities that take place during learning affect memory. In the last chapter of this first section, chapter 5, "Retrieval Processes," we explore factors that control recognition and recall as we retrieve information from memory.

By the time you have completed the first part of this text, you should have a clear sense of the basic concepts and perspectives of cognitive psychology and some feeling for what it has to offer education. Part II, "Beliefs and Cognition," tracks the evolution of cognitive psychology as it has expanded into important new areas, such as learning strategies, self-regulated learning, motivation, and the role of beliefs in learning. Part III, "Fostering Cognitive Growth," links cognitive psychology with the processes that many educators would place highest among their goals for students—the ability to think critically about issues, reflect wisely on them, and choose effective solutions for problems. The general perspective of this section is the contextual nature of cognition, as we emphasize roles that classroom processes and well-designed technology can play in nurturing "ways of thinking." Part IV, "Cognition in the Classroom," closely examines the key cognitive skills that apply across all subject areas—language use, reading, and writing—and examines how cognitive psychology has begun to transform mathematics and science instruction.

Summary

For most of this century, associationism was *the* American psychology. Working within this tradition, American psychologists attempted to derive basic laws governing learning and memory by studying these phenomena in simplified, rigorously controlled experimental settings. As this research became more and more focused, however, much of it seemed to lose its relevance.

Researchers could not find the general laws they were seeking. Nonetheless, one branch of stimulus–response psychology—radical behaviorism, which focused on observable responses and environmental design—had a powerful impact on education that continues today. Behaviorism generally has deemphasized the need to understand learners' mental processes, instead concentrating on the relationships between environmental conditions and learners' performance.

In psychology itself, however, was a growing dissatisfaction with strict stimulus–response theories, which increasingly were judged deficient for understanding complex mental events. Memory researchers were frustrated as they attempted to use associationistic theory and experimental studies of rote learning to explain the complexities of human memory, especially meaningful learning. The behavioral perspective was attacked by linguists, who questioned its accounts of language development, and by others who criticized the idea of behavioral control and feared a technology of behavior management.

Today, American psychology is cognitive. Cognitive psychology portrays humans as information processors. The computer metaphor is reflected in both the theorizing and the methods of many cognitive psychologists. Drawing on a contextualist, as well as a mechanistic philosophy, cognitive psychology also stresses the importance of learners' activities, strategies, and mental structures in comprehending and creating meaning. As cognitive psychology matures, it increasingly is focusing on the interplay among beliefs, goals, and cognition and how cognition develops in a social context.

Although cognitive views long since have become dominant in psychology, their application to education still is only partially realized. Our goal, therefore, is to present the concepts, principles, and perspectives of current cognitive psychology in detail and to help you explore their implications for educational practice.

Suggested Readings

Anderson, J. R. (2000). *Cognitive psychology and its implications* (5th ed.). New York: Worth. This is the fifth edition of a textbook by J. R. Anderson, a widely respected cognitive researcher and theorist. First published in 1980, Anderson's book provides a good overview of cognitive psychology, covering topics as diverse as attention and perception and problem solving and reasoning.

Bransford, J. D., Brown, A. L., & Cocking, R. R. (2000). *How people learn: Brain, mind, experience, and school.* Washington, DC: National Academy Press. An edited volume that summarizes a project of the National Research Council evaluating current learning sciences, this book highlights key cognitive principles and shows how they can be applied to the design of learning environments.

Sensory, Short-Term, and Working Memory

Humans have always been fascinated by memory. The scientific study of memory is a recent matter, however, tracing back little more than a century to the pioneering work of Hermann Ebbinghaus (1850–1909), *Uber das Gedächtnis,* first published in 1885. Ebbinghaus's genius was to reduce the study of memory to its most elementary forms—namely lists of nonmeaningful syllables, or so-called nonsense syllables (e.g., *FOH* and *TAF*). Ebbinghaus carefully tested his learning at regular intervals, noting how much he remembered and forgot and how easy it was to relearn forgotten information.

The tradition of memory research begun by Ebbinghaus dominated the study of memory for nearly a century (MacLeod, 1988). Today, our conception of what constitutes the valid study of memory has broadened considerably. Memory research has transcended the painstaking study of words and isolated facts and focuses instead on memory for complex chunks of information, such as the gist of a newspaper article or a technical chapter such as the one you are reading now.

Memory research also has developed several distinct branches since the early 1970s. One of these focuses on memory performance during the act of learning. Most researchers refer to this as **working memory.** We examine this research and its implications for learning in detail in this chapter. A second strand focuses on the contents and functioning of information in permanent store, often referred to as **long-term memory.** We examine this research in chapter 3. A third strand of research focuses on the relationship between memory and brain physiology. Although fascinating and important, much of this research lies beyond the scope of this book.

In this chapter, we introduce a general model of memory that we refer to as the **modal model** (Healy & McNamara, 1996). The modal model includes several different memory components that each perform a specific task, much as different gears perform different tasks in an automobile. Our first goal is to provide an overview of the modal model and why it is important to the study of learning. Next, we discuss **sensory memory,** the initial memory component that perceives, recognizes, and assigns meaning to incoming stimuli. Then, we consider **short-term memory,** the so-called mental workbench, and describe how the concept of short-term memory has been supplanted by the concept of working memory. Finally, we consider the practical implications of working memory research for learning.

Chapter 2 focuses on sensory memory and short-term memory because both are limited-capacity, brief-duration memory systems. In contrast, long-term memory holds a large amount of information indefinitely. We believe that three obstacles stand in the way of effective learning. One is the information bottleneck that occurs in sensory and short-term memory (only a small amount of information can be processed at one time). The second is acquiring and organizing a knowledge base in long-term memory. Third is constructing metacognitive knowledge (knowledge about the contents and regulation of memory) that enables learners to use their memory with optimum efficiency. This chapter focuses on the first of these problems, chapter 3 focuses on the second, and chapters 4 and 5 focus on the third.

The Modal Model

Traditionally, memory researchers have divided memory processes into stages of acquisition, storage, and retrieval. For a memory to be made, new information somehow must be acquired and brought into the system. Information must also be stored within the system and retrieved when it is needed. In the 1950s, cognitive scientists began creating models that acknowledged these stages; their models also clearly reflected the increasing influence of the computer as a metaphor for human cognition. The models came to be known collectively as **information processing models** (e.g., Atkinson & Shiffrin, 1968; Waugh & Norman, 1965) and their common features as the modal model. Although new memory models continue to evolve, the modal model provides a useful organizer for thinking about memory.

Figure 2-1 presents a schematic diagram of the modal model. The main assumption of the model is that information is processed via a series of discrete memory systems, each serving a specific function. Although this view dates back to William James's distinction between primary and secondary memory, it did not achieve central importance in information processing theory until the publication of George Miller's (1956) landmark article "The Magic Number Seven, Plus or Minus Two." **Sensory memory** in this framework refers to initial perceptual processing that identifies incoming stimuli. Information that has been processed in sensory memory is then passed to short-term memory, where it receives additional meaning-based processing. Information that is relevant to one's goals is then stored indefinitely in long-term memory until it is needed again.

Clarifying the role of different memory systems is only part of our goal. We also want to understand how information is transferred between the memory systems. It turns out that skilled learners use a variety of information processing strategies to move new information from short-term to long-term memory. These processes collectively are

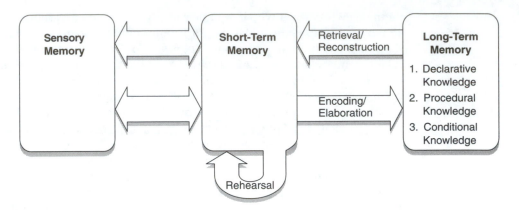

Figure 2-1
The Modal Model

known as *encoding processes* and are discussed in detail in chapter 4. Similarly, processes used to access information in long-term memory for use in short-term memory are known as *retrieval processes* and are discussed in chapter 5.

Recent versions of the information processing model have added more components. One addition is that short-term memory has been replaced by working memory (Baddeley, 1998, 2001), which makes an important distinction between subprocesses in short-term memory that passively maintain versus actively process information. A second addition is a loop connecting long-term and sensory memory. This loop enables information in permanent memory to influence initial perceptual processing. A third addition is metacognition, which guides the flow of information through the three "lower" memory systems. These additions are important because they allow us to use what we already know to learn new information, a phenomenon known as top-down processing. In the original version of the model, information processing was bottom-up because none of the "higher" components of memory, such as long-term memory and metacognition, affected initial processes in "lower" components, such as sensory memory. In the revised model, initial sensory processing is affected by short-term, long-term, and metacognitive processes simultaneously.

It may be helpful to consider some main assumptions of contemporary information processing theory that pertain specifically to sensory and short-term memory.

1. *Memory systems are functionally separate.* All information processing accounts of cognition postulate two or more global memory systems that perform specific functions. These systems originally were assumed to be metaphorical in nature; that is, they corresponded neither to specific neurological regions in the brain nor to specific neurobiological processes. Recent research on humans and other animals suggests that the functional distinctions proposed by information processing theorists may have biological analogues as well (Rose, 1992).

2. *Attention is limited.* The ability to perform mental work is limited in several ways. One is **attention,** or the mental energy used to perceive, think, and understand.

Although individual differences exist, everyone's attentional capacity is extremely limited (Just & Carpenter, 1987). Cognitive psychologists refer to this phenomenon as limited processing capacity. It is important to note, however, that the limits of information processing can be stretched in amazing ways by using "capacity-saving" strategies such as chunking, categorization, and elaboration (Ericsson, Chase, & Faloon, 1980; Reynolds, 1992).

3. *Processes are both controlled and automatic.* Skilled cognition is the result of using one's limited resources efficiently. Some tasks require more resources than others, in part, because of the complexity of the task but also because of how automatic one is at performing it. **Automaticity** refers to performing any cognitive activity (e.g., retrieving word meanings, driving a car) in an automatic fashion. Automated processes require very little attentional capacity; thus, we get something for nothing when we are automated (Chandler & Sweller, 1990; Stanovich, 1990, 2000; Sweller, 1999).

In contrast with automated processes, **controlled processes** require some portion of our limited attentional resources. One further assumption is that controlled processing can be allocated to higher order tasks (e.g., constructing inferences when reading) only when basic cognitive processes (e.g., decoding words and grammatical parsing) are automated. One of the best examples of a controlled process is selective attention, or the process by which we allocate all of our limited resources to the most important information before us.

4. *Meaning is constructed.* Information processing is more than just translating information from physical stimuli to a symbolic mental representation. Almost all information is transformed in the process (Kintsch, 1998). Meaning is constructed on the basis of prior knowledge and the context in which the task occurs. Even though the construction of meaning is supported by all components of the information processing system, much of it takes place in short-term memory. Research suggests that once meaning is constructed and forwarded to long-term memory, much of the original form of information is lost.

The modal model has proved highly useful to researchers and educators for several reasons. First, the model helps us better understand the specific role of different memory components. Second, the model has generated massive amounts of research that contribute to theory and practice. Indeed, many ongoing changes in the modal model are a result of this research. Third, the modal model makes an important distinction between memory *structures,* such as short-term memory, and memory *processes,* such as encoding and retrieval that enable us to move information around in memory.

The modal model also has its critics. One criticism is that the model proposes three separate structures in memory corresponding to sensory, short-term, and long-term memory. Many researchers question this assumption for theoretical and empirical reasons. A better assumption is that memory consists of many small interrelated parts. A second criticism is that the modal model implies that information flows through memory in a linear, unidirectional manner. That is, information enters in sensory memory, proceeds to short-term memory for additional processing, and then proceeds to long-term memory. In fact, research indicates that information processing is much more dynamic. Information in long-term memory often influences initial processing, and there is reason to believe that information is processed simultaneously in short-term and long-term memory (Neath, 1998). A third criticism is that the modal model does not correspond to the neurological structure of the brain. Recent theories have opted for an entirely different metaphor in which memory is viewed as one integrated network of connected neurons. These theories are referred to as connectionist models and are discussed in chapter 3.

Notwithstanding these criticisms, we believe there is a great deal of practical utility in using the modal model as a metaphor for understanding different aspects of memory. Keep in mind that the modal model is just one way to think of memory and that many alternative models could be proposed as well.

Sensory Memory and Perception

The modal model views memory as a collection of holding systems. **Sensory memory** is a system that briefly holds stimuli in sensory registers so that perceptual analyses can occur before that information is lost. The first step in this process is **perception,** which enables us to detect incoming perceptual stimuli by allocating attention to them. The next step is **pattern recognition,** which enables us to associate perceptual information with a recognizable pattern. Once stimuli are perceived and recognized, they are forwarded to short-term memory for additional processing. Research on sensory memory attempts to answer three main questions that pertain to how we perceive incoming stimuli, how we recognize those stimuli, and how we allocate our attention during perception. We explore each of these questions in more detail in the following discussion.

Think for a moment about what is required for perception to occur. First, some aspect of the environment—some stimulus—has to be detected by the person (e.g., has to be seen or heard but not necessarily understood). That stimulus then somehow must be transformed and held. This process usually is referred to as **storage.** Next, a body of knowledge has to be available and brought to bear on the stimulus in the process referred to as **pattern recognition.** Finally, some decision has to be made regarding its meaning. This process is referred to as **assignment of meaning.**

The very common phenomenon of identifying the letter *a* seems far more complex when we consider what may happen during the process of perception. One important observation is that perception takes time. The fact that perception requires time and effort leads to a problem of sorts. Because environments may change rapidly (e.g., when watching a film or driving a car), a stimulus could stop being available before a meaning was assigned. (Imagine seeing DOOR projected by a slide projector for, say, one tenth of a second.) Unless we can "hold" that stimulus for a while, our perceptual processes would stop in midstream (Fisher, Duffy, Young, & Pollatsek, 1988). The experience of watching a movie, for example, would be terribly frustrating if stimulus after stimulus disappeared before we could interpret their meanings. Our experience, however, tells us that such breakdowns in our perceptual processes occur infrequently. This is because our cognitive systems are equipped with sensory registers.

Sensory Registers

One of the wonders of our cognitive system is that the system can temporarily retain environmental information after it has disappeared (DiLollo & Dixon, 1988). Even though each of our senses has this ability—a **sensory register**—research has focused almost entirely on vision and hearing. Here, we discuss the visual and auditory sensory registers to give you a flavor of this research.

Visual Registers   The classic work on the visual registers was performed over 40 years ago by George Sperling (1960). Sperling was engaged in basic perception research, attempting to identify the nature of the visual registers. As a part of his study, he showed subjects slides depicting arrays of letters, such as the one shown in Figure 2-2.

Sperling noted that when subjects were shown this kind of array for less than 500 milliseconds (1 second consists of 1,000 milliseconds), they could recall about 4 of the letters. This number did not change, regardless of whether Sperling altered the length of time subjects saw the array (from 15 to 500 ms) or altered the number of letters they saw from 4 to 12. He developed two hypotheses that could account for his results. One hypothesis was that it was possible that only the 4 letters reported by subjects were registered; that is, subjects saw only 4 letters and could recall no more because they had never registered. The second hypothesis was that it might have been that all 12 letters were registered but somehow were lost before they could be reported.

To test these hypotheses, Sperling developed what has come to be called the *partial report method*. He reasoned that if subjects had more information available than they could report, he could sample their knowledge. So, rather than ask subjects to report all they saw, he asked them to recall only one of the rows of letters in the arrays they were shown (see Figure 2-2).

Sperling's partial report procedure was very clever. Participants were told that after the array of letters disappeared from the screen, they would hear a tone. If the tone

Figure 2-2
Stimulus Array Similar to That Used
by Sperling

C	Z	K	L
D	P	M	B
R	L	X	N

was of high pitch, subjects were to recall the top row. If the tone was of middle-range pitch, they were to recall the middle row. If the tone was of low pitch, they were to report the bottom row. Because the subjects had no way of knowing which row they would be asked to recall until after the array disappeared from view, the number of letters they recalled could be used as an estimate of the total number of letters they actually had available when they began their recalls. By varying the delay between the disappearance of the array and the tone, Sperling was able to estimate how long such information was retained.

The results of Sperling's study are summarized in Figure 2-3. When the tone occurred immediately after the array was terminated, the subjects were able to remember about three of the four letters in the row for which they were cued. The value of 9 in Sperling's graph in Figure 2-3 is obtained by multiplying the average number of letters recalled in a row by the number of rows (3) to obtain an estimate of the total number of available letters. The longer the tone was delayed, however, the fewer letters were recalled. This decrease was very rapid. After only a 0.5-second delay, subjects recalled an average of slightly more than one letter per row overall, indicating that about four letters were available.

The data thus supported Sperling's second hypothesis; all or most of the letters in the arrays were registered, but most were lost before they could be reported.

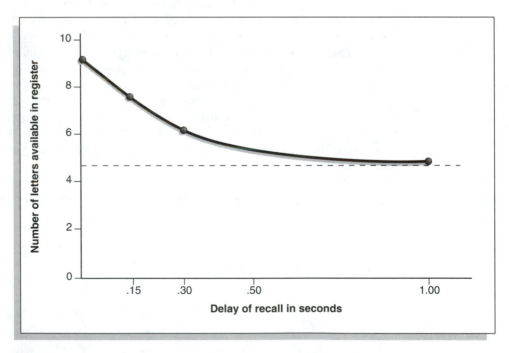

Figure 2-3
Results of Sperling's 1960 Experiment. This graph, which is based on that presented by Sperling, represents recall without sampling by the dashed line.

Apparently, Sperling's subjects were able to hold visual information for about 0.5 second. After that time, it no longer was available, having decayed in sensory memory.

The answer to Sperling's question was clear: People register a great deal of the information they see in brief presentations. After the information is removed from sight, however, it is available only briefly—about 0.5 second. By the time Sperling's subjects could say the letters from one row (e.g., *c*, *z*, and *k*), the rest of the information was gone.

Another question that Sperling addressed in his 1960 article was whether meaning had been assigned to information in the visual sensory register (or **icon,** as it has been called). To examine this question, Sperling (see also Sperling, 1983; Von Wright, 1972) presented arrays, such as the one in Figure 2-2, containing both numbers and letters. Participants in the study then were given cues indicating that they were to recall either numbers or letters. Such cues would work only if meaning (number or letter) had been assigned to the information in the array. The results indicated that unlike the location cues we described earlier, number/letter cues were ineffective. This outcome strongly suggests that the information in the icon is held with limited processing. Had the arrays been processed (if meaning had been assigned), then the number/letter cues would have made a difference.

Collectively, these findings suggest that visual sensory memory is very limited. Only seven to nine pieces of information are processed at any given time, and much of that decays rapidly. Information held in visual sensory memory receives only limited processing.

Auditory Registers   Although the majority of research on sensory registers has centered on the icon, considerable work also has been devoted to understanding the auditory register (the echo; for reviews, see Deutsch, 1987; Handel, 1988; Hawkins & Presson, 1987; Scharf & Buss, 1986; Scharf & Houtsma, 1986; Schwab & Nusbaum, 1986). A particularly helpful study in the area is one by Darwin, Turvey, and Crowder (1972), which replicated Sperling's work on the icon but used auditorily presented information.

Darwin et al., (1972) presented the participants in their study with three brief lists containing numbers and letters. The lists were presented simultaneously over headphones so that it seemed one list came from the right, a second list from the left, and a third list from behind. After hearing the lists, subjects were given position cues to remember one of the lists. Darwin et al., delayed these cues from 0 to 4 seconds after the lists were presented. The results closely resembled those reported by Sperling for the icon; that is, as the cue delay increased, recall performance decreased, until, at about 3 seconds after the presentation, subjects' recall with cues was no better than without cues. When Darwin et al., contrasted number/letter cues with position cues, they found the number/letter cues to be relatively ineffective. So, much like the icon, it appears that an echo exists that holds relatively unprocessed information while perceptual processing begins.

Comparisons of the visual and auditory sensory stores indicate some interesting differences (see Ashcraft, 1994; Handel, 1988). The most obvious is the length of time information is stored in the registers: less than 0.5 second in the icon and slightly more than 3 seconds in the echo (see Chase, 1987; Hawkins & Presson, 1987). This greater ability of the echo to retain information seems related to the processing of language (see Schwab & Nusbaum, 1986).

Implications of Research on the Sensory Registers   Our brief review of research on the icon and the echo suggests some direct implications for teaching. First, there are limits to the amount of information that can be perceived at any one time. The short duration of memory in the sensory registers should remind us of the need for teachers to limit the amount of information they present to students. Further, some work on developmental differences in cognition (e.g., Case, 1985) suggests that the size of the sensory registers increases with age. Children's sensory registers have more stringent constraints than those of adults. Especially with early elementary-age children, teachers must be aware of the need to manage the amount of information that children are expected to perceive at any one time.

Second, there may be real benefits to presenting information both visually and auditorily. Given the limits of students' ability to hold information in their sensory registers, we would expect that information presented both visually and auditorily would have a higher likelihood of being perceived than information presented only in one format. Using visual aids for auditory presentations and discussing visual materials seem to be reasonable approaches to increasing the likelihood that instructional materials will be perceived. It also is reasonable to assume that tactile, gustatory, and olfactory stimulation may enhance learning.

The Role of Knowledge and Context in Perception

Prior knowledge directly influences perception, pattern recognition, and the assignment of meaning (Adams, 1990). Knowing what we see (or hear) and even how to look (or listen) depends on the knowledge we have (see McCann, Besner, & Davelaar, 1988). An expert chess player, for example, perceives the pieces of a chess game in progress very differently from a person who has never played the game. The expert immediately recognizes that a king is in check, that a certain style of defense is being played, and so on, whereas a nonplayer merely perceives pieces she or he may not even be able to name on a checkerboard playing surface.

Knowledge also influences how we look for things to perceive. For example, an accomplished baseball fan knows the need to watch the shortstop's behavior to determine whether the pitcher is going to throw a fastball, curveball, or slider. A nonfan may have no inkling why the shortstop takes steps right or left as soon as the pitcher releases the ball. Similarly, an accomplished debater understands what to look for in evaluating other debaters, much as an expert welder knows what to examine in judging another welder's work.

It is clear, then, that knowledge permits perception to occur and guides our perception of new information (see Mandler, 1984). As is shown in chapter 3, one compelling way to envision our knowledge is by means of **schemata** (sing. **schema**). Schemata are domain-organized knowledge structures in long-term memory that contain elements of related information and provide plans for gathering additional infor-

Figure 2-4
Context Effects in Perception

A B C   I2 I3 I4

mation (R. C. Anderson, 1984; Mandler, 1984; Rumelhart, 1980). Schemata incorporate the prototypes, feature analyses, and structural descriptions described earlier. For example, a person's schema for "tree" will contain not only its structural description but also information about the nature of trees (they take in carbon dioxide and give off oxygen), where trees are found (not above certain elevations or in areas that are too dry or cold), and the care of trees (they must be pruned and watered).

In some situations, appropriate schemata seem to be activated because of the results of pattern recognition processes. For example, if you are sitting quietly in your office and smell smoke, schemata for reacting to that situation are activated by the data (a fire!). Activation of the schemata results primarily from the analysis of an environmental event. In such instances, schemata allow us to make sense of what we encounter and prepare us for continued analyses of the environment.

Context affects what we look for and perceive as well. Consider the following sentences:

The man walked into the quiet *wood*.
The man threw the *wood* into the fire.
The man got good *wood* on the ball.
The man was made of *wood*.

In each instance, the word *wood* is understood differently because of the sentence context. Research indicates that skilled readers automatically retrieve the appropriate meaning of a word without activating inappropriate meanings, provided the context is sufficiently rich.

Now look at Figure 2-4. In this case, what first appears as the letter *B* turns out to be an equally acceptable *13* in a different context. Most readers probably have no difficulty understanding the appropriate meaning in either case even though the physical stimulus is identical in both settings. The moral to this story is that perception is a relative, rather than an absolute, phenomenon. Two people can interpret the same stimulus in two ways, depending on what they know and the context in which they encounter a stimulus!

Attention

Interwoven with perception is **attention**—a person's allocation of cognitive resources to the task at hand. In general, the research on attention shows that human beings are severely limited in the number of things they can pay attention to at a given time (e.g., Friedman, Polson, & Dafoe, 1988; Spear & Riccio, 1994). This phenomenon is usually referred to as limited processing capacity. Although there are individual differences in this regard, most people cannot do more than one or two things at the same time. Multitasking has its downside. Eventually, a person can try to do too much at once and wind up doing everything poorly.

Attention is the mind's most valuable resource with the possible exception of knowledge! Attention is the fuel on which the mind runs. Thinking about attention as a kind of mental fuel reveals that there are three ways to improve learning. These include increasing the amount of attention at one's disposal, decreasing the amount of attention each task consumes, or allocating one's limited attention as carefully as possible on the most important information one needs to learn.

Because students must learn a large amount of information in school, they need to select what they attend to. A sixth-grader might begin to pay careful attention to her or his teacher's explanation of an arithmetic problem but then shift her or his attention to a whispered conversation across the aisle. Her or his attention then might wander to the aroma drifting into the room from the cafeteria and later to the sight of the snow falling outside. As a result, the explanation for how to work the new set of mathematics problems may not be remembered.

Research on attention has a long, contentious history. The main debate focuses on how learners allocate their attention. Some theories suggest that attention is allocated early, while others suggest that attention is allocated late. Contradictory findings have appeared frequently in the research literature, making it difficult to construct a clear understanding of the attention allocation process. However, researchers eventually realized that different experiments led to different results because attention allocation is highly sensitive to the type of task being performed. This led several researchers to distinguish between what are known as resource-limited and data-limited tasks (Norman & Bobrow, 1976; Nusbaum & Schwab, 1986).

In this context, **resource-limited tasks** are those in which performance will improve if more resources are shifted to them (Chandler & Sweller, 1990). For example, if you are watching television as you read this chapter, the chances are good that you will not be allocating enough of your attention to understanding the chapter's main points. Turning off the television and concentrating on the book should improve learning greatly!

Data-limited tasks are those in which performance is limited by the quality of data available in the task. Above some minimal amount of resources needed to perform the task in the first place, allocating more resources to a data-limited task will not improve performance. Trying to make sense of a poor-quality tape recording is an example of a data-limited task. If the tape is bad, after a certain amount of resources have been assigned to the task, no amount of additional effort will help. For many students, following complicated instructions or "analyzing" Shakespearean sonnets may fit into the category of data-limited tasks; no matter how many resources they assign to the job, performance will not improve. Most serious, however, is when the data to complete a task do not exist—for example, when the first-semester calculus student has little prior knowledge of key mathematical concepts from algebra and trigonometry.

Resource-limited tasks are difficult if we do not have enough attention to allocate to them. For example, remembering three numbers such as 7, 3, and 5 is easy, unless you also are asked to count backwards by 3s from 100! Each of these tasks are relatively easy in isolation, but once combined, we do not have ample resources to do both. In contrast, data-limited tasks are difficult regardless of how much attention we allocate. For example, sometimes car radio reception is just too poor for us to make out the voice we hear in the distant night.

The important point to carry away from this discussion is that attention is allocated differently depending on situational demands. Skilled learners become adept at allocating the right amount of attention to a learning task at the right time. When information is important, skilled learners selectively attend to it (Fisher et al., 1988; Reynolds, 1993). Skilled learners do not waste their attentional resources unnecessarily. In addition, skilled learners rely on many automated skills to conserve resources.

Automatic Processes

One of the major themes of this text is the importance of automatic cognitive processes (see chapter 1). Because automatic cognitive processes require fewer resources than nonautomated processes (see Stanovich, 1990, for a review), learners need fewer resources to perform tasks where their skills are automated than those tasks requiring conscious attention and thought. The notion of automatic processes, or **automaticity,** was first conceived of by Neisser (1967) and elaborated by Laberge and Samuels (1974), Shiffrin and Schneider (1977), Neves and Anderson (1981), and Nusbaum and Schwab (1986). Although opinions differ concerning the specifics of automatic processes, it is generally agreed that they (1) require little or no attention for their execution and (2) are acquired only through extended practice.

The existence of automatic processes helps us explain why people can carry out complex tasks and perform different tasks simultaneously. Examples of automatic processes are decoding by good readers, shifting gears by accomplished drivers, punctuating of sentences by skilled writers, and the placing of fingers by expert typists and piano players. Each of these processes appears to require few cognitive resources (e.g., being able to downshift into second gear while also talking to your passenger, watching traffic, and making a turn) and little or no conscious attention (e.g., how often have you thought about the process of shifting gears while doing it?).

It is easy to see how automatic processes are related to how students allocate their attention to tasks. For example, if a student could not perform most of the processes of division automatically, resources could not be devoted to making estimates and evaluating. Similarly, good readers can devote their attention to reading for meaning because decoding the words no longer requires much in the way of cognitive resources. Poor readers, in contrast, may have trouble with meaning because so many of their resources have to be used for decoding words, not because they lack poor comprehension skills (Samuels, 1988; Stanovich, 2000). Perhaps you have experienced this yourself when reading in a foreign language.

Research on development of automaticity has shown that in the beginning, performance on any cognitive activity will be awkward and slow. As learning proceeds, however, knowledge of facts can become knowledge of *how to use those facts.* This "proceduralized knowledge" is much more readily and quickly available for use and greatly reduces the demands on our limited processing resources during routine tasks such as reading.

In fact, there is a startling consistency in the research findings on skill acquisition in a wide range of tasks. Although performance initially may be halting, it soon improves to a reasonable level of competence. In most areas in which "expertise" has been investigated, however, performance continues to improve even after hundreds and even thousands of hours of practice! Such findings have been shown in studies as diverse as Crossman's (1959) classic investigation of cigar rolling (in which performance continued to improve over almost three million trials and 2 years!), the reading of inverted text after hundreds of pages (Kolers, 1975), and the continued learning of a card game after hundreds of hands (Neves & Anderson, 1981). Consider, for example, students' efforts to improve their skiing, to ride a skateboard, or to develop fluency in a foreign language. Careful examination of their performance, even after many hours of practice, reveals continuing skill improvement.

Summary of Sensory Memory Processes

Sensory memory briefly processes a limited amount of incoming stimuli. Visual registers hold about seven to nine pieces of information for about 0.5 second. Auditory registers hold about five to seven pieces of information for up to 4 seconds. Incoming stimuli are first perceived, then matched to a recognizable pattern, and then assigned a meaning. How much information we can process depends on two things: (1) the complexity of the information and (2) our available resources. Automated tasks are easy to perform because they require fewer attentional resources. Resource-limited tasks can be improved if we selectively allocate more attention to them. Data-limited tasks are difficult no matter how much attention we allocate because the information itself is deficient.

Short-Term and Working Memory

Short-term memory refers to the place where information is processed for meaning. In the modal model (see Figure 2-1), information is assumed to enter short-term memory once it has received initial processing in sensory memory. Like sensory memory, short-term memory is limited with respect to capacity and duration. Researchers also have investigated how information is accessed from short-term memory. More recently, the very notion of short-term memory as a unitary system has been questioned. Many researchers now prefer the name **working memory,** which consists of three component subsystems, each performing a highly specialized function (see Baddeley, 2001, and Healy & McNamara, 1996).

Capacity and Duration

The first serious discussion of short-term memory as a separate cognitive entity was George Miller's (1956) classic article "The Magic Number Seven, Plus or Minus Two: Some Limits on Our Capacity for Processing Information." Miller argued that information processing is constrained by a severe "bottleneck" in the memory system. Under most circumstances, people can hold no more than seven or so **chunks** (meaningful units of information) in memory at one time. One way to process information more efficiently, according to Miller, is to increase the size of chunks of information. For example, although the number *4727211* may be meaningless to you and therefore remembered as seven chunks of information, we remember it as the main switchboard number at one of our universities, usually as three chunks as follows: *472, 72,* and *11*. The most provocative part of Miller's article, however, was that short-term memory is sensitive only to the number of chunks, not their size. As a result, people can hold large amounts of information in memory and therefore improve information processing dramatically simply by chunking information into larger and larger units of meaning. Numerous studies during the past 4 decades have supported this view. Some have shown that ordinary people can be taught to use chunking strategies to improve the capacity of short-term memory (Ericsson et al., 1980).

Another important aspect of short-term memory is the duration of information. Early studies by Peterson and Peterson (1959), using what is now known as the *Brown–Peterson paradigm,* showed that information is forgotten very quickly from short-term memory. The Petersons asked college adults to study a list of three unrelated syllables and then to count backward from 100 by threes (i.e., *100, 97, 94,...*). When tested after 3 seconds, people already had forgotten about half of the information. After 18 seconds, almost everything had been forgotten. Originally, forgetting in short-term memory was attributed to decay—that is, information fading from memory as a function of time. Subsequent studies revealed that forgetting was less a result of the passage of time than of *interference* caused by other information (Greene, 1992). For example, Waugh and Norman (1965) varied the amount of intervening information within a fixed time interval after studying the target list. Their results confirmed that the amount of information that intervened increased forgetting regardless of time. This result and others like it led researchers to conclude that forgetting is a result of interference rather than of time-related decay.

Taken together, many studies conducted between 1956 and 1970 suggested that the capacity of short-term memory is limited to seven or so chunks as Miller had predicted. Information also is forgotten quite rapidly, particularly when new information follows it in the information processing cycle. Thus, although evidence suggests that information decays in short-term memory, strong evidence supports the idea that forgetting typically is a result of interference and capacity overload.

Accessing Information

Researchers soon began to address how we search through information that is held temporarily in short-term memory. In a now-famous set of studies, Saul Sternberg (1975) asked people first to learn a short list of unrelated letters (e.g., *BVGK*) and then to identify whether a target letter matched any of the letters included in the original list. The rationale of this technique was that letters included in the list should be judged faster than those not in the list. Sternberg addressed two specific questions related to subjects' decision making. The first was whether letters in the list were searched in a *serial* (one by one) or *parallel* (simultaneously) manner. The second was whether search was *self-terminating* (the search ended when the letter was found in the list) or *exhaustive* (the entire list was searched even when the letter was found prior to the end of the list). Contrary to intuition, Sternberg argued that people search the contents of short-term memory in a serial, exhaustive fashion. The main evidence on which Sternberg relied was that decisions took longer when the size of the original list increased, regardless of where the target letter was located in the list. Sternberg argued that self-terminating, parallel searches, which at face value appear much more efficient, are impossible because of (1) the speed at which decisions are made and (2) the fact that the entire search process is completely automated (and therefore not under conscious control).

Working Memory

By the 1970s, researchers were becoming increasingly disenchanted with the idea of short-term memory. The main complaint was that many different kinds of activities were attributed to short-term memory without specifying how these activities occurred. To illustrate, imagine that you are given the letters *I, N, R,* and *U* and are asked to decide whether they form a meaningful word. After a few moments, you retrieve the word *ruin.* But what does it take to perform these simple mental operations in short-term memory? On the one hand, you need to store the letters *inru* temporarily while, on the other, you permute these letters to determine whether they match lexical entries elsewhere in memory. Of course, to do so, you evoked general knowledge about the structure of words and subsequently searched lexical memory (memory for words) in a highly strategic fashion (e.g., alphabetically). The point of this exercise is that you did several very different kinds of activities just to perform a very simple lexical decision task in short-term memory.

The complexity of operations in short-term memory led a number of theorists, most notably Baddeley (1986), to propose a model of working memory. Baddeley's model included three main components, shown in Figure 2-5. The *executive control system* is assumed to be a limited capacity control system that governs what enters short-term memory. A second important function is to select strategies necessary to process information—for instance, deciding to search lexical memory alphabetically. The central executive also controls two "slave systems," the *visual-spatial sketch pad* and the *articulatory loop.* The former enables us to hold visual-spatial information in short-term memory and to perform a variety of computations on that information (e.g., mental rotation of an object). The latter is the verbal analog to the sketch pad. It enables us to hold acoustic information temporarily via rehearsal, usually for 2 to 4 seconds. Together, these three subsystems perform the mental operations usually assigned to short-term memory.

The working memory model proposed by Baddeley and Hitch (1974) and developed more fully by Baddeley (1986, 2001) makes assumptions about the three subsystems described above. One assumption is that each of the three subsystems possesses its own limited attentional resources. This means that, under normal information processing loads, each subsystem can perform mental work without taxing the

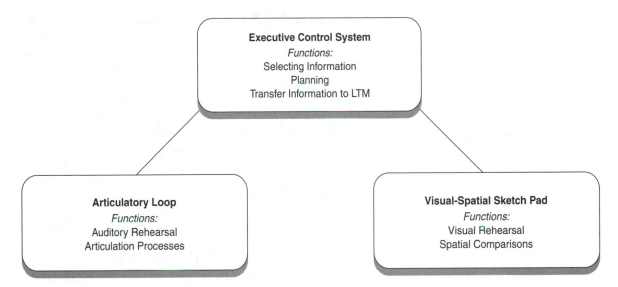

Figure 2-5
A Model of Working Memory

resources of the remaining subsystems. A second assumption is that the central executive regulates the activities of the two slave systems. Presumably, the more purposeful and strategic the central executive, the more efficient the slave systems.

Questions remain, however, about the exact nature of the working memory system (Hulme & Mackenzie, 1992). One question is the degree to which the three subsystems have access to their own unique pool of resources or compete for a shared pool. A second question is the specific role of the central executive, which at times appears to take on the duties usually performed by the lower slave systems. A third question is the extent to which information in the articulatory loop is stored temporarily with or without some kind of elaborative rehearsal.

Meanwhile, as the debate continues, more and more models of working memory have appeared in the literature (MacDonald & Christiansen, 2002). Some of these models are similar to Baddeley's three-component model shown in Figure 2-5 and some are not. Experts also have invested a great deal of time developing tests of working memory (Daneman & Merikle, 1996; Miyake, 2001). Some of these tests involve memory for random numbers (e.g., *4, 3, 7, 1, 8*) or letters (e.g., *D, X, Z, P*). Others involve what is known as digit or letter recoding, in which an individual hears a string of random digits and then recalls them in ascending numeric order. More recent tests involve counting objects, pointing to a designated square, or judging whether complex sentences are grammatically acceptable. Tests of working memory generally are good predictors of learning and are correlated with academic achievement and intelligence test scores. Some experts have even argued that working memory is the key factor in intelligence (Engle, Kane, & Tuholski, 1999; Kyllonen & Christal, 1990).

Despite the ongoing debate about the structure and importance of working memory, there are a number of points that most experts agree on (Miyake, 2001; Miyake & Shah, 1999). One is that working memory is not a physically separate component in the cognitive system as suggested by Baddeley's model (2001) and Figure 2-1. Research indicates that working memory is closely tied to long-term memory and is greatly affected by it; thus, what we already know has a direct impact on current processing. A second point of agreement is that working memory is responsible for active information processing rather than strictly passive short-term maintenance of information. Said differently, working memory is the place where meaning is made in the information processing system. A third point is that working memory is essential for skilled self-regulation of learning and memory, a point discussed further in chapter 6. A fourth theme is that working memory is best viewed as a domain-specific rather than domain-general phenomenon. This is, working memory is not equally efficient across different academic tasks or domains such as reading, writing, mathematics, and science. How well one uses working memory depends on how much one already knows about a domain, as well as the degree to which the skills in that domain are automatized. A fifth point of consensus is that working memory develops over time. Most experts believe that two changes occur. One is due to naturally occurring biological maturation (Case, 1985). A second is due to improve use and regulation of working memory skills (Engle et al., 1999). Last, there is growing consensus that emotional factors play a role in the efficiency of working memory. For example, anxiety reduces efficiency because it competes for limited resources that might otherwise be used to solve problems. Negative emotions may lead to blocking or traumatic persistence of memories (Schacter, 2001). In contrast, positive mood appears to enhance working memory (Oaksford, Morris, Grainger, & Williams, 1996).

Working Memory and Learning

A number of applied educational researchers, especially those working with technology (see chapter 10), have taken Baddeley's model of working memory to heart and developed it into what is known as **cognitive load theory** (Chandler & Sweller, 1990; Kalyuga, Chandler, Tuovinen, & Sweller, 2001; Mayer & Chandler, 2001; Mousavi, Low, & Sweller, 1995; Sweller, 1994, 1999; Sweller, van Merrienboer, & Paas, 1998). Cognitive load theory assumes that some learning environments impose greater demands than others and, as a consequence, impose a higher information processing load on limited cognitive resources in working memory (Sweller et al., 1998). Cognitive load may vary due to intrinsic or extraneous demands. According to cognitive load theory, **intrinsic cognitive load** is caused by the inherent properties of the to-be-learned information and is unalterable other than by schema acquisition (Sweller, 1994), whereas **extraneous cognitive load** results from the manner in which to-be-learned information is presented or from activities required of the learner. Intrinsic cognitive load cannot be changed because it is due to the complexity of the information itself. In contrast, extraneous cognitive load can be changed in a variety of ways, such as using adjunct aids, providing specific learning instructions, or enhancing the organization of to-be-learned information.

In essence, cognitive load theory states that there are three constraints on the efficiency of learning. The first includes *characteristics of the learner,* but especially working memory capacity, task-relevant conceptual knowledge in long-term memory (i.e., schemata), and the extent to which the learner has automatized basic learning processes. Research suggests that individuals who are automated and knowledgeable in a domain use their working memory resources efficiently. A second constraint is the *complexity of the to-be-learned information.* Information including concepts that can be learned in isolation imposes a smaller cognitive load than information consisting of concepts that must be learned simultaneously. A third constraint is the *instructional environment.* Learning can be enhanced by providing helpful instructions; segmenting a learning task so that it reduces load or enables the learner to manage the load more efficiently; or by providing adjunct aids such as advance organizers, notes, and summaries. In addition, learning improves when information processing is distributed across two modalities in working memory. For example, Mousavi et al., (1995) found that students solved geometry problems more efficiently when they involved words and pictures rather than just words or just pictures. Increased efficiency was attributed to the fact that the verbal and spatial slave systems in working memory increase total processing capacity.

Recently, Mayer and Moreno (2003) have used cognitive load theory to distinguish between three different types of cognitive demands during learning. *Essential processing* refers to cognitive processes that are absolutely necessary in order to understand the information. These include understanding main ideas, generating inferences that link these ideas together, and relating them to related information in memory. *Incidental processing* refers to information processing that is not absolutely necessary even though it may enhance understanding. For example, a student may take detailed notes of a passage she already understands quite well. *Representational holding* refers to temporarily holding information in memory while other information is being processed. For example, it may be necessary for a reader to look back at information in order to understand a graph she is studying.

Mayer and Moreno (2003) suggest that learning is most efficient when individuals focus all of their resources on essential learning and few or none of their resources on incidental learning and referential holding. They have described several scenarios in which additional incidental learning or referential holding lead to cognitive overload and poor learning. One overload situation occurs when an individual is forced to do too much essential processing simultaneously. One possible solution is *segmenting,* in which the learner is allowed time between successive presentations to manage the information more efficiently. Another solution is *pretraining,* in which the individual receives instruction designed to automate essential skills. A second overload scenario occurs when the individual is overloaded with some combination of essential and incidental processing. One solution is *weeding,* in which the learner eliminates all but essential processing through either instruction or periodic feedback. Another solution is *eliminating redundancy,* which reduces incidental processing. A third overload scenario occurs when individuals are forced to hold information in memory while engaged in some other information processing task. One solution is providing *adjunct spatial displays* that eliminate the need for representational holding. An alternative is *synchronizing,* which enables the learner to reduce the amount of information or amount of time that information is held in memory while other cognitive processing takes place.

Research on working memory has made a tremendous contribution to our understanding of learning from both a theoretical and practical perspective. Experts agree on a number of important points, including that working memory has limited capacity, oversees a variety of different learning activities, and is closely involved in self-regulated learning. Cognitive load theory has enabled educators to apply working memory theory to the design of instruction. Students find it difficult to learn because they lack knowledge, the to-be-learned information is too difficult, or the instructional environment does not adequately support learning. Cognitive load theory has increased our awareness of problems due to redundancy, divided attention, and information complexity.

Implications for Instruction: Guiding and Directing Attention

The information presented in this chapter, given its highly theoretical nature, might seem to some readers to be unrelated to educational practice. The material in this chapter has a number of very important implications for learning and instruction, however. We now present seven implications that we consider to be the most important.

1.   *Information processing is constrained by a "bottleneck" in sensory and short-term memory.* Because there are rather severe limits on sensory and short-term memory, students need to allocate their resources to important information as selectively as possible. Indeed, students who selectively focus their attention remember more important information without spending more time or effort studying (Reynolds, 1993). One way to help students focus their attention is to inform them prior to study which information is most important. Another powerful constraint on selective attention is prior knowledge. Students who know more about a topic find it easier to identify and focus on important information. For this reason, choosing a text wisely may greatly facilitate learning.

2.   *Automaticity facilitates learning by reducing resource limitations.* Automatic processes allow students to use fewer cognitive resources in completing the same task. Teachers need to remember that cognitive processes become automatic only after extensive practice. Practice should be regular and varied; for example, you would not want to practice driving only in your driveway under ideal conditions. Achieving true automatic processing even on simple skills requires hundreds of hours of practice.

3.   *Perception and attention are guided by prior knowledge.* What we already know greatly affects the stimuli we perceive, how easily we recognize these stimuli, and even what meaning we give them. Students should be encouraged to use what they know to help themselves process new information. One way to do so is to provide preteaching "organizers" that activate existing knowledge (see chapter 4). Another approach is to allow students to share knowledge in small-group discussions prior to beginning a new and possibly unfamiliar task.

Moreover, teachers should carefully match instructional activities with students' current levels of knowledge. Perception is apt to be no better than the knowledge base that supports it. In those cases in which sophisticated perceptions are the goal (e.g., noting different textures in chemicals and hearing when a clarinet is slightly out of tune), an extensive knowledge base, as well as extensive practice, is crucial.

4. *Perception and attention are flexible processes.* Although our ability to process new information has limits, information processing capacity is not as fixed as it might appear. Skilled learners are able to overcome these limits in a number of ways. One way is to be automatic at a task. Automaticity increases the rate at which information is processed because perception and attention require fewer cognitive resources. In a sense, automaticity is equivalent to increasing the flow of water through a garden hose of fixed capacity; we cannot increase the diameter of the hose (processing capacity), but we can accelerate the flow of water (information). A second way to enhance processing flexibility is to attend selectively to what is important. The key is to understand that perception and attention are under the partial control of learners rather than the other way around. Any way that a teacher helps a student control these processes is a big step forward to independent learning. A third way is to distribute the information processing load strategically across visual and auditory channels.

Although they acknowledge the existence of physiological differences in information processing, they seem to us as much less important than strategic differences (see Brody, 1992, for alternative views). Educators can do very little about differences in innate ability, but they often have a substantial impact on students' strategic use of their cognitive resources. Learners are remarkably flexible and adaptive and even more so with help from parents, peers, and teachers.

5. *Resource and data limitations constrain learning.* Not all learning tasks are the same. Sometimes we are limited by our resources. Trying to monitor two conversations while driving in heavy traffic probably is not a good idea for most drivers. Teachers should recall that some tasks are too demanding for some students to master all at once; that is, students may lack the cognitive resources to process the amount of information they are expected to learn. If you suspect that a student lacks the necessary resources for a learning task, break the task into smaller, more manageable parts; provide an easier task; or make some kind of peer–tutor assistance available to the student. Expecting students to perform beyond their limitations undoubtedly will have negative effects on learning.

Sometimes learning is limited by the information to be learned. One example is when a student is asked to learn just too much information in too short a time. In this case, selectively attending to what is most important is an excellent strategy. But what about a situation where there is too little information? For instance, textbooks often omit information that is important or even essential. When this happens, students are forced to provide this information themselves by checking other sources, asking for information, or making their own inferences (which consume precious resources). Unfortunately, many students simply give up because they cannot cross the gulf created by insufficient data. We encourage teachers to examine carefully the information that students are expected to learn to ensure that too much or too little information does not create a problem.

6.   *All students should be encouraged to "manage their resources."* Good learners are self-regulated, a concept discussed in more detail in chapter 4. Being self-regulated means that a learner has appropriate knowledge, a repertoire of strategies to perform required tasks, and the motivational will to do so. At the heart of self-regulation is the willingness to manage one's limited cognitive resources in the most strategic way possible. Research suggests that even college students fail to manage their resources effectively, in part, because they lack knowledge and, in part, because they lack the desire to do so (Wade, Trathen, & Schraw, 1990). In our opinion, helping students to be more strategic, to identify important information, and to use prior knowledge is an essential part of teaching.

7.   *Information processing is easier when to-be-learned information is distributed in working memory.* Baddeley's three-component model of working memory suggests that visual and auditory loads are processed separately in working memory. Presenting some information to one modality may reduce the burden on another (Mousavi et al., 1995). By using their working memory system more efficiently, students may actually process more information with less stress.

Summary

This chapter reviewed the processes of perception and attention. Perception is the assignment of meaning to incoming stimuli; attention is the allocation of cognitive resources to the tasks at hand.

Perception begins with the sense receptors. Each of our senses apparently has a sensory register. The majority of research, however, has focused on the visual sensory register (icon) and the auditory sensory register (echo). The sensory registers are brief repositories of unprocessed information. They allow analyses of incoming stimuli to occur at the outset of the perception process.

Research indicates that attention is allocated in a flexible manner. Skilled learners selectively focus on what is important to learn. Some tasks are difficult because they are resource-limited; that is, we may not have adequate resources to allocate to them. Other tasks are difficult because they are data-limited; that is, the information is degraded or insufficient.

Like sensory memory, the capacity and duration of short-term memory are quite limited. Miller (1956) suggested that we hold approximately seven pieces of information in working memory at a time. This information is forgotten quickly because of interference, decay, and replacement by new information. Research by Sternberg (1975) indicated that we search information in short-term memory in a serial, exhaustive manner.

We also described the transition from short-term memory to working memory. The latter includes a central executive, articulatory loop, and visual-spatial sketch pad. The central executive coordinates the two remaining slave systems, which are responsible for maintenance of verbal and spatial information. Research suggests that each subsystem possesses some unique resources that enable individuals to distribute information processing load.

Cognitive load theory has used Baddeley's model of working memory to better understand learning. Cognitive load theory states that learning is constrained by limited processing capacity. The higher the cognitive load of the to-be-learned information, the harder it is to learn that information. Researchers have considered a number of ways to reduce cognitive load through either the design of better learning materials or instructional methods that enable learners to use limited resources more efficiently.

Suggested Readings

Greene, R. (1992). *Human memory: Paradigms and paradoxes.* Mahwah, NJ: Erlbaum.

> This book provides an extremely well-written overview of memory research over the past 40 years.

Mayer, R. E., & Moreno, R. (2003). Nine ways to reduce cognitive load in multimedia learning. In R. Bruning, C. Horn, & Lisa PytlikZillig (Eds.), *Web-based learning: What do we know? Where do we go?* Greenwich, CN: Information Age.

> This chapter summarizes cognitive load theory, describes a variety of scenarios that create cognitive overload, and discusses ways to reduce overload.

Reynolds, R. E. (1993). Selective attention and prose learning: Theoretical and empirical research. *Educational Psychology Review, 4,* 345–391.

> Reynolds comprehensively reviews the past 2 decades' research on attention.

Rose, S. (1992). *The making of memory: From molecules to mind.* New York: Anchor Books.

> Rose summarizes trends in human and animal memory research, with a special emphasis on the contribution of molecular processes.

Stanovich, K. E. (1990). Concepts in developmental theories of reading skill: Cognitive resources, automaticity, and modularity. *Developmental Review, 10,* 72–100.

> In this article, Stanovich considers the effects of resource limitations and automaticity on information processing.

Sweller, J., van Merrienboer, J., & Paas, F. (1998). Cognitive architecture and instructional design. *Educational Psychology Review, 10,* 251–296.

> This article provides a detailed overview and experimental test of cognitive load theory.

Long-Term Memory: Structures and Models

A Framework for Long-Term Memory ■ *The Building Blocks of Cognition* ■
Another Dimension of Long-Term Memory: Verbal and Imaginal Representation ■
Evolving Models of Memory ■ *Implications for Instruction* ■ *Summary* ■
Suggested Readings ■

IN CHAPTER 2, we presented a model that portrays how information enters memory, is stored, and is retrieved. We focused especially on the first two parts of the model: sensory memory and working memory. Here in chapter 3, we turn our attention to the third part of the model, **long-term memory (LTM).**

When we talk about sensory and working memory, we typically are examining events recently experienced or currently in consciousness. LTM, in contrast, involves memory traces developed over periods of days, weeks, months, and years. LTM is the permanent repository of the lifetime of information we have accumulated. Also encoded in our LTM is the memory that lets us recognize familiar people and objects, drive a car, brush our teeth, or type a letter.

Constant rehearsal and repetition, so crucial for keeping information in working memory, are less critical for LTM. For instance, we can state our uncles' names; name a large city on the East Coast; or easily give examples of large, hairy animals without having to rehearse any of this information—despite the fact that we may not have thought of these topics for months or even years. More important for LTM are meaning and organization. Recall depends on our understanding what information means and being able to find it.

When you consider our first theme for cognitive education, that learning is a constructive process where knowledge is created and re-created on the basis of previous learning, the importance of LTM to learning becomes clear. Understanding how LTM works allows us to find ways to help students access and use their prior knowledge to create new knowledge. Just as cognitive research has helped us understand a great deal about how information initially enters our cognitive systems, it also has given us a vast amount of knowledge about how the information we process is organized, stored, retrieved, and used.

This chapter is the first of three devoted to the topic of LTM. In this chapter we begin by presenting a general framework that represents how different kinds of knowledge are organized in LTM. We then describe several units that cognitive theorists have proposed as "building blocks of cognition," highlighting features that qualify each as a useful way of thinking about memory and thought, including the role of imagery. A description of important new developments in memory research follows and, in the final section, we lay out the implications of long-term memory research for education.

A Framework for Long-Term Memory

Cognitive psychologists have found it useful to distinguish between the types of knowledge in memory. The classifications they make have both a common sense and a neurophysiological base (e.g., see Eichenbaum, 1997). Perhaps the most basic distinction is the one between declarative knowledge and procedural knowledge (J. R. Anderson, 1983a, 1993; Squire, 1987; Woltz, 1988). **Declarative knowledge** is factual knowledge, "knowing what." Some examples of declarative memory are recalling that Sakhalin is an island off the coast of Siberia, that Ebbinghaus studied memory by using nonsense syllables, and that you had Oat Squares for breakfast. **Procedural knowledge,** in contrast, is "knowing how" to perform certain activities. Our procedural knowledge allows us to make coffee, drive a car, use a computer, and perform a host of other actions. A young child who has learned how to unlock a door, turn on a faucet, brush his or her teeth, and open a book is demonstrating his or her recall of procedural knowledge.

A third category of knowledge—conditional knowledge—is increasingly grouped with declarative and procedural knowledge (see Figure 3-1) and emphasized as a vital goal for learning. **Conditional knowledge** is knowing *when* and *why* to use declarative and procedural knowledge. For example, students may have learned basic concepts of algebra (e.g., representing numbers by letters and expressing numerical relationships by algebraic expressions) and be able to reliably perform certain procedural operations (e.g., simplifying an algebraic expression), but still be unable to apply this knowledge to real-world problems, such as figuring out driving time on a trip or buying the right amount of tile for a bathroom floor. Conditional knowledge is needed to help students make effective use of their declarative and procedural knowledge.

Most learning involves interplay among declarative, procedural, and conditional knowledge. A concert pianist learning a new song by Domenico Scarlatti, for instance, may search her memory for declarative knowledge about that composer's preferred method of executing certain embellishments, such as the *appoggiatura, mordent, and trill*—declarative knowledge that will be used in the development of procedural and conditional knowledge. Her procedural and conditional knowledge about performing, in turn, give substance to the declarative knowledge she possesses (e.g., "Scarlatti intended for the mordents to be played according to the basic tempo of the passage. That would mean there should be thirty-second notes here.") and allow her to use her knowledge in her performance.

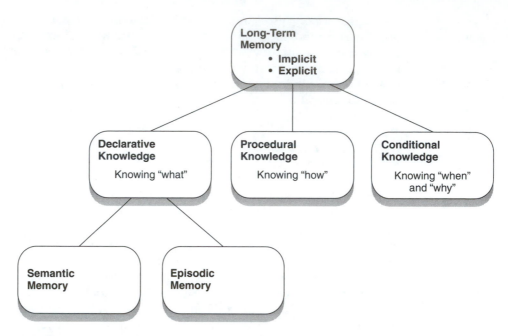

Figure 3-1
The Knowledge in Long-Term Memory

The declarative-procedural-conditional knowledge distinction is valuable for helping educators think about our goals for student learning. Novice students in a teacher education program, for instance, may memorize and recite a principle of cooperative classroom learning (e.g., "Establish an atmosphere of shared decision making and trust") as declarative knowledge but have little or no notion of how, why, and when actually to use this principle in the classroom (i.e., they lack procedural knowledge and conditional knowledge). As important as declarative knowledge is, we almost always will benefit from thinking beyond it to include both procedural and conditional knowledge goals.

For example, one of the most important aims of education is to help students develop relatively large, stable, and interrelated sets of declarative knowledge. As educators, we expect students to be "knowledgeable" in domains as diverse as mathematics, science, literature, and history. Yet we also need to place a considerable premium on knowing "how," "when," and "why." The reason is that almost all learning combines declarative, procedural, and conditional elements. No matter what the content domain, declarative knowledge—although a basic building block of all expertise—is most valuable when linked appropriately to actions. In settings ranging from elementary students reading and writing to students in the professional schools of journalism, architecture, teaching, business, and medicine, procedural and conditional knowledge are critical outcomes of the educational process.

Beginning in chapter 4 with our *introduction of the concepts of metacognition* and *learning strategies* and continuing throughout the remaining chapters, we frequently revisit and elaborate on the importance of conditional knowledge. Here, however, we focus primarily on the role of declarative and procedural knowledge in cognition. We begin by discussing two subcategories of declarative knowledge, semantic and episodic memory.

Semantic and Episodic Memory

Within the category of declarative knowledge, Tulving (1972, 2002) and others (e.g., Squire, 1987) have distinguished further between memory for general knowledge, called semantic memory, and memory of personal experiences, called episodic memory.

Semantic memory refers to memory of general concepts and principles and the associations among them. Semantic memory contains such information as the facts that lemons are yellow and that computers contain chips. Also in semantic memory is the organized knowledge we have about words and concepts and how they are associated. For instance, areas such as English literature and American history represent vast networks of semantic information that we encode, organize, and have available for retrieval. Recalling word meanings, geographic locations, and chemical formulas requires searches of semantic memory.

Episodic memory refers to storage and retrieval of personally dated, autobiographical experiences (Tulving, 1983, 1985). Recalling childhood experiences, recollecting the details of a conversation with a friend, and remembering what you had for dinner last evening all fall within the realm of episodic memory. Episodic memories are retrieved using "personal tags," associations with a particular time or place linked to the memory. Obviously, a great deal of what we must recall to function effectively in our personal lives is episodic.

An ongoing disagreement exists among psychological researchers about the distinction between semantic and episodic memory. Some researchers, such as McKoon and Ratcliff (1986), Howe (2000), and Craik (2000) believe that there is no division between the two; rather each is simply a different type of remembering. Others, such as Squire (1987), see the distinction as reflecting separate memory systems in the brain. Work with amnesiacs who have lost their episodic memory and studies using functional neuroimaging of brain activity supported the two-system theory (Tulving, 2002). Other recent studies showed that semantic and episodic memory systems are not absolutely separate, but sometimes work in tandem (Klein, Cosmides, Tooby, & Chance, 2002). Certainly the two-system distinction is useful for helping us think about the types of information we—and our students—must remember and the cognitive procedures that learners use (Roediger, 1990). On the one hand, we need a broad knowledge base to think and reason effectively. On the other hand, our episodic memories must function well enough for us to locate ourselves in time and space and to have a reasonably accurate picture of our experiences.

The recent interest in episodic memory has in part been rekindled by research on the topic of **implicit memory,** an unintentional, nonconscious form of retention, such as that underlying playing a piece on the piano or tying your shoes (e.g., see Roediger, 1990; Schacter, 1993, 1996a; Schacter & Cooper, 1993).

Implicit Memory: Retention Without Remembering

When we think of memory, we usually think about bringing a past experience to mind. Whether the memory is voluntary (a conscious search for information) or involuntary (thoughts pop into our heads), we recognize it as corresponding to some past event. This kind of memory, involving conscious recall or recognition of previous experiences, is called **explicit memory.** Explicit memory has been studied for many decades by memory researchers; it usually is tested by recall and recognition tasks that require intentional information retrieval.

Yet often the record of our earlier experience is not available to our consciousness, but still affects our behavior. This kind of memory is called **implicit memory.** Implicit memory is an unintentional, nonconscious form of retention in which our actions are influenced by a previous event but without conscious awareness (Jacoby & Witherspoon, 1982). Many of our daily performances, for example, reflect prior learning but resist conscious remembering. In skills as diverse as using computers, tying our shoes, and driving a car, conscious remembering seems to play little part. In fact, when a person tries to reflect on how these skills are being performed, performance often deteriorates (Roediger, 1990).

Memory researchers dating back to Ebbinghaus have recognized the phenomenon of implicit memory, but systematic research on the topic dates back only to the 1980s (Graf & Schacter, 1985; Jacoby, 1983; Jacoby & Witherspoon, 1982). Since the early 1990s, this topic has moved from obscurity to a position of central importance in cognitive psychology (Greene, 1992; Ratcliff & McKoon, 1996; Roediger, 1990; Schachter & Cooper, 1993).

Interest in the topic of implicit memory first developed among cognitive neuroscientists working with *amnesiacs,* individuals with certain forms of brain injury that make them unable to remember verbal materials, such as words or names, for more than a very brief period. Other functions, however, such as perceptual abilities and motor skills, remain intact.

The early conclusion was that the inability of such individuals to transfer verbal materials from STM to LTM played a critical role in their amnesia. That view proved to be too simple, however, as researchers demonstrated that some kinds of long-term verbal memory in amnesics were not impaired at all. Instead, the crucial dimension was whether explicit or implicit memory was being tested.

A representative early experiment by Jacoby and Witherspoon (1982) comparing amnesic and normal subjects provides an excellent example of the experimental procedures that have been used to contrast explicit and implicit memory performance. They used homophones (e.g., *read/reed*) as their experimental materials. In Phase 1, all subjects were asked questions (e.g., Name a musical instrument that employs a *reed*) to bias the interpretation of the target homophones toward their less frequent interpretation. Hearing the word in isolation, most subjects would think of *read,* not *reed*. The question prompts the less frequent choice. In Phase 2, subjects were asked to spell words, a task that for the subjects seemed totally unrelated to Phase 1. The list of words to be spelled, however, contained some homophones previously presented and some not. Although the experimenters made no connection between Phases 1 and 2, how subjects chose to spell the homophones was the key measure of effects of earlier encounters with some of the homophones. If the prior presentation influenced later interpretation, the lower probability spelling (e.g., *reed*) would be more probable for the homophones encountered earlier. As Jacoby and Witherspoon (1982) pointed out, an influence of memory on spelling does not necessarily require awareness of remembering. Awareness, however, was indeed necessary in a recognition task presented in Phase 3 of the experiment, which required subjects to indicate whether they had seen words before. Words from Phase 1 were mixed into the set of words in Phase 3.

Predictably, the probability of correctly recognizing whether they had seen a word before (the Phase 3 measure) was much lower for amnesics (.25) than for normal controls (.76). As expected, amnesics' explicit memory was very poor. But the amnesics' spelling performance was startling. It revealed very strong effects of their earlier encounters with the words primed by the questions even though they had no awareness of the impact; that is, the spellings they chose (e.g., *reed,* not *read*) reflected their implicit memory from encountering the words in the questions they had answered in Phase 1. In fact, although both groups showed the influence of implicit memory, their probability of choosing the low-frequency spelling was even higher than that of normal controls (.63 vs. .59)!

Since that time, implicit memory effects have been demonstrated in both amnesic and normal subjects by using a variety of experimental methods. These have been as diverse as better performance on completion tasks, in which subjects are shown partial stimuli and asked to complete them (e.g., having seen the word *flower* before, guessing the word FLOWER more easily when shown –L–WER) and decision tasks, in which subjects make more favorable judgments (e.g., of liking or preference) about individual members of pairs to which they earlier had been exposed. Researchers also have demonstrated that effects of implicit memory extend to nonverbal materials, such as novel visual patterns and shapes (see Schacter & Cooper, 1993).

For memory theorists, two aspects of implicit memory research have been especially intriguing. First was the emergence of unequivocal evidence that behavior can be influenced by memory of past events even without conscious awareness. Second, and even more exciting for many theorists, was the fact that implicit and explicit memory tasks sometimes elicit **functional dissociations,** in which implicit and explicit memory performances are unrelated. In Jacoby and Witherspoon's (1982) research, for instance, explicit memory performance as demonstrated by word recognition greatly favored normal subjects, but implicit memory performance on the spelling task did not. Weldon and Roediger (1987; see also Roediger, 1990) similarly showed a dissociation between explicit and implicit memory tasks. When a mixed list of pictures and words was studied and subjects' recall was tested later in explicit free recall, the names of the pictures were better recalled than the words. On an implicit word-fragment completion test (see example above), in which some fragments corresponded to presented words and some to names of pictures, prior study of words produced far greater effects than study of pictures.

Findings of dissociations like these are extremely interesting to memory theorists, some of whom (e.g., Squire, 1987) have proposed distinct memory systems to account for them. These theorists, who tend to be those working in the neuroscience tradition, argue that the declarative memory system is responsible for performance on explicit tests of retention, whereas the procedural system underlies implicit memory. Other theorists, such as Roediger and Jacoby, assert the more straightforward explanation that explicit and implicit memory tasks require different cognitive operations. They contend there is no need to propose different memory systems. As yet, however, neither the multiple memory systems nor the processing accounts (Greene, 1992) have proven wholly satisfactory in explaining all of the experimental results.

What has been learned in a few years nonetheless is quite remarkable. Researchers are exploring systematically a completely new class of memory tasks and have acquired much basic knowledge about how implicit memory affects behavior. The finding that implicit and explicit memory may be dissociated from each other may have important implications for understanding memory performance in special groups, such as very young children and the elderly. Research examining developmental patterns for implicit and explicit memory is increasing (see, e.g., Drummey & Newcombe, 1995; Hayes & Hennessy, 1996) and likely will produce revisions of our theories of memory development. Similarly, we will better understand memory processes associated with aging or memory loss as a result of injury because of the empirical and theoretical advances in this area.

The Building Blocks of Cognition

One challenge for the science of cognition is to find the most meaningful "units" for describing cognitive operations. In the previous section, we presented a framework for describing the contents of LTM. In this section, we elaborate on that framework by describing five concepts proposed by theorists as "building blocks of cognition" that make up the information stored in LTM. These concepts have common features, but each of them represents a somewhat different view of how best to conceptualize the information stored in memory. Three of them—*concepts, propositions,* and *schemata*—have been related most closely to declarative knowledge (see Figure 3-1) and, though equally relevant for understanding episodic memory, have been studied most extensively in the context of semantic memory. The fourth and fifth concepts—*productions* and *scripts*—have been used primarily to explain procedural knowledge. Each of the five illuminates somewhat different aspects of LTM and is important in thinking about memory and cognition.

Concepts

One major way we deal with the bewildering array of information in the world is to form categories. In science, for example, Chi, Slotta, and de Leeuw (1994) have proposed that students' concepts about science fall into three primary categories:

matter (e.g., *animals* and *minerals*), *processes* (e.g., *osmosis* and *acceleration*), and *mental states* (e.g., *curiosity* and *doubt*). Our language in general reflects conceptual categories: The words *grandfather, exercise, bird, psychology, blue, dog,* and *cheerful* each represent a category meaningful to most of us. **Concepts** are the mental structures by which we represent meaningful categories. Particular objects or events are grouped together on the basis of perceived similarities; those that "fit" the category are examples, or instances of the concept; those that do not fit are nonexamples. The similar features across examples of a concept (e.g., all oceans contain water and are large) are called **attributes;** features essential to defining the concept are called **defining attributes.** Learning a concept involves discovering the defining attributes and discovering the rule or rules that relate the attributes to one another.

Rule-Governed Theories of Conceptual Structure   There is a rich tradition of psychological research on how we identify and acquire concepts. One such tradition, exemplified by the early work of Bruner et al. (1956), focused on **concept identification.** Bruner et al. presented students with an array of simple objects or stimuli, such as triangles and squares, for which there were only four defining features: number, size, color, and form. The task was to discover the unknown concept.

The experimenters had predetermined the rules defining the concepts, which could be either relatively simple (e.g., "All green objects are examples") or quite complex (e.g., "Either green patterns or large patterns are examples"). A single stimulus (e.g., a green triangle) within the array was specified as a positive instance of the unknown concept to be discovered. On the basis of that example, the subjects were asked to formulate their best guesses—their hypotheses—about the unknown concept. They then were allowed to pick another stimulus from the array and to ask whether it was a positive or negative example of the concept, to which the experimenter responded truthfully. The procedure continued until subjects were confident they could identify the concept.

Bruner et al.'s (1956) work showed quite clearly that most individuals quickly formulate hypotheses about relevant attributes and choose stimuli accordingly. A sizable number of individuals adopt what is called a **conservative focusing strategy** to test their hypotheses where their first hypothesis is quite global. Here is a protocol:

> This is a single large, green triangle. I can't rule out any of these things. But I can rule out examples with two and three objects, small- and medium-size objects, red and blue objects, and circles and squares. Now, I'll pick a new example that differs in one and only one attribute from the first; in that way, I'm guaranteed to get new information.

Others adopt a strategy called **focus gambling,** in which they vary more than one attribute of a stimulus at once. In this strategy, subjects may shortcut the methodical steps of conservative focusing but also run the risk of getting no information at all by their selection. Still others use **scanning strategies,** in which they attempt to test several hypotheses at once, a technique that puts some strain on subjects' ability to remember and process information.

The early work of Bruner et al. (1956) and others (e.g., Haygood & Bourne, 1965; Neisser & Weene, 1962) showed that individuals typically solve concept identification problems by trying to discover the rules relating the concept attributes. In general, concepts with more difficult rules are more difficult to learn. The simplest rules involve affirmation (e.g., any green object) and negation (e.g., any object that is not green), which apply if only one attribute is being considered. But most concepts involve more than one relevant attribute and require more complex rules. Among the most common are **conjunctive rules,** in which two or more attributes must be present (e.g., any triangle that is green), and **disjunctive rules,** in which an object is an example of a concept if it has one or the other attribute (e.g., either a triangle or a green object).

Bourne's work (e.g., Bourne, 1982) has represented the clearest statement of rule-governed conceptual structure. In his view, concepts are differentiated from one another on the basis of rules such as the above. These rules can be learned either through instruction or through experience with instances that either are members of the class (positive instances) or are not (negative instances). One learns to classify a set of animals as birds or nonbirds by acquiring rules for combining characteristic attributes of birds (e.g., wings, bills, and feathers). Using these rules one can unambiguously classify a new instance as either a bird or a nonbird. This works fine with a very simple classification, where a new instance either is a bird or not a bird. But such a rule-based conceptual system is not always adequate.

Most natural or real-world concepts are "fuzzier" and differ qualitatively from those studied in the laboratory. Consider the concept of *furniture*. We would all quickly agree that tables, chairs, sofas, and floor lamps are furniture, and we can describe many rules that differentiate articles of furniture from other objects. But some of our attempts at rule formation quickly run into trouble. Presence of legs? What about some floor lamps? What about a table or a desk? Is a rug furniture? Some would say it is but would wish to include a qualifying statement or **hedge;** it is like furniture, but not exactly like it. What is the set of rules that unambiguously determines which objects are members of the concept class *furniture?*

Logical efforts to determine such sets of rules mostly have been unsuccessful, especially with ambiguous examples such as a rug. Rosch and Mervis (1975), dissatisfied both with the artificiality of laboratory work on concept formation and with the difficulties of classifying concepts with rule-governed approaches, proposed an alternative view based on "degree of family resemblance" to a **prototype**—a highly typical instance of the concept.

Prototype Theories of Conceptual Structure   Prototype theories of concepts, in contrast with rule-governed theories, do not assume an either–or, member-nonmember process of concept identification. Instead, prototype theorists (Rosch, 1978; Rosch & Mervis, 1975) have argued that conceptual class membership is determined by the degree to which an example is similar to a known instance in memory—one that seems to best exemplify the concept. As stated in chapter 2, this line of reasoning is similar to that employed by perception theorists in accounting for pattern recognition in perception. Wattenmaker, Dewey, Murphy, and Medin (1986) have

Table 3-1
Typicality of Members in Six Superordinate Categories

Item	Furniture	Vehicles	Fruits	Weapons	Vegetables	Clothing
1	Chair	Car	Orange	Gun	Peas	Pants
2	Sofa	Truck	Apple	Knife	Carrots	Shirt
3	Table	Bus	Banana	Sword	String beans	Dress
4	Dresser	Motorcycle	Peach	Bomb	Spinach	Skirt
5	Desk	Train	Pear	Hand grenade	Broccoli	Jacket
6	Bed	Trolley car	Apricot	Spear	Asparagus	Coat

Source: Adapted from "Family Resemblance: Studies in the Internal Structure of Categories," by E. Rosch and C. B. Mervis, 1975, *Cognitive Psychology, 7*, pp. 573–605. Copyright 1975 by Academic Press, Inc. Reprinted by permission.

suggested that the majority of "natural" or real-world concepts are structured in terms of sets of typical features.

Particular instances of concepts in the real world do not have all the defining features, but rather have a family resemblance. So, for North Americans, robins or bluejays often are prototypes of birds. We also might classify animals such as emus or penguins as "birds," but with less assurance. In those instances we frequently **hedge,** or qualify, what we say with a statement such as "Well, they are birds, but not the best examples of birds." The hedge is necessary because the emu and the penguin do not exhibit a particularly strong family resemblance to robins or bluejays, yet they do have some resemblance. Rosch (1978) and others have provided evidence that young children learn category memberships for prototypical and near-prototypical instances (see Table 3-1) before they learn the less typical ones.

Both rule-governed and prototype conceptual theories correctly classify many simple, naturally occurring phenomena, but both have difficulty developing clear categorizations for abstract concepts, such as *wisdom, justice,* and *equality*. What are the rules for defining a particular act as "wise" or "just"? Most of us find making such distinctions quite difficult because, in most cases, we can only categorize whether an act fits these categories if we understand the context in which the act occurred. As a result, theorists have suggested that both rule-governed and prototype theories of concepts are inadequate. They propose a *probabilistic* view, in which a sufficient number of attributes must be present to reach a "critical mass"—the number sufficient to make a category judgment. This view incorporates some characteristics of rule-governed approaches but retains the "naturalness" of prototype views.

Probabilistic Theories of Conceptual Structure   Some theorists (e.g., Tversky, 1977; Wattenmaker et al., 1986) have suggested that concept learning involves weighing probabilities. When faced with a new instance, the learner searches it for characteristic, but not necessarily defining, attributes (e.g., observing flying and singing in an animal that looks like a bird). Whether it is a bird is determined by the summing of evidence for category membership against criteria stored in memory. If a particular instance reaches a critical sum of properties consistent with category membership, it is classed as an example of that concept. The emu, though it does not fly or sing melodiously, lays and hatches eggs, feeds its young in "birdlike" ways, and in general looks like a bird. It exhibits enough characteristics to be classified as a bird.

In general, the greater the sum beyond the critical value, the quicker the classification. On the one hand, robins and bluejays are identified quickly as birds and not mammals because they have many characteristics of birds and relatively few of mammals. On the other hand, emus and penguins have comparatively fewer bird characteristics and so are less likely to be identified quickly as birds. These expectations are similar to those of prototype theory. Note that the "critical sum" approach also has some characteristics of rule-governed conceptual behavior because the learner must have a "rule" for determining when a set of features reaches the critical value.

We emphasize that the greater difficulty of categorizing emus and penguins as birds is probably, at least in part, because of our lack of familiarity with these animals. Nevertheless, probabilistic models emphasize that those exotic birds exhibit sufficient attributes common to birds that they are so classified. In the same way, a rug, though not exactly like "a piece of furniture," is classified as furniture by virtue of its being used as furniture, its presence in homes, and so on.

Summary of Concepts   Concepts are one way we structure the huge amount of information that we acquire and store in our LTM. This structuring of knowledge is one of the important cognitive themes for education we outlined in chapter 1. Whether concepts are conceived of in terms of rules, prototypes, or probabilistic judgments, each of the theories of concept learning suggests that different cultures may define concepts in different ways, depending on the set of properties used to characterize the concept. For instance, Schwanenflugel and Rey (1986) compared Spanish- and English-speaking individuals on prototype tasks similar to those Rosch used and found clear cultural differences even in such simple tasks as determining prototypical birds. One would expect even greater differences in classifying abstract concepts, in which the relevant attributes are much less obvious. Classifications of abstract concepts such as just or wise could be expected to reflect strongly the cultural context in which they are used.

Medin, Wattenmaker, and Hampson (1987) suggest that simple rule-governed or prototype conceptual sortings are common in memory and are used widely when conceptual categorizations are easy to make. But when objects contain attributes from multiple categories or are influenced heavily by the context within which they occur (e.g., "ethical behavior"), people may make categorizations probabilistically. It should be clear from the above that no unambiguous evidence exists supporting a single view of the nature of concepts. Some consensus, however, appears to be emerging concerning a probabilistic view.

Propositions

Suppose you read the following sentence:

> The trainer of the Kentucky Derby winner Alysheba was Jack Van Berg, who always wore a brown suit.

How can its meaning be represented in LTM? The most common way cognitive psychologists have represented declarative knowledge, especially linguistic information, is by propositions (J. R. Anderson, 1996; Kintsch, 1974; Rumelhart & Norman, 1978). A **proposition** is the smallest unit of meaning that can stand as a separate assertion. Propositions are more complex than the concepts they include. Where concepts are the relatively elemental categories, propositions can be thought of as the mental equivalent of statements or assertions about observed experience and about the relationships among concepts. Propositions can be judged to be true or false (J. R. Anderson, 2000).

Propositional analysis has been used extensively in analyzing semantic units such as sentences, paragraphs, and texts. When we analyze the example sentence above, for instance, we see that it can be broken into the following simpler sentences or "idea units":

1. Jack Van Berg was the trainer of Alysheba.
2. Alysheba won the Kentucky Derby.
3. Jack Van Berg always wore a brown suit.

These simple sentences are closely related to the three propositions underlying the complex sentence above. Each represents a unit of meaning about which a judgment of truth or falsity can be made. If any of these units of meaning are false, then of course the complex sentence is false. Propositions are not the sentences themselves; they are the meanings of the sentences. Memory contains the *meaning* of information, not its exact form.

Now examine the following two sentences without looking back. Have you seen either of them before?

1. The Kentucky Derby was won by Alysheba.
2. Jack Van Berg always wore a blue suit.

Most individuals readily will reject having seen sentence 2; after all, we have just read that Jack Van Berg always wore a brown, not blue, suit. But many will "recognize" sentence 1, even though they have not seen it. We remember the sense of oral and written statements; the meaning of propositions is what is preserved. In contrast, the surface structure of the information (e.g., whether the first sentence above read *Alysheba won the Kentucky Derby* or *The Kentucky Derby was won by Alysheba*) usually is lost quickly unless we make a special effort to attend to it.

Propositions usually do not stand alone; they are connected with one another and may be embedded within one another (see J. R. Anderson, 1996). Kintsch (1986, 1988) has shown that texts can be viewed as ordered lists of propositions. In Kintsch's formal system of analysis, each proposition consists of a **predicate** and one or more

arguments. Several examples are written below, using Kintsch's notation, in which predicates always are written first and propositions are enclosed by parentheses:

1. John sleeps. (SLEEP, JOHN)
2. A bird has feathers. (HAVE, BIRD, FEATHERS)
3. If Mary trusts John, she is a fool. IF, (TRUST, MARY, JOHN) (FOOL, MARY)

Kintsch and others have done propositional analyses of many texts, transforming them into **text bases,** which are ordered lists of propositions. Using such propositional analyses, Kintsch has shown that the reading rates in expository texts are directly related to the number of propositions in the texts. Moreover, Kintsch and others (e.g., Kintsch, 1988; Meyer & Rice, 1984) also have demonstrated experimentally that free recall patterns reflect the hierarchical propositional structure of the text (see chapter 12, "Reading to Learn," for further discussion of Kintsch's theory).

What implications do propositions have for LTM? Cognitive theorists have hypothesized that propositions sharing one or more elements are linked with one another in **propositional networks.** As is shown, the notion that ideas—whether concepts, propositions, or schemata—are linked in large networks is very useful for thinking about how information is stored in and retrieved from memory. Students' ability to comprehend information and to use it effectively in cognitive operations such as problem solving hinges on the quality of the networks they are able to create.

Schemata

Many cognitive theorists are interested in how memory is organized and how knowledge is used to interpret experience. One of the most potent theories is that of **schemata**—mental frameworks that we use to organize knowledge. Schema theorists have proposed that knowledge is organized into complex representations called schemata (sing., schema) that control the encoding, storage, and retrieval of information (Marshall, 1995; Rumelhart, 1984; Seifert, McKoon, Abelson, & Ratcliff, 1986).

As described by Rumelhart (1981), schemata are hypothesized data structures that represent the knowledge stored in memory. Schemata are presumed to serve as "scaffolding" (R. C. Anderson, Spiro, & Anderson, 1978; Ausubel, 1960; Rumelhart, 1981) for organizing experience. Schemata contain **slots,** which hold the contents of memory as a range of slot values. In other words, knowledge is perceived, encoded, stored, and retrieved according to the slots in which it is placed. Schemata are fundamental to information processing. Some schemata represent our knowledge about objects; others represent knowledge about events, sequences of events, actions, and sequences of actions (Rumelhart, 1981).

Whenever a particular configuration of values is linked with the representation of variables of a schema, the schema is said to be **instantiated** (Rumelhart, 1981). Much as a play is enacted whenever actors, speaking their lines, perform at a particular time and place, so schemata are instantiated by concepts and events. A "teaching" schema may be instantiated when you view a situation where enough of the requisite values— a teacher, some students, and a transaction between them—are present to activate the

schema. Once schemata are instantiated, their traces serve as a basis of our recollec-
tions (Rumelhart, 1981)—they are part of our long-term memory.

Before 1970 or so, the notion of schemata was an obscure one in experimental psychology, appearing in historical perspective in the early work of Bartlett (1932) and in
the work of the 18th-century philosopher Immanuel Kant, who referred to the "rules
of the imagination" through which experience was interpreted. But by the mid-1970s
many leading cognitive theorists and researchers (e.g., Bobrow & Norman, 1975;
Minsky, 1975; Rumelhart, 1975; Rumelhart & Ortony, 1977; Schank & Abelson, 1977;
Winograd, 1975) had become tremendously interested in schema theory. Why did this
perspective assume such importance?

In our judgment, the reason schema theory came to the fore so rapidly had to do
with its extraordinary power to explain memory and other cognitive phenomena. To
get a better feel for the power of schemata, consider the following paragraph. Read it
carefully a time or two.

Death of Piggo

The girl sat looking at her piggy bank. "Old friend," she thought, "this hurts me." A tear
rolled down her cheek. She hesitated, then picked up her tap shoe by the toe and raised
her arm. Crash! Pieces of Piggo—that was its name—rained in all directions. She closed
her eyes for a moment to block out the sight. Then she began to do what she had to do.

Think now about some of the things you need to know in order to comprehend this
passage, one with fairly simple sentence construction, no rare words, and dealing with
a topic—piggy banks—familiar to most. Let's start with piggy banks. What do we know
about them? A short list follows. Piggy banks

- are representations of pigs
- hold money
- usually hold coins
- have a slot to put the money in
- are hard to retrieve money from
- have fat bodies
- are not alive
- usually are made of brittle material
- can be shattered by dropping or a blow
- look friendly
- usually are smaller than real pigs
- once broken, usually stay that way
- etcetera

This list of "piggy bank facts" could be continued almost indefinitely. Note that the list
does not define the concept of *piggy bank* (a piggy bank is . . .), but rather is a partial
description of our overall conception of piggy banks—how they look, work, and so
on. Our overall mental representation, or schema, of even a single concept like *piggy
banks,* we discover, is an immensely complex array of information and its interrelationships. Within and related to this global schema are embedded many other

schemata—for instance, schemata for "tap shoe," "striking something with a hard object," "saving money," and so on.

If you turn again to "Death of Piggo" and examine it closely, you quickly see the vital role your schemata for piggy banks and many other objects and events played in comprehending this paragraph. The notions that piggy banks hold money, that they can be shattered, that shattering is necessary to retrieve their contents, and that they are friendly looking—*none of this information actually is stated in the passage*. Yet, all of it must have been activated automatically as you read, or else you could not have understood what you read. You somehow "filled in" the information.

In Rumelhart's terms, the slots in your schemata had default values assigned to them when they were activated. Although specific information actually was not presented on the piggy bank containing money or its brittleness, we assumed these to be true from our general knowledge of piggy banks. Even the simplest event or message has an infinite number of features that could be attended to. Yet as was shown in chapter 2, only a few of these actually become a part of memory. One critical function of schemata is guiding attention. Pichert and Anderson's (1977) "home buyer" and "burglar" study (described in chapter 1) shows this guiding function. "Home buyers" tended to recall information about a picture of a house that was relevant to their perspective, such as number of bedrooms, newly painted rooms, and a nursery. "Burglars" showed significantly better recall for such details as the presence of 10-speed bicycles in the garage, a valuable painting, and a color television. Pichert and Anderson (1977, p. 314) commented on their findings as follows:

> The striking effect of perspective on which elements of a passage were learned is easily explained in terms of schema theory. A schema is an abstract description of a thing or event. It characterizes the typical relations among its components and contains a slot or placeholder for each component that can be instantiated with particular cases. Interpreting a message is a matter of matching the information in the message to the slots in a schema. The information entered into the slots is said to be subsumed by the schema.

Because "home buying" and "burglary" represent quite different schemata, information more likely to instantiate important variables in one was less likely to instantiate the other. The information individuals paid attention to and subsequently recalled was that most consistent with their currently activated schema. Schemata play several other critical roles, including guiding interpretation. For example, given sentence 1 below, most people later will recall sentence 2.

1. The paratrooper leaped out the door.
2. The paratrooper *jumped* out of the plane.

Or, to take a second example, the first sentence below often is recalled as the second.

1. The student spoke to the department chair about her instructor's sexist comments.
2. The student *complained* to the department chair about her instructor's sexist comments.

Recall is transformed, often subtly, by schemata. Especially if information is general or vague, instantiation molds it into familiar form, as demonstrated by the following passage, used in early research by Bransford and Johnson (1972, 1973) and Dooling and Lachman (1971):

> The procedure is actually quite simple. First you arrange items into different groups. Of course one pile may be sufficient depending on how much there is to do. If you have to go somewhere else due to lack of facilities that is the next step; otherwise, you are pretty well set. It is important not to overdo things. That is, it is better to do too few things at once than too many. In the short run this may not seem important but complications can easily arise. A mistake can be expensive as well. At first, the whole procedure will seem complicated. Soon, however, it will become just another facet of life. It is difficult to foresee any end to the necessity for this task in the immediate future, but then, one never can tell. After the procedure is completed one arranges the materials into different groups again. Then they can be put into their appropriate places. Eventually they will be used once more and the whole cycle will then have to be repeated. However, that is part of life. (Bransford & Johnson, 1972, p. 722)

Most individuals asked to read and recall Bransford and Johnson's passage have poor comprehension and subsequent recall. But simply adding the title "Washing Clothes" improves both comprehension and recall significantly by adding an appropriate context for the information. When schemata are not or cannot be activated during learning, new knowledge cannot be assimilated easily.

Schema theory provides an explanation for several memory phenomena. Because the contents of memory consist of representations of knowledge, rather than exact copies of it, encoding will vary according to the schemata activated at the time of encoding. In this way schema theory supports a constructivist view of learning and an explanation for the effect of context in memory storage, two of the major cognitive themes we discussed in chapter 1. Recall is seen as a reconstructive activity (Spiro, 1980), with schemata providing frameworks that direct the recall process (e.g., "Who *is* the author of *The Polar Express*? Let's see, wasn't that book a Caldecott Medal winner? That guy also wrote *Jumanji*. Just give me a minute; I'll think of his name!"). Recall is not simply remembering stored information, but rather is *re-creating* information and events. Memory, in this view, is not so much reproductive as constructive and reconstructive.

Because it emphasizes the application of what learners already know, schema theory has been tremendously appealing to both cognitive theorists and educators. It helps us understand that many recall and recognition "errors" are not so much errors as they are constructions logically consistent with the learner's mental structures. In general, schema theory portrays learners in a dynamic, interactive way. Although schema theory has been criticized for its generality and vagueness (Alba & Hasher, 1983), cognitive research (see, e.g., Marshall, 1995, who has applied schema theory to problem solving and decision making) has continued to reflect schema-based conceptions of perception, memory, and problem solving.

Productions

Whereas concepts, propositions, and schemata are ways of representing declarative knowledge, productions and scripts are ways of representing procedural knowledge. **Productions** can be thought of as condition-action rules—if/then rules that state an action to be performed and the conditions under which that action should be taken (J. R. Anderson, 1983a, 1993). The idea of productions can be illustrated by the following set of instructions and actions for unlocking a car door:

Production A: If car is locked, then insert key in lock.
Production B: If key is inserted in lock, then turn key.
Production C: If door unlocks, then return the key to vertical.
Production D: If key is vertical, then withdraw key.

In general, productions are seen as having the capability of "firing" automatically: If the specified conditions exist, then the action will occur. Memory for productions ordinarily is implicit memory, discussed earlier in this chapter. Conscious thought typically is not involved. Outcomes of productions supply the conditions, as in the example above, to fire other productions in a sequence of cognitive processes and actions.

The idea of productions has been a useful one. It not only captures the automatic nature of much of cognition but also lends itself to modeling many cognitive processes on the computer. Productions and the rules they embody can be specified formally as instructions in computer programs that operate on data and simulate cognitive processes. In reading, for example, Just and Carpenter (1987) incorporated the idea of productions in an elaborate computer model (READER) to simulate various aspects of reading. In this model there are productions such as the following:

If the word *the* occurs, assume a noun phrase is starting.

If READER encountered the word *the* in a text it was analyzing, this production would fire (an instruction is triggered in READER), leading READER to "infer" that it currently was processing a noun phrase.

Like propositions, productions are organized in networks called **production systems.** In a production system, multiple productions may be active at a given time. Outcomes of the productions modify memory and activate knowledge, which in turn may activate new productions and new knowledge. Cognition moves ahead from state to state until its ultimate goal is accomplished.

Production systems enable us to represent the dynamic, changing aspects of cognitive processes. For instance, Just and Carpenter (1987) pointed out that, in reading, conceptualizing certain cognitive processes as production systems nicely captures the "automatic side" of reading. In reading, as in many of our cognitive functions, we do not necessarily think about what we are doing; we simply do it, an example of the "automaticity" described in chapter 2. Similarly, J. R. Anderson (1993, 1996; J. R. Anderson & Matessa, 1997) has used production systems and the concept of **production rules** in modeling automatic processes in tasks as diverse as list learning and problem solving (see the discussion of Anderson's theory later in this chapter; see also chapter 8). Knowledge, once in production form, is seen as applying much more rapidly and reliably. In Anderson's view, the critical productions of problem solving are those that recognize general goals and conditions and translate them into a series of subgoals.

Scripts

Just as schemata organize our declarative knowledge, *scripts* provide the underlying mental frameworks for our procedural knowledge. Simply, **scripts** are schema representations for *events*. In proposing the concept of scripts, Schank and Abelson (1977) were attempting to account for our comprehension of commonplace events such as going to a restaurant or a movie. When actions such as these are done repeatedly, the researchers argued, our knowledge becomes encoded in scriptlike mental structures. These mental structures contain not only action sequences and subsequences but also the actors and objects characteristic of that setting. In a restaurant, for example, one typically enters, orders, eats, gets and pays the bill, and leaves. As predicted by script theory, people's knowledge, inferences, and recall do closely conform to stereotypical patterns of activity.

Another Dimension of Long-Term Memory: Verbal and Imaginal Representation

"A picture is worth a thousand words." Although the validity of this aphorism may be debatable, there is little doubt that humans have extraordinary capabilities for remembering visual information. For example, Standing, Conezio, and Haber (1970), in an early study of visual recognition memory, showed subjects 2,500 slides for 10 seconds each. Recognition, estimated from a test on a subset of these slides, was over 90%! In a study by Standing (1973), participants viewed an even larger number of pictures—10,000—over a 5-day period. From the test performance, Standing estimated subjects' memory at 6,600 pictures, remembered in at least enough detail to distinguish these pictures from ones they had not seen before. Given evidence such as this, there is little doubt that pictorial information can be represented in our memories quite well. Most of us can easily conjure up images of a book, a soaring bird, a train wreck, or a walk in the woods.

One major contribution of cognitive psychology has been a revitalization of interest in mental imagery. Once largely banished from experimental psychology as subjective, mentalistic, and therefore unscientific (Watson, 1924), imagery has come to play a significant role in cognitive theory and research.

Alan Paivio (1971, 1986a) has proposed that information is represented in two fundamentally distinct systems: one suited to verbal information and the other to images. The **verbal coding system** is adapted for linguistically based information and emphasizes verbal associations. According to Paivio, words, sentences, the content of conversations, and stories are coded within this system. In contrast, nonverbal information, such as pictures, sensations, and sounds, are stored within an **imaginal coding system** (Paivio, Clark, & Lambert, 1988).

Paivio's theory has been called a **dual coding theory,** because incoming information can be coded within one or both of the systems. Information that can be coded into both systems will be more easily recalled than information coded only in the verbal or imaginal system. In Paivio's view, the verbal and nonverbal codes are functionally independent and "contribute additively to memory performance" (1986a, p. 226). Paivio also has hypothesized that image-based memory traces generally are stronger than verbal memories.

Much of Paivio's early work demonstrated the effects of the abstractness of materials on their memorability and relating these results to dual coding theory. For instance, some words (e.g., *bird, star, ball,* and *desk*) have concrete referents and presumably are highly imaginable. When presented with such words, both the verbal (e.g., the linguistic representation of the word *bird,* its pronunciation, and its meaning) and the imaginal (e.g., an image of a bird soaring) representations are activated simultaneously. Other, more abstract words (e.g., *aspect, value,* and *unable*), are far less readily imaginable and activate the nonverbal system only minimally. In Paivio's view, memory for abstract materials should be poorer because such materials are represented only within a single system. Pictures, because they tend to be labeled automatically and are dual–coded, should be more memorable than words (Paivio, 1986a).

Words, even concrete ones, are not necessarily automatically imaged (see also Svengas & Johnson, 1988). In many experimental studies, Paivio and his associates (e.g., Paivio, 1971; Paivio & Csapo, 1975; Paivio, Yuille, & Madigan, 1968) demonstrated beneficial effects of imagery on learning and memory that were consistent with his predictions. Words that are rated high in imagery also are better remembered in free recall, serial learning (a series of words recalled in order), and paired-associate learning (the "associate" of a word must be recalled when the word is presented). Also, when subjects are instructed to "form images," their memory is enhanced.

Although considerable debate has surrounded the exact mechanisms by which imagery functions (e.g., Intons-Peterson, 1993; Kosslyn, 1994; Pylyshyn, 1981), there is little doubt that imagery is important to memory and cognition. In reading and text recall, for example, effects of concreteness and imagery are well-documented (e.g., Goetz, Sadoski, Fatemi, & Bush, 1994; Sadoski, Goetz, & Rodriguez, 2000). A large body of evidence shows that materials high in imagery are more memorable and that learners instructed to create images will enhance their learning. As educators, the distinction between verbal and imaginal information should remind us not to rely too heavily on verbal instruction. Just as in chapter 2, when we discussed the use of auditory and visual material to enhance working memory, we should remember the potential that visual images hold for storage and recall in LTM.

Evolving Models of Memory

Through the 1960s and well into the 1970s, the prominent model of memory was the modal model, exemplified by the "stage" models of Waugh and Norman (1965) and Atkinson and Shiffrin (1968). As shown in chapter 2, these models portray human cognition as computerlike and emphasize sequential steps in information processing. Information moves from the sense receptors and sensory registers into short-term/working memory and, depending on the success of the processing there, into long-term memory.

The importance of the distinction between short-term/working memory and LTM has diminished as memory models shifted from a "storage" to a "processing" emphasis (e.g., Collins & Loftus, 1975; Craik & Lockhart, 1972; Jenkins, 1974; see also Ericsson & Kintsch, 1995). This processing emphasis is retained in most current models (see J. R. Anderson, 1993, 1996; Collins, Gathercole, Conway, & Morris, 1993). As discussed in chapter 2, rather than being conceived of as a "place" where information is held for brief periods, the concept of STM has broadened into the idea of **working memory,** which better reflects the many ways in which we process and transform information. For example, J. R. Anderson's ACT model, discussed later in this chapter, incorporates a working memory and a long-term memory. These two are not emphasized as "separate places" but rather as closely interrelated. The current contents of consciousness set up a pattern of activation in LTM; this activation of LTM, in turn, "reverberates" back into working memory.

Obviously, all components of memory—sensory memory, working memory, and long-term memory—are highly interactive. Although information plainly does move through sensory memory and working memory to LTM, the contents of LTM simultaneously are exerting a powerful influence on what we perceive, pay attention to, and comprehend (Ericsson & Kintsch, 1995; Kintsch, 1998). Although the modal model has been useful in drawing our attention to important dimensions of our memory systems, it should not be taken as implying that cognition is neatly separable into a set of sequential steps. The "early" process of perception, for instance, plainly is guided by semantic memory from the supposedly "later" stage of LTM. Also, many cognitive activities are highly automatic, driven by the information coming in, and seem to depend only minimally on "central processing."

Researchers have continued to develop new models aimed at better portraying the active, dynamic nature of cognition and its ability to interpret and restructure incoming information. Memory models continue to evolve, with earlier models contributing key elements to those that follow. In this section we describe three of the most prominent of these models—the network model, the ACT model, and the connectionist model—and their evolution.

Network Models

In **network models of memory,** knowledge is represented by a web or network and memory processes are defined within that network (J. R. Anderson, 1983b, 1993, 1996). In most such models, the networks are hypothesized to consist of **nodes,** which consist of cognitive units (usually either concepts or schemata), and **links,** which represent relations between these cognitive units.

Quillian (1968) and Collins and Quillian (1969) proposed an early network model, called the **Teachable Language Comprehender (TLC),** as a model for semantic memory. Devised as a computer program, TLC was based on the assumption that memory could be represented by a semantic network arranged into a hierarchical structure. In this hierarchy, the nodes are concepts arranged in superordinate-subordinate relationships. Properties of each concept are labeled **relational links,** or

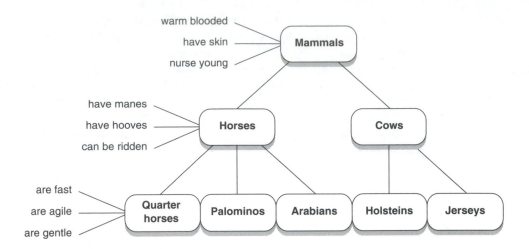

Figure 3-2
A Network Model of Memory
Source: This sample of a network is modeled after those developed by Collins and Quillian (1969).

pointers going from the node to other concept nodes. An example of such a network is presented in Figure 3-2.

Quillian proposed five kinds of links: (1) superordinate (ISA) and subordinate links, (2) modifier (M) links, (3) disjunctive sets of links, (4) conjunctive sets of links, and (5) a residual class of links. These links can be embedded in one another. In Figure 3-2, the links from *are fast, are agile,* and *are gentle* to *quarter horses* are **M** (modifying) links; the links between *quarter horses* and *horses* and between *horses* and *mammals* are **ISA** (superordinate) links. In general, properties particular to a concept were assumed to be stored along with the concept (e.g., *are gentle* is stored with *quarter horses*). Those not unique to that concept (e.g., *have manes* and *have hooves*), however, are assumed to be stored with more general concepts higher in the hierarchy.

When memory is searched, activation moves along the links from the node that has been stimulated (say, by reading the word *horse*). This **spreading activation** constantly expands, first to all the nodes directly linked with the concept (in our simple model, from *horses* to the superordinate concept of *mammal* and to the subordinate concepts of *Arabians, palominos,* and *quarter horses*) and then to the nodes linked with these nodes and so on (Collins & Loftus, 1975). As activation moves forward through the nodes, an activation tag is left at each. When a tag from another starting node is encountered, an *intersection* has been found. By tracing the tags backward from the intersection to their sources, the path linking the starting nodes can be reconstructed. The question *Are quarter horses mammals?* would trace a path in the network from the starting nodes *quarter horses* and *mammals* through the node for horses.

According to this model, language comprehension consists of path evaluation to see whether it is consistent with the constraints imposed by language. For instance, the starting point in comprehending the question *Are quarter horses mammals?* is activation of the paths from *quarter horses* to *horses* and from *horses* to *mammals*. The memory search is presumed to begin at the concepts included in the input question (*quarter horses, mammals*). Beginning with the concept of quarter horses, this search would arrive in one step (link) at the properties *are fast, are agile,* and *are gentle* and at the superordinate concept of *horses*. A second step takes the search to *mammals*. If the relationship between the two nodes is permitted by the syntax and context of the question, the question can be comprehended.

Collins and Quillian tested a number of hypotheses based on their model, including the hypothesis that the more links needing to be traversed in accessing memory (e.g., deciding whether a Holstein is a mammal vs. deciding whether a cow is a mammal; see Figure 3-2), the longer the process will take. This prediction usually was borne out, although, like all models, Collins and Quillian's model had trouble accounting for some results, such as familiarity effects (e.g., deciding whether a palomino is a horse is easier than deciding whether a tarpon is a horse simply because most of us are more familiar with palominos than tarpons). To account for such findings and their own accumulating data, Collins and Loftus (1975) extended the model, including several assumptions to make the model less "computerlike" and more "human." (Quillian's original theory was developed as a program for the computer, which imposed constraints that he thought were unrealistic.) Spreading activation remained a key assumption, but with activation decreasing over time. In addition, Collins and Loftus proposed the existence of a separate **lexical network,** in which concept names were stored. Links in this lexical network could serve as an alternative source of entry into memory (e.g., "words that sound like *horse*"). Collins and Loftus's revised network model accounted for results from a variety of studies and dealt with many criticisms of the original model.

Collins's network models, although superceded by other models in recent years, have contributed key concepts, especially the conceptualization of memory as organized into networks of nodes and links and the idea of spreading activation, to current theories and models of memory. Arguably the most prominent of these is J. R. Anderson's ACT Model.

The ACT Model

Perhaps the most comprehensive current model of memory and cognition is the ACT model (J. R. Anderson, 1976, 1983a, 1983b, 1993, 1996). Growing out of an early model called *human associative memory (HAM)* (J. R. Anderson & Bower, 1973), ACT is broader than the models of Collins and Quillian (1969) and Collins and Loftus (1975). In formulating and revising ACT, Anderson's ambitious intention has been to provide a unifying theoretical framework for all aspects of thinking, one that includes initial encoding of information and then information storage and retrieval and encompasses both declarative and procedural knowledge.

In the latest version of ACT, called *ACT-R* (J. R. Anderson, 1996; J. R. Anderson & Matessa, 1997), declarative knowledge is represented by schemalike structures or chunks that encode the category and contents of the information. Procedural knowledge, such as the ability to solve mathematics problems, is represented by productions. Production rules specify the conditions and actions of productions—that is, the conditions under which the action will take place and the outcome of the production, which can include creating new declarative information. Production rules respond to goals of the situation (e.g., the need to solve a word problem in algebra), often by creating subgoals (e.g., converting linguistic information in the word problem into symbolic representations).

In ACT-R, declarative and procedural knowledge are intimately connected. Production rules specify how chunks are transformed and apply only when a rule's conditions are satisfied by the knowledge available in declarative memory. In short, declarative knowledge provides the context in which cognitive processes, as represented by production rules, take place.

As in most network models, the concept of *spreading activation* is a key feature of ACT. Spreading activation is seen as determining the level of activity in long-term memory. Of course, activation must begin somewhere; the points where activation begins are called **focus units.** Once focus units are activated—either externally from perception (e.g., by reading a sentence) or from working memory (e.g., by thinking about what has been read)—activation spreads to associated elements. When you read the word *hot,* elements for *cold, warm, water,* and other related items likely would be activated automatically. Any item's activation is a function of prior experience—the extent to which an item has been useful in the past—and the odds that it will be useful in the current context. In Anderson's words, "[T]he mind keeps track of general usefulness and combines this with contextual appropriateness to make some inference about what knowledge to make available in the current context" (1996, p. 360). Attention determines the continued activation of the network; when the source of activation for the focus unit drops from attention, activation decays.

Because working memory and LTM overlap extensively, activation spreads easily from working memory to associated elements in LTM. From there, activation can "reverberate back" to nodes in the network. If Node 1 activates Node 2, then activation from Node 2 also can spread to Node 1. Retrieval occurs when focus units are reactivated. Activation is cumulative: The more units activated, the more likely an item will be retrieved. In the classroom, a student who may not be able to recall a fact when first questioned may remember the information if the teacher rephrases the question or supplies "hints" that activate additional pathways, stimulating recall.

In ACT, well-learned concepts are seen as producing more activation and so are more easily retrieved than less well-learned concepts. Well-learned information has wide-ranging activation and many associations that permit access through multiple routes. Also, the ACT model implies that more activation occurs on paths leading to stronger nodes. Anderson's model would predict that students who are helped to relate new information to existing, well-learned knowledge will have superior recall.

The ACT model has generated a great deal of research. Because of its breadth, ACT has been adapted not only to the study of memory but also to modeling high-level cognitive processes, such as problem solving and decision making (J. R. Anderson, 1993, 1996). Because it can account for a wide variety of data and addresses many important aspects of cognition, this model is likely to play an important role in directing cognitive research in the foreseeable future.

Connectionist Models

Throughout much of its history, cognitive psychology has been dominated by a computer metaphor. Human cognition, cognitive scientists have argued, is computerlike. Information is taken in, processed in a single central processor of working memory, and stored in and retrieved from long-term memory. The computer metaphor has generated models of memory (e.g., Atkinson & Shiffrin, 1968), knowledge representation (e.g., Kintsch, 1986, 1988), and problem solving (e.g., Newell & Simon, 1972). Beyond providing a metaphor for cognition, computers have provided a mechanism for simulating cognition and for testing cognitive theories.

Most computer architecture requires sequential or **serial processing.** Computer programs typically are a series of instructions the computer executes very rapidly, one after the other. One serious problem in modeling cognition is that this kind of serial information processing is not very "brainlike." Where digital computers are quick and precise, executing millions and even billions of operations in sequence per second, human information processing is far slower. Yet although our brains are slower, they are much better suited and far more powerful than computers for most kinds of "messy" everyday cognitive tasks, such as recognizing objects in natural scenes, understanding language, searching memory when given only fragmentary information, making plans, and learning from experience.

Also in contrast with most computer programs, our cognitive systems can operate under multiple constraints. Although some cognitive tasks require serial processing, many require **parallel processing,** with processing occurring simultaneously along several dimensions. For instance, in a famous example from Selfridge (1959), the interpretation of the middle letter in the words CAT and THE is determined by the context in which it appears. Similarly, we have little trouble identifying the words in Figure 3-3 even though parts of key letters are obscured. Our perceptual system somehow explores possibilities simultaneously without committing itself to one interpretation until all constraints are taken into account. The identity of each letter is constrained by all the others. Most cognitive tasks, including physical performances (e.g., hitting a ball, typing, playing a piano) and language use (e.g., oral language comprehension, reading and understanding stories), involve resolving multiple constraints.

Given the characteristics of the brain and its tremendous adaptability, some cognitive theorists (e.g., McClelland, McNaughton, & O'Reilly, 1995; McClelland, Rumelhart, & Hinton, 1986; Rumelhart & Todd, 1993) have proposed replacing the "computer metaphor" with a "brain metaphor," a so-called **connectionist model of memory** or **parallel distributed processing (PDP) model.** The reason human beings are better

Figure 3-3
Examples of Information Processing with Multiple Constraints

at many tasks than conventional computers, they contend, is that the brain has an architecture that better fits natural information processing tasks. What humans do so exceedingly well, far better than any computer, is to consider many pieces of information simultaneously. Processing occurs in *parallel,* along many dimensions at the same time. Although any single bit of information may be imprecise or ambiguous, the system's parallel processing capabilities make it possible to make judgments and decisions with a high level of confidence.

According to McClelland (1988), the major difference between connectionist models and other cognitive models is that, in most models, knowledge is stored as a static copy of a pattern. When access is needed, the pattern is found in long-term memory and copied into working memory. In a connectionist model, however, the units themselves are not stored. What is stored are the connection strengths among simple processing units. These connection strengths allow the patterns to be re-created when the system is activated. Figure 3-4, from McClelland et al. (1995), contrasts a connectionist network with a semantic (propositional) network of the type traditionally used to model the organization of knowledge in memory. Note the close correspondence of the semantic network with the Collins and Quillian (1969) model presented in Figure 3-2. In the connectionist model, a subset of one used by Rumelhart (1990) to "learn" the relationships in the semantic network, inputs consist of concept-relation pairs and activation spreads

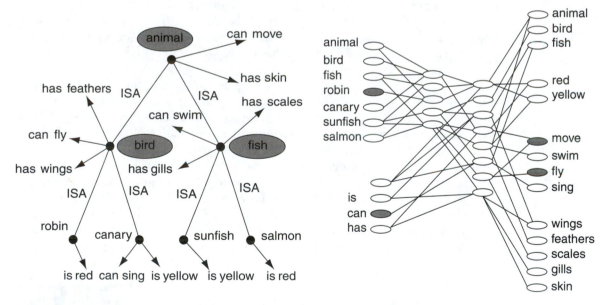

Figure 3-4
Contrast Between Network (left) and Connectionist (right) Models of the Knowledge in LTM
Source: Adapted from "Why There Are Complementary Learning Systems in the Hippocampus and Neocortex: Insights from the Successes and Failures of Connectionist Models of Learning and Memory," by J. L. McClelland, B. L. McNaughton, & R. C. O'Reilly, 1995, Psychological Review, 102, 419–457. Copyright 1995 by the American Psychological Association. Used by permission.

from left to right. Over time, the network can be "trained" to turn on all of the output units (those on the right side) that are correct completions of the input pattern. What the network learns are connection weights linking inputs and outputs.

Because processing is parallel in connectionist models, it can proceed along many dimensions at the same time. In reading, for instance, the cognitive processes are not portrayed as moving through steps from "lower levels," such as decoding, to "higher levels," such as comprehension. Instead, processing moves ahead on many levels at once; as we read, we simultaneously depend on feature extraction processes (e.g., recognizing lines, curves, and angles in letters), letter and word recognition processes, syntactic assignment processes (e.g., is *feature* a noun or a verb?), and schema activation. These processes trigger and inhibit one another as processing moves forward. Top-down, bottom-up, and interactive (a combination of top-down and bottom-up) processing all can occur within such a system (McClelland et al., 1995). As is shown in chapters 11 and 12, this conception of reading seems to fit well with the data.

Another key concept in connectionist models is that of **distributed representation.** As we have indicated, in a connectionist model knowledge is stored in the strengths of connections between processing units, not in the units themselves. Researchers such as McClelland and his associates argue that connectionist models can provide a better account of how semantic networks, such as that in Figure 3-4, are acquired and can help us understand how knowledge is transferred. Knowledge of any specific pattern (e.g., oaks, trees, plants, and living things) does not reside in a special processing unit reserved just for that pattern, but instead is distributed over the connections among a very large number of simple processing units. Our understanding of *bark* in the sentence "Marty's dog let out a loud *bark!*" arises through activation of connections among a host of processing units, including those for letter perception, word meanings, and syntactic roles and those relating to the context in which the sentence was uttered. We comprehend automatically that *bark* is something Marty's dog did, not what covers the oak tree outside our window.

In connectionist models, processing units are roughly analogous to neurons or assemblies of neurons, and the connections by which units are linked are seen as roughly analogous to synapses. These parallels make them particularly attractive in helping researchers understand brain structures and functions (see, e.g., McClelland et al., 1995; McClelland & Seidenberg, 2000). When stimulated by the environment, input units cause other units to be activated via their connections—the familiar spreading activation from Collins and Quilian's early network model. Eventually, activation spreads to those units associated with responses.

"Brainlike" models of information processing now are appearing more frequently in computer hardware and software. The computer world has long recognized that the conventional, single-central-processor design has inherent limitations. Because instructions must be operated on serially, a bottleneck eventually will occur in the central processor no matter how fast the computer. The newest super computers are based on parallel distributed processing and may contain hundreds of dedicated processor systems linked by a high-speed network—a brainlike, connectionist system that enables these computers to do advanced simulations and modeling not possible with serial processing.

Connectionist models continue to have some intriguing applications in cognitive psychology. Because of their higher degree of correspondence to brain characteristics and their ability to match more closely aspects of human cognition, including learning, they seem likely to make a major contribution to cognitive psychology and to the understanding of human learning and memory.

Implications for Instruction

The models of memory and the memory-related concepts we have explored provide us with several powerful conceptions about the nature of learning and memory. These have important implications for educators.

1. *Recognize that the starting point of learning is what students already know—their prior knowledge.* Students understand what they read, hear, and see through the filters of their experiences in their families and cultures. The models of memory we have examined in this chapter all stress the role of prior knowledge in information processing and memory. What can be learned depends substantially on what learners already know. In the modal model, for instance, we see knowledge from LTM affecting perception and attention. Schema research has dramatically illustrated how knowledge structures guide information processing and influence what we learn and remember. As discussed in chapter 1, learning is a constructive process. A starting point of instruction should be the recognition that much of what students learn is constructed from the prior knowledge in their long-term memory.

2. *Help students activate their current knowledge.* Having relevant knowledge is one thing; using it in new learning is another. From a schema theory standpoint, new information needs to be instantiated within learners' schemata. From an instructional perspective, this implies that teachers need to ensure that students have activated relevant knowledge. Using the framework of ACT, we can see that knowledge activation provides more and stronger links for embedding new declarative and procedural knowledge within existing networks. As teachers, we need to take maximum advantage of the relationship between prior and new knowledge. Stimulating students' recall of related information, providing analogies and schema activation, and probing both intellectual and emotional reactions to materials and activities are only a few of many ways in which what students already know can be acknowledged and used to improve instruction.

3. *Help students organize new information into meaningful "chunks."* As shown in chapter 2, the research on STM/working memory highlighted our ability through organization to increase the size of information "chunks" and so hold more information in memory. If anything, organization plays an even more critical role in LTM. Organizing and linking information makes units of memory larger and more meaningful. When students are helped to discover relationships, to group related concepts and ideas, and to see how information can be used in their lives, comprehension increases and recall is enhanced.

4. *Aid students in proceduralizing their knowledge and linking it to conditional knowledge.* A frequent challenge to educators is to make knowledge useful for students. Although it is important that we build students' declarative knowledge, particularly organized declarative knowledge, we usually want to go well beyond this. We hope the knowledge that students acquire will become a vital, working part of their lives. In J. R. Anderson's view (1993), declarative knowledge needs to be **proceduralized,** which is a function of practice. Solving mathematics problems is an example. Once a student knows the steps to solving a problem (the knowledge is proceduralized) and understands when and where it can be used (conditional knowledge), it can be applied rapidly and reliably across a variety of situations. We can help students develop working knowledge by providing experiences in which they use information to solve real-life problems, or practice and integrate their skills in complex performances.

5. *Provide opportunities for students to use both verbal and imaginal coding.* Most classroom transactions are verbal: Teachers and students spend their days talking, listening, reading, and sometimes writing. Images—generated by pictures, touch, activities, and imagination—are less often the focus of classroom processes. When we exclude images, we may be neglecting some of the most important goals for learning. Imagery can be a powerful tool for increasing memorability of information that students need to acquire, as Paivio and others have shown. It also is a key to creative imagination.

Summary

Memory is one of the most important concerns of cognitive psychologists, playing a major role in two of our cognitive themes in education: that learning is a constructive process and that mental structures organize memory and guide thought. The earliest scientific studies of memory were experimental investigations of rote learning and set the course of memory research for most of the 20th century. This changed with the advent of cognitive psychology, as memory theorists made immense strides in describing the encoding, storage, and retrieval of meaningful information in real-life settings.

The basic or modal model of memory, which was introduced in chapter 2, portrays memory as composed of three major components: sensory memory, STM or working memory, and LTM. LTM, the focus of this chapter, is the permanent repository for information and seems to have virtually unlimited capacity. LTM represents the prior knowledge that is used for constructing much of our learning. As cognitive theorists have shifted to studying meaningful learning, they have made distinctions that are useful for educators. These include contrasts between declarative and procedural knowledge, episodic and semantic memory, implicit and explicit memory, and verbal and imaginal representation. They also have defined mental structures and cognitive units—such as concepts, propositions, schemata, productions, and scripts—that organize memory and guide thought. These units are the building blocks in comprehensive models of memory, such as Anderson's ACT model.

Early models of memory that were based on a computer metaphor have evolved, as computer science itself has, from a stepwise, serial processing-type model to a more brainlike connectionist model. The connectionist model offers a closer match to aspects of human cognition, especially learning, and may offer new ways to enhance our students' abilities to learn and to recall and use their knowledge.

Suggested Readings

Anderson, J. R. (1993). Problem solving and learning. *American Psychologist, 48,* 35–44.

This short article is a very readable description of J. R. Anderson's ACT model (ACT* version) and its potential for understanding the phenomenon of problem solving.

Anderson, J. R., & Matessa, M. (1997). A production system theory of serial memory. *Psychological Review, 104,* 728–748.

This review article provides a good description of the ACT-R (adaptive character of thought-rational) version of J. R. Anderson's theory and applies it to an area long studied by memory researchers, serial list learning (e.g., learning to say items in a list in order).

Although somewhat technical, the review nicely describes how the assumptions and procedures of a theoretical perspective are applied to a specific domain of memory research.

Tulving, E. (2002). Episodic memory: from mind to brain. *Annual Review of Psychology, 53,* 1–25.

This review article gives an excellent, easily understandable overview of episodic memory, how it has changed since its inception, criticisms of it, and new supporting evidence of its existence as a separate memory system. The new evidence provided by memory-impaired patients and the recent work in neuroimaging is intriguing.

Encoding Processes

IN CHAPTER 2, we reviewed perception, attention, and working memory and noted how all three were powerfully affected by people's knowledge of the world. In chapter 3, we introduced the topic of long-term memory and how knowledge is stored. The topic of this chapter is the process involved in placing information into long-term memory. This process usually is referred to as *encoding* (see Figure 2-1). As you might expect, encoding has a major impact on other cognitive processes, such as *storage* (how information is kept in memory) and *retrieval* (how information is retrieved from memory). Chapter 5 addresses retrieval and its relationship to encoding and storage. In this chapter, we focus on strategies that help us encode information.

Not all of the information we want to learn is the same. Some is straightforward, such as the capital of Nebraska, the atomic structure of hydrogen, the names of the oceans, or even the quadratic formula. But much of what we encounter and need to learn is more complex and inferential. For example, if you are using this text as part of a course, you could be expected to read this chapter and take a test on it. You might need to know specific facts, technical terms, and perhaps some dates. More important, however, is understanding what the chapter means in both a theoretical and an applied sense. Presumably, a theory of encoding is presented in this chapter. Your task is to understand this theory, identify component parts of it, understand the relationships among these parts, and apply them to your everyday and professional life.

Traditionally, psychologists have separated simpler from more complex forms of learning (Bransford, Brown, & Cocking, 2000; Sternberg & Ben-Zeev, 2001). Learning, say, to link states with their capitals or Civil War battles with their dates does, in fact, seem quite different than explaining why state capitals often are not located in major cities or arguing whether social or economic factors were more important in causing the Civil War. The former examples seem more a matter of associating terms and acquiring them through rehearsal, whereas the latter involve understanding, reasoning, and critical thinking.

Much early research on cognitive strategies involved experimental studies of the simpler kinds of learning and identifying strategies students could use to better encode and retrieve information. Most applications of cognitive theory, however, have tended to focus on helping students better *understand* concepts and ideas and use them to reason and solve problems. Strategies for acquiring simple information actually turn out to be quite useful in helping students master more complex cognitive tasks, but need to be combined and used thoughtfully.

The way we have organized the chapter, therefore, is in three parts. In the first part, we discuss research-based strategies that have proven to be very useful in encoding and making simpler kinds of information more memorable. In the second part, we focus on the role of meaning in students' understanding and using more complex kinds of information. Our third section begins our discussion of conditional knowledge in earnest. There we introduce the concept of *metacognition*—the knowledge that students have about their own thought processes. What we will see is that the more students are aware of their own cognitive processes and strategic in encoding information, the more likely they will be to use what they learn. A final section summarizes implications for instruction.

Encoding Simple Information

How we encode to-be-remembered information makes a huge difference in how well we remember it. One very important dimension of encoding is rehearsal. As a means of examining rehearsal more closely, let's look at two sixth graders studying for a spelling test. For our purposes, let's assume that the two children are of equal ability, save for how they rehearse the spelling words. Susan starts at the top of the list, reads the first word, and spells it to herself over and over *("familiar—f, a, m, i . . .")*. She does this six times for each of the 25 words on the list and then sets the list aside. Perlita also starts by reading the first word on the list, but she rehearses the information differently by breaking the words into smaller words and syllables she already knows how to spell *("familiar—fam, i, liar*. That's *fam—f, a, m; i—I,* and *liar—l, i, a, r")*. Perlita also cycles through her list six times for each word.

If we give Susan and Perlita a test of the spelling words after they finish studying, the odds are extremely good that Perlita will obtain a higher score than Susan. The reason for this difference is obvious to us, if not to the sixth graders: The way the information was rehearsed influenced its memorability.

Typically, the kind of rehearsal Susan engaged in is called **maintenance rehearsal** (Craik, 1979). Maintenance rehearsal is the direct recycling of information in order to keep it active in short-term memory. It is the sort of rehearsal we perform when we look up a telephone number and want to retain it just long enough to dial the number (e.g., repeating 555–2225 over and over until the number is dialed). The results of such maintenance rehearsal seldom last long (McKeown & Curtis, 1987). For example, have you ever repeated a telephone number to yourself until you dialed it, obtained a busy signal, and then had to look up the number two minutes later to call again?

Several studies have examined maintenance rehearsal (e.g., Schweickert & Boruff, 1986). In general, it seems that it is highly efficient for retaining information for a short time without taxing a person's cognitive resources. For example, you can cycle 555–2225 over and over while looking for a pencil and a pad of paper, picking up the telephone, and thinking about what you are going to say once you reach the person at 555–2225. Maintenance rehearsal also can enhance long-term memory (Glenberg, Smith, & Green, 1977), but it is quite effortful and inefficient.

In contrast with maintenance rehearsal is **elaborative rehearsal.** Elaborative rehearsal is any form of rehearsal in which the to-be-remembered information is related to other information (Craik & Lockhart, 1986). Later in this chapter, we discuss *levels of processing,* which refers to the ways information can be elaborated. In terms of the levels-of-processing framework, elaborative rehearsal amounts to deeper or more elaborate encoding activities, whereas maintenance rehearsal can be seen as shallow encoding.

Perlita's rehearsal of the spelling words is a clear example of elaborative rehearsal. Rather than merely recycle the spelling words over and over, she broke them into components and elaborated (related) the to-be-remembered information to what she already knew. In contrast with Susan's, Perlita's encoding activities are much more likely to lead to high levels of recall.

Another example of elaborative rehearsal in the learning of spelling words can be seen in how the fourth-grade daughter of one of the authors learned to spell *respectfully*. While getting ready to study her spelling, she heard an old rock song in which the word *respect* is spelled out in the lyrics to a very strong beat. Later, when her father walked by, the fourth grader had her spelling list turned out of sight and was mimicking the singer's lyric line: *r, e, s, p, e, c, t, fully*.

Research suggests that elaborative rehearsal is far superior to maintenance rehearsal for long-term recall but that it tends to use considerably more of a person's cognitive resources than maintenance rehearsal (Craik, 1979). It also suggests that maintenance and elaborative rehearsal need to be thought of as representing opposite ends on a continuum of rehearsal. At one extreme of the continuum would be the minimal processing needed to repeat a term over and over; at the other end would be processing activities in which the to-be-learned information was linked with several bits of information already in memory.

One implication of research on rehearsal is that different types of rehearsal are appropriate for different tasks. When long-term memory is desired (e.g., when a student will be tested over content or when the information will be important for later understandings), some form of elaborative rehearsal should be employed. As you might suspect, many encoding strategies employ elaborative rehearsal, and we review several of them in the next few pages.

Mediation

One of the simplest elaborative encoding strategies is **mediation.** Mediation involves tying difficult-to-remember items to something more meaningful. The original research on mediation in memory was based on the learning of paired nonsense syllables (e.g., BOZ and BUH). Although we hope none of what we teach is at the level of nonsense syllables, the strategy has some implications for instruction.

In early research on mediation (Montague, Adams, & Kiess, 1966), it became apparent that subjects who used mediators in committing pairs of nonsense syllables to memory outperformed subjects who used no mediators; that is, when subjects could devise a mediator such as *race car* when faced with a pair of nonsense syllables (e.g., *RIS-KIR*), they were able to tie their memory for the meaningless information to something meaningful and greatly ease their memory task.

Although mediation is a very simple and easily learned technique to enhance memory for a limited range of information, it is congruent with the theme of this chapter; that is, what people do with to-be-learned information determines how it will be remembered. Even at its simplest levels, learning proceeds better as a constructive than as a receptive process. Mediation results in deeper, more elaborate encoding than simple repetition of new content.

Imagery

Our emphasis up to this point has been on the encoding of verbal information. One powerful adjunct to verbal encoding is the use of imagery. (See chapter 3 for a discussion of imagery and Paivio's dual coding theory.) Consider the fourth grader who conjures up an image of an emperor (complete with rich robes, a crown, and a jewel-encrusted scepter) when trying to learn the meaning of the word *czar*. Finally, think about the chemistry student who shuts her eyes and visualizes a three-dimensional picture of the bromination of benzene as she studies for a quiz. In each of these examples, imagery is an important part of encoding information.

As shown in chapter 3, imagery usually leads to better memory performance. Some provisos should be considered, however, when we discuss the facilitative effects of imagery. One is the imagery value of various to-be-learned materials. For example, the word *car* much more easily leads to an image than does, say, the word *truth*. Similarly, the word *turban* leads easily to a clear picture, whereas the word *freedom* does not.

Easily imaged words tend to be remembered more readily than hard-to-image words, even in the absence of instructions to use imagery (Paivio, 1986a, 1986b). When subjects are instructed to use imagery, the difference is even more pronounced. Even subjects' memory for nonsense syllables is enhanced when they use imagery in learning.

Imagery value should not be thought of as being restricted to individual words (Paivio, 1986a, 1986b). The idea can be extended to the imagery value of concepts (e.g., compare internal combustion to entropy), people (e.g., compare Theodore Roosevelt with Calvin Coolidge), and whole segments of information (e.g., compare *Macbeth* with 99 percent of the situation comedies ever produced). Simply, some sets of information are easier to image than others.

A second issue to be considered when we discuss imagery is the likelihood of individual differences among students in their ability to image information (Ahsen, 1987; Scruggs, Mastropieri, McLoone, Levin, & Morrison, 1987). Even though very little research has been conducted on this question, results suggest that some students are better able to employ imagery than others and that these differences seem to lead to differences in memory performance. Unfortunately, no evidence points to whether ability to image is learned or can be improved with practice. Still, even students who score very low on measures of ability to image do show improved memory performance when they employ imagery (Scruggs et al., 1987).

A third factor associated with imagery concerns the nature of the images that people conjure up. Many memory experts have argued that the best images are bizarre, colorful, and strange. For example, if you wanted to remember that one of J. P. Morgan's characteristics was greed, you could imagine J. P. Morgan as a hog wearing a business suit with a watch fob, chomping on a large black cigar, and fighting with other industrialists for a share of the spoils. Similarly, if you wanted to remember that the word *peduncle* refers to the stem bearing a flower, you could imagine a garish flower being carried by its stalk with the word *peduncle* pictured on each side of the stalk.

Research on the value of bizarre imagery, however, has been inconclusive. Early work (e.g., Collyer, Jonides, & Bevan, 1972) sometimes found no advantage for bizarre imagery, as opposed to mundane imagery (e.g., trying to remember *peduncle* by picturing a daisy) and sometimes found it to be valuable (Furst, 1954). Studies reporting conflicting findings have continued to appear (e.g., Clark & Paivio, 1991).

By itself, imagery has considerable value in helping make information memorable. In conjunction with a group of techniques for enhancing memory called *mnemonics,* it can be a powerful tool for improving memory performance.

Mnemonics

Mnemonics (nih-MAH-niks) are memory strategies that help people remember information. Typically, mnemonics involve pairing to-be-learned information with well-learned information in order to make the new information more memorable. Mnemonics help us learn new information by making it easier to elaborate, chunk, or retrieve it from memory.

Mnemonic techniques include the use of rhymes ("*i* before *e* except after *c*"), sayings ("thirty days has September, April, June, and November"), gestures (the "right-hand rule" in physics is a mnemonic for determining the flow of a magnetic field around an electrical current—merely put the thumb of the right hand in the direction of the current and the curl of the fingers around the conductor will show the direction of the magnetic field), and imagery. Teachers often use mnemonics as a part of their instruction (Higbee & Kunihira, 1985). For example, music teachers may instruct students in the use of "Every Good Boy Does Fine" to help them remember the lines of the treble clef and "FACE" to remember the spaces. Students report that they often use mnemonics without being instructed to do so (Schneider & Pressley, 1997). As might be expected, some mnemonics are more effective than others (Levin, 1993), and different mnemonics seem especially suited to specific forms of learning. In the remainder of this section, we examine several mnemonic techniques and see how they may be implemented in instruction.

The Peg Method   In the **peg method,** students memorize a series of "pegs" on which to-be-learned information can be "hung" one item at a time. The pegs can be any well-learned set of items, but the most popular approach involves the use of a very simple rhyme.

> One is a bun.
>
> Two is a shoe.
>
> Three is a tree.
>
> Four is a door.
>
> Five is a hive.
>
> Six is sticks.
>
> Seven is heaven.
>
> Eight is a gate.
>
> Nine is a pine.
>
> Ten is a hen.

Students who have mastered this rhyme can use it to learn lists of items, such as the names of authors, politicians, or terms in a social studies course. The technique is simple and effective. Its use can be seen, for example, in the learning of the following grocery list: pickles, bread, milk, oranges, and lightbulbs.

If you actually were to use the rhyme, the first step is to construct a visual image of the first thing on the to-be-learned list interacting with the object named in the first line of the rhyme. For instance, to remember pickles, we could imagine a very large pickle stuffed into the center of a bun. Next, a loaf of bread could be imagined shoved into a shoe as it sits in the closet. The third item, milk, could be visualized as a milk tree—a large tree with quarts of milk, rather than fruit, hanging from it. Oranges could be remembered by picturing the knob of the door to be an orange, and when the door is opened, it opens into a closet filled with oranges that then fall out all over the person opening the door and roll across the floor. Finally, lightbulbs readily could be seen as interacting with a beehive, such as picturing a beehive with a flashing lightbulb on its top, with additional lightbulbs lighting a doorway to the hive.

After each item on the list has been carefully imagined interacting with the corresponding item in the rhyme, the learner is finished until time for recall. At recall, the learner simply recites the rhyme. Each image is retrieved as the recitation proceeds, and so recall of the list follows.

When it is well learned, the peg method has been shown to be effective with word lists of various sorts (Bugelski, Kidd, & Segmen, 1968). It also has been shown to be helpful in learning written directions (Glover, Harvey, & Corkill, 1988) and learning steps in complex procedures (Glover, Timme, Deyloff, Rogers, & Dinnel, 1987). Interestingly, the peg method can be used over and over without losing its effectiveness. It is not clear why, but previous uses of the peg method (e.g., the grocery list we gave) do not seem to diminish the effectiveness of the system when it is reused.

The Method of Loci   One of the best-known mnemonic procedures dates back to the ancient Greeks. According to Bower (1970) and Schacter (1996b), the **method of loci** got its name from an event where the poet Simonides, attending a banquet, was called outside. While Simonides was outside, the roof of the banquet hall collapsed, killing everyone left inside. The disaster was especially cruel because the bodies were so badly mangled that not even the victims' loved ones could identify them. Simonides, however, was able to remember each person on the basis of where the person sat at the banquet table. Hence, the name "method of loci" came from Simonides's use of location to recall information.

To use the method of loci to learn new information, a very imaginable location, such as one's home or the path one walks to school, must be learned flawlessly. The location then is practiced so that the person can easily imagine various "drops" in the location, such as the sofa, coffee table, window, television, and armchair in a living room. These drops must be learned such that they are recalled in exactly the same order each time.

Once the location and its drops have been overlearned, the system is ready for use as a mnemonic. Let's suppose a student must recall five famous poets: Spenser, Keats, Sand, Dickinson, and Eliott. We could imagine Spenser sitting on the sofa, Keats with his boots propped up on the coffee table, Sand looking out the window, Dickinson tuning the television, and Eliott sitting in the armchair. If our list were longer, we could continue to place people in locations until we completed the list.

At the time of recall, we would take our mental walk back through the location, and each drop would lead to the image of the to-be-remembered person. As with the peg method, the method of loci can be used over and over without losing its effectiveness. It also can be employed to help students remember a wide variety of information. Both methods, however, exact a price—the effort required to learn the original "base" on which the mnemonic depends. Students sometimes balk at giving the effort needed to develop one of these mnemonics, but they almost always report that the effort was well worth it after they begin using them (Kilpatrick, 1985).

The Link Method   Relatively little research has been done on the link method. Memory experts, however, report using it (Neisser, 1982), and it has the advantage over the method of loci and the peg method of not needing an external system or previously learned set of materials.

In the **link method,** which is best suited for learning lists of things, the student forms an image for each item in a list of things to be learned. Each image is pictured as *interacting* with the next item on the list so that all of the items are linked in imagination. For example, if a student needed to remember to bring her homework, lab notebook, chemistry text, goggles, lab apron, and pencil to class tomorrow, she could imagine a scene in which the homework papers were tucked inside the lab notebook. The lab notebook then could be placed into the textbook, with her goggles stretched around it. Next, the total package could be wrapped up in the lab apron, with the ties of the apron wrapped around a pencil to make a nice bow. The next morning, when she attempted to recall what she must take to class, she would recall the image and mentally unwrap it. The interactive image makes it probable that recall of any item on the list will cue recall of the others.

Stories   Another simple mnemonic is the use of **stories** constructed from a list of words to be remembered. In this method, the to-be-learned words in a list are put together in a story such that the to-be-learned words are highlighted. Then, at recall, the story is remembered and the to-be-remembered words are plucked from the story.

For example, let's suppose a student is expected to remember to bring scissors, a ruler, a compass, a protractor, and a sharp pencil to school. Our student could construct the following story to help her or him remember these items: "The king drew a *pencil* line with his *ruler* before he cut the line with *scissors*. Then he measured an angle with a *protractor* and marked the point with a *compass*."

The story method is simple but effective. An early study by Bower and Clark (1969) gave experimental subjects in two conditions 12 lists of 10 words each. The subjects in one condition were asked merely to learn the words in each list, as they would be tested over the words at a later point. Subjects in the other condition, however, were asked to construct stories around each list of 10 words. Holding study time equal in the two conditions, Bower and Clark tested for recall after each list was presented and found no difference in recall between the two conditions. When they tested subjects for recall of all 120 words on completion of the entire experiment, however, there was a very large difference indeed—subjects in the story condition recalled 93 percent of the words, whereas subjects in the control condition recalled only 13 percent.

The First-Letter Method   Among all mnemonics, the one that students most often report using spontaneously is the **first-letter method** (Boltwood & Blick, 1978). This method is similar to the story mnemonic, except it involves using the first letters of to-be-learned words to construct acronyms or words. These acronyms or words then function as the mnemonics. At recall, students recall the acronym and then, using its letters, recall the items on the list.

For example, let's suppose a high school student is trying to remember that borax is made of boron, oxygen, and sodium. The student could take the first letter of each component and construct a word, *bos,* as a mnemonic. Then, when she or he attempts to recall the constituents of borax on a test, she or he would remember the word *bos* and generate the constituents from the first letters. Similarly, if we asked you to remember a grocery list consisting of cheese, ham, eggs, radishes, razor blades, and yogurt, the word *cherry* could be constructed from the first letter of each item on the list. Then, when you visit the store, if you remember the mnemonic *cherry,* you should be able to use the letters in the word to reconstruct the items in your list.

As straightforward as their appeal might be, the results of research on first-letter mnemonics have been mixed (Boltwood & Blick, 1978; Carlson, Zimmer, & Glover, 1981). On the one hand, students who are already familiar with their use do seem to benefit from the strategy. On the other hand, students who have not previously used first-letter mnemonics on their own seem to receive little benefit from using the procedure (Carlson et al., 1981). To this point, however, it is difficult to draw conclusions about first-letter mnemonics because of the sparsity of research on the technique. It would seem that students who use the procedure should be encouraged to continue, but there is no compelling evidence for teaching the method.

The Keyword Method   Of all the mnemonic techniques, probably the most flexible and powerful is the **keyword method** (Carney & Levin, 2000; Levin, 1993). This method was developed originally to facilitate vocabulary acquisition, but it has many other uses. As in the link method, the method of loci, and the peg method, imagery is critical to the effectiveness of the keyword method. The use of imagery in the keyword method, however, varies considerably from how imagery is used in the other techniques.

The keyword mnemonic consists of two separate stages: an acoustic link and an imagery link. In vocabulary learning, for example, the first stage—the acoustic link—requires the identification of a "keyword." The keyword sounds like a part of the to-be-learned vocabulary word and furnishes the acoustic link necessary to the method. The second stage—the imagery link—requires the learner to imagine a visual image of the keyword interacting with the meaning of the to-be-learned vocabulary word. At the time of recall, the original vocabulary word on a test should evoke the interactive image in memory, which will allow for recall of the word's meaning.

An example will clarify these stages. Let's suppose a sixth grader has the assignment of learning 10 vocabulary words in a language arts unit. Among these words is *captivate*. Although our sixth grader has a fine vocabulary, *captivate* is not in it. So he decides to use the keyword method to help remember this word. First, he searches for a keyword within the to-be-learned word and settles on *cap,* which he can picture readily in imagination. He then links his keyword with an image—in this case, his Uncle Bill, who always wears a cap and, whenever he visits, holds everyone's attention with outrageous stories. So the student's image linked with the word's meaning is of his Uncle Bill captivating him with a story. If all goes well, when he has his test and sees the word *captivate,* he will remember his keyword, *cap,* and remember his image of Uncle Bill and the word's meaning.

The keyword method does not depend on a perfect match of the keyword with the vocabulary word. For example, the word *exiguous* does not contain an easily located keyword. With a little Kentucky windage worked in, however, the keyword *exit* (rather than *exig*) can be selected. Then, if you imagine an extremely tiny exit (ours is in a darkened movie theater with red neon letters spelling out *exit* on a mouse-sized sign above it), you should have a workable interactive image. Next time you see *exiguous,* find the *exig* or *exit* and recall the image of the miniature exit. This should be all you need to remember that exiguous means "small" or "meager."

The keyword method was developed originally for the acquisition of foreign-language vocabulary (Atkinson, 1975). Consider, for example, the Spanish word *caballo,* which means "horse." The keyword *ball* can be picked out easily, and an image of a horse balancing on a ball readily comes to mind. Alternatively, the keyword *cab* could be chosen, and the interactive image could be of a horse driving a cab on Chicago's Wabash Avenue.

Since 1975, a very large amount of research has been done on the keyword method. In general, results have been positive among students of all ages (J. R. Levin, 1986, 1993; Pressley, Levin, & Delaney, 1982) and across several languages (e.g., Atkinson & Raugh, 1975; Pressley, 1977); the keyword method has been exceptionally effective in improving the learning of students with mild retardation and learning disabilities (Mastropieri & Scruggs, 1989). The method also has been an effective means of enhancing memory for facts other than vocabulary (Levin, 1993), for increasing learning from text (Mastropieri & Scruggs, 1989), and even for matching artists with their paintings (Carney & Levin, 2000)

Even though study after study has shown the benefits of the keyword method, recommendations for its use have not yet made their way into most teaching-method textbooks. The method is easy to teach and readily learned by even the youngest children, and students generally enjoy using it. Because students generate their own keywords and images, probably the major challenge for teachers is to help students learn to use the keyword method flexibly and to apply it to new situations (Levin, 1993).

Summary of Mnemonics   Mnemonics are rhymes, sayings, and other procedures designed to make new material memorable. They help create more elaborate encoding of new materials and strong memory traces. The peg method and the method of loci both depend on a well-learned base to which to-be-learned information is related. The link and story methods put to-be-learned items together in a list and rely on the recall of the overall image or story to facilitate recall. The first-letter mnemonic chains items together by forming a word or acronym from the first letters of the words in a to-be-learned list. The most powerful and flexible mnemonic is the keyword method, which employs interactive imagery to form an acoustic and a visual link.

Encoding More Complex Information

Even though mnemonics have a relatively broad range of applications, their use generally has been limited to learning lists of facts, sets of vocabulary items, groups of ideas, or steps in a skill (although see Carney & Levin, 2000). Many of our instructional goals are much broader in scope, such as helping students learn about John Steinbeck's portrayal of human nature, Isaac Newton's laws of physics, or American foreign policy in the 1990s. Cognitive psychologists have given a great deal of thought to how students' encoding of such complex materials can be facilitated, and a general consensus has been emerging during the past decade.

In the following sections, we discuss ways students can elaborate and enrich complex information. Consistent with a key theme of this text, the point is that effective learning needs to be an active, not a receptive process. The sheer bulk of information learners now need to cope with—whether from texts, the internet, or a teacher's presentation—requires them to focus selectively on what is most important, grasp its meaning, make high-level inferences across main ideas, and represent this information in long-term memory. Of course, meaning may be constructed in many ways and effective learners use a variety of approaches to organize, enrich, and add to new information. Here, we review three general frameworks and associated methods for improving active learning: schema activation, guided questioning, and levels of processing.

Schema Activation

Schema activation refers to various methods designed to activate students' relevant knowledge prior to a learning activity (Pearson, 1984). For instance, before a lesson on internal combustion engines, seventh-grade students can be asked to describe the characteristics of their parents' cars or lawn mowers, their own model cars or airplanes, and city buses in order to activate relevant concepts and schemata. Similarly, high school students preparing for a lesson on the Holocaust can be asked to talk about their own experiences with prejudice, racism, and "scapegoating" in order to activate relevant schemata. Fourth-grade students, as another example, can be led in a discussion of various animals they have seen in their neighborhood to introduce a lesson on the characteristics of mammals. The central idea underlying schema activation is that new knowledge always builds on prior knowledge; that is, a foundation of well-understood information will help students comprehend new information and will guide their thinking about the new topic.

Methods using the idea of schema activation are based on the assumption that students at any age will have some relevant knowledge to which new information can be related. A class of fourth graders we know, for example, began to learn about heat conduction and the relationship of a substance's density to its heat conductivity by first thinking of examples of objects that carried heat (e.g., the handle of a metal frying pan, the outside-facing wall of a room on a cold day, and the end of a burning match) and then doing a simple but carefully supervised experiment in which several rods of different materials (e.g., iron, glass, and wood) but of the same length and diameter were put into a flame. The students then discussed why some rods became warm rapidly, whereas others seemed to remain cool, and related the results of the experiment to their own experiences. (One girl camped out frequently and knew that a metal frying pan over a fire very quickly would become too hot to touch, whereas even a burning stick would remain comfortable to the touch at the nonburning end. One boy noted how his metal cup would burn his lips when it was filled with hot chocolate but the same hot chocolate in a ceramic cup would not make the cup too hot.)

With their own schemata for "heat conduction" presumably activated, the students weighed the various rods on a balance and recorded the masses, noting next to each whether it had become hot rapidly or slowly. Then, the students were asked to guess why some of the rods conducted heat more readily than others. Finally, the teacher gave a brief lesson about density, heat conduction, and the relationship of the two.

The relationship of density to heat conduction is, of course, a fairly sophisticated concept that many adults do not clearly understand. By carefully activating her students' relevant schemata, however, the teacher in our example was able to help her students learn and remember a difficult concept.

Schema activation is a general procedure for enhancing students' encoding of new information by activating their prior knowledge. It can involve having students describe examples from their experiences, perform experiments, review previous learning, or use the context in which new material is presented (Pearson, 1984). Overall, any teaching procedure that helps students form conceptual bridges between what they already know and what they are to learn can be considered a form of schema activation.

Guided Questioning

Asking and answering questions about a text or teacher-presented information can greatly improve comprehension (see King, 1992, and Rosenshine, Meister, & Chapman, 1996, for reviews), especially when those questions prompt students to think about and discuss material in specific ways, such as comparing and contrasting, inferring cause and effect, evaluating ideas, explaining, and justifying (King, 1994; King, Staffieri, & Adelgais, 1998). Comprehension presumably improves because asking and answering such questions helps learners build elaborated and integrated links among the ideas in the materials that make their mental representations more durable and provide more cues for recall (King & Rosenshine, 1993). In research by King and her associates (King, 1994; King & Rosenshine, 1993), for example, students were taught a procedure called **guided peer questioning.** Working in pairs, students were trained both to ask and answer specific thought-provoking questions on the material to be learned (e.g., "What causes . . . ?", "What could happen if . . .", and "How does . . . tie in with what we learned before?"). When they used this procedure, their learning was significantly enhanced. As King et al. (1998) pointed out, this approach to structuring peer interaction is successful because it ". . . ensures that partners carry out specific cognitive activities known to promote learning, such as rehearsing orally, accessing prior knowledge, making connections among ideas, elaborating ideas, assessing accuracy of responses, and monitoring metacognitively" (p. 135). In general, teaching students to generate their own questions before or after reading is likely to produce favorable learning outcomes (Palincsar & Brown, 1984; Raphael & McKinney, 1983; see also chapter 12). One example is when students generate questions that can be answered only by making inferences across the text or by using prior knowledge. For example, **text-explicit questions** can be answered by information presented explicitly within one sentence in the text (Raphael & McKinney, 1983). **Text-implicit questions** can be answered by information from the text that occurs across two or more sentences; in other words, an inference is required. **Script-implicit questions** require answers that depend, in part, on text-implicit inferences plus information from prior knowledge that was not included in the text. Generating and answering text- and script-implicit questions facilitates comprehension significantly.

Evidence also suggests that answering questions while performing a task is more useful than answering questions while learning about a task (Fishbein, Eckart, Lauver, Van Leeuwen, & Langmeyer, 1990). This may occur because students fail to integrate information completely or are not fully prepared for inference-type questions until they actually attempt to perform the task. Questions asked during performance appear to be most effective when they focus on salient properties of problem solving. King (1991) found that students trained to answer guided questions during problem solving solved problems more accurately, asked more strategic questions, and provided more elaborated explanations of their performance than a control group.

Levels of Processing

A third general framework for thinking about how different kinds of encoding activities influence memory was developed by Craik and Lockhart (1972). Reacting to the mechanistic nature of computer models of human memory and providing an early argument for a constructivist view of learning, Craik and Lockhart argued that memory depends on what learners do as they encode new information (see also Jenkins, 1974).

In the **levels of processing** view, memory for new information is seen as a by-product of the learner's perceptual and cognitive analyses performed on incoming information. On the one hand, if the semantic base or meaning of the new information is the focus of processing, then the information will be stored in a semantic memory code and will be well-remembered. On the other hand, if only superficial or surface aspects of the new information are analyzed, the information will be less well-remembered. In Craik and Lockhart's terms, memory depends on *depth* of processing. *Deep processing* is seen as that processing centered on meaning. *Shallow processing* refers to keying on superficial aspects of new material.

These two levels of processing may be seen in two common classroom assignments. In the first, students are asked to underline a set of vocabulary words in a brief essay. In the second, students are asked to read the same essay and be prepared to tell the class about it in their own words. If the students follow directions, the first assignment is a clear example of shallow processing; all they have to do is find the words in the essay and underline them. To perform this task, students do not have to think about the meaning of the essay and perhaps not even with the meaning of the words. Not surprisingly, if we tested these students for their understanding of the contents of the essay, the odds are they would remember relatively little.

In contrast, if the students who were asked to explain the essay to their classmates followed instructions, we would likely see a very different outcome. Putting an essay into one's own words requires thinking about the meaning of the content. In so doing, the students would have had to carefully analyze and comprehend the material. If we were to surprise these students with a test measuring their understanding of the essay, they almost certainly would remember far more of its contents than could the group that underlined vocabulary words.

It can be argued that the two assignments described above were given for different instructional purposes. In fact, the vocabulary word group might remember more vocabulary words (but probably not their meanings) than the group asked to read and explain the materials. In this instance, students' recall would be appropriate to the type of processing in which they engaged (see Moeser, 1983), a topic we examine in more detail a bit later. In any event, students in the underlining group engaged in an activity almost guaranteed not to result in memory for the essay.

Another example of levels of processing can be seen in an *incidental learning paradigm* (one in which individuals are not directed to learn material but in which their memory for that material is unexpectedly tested). Let's suppose that one group of students is asked to count the number of *i*'s in a list of words (e.g., "festive," "colic," and "delight"), and another group is asked to rate the pleasantness of the same words on a scale from 1 to 5. If, after both groups finish their tasks, we give them a surprise test and ask them to recall as many words on the list as possible, the probability is very high that the group that rated the pleasantness of the words will recall far more than the group that counted the number of *i*'s. The reason for this difference in performance is quite simple: Rating the pleasantness of words requires students to think about the meanings. In contrast, counting the number of *i*'s merely requires a superficial analysis (see Hyde & Jenkins, 1969).

The levels-of-processing framework is intuitively appealing and has led to a great deal of research emphasizing educationally relevant applications (see Andre, 1987b, for an extensive review). The "levels" position, however, has been criticized on the grounds of not having an independent measure of "depth" and the apparent circularity of the depth formulation (Baddeley, 1978; Loftus, Green, & Smith, 1980; Nelson, 1977; Postman, Thompkins, & Gray, 1978); that is, saying that something is well remembered because it was deeply processed does not tell us how we may ensure deep processing in students.

In response to these criticisms, Craik and his associates developed two variants of their original "levels" perspective: distinctiveness of encoding (Jacoby & Craik, 1979; Jacoby, Craik, & Begg, 1979) and elaboration of encoding (e.g., Craik & Tulving, 1975). By the late 1980s, the elaboration position clearly was dominant (see Walker, 1986, for a critical discussion), but both are useful in considering the applications of the levels framework. We examine each of these positions next, as well as an alternative position offered by Bransford and his associates.

Distinctiveness of Encoding   The **distinctiveness of encoding** position states that the memorability of information is determined, at least in part, by its distinctiveness (Jacoby & Craik, 1979; Jacoby et al., 1979). In a series of experiments in which distinctiveness was defined by the difficulty of decisions required of students during various learning episodes (more difficult decisions were equated with more distinctive encoding), Jacoby et al. (1979) found that materials requiring more difficult decisions at the time of encoding were better recalled than materials requiring less difficult decisions.

The experiments conducted by Jacoby et al. led to a series of studies focusing on distinctiveness of encoding in reading and mastering various learning tasks (Benton, Glover, Monkowski, & Shaughnessy, 1983; Glover, Bruning, & Plake, 1982; Glover, Plake, & Zimmer, 1982). These studies were designed to determine how students' decision making during reading affected recall and to examine the possibility that an independent means of specifying depth of processing (or, in this case, distinctiveness) could be developed. In general, requiring students to make decisions about what they read leads to greater recall than when no decisions are required. Also, when students were asked to make more difficult decisions, they recalled more than if their decisions were easier. In other words, as students make more complex and difficult decisions during encoding, they remember the content better.

Elaboration of Processing   The **elaboration of processing** perspective was outlined first by Craik and Tulving (1975) and specified further by J. R. Anderson and Reder (1979), J. R. Anderson (1983a), and Walker (1986). This position was articulated most clearly by Anderson and Reder, who stated the following:

> The basic idea is that a memory episode is encoded as a set of propositions. This set can vary in its richness and redundancy. At the time of recall, only a subset of these propositions will be activated. The richer the original set, the richer will be the subset. Memory for any particular proposition will depend on the subjects' ability to reconstruct it from those propositions that are active. This ability will in turn depend on the richness of the original set and hence the amount of elaboration made at study. (J. R. Anderson & Reder, 1979, p. 388)

Considerable research on the acquisition of educationally relevant material has been performed, showing generally that as the elaborateness of students' encoding of information increases, so does their memory for the content (see McDaniel & Einstein, 1989, for a review). Elaborate processing is not merely reprocessing the same information, but rather it is encoding the same content in different but related ways. For example, in an explanation of how to solve a specific type of problem, students are far more likely to remember the explanation if different examples are given than if the same example merely is restated. Similarly, when students read about a famous person, their ability to recall information about that person is strongly related to the number of details provided (Dinnel & Glover, 1985).

Transfer-Appropriate Processing   Morris, Bransford, and Franks (1977) reacted to the original levels perspective by offering an alternative. In their view, differences in memory are the result of what is contained in various semantic memory codes and whether what is encoded matches or can be transferred to the retrieval context (see Glover, Rankin, Langner, Todero, & Dinnel, 1985, and Moeser, 1983, for extended contrasts of the original levels position with transfer-appropriate processing). From a transfer-appropriate processing perspective, shallow processing leads not to the encoding of, say, the image of the letter *i* if people are seeking the number of *i*'s in a passage. Instead, a semantic memory is produced (e.g., "Forty-three *i*'s were in the passage"), but one that does *not* contain information about the meaning of the content. In Morris et al.'s view, deep processing differs from shallow processing primarily because the semantic memories formed in deep processing contain the meaning of the content that students encounter (e.g., the main idea in a paragraph).

Transfer-appropriate processing is an interesting alternative to the original levels perspective, and it does seem clear that students' memories for to-be-learned information almost inevitably are semantic (see Bransford et al., 1982). For instance, in the example we first used to show the difference between deep and shallow processing, one group of students read to find key words and another group read to be able to explain the contents of the material. In the original levels perspective, differences in memory performance between these two groups are a result of different kinds of memory codes brought about by different levels of analysis. In contrast, transfer-appropriate processing holds that both groups of children form semantic memory codes. The differences in memory are a result of the contents of those memories; the vocabulary group's codes likely would contain little more than some of the words, whereas the "explanation" group's codes would contain information about the topic of the reading passage. Finally, a related development in this area has been the concept of **material-appropriate processing** (see McDaniel & Einstein, 1989). From this point of view, deep or elaborate processing activities depend on what learners do and on the type of material they encounter. In McDaniel and Einstein's view, for example, prose requires different activities for elaborate, deep processing different than does poetry.

Summary of Encoding Processes

In this and the previous sections, we reviewed several frameworks for encoding simpler and more complex information. Rehearsing, categorizing, and using special mnemonics techniques are helpful ways to encode new information that is important but not yet particularly meaningful. As you have seen, many mnemonic techniques rely on distinctive visual images or auditory processes. We also considered the encoding of more complex information. Much of the research conducted in this area is related to the theoretical frameworks of schema activation and levels of processing. Both of these strongly emphasize the importance of what students do while encoding information. To the extent that students are helped to use their prior knowledge and required to deal with the meaning of content, their memories improve. Tasks focusing on superficial or surface aspects of to-be-learned materials are unlikely to result in understanding or long-term recall. Our discussion suggests a variety of ways to encode information at deeper levels. One is to relate new information to background knowledge at the time of encoding, another is ask and answer questions relating to meaning, a third is to increase its distinctiveness and elaborate its meaning as much as possible. Also, we should keep in mind that techniques such as rehearsing information and creating images, although most often researched and discussed earlier in connection with simpler forms of learning, are also applicable for more complex forms of learning. Rehearsal is needed to make processing more automatic and to build stable memories for new vocabulary and concepts. Similarly, the ability to generate images can aid in the understanding of text materials (e.g., Sadowski, Goetz, & Rodriguez, 2000).

      In the next section, we turn our attention to a third aspect of encoding—the role learners themselves play in managing their own encoding, storage, and retrieval. As we have seen, what learners do as they encode information is very important to their understanding and recall. The question we now address is how to help them learn to guide their own cognitive processing effectively. The starting point, it seems, is becoming aware of their own strengths and weaknesses as learners. The goal, however, is having the conditional knowledge needed to use powerful strategies for encoding as needed in any learning situation. Both of these fall under the general framework of metacognition, the knowledge that people have about their own thought processes and how to manage them effectively.

Metacognition: Thinking About Thinking

Metacognition refers to knowledge people have about their own thought processes. A teacher who knows she does not remember names well, for example, and has her new students wear nametags for several days is showing her metacognitive knowledge about her memory. Similarly, a student is revealing her metacognition when she listens to a teacher's explanation of how to solve a problem and takes notes only on those points she thinks will be difficult. Still another example is a student asking a teacher whether an upcoming test will be essay or multiple-choice. Each example shows the person's awareness of her or his own cognition and either shows or hints at a strategy for managing learning based on this awareness (i.e., the teacher having her students wear name tags, the first student taking selective notes, the second student presumably studying somewhat differently based on the kind of test she will have).

Since the term was first coined in the early 1970s, metacognition has been viewed as an essential component of skilled learning because it allows students to control a host of other cognitive skills. In a way, metacognition is like the "mission control" of the cognitive system. It enables students to coordinate the use of extensive knowledge and many separate strategies to accomplish learning goals, just as a real mission control coordinates the myriad of functions necessary for a successful space flight. This does not imply a single place in our minds where metacognition takes place; rather, we simply want to suggest that metacognition is a part of our cognition that controls other lower level cognitive functions, such as perception and attention.

One of the clearest descriptions of metacognition is that by Ann Brown. According to Brown (1980, 1987), metacognition includes two related dimensions: *knowledge of cognition* and *regulation of cognition*. The former refers to what we know about cognition; the latter refers to how we regulate cognition. **Knowledge of cognition** usually is assumed to include three components (Brown, 1987; Jacobs & Paris, 1987). The first involves *declarative* knowledge about ourselves as learners and knowing what factors influence our performance. For example, most adult learners know the limitations of their memory and can plan accordingly for a task based on this knowledge. The second component is *procedural,* knowledge about cognitive strategies. For instance, most older students possess a basic repertoire of useful reading comprehension strategies, such as taking notes, slowing down for important information, skimming unimportant information, using imagery, summarizing main ideas, and using periodic self-testing. The third component is *conditional* knowledge, knowing when or why to use a strategy. One example of this kind of conditional knowledge would be studying differently for essay versus multiple-choice tests; another would be "overrehearsing" the key points that you want to make in a talk, because you realize you may be a bit nervous and distracted.

Ann Brown has argued that knowledge of cognition is usually statable and late developing. Research suggests that these assumptions are reasonable when considering the metacognitive activity of older students but probably not for preadolescents (Flavell, 1992; Garner & Alexander, 1989). For example, research by Paris and colleagues (Paris, Cross, & Lipon, 1984; Paris & Jacobs, 1984) found that instructional training programs enhance the development and use of metacognitive knowledge among elementary-age children, who ordinarily cannot recognize and describe their metacognitive abilities. Studies comparing expert performance among adults, however, are consistent with Brown's assumptions (cf. Glaser & Chi, 1988).

Regulation of cognition also typically is seen as including three components: planning, regulation, and evaluation (Jacobs & Paris, 1987; Kluwe, 1987). *Planning* involves selecting appropriate strategies and allocating resources. Planning frequently includes setting goals, activating relevant background knowledge, and budgeting time. *Regulation* involves monitoring and self-testing skills necessary to control learning. Activities such as making predictions or pausing while reading, strategy sequencing, and selecting appropriate repair strategies also belong in the category. *Evaluation* involves appraising the products and regulatory processes of one's learning. Typical examples are reevaluating one's goals, revising predictions, and consolidating intellectual gains.

Brown has argued that regulation of cognition, unlike knowledge of cognition, often may not be conscious in many learning situations. One reason is that many of these processes are highly automated, at least in adults. A second reason is that some of these processes have developed without any conscious reflection and therefore are difficult to report to others. In addition, Brown has drawn an important distinction about the relationship of age to metacognitive regulation and abstract reflection, arguing that regulatory mechanisms, such as planning, are independent of age, whereas reflection is not (A. Brown, 1987). Thus, like metacognitive knowledge, conscious use of regulatory processes may be related to limitations in one's ability to reflect rather than in one's ability to regulate.

Research on Metacognitive Processes

A wealth of research on metacognition and on instructional practices aimed at developing metacognitive strategies has been conducted since the mid-1970s (e.g., see Block & Pressley, 2002; Boekaerts, Pintrich, & Zeidner, 2000; Harris & Graham, 1996; Harris, Graham, & Deshler, 1998; Pressley & Woloshyn, 1995). A number of important findings have appeared. One is that metacognition is late developing (Alexander et al., 1995). In a variety of studies, children between kindergarten and sixth grade consistently show an inability to monitor their comprehension accurately and, just as important, to describe their own cognition (Baker, 1989, 2002). In one study, Markman (1979) found that even skilled readers were unable to identify information that was inconsistent with the text's meaning. Older students and adults, however, are better able to describe their own cognitive processes.

Recognizing the need to remember also develops slowly throughout childhood (Pressley & Schneider, 1997; Schneider & Pressley, 1997). Whereas preschoolers may have to be told to remember certain things, older children have learned that some information is likely to be important to remember (e.g., directions for where to meet a friend and tips for assembling a bicycle). By the time students reach high school, most know a great deal about what should be remembered and are very selective about what they will and will not try to remember. Developmental trends also are present in the ability to assess the difficulty of various memory tasks. As adults, we understand that the sheer amount of material to be remembered makes a difference. For instance, we know that learning one telephone number is considerably less demanding than committing 10 new telephone numbers to memory. Similarly, we know that learning, say, 5 new psychological terms will take less effort than learning 30 of them. In contrast with adults and older children, younger children typically have only a rudimentary knowledge of the factors influencing task difficulty. Their diagnostic skills are immature and develop slowly (Alexander et al., 1995; Pressley & Schneider, 1997). Teachers still can make an important difference in children's diagnostic skills by providing instruction in how to make estimates of task difficulty, prompting children to make such estimates and providing practice in making diagnoses.

Monitoring skills also improve as children mature (Butler & Winne, 1995). These changes presumably reflect important differences in how one monitors, as well as increased knowledge about what one monitors. This is not to say that adults are skilled monitors or have conscious access to metacognitive knowledge. Even college students have much difficulty monitoring their performance prior to a test (Schraw, 1994). Although college students are better able to monitor their test performance during or after the test, it still is far from perfect (see chapter 11).

The reason for poor monitoring among adults is becoming increasingly clear. Monitoring accuracy appears to be related to two dimensions of performance: *task difficulty* and *prior knowledge*. When a task is difficult, students are more likely to be overconfident in their performance (Schraw & Roedel, 1994). Although you might expect monitoring accuracy to improve as prior knowledge increases, the opposite appears to be true. Glenberg and Epstein (1987) found that music majors monitored their performance more poorly after reading a passage about music than one about physics. A subsequent study by Morris (1990) clarified this relationship further. Prior knowledge aids performance, but it does not contribute to more accurate monitoring. Thus, older students monitor accurately when they possess enough knowledge to perform well; in turn, performing well reduces overconfidence.

Metacognitive monitoring also appears to be unrelated to aptitude. For example, Pressley and Ghatala (1988) found that college students of different verbal ability levels monitored with similar accuracy. Swanson (1990) reported that metacognitive knowledge as measured on a verbal self-report interview was not limited by intellectual aptitude. On the contrary, metacognitive awareness sometimes compensated for lower levels of ability in that low-aptitude/high-metacognitive-knowledge students outperformed high-aptitude/low-metacognitive-knowledge students with respect to the number of moves necessary to solve pendulum and fluid combination problems. Overall, low-aptitude/high-metacognition students required 50 percent fewer moves. Low-aptitude/high-metacognition students also used fewer domain-specific problem-solving strategies than high-aptitude/high-metacognition students, however, suggesting that domain-specific knowledge alone could not account for the low-aptitude/high-metacognition group's performance, a finding consistent with Morris (1990).

Many instructional studies suggest that metacognition can be improved by direct instruction and modeling of metacognitive activities. For example, Paris and colleagues' *Informal Strategies for Learning Program* (ISLP; Paris et al., 1984; see also Jacobs & Paris, 1987) instructed children in knowledge about and the use of metacognitive reading strategies in several ways. Gains during an academic school year were particularly impressive with respect to reading awareness and evaluating the effectiveness of reading strategies.

Delclos and Harrington (1991) examined fifth and sixth graders' ability to solve computer problems after assignment to one of three conditions. The first group received specific problem-solving training, the second group received problem-solving plus self-monitoring training, and the third group received no training. The self-monitoring problem-solving group solved more of the difficult problems than either of the other groups and took less time to do so.

These studies suggest several general conclusions about metacognition. First, younger students may have only a limited amount of metacognitive knowledge at their disposal. This knowledge improves performance; moreover, metacognitive knowledge appears to be highly trainable even in younger students. Second, aptitude and knowledge constrain metacognitive knowledge far less than one might expect. Thus, rather than reserve metacognitive training for more advanced students, teachers should make a special effort to provide training to students who appear to lack it regardless of relative achievement level. Third, evidence suggests that metacognitive awareness can compensate for low ability and insufficient knowledge. Developing metacognitive skills should be particularly helpful for students attempting to learn unfamiliar content.

Becoming a Good Strategy User

Interest in strategies and metacognition has given rise to the concept of a good strategy user. What might such a student look like? Pressley, Borkowski, and Schneider (1987) suggested five criteria: (1) a broad repertoire of strategies; (2) metacognitive knowledge about why, when, and where to use strategies; (3) a broad knowledge base; (4) ability to ignore distractions; and (5) automaticity in the four components described above.

Regarding the first of these five criteria, Pressley et al. distinguished between two types of strategies. The first of these is a *domain-specific strategy* (e.g., applying the quadratic formula), which is of little or no use outside that domain. A second type of strategy is a *higher order strategy,* which is used to control other strategies. One example is how a skilled reader sequences strategies while reading—perhaps skimming before beginning to read, then selectively attending to important information, then monitoring, and finally reviewing. Having knowledge about how to orchestrate related strategies enables good strategy users to regulate their learning efficiently.

The second criterion described by Pressley et al. emphasizes a key theme of our text—that cognitive ability is greatly enhanced by *self-awareness and the ability to self-regulate*. As has been shown, knowing *how* to do something is of little practical good if you do not have the conditional knowledge of knowing *when* or *where* to use it. For example, you can study for a test for several hours and still do poorly if you do not focus on the information that appears on the test. Being able to size up a test in advance, to determine what it will include and how you can best prepare, illustrates nicely the value of conditional knowledge.

By this point, we hope that we also have convinced you that the third criterion—*a broad knowledge base*—is one of the most important components of learning. Pressley et al. have argued that encoding and representing new information in memory without some existing knowledge base as an anchor make efficient learning almost impossible. But existing knowledge also is important because it promotes strategy use and, at times, compensates for lack of strategies. For example, elementary-age children have been found to learn categorizable lists without using strategies because of their ability to activate knowledge about the category (e.g., *kitchen utensils* includes *spoons, forks,* and *knives*).

The fourth criterion of a good strategy user is what Pressley et al. refer to as *action control*. This means that students are able to motivate themselves, tune out distractions, and correctly attribute their progress to effort rather than to ability (see chapter 7). Even very young children show signs of controlling their learning and directing their attention (Alexander et al., 1995), although there is steady improvement into early adulthood.

The fifth criterion is that good strategy users accomplish all of these things *automatically*. As is shown in chapter 2, automaticity is the ability to activate knowledge or perform a task with minimum drain on our limited processing resources. Being automatic is essential to good strategy use because, without it, we are unable to allocate our resources to higher order regulation of our learning. In fact, nonautomated students allocate most of their resources to basic cognitive tasks such as perception, attention, accessing information from long-term memory, and selecting strategies. In contrast, good strategy users accomplish these basic tasks with much less cognitive load, freeing up valuable resources for constructing meaning and overseeing their learning.

Research on Strategy Instruction

Research on strategy instruction has been an important part of educational research for 2 decades. Two especially good analyses of this research have been conducted by Hattie, Biggs, and Purdie (1996) and Rosenshine et al. (1996). Their reviews generally support the following claims:

• *Strategy instruction typically is moderately to highly successful regardless of the strategy or instructional method*. This means that students usually benefit from strategy instruction, whether on single strategies or combinations of strategies. Strategy instruction appears to be most beneficial for younger students, as well as for low-achieving students of all ages. One reason may be that younger and lower achieving students know fewer strategies and therefore have far more room for improvement.

• *Programs that combine several interrelated strategies are more effective than single-strategy programs* (Hattie et al., 1996; see also Pressley, 2002). One reason may be that no single strategy is enough to bring about a substantial change in learning, because most learning is typically complex. A repertoire of four or five strategies that can be used flexibly, however, may be quite effective in this regard. Interested readers are referred to the work of R. Brown et al. (1996) for a more detailed description of a typical (and highly successful) cognitive strategy program.

• *Strategy instruction programs that emphasize the role of conditional knowledge are especially effective.* One explanation is that conditional knowledge enables students to determine when and where to use the newly acquired strategy.

• *Newly acquired strategies do not readily transfer to new tasks or unfamiliar domains.* We often overestimate our students' abilities to use strategies in new situations. Thus, it almost always is a good idea to teach specifically for transfer of strategies. Two ways of accomplishing this are to help students make the link between strategies and their application (Duffy, 2002) and having them apply strategies in a variety of settings (Mayer & Wittrock, 1996). Research also indicates that the more automatic a strategy, the more likely it is to transfer (Cox, 1997).

Research also has addressed whether strategy instruction is more effective in teacher-centered or student-centered learning environments. Neither type of setting appears to increase the effectiveness of the interventions. Specifically, Rosenshine et al. (1996) reported that student-centered approaches, such as reciprocal teaching and cooperative learning, were no more effective than direct instruction approaches. Unfortunately, well-controlled comparisons of different approaches are few. For this reason, debate continues regarding how strategies should be taught to students.

Another question of interest is what kinds of strategies are most important to teach. Hattie et al. (1996) compared rank orderings for approximately 25 learning strategies across three cultures (Japanese, Japanese–Australian, and Australian). Results indicated that a handful of general learning strategies were rated as most important among all cultures. These included, in order of importance, self-checking, creating a productive physical environment, goal setting and planning, reviewing and organizing information after learning, summarizing during learning, seeking teacher assistance, and seeking peer assistance. Not surprisingly, most of the commonly used strategy instruction programs incorporate these skills (see Pressley & Wharton-McDonald, 1997, for an excellent review of strategy instruction and summary of programs).

Implications for Instruction

1. *Match encoding strategies with the material to be learned.* This chapter describes a wide variety of strategies for encoding simple and more complex information. Students should match their strategy use with the materials, goals of learning, and kind of evaluation as much as possible. For example, students learning a list of five recent American presidents for a recognition test is a much different learning goal than

their using this knowledge in short essay contrasting these presidents' contributions to foreign and domestic policy.

Our goal should be to help students be as *strategic* and *flexible* as possible when encoding information. Sometimes this means using maintenance rehearsal rather than deep processing, although usually it means the opposite. Encouraging material appropriate processing should be a goal of every teacher. Of course, to do so successfully requires students to possess a repertoire of strategies, as well as the metacognitive knowledge to use them.

2. *Encourage students to engage in deeper processing.* The deeper students' processing, the better their memory for meaning of to-be-learned information. One way that students can process information more deeply is to make connections to their prior knowledge and the learning context. Encouraging affective responses is another way to promote deeper processing. A third way—answering questions about to-be-learned information or generating them yourself—clearly facilitates inferential processing of that information.

3. *Use instructional strategies that promote elaboration.* Teachers can do much in the classroom to promote elaborative encoding. Most important is that teachers encourage students to give meaning to what they are learning in terms of their own knowledge, goals, and uses of information. Making students more active in this way and helping them take responsibility for their learning will do more than anything else to improve learning.

One structured technique for teachers to use is *schema activation,* which refers to finding ways to activate what students already know: things such as preteaching class discussions, brainstorming, and clarifying salient concepts. Another method is to encourage students to categorize and organize new information. A third method is to promote knowledge construction through cooperative social practices. This topic is discussed in detail in chapter 9, "Classroom Contexts for Cognitive Growth."

4. *Help students become more metacognitively aware.* Having declarative and procedural knowledge is only part of effective learning; knowing one's own cognitive strengths and weaknesses and using one's knowledge strategically are equally important. Educational psychologists became interested in metacognition as it became evident that good learners are highly aware of their own thinking and memory and use this information to regulate their learning. Their knowledge includes the *how, why,* and *when* of learning. Teachers should make a special effort to model their own conditional knowledge for their students. A second component is regulation of cognition. Students need to learn basic regulatory skills such as planning and monitoring and, most important, how to coordinate them.

The first step is to make students aware that metacognition is vital to good learning. Metacognitive skills should be taught and discussed in every classroom (Pressley & Schneider, 1997). These discussions should be between students and other students, as well as teachers. Peer tutoring or small cooperative learning groups are an especially effective way to share and develop metacognitive knowledge and strategies (see chapters 6 and 9).

The second step is to develop some level of basic automaticity with metacognitive skills. One way to do so is to use monitoring checklists in which students check off component steps in monitoring one's learning (Schraw, 1998). The following checklist provides an example:

1. What is the purpose for learning this information?
2. Do I know anything about this topic?
3. Do I know strategies that will help me learn?
4. Am I understanding as I proceed?
5. How should I correct errors?
6. Have I accomplished the goals I set myself?

Studies that have used checklists and related methods such as cue cards report favorable findings (Delclos & Harrington, 1991; King, 1994; King et al., 1998), especially when students are learning difficult material. We recommend that a variety of prompts for using strategies be used consistently until students become automatic at using them.

5. *Make strategy instruction a priority.* Strategy instruction should be an integral part of every class (Pressley & Wharton-McDonald, 1997). Research clearly shows that the strategic use of knowledge, rather than the mere possession of it, improves learning. Teaching students strategies not only produces learning gains but also empowers them psychologically by increasing self-efficacy (see chapter 6). We recommend that teachers target age-appropriate strategies at each grade by thinking about their most and least successful students. The chances are good that highly successful students rely on strategies that struggling students do not use. Modeling instruction with these strategies will, no doubt, enhance all your students' ability to learn more effectively.

Pressley and Wharton-McDonald (1997) recommend that strategy instruction is needed before, during, and after the main learning episode. Strategies that occur before learning include *setting goals* and *determining how much information to learn, how new information relates to prior knowledge,* and *how the new information will be used.* Strategies needed during learning include *identifying important information, predicting, monitoring, analyzing,* and *interpreting.* Strategies used after learning include *reviewing, organizing,* and *reflecting.* Good strategy users should possess some degree of competence in each of these areas to be truly self-regulated.

Helping your students become good strategy users demands a fair amount dedication and diligence on your part. For students to use strategies independently and capably requires that they not only use strategies well and automatically but also believe in their value and know when and where to apply them. The instructional sequence below, which aims at these goals, draws heavily on strategy research by Palincsar and Brown (1984); Pressley and his associates (Brown et al., 1996; Collins & Pressley, 2002; Pressley & Woloshyn, 1995; Poplin (1998); and Harris, Graham, and Deshler (1998) in addressing these issues. Much if not most of this instruction can occur as students work in groups, with members using the strategies to construct meaning jointly.

STEP 1. *Discuss and explain the value of strategies.* Students should understand why they are being asked to learn strategies, what instruction will be like, and how they will use them. In addition to understanding the obvious benefits for learning, students need to know that strategies can help them overcome lack of prior knowledge and domain-specific ability. Another reason is that strategies positively affect their self-confidence and learning expectations (see chapters 7 and 8).

STEP 2. *Introduce one or at most a very few strategies at a time.* Students can be overwhelmed easily. The best chance of teaching students strategies that are useful to them is to limit their number to perhaps two or three (e.g., summarization, creating mental images, and generating questions) over a several-week period of instruction. A single strategy can usually be taught in 10 hours or less, including time to practice applying it (Pressley & Woloshyn, 1995), but students need the time and opportunity to use it in a variety of situations before the strategy is really "theirs" and they can use it flexibly.

STEP 3. *Continue practice over an extended period.* Teachers should plan on 6 to 10 weeks for instruction, modeling, and practice of a new strategy. Effective strategy instruction occurs throughout the school year; ideally, it should even continue across school years (Pressley & Woloshyn, 1995). Periodic follow-ups also are helpful to ensure that the strategy has been maintained.

STEP 4. *Explain and model strategies extensively.* Even when students understand why they are learning a strategy and how to use it, they need to see strategy use modeled by a teacher (or other expert). Modeling should include at least two components: (1) how the strategy is used in a variety of settings to accomplish different learning objectives and (2) when and why the teacher uses the strategy. The former will convey declarative and procedural knowledge to the student; the latter conveys conditional knowledge. Of course, teachers are not the only models for using strategies. Students also should be coached to model strategy use for each other—for example, thinking aloud as they read or prepare to write.

STEP 5. *Provide feedback to students about strategies* (Butler & Winne, 1995). One way for teachers to share their expertise with students is to provide feedback on which strategy works best for which task. Feedback helps students apply the strategy in the best way and evaluate its effectiveness, that is, whether it has improved performance or increased efficiency.

6.   *Look for opportunities to help students transfer strategies.* A common failing of strategy instruction is that students do not use strategies learned in one setting in new ones. Ways to combat this problem are teachers' modeling flexible strategy use, thinking aloud as they do (Duffy, 2002), and providing opportunities for students to practice strategies across the curriculum (see Mayer & Wittrock, 1996, for a review). In our view, it is better to teach fewer strategies and have students use them in every content area than it is to bombard them with new strategies in every class. For older students, of course, this approach will require coordination among different content instructors.

7.   *Encourage reflection on strategy use.* The way students become metacognitively aware and, in turn, self-regulated is to think and talk about their learning. Everyone who goes to school, no matter how young, should be encouraged to do so. Older students should be given regular time in school to reflect on using strategies by means of small-group discussion, journals, and essays. Younger students should be helped to understand how older students and adults think about their learning. Careful teacher modeling helps accomplish this goal, along with coaching students to ask questions, use strategies, and express their ideas.

Summary

This chapter focused on encoding strategies and how effective learners adopt strategies relevant to the kind of information they are learning. Some strategies have been studied extensively in relation to learning simpler kinds of information, such as vocabulary, lists of things, and procedural steps. Others typically are applied to more complex information.

Rehearsal, mediation, mnemonics, and the use of imagery are examples of strategies that often are used in acquiring simpler kinds of information. A distinction was made between maintenance and elaborative rehearsal. Maintenance rehearsal refers to the recycling of information for brief periods of time to keep it ready for use, such as when a person repeats a telephone number over and over while getting ready to dial. Elaborative rehearsal, in contrast, is the recycling of information in ways that relate it to other, previously learned knowledge. In general, elaborative rehearsal results in superior memory performance, but both types of rehearsal have distinct uses. One form of elaborative rehearsal involves mediation, in which difficult-to-remember items are converted into something more meaningful and are easily remembered.

One approach used to improve learning is mnemonics, memory aids designed to help people remember information. They include the peg method, the method of loci, the link method, stories, first-letter mnemonics, and the keyword method. The various mnemonics differ, but all use familiar information to facilitate remembering unfamiliar information, and most use imagery in one form or another. Mnemonics generally are easy to teach and students enjoy using them. In our view, mnemonics are best seen as adjuncts to regular classroom methods.

We introduced three general frameworks for understanding complex information—schema activation, guided questioning, and the levels of processing view. All three of these perspectives hold that what students already know and what they do while encoding determine the quality of what they remember. Activities that focus students on the meaning of to-be-learned information almost always will result in better memory performance than activities that center on superficial aspects of to-be-learned materials.

The nature of the materials that students encounter also influences memory. Well-organized materials tend to be better recalled than poorly organized ones. In the absence of organization, students impose their own organization on to-be-remembered information. Complex materials are best encoded by using meaning-oriented procedures that help students relate new information to what they know already.

Finally, we considered the role of metacognition in learning and saw that skilled students are aware of their mental processes and have the conditional knowledge to regulate their learning. Metacognitive abilities can help students compensate for low domain knowledge and a limited strategy repertoire.

Metacognition can improve with instruction; a powerful example is teaching students to use learning strategies. We explored what it means to be a good strategy user and how to make strategy instruction most effective. We observed that good strategy users possess more strategies, use them more flexibly, are more automatic, and control their motivation to learn. Because these skills are teachable and improve substantially with practice, all students have the potential to become good strategy users.

Suggested Readings

Pressley, M., Woloshyn, V., & Associates. (1995). *Cognitive strategy instruction that really improves children's academic performance* (2nd ed.). Cambridge, MA: Brookline Books.

This very readable book, now in a second edition, outlines strategy instruction for all grades in most content areas.

Siegler, R. (1998). *Children's thinking* (3rd ed.). New York: Guilford.

This text, by a leading scholar in children's cognitive development, includes an excellent discussion of how children's approaches to encoding and remembering become more strategic over time.

Chapter 5

Retrieval Processes

Encoding Specificity ■ *Recognition and Recall* ■ *Reconstruction* ■
Recalling Specific Events ■ *Relearning* ■ *Implications for Instruction* ■
Summary ■ *Suggested Readings* ■

IN CHAPTERS 3 AND 4, we examined the nature of memory, its structure, and the processes involved in encoding. Our description of human memory is not complete, however, until we describe the processes involved in retrieving information from memory. Our focus in this chapter is on retrieval, the process involved in accessing and placing into consciousness information from long-term memory (see Figure 2-1). We begin our discussion by illustrating some common retrieval phenomena through the following story:

> Mrs. Thompson has just finished handing out her American history test. Most students begin writing immediately, but Ronald reads the first question and feels a cold shiver run up his spine. Not only can he not remember the answer, but he also cannot even remember that the topic was ever talked about. He gulps and proceeds to the next question.
>
> Laura, in contrast, reads the first question and smiles to herself, remembering a joke Mrs. Thompson told on the day she covered the material. Laura starts to write her answer and finds that the words come easily. For Laura, the question is a perfect cue for remembering.
>
> Aisha, meanwhile, writes part of the answer and then stops. She knows that she knows the rest of the answer, but somehow the words do not come to her. She raises her hand, and Mrs. Thompson drifts over to Aisha's desk. Mrs. Thompson briefly clarifies the question. After hearing just a sentence from her teacher, Aisha has a powerful "aha!" feeling, and she returns to her writing, confident that she can answer Mrs. Thompson's question.
>
> Across the room, Scotty is having trouble remembering the answers to the test. Finally, he flips the test over and scratches out the outline he used to organize his studying the night before. Then he uses his outline to help him remember what to say. Mrs. Thompson watches Scotty bemused because he so often seems to provide his own cues for her tests.

The experiences of the four students in Mrs. Thompson's history class were varied, but the probability is high that we all have shared similar experiences. Sometimes our retrieval processes seem very ineffective and, like Ronald, we draw a blank. At other times, we marvel at our own abilities to retrieve information in great detail. At still other times, we do retrieve the information we need, but not without a struggle.

Research on human memory has focused primarily on understanding encoding and storage. Still, many important issues related to retrieval have come to light in recent years. We begin our discussion of retrieval processes by examining a phenomenon that has come to be known as encoding specificity.

Encoding Specificity

In our discussion of encoding, we pointed out that the organization of material and the context in which it is learned have considerable influence on how well the material is remembered. For years, psychologists have wondered whether this organization was important only at the time of encoding, only at the time of retrieval, or at both times. In an important early study, Tulving and Osler (1968) addressed this question.

Tulving and Osler divided their group of subjects into two conditions. In one condition, the subjects merely were presented a 24-item word list to learn. In the second condition, the subjects received the same word list, but in this instance each of the 24 to-be-learned words was paired with a weak associate (e.g., for boy–child, a strong associate pair would be boy–girl). Then, when the subjects were tested for their ability to remember the words, the two conditions were divided further. Half of the subjects in both original conditions simply were asked for free recall of the 24 words. The remainder also were asked to recall the 24 words, but these subjects were given the 24 weak associates that originally were given only to the subjects in the weak-associates condition. In this way, Tulving and Osler constructed four groups: (1) word list to learn without associates, test without associates; (2) word list to learn without associates, test with associates; (3) word list to learn with associates, test without associates; and (4) word list to learn with associates, test with associates.

Results of the study indicated that the weak associates or cue words facilitated memory performance only when they were available to the subjects both at encoding and at retrieval. Having cues present at encoding only or at retrieval only did not enhance memory performance. The conclusion is that cues indeed make a difference in memory performance but only when cues present at encoding are reinstated at retrieval. The phenomenon that Tulving and Osler observed in their experiment is known as **encoding specificity,** and it has become one of the basic principles of memory performance.

One implication of the encoding specificity principle is that remembering knowledge is enhanced when conditions at retrieval match those present at encoding. If such a match occurs, contextual cues help individuals perform an efficient search of memory. More often, however, our goal is to broaden the range of cues linked to both encoding and retrieval so that students can retrieve and use what they know in the widest possible range of situations. When retrieval cues differ substantially from those present at encoding, an efficient search of memory may be impossible.

Thus, a number of studies have investigated encoding activities that are designed to create a richer context for retrieval. These studies include research on the *generation effect, elaborative interrogation, guided peer questioning,* and *state-dependent learning.*

The **generation effect** refers to the finding that verbal material self-generated at the time of encoding is better remembered than material that students merely read at encoding (see our discussion of distinctiveness of encoding in chapter 4). For example, Rabinowitz and Craik (1986) presented subjects with 56 words to learn. Each word in the list was paired with an associated item. Half of the to-be-learned or target words merely were read by the subjects. The remaining target words had letters deleted from them that were replaced with blanks. As the subjects encoded these words, they had to generate the missing letters from memory. At the time of the test, half of the target words subjects read were cued by the original associates; the other half were cued by different words that rhymed with the target words. The target words that students had to generate also were split at the time of test so that half received the original cue and half got a rhyming cue.

Results were striking. As Rabinowitz and Craik had predicted from the generation effect literature (see Jacoby, 1978; McElroy & Slamecka, 1982; Slamecka & Graf, 1978; Slamecka & Katsaiti, 1987), a large generation effect was observed. Students remembered far more words for which they had to generate missing letters than words they merely read. The generation effect only worked, however, when the cues present at encoding also were present at recall. Apparently, even one of the most durable phenomena known to memory researchers—the generation effect—is governed by the principle of encoding specificity.

More recent studies have investigated the effect of generation on implicit and explicit memory (Segar, 1994). In chapter 3, we learned that implicit memory occurs when individuals remember information without conscious awareness (Berry & Dienes, 1993). A wide variety of studies have found that shallow processing typically affects implicit memory without any corresponding effect on explicit memory. In contrast, generating information typically has a positive effect on explicit memory, as well as transfer of information to new settings (Toth, Reingold, & Jacoby, 1994).

Other researchers have examined whether the generation effect occurs when reading longer texts and in classroom discussions. For example, Pressley and colleagues (Martin & Pressley, 1991; Pressley, Symons, McDaniel, Snyder, & Turnure, 1988; Willoughby, Waller, Wood, & McKinnon, 1993) have investigated the technique of **elaborative interrogation,** in which students are asked to answer "why" questions about information they have just read. As discussed in chapter 4, work by King and her associates (e.g., King, 1994; King, Staffieri, & Adelgais, 1998) similarly has shown that the technique of **guided peer questioning**—having students ask and answer thought-provoking questions about class content—significantly enhances their learning and recall. Studies consistently have shown that these approaches improve learning for text and teacher-presented information, especially when they prompt learners to activate relevant prior knowledge they would not activate otherwise and to carry out other cognitive activities (e.g., connecting ideas and monitoring metacognitively) known to promote learning.

The research on elaborative interrogation and guided peer questioning answers some questions about why the generation effect occurs. One explanation is that learners are more apt to integrate new information with what they already know; thus, elaborated information is easier to store in memory. A second explanation is that elaboration helps students "enrich" incoming information in a variety of ways; that is, information is learned better not only because it is easier to categorize and store (as suggested above) but also because it is "reconstructed" in a way that makes it more meaningful.

Another instance of research on encoding specificity can be seen in a study by Corkill, Glover, and Bruning (1988) that focused on some factors that make for an effective advance organizer. Advance organizers are materials given to students prior to reading that are designed to tie the to-be-learned material in an upcoming passage into what students already know (see chapter 10). In their Experiment 3, Corkill et al. sorted students into conditions on the basis of whether they read an advance organizer prior to reading a chapter on astronomy. Then, at recall, Corkill et al. examined the effects of presenting advance organizers as cues for retrieval. In contrast with no cue conditions and other conditions (in which other types of cues were furnished to students at time of retrieval), giving readers the advance organizer as a retrieval cue led to significantly greater levels of recall of the passage content. However, presenting the advance organizer as a retrieval cue worked only if the students had read the advance organizer prior to reading the chapter on astronomy. Students who merely read the chapter on astronomy without an advance organizer obtained no benefit from having the advance organizer presented to them at the time of retrieval. Apparently, even the recall of long reading passages can be facilitated when students are given cues at retrieval that were present when they first activated schemata for reading the material.

The type of cues used in studies of encoding specificity seems to make little difference as long as the cues are present both at encoding and at retrieval. Tulving and his associates (Tulving, 1983; Sloman, Hayman, Ohta, Law, & Tulving, 1988), for example, examined encoding specificity with both semantic and episodic elements of memory (see chapter 3) As you recall, *semantic memory* refers to memory for general knowledge (e.g., that canaries are yellow and that Greenland has an ice cap) *not* tied to a specific occurrence in a person's lifetime (e.g., to remember that Pluto's moon is named Charon, it is unlikely that we remember any personal experience related to this knowledge, at least until well after we have retrieved the information). In contrast, *episodic memory* refers to our memories for specific events in our lives (e.g., once, one of the authors' daughters caught a 2-pound bass and this morning, one of the authors had wheat toast for breakfast). Apparently, both semantic and episodic information may be used as effective retrieval cues. For example, a teacher could construct an item that used episodic information as a cue (e.g., "As you recall from our class demonstration in which Sharmar bent the glass tubes . . .") or an item that used semantic information (e.g., "As you recall, many historians have argued that Hoover actually laid the groundwork for recovery from the Depression. What were the . . ."). Either of these retrieval cues could facilitate retrieval as long as it is present at encoding.

One interesting aspect of encoding specificity is its generality. Researchers have discovered that retrieval is more efficient when it matches encoding conditions even when unusual affective or psychological states are involved. This phenomenon often is referred to as **state-dependent learning** (Overton, 1985; Schramke & Bower, 1997). In one study, Bower (1981) found that students who learned information when they were sad recalled that information better when they were in a similar state versus when they were happy. Godden and Baddeley (1975) found similar differences when individuals learned information on land or under water! These results suggest a very strong relationship between the conditions at encoding and those at retrieval. The more these conditions match, the more likely it is that retrieval will be successful.

Results of studies focusing on encoding specificity are important for educators because they underscore the importance of context in memory. In these studies, the context of retrieval situations is varied by the presence or absence of cues available to students at encoding. The effects of context on retrieval, however, go beyond the presence or absence of study cues. Smith (1986) and Smith, Vela, and Williamson (1988), for example, showed that even the general environmental context in which encoding and retrieval occur influences memory. It turns out that students' memory for information depends not only on study cues but even on the classroom in which students study; that is, when students are tested in the same room in which they study, their memory performance is better than if they are tested in a room different from the one in which they studied.

Studies of the influence of context on retrieval and the principle of encoding specificity have become integral to our understanding of memory. Encoding specificity helps us explain why some test items seem to facilitate our recall and others do not. In short, test items (whether multiple-choice, true–false, or essay) that reinstate cues that were present at the time of encoding facilitate students' retrieval of the content. Test questions that do not provide cues from encoding are less able to enhance recall.

The principle of encoding specificity also is important because it highlights the relationship between different stages of information processing. We now know that activities that improve the encoding of information will improve retrieval as well. Although it is convenient occasionally to distinguish among encoding, storage, and retrieval, it is even more important to remember that all memory functions are integrated.

Encoding specificity also helps us explain everyday memory experiences. For example, all of us have had the experience of hearing an old song on the radio and then remembering things we have not thought of in years (recall our discussion of episodic memory). Similarly, most of us have experienced a rush of memories we thought were forgotten when we met an old college roommate or a friend from our high school days. In these examples, the music or the sight of the old friend reinstates cues present when we encoded information. Without the cues, retrieval may be very difficult. With the cues, retrieval becomes much easier.

Encoding specificity emphasizes the situated nature of our cognitive processes (Wortham, 2001) and importance of context in cognition. Students' memories do not function like tape recorders or videotape machines; students cannot simply replay events at their choosing. Instead, retrieval depends on the cues they have available to call forth memory and the degree of match between encoding and retrieval contexts. A rich context providing multiple cues for retrieval almost always will lead to better memory performance, while a context with few or no retrieval cues is apt to give us little indication of what students actually know.

One way that context at retrieval may be varied is by the demands we place on students at the time of testing. For instance, on the one hand, we could provide students with some information and ask them whether they recognize it, such as when a simple multiple-choice or true–false item is used. On the other hand, we could ask that students supply information from memory, such as when we ask them to discuss two important social consequences of the Vietnam War. In these situations, we are asking students to recall information. A good deal of attention has focused on how recognition and recall operate. In the following section, we review each of these approaches to retrieving information from long-term memory.

Recognition and Recall

Imagine you are preparing to take your midterm examination for this course. The professor has announced that the test will be multiple-choice (recognition), and so you work hard readying yourself to recognize pertinent ideas on the test and to discriminate important facts from other material. You finally finish studying at 4 in the morning—exhausted, but happy in the knowledge that you have mastered the content. Unfortunately, your happiness lasts only until you walk into the testing room and see that the instructor has had a change of heart: The test will not be multiple-choice, but instead will be an essay, which requires you not just to *recognize* information, but to *recall* it.

The events described above are not especially uncommon (even though they represent poor pedagogical practice). Even so, studies find that switching the type of test students are to take from one form to another to be upsetting (whether from multiple-choice to essay or vice versa). The reactions that students have to changing the type of test they expect would lead us to believe that significant differences exist between recall and recognition.

Further evidence for a difference between recall and recognition comes from research on how students prepare themselves for tests. In laboratory settings, students who expect recall tests tend to focus on the organization of material, whereas those who anticipate recognition tend to emphasize discriminating items from each other so that they can pick out the relevant items from the distractors on the test (Kintsch, 1986). These different methods of preparation lead to test-taking performances shaped to the type of test expected. Students who are tested in a manner consistent with their expectations for testing far outperform students who receive a type of test they did not expect (Glover & Corkill, 1987).

Students' actual study habits bear out the laboratory work. Typically, students prepare differently for essay tests than for recognition tests. They report that when they study for an essay examination, they emphasize organizing content, relating important ideas to each other and practicing the recall of information. In contrast, when students prepare for a recognition test, they report focusing on becoming familiar with the material and discriminating the to-be-learned information from other materials. They also recall studying harder for essay tests than for recognition tests. This latter difference makes especially good sense because laboratory studies indicate that recognition is easier than recall. In almost all situations, students' performance is better on recognition tests than on recall tests (Hamilton & Ghatala, 1994; Mitchell & Brown, 1988).

Despite the overwhelming array of circumstantial evidence indicating, almost certainly, important process differences in recall and recognition, the exact nature of these differences has been very elusive (see Nilsson, Law, & Tulving, 1988). An early hypothesis offered to account for differences in recall and recognition was put forward by McDougall a century ago. This "threshold" hypothesis held that both recognition and recall performance depend on the strength of information in memory. Further, the hypothesis held that a bit of information must have a specific strength before it can be recognized, the so-called **recognition threshold.** The threshold hypothesis also held that a greater amount of strength is necessary for information to be recalled, the **recall threshold.**

The implications of the threshold hypothesis were very clear and seemed to account for most data from studies that contrasted recognition and recall. This hypothesis predicted that some bits of very well-learned information would be both recognized and recalled because the strength of that information in memory would be above both the recognition threshold and the recall threshold. When information was poorly learned, however, it would be neither recalled nor recognized because its strength in memory was below the recall and recognition thresholds. The threshold hypothesis also predicted that some information would be recognizable, but not recallable, because its strength was above the recognition threshold but below the recall threshold.

As appealing as the threshold hypothesis was for more than a half-century, it no longer is accepted by cognitive psychologists. The threshold hypothesis was abandoned for two reasons. First, it is quite possible for some items in memory to be recalled but not recognized. The hypothesis would hold that this was not possible. Second, the threshold hypothesis never offered an explanation for how recall or recognition operated. Instead, it was a hypothesis to account for why recall seemed more difficult than recognition.

The threshold hypothesis has been replaced by more contemporary perspectives. One, typified by the work of Tulving and his colleagues (e.g., Nilsson et al., 1988; Tulving, 1983, 1985), argues that differences in recall and recognition are a part of larger contextual phenomena in memory akin to encoding specificity; that is, Tulving contends that the match of the encoding and retrieval operations determines performance. Tulving's argument is less of an attempt to examine the processes involved in recall and recognition than it is an attempt to account for performance differences in recall and recognition. A second contemporary perspective on recall and recognition is referred to as the **dual process model of recall.** This view holds that recall and recognition essentially are the same, save that a much more extensive memory search is required in recall than in recognition (see Greene, 1992, for a further discussion).

To understand how recall and recognition searches differ (see chapter 3 for a detailed discussion of memory searches), we employ J. R. Anderson's (1985, 1993) model. Consider, for example, the following two questions, modeled on similar questions posed by Anderson:

1. Who was president after Madison?
2. Was Monroe the president after Madison?

The first question ("*Who was* . . .") is a recall question; the second ("*Was Monroe* . . .") is a recognition question. Figure 5-1 pictures the kind of propositional network that Anderson (1983b, 1993) believes is involved in representing the information that Monroe was president after Madison.

The recall question gives students *Madison* as a point of access from which to begin a memory search. From Anderson's perspective, such a question requires that readers enter memory at *Madison* and search to *Monroe*. To accomplish this, a student first would activate the *Madison* node and have activation spread until it reached *Monroe*. If, however, the link between the second and third proposition were weak or if it could not be sufficiently activated, then recall would fail.

In contrast with the recall question, the recognition question provides two points of access in memory from which activation could spread: *Madison* and *Monroe*. Presumably, if students cannot activate the appropriate link from *Madison*, they might do so from *Monroe*. In Anderson's opinion, recognition questions typically are easier than recall questions because they offer more ways to search memory. Otherwise, however, recognition and recall essentially are the same process.

Most contemporary psychologists take a position midway between Anderson's and the context-dependent position exemplified by Tulving. Craik (1979; Craik & Lockhart, 1986), for example, argues that similar processes probably do operate in recall and recognition but that the requirements of retrieval differ; that is, Craik holds that, in recognition, an item is presented but information related to the item must be retrieved to allow for discrimination of the item from distractor items. For example,

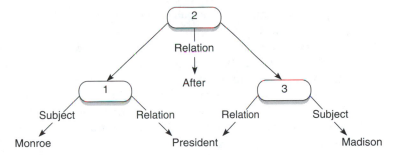

Figure 5-1

A Propositional Network. The figure illustrates a propositional network of the information that Monroe followed Madison as president of the United States.

Source: Based on a similar figure in Cognitive Psychology and Its Implications *(2nd ed., p. 158), by J. R. Anderson, 1985, New York: Freeman.*

Did Smith perform research on (a) context-dependent retrieval, (b) the generation effect, or (c) keyword mnemonics? The item is given: *On what did Smith perform research?* To answer the question, you must retrieve information about Smith so that you can distinguish among the three alternatives. In this case, the answer is *context-dependent retrieval.* The demands of recall, in Craik's view, differ from those of recognition in that a to-be-recalled item is presented (e.g., *Who was known as the "angel of the battlefield"?*) and the person must retrieve the item (*Clara Barton*).

A full theoretical analysis of potential differences between recall and recognition is beyond the scope of this text. Our brief discussion of these processes may tend to imply that retrieval, provided students are given the proper cues, is a matter of searching for the appropriate memory, finding it, and then just reading it off. Thus, if you were to sit down to take a test over this content, it might seem that all you need to do is find where you stored your memories and then merely read them off. This view of memory would be incorrect, however. It presumes that the entire content of a memory event (e.g., the results of studying this chapter) is stored and that it is stored in the same spot. Further, it assumes that all that must be done is to locate the memory event and read it off. If memory indeed were stored in this fashion, each of us would need a warehouse to hold our memories. We simply encounter far too much information during a lifetime to allow for such massive storage.

Reconstruction

If retrieval is not just a straightforward reading out of memory, what is it? Considerable evidence suggests that retrieval is **reconstructive memory** (e.g., Greene, 1992; Spiro, 1980; Welch-Ross, 1995), just as encoding is constructive memory. In other words, rather than remembering the entirety of a memory event, only key elements of an episode are stored, guided by schemata (see chapter 3). At retrieval, we bring up these key elements and put them together with general knowledge (both domain-specific and general) to reconstruct what we encountered. This process allows us to "handle" far less information than if we encoded and retrieved all of the information we encounter.

For example, suppose you witness an automobile accident this afternoon. Later, when a police officer asks you to tell what happened, you probably will retrieve some key elements of the event and reconstruct the rest. For instance, you can recall clearly that the pickup truck broadsided the Mercedes in the intersection. You also can recall that you were waiting for the "Walk" sign to come on. But you may not actually have been in a position to see the traffic lights. So, to describe which vehicle ran the red light, you work from what you know to conclude that the pickup must have ignored a red light. For all you know, though, the traffic lights could have been stuck so that both vehicles had green lights.

Mistakes such as which vehicle ran a light are common when we retrieve events from memory. Students make similar errors when recalling text and lecture information. They may write about George Washington having been elected the first president of the United States and note that John Adams ran with him as vice president. In fact, Adams finished second in the race for president and so became vice president. The election laws that set up our current system of "running mates" for president and vice president were not formulated until well after Washington's time. In this instance, students remember who was president and who was vice president but reconstruct how the vice president came to office. A similar phenomenon often occurs when psychology students describe John B. Watson's famous study of Little Albert. As you know, Watson conditioned a fear response in the child Albert by pairing a loud noise with white objects until the white objects themselves elicited the fear response. However, we have seen several students who went on to state that Watson then "unconditioned" Little Albert and removed the fear response. In fact, no such thing happened. Students use their knowledge of contemporary approaches to psychology research to reconstruct a plausible ending for the story.

As can be seen from our examples, a reconstructive memory system should be far less demanding of memory "space" than a "readout" system. Only key elements need to be remembered about a memory event when general knowledge can be used to reconstruct events. Of, course, a reconstructive system also will be open to far more errors that give evidence of improper reconstruction. In fact, errors of just this type have convinced many psychologists of the reconstructive nature of memory (see Ceci & Bruck, 1993, and Welch-Ross, 1995, for reviews).

Two classic studies performed in the 1930s have been central to arguments for the reconstructive nature of human memory. Each has been replicated several times, and results remain consistent (see Schwartz & Reisberg, 1991). The better known of the two studies was reported in Bartlett's excellent book, *Remembering* (1932). Bartlett, an English psychologist, had subjects read a very brief story titled "The War of the Ghosts." This particular story was an abstraction of a North American Native legend that was firmly grounded in that culture. Bartlett's subjects, however, were British and had little, if any, cultural background for the story.

After the subjects read the story, Bartlett assessed their recall at differing time intervals. Bartlett noted that recall for the passage was poor even at short intervals. More important, Bartlett observed that subjects seemed to recall only the gist or theme of the story. From this gist, they constructed a reasonable story that made a kind of sense out of the information recalled. Not surprisingly, the reconstructed stories often contained errors and distortions that made the story fit the general cultural knowledge possessed by the British subjects (see Box 5-1).

In the same year Bartlett's book was published, Carmichael, Hogan, and Walter (1932) reported convincing evidence for reconstructive processes in subjects' memories for drawings. In their experiment, all of Carmichael et al.'s subjects were shown a set of line drawings similar to those pictured in Figure 5-2. The subjects were grouped into three conditions on the basis of the labels they received with the drawings. The subjects in the control condition received no labels; they merely were shown the drawings. The subjects in one experimental condition received the labels shown in List A in Figure 5-2. The subjects in the second experimental condition were provided the labels pictured in List B in Figure 5-2. For example, the subjects in one experimental condition saw the two circles connected by a straight line labeled as "dumbbell," whereas the subjects in the other condition saw this drawing labeled as "eyeglasses."

Box 5-1

Bartlett's Story "The War of the Ghosts" and One Student's Protocol

The War of the Ghosts

One night two young men from Egulac went down to the river to hunt seals, and while they were there it became foggy and calm. Then they heard war cries, and they thought: "Maybe this is a war party." They escaped to the shore, and hid behind a log. Now canoes came up, and they heard the noise of paddles, and saw one canoe coming up to them. There were five men in the canoe, and they said:

"What do you think? We wish to take you along. We are going up the river to make war on the people."

One of the young men said: "I have no arrows."

"Arrows are in the canoe," they said.

"I will not go along. I might be killed. My relatives do not know where I have gone. But you," he said, turning to the other, "may go with them."

So one of the young men went, but the other returned home.

And the warriors went on up the river to a town on the other side of Kalama. The people came down to the water, and they began to fight, and many were killed. But presently the young man heard one of the warriors say: "Quick, let us go home: that Indian has been hit." Now he thought, "Oh, they are ghosts." He did not feel sick, but they said he had been shot.

So, canoes went back to Egulac, and the young man went ashore to his house, and made a fire. And he told everybody and said: "Behold, I accompanied the ghosts, and we went to fight. Many of our fellows were killed, and many of those who attacked us were killed. They said I was hit, and I did not feel sick.

He told it all, and then he became quiet. When the sun rose he fell down. Something black came out of his mouth. His face became contorted. The people jumped up and cried. He was dead.

Student's Protocol

Two youths were standing by a river about to start seal-catching, when a boat appeared with five men in it. They were all armed for war.

The youths were at first frightened, but they were asked by the men to come and help them fight some enemies on the other bank. One youth said he could not come as his relations would be anxious about him; the other said he would go, and entered the boat.

In the evening he returned to his hut, and told his friends that he had been in a battle. A great many had been slain, and he had been wounded by an arrow; he had not felt any pain, he said. They told him that he must have been fighting in a battle of ghosts. Then he remembered that it had been queer and he became very excited.

In the morning, however, he became ill, and his friends gathered round; he fell down and his face became very pale. Then he writhed and shrieked and his friends were filled with terror. At last he became calm. Something hard and black came out of his mouth, and he lay contorted and dead.

From *Remembering: A study in experimental and social psychology* by F. C. Bartlett, 1932, Cambridge, England: Cambridge University Press. Pp 23–26.

When the subjects in Carmichael et al.'s study were asked to draw the figures from memory, some interesting differences among the conditions appeared. The subjects in the control condition most accurately depicted the drawings as originally shown. The experimental group given the labels in List A tended to bias their drawings

Figure 5-2

Figures Similar to Those Used by Carmichael, Hogan, and Walter (1932).

Source: The drawings are based on those used in "An Experimental Study of the Effect of Language on the Reproduction of Visually Perceived Forms," by L. Carmichael. H. P. Hogan & A. A. Walter, 1932, Journal of Experimental Psychology, 15, 73–86.

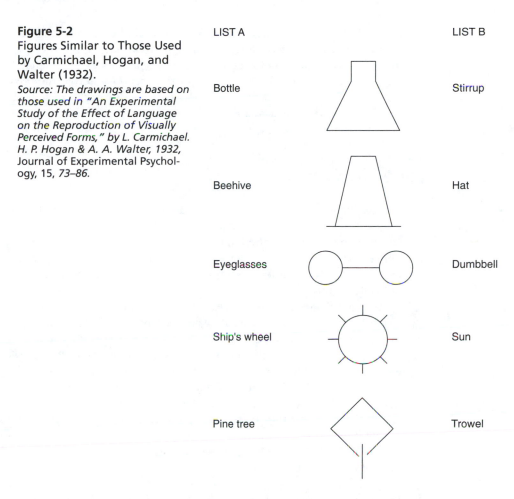

LIST A		LIST B
Bottle		Stirrup
Beehive		Hat
Eyeglasses		Dumbbell
Ship's wheel		Sun
Pine tree		Trowel

systematically so that they fit the labels. In a classroom demonstration in which we repeated the Carmichael et al. experiment, one student drew nosepieces and bands on the "eyeglasses." Similarly, the subjects shown the labels in List B also biased their reproductions to fit the labels they saw. In our use of these materials, we have seen students who drew a cowboy hat for "hat" and another who put grips on the handle of the "trowel."

Although the results of Bartlett's and Carmichael et al.'s studies clearly demonstrated that memory is reconstructive, their explanations for how reconstruction operated were vague and not well-accepted. Not until the 1970s, with the increasing acceptance of schema theory, did more sophisticated theoretical accounts of reconstructive memory began to appear. In general, the view of reconstructive processes in memory emphasizes students' assimilating new information into existing memory structures. Rather than remember all of the details in an episode, students remember the gist of an event (e.g., Washington and Adams were the first president and vice president) and then use their general knowledge about similar events (e.g., students' schemata for "presidential elections") to reconstruct the information at the time of test. The rarity with which we see reconstructive memory in recitations of information committed to rote memory (e.g., the Pledge of Allegiance and Hamlet's soliloquy) also suggests that reconstructive memory is most likely when students learn meaningful information—information for which knowledge structures are readily available.

Recalling Specific Events

Our discussion above indicates that people tend to reconstruct the meaning of a story when they retrieve that information from a general knowledge store—something like semantic memory described in chapter 3. But what happens when we try to remember very specific events that have happened to us? These events probably are retrieved from a somewhat different representational schema in memory—something like episodic memory.

Among the questions that researchers have studied are whether episodic events are easier to retrieve and whether they are reconstructed to the same degree as semantic information. Most of us believe that we can retrieve specific events from memory with a great deal of ease and accuracy. For example, many older Americans remember exactly where they were and what they were doing when President John Kennedy was assassinated. Others have similar memories regarding the death of Beatle John Lennon or the loss of the space shuttles *Challenger* and *Columbia*. The images of the World Trade Center tragedy now are fixed in virtually everyone's mind. Memories of highly specific events of this kind often are referred to as **flashbulb memories** (R. Brown & Kulik, 1977). Memories for a traffic accident we witnessed or for your sister's wedding also would fall into this category.

Researchers have discovered startling things about flashbulb and other "less photographic" episodic memories. Flashbulb memories are not as accurate as one might think, and certainly they are not "photographic" memories in most cases. One example is the work of Loftus and Loftus (1980), who examined the accuracy of eyewitness testimony. In related studies, the Loftuses reported that eyewitness testimony is often highly inaccurate and, more important, that it is subject to constraints imposed at retrieval. For instance, asking a witness to recall how fast the car was traveling when it *smashed* into the other car is more likely to elicit an overestimate than a more neutral word such as *struck*. These findings strongly suggest that information is subject not only to serious distortion at retrieval because of learner-induced reconstruction but to situationally induced retrieval cues as well.

Studies of flashbulb memories report similar findings. In one case, McCloskey, Wible, and Cohen (1988) asked college students to fill out a questionnaire about events surrounding the explosion of the space shuttle *Challenger* 3 days after the disaster. McCloskey et al. reported that most individuals had strikingly vivid memories of where they were, what they were doing, and how they felt at the time of the accident. Interviews with the same individuals 9 months later, however, revealed inaccuracies between initial and delayed memory for the event, with only about 65% of subjects' reports matching their original versions.

These studies reveal that retrieval is not as straightforward as one might expect, even for vivid and emotionally charged information. Retrieval errors fall into two categories: (1) those that are self-induced, as in Bartlett's study; and (2) those that are situationally induced, such as a lawyer's "leading questions" in a courtroom. These errors occur because we try to store as little information as we need, making for a more efficient cognitive system.

Most reconstructive errors are of little importance, although some may be highly important and lead to serious consequences. For example, eyewitness testimony in a courtroom setting may have important consequences for victims and the accused. Most adults are far less accurate than they suspect when monitoring their own memories (Johnson, Hashtroudi, & Lindsay, 1993). Memory monitoring is even less accurate when it comes to autobiographical memories, in part because most people can be quite overconfident when assessing their own memories. Children are especially poor in this regard (Ceci & Bruck, 1993), often failing to distinguish between actual events that happened versus events that were suggested by credible adults and peers.

Relearning

At times, information we once knew fairly well seems forgotten forever. One of the authors, for example, had 3 years of college French and some 20 years later stated that he remembered only *un peu*. Apparently, three years of study had disappeared somewhere, as recognition and recall of the French language seemed impossible. When the author recently visited Montreal, however, he found himself relearning basic French very rapidly—at least to the point that he was able to shop, ask simple directions, and even get the gist of the day's report on the Montreal Expos baseball team. Apparently, the knowledge of French only *seemed* to be forgotten because the relearning was far easier than the original learning had been.

The most sensitive measure of memory is not recall, recognition, or the ability to reconstruct events. Instead, it is the memory savings that people experience when relearning information (MacLeod, 1988). The relearning method was the favorite of the pioneer memory researcher Hermann Ebbinghaus (1885). In Ebbinghaus's use of the approach, he first practiced a list of nonsense syllables until he obtained one error-free recitation. Then, after varying delays, Ebbinghaus would relearn the materials to the same criterion. He determined the level of memory savings by comparing the number of trials he needed in the first and second learning sessions. The existence of any savings (if fewer trials were required on the second than on the first session), even when recognition or recall was not possible, indicated that some parts of the information had been remembered between the first and second learning sessions.

Even though psychologists are aware that the memory savings approach is the most sensitive measure of memory, the method is seldom used. A major reason is that the method often does not seem to be appropriate for complex stimulus materials. Further, a criterion of one error-free verbatim recall might seem reasonable for a list of nonsense syllables, but it hardly seems workable for the contents of a chapter on American history, a lecture on basic genetics, or a discussion of *The Grapes of Wrath*. In addition, after-the-fact attempts to measure savings in learning appear extraordinarily difficult and seldom have been attempted.

Nelson (1985) and MacLeod (1988) developed variations on Ebbinghaus's classic procedure. In their studies, individuals learned a list of paired associates, with nouns paired with numbers. Initially, they worked until they attained one error-free pass through the list in which they elicited the nouns paired with the provided numbers. After a lengthy delay (weeks or months in Nelson's work), a second session was conducted. This second session had two phases. The first was a test of recall in which individuals were given the numerical cues and attempted to remember as many nouns as they could. In the second phase, subjects were asked to relearn the unrecalled items and an equivalent number of previously unseen items on a single trial. Differences then seen in the immediate recall of previously studied and new items were taken as indications of memory savings.

Although relearning procedures seem to hold promise for research (see MacLeod, 1988, for a discussion), results to this point are sketchy. What is clear is that we remember far more than we are able to recall, recognize, or even reconstruct. The form of these memories and exactly how relearning differs from original learning are topics of future research.

One factor that affects both initial learning and relearning is the type of practice in which one engages (Ericsson, 1996). **Distributed practice** refers to regular periods of practice (e.g., daily piano practice). **Massed practice** refers to irregular periods of intense practice (e.g., cramming for a test). Distributed practice appears to be more efficient than massed practice (Ashcraft, 1994). For example, learning 5 new words each day for 30 days requires less learning time than learning those same 150 words in a 3-day interval. Distributed practice appears to be more beneficial when learning declarative, rather than procedural, knowledge (Mumford, Costanza, Baughman, Threlfall, & Fleischman, 1994). Distributed practice also facilitates learning higher order concepts, which typically require more time or effort to learn than simple facts.

Implications for Instruction

This chapter has suggested ways that information retrieval can be made more effective. One way is to provide a match between encoding and retrieval conditions. A second way is to provide relevant cues at retrieval. A third way is to use prior knowledge to reconstruct missing information. Implications of these three retrieval strategies are discussed below.

1. *Encoding and retrieval are linked.* The literature on encoding specificity clearly indicates that students' ability to remember information is related strongly to

their ability to encode it in a meaningful fashion. When information is elaborated at encoding and when information present at encoding is used to prompt retrieval, students remember more information than if "encoding-specific" information is not present.

At a broader level, encoding specificity reaffirms the highly interactive nature of our cognitive system. Learning information does not occur in isolated acts such as "encoding" or "retrieval" but rather is the result of all of these processes. Problems in one area lead to problems in another. All of us need to bear in mind the continuous, interactive nature of learning when planning instruction. This requires us to plan ahead so that our instructional goals for students are matched with effective review and testing. Even more importantly, we need to ask whether they are matched to the contexts in which our students will need to retrieve and *use* what they have learned.

2. *Learning always occurs in a specific context that affects encoding and retrieval.* One way to improve learning is to situate it in a context that provides useful structure to the student (see Lave & Wenger, 1991). Specifying the purpose of the learning task is one excellent means for doing so. Another useful strategy is to activate students' prior knowledge or to provide some schematic framework prior to instruction (see chapter 4). Last, information should be presented and worked with in ways that reflect how students will be asked to use it in their everyday lives.

3. *Retrieval is state-dependent.* Few teachers or students ever consider that their ability to remember information depends on their emotional state or physical location. Nevertheless, a large body of research indicates that the ability to remember information is related to our mood and the conditions under which we learned that information. One implication is that testing conditions should match learning conditions. Herding students into an unfamiliar room at a different time of day than their regular class may negatively affect test performance. Conducting final exams in a new time or location, as is often done at universities, may be ill-advised as well. Indeed, one way that teachers can help students is to teach them to prepare for important tests, such as the Scholastic Aptitude Test (SAT), in "states" that approximate actual testing conditions as closely as possible.

4. *Memory is reconstructive.* Retrieval is more than playing back an event from memory. Students often retrieve main ideas and use them and their general knowledge to construct a reasonable response. Overall, it seems that as the richness and quantity of cues at retrieval increase, reliance on reconstruction decreases. Regardless of how supportive a retrieval context is provided, however, recall will vary from student to student on the basis of their world knowledge. Two students with the "same" amount of learning may write very different essays, not because one knows more than the other, but because of differences in knowledge available to support reconstruction.

Recalling a key theme of this text, we should never lose sight of the fact that learning is a highly constructive process. In chapters 3 and 4, we saw how learners construct meaning by elaborating it with respect to their prior knowledge or processing it at a deeper level. The analog to constructive processes at encoding is reconstructive processes at retrieval. Some teachers look at constructive and reconstructive processes in a negative light, perhaps assuming that students should focus on explicit facts and concepts in their textbooks instead of making their own meaning. We disagree strongly with this view. Research has shown consistently that students learn more and remember it better when they are active (constructive) learners (see chapter 12, "Reading to Learn"). Although constructing or reconstructing meaning may seem to lead to more errors than a verbatim translation of to-be-learned material, these errors are usually insignificant, whereas the cost paid for learning information in a rote, nonconstructivist way is very high.

5.   *Learning increases when students generate their own contexts for meaning.* Research on the generation effect, elaborative interrogation, and guided peer questioning consistently has shown that learning improves when students make, rather than take, meaning. For example, generating an antonym to the word *stop* (e.g., *go*) will improve memory for the word *go* compared with simply reading it from a list or seeing it paired with *stop*. Answering questions about to-be-learned information (e.g., using methods such as elaborative interrogation and guided peer questioning) will also improve remembering. One explanation is that students are more apt to remember encoding conditions when they attempt to retrieve information if they themselves have created these conditions. Although cues provided by the text or teacher can be effective, those generated by students themselves are much more likely to be available and effective.

6.   *Recall and recognition are not the same.* Evidence suggests that recall and recognition tests require different retrieval processes and elicit different study patterns. Because of this, students' retrieval performance is best when the form of assessment is "as advertised." Students expecting a multiple-choice test will perform best on a multiple-choice test; students who have prepared for a true–false test will perform best on a true–false test; and so forth. Knowing what kind of information will be included on the test also helps students study more effectively.

7.   *Retrieval is fallible.* Retrieval is subject to error under the best of circumstances. One main reason for poor retrieval is that information was not encoded adequately in the first place. Errors occur in reconstruction as well. Although one might expect this to be less of a problem when retrieving specific facts or events, reconstructive errors are still common even for highly memorable events such as flashbulb memories. Some reconstructive errors are a result of our inclination to "bend" information to make it fit our existing schemata, whereas others are a result of new cues not available at encoding. Thus, reconstructive errors are more likely to occur when either the context or cues present at encoding are unavailable or have been changed.

8.   *Distributed practice is more efficient than massed practice.* Distributed practice helps students learn declarative knowledge more efficiently. Distributed practice appears to be most effective when organizing knowledge into higher order frameworks such as schemata. Ericsson (1996) also has argued that distributed versus massed practice is more likely to positively affect motivation for performing a task.

Summary

The context of retrieval has a powerful influence on memory performance. Generally speaking, for cues to be effective at retrieval, they must be present at the time of encoding. A major implication of the principle of encoding specificity therefore is that contexts for learning should match those likely to be present when information needs to be retrieved and used. One important aspect of the context of retrieval is the type of test—recall or recognition—given at the time of retrieval. In general, students will perform better on recognition tests, but it should be kept in mind that performance is best when there is a match between the type of test actually given and how students expect to be tested. A more important goal, however, is for students to have their knowledge and skills available for use in the widest possible range of contexts. This goal is best accomplished by helping them encode what they are learning in as many ways as possible with the broadest range of cues.

Suggested Readings

Baddeley, A. D. (1998). *Human memory: Theory and practice*. Boston: Allyn & Bacon.

   This is a text by a leading authority that is devoted entirely to the topic of memory.

Lave, J., & Wenger, E. (1991). *Situated learning: Legitimate peripheral participation*. New York: Cambridge University Press.

   This book addresses constraints on thinking and learning within a broader context and raises many questions central to the constructivist view of memory.

Chapter 6

Beliefs About Self

Bandura's Social Cognitive Learning Theory ■ *Attribution Theory* ■
Autonomy and Control ■ *Summary* ■ *Suggested Readings* ■

Tᴴɪꜱ ᴄʜᴀᴘᴛᴇʀ ᴇxᴀᴍɪɴᴇꜱ ᴛʜʀᴇᴇ ᴘᴇʀꜱᴘᴇᴄᴛɪᴠᴇꜱ on why students succeed and fail in the classroom: Bandura's social cognitive theory, attribution theory, and the role of student control and autonomy. The first of these theories considers how self-confidence affects academic learning. The second examines how students explain their academic success and failure to themselves. The third considers how students' and teachers' expectations create a controlling or autonomy-producing environment in the classroom.

These perspectives are by no means exhaustive, although we believe that they provide a sound basis for why some students succeed and others do not. Indeed, one reason that we selected these particular theories is they are comprehensive and cover most aspects of life in the classroom. We believe that most everyday motivational issues of special importance to teachers can be addressed by these theories.

Bandura's Social Cognitive Learning Theory

Most of us realize that self-confidence is essential to success in any discipline. Few of us, however, have thought carefully about what self-confidence is, where it comes from, or how it can be improved. Albert Bandura (1986, 1997) has developed an extensive theory since the early 1970s that has examined people's self-confidence in a variety of settings; how confidence develops; and how it affects behavioral outcomes, such as persistence and effort.

At the heart of Bandura's theory is the idea of reciprocal determinism (Schunk, 1991). As the name implies, reciprocal determinism suggests that learning is the result of interacting variables. Figure 6-1 shows the relationship among three basic components described by Bandura: personal, behavioral, and environmental factors. Personal factors include beliefs and attitudes that affect learning, especially in response to behavioral and environmental stimuli. Behavioral factors include the responses one makes in a given situation—for example, whether one responds to a poor test score with anger or with increased effort. Environmental factors include the role played by parents, teachers, and peers.

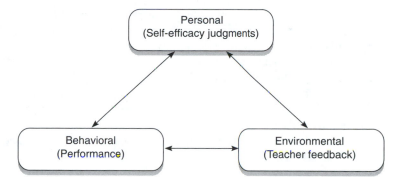

Figure 6-1
Bandura's Model of Reciprocal Determinism
Source: Adapted from Social Foundations of Thought and Action: A Social Cognitive Theory, *by A. Bandura, 1986, Upper Saddle River, NJ: Prentice Hall. Adapted by permission of Prentice Hall.*

The idea of reciprocal determinism suggests that personal factors, such as one's self-beliefs, affect behaviors and the interpretation of environmental cues. One way that personal factors are related to behaviors and environmental cues is through mediated responses—that is, how events are interpreted cognitively prior to a response. In one case, poor performance on a test may elicit anxiety in one student and increased effort in another because the same event (a poor grade) is interpreted differently.

The fact that beliefs and attitudes affect behaviors and environmental cues gives special importance to personal factors in Bandura's model. Two personal factors provide especially powerful influences on behavior. One is self-efficacy, or the degree to which an individual possesses confidence in her or his ability to achieve a goal. Self-efficacy has been related to many behavioral outcomes that we explore in greater detail later in this section. A second factor is outcome expectancy, or the perceived relationship between performing a task successfully and receiving a specific outcome as a consequence of that performance.

Consider the plight of African American baseball players prior to 1946, the year that Jackie Robinson became the first African American player to play in the major leagues. Prior to this time, two particularly talented African American players—Satchel Paige and Josh Gibson—were excluded from the all-White major leagues. Both of these players undoubtedly had very high degrees of self-efficacy concerning their baseball skills. In fact, both eventually were elected to the Hall of Fame long after their active careers were over. Neither, however, had high outcome expectancies for playing in the major leagues during their careers because, as a result of racial bias, no amount of talent would guarantee admittance. We return to the topic of self-efficacy in greater detail later in this section. First, however, let's examine how learning is portrayed in Bandura's model.

Enactive and Vicarious Learning

Learning occurs in two ways, according to Bandura (1997). The first—enactive learning—occurs when one learns a task by doing it. Bandura has argued that enactive attainments are the most important form of learning because they provide direct feedback about one's performance. Performing a task successfully over many occasions gives rise to a high level self-efficacy that is unaffected by occasional failures. The second type of learning—vicarious learning—occurs when one learns about a task by observing others perform or discuss it.

Both types of learning appear to be extremely important. Enactive learning enables us to develop the basic procedural knowledge necessary to perform a task, whereas vicarious learning allows us to observe the subtle nuances of expert performance long before we are capable of such performance ourselves. Vicarious learning, especially when it involves a skilled model, is useful for several reasons (Bandura, 1997). First, observing a model allows us to allocate all of our resources to learning about the task rather than to performing it. Second, vicarious learning enables us to see expert strategies performed without interruption. Third, observing others provides motivation to less skilled observers.

Schunk (1991) has identified three influences on the effectiveness of learning and performance. One is the developmental status of the individual. For example, students differ with respect to reasoning skills and working memory capacity at different ages. Children may also lack the physical ability or knowledge base to perform a task modeled by a skilled adult. A second influence is the prestige of the model. Models with a high functional value (those judged to be more credible) exert a stronger influence on learning. The effects of model prestige also extend to other skills in which the model is not necessarily expert. For instance, some aspiring basketball players may be more apt to eat a particular breakfast cereal because Shaquille O'Neal's picture is on the front of the cereal box. A third influence is one's ability to set an attainable goal, often with standards provided by a model. Goals do not necessarily improve learning but rather offer incentives to students. Goals that are specific, attainable within a limited amount of time, and of moderate difficulty appear to provide the greatest incentives.

Self-Efficacy

Self-efficacy should not be confused with general self-esteem. According to Bandura (1997), self-efficacy is a judgment of one's ability to perform a task within a specific domain. High efficacy in one setting does not guarantee high efficacy in another. Within a specific domain, however, self-efficacy is linked reciprocally with behavioral outcomes and environmental cues (see Figure 6-1). High self-efficacy positively affects performance, whereas good performance, in turn, positively affects one's sense of self-efficacy. Self-efficacy also indirectly affects future learning by predisposing students to engage in challenging tasks and to persist longer despite initial failures (Maddux, 2002; Pajares, 1996).

Judgments of self-efficacy differ along three dimensions related to performance. One dimension is the level of task difficulty. Even students with high efficacy in a domain may be reluctant to take a challenging graduate class. One reason is that the general level of expertise in such a class is much higher than what the students are used to. Another reason is that students may lack prior knowledge or strategies necessary to do well in the class.

A second dimension is the generality of one's self-efficacy. Some individuals feel able to perform well in almost any academic setting. Others feel confident in only one or two settings. Still others have very little self-efficacy in any domain. Generally speaking, self-efficacy in one domain is unrelated to efficacy in another domain. This does not mean, however, that some individuals do not have high self-efficacy in general. Rather, it suggests that they have reason to believe they can perform competently in many domains. In some cases, self-efficacy may generalize from one domain to another. Shell, Colvin, and Bruning (1995) found that elementary and high school students with high self-efficacy in reading also had high self-efficacy in writing.

A third dimension is the strength of one's efficacy judgments. Weak perceptions of efficacy are more susceptible to disconfirming evidence (observing someone else fail at a task) or to poor performance. Individuals with strong senses of self-efficacy persevere in the face of disconfirming evidence and poor performance. Thus, two people may receive the same low grade on a chemistry test, with very different effects on their efficacy. All other things being equal, the student with the higher efficacy will be more inclined to persist and to maintain self-confidence, whereas the other student will not.

Research by Bandura and colleagues (see Bandura, 1993; Goddard, Hoy, & Hoy, 2000; Pajares, 1996; and Welch & West, 1995, for reviews) indicates that self-efficacy is linked closely with initial task engagement, persistence, and successful performance. Bandura (1986) has identified four influences on the level, generality, and strength of self-efficacy. One influence is enactive information acquired during the performance of a task. Successful performance leads to higher self-efficacy; failure leads to lower efficacy. A second influence is observation of others; it often improves efficacy, especially when the model is judged to be similar in ability to the observer. Vicarious influences are strongest when observers are uncertain about the difficulty of the task or their own ability. A third influence is verbal persuasion. Although the effect of persuasion often is limited, it may facilitate engagement in an otherwise forbidding task that, in turn, leads to enactive feedback. Self-efficacy is judged, in part, by a fourth influence—one's psychological state. Sleepiness or physical fatigue often lowers efficacy even though it may be unrelated to the performance of a task. Strong emotional arousal also often reduces efficacy, chiefly by invoking fear-inducing thoughts.

Research on Student, Teacher, and School Self-Efficacy

Bandura's social cognitive theory has attracted much attention from educational and psychological researchers. One reason is that self-efficacy is a concept that applies to successful task engagement and performance in any domain, whether mathematics, history, waterskiing, or social events. Virtually all of this research reports the same findings; thus, we focus our attention on research most relevant to educators.

Student Efficacy   The most important and consistent finding in the research literature is that student self-efficacy is strongly related to critical classroom variables such as task engagement, persistence, strategy use, help seeking, and task performance.

High self-efficacy is associated with greater flexibility, resistance to negative feedback, and improved performance (Pajares, 1996).

For example, Collins (reported in Bandura, 1993) examined the way children used mathematics skills. She compared mathematics performance across high-, average-, and low-ability students who exhibited either high or low self-efficacy. Students with high self-efficacy at each level discarded unproductive strategies more quickly than their low-efficacy counterparts. High-efficacy students also were more likely to re-work problems they missed originally. High-efficacy students at each level outper-formed their low-efficacy counterparts.

This study highlights two important conclusions. First, efficacy improves perfor-mance and strategy use among students even when their ability level is controlled. Sec-ond, low-ability students may have the same degree of self-efficacy as some high-ability students. When they do, they tend to perform as successfully as their high-ability/low-efficacy counterparts.

Bandura and Wood (1989) found that self-efficacy is related to perceived control of one's environment. Higher self-efficacy was positively related to two kinds of control. The first concerns the belief that control can be achieved through effortful use of one's skills and resources. The second addresses the degree to which the environment can be modified. Those with higher efficacy were more apt to feel greater control and, in turn, persist in the face of performance failures.

Higher levels of self-efficacy have been linked as well with the way individuals ex-plain their success and failure in a particular situation (causal attributions). Self-efficacious individuals are more likely to attribute their failure to low effort than to low ability, whereas low-efficacy individuals attribute their failure to low ability.

Research reviewed by Bandura (1993) and Pajares (1997) points to other ways that self-efficacy may help students. One way occurs when students have high self-efficacy for controlling their own thoughts. Students who believe that they have control are less likely to experience stress, anxiety, and depression when goals have not been met. Another way occurs when students demonstrate a strong sense of self-efficacy for coping with anxiety-producing situations in the classroom or at home. Students who believe that they cope well are less apt to engage in avoidant behaviors.

Schunk (1989) also reviewed important consequences of self-efficacy on class-room behavior and performance. One consequence is that self-efficacious students are better goal setters, in part, because of their willingness to set "close" rather than "distant" goals. Another is that self-efficacious students are better at setting their own goals. Ironically, the ability to set one's own goals has been shown to enhance self-efficacy!

Teacher Efficacy   Teachers' expectations and behaviors also are affected by self-efficacy judgments (Calderhead, 1996). Teachers appear to evaluate their perfor-mances by using two independent efficacy assessments (Woolfolk & Hoy, 1990). One is teaching efficacy, which refers to the belief that the process of education affects stu-dents in important ways. The second is personal teaching efficacy, which refers to the belief that the teacher can enact significant change in her or his students. Woolfolk and Hoy found that the relationship between teaching efficacy and controlling attitudes among teachers is negative; that is, teachers high on this dimension are more likely to value student control and autonomy. This is true especially when teachers also show high personal teaching efficacy.

Other studies have investigated teacher efficacy by using only a single dimension similar to what Woolfolk and Hoy (1990) refer to as "personal teaching efficacy." A review of these studies by Kagan (1992) found that self-efficacious teachers were more apt to use praise, rather than criticism, to persevere with low-achieving students, to be task oriented, to be more accepting of students, and to raise their achievement levels. In contrast, low-efficacy teachers devoted less class time to class-related activity, spent more time criticizing students, and gave up on "problem students" more quickly. Studies by Poole, Okeafor, and Sloan (1989) and Smylie (1988) also found that self-efficacious teachers were more likely than low-efficacy teachers to use new curriculum materials and to change instructional strategies.

Since the early 1990s teacher efficacy has become something of a touchstone. A number of reviews have appeared (Goddard et al., 2000; Herbert, Lee, & Williamson, 1998; Tschannen-Moran, Hoy, & Hoy, 1998) and more attention has been focused on ways of improving teacher efficacy (Alderman, 1999; Coladarci & Breton, 1997; Guskey & Passaro, 1994). Researchers also have focused on better ways to measure teacher efficacy (Brouwers & Tomic, 2001; Henson, Kogan, & Vacha-Haase, 2001; Rich, Smadar, & Fischer, 1996) that suggest that as teachers' efficacy improves, teacher decision making and students' efficacy (Schoon & Boone, 1998) improve as well.

Alderman (1999) provides an excellent summary of attitudes and practices associated with high and low teacher efficacy, as well as ways to improve it. High-efficacy teachers possess a greater sense of personal accomplishment, convey more positive expectations to their students, and are more likely to take personal responsibility for their choices and decisions (Ghaith & Yaghi, 1997). High-efficacy teachers also teach more strategies to their students. There is higher student accountability and more time focused on academic learning. High-efficacy teachers also show more confidence in working with parents.

Alderman (1999) suggests several ways to increase teacher efficacy. One is social support, which includes support from the administration as well as a close personal relationship with other teachers. A second category is teacher planning, which includes seeking feedback from other teachers and using this information to state goals, plan, and evaluate in a systematic fashion. One particularly important way to enhance teacher efficacy is to encourage teachers to maintain ongoing assessment of student progress.

One disturbing finding, however, is that the number of years teachers spend in the classroom negatively affects their efficacy (Brousseau, Book, & Byers, 1988). Research suggests that experienced teachers are more likely to adopt a custodial view of classroom control in which rigid rules and standards are used to maintain discipline. In contrast, teachers with fewer years of experience or those who maintain high self-efficacy regardless of years of experience are more inclined to adopt a humanistic view of control in which student individuality and classroom diversity are used.

School Efficacy   Research reviewed by Bandura (1993) suggests that schools differ with respect to self-efficacy. School communities that collectively judge themselves powerless to improve student learning negatively affect both students and teachers. Within this context, individual teachers with low self-efficacy appear to lower the efficacy of their students, especially when students view themselves as having low ability. Factors that appear to affect school efficacy negatively are the stability of the student body and their relative socioeconomic status. The length of teaching experience of the teaching staff is negatively related to school efficacy as well, although it is positively related to students' academic achievement. Not surprisingly, students' prior academic achievement is positively related to school efficacy.

Modeling

Modeling is the demonstrating and describing of component parts of a skill to a novice. It is an extremely important component in the development of self-efficacy. Bandura (1997) proposed that positive instances of modeling are effective because they raise expectations that a new skill can be mastered, can provide motivational incentives, and can provide a great deal of information about how a skill is performed. Not all models are the same, however. Peer models are usually the most effective because they are most similar to the individual studying the model. For example, third-grade mathematics students will not be convinced they can develop mathematical competence just by observing a teacher solve difficult mathematics problems. Indeed, they are most likely to improve their self-efficacy vicariously when observing a student who is similar in age and especially perceived ability (Schunk, 1991).

This is not to say that teachers are not important classroom models. Often, the teacher is the only person in the classroom who can model a complex procedure adequately. One of the most effective ways to do so is through cognitive modeling (Meichenbaum, 1977), which includes the following six steps:

1.   *Create a rationale for the new learning skill.* Explain to students why acquisition of this skill is important. Provide examples of how, when, and where this skill will be used (establish outcome expectancies).

2.   *Model the procedure in its entirety while the students observe.* For example, a piano teacher plays an entire piece of music without interruption.

3.   *Model component parts of the task.* If the task can be broken into smaller parts (e.g., using the "integration by parts" method in a calculus class), model each part by using different problems or settings.

4.   *Allow students to practice component steps under teacher guidance.* For example, a music student may practice only the first eight measures of a piece of music, receiving feedback on each occasion from her piano instructor.

5.   *Allow students to practice the entire procedure under teacher guidance.* Component steps eventually are merged into a single, fluid procedure that is performed intact.

6.   *Have the student engage in self-directed performance of the task.* Research suggests that modeling is a highly effective way to improve simple and complex skills learned in the classroom. New skills may be modeled in many ways other than teacher-directed instruction. One method is reciprocal teaching, in which two to four students work in cooperative learning groups (Palincsar & Brown, 1984). A variety of other methods are described in Schmuck and Schmuck (1992).

Regardless of which method is used, however, feedback should be an essential part of the modeling process. Recall that Bandura's model of reciprocal determinism postulates a strong relationship between performance and environmental cues and learning. Feedback provided to students directly from the teacher improves both performance and self-efficacy. Feedback provided to students from other students appears to be equally effective in many situations. Perhaps the most effective type of feedback is self-generated by the student. Self-generated feedback is important because it enables students to self-regulate their performance without teacher or peer-model assistance (Butler & Winne, 1995).

Previous research indicates that different types of feedback exert different influences on performance (Hogarth, Gibbs, McKenzie, & Marquis, 1991). Outcome feedback provides specific information about performance and has little effect on initially correct or subsequent test performance (Lhyle & Kulhavy, 1987). Cognitive feedback, which stresses the relationship between performance and the nature of the task, appears to exert a more positive influence on subsequent performance by providing a deeper understanding of how to perform competently (Balzer, Doherty, & O'Connor, 1989). In a study by Schraw, Potenza, and Nebelsick-Gullet (1993), outcome feedback did little to improve students' comprehension monitoring, whereas incentives to use self-generated cognitive feedback improved both monitoring accuracy and performance.

Self-Regulated Learning Theory

Since the early 1990s, researchers have attempted to integrate the key components of Bandura's learning theory with findings from other areas of cognitive psychology. These attempts have led to the development of self-regulated learning theory (Pintrich, 2000; Schunk & Zimmerman, 1994; Winne, 1995; Winne & Perry, 2000; Zimmerman, 2000). Self-regulated learning refers to the ability to control all aspects of one's learning, from advance planning to how one evaluates performance afterward.

Most theories of self-regulation include three core components: metacognitive awareness, strategy use, and motivational control (Zimmerman, 1990). In chapter 4, we discussed how metacognition includes knowledge about, and regulation of, cognition. These different kinds of knowledge enable students to select the best strategy for the occasion and to monitor its effectiveness with a high degree of accuracy. An especially important part of metacognition is what we refer to as the planning sequence, in which students set goals, plan how to reach those goals, and periodically assess the extent to which goals were achieved. Students who engage in effective planning generally do quite well (Pintrich, 2000; Zimmerman, 2000).

Strategies are an essential part of self-regulation because they provide the means by which learners encode, represent, and retrieve information (see chapters 4 and 5). Skilled learners choose strategies selectively and monitor their effectiveness throughout the learning process (Zimmerman & Martinez-Pons, 1990). In turn, strategies enable skilled learners to use their limited resources as efficiently as possible. Randi and Corno (2000) provide a comprehensive list of study strategies that is consistent with those discussed in chapter 4. These include planning, focusing one's resources on important goals, persistence, emotional control, effective use of available external resources, and seeking help when needed.

Motivational control refers to the ability to set goals, evoke positive beliefs about one's skills and performance, and adjust emotionally to the demands of studying and learning. Skilled learners understand the role of effort and strategies in learning and are less likely than unskilled learners to attribute poor performance to uncontrollable causes, such as ability and luck. Skilled learners also are more adept at blocking out disturbances while studying (Pressley et al., 1987).

Self-regulated learning represents an important step forward in understanding how learners develop intellectual independence. Randi and Corno (2000) describe four aspects of teaching that help students achieve their best. One is providing students with choice that facilitates autonomy (Flowerday & Schraw, 2000; Ryan & Deci, 2000). A second is community building with a special emphasis on collaborative instruction. A third is explicit scaffolded instruction that carefully models complex skills and provides teacher support during the acquisition of new skills. A fourth is ongoing assessments that include teacher and peer feedback to students, as well as regular performance-based assessments of critical learning skills.

Research suggests that students who receive quality instruction are motivated to learn and succeed. Teachers help encourage self-regulation through modeling and efficient instruction. Students also observe other students engage in self-regulated learning. Teachers and other students model self-efficacy and strategy use for less regulated students (McInerney, 2000). Students also benefit from feedback. Collectively, students become self-regulated because of skilled teachers and students who demonstrate critical skills which, in turn, are incorporated into their own learning repertoire.

Implications: Improving Self-Efficacy

Research indicates that self-efficacy is affected by self-assessments, behavioral feedback, and environmental cues. Self-efficacy strongly influences many classroom behaviors, including task engagement, performance, anxiety, stress, persistence, and use of academic or social coping strategies. Because self-efficacy is changeable, teachers and parents bear a special responsibility for providing an environment conducive to improving efficacy. Several suggestions for doing so follow:

1.   *Increase students' awareness of the self-efficacy concept.* Many teachers and students underestimate the importance of self-efficacy. Emphasizing the positive consequences of high efficacy, describing how efficacy develops and deteriorates, and promoting positive efficacy messages in the classroom are goals every teacher should

adopt. Teachers may wish to communicate to parents the role of efficacy to help promote an efficacy-producing environment at home.

2. *Use expert and inexpert modeling.* Self-efficacy is domain-specific. One way to improve efficacy is by exposing students to expert and intermediate-level models. The former provide examples of expert performance that are motivational and informative. The latter illustrate that expertise develops slowly and is attainable through effort and use of strategies. In many settings, peer models appear to be especially effective.

3. *Provide feedback.* Behavioral and environmental feedback are two of the most important influences on self-efficacy. Students should be helped to evaluate their own performance to enhance this function. Teachers should also provide prompt, in-depth "performance" and "cognitive" feedback. For example, teachers should emphasize not only whether a strategy succeeded or failed but also why it did. The most effective kind of feedback relates performance outcomes to activities that cause those outcomes.

4. *Build self-efficacy rather than reduce expectations.* Bandura (1993) has stressed the importance of improving self-efficacy by incorporating efficacy-increasing experiences in the classroom rather than by decreasing task difficulty (see also Stevenson & Stigler, 1992). Indeed, the latter may decrease efficacy if students perceive that the teacher has little confidence in them. Teachers should consider ways in which class content is challenging yet attainable. One effective method is to incorporate small, cooperative groups. Another is to allow ample time for students to achieve mastery of the material.

5. *Encourage self-regulation.* Educators should be mindful that teaching individual skills, such as metacognitive awareness and strategies, is only one aspect of the educational process. A more important aspect is to help students integrate all of these skills in a manner that enables them to become self-regulated learners once they leave school. Doing so presents a tremendous challenge to parents, teachers, and society. Although no easy paths lead to this goal, careful planning and reflection on what it means to be self-regulated no doubt will benefit students and teachers alike.

Attribution Theory

Every day, events take place in our lives that can be interpreted in several ways. Consider two college students who receive the same mediocre score on a history test. One student becomes angry and decides to drop the class because, according to her, the professor is a poor teacher who has written an unfair test. The second student resolves to work harder to learn the material. Clearly, these students have interpreted their experiences in very different ways despite similar levels of performance.

But what separates these two students? Why does one drop the class, whereas the other increases her effort? One explanation is that the two students have made different attributions about their poor test performance. The first student attributes her poor showing to the teacher, although she secretly may believe that it is because of low ability. The second student attributes her poor performance to lack of effort.

Attribution theory is the study of how individuals explain events that take place in their lives. An **attribution** is a causal explanation of one of those events. Attribution theory provides a framework for understanding why people respond so differently to the same outcomes (for reviews see Eccles & Wigfield, 2002; Graham & Weiner, 1996; Stipek, 1996). Some of these causal explanations may predispose individuals to negative emotions or decrease the likelihood of future task engagement. Other explanations may provide individuals with reasons to persist or to work even harder.

In this section, we describe some main assumptions of attribution theory. To do so, we must consider what causes people to make certain kinds of attributions, what the most common attributions are that people make, what kinds of affective responses attributional judgments elicit, and how attributional judgments affect our behavior. We refer to these steps as the attributional process. We turn now to this process.

The Attributional Process

One way to think about the attributional process is the model shown in Figure 6-2. Four components are included in this model. One is *outcome evaluation,* the process by which we assess whether an outcome (e.g., a test score) is favorable or unfavorable. The second is *attributional responses,* in which we attribute this outcome to a particular cause. The third is some kind of *affective response,* in which the attributional response elicits an emotional reaction. The last is a *behavioral response,* in which we respond to the outcome in a particular way.

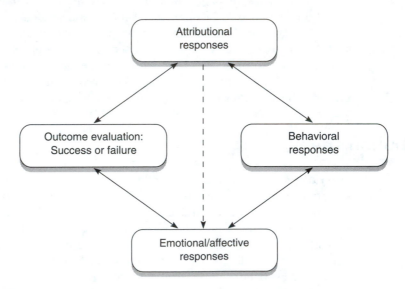

Figure 6-2
The Attributional Process
Source: Adapted from Learning and Instruction: Theory into Practice *(2nd ed.), by M. E. Gredler, 1992, Upper Saddle River, NJ: Merrill/Prentice Hall. Adapted with permission.*

The key aspect of Figure 6-2 is that events do not elicit behavioral reactions *directly,* but do so only after being *mediated* by some form of cognitive interpretation. This model is similar in many regards to the basic assumptions of Bandura's social cognitive learning theory. One important difference, however, is that self-efficacy judgments pertain to future events, whereas attributional judgments pertain to past events (Graham, 1991).

Outcome Evaluation   Outcome evaluations are made by using several criteria. One is the individual's prior history with similar outcomes. For example, if a student consistently performs poorly in history class, even an average grade on an essay test may seem favorable. A more important constraint, however, is performance feedback. Typically, performance that falls below a preestablished standard is viewed unfavorably. Whether an outcome is viewed favorably also depends on characteristics of the person, such as the need for achievement, the perceived importance of the task, and the expectations of others. Last, outcomes are evaluated, in large part, on the basis of cues from others. For example, students who usually do quite well in class may be chided by instructors for submitting an average paper, whereas other students performing the same level of work may be praised because instructors expect less from them.

Attributional Responses   Attributional responses vary along three causal dimensions (Weiner, 1985, 1986). The first dimension is **locus of control,** which defines the cause of an outcome as either internal or external to the individual. Mood, for example, is an internal cause even though it may be affected by external variables. In contrast, parents and teachers are external causes of success or failure. The locus of control dimension frequently is linked with the kind of affective responses individuals experience after an outcome. For example, pride and confidence are associated with internal causes of academic success, such as ability, expert knowledge, and effort. Shame and anxiety are associated with external causes, such as unsolicited teacher help.

The second dimension described by Weiner is **stability.** Some causes of success, such as ability, usually are assumed to be stable, although considerable debate surrounds this issue (see chapter 7). Other causes, such as effort, are less stable. Still other external causes, such as luck, are completely unstable. The stability dimension usually is linked with a person's success expectancy. If success is attributed to a relatively stable trait, such as ability or knowledge, it seems reasonable that past success would be repeated. In contrast, if success is attributed to highly unstable causes, there is little reason to believe that success will occur again.

The third dimension is **controllability.** Some causes of success, such as effort and strategy use, are highly controllable; others, such as ability or interest, are not. Uncontrollable factors, such as task difficulty and luck, obviously fail to promote confidence in one's ability to succeed again. The controllability dimension often is related to the amount of effort and persistence an individual devotes to a task. Outcomes viewed as uncontrollable often promote anxiety and avoidance strategies, whereas those under control lead to increased effort and persistence.

Table 6-1
Three Dimensions of Weiner's Attribution Theory

	Internal		External	
	Stable	Unstable	Stable	Unstable
Controllable	Typical Effort	Specific Effort	Teacher Responses	Help
Uncontrollable	Ability	Interest	Task Difficulty	Luck

The three dimensions described above can be used to create a locus (stability) controllability matrix that is shown in Table 6-1. As this table reveals, causal attributions must be categorized along all three dimensions simultaneously because two different causes, such as effort and ability, may share two common dimensions but differ along a third. According to Weiner (1985), the unique configuration of each attributional cause elicits different emotional and behavioral responses in people.

Affective Responses   Different attributional configurations give rise to different, though highly predictable, affective responses (Curren & Harich, 1993; Weiner, 1991). Positive affective responses, such as pride and confidence, are most likely to occur when an event is attributable to an internal, controllable, and stable factor, such as general effort. This is especially true for average- and low-achieving students because effort allocation is under their direct control, whereas ability and task difficulty are not. Other positive emotions, such as gratitude, are most likely to occur when an event is attributable to an external, uncontrollable, and unstable factor, such as help from individuals who are not expected to provide it.

Negative emotions, such as anger, are most likely when an event has external, controllable, and stable causes. In contrast, humiliating emotions, such as shame, guilt, and embarrassment, have internal causes that vary along other dimensions. For example, students are most likely to feel shame when an outcome (e.g., low mathematics performance) is caused by an internal, uncontrollable, and stable trait (e.g., low mathematics ability). By the same token, pity is most apt to be elicited from others under the same conditions, wherein observers view the individual as helpless. Emotions such as guilt are most likely to occur when a cause is internal, controllable, and unstable. For instance, failing to complete one's homework or engaging in occasional inappropriate behavior produces such feelings.

Behavioral Responses   One basic tenet of attribution theory is that the interpretation of an outcome (causal attribution) will determine the kind of behavioral response an individual makes. As we have seen, attributions in which stability is the critical dimension frequently give rise to higher success expectancies and, in turn, higher levels of task engagement, challenge seeking, and performance. Attributions in which controllability is the critical dimension lead to greater effort and more persistence. Attributions in which internal locus of control is critical lead to feelings of confidence, satisfaction, and pride, whereas an external locus results in positive responses, such as help seeking, as well as negative reactions, such as helplessness, avoidance, and lack of persistence (Graham, 1991; Gredler, 1992).

Attributions in the Classroom

Studies have examined the kind of attributions that students make and why they make them. One of the most important findings from this literature is that different students make very different kinds of attributions. Some differences are related to gender; others are related to students' perceptions of ability. Still others are related to the ways teachers respond to students (Stipek, 1993).

A review by Peterson (1990) found that students' negative attributional styles (e.g., attributing failure to ability and teachers) are related to low grades, less help seeking, vaguer goals, poorer use of strategies, and lower performance expectations. Studies focusing on help-seeking behaviors in particular have reported that many students do not seek help because doing so provides an explicit low-ability cue to one's peers.

In a study by Karabenick and Knapp (1991), help seeking among college students was positively related to global self-esteem but negatively related to the perceived psychological risk of help seeking. One plausible explanation of these findings is that high-self-esteem students were more likely to attribute their success to controllable causes, including asking competent individuals for help. In addition, students who were more likely to seek help were more likely to use cognitive and metacognitive learning strategies even after the effect of perceived risk was controlled statistically.

Newman and Goldin (1990) reported similar findings in a study of elementary-age children. One interesting outcome was that children were more reluctant to seek help from peers, compared with adults (including teachers), because they were afraid to "look dumb" in the eyes of their classmates. Girls were more concerned about public appearances than boys, especially in mathematics classes, compared with reading classes. Help seeking was related also to academic achievement in that low achievers sought less help. Last, the more the children thought help seeking would benefit them, the more likely they were to ask.

These studies suggest that low-achieving students are less likely to seek help because doing so provides a low-ability cue. Research by Barker and Graham (1987) and Graham and Barker (1990) has investigated low-ability cues in more detail. Barker and Graham (1987) found that teachers transmitted low-ability information to other students by way of the type and amount of praise and/or blame. Students praised for average achievement were judged by other students as having lower ability than students praised only for outstanding performances. Similar results were found when teachers blamed students for mistakes on simple versus complex tasks.

Graham and Barker (1990) extended these findings to teachers' offers of help in the classroom. Students who were quick to be helped by teachers were judged as having lower ability. The amount of teacher help also provided a low-ability cue. These cues were most apt to be detected among older (12-year-old) versus younger (5-year-old) students, although cues were salient at times even among the youngest students.

Together these studies suggest that teacher–student interactions provide a great deal of unintended information to other students (Weiner, 1995). Several studies indicate that reluctance to seek help is caused by low-ability cues provided inadvertently by teachers! Ironically, students labeled as low ability may be less likely to solicit teacher help in the future and may try to decline help even when it is offered spontaneously by teachers and despite the fact that seeking help is related to improved performance and higher academic achievement.

Attributional Retraining

Attributional retraining refers to helping individuals better understand their attributional responses and develop responses that encourage task engagement. A review by Försterling (1985) found that the majority of attributional retraining programs are quite successful. The general sequence is as follows: (1) Individuals are taught how to identify undesirable behaviors, such as task avoidance, (2) attributions underlying avoidant behavior are evaluated, (3) alternative attributions are explored, and (4) favorable attributional patterns are implemented.

Försterling reported that most programs emphasize a shift in "unfavorable" attributions based on ability to "favorable" attributions based on effort. Shifting attributions from ability to effort appears to be effective because effort is a controllable variable, whereas ability is not. Programs adopting this strategy frequently report an increase in task persistence and achievement levels.

In a series of studies by Schunk and colleagues (Schunk, 1983, 1987; Schunk & Cox, 1986), attributional feedback provided to students while they were engaged in a task increased self-efficacy and performance. Feedback about effort frequently improved task persistence, especially when it was given early in the learning cycle. To be effective, however, attributional feedback must be credible.

In contrast, Schunk (1984) found that sometimes feedback about ability has a stronger effect than feedback about effort. One group of students in this study received effort-only feedback, a second group received ability-only feedback, and two other groups received either effort-ability or ability-effort feedback. Schunk found that those who received ability feedback before effort feedback performed better and reported higher self-efficacy than those who received effort-only feedback or those who received effort feedback prior to ability feedback. Apparently, information regarding ability is linked more closely with one's sense of efficacy than is information about effort.

These findings suggest that attributional training should not focus exclusively on effort. In some cases, students may need to be reminded that their success is a result of high ability. In other cases, especially when students lack basic skills necessary for task completion, emphasizing the role of effort may increase persistence and task performance.

In addition, attributional training programs may be more effective for some individuals than others. Perry and Penner (1990) found that college students with an external orientation (those who perceived their success as having external causes)

benefited more from attributional retraining than students with an internal orientation. Externally oriented students receiving the training earned higher achievement
scores in course work than externally oriented students without training and all internally oriented students.

Overall, the attributional retraining literature provides clear evidence that increasing students' awareness about the attributions they make and helping them make
more favorable attributional responses improve self-efficacy and learning while reducing achievement-related anxiety. For this reason, we believe that teachers should
discuss the role of attributions in learning and provide some degree of retraining for
students who make inappropriate attributions.

Implications: Improving Student Attributions

1. *Discuss the effects of attributions with students.* Teachers can help students
better understand the learning process by explaining the role that attributions play in
it. Research indicates that some students struggle unnecessarily because they incorrectly attribute failure to ability rather than to lack of effort or undirected effort. Explaining these subtle differences to students is neither time-demanding nor difficult
yet may improve learning and confidence greatly.

Studies also reveal that children younger than age 10 often do not distinguish between
different attributional responses to the same extent as older children, adolescents, and
adults (Schunk, 1991). For this reason, younger students may need explicit instruction
(retraining) to help them understand and redirect their attributional responses.

2. *Help students focus on controllable causes.* Most attributional retraining programs attempt to shift one's emphasis from ability to effort judgments. Attributing
success or failure to effort is not as damaging psychologically because effort is controllable. In general, emphasizing controllable factors in the learning process increases task engagement, persistence, and performance. Emphasizing uncontrollable
causes, such as ability, mood, task difficulty, luck, and characteristics of other students, increases anxiety and decreases challenge seeking.

3. *Help students understand their emotional reactions to success and failure.*
Attribution theory provides a framework for understanding not only how we explain
success and failure but also how we feel about it. Students who make certain types of
attributions after failure experience predictable types of emotional responses. For instance, attributing failure to ability elicits some degree of humiliation in most students,
whereas attributing failure to lack of effort leads to embarrassment. Clearly, some
emotions are more denigrating than others. Parents and teachers can do students a
great service by helping them understand their emotional reactions to success and
failure. More important still, students can be shown how to change these emotions by
redirecting their attributional thinking.

4. *Consider alternative causes of success and failure.* Most attributional studies
investigate a core set of responses, including ability, effort, teacher help, and luck. Curiously, many students struggle in class for different reasons, but especially because
they lack prior knowledge, appropriate strategies, monitoring skills, and automaticity.

Fortunately, all of these factors are controllable (changeable) even though it may take some time to change them. Students should recognize that many difficulties in the classroom are attributable to these factors, instead of to low ability or lack of effort. Doing so may help remove blame from students for poor performance or for difficulty mastering new information.

5. *Be mindful of inadvertent low-ability cues.* Sometimes teachers provide low-ability cues about students even when they do not intend to. Unfortunately, some of these cues are transmitted while teachers are engaged in otherwise "positive" activities, such as praising and helping students. We recommend that teachers carefully consider the kind of information they communicate to their class by the way they offer help and praise and the way they reprimand students. Offering praise or help privately or through written feedback may be more beneficial for low-achieving students or for students who are prone to low self-esteem. Similarly, praising high-achieving students privately for normatively high performance may reduce the number of performance-oriented expectations they impose on themselves.

Autonomy and Control

The question of student autonomy is an important one, particularly as it pertains to real and imagined success in the classroom. To examine this question in more detail, however, we first must consider what it means to be motivated and how motivation affects behavior and a student's sense of control. In this section, we review important frameworks for understanding motivation, examine how motivation is related to behavior, and explore how controlling versus uncontrolling environments affect motivation.

One way to think of motivation is to distinguish between internal and external constraints on behavior. **Intrinsic motivation** refers to behaviors that are engaged in for their own sake (Deci, Vallerand, Pelletier, & Ryan, 1991; Ryan & Deci, 2002). When an individual is intrinsically motivated, tasks are performed for internal reasons, such as joy and satisfaction, rather than for external reasons, such as reward, obligation, or threat of punishment. Thus, a student is intrinsically motivated when she or he solves unassigned math problems because they interest her or him. **Extrinsic motivation** refers to behaviors that are performed to achieve some externally prized consequence, not out of interest or a personal desire for mastery. Solving mathematics problems that one does not enjoy because they were assigned as homework is one example.

Studies have shown that even young children distinguish between intrinsic and extrinsic sources of motivation (see Deci et al., 1991, for a review). Gottfried (1990) found that intrinsic motivation at age 7 was correlated with intrinsic motivation 2 years later, was positively related to intellectual ability, predicted current and future academic achievement, and was positively correlated with students' grades. Vallerand, Blais, Briere, and Pelletier (1989) reported that high intrinsic motivation was related to school satisfaction and more positive emotions in the classroom. More recent research has replicated this effect with older students up through college students (Black & Deci, 2000; Reeve, 2002).

At first glance, one might conclude that promoting intrinsic motivation would be sufficient for high levels of task engagement, persistence, and satisfaction. Unfortunately, the relationship between intrinsic motivation and classroom success is not as straightforward as it seems. Deci and Ryan (1985, 1987) have argued that a more fundamental distinction can be made between actions that are **self-determined** and **controlling.** The former actions include behaviors that individuals choose to engage in for intrinsic reasons. The latter are behaviors that individuals engage in because of internal or external pressure to conform to a set standard or to meet a particular expectation. For example, one student may choose to complete her homework because she enjoys the topic and takes pleasure in learning the material. Another student may choose to complete the same assignment to avoid a failing grade or because failure to complete the assignment would jeopardize his eligibility on the swim team. Although both students technically "choose" to complete the assignment, the degree of choice clearly is not the same.

According to Deci and Ryan, the distinction between autonomous and controlled actions is an important one because the degree of perceived choice determines one's behavioral response within a particular context. To be autonomous, a behavior must be both chosen without pressure and self-determined. In contrast, a controlled behavior may be chosen, but it will never be self-determined. As the example provided above illustrates, the same behavior in two individuals may be autonomous or controlling, depending on each person's understanding of why the behavior is performed and what the internal and external consequences are for performing or not performing the behavior. The subjective perception of why an action takes place is referred to as its **functional significance.** Individuals may attach different functional significance to the same event because "a person's perception of an event is an active construction influenced by all kinds of factors" (Deci & Ryan, 1987, p. 1033).

Control in the Classroom

Deci and Ryan have identified two types of environments: autonomy-supporting and controlling. A growing body of research has investigated some factors that promote autonomy and control, as well as their effects on task engagement, persistence, and learning. The most important of these factors are the nature of the to-be-learned materials, task constraints, teacher expectations, student expectations, evaluation, and rewards. We examine in the following sections how each of these factors affects intrinsic motivation and a variety of other behavioral measures.

Nature of the Materials   One of the most important motivational characteristics of materials is their difficulty. Materials that are too difficult for students promote a controlling environment, reduce intrinsic motivation, and promote resistance to the task in many students. Materials may be difficult for several reasons, including their grammatical complexity and their relative familiarity. Information that students know little about typically will require more time and effort to learn and will be more difficult to remember because they lack existing background knowledge.

Another important dimension is the interestingness of materials. Research suggests that students find it easier to learn and remember more when they are interested in what they are studying. This is true especially of children and adolescents (Schiefele, 1991). For example, Guthrie et al. (1996) found that high intrinsic motivation and interest were correlated with strategy use (.80) among fifth- and seventh-grade students. One reason is that interesting materials may increase intrinsic motivation to learn. A second reason is that interesting materials are more likely than uninteresting materials to be familiar to students. Not all interesting materials improve learning, however. Garner, Gillingham, and White (1989), for example, found that seductive details (information that was highly interesting but unrelated to the main topic of the story) interfered with learning main ideas. Wade, Schraw, Buxton, and Hayes (1993) reported that seductive details attract a great deal of readers' attention that would be spent more profitably on nonseductive main ideas.

Surprisingly, several recent studies suggest that individuals may regulate how much interest they have in materials. Sansone, Weir, Harpster, and Morgan (1992), for example, found that college students conceptually redefined boring tasks (e.g., copying information in different typefaces) that were viewed as important to complete. Whether younger students spontaneously adopt strategies to make boring tasks more exciting and intrinsically rewarding remains to be seen. In a study by Schraw and Dennison (1994), students read a story from one of two assigned perspectives. Information relevant to the assigned perspective but not to the other unassigned perspective was judged as more interesting and was remembered better.

In general, materials are most apt to promote autonomy and to be remembered when they are student selected or generated, of moderate difficulty, personally interesting, and familiar. Research also has shown that relating newly learned material to real-life experiences increases interest in that material, facilitates learning, and promotes autonomy.

Task Constraints   The nature of the task affects whether individuals perceive it to be autonomy producing or controlling. One obvious constraint frequently overlooked is whether the purpose of the task is clearly understood. A study by L. Anderson (1981) suggests that low-achieving elementary-age children often do not understand the purpose of a task. Although higher achieving students within the same age-group have a better understanding of the immediate purpose, they lack broader knowledge of the task, such as what skills the task will help them develop and how successful performance of the task is related to performance outside school.

Another factor is the task's difficulty. Tasks of moderate difficulty appear to be the most challenging and satisfying for students. For this reason, accelerating the difficulty of a task to keep abreast of student development has a beneficial effect on learning and motivation. Nonaccelerated tasks have been shown to promote within-class performance comparisons that, in turn, adversely affect intrinsic motivation.

One problem that teachers often face, however, is how to increase task difficulty in a heterogeneous group. Stipek (1993) describes several strategies for meeting this challenge. One strategy is to divide a class into smaller groups based on course achievement or task expertise. A second strategy is to use individual mastery programs in which students work at a pace that is comfortable for them until each has mastered the core material included in a unit. Learning centers where students work individually or in small groups are good examples. A third strategy is that teachers may use peer tutors (including parent and volunteer aides) from either the same class or other classes. Research reveals that peer tutoring leads to higher motivation and learning in both tutors and tutorees.

The pace and variability of tasks is important as well. Tasks that require active student participation tend to increase intrinsic motivation and learning. Question-asking activities before, during, and after class discussions are one avenue for involving students. Similarly, encouraging students to use deeper, more elaborative strategies, such as those described in chapter 4, leads to more active learning.

Varying the types of tasks to which students are exposed increases interest and learning. Tasks that require students to engage in problem solving, to consider unusual applications, or to think divergently about material not only encourage more active processing but also give students autonomy by allowing them to self-regulate their goals and strategy use.

Finally, research suggests that responses to different types of classroom tasks may depend on expectations established prior to beginning the task. Sansone, Sachau, and Weir (1989) found that students responded more favorably to instruction when it matched students' perceived academic goals. In one study, Sansone et al. emphasized either skill acquisition or fantasy while learning a computer game. Students in the skill-acquisition condition responded more favorably to instruction intended to facilitate skill acquisition, whereas the reverse was true of the fantasy condition. These findings suggest that responses to a learning task, as well as receptivity to instruction, depend, in part, on student- and teacher-imposed expectations.

Teacher Expectations   Teachers create either an autonomy-producing or controlling environment in the classroom by their actions and responses to students (Black & Deci, 2000; Reeve, Bolt, & Cai, 1999; Reeve, 2002). Studies have revealed some ways teachers intentionally or unintentionally affect student motivation. Providing enjoyable and challenging tasks, making favorable attributional responses that emphasize the role of effort and strategies while minimizing the role of ability, and evaluating in a nonthreatening manner are all ways that teachers promote intrinsic motivation and autonomy.

Research suggests that it is not so much what a teacher does but how she or he does it that matters most to students. For example, different "lesson-framing statements" can promote either an autonomous or a controlling environment. Statements that emphasize performance aspects of the task, such as "I want you to learn this material so that you will do well on the test," are more apt to decrease intrinsic motivation, compared with statements that emphasize learning aspects of the task, such as "Reading this passage will really help you understand the concept better." In one recent study, Williams and Deci (1996, p. 767) reported that "students who perceived their instructors as more autonomy-supportive became more autonomous."

Grolnick and Ryan (1987) studied different lesson-framing statements. Students in the controlling condition were told that they would take a test after reading a passage and that they were expected to do well on it. Other students read the same passage after being told to read however they wanted to read. Students in the controlling group reported greater interest in the passage and outperformed the noncontrolling group on a measure of conceptual learning. These effects also were observed 1 week later.

In another study, Flink, Boggiano, and Barrett (1990) investigated the effect of teacher pressure on student performance. Teachers were either pressured to maximize student performance or encouraged to teach in a style comfortable to them. Students of pressured teachers also were more pressured, compared with students taught by nonpressured teachers. The nonpressured students outperformed their pressured counterparts. In addition, pressured teachers made fewer personal disclosures and laughed less.

Another way teachers promote autonomy or control in the classroom is by the type of feedback they provide to students. **Performance-oriented feedback** emphasizes how well a student has performed in relation to other students. **Information-oriented feedback** emphasizes how performance can be improved. Studies indicate that informational feedback leads to greater intrinsic motivation, task engagement, and persistence than performance feedback. Written informational feedback has been found to be especially effective.

In addition, teachers elicit very different student responses based on their expectations. Teachers form expectations based on factors that include in-class performance and behavior, information provided by other teachers, and contact with siblings (Alderman, 1999). In general, the more controlling a teacher's expectations, the more likely it is that students will have low intrinsic motivation. Ironically, performance expectations communicated to students in a controlling manner tend to lower student performance rather than improve it (cf. Flink et al., 1990).

Good and Brophy (1986) provide a useful framework for understanding teacher expectations. *Proactive* teachers do not allow their expectations to interfere with student interactions. Instead, they communicate beliefs and expectations openly, provide opportunities to all students, incorporate accelerated tasks, and offer genuine praise. *Reactive* teachers, however, are more likely to act on erroneous beliefs about students and to impose controlling expectations. Research surprisingly indicates that proactive teachers set performance standards that are as high or higher than those of reactive teachers even though they provide students with more choices and options for achieving those standards. Proactive teachers also may be less likely to establish teacher's pets (Tal & Babad, 1990).

Jussim (1989) and Jussim and Eccles (1992) asked whether teachers' expectations cause students to behave in a manner consistent with those expectations. Contrary to many earlier studies (e.g., Rosenthal & Jacobson, 1968), Jussim found that teachers' expectations tended to be quite accurate and showed little evidence of creating a "self-fulfilling prophecy." Of course, this does not mitigate the effect of some teachers' controlling behaviors and expectations. Jussim and Eccles (1992), for instance, reported that teachers' expectations were unrelated to standardized test performance but were related to systematic bias in the grades they gave to students. Thus, it appears that expectations may affect teachers' views of students and influence students' motivation negatively by controlling expectations. This does not mean, however, that a teacher's expectations actually cause a student to act in accord with those expectations.

Last, teachers' expectations are shaped, in part, by ability and gender variables (for a review see Eisenberg, Martin, & Fabes, 1996). Oakes (1990) reported that teachers of low-ability classes put less emphasis on basic concepts, complex problem-solving skills, and preparation for future course work in the same area. In contrast, teachers of high-ability classes attempted to provide students with more in-class control and greater autonomy. Similarly, Kimball (1989) reported that females receive less teacher contact in middle school and high school settings despite no differences in the number of student-initiated interactions. Females also received less praise and more criticism than males.

Student Expectations   Students create their own autonomous and controlling environments by the expectations they hold for themselves. Bandura (1993) identified two ways that beliefs promote autonomy. One way concerns the strength of personal self-efficacy. As efficacy increases, individuals feel a greater sense of control, which leads to less anxiety, greater persistence, more task-related effort, and better use of feedback. A second way pertains to the modifiability of the environment. Individuals with low self-efficacy are more likely to view their environment (as well as personal traits) as fixed rather than as changeable. This belief has been associated with a greater sense of futility, lower aspirations, and less ingenuity.

Other researchers have distinguished between a desire for control and perceived control. Desire for control among older students is related to increased effort, challenge seeking, persistence, and positive attributional response patterns, such as attributing success to effort rather than to luck (Burger, 1985). Perceived control is positively related to academic achievement. Skinner, Wellborn, and Connell (1990) found that beliefs of elementary-age students were related to task engagement and grades. One type of belief pertained to *capacity;* that is, whether a student has the resources to accomplish a challenging goal. A second type of belief pertained to *control;* that is, whether a student could control her or his own academic progress. Skinner et al. reported that both capacity and control beliefs were significantly related to engagement and grades. In addition, teacher ratings of students' task engagement were significantly related to students' grades.

Boggiano, Main, and Katz (1988) investigated whether children's perceptions of academic control were related to academic competence and intrinsic interest. As predicted, children with a greater sense of personal control in the classroom reported more intrinsic interest in school activities, more academic competence, and a greater preference for challenge. These findings closely mirror those reported by other researchers (see chapter 6 in Stipek, 1993, for a review of this area).

Classroom factors increase intrinsic motivation as well. One factor is to provide students with a choice of materials and in-class tasks. Students allowed to choose relevant and pleasurable tasks usually select more challenging tasks and engage in them for longer periods of time. Setting personal learning goals also has a positive effect on motivation and learning. Studies show that **proximal goals** (short-term goals that can be achieved within several learning sessions) increase intrinsic motivation, provide more feedback, and increase feelings of competence and personal control compared with **distal goals** (long-term goals that require a great deal of time and effort to achieve).

Students also feel a greater sense of control when they are active participants in learning and classroom management. Teachers who allow students to set rules and to choose appropriate consequences for violating those rules experience fewer behavioral problems. Similarly, when students generate their own materials, select learning strategies they feel most comfortable with, and ask questions of other students and teachers, they are more likely to persist and to report greater interest in a task.

Evaluation   One area of academic life that imposes a strong perception of control is testing and evaluation. Not all types of evaluation elicit the same reactions in students, however. **Norm-referenced evaluation** (students compete against other students) often reduces intrinsic motivation for average and low-achieving students. In contrast, **criterion-referenced evaluation** (students compete against a predetermined standard) may increase intrinsic motivation (Stipek, 1993). Achieving a preestablished standard is especially motivating when the standard is related to the student's personal goals, signifies improvement, and is reached through effort rather than through normatively high ability. Along these lines, Covington and Omelich (1984) found that college students perceive criterion-referenced evaluation as fairer and better able to detect student effort.

Research further indicates that written evaluation serves a very useful function and frequently increases intrinsic motivation and performance. Comments that provide formative and/or diagnostic information help students identify the source of their errors, the nature of the errors, and how to correct them in subsequent assignments. In contrast, controlling feedback, such as negative remarks; excessive amount of red ink; or, worst of all, a poor grade without any comments, unequivocally reduces intrinsic motivation, task engagement, and persistence.

Another aspect of evaluation that strongly affects motivation is how teachers deal with errors. In a performance-oriented class, errors reduce motivation. Emphasizing the informational value of errors through written feedback or conferences, however, increases intrinsic motivation. Studies indicate that errors need not undermine performance, provided teachers believe that errors are potentially useful (Poplin, 1988). Using errors to evaluate the "process" rather than the "product" components of performance is helpful. Moreover, praising correction of errors frequently increases intrinsic motivation because it rewards student effort. One helpful rule of thumb for increasing intrinsic motivation is to allow students, whenever possible, to redo work that contains errors.

In addition, teachers should consider the relative merits of private versus public evaluation. Most motivation theorists do not advocate public evaluation because it orients students to normatively high performance, rather than to improvement, and typically benefits only the top 15 to 20 percent of students. If public evaluation is used, teachers must ensure that all students are capable of competing with other students for high grades.

Private evaluation has important advantages from a motivational perspective. One advantage is that private evaluation does not provide ability cues to other students in the class. A second is that private evaluation is more apt to encourage students to engage in challenging assignments. It also enables students to track their progress actively by using charts and records in journals.

Rewards   Rewards have been part of classroom life since education began, and they continue to spark tremendous debate among practitioners and theorists (Cameron & Pierce, 1994; Eisenberger & Cameron, 1996; Kohn, 1996; Lepper, Keavney, & Drake, 1996; Ryan & Deci, 1996). Unfortunately, from our perspective, the most commonly used type of reward has been for compliant behavior or normatively high performance. Many teachers and parents use rewards on a regular basis to motivate students. Indeed, many school programs use token economies and other sophisticated reward systems to encourage learning and good behavior. Others rely on the first cousin of rewards—some form of threat or punishment. Many teachers give students in-class choices as a reward (Flowerday & Schraw, 2000; Schraw, Flowerday, & Reisetter, 1998).

But how effective are rewards at motivating students and improving performance? Deci and colleagues (Deci & Ryan, 1985, 1987; Deci et al., 1991) have identified two kinds of rewards: **informational** and **controlling.** Rewards that provide useful information or feedback to students generally increase intrinsic motivation and learning, whereas rewards that attempt to shape or control student behavior and performance generally decrease it. Moreover, controlling rewards invariably lead to poorer performance and reduced task engagement and interest *once they are terminated* (see Kohn, 1993, for a book-length review).

The potentially deleterious effects of rewards have been observed in a wide variety of settings. Newby (1991) found that first-year teachers' use of rewards and threats was negatively correlated with on-task behaviors, whereas confidence-building strategies, such as verbal encouragement, explicit instruction with examples, and favorable comments about mistakes, were positively correlated with the same behaviors. Hennessey and Amabile (1988) found that rewarding children for artistic performance had little immediate effect on the quality of artistic productions. When rewards were curtailed, however, students reported less interest in artistic endeavors and produced lower quality artistic productions. Similar negative effects were found when students were given strong criticism, received controlling rather than informational feedback, or were forced to compete with other students. In many cases, mere surveillance was sufficient to reduce intrinsic motivation and to impair performance (Deci & Ryan, 1987).

The "reward withdrawal" effect described above seems universal in scope. Rewards decrease intrinsic motivation even though they do increase extrinsic motivation when intrinsic motivation is lacking. For this reason, rewards should be used only when individuals are not intrinsically motivated to perform a task. When rewards are used, negative effects are most likely to occur when they are expected, salient, and contingent on engagement rather than when meeting a criterion-referenced performance standard is expected (Deci & Ryan, 1987). Curiously, providing a reward after the fact, when it is not expected, has few negative effects on motivation and performance. Thus, the *anticipation* of the reward, rather than the reward itself, impairs motivation.

For those who prefer to use limited rewards, the following tips may be helpful. First, use rewards sparingly. Rewards help motivate students, albeit extrinsically, in many tasks they would not engage in otherwise because of indifference or anxiety. Second, make sure all students are capable of meeting the criteria for earning the reward. Third, eliminate rewards once they are no longer needed, while simultaneously modeling positive, intrinsic reasons to engage in tasks (e.g., reading is relaxing and entertaining). Last, avoid threats, deadlines, and other constraints that could be construed as punishments. Often, punishments fail to elicit compliance and may impair performance and reduce intrinsic motivation.

Implications: Fostering Student Autonomy

Research reveals many ways to promote either an autonomy-producing or controlling environment. Deci et al. (1991) and Lepper (1988) are particularly good references on this topic. Below, we summarize some main points to consider when trying to promote student autonomy.

1. *Let students make meaningful choices.* The more options students are given, the more likely they will be to engage in, persist in, and enjoy a task. Parents and teachers should provide students with at least some choice regarding the materials, tasks, and kinds of evaluations used in the classroom. Allowing students to help select the tasks they undertake, to establish rules democratically, and to set appropriate consequences for violating rules helps promote better classroom discipline.

2. *Scrutinize teacher and student expectations.* Students often are unaware of teachers' and their own expectations. Taking some time at the beginning of the school year and periodically throughout the year to clarify expectations may be helpful. Low expectations or those that intentionally or unintentionally impose control have been shown to affect the performance of everyone in the classroom in negative ways. Teachers' expectations are especially important because students may form self-expectations based on these messages.

3. *Minimize extrinsic rewards.* Extrinsic rewards should be used thoughtfully and sparingly. Intangible rewards, such as genuine praise and attention, usually have a positive influence on students *provided* they are genuine, not overused, and accessible to all students. Tangible rewards, such as money, tokens, gifts, and free time, may reduce intrinsic motivation and interest in tasks while they are being performed and frequently decrease task engagement, persistence, and quality of performance once they are curtailed. Both tangible and intangible rewards, however, can promote task engagement when intrinsic motivation is low.

For these reasons, extrinsic rewards should be used only when students have no other reason to engage in the task. Using rewards as a long-term motivator may be disastrous unless the rewards are continued indefinitely. Using threats, punishment, or surveillance also is ill-advised because these methods rarely accomplish their purpose and may lower intrinsic motivation. In particular, essential academic skills, such as reading, writing, and mathematics, should never be used as punishments (e.g., writing essays after school for being late). Doing so gives students many reasons not to be intrinsically motivated in these activities in the future.

One final point: Rewards often can be used effectively without any of the negative consequences described above, provided they are not contingent on some type of performance outcome. Rewards offered spontaneously, when they are not expected, do not reduce intrinsic motivation and performance as a rule.

4. *Incorporate criterion-referenced evaluation.* Evaluation that reduces the amount of direct competition while increasing the amount of informational or cognitive feedback to students usually increases intrinsic motivation and other task-engagement variables. In most instances, criterion-referenced evaluation satisfies these constraints more readily than does norm-referenced evaluation. Examples of the former include "mastery learning," in which students work toward a preestablished standard that does not depend on the performance level of other group members; multiple-choice and essay tests that allow students to revise or justify their responses to improve their grade; portfolio assessment; and most forms of ongoing (formative) evaluation.

5. *Provide intrinsically motivating reasons for performing a task.* Providing students with an explicit or implicit rationale for engaging in an activity is a powerful instructional technique. Teachers who read more and model their own intrinsic enjoyment of reading to their students usually have students who read more inside and outside class. Similarly, explicitly highlighting positive aspects of reading may help offset feelings of low self-efficacy or anxiety in some students.

Summary

This chapter described three frameworks for understanding self-beliefs and how they can affect self-determination in the classroom. Bandura's learning theory emphasizes the reciprocal relationship among self-beliefs, performance, and environmental feedback. We focused in detail on one type of belief—self-efficacy—which is related to task engagement and academic achievement. Self-efficacy is domain-specific and subject to change through modeling, feedback, and self-statements.

Whereas self-efficacy beliefs are judgments about future events, attributions are judgments about past events. Attributions are causal explanations of our success and failure experiences in the classroom. Attributions vary along three dimensions: locus of control, stability, and controllability. Each dimension is associated with a particular type of emotional response. Research indicates that students' attributional patterns strongly affect their task engagement, persistence, and achievement. Undesirable attributional patterns can be changed with the help of attributional retraining programs.

We also considered the role of student autonomy in the classroom and how intrinsic motivation promotes feelings of autonomy. Students who feel a sense of control are more likely to seek challenge, persist at difficult tasks, and perform better than teacher-controlled students. Teachers who experience a sense of control also interact with students more favorably. Factors were discussed that affect students' sense of control, including classroom materials, task constraints, teacher and student expectations, evaluation strategies, and the use of rewards. Providing choices to students is an important means for increasing feel- ings of control and intrinsic motivation. Using extrinsic rewards, such as money or praise, gen- erally decreases intrinsic motivation.

Suggested Readings

Alderman, M. K. (1999). *Motivation for achievement: Possibilities of teaching and learning*. Mahwah, NJ: Erlbaum.

This book covers all the topics discussed in chapters 6 and 7. Alderman focuses on day-to-day educational implications of motivation research.

Bandura, A. (1993). Perceived self-efficacy in cognitive development and functioning. *Educational Psychologist, 28*, 117–148.

This review provides a good summary of self-efficacy theory.

Deci, E. L., Vallerand, R. J., Pelletier, L. G., & Ryan, R. M. (1991). Motivation and education: The self-determination perspective. *Educational Psychologist, 26*, 325–346.

This review provides a thorough discussion of in- trinsic and extrinsic motivation.

Eccles, J. S., & Wigfield, A. (2002). Motivational beliefs, values, and goals. *Annual Review of Psychology, 53*, 109–132.

This article reviews recent research on motivation, including self-efficacy, self-regulation, and attribu- tional research.

Reeve, J. (2002). Self-determination theory applied to educational settings. In E. L. Deci & R. M. Ryan (Eds.), *Handbook of self-determination research* (pp. 183–203).

Rochester, NY: University of Rochester Press.

This article describes implications of self-determination theory in the classroom.

Beliefs About Intelligence and Knowledge

THIS CHAPTER EXAMINES THE ROLE that beliefs about intelligence and knowledge play in thinking and problem solving. Often, we are unaware that we hold these beliefs even though they predispose us to respond or think in a certain way. Research suggests that individuals who reflect on their beliefs are more apt to change them.

The beliefs we hold, whether they are implicit or explicit, affect our behavior in many ways. In chapter 6, we found that individuals with high self-efficacy are more willing to try a difficult task. By the same token, people who hold certain beliefs about the changeability of intelligence are more likely to persist when faced with difficulty, and those who view knowledge as certain only within a particular context are more likely to engage in skilled reasoning than those who view knowledge as absolutely certain. Before we discuss beliefs about intelligence and knowledge in more detail, let's first look at implicit beliefs.

Understanding Implicit Beliefs

What makes us think and act the way we do? At some point, most of us find ourselves voicing opinions that at another time and upon reflection we do not agree with. Sometimes, we realize quite unexpectedly that we are not sure what we believe about a controversial issue; at other times, we may articulate strong beliefs about important social topics without having any conscious awareness of where these beliefs came from or why we believe them. Researchers are beginning to understand that much of our behavior is shaped by unconscious beliefs about key aspects of learning, such as intelligence and knowledge. Beliefs of this type often are referred to as **implicit beliefs** because they represent unconscious, personal beliefs about the world that evolve slowly over time (see chapter 3 for a discussion of implicit memory). No one is certain how or when these beliefs begin to develop. There is considerable agreement, however, that implicit beliefs have a significant effect on the way we view ourselves as learners and how we operate in the classroom (Dweck, 1999; Hofer, 2001; Rhodewalt, 1994; Schraw, 2000; Sinatra, 2001).

Implicit beliefs often give rise to an **implicit theory;** that is, a set of tacit assumptions about how some phenomenon works. To illustrate, let's compare two typical students in a beginning algebra class. Imagine that both are talking after a difficult test and that Akira says, "It doesn't surprise me that I'm no good in math. Nobody in my family was good at it either!" Presumably, Akira believes (at least implicitly) that success in a mathematics class is, in large part, attributable to genetic inheritance; otherwise, his family's mathematics ability should have nothing to do with his own success or failure. Now compare Akira with Alonzo, who responds, "At first, I struggled in this class, but then I went to the math lab, and the work I did there really helped me improve!"Alonzo appears to believe that his success in a mathematics class is attributable more to effort than to ability. Of equal importance, Alonzo implicitly endorses the view that his ability to learn mathematics is changeable.

Alonzo seems to hold a very different view about his ability than does Akira about his. Their beliefs about their abilities form the basis of "theories of intelligence." These theories almost certainly are implicit. If Akira and Alonzo were asked to state their "theories of intelligence" explicitly, they would find it difficult to do so (Schraw & Moshman, 1995). Moreover, the theory that each actually describes may be at odds with the implicit beliefs echoed in their conversation.

Although at first glance the study of implicit theories may appear to have little to do with effective learning and teaching, a good argument can be made that understanding and clarifying students' implicit theories may be just as important as providing basic content knowledge or strategy instruction. One reason is that research has shown that students with differing implicit beliefs differ in their willingness to use strategies while learning (Ames & Archer, 1988; Schraw, Horn, Thorndike-Christ, & Bruning, 1994). Another reason is that students with differing implicit beliefs appear to think and reason in very different ways, some of which are far more conducive to effective learning (Kardash & Scholes, 1996; Kuhn & Weinstock, 2002; Ryan, 1984).

At this point, you may be asking yourself what kinds of implicit theories you have and how they affect your learning. The answer to this question is that all of us have many implicit beliefs, or in some cases explicit beliefs, about all kinds of everyday intellectual phenomena. Consider your attitudes about intelligence. What is intelligence? Do you believe that your intellectual aptitude is fixed and that no amount of effort, strategy use, or metacognitive awareness will improve it, or do you believe, as does Sternberg (1999a), that intelligence is changeable by improving the kinds of intellectual skills that are necessary for classroom success?

Now, consider your views on creativity. Are some people born creative, whereas others are not? Is creativity teachable and, if so, to whom? Next, consider knowledge. Is there an ultimate, knowable truth in the universe that humans eventually will discover? Is knowledge relative? Does "truth" exist, and if it does, is it fixed and certain?

These examples illustrate the scope and importance of implicit beliefs on thinking and learning. The chances are good that you found these questions difficult to answer.

The chances are also good that you have spent little time trying to reach definitive answers to these questions. Nevertheless, the "hidden assumptions" that underlie our thinking and behavior exert a very powerful influence.

Understanding implicit beliefs is an important first step in becoming self-regulated. Let's begin by examining some specific implicit beliefs in greater detail.

Beliefs About Intelligence

Dweck and colleagues (Dweck, 1999; Dweck & Leggett, 1988) proposed a highly influential social-cognitive model of motivation based, in large part, on the kinds of implicit theories that people hold about intelligence. Two types of implicit theories are proposed in their framework. The first is referred to as an **incremental theory,** owing to the assumption that intelligence is changeable and improves incrementally. In contrast, individuals holding an **entity theory** of intelligence tend to believe that intelligence is fixed and unchangeable. According to Dweck and Leggett, most individuals can be characterized by one of these basic belief orientations. Individuals holding incremental and entity theories view the world in very different ways that affect how they react to challenging situations.

One interesting aspect of the Dweck and Leggett model is that incremental and entity views of intelligence seem to be independent of a person's true intellectual ability (Dweck, 1999; Pintrich, 2000a). Several studies support this view, indicating that high-ability students are no more likely than low-ability students to adopt incremental theories (Miller, Behrens, Greene, & Newman, 1993; Schraw et al., 1994). This finding holds promise for educators because it suggests that students' beliefs about intelligence need not be compromised on the basis of their true ability. Even those who struggle in the classroom can change the way they think about intelligence, which in turn may have a positive effect on their classroom achievement.

Holding either incremental or entity views also appears to have important consequences for personal academic goals. Incremental beliefs give rise to the development of **learning goals** (also commonly referred to as mastery goals), in which individuals seek to improve their competence. Entity beliefs give rise to **performance goals,** in which individuals seek to prove their competence. Research indicates that children and adolescents attuned to learning goals persist longer in the face of task difficulty; are more likely to attribute success to internal, controllable causes, such as strategy use and effort; and have an overriding concern for personal mastery (Greene & Miller, 1996; Harackiewicz, Barron, Tauer, Carter, & Elliot, 2000; Kaplan & Maehr, 1999). Children attuned to learning goals also show a preference for challenge and risk taking (Ames, 1992) and spend more time on-task (Butler, 1987; Midgley, Kaplan, & Middleton, 2001). In contrast, individuals attuned to performance goals are more apt to become frustrated and defensive when confronted with a challenging task; tend to attribute failure to external, uncontrollable causes, such as luck or teachers, or to internal, uncontrollable causes, such as lack of ability; and show an undue concern for demonstrating high performance, compared with others (Blumenfeld, 1992; Dweck, 1986).

More recently there has been debate about the specificity of performance goals. Researchers have distinguished between performance-approach and performance-avoidance goals (Midgley et al., 2001; Pintrich, 2000a). Performance-approach goals are those in which a student willingly approaches a task to prove his or her competence and high ability. Performance-avoidance goals are those in which a student attempts to avoid a task in which he or she looks incompetent. Pintrich (2000) suggests that performance-approach goals may facilitate adaptive behaviors such as strategy use and positive feelings over and above the effects of mastery goals. In contrast, Midgley et al. (2001) suggest that performance-approach goals do not facilitate learning and achievement. Although the jury is still out on this debate, all of the relevant research on goal orientations agrees that learning goals facilitate learning and achievement and that performance-avoidance goals interfere with them.

Table 7-1 presents some important characteristics of individuals with learning and performance goals. Individuals with learning orientations tend to be most interested in academic improvement and, as a consequence, may be more apt to focus on the *process,* rather than on the *products,* of learning (Stipek & Gralinski, 1996; Urdan, Midgley, & Anderman, 1998). These students enjoy learning for its own sake and feel comfortable asking for help when they do not understand something. Another important characteristic of learning-oriented students is that they enjoy intellectual challenge and usually will work harder when they encounter challenging materials. When students with learning goals fail a quiz, they correctly recognize that many reasons can account for failure and that most of these reasons are changeable. They do not tend to attribute failure to low ability, as do students with strong performance goals. This characteristic, more than any other, may give learning-oriented students a distinct advantage because academic challenge or even failure may increase their motivation.

Students with learning goals differ from those with performance goals in several other important ways. One difference is that learning-oriented students are more

Table 7-1
Characteristics of Learning and Performance-Oriented Students

Learning Orientation	Performance Orientation
Improving competence	Providing competence
Seeks challenge	Avoids challenge
Persists	Quits
Attributes success to effort	Attributes success to ability
Positive response to failure	Negative response to failure
Uses strategies effectively	Uses inappropriate strategies
Self-regulated	Helpless

Source: From "A Social-Cognitive Approach to Motivation and Personality," by C. S. Dweck and E. S. Leggett, 1988, *Psychological Review, 95,* 256–273. Copyright 1988 by the American Psychological Association. Adapted by permission.

likely to adopt more complex strategies once they begin to fail at a task, whereas performance-oriented students resort to inappropriate strategies (Diener & Dweck, 1978). A second difference is that individuals characterized by a learning orientation are more apt to engage in adaptive behaviors, such as persistence, focusing attention, and appropriate help seeking (Archer, 1994; Newman & Schwager, 1995; Schunk, 1996). For example, Miller et al. (1993) found that college students characterized by a strong learning orientation were significantly more likely to persist when confronting difficult material in an introductory statistics class. One explanation of this finding is that students with learning orientations maintain a higher sense of self-efficacy while engaged in a difficult task (Bandura, 1993).

In contrast, performance-oriented students often adopt a maladaptive response pattern to failure. One type of maladaptive response occurs when students assume that they do not have the ability to succeed and refuse to continue working on a difficult task once they begin to fail (Solmon, 1996; Urdan, 1997). A second maladaptive response occurs when performance-oriented students become verbally defensive after experiencing difficulty on a task: These students may change the focus of conversation unexpectedly and describe in detail their competence at skills totally unrelated to the task at hand. For example, after failing a mathematics task, a performance-oriented student may boast about his or her skill at singing. A third behavior occurs when individuals refuse to engage in a task on the assumption that they will fail. In some cases, **learned helplessness** is a defense against perceived incompetence (Dweck, 1975).

In general, individuals with performance orientations often seem overly concerned with doing better than others and may show far greater concern for the grade they receive than for the amount of information they learn. These students see their success or failure as the direct consequence of their intellectual ability yet do not see their ability as controllable. Performance-oriented students do not enjoy challenge to nearly the same degree as their mastery counterparts. For this reason, they may be less likely to show interest in topics they know little about or may fail at. They also may be less willing to try new strategies or to investigate novel solutions to a problem. One particular concern is that performance-oriented students are more likely to quit when faced with a difficult task.

As you might expect, students with learning and performance goals also differ noticeably in the types of attributions they make for academic success and failure. Results of a correlational study conducted by Ames and Archer (1988) are presented in Table 7-2. In this study, approximately 200 middle school and high school students were classified according to their goal orientations (see Roedel, Schraw, & Plake, 1994, for a similar study using college students). Students with learning and performance orientations were compared on several dimensions, including self-reported strategy use, responses to task challenge, and attributions for classroom success and failure. Results of the Ames and Archer study suggest some important and startling differences, which are summarized in Table 7-2. According to this study, students with learning goals tend to attribute their success in the classroom to effort, strategy use, and teachers.

Learning and performance-oriented students also differ with respect to academic self-efficacy and self-regulation (Midgley, Anderman, & Hicks, 1995). Schunk (1996) and Roeser, Midgley, and Urdan (1996) reported that students with strong learning

Table 7-2
Attributions for Classroom Success and Failure for Students with Learning and Performance Orientations

	Learning Orientation	Performance Orientation
Reasons for success	Effort (.37) Strategy use (.22) Teacher assistance (.47)	Effort (.14) Strategy use (.24)
Reasons for failure	Teachers (−.29)	Low ability (.21) Task difficulty (.29) Lack of strategy use (.16)

Note. Numbers in parentheses indicate statistically significant correlations.

Source: From "Achievement in the Classroom: Student Learning Strategies and Motivational Processes," by C. Ames and J. Archer, 1988, *Journal of Educational Psychology, 80,* 260–267. Copyright 1988 by the American Psychological Association. Adapted by permission.

goals are more efficacious. Archer (1994) and Schraw et al. (1994) reported similar findings among college students. Bouffard, Boisvert, Vezeau, and Larouche (1995) found that college students who reported strong learning and performance goals attained the highest levels of academic self-regulation.

Learning-oriented students also appear to have better relationships with teachers compared with performance-oriented students. In fact, of all the variables considered in the Ames and Archer (1988) study, learning-oriented students considered teachers to be of greater importance to academic success than ability, effort, or strategy use! Performance-oriented students, however, saw no relationship between teacher assistance and academic success. One important consequence of these differences is that learning-oriented students may be more inclined to ask for help from teachers or other students when they begin to struggle.

A comparison of performance-oriented students reveals a rather different picture. Although these students appropriately attribute classroom success to effort and strategy use, they also view failure as the consequence of low ability, task difficulty, and poor teacher-student interactions. This pattern of attributions captures the essence of performance goals—the belief that success and failure in the classroom depend, in large part, on one's ability rather than on effort, strategy use, or teachers. Ironically, students with performance goals are more apt to quit when faced with a difficult task, on the assumption that they lack the ability needed to succeed even though they do not differ in ability, compared with students with learning goals.

Constraints on Classroom Behaviors

One might ask at this point what classroom factors, if any, are known to affect students' goal orientations positively. The work of Dweck (1999) and other researchers (Church, Elliot, & Gable, 2000; Harackiewicz et al., 2000; Midgley et al., 2001; Pintrich, 2000a;

Urdan et al., 1998) suggests two important components: situational factors, such as classroom climate or home environment, and dispositional factors, such as basic personality makeup. Unfortunately, little is known about the relative contribution of each of these factors, although many researchers working in this area believe that the type of goal orientation a student adopts depends on a complex interaction between the two (Cain & Dweck, 1989). The work of Dweck and colleagues generally places a greater emphasis on dispositional factors that the student brings to the classroom. Ames and Archer (1988), however, have argued that learning and performance orientations are largely the result of classroom structure. Classes that place normatively high emphasis on ability and performance within the classroom peer group appear to promote a performance orientation among the majority of students, whereas classes that place high value on improvement, strategy use, persistence in the face of difficulty, and effort may promote learning goals even among students who are otherwise rather performative. From a practical viewpoint, all theorists agree that goal orientations are changeable, given careful consideration on the part of the teacher and an awareness by students of the consequences of adhering to different types of goals.

Clearly, educators should think carefully about the kind of environment they create in their classrooms because situational factors are known to affect interest and motivation (Schiefele, 1991). Careful consideration should be given also to the role of ability, effort, and strategy use in successful learning. Emphasizing daily academic improvement while simultaneously deemphasizing the importance of ability are central to establishing a learning-oriented environment. The results of Sansone et al. (1989) also suggest that instruction is most effective when skill acquisition is emphasized from the onset.

Is Intelligence Changeable?

The work of Dweck and colleagues (Dweck, Chiu, & Hong, 1995; Dweck & Leggett, 1998; Elliott & Dweck, 1988) raises interesting questions about the controllability of such traits as intelligence and personality. Attributional theorists, such as Weiner (1986) and Graham (1991), suggest that intelligence is defined as an internal, stable, and uncontrollable trait, a view quite consistent with the beliefs of entity theorists (see chapter 6). In contrast, other theorists believe that intellectual ability is changeable and therefore partially under the control of the learner (Lohman, 1993; Perkins, 1995).

The idea that one's intelligence is controllable may seem foreign to some readers. Whether intelligence is controllable and, if it is, to what extent it can be changed remain hotly debated. Some experts working in the area of human intelligence support the entity view (Jensen, 1992); others, such as Robert Sternberg (1986), have proposed theories consistent with an incremental theory. In Sternberg's view, individuals can improve their intellectual performance in any given situation by adapting to the demands of the situation as strategically as possible.

Ultimately, whether intelligence is fixed or changeable depends on how one defines intelligence. If *intelligence* means "the ability to adapt successfully to an environment," then surely it is changeable. In chapter 4, for instance, we described helpful learning strategies that are known to improve learning by helping individuals use their cognitive resources more efficiently. In chapter 6, we described the many ways that academic performance and reasoning ability are improved by a concomitant change in self-efficacy (see Bandura, 1993, for a further discussion of changeable ability). Our own view is that successful learning depends far more on how one uses one's resources than on how many resources one has. Although it is unknown whether the amount of resources one has can be changed, it is well known that how effectively one uses them can be changed quite dramatically.

Guidelines for Fostering Adaptive Goals

Dweck and Leggett's (1988) theory suggests that individuals with learning orientations are more likely to feel comfortable and to succeed in an academic setting. This suggestion raises the question how teachers and parents can create an environment conducive to the development of learning goals. We offer these suggestions.

1.   *Promote the view that intellectual development is controllable.* The basic distinction made in Dweck and Leggett's framework is between individuals who believe that intelligence is fixed or changeable. Those who believe that it is changeable report more satisfaction with school and persist longer on a difficult task without succumbing to frustration. Promoting the view that intellectual performance is controllable may lead to the kinds of adaptive behaviors described above.

2.   *Reward effort and improvement while deemphasizing native ability.* Students clearly differ in ability. Basing class grades or recognition on ability, however, may promote a performance orientation, especially if carried to an extreme. In contrast, rewarding effort and improvement emphasizes the incremental nature of learning.

3.   *Emphasize the process, rather than the products, of learning.* Focusing on the process of learning highlights its incremental nature, whereas focusing on the products emphasizes the outcome of that process. Research suggests that feedback acquired about the process of learning is especially important to learners.

4.   *Stress that mistakes are a normal (and healthy) part of learning.* Everyone makes mistakes when learning a new skill. How teachers respond to these mistakes sends a powerful message to students. When mistakes are viewed positively, receive corrective attention, and are used to provide feedback to students, students learn more than when mistakes are viewed in a negative light (Poplin, 1988). Using mistakes constructively also highlights the incremental nature of learning, a view consistent with a learning orientation.

5.   *Encourage individual, rather than group, evaluative standards.* Much of the evaluation that occurs in education, especially among high school and college students, is **norm-referenced** (each student's performance is compared with the group's average performance). Group-based grading may lead to the adoption of a performance orientation, given that each student is compared directly with the group norm. In contrast, encouraging individual standards (e.g., portfolio evaluation) is more likely to promote the development of a learning orientation.

Beliefs About Knowledge

Our discussion thus far has focused on the classroom consequences of implicit beliefs about intelligence. Researchers have also discovered that students' beliefs about the nature of knowledge have important consequences for academic performance and critical thinking (DeJong & Ferguson-Hessler, 1996; Farnham-Diggory, 1994). Historically, beliefs about the origin and nature of knowledge, or **epistemological beliefs,** have been of interest since the Greek philosophers. Recent studies of epistemological beliefs have attempted to isolate more precisely the consequences of holding particular beliefs (for recent reviews see Cunningham & Fitzgerald, 1996; Hofer, 2001; Hofer & Pintrich, 1997). This research has investigated the developmental sequence that individuals pass through on their way to mature reasoning about knowledge.

One of the earliest educators to investigate this phenomenon was Perry (1970), who proposed a model in which students pass through several distinct, ordered stages in the development of beliefs about knowledge. In the early stages, students adopt what Perry refers to as a *dualist* perspective, in which knowledge is viewed as either right or wrong. Students in this stage tend to view knowledge as being absolute, universally certain, and accessible only to authorities. Individuals at this level of reasoning may assume, for example, that only prominent theologians have a true understanding of life's basic truths. Rather than question this authority, dualists accept these truths on the assumption that understanding such matters is beyond their intellectual grasp and must be accepted on faith. In later stages, however, students progress beyond the dualist mode of thinking to a more relativist stage, in which knowledge is viewed as uncertain and relative. *Relativists* hold the view that knowledge must be evaluated on a personal basis by using the best available evidence.

Ryan (1984) provided an experimental test of Perry's basic framework and concluded that relativists not only hold different beliefs from dualists but also approach learning in a more sophisticated way. To test the dualist–relativist distinction, Ryan first grouped college students into the two categories described above. Next, he asked them to describe the strategies they used to monitor their comprehension while reading. Finally, he tracked students through a semester-long psychology class and recorded their final grades.

Results of this study suggest some important findings. First, dualists do not do as well as relativists when final grades are considered. An analysis of comprehension-monitoring standards suggests why: Dualists tend to search for fact-oriented information while studying, whereas relativists tend to search for context-oriented information. Dualists generally rely on remembering information reported explicitly in the text, whereas relativists are more likely to construct a meaning from the text, to paraphrase, or to create an overall framework that summarizes the main ideas presented in the chapter. Surprisingly, these differences were found even when academic aptitude (Scholastic Assessment Test scores) and academic experience were taken into consideration. These latter findings suggest that the performance differences observed between dualists and relativists are attributable to beliefs about knowledge and how these beliefs affect study strategies.

Responses to Ryan's work have been mixed, however. Schommer (1990) argued that Ryan's dichotomous view is too simple to describe accurately the complexity of epistemological beliefs. To test this view, Schommer developed a self-report inventory in which students responded to 62 true–false questions on their beliefs about the nature of knowledge. Three of the questions included in this instrument are "Truth is unchanging," "Scientists can ultimately get to the truth," and "Successful students learn things quickly."

Schommer's study suggests that people hold extremely complex beliefs about knowledge that vary across four separate dimensions. The first dimension, *simple knowledge,* refers to the belief that knowledge is discrete and unambiguous. Students who score high on this dimension believe that learning is equivalent to accumulating a vast amount of factual knowledge in an encyclopedic fashion. Schommer's second dimension, *certain knowledge,* pertains to the belief that knowledge is constant: Once something is believed to be true, it remains true forever. The third dimension is *fixed ability;* that is, the belief that one's ability to learn is inborn and cannot be improved through either effort or strategy use. Like Dweck and Leggett's (1988) entity theorists, these individuals may believe that intelligence is fixed and personally uncontrollable. The final dimension, *quick learning,* refers to the belief that learning occurs quickly or not at all. Students scoring high on this dimension assume (inappropriately) that limited failure is tantamount to permanent failure. If a problem cannot be solved within 10 minutes, for example, it will never be solved. A number of recent studies have replicated these dimensions (Hofer, 2000; Schraw, Bendixen, & Dunkle, 2002).

Schommer's work is unique in that it is one of the first studies to examine closely the underlying complexity of beliefs about knowledge. But Schommer's research did not stop there. After identifying the four component beliefs described above, she next investigated their relationship to socioeconomic variables and information processing skills (for reviews see Schommer, 1994; Schommer-Aikins, 2002). One of the more interesting findings is that the amount of higher education that students receive is inversely related to their belief in certain knowledge. All other things being equal, the longer students attend college, the more likely they are to believe that knowledge is tentative and subject to personal interpretation. One important implication of this finding is that better educated people may be more willing to adopt a constructivist approach to learning because believing that knowledge is certain should rarely lead one to question the legitimacy of that knowledge. This finding also suggests that encouraging individuals to further their education beyond high school may have a profound effect on their beliefs about knowledge (Baxter-Magolda, 1999, 2002; Kuhn, Cheney, & Weinstock, 2000).

Another interesting finding is that females are more likely to believe that learning is gradual rather than quick. This belief may lead females to stick with a difficult-to-learn subject longer than males and to feel less frustrated when an answer does not occur immediately. Quick learning was related as well to other socioeconomic indicators: the student's year in school, the father's educational level, and how much independent discussion was allowed at home. Those with less education were more apt to believe that acquiring new knowledge occurs in an all-or-nothing fashion; those with more college experience tended to view knowledge as tentative. Simple knowledge was related to the strictness of the home environment: Stricter standards led to the belief that knowledge is unambiguous, whereas greater tolerance led to the belief that knowledge is complex and subject to interpretation. Encouragement toward independence in the family structure also had positive effects on beliefs about simple knowledge and quick learning.

An analysis of the relationship between beliefs about knowledge and information processing strategies showed that quick learning predicted oversimplified conclusions when students were asked to provide a written conclusion to a chapter on theories of aggression. Prior knowledge also was related to the type of conclusions students drew in that more knowledge about the topic was associated with broader conclusions. A belief in quick learning also led to poorer performance on a summative mastery test of the material, as well as greater overestimation of understanding of the passage.

More recently, Schommer, Crouse, and Rhodes (1992) reported that beliefs in simple knowledge negatively affected complex problem solving. As beliefs in complex, incremental knowledge increased, problem solving improved. Jehng, Johnson, and Anderson (1993) found that epistemological beliefs differ across academic disciplines among college undergraduate and graduate students. Students in "soft" disciplines, such as the humanities, were more likely to believe that knowledge is uncertain than students in "hard" disciplines, such as physics. Compared with undergraduates, graduate students were more likely to believe that knowledge is uncertain and develops incrementally (they did not believe in quick learning). Bendixen, Schraw, and Dunkle (1998) found that epistemological beliefs were related to moral reasoning among adults. Individuals adopting beliefs in complex, incremental knowledge reasoned at a higher level on the Defining Issues Test. Kardash and Scholes (1996) reported that beliefs in certain knowledge were associated with lower scores on the Need for Cognition Scale and in written measures of cognitive reasoning.

Kuhn and colleagues (Kuhn 1991, 1992; Kuhn et al., 2000) found that epistemological beliefs are related to one's ability to argue persuasively. In this study, individuals were classified as an *absolutist* (one who believes that knowledge is absolutely right or wrong), a *multiplist* (one who believes that knowledge is completely relative), or an *evaluative* theorist (one who believes that knowledge, though relative, is constrained by situational factors such as commonly accepted rules) on the basis of their beliefs about the certainty of knowledge. Evaluative theorists were more likely than absolutists to provide legitimate evidence in support of an argument. In addition, compared with absolutists, evaluative theorists generated a greater number of plausible alternative theories and provided better counterarguments.

Elsewhere, Schoenfeld (1983) investigated consequences of quick learning. Schoenfeld reported that even experienced students who were asked to solve mathematics problems gave up after 5–10 minutes on the assumption that if they failed to solve the problem during this time, the problem could not be solved. One interesting question raised by this research is whether students who are prone to quit after a brief period are more likely to hold entity theories of learning that predispose them to failure avoidance.

Together, these studies indicate that beliefs about knowledge and the knowing process affect the way one reasons, how long one persists at a difficult task, and perhaps what academic discipline one enters (Schraw, 2001). They also indicate that epistemological beliefs are affected by one's home environment and, in particular, by one's educational level. More education seems to translate into a more relativist viewpoint—a fact that has not escaped the attention of some civic and religious leaders who view universities suspiciously as bastions of "secular humanism" (cf. Moshman, 1981). Ironically, when using objective criteria such as amount and kind of evidence at one's disposal, virtually all studies indicate that relativist thinking leads to better reasoned conclusions (see Kuhn, 1991, for a comprehensive review).

Reflective Judgment

Another framework for studying beliefs about knowledge and how they affect behavior is that of Kitchener and King (King & Kitchener, 1994, 2002; Kitchener, 1983; Kitchener & King, 1981; Kitchener, King, Wood, & Davidson, 1989). The focus of this research is somewhat different from Perry's in that its emphasis is on examining differences in the way people resolve dilemmas rather than differences in their beliefs per se. In their initial study, Kitchener and King (1981) developed a seven-stage developmental model of *reflective judgment*. Table 7-3 presents the characteristic reasoning processes and assumptions of each of these stages.

Reflective judgment is a term used by Kitchener and King (1981) to refer to one's ability to analyze critically multiple facets of a problem, reach an informed conclusion, and justify one's response as systematically as possible. Previous research suggests that reflective judgment depends on a set of epistemological assumptions that develop slowly in a predictable, developmental sequence (Kitchener, 1983; Kitchener & King, 1981; Kitchener et al., 1989). For example, abandoning the belief that knowledge can be known with absolute certainty appears to improve the quality of one's reasoning (Kitchener & Fischer, 1990). Other studies reveal that reflective judgment develops throughout early adulthood (Kitchener & King, 1981; Kitchener et al., 1989) and is related to age and education (King, Wood, & Mines, 1990) and critical thinking ability (King et al., 1990) but is independent of measures of cognitive ability, such as verbal fluency (Kitchener et al., 1989).

Kitchener and colleagues (Kitchener & King, 1981; Kitchener et al., 1989) have identified seven developmental stages of reflective judgment that can be distinguished on the basis of three criteria. One criterion is the *certainty* of a knowledge claim (King et al., 1990). Individuals in Stages 1 through 3 of the Kitchener et al. (1989) taxonomy believe that knowledge is certain and permanent even though knowledge may be known to only a select few. Individuals in Stages 4 and 5 view knowledge as almost totally uncertain. Individuals in Stages 6 and 7 view knowledge as context-dependent; some things are knowable, at least temporarily, even though one's views on a particular topic may change in the light of new information or a different set of evaluative criteria.

Table 7-3
Stages in Kitchener and King's Reflective Judgment Model

Stage 1:	Knowledge is unchanging, absolute, and accessible
	• beliefs are based on personal observation
	• knowledge exists absolutely and concretely
Stage 2:	Knowledge is certain but may not be accessible to everyone
	• knowledge is certain
	• knowledge is accessible only to authorities
Stage 3:	Knowledge is certain, though it may be accessible to anyone
	• knowledge exists absolutely
	• no rational way to justify beliefs
Stage 4:	Knowledge is uncertain and idiosyncratic
	• truth varies from person to person
	• knowledge is interpreted subjectively
Stage 5:	Knowledge is uncertain, though contextually interpretable
	• objective knowledge does not exist
	• beliefs can be justified by using "rules of inquiry"
Stage 6:	Knowledge is relative yet justifiable on the basis of rational arguments
	• knowledge is personally constructed
	• beliefs are justified by comparing evidence
Stage 7:	Knowledge is relative, though some interpretations have greater truth
	• knowledge is constructed
	• beliefs are justified probabilistically

Source: Adapted from "Reflective Judgment: Concepts of Justification and Their Relationship to Age and Education," by K. S. Kitchener and P. A. King, 1981, *Journal of Applied Developmental Psychology*, 2, 89–116. Adapted with permission.

A second criterion is the *process by which we acquire knowledge*. Individuals in Stages 1, 2, and 3 emphasize the defining role of direct observation or authority figures; that is, knowledge is encoded directly from external sources. Those at Stage 4 rely chiefly on personal, idiosyncratic processes, such as personal opinion. Individuals at higher stages of reflective judgment show an increasing proclivity to rely on objective, consensual processes, such as critical debate and hypothesis testing, that are tempered by personal reflection.

A third criterion is the *type of evidence* used to justify one's views of the world. Individuals at Stage 1 typically view justification as self-evident. Thus, a Stage 1 reasoner may assert that evidence that God exists "is all around us." Those at Stages 2 and 3, in contrast, are apt to cite a specific authority, such as an eminent theologian, book, or expert. Individuals at Stages 4 and 6 tend to rely on idiosyncratic evidence. For these individuals, a belief in God would be justified on the basis of the individual's personal beliefs, whereas those in Stages 5 and 7 rely on consensual forms of evidence, such as laws, scientific facts, and the opinions of a diverse body of experts.

The work of Kitchener and colleagues suggests that two primary mechanisms affect the development of reflective judgment. One mechanism is *experience*. Previous research has found that age, education, and home environment all provide a statistically significant prediction of reflective judgment skills (Kitchener & King, 1981). Related research also suggests that reflective judgment may be affected by the type of intellectual discipline one enters (King & Kitchener, 2002; King et al., 1990). A second mechanism is one's *belief system*. In this regard, Kitchener and King (1981, p. 90) state, "Differences in concepts of justification . . . are derived from different assumptions about reality and knowledge." What these assumptions are and how they differ across individuals remain unclear, however. No doubt, some are related to epistemological beliefs about the certainty, complexity, and permanence of knowledge; others may be related to a broader set of beliefs that include assumptions about the role of innate ability (Dweck & Leggett, 1988) and the legitimacy of constructivism in the knowing process (Chandler, Boyes, & Ball, 1990).

Stages in Reflective Judgment

Reflective judgment is assumed to develop in a sequential fashion; that is, individuals progress from Stage 1 to higher levels without skipping stages. This does not mean that each person reaches the highest stages or that two people progress at the same rate. Rather, development of reflective judgment is highly idiosyncratic.

Each stage is associated with a unique set of assumptions about reasoning. These assumptions pertain to the certainty of knowledge, the processes by which one acquires knowledge, and the kinds of evidence used to evaluate one's claims about knowledge. These criteria are shown in Table 7-4.

Individuals in Stage 1 are characterized by the belief that knowledge is certain, absolute, and indistinguishable from one's beliefs. Beliefs are either right or wrong within this framework, but they are never ambiguous. Individuals in this stage are prone to accept apparent truths at face value, without a great deal of scrutiny. Justification of truth or knowledge is not required, owing to the close relationship between knowledge and direct observation. In many ways, Stage 1 thinkers lack the ability to make reflective judgments because they believe that knowledge is predetermined and absolute.

Stage 2 reasoners differ from those in Stage 1 in that they believe that knowledge, though assumed to be absolute and predetermined, is limited to authorities and experts. Individuals at this level implicitly live by the motto "When in doubt, ask an authority." Of course, this approach to resolving complex moral and ethical issues can have disastrous consequences because there is no reason to believe that reflective judgment will improve as long as one believes that only experts are capable of skilled reflective reasoning; that is, excessive faith in "omniscient authorities" may undermine the subsequent development of reflective judgment!

Stage 3 differs from either of the stages described above; individuals in this stage recognize that even authorities may lack answers to difficult dilemmas. In this view of reflective judgment, individuals may come to the initially disconcerting conclusion that no one is capable of ever reaching the truth about a complex issue. Typically, however, the belief that truth ultimately will be identified empirically is still maintained. According to Kitchener and King (1981), beliefs at this level are justified by what feels right to the individual.

Table 7-4
Evaluative Criteria for Each of the Seven Stages of Reflective Judgment

Level	Performance	Certainty	Justification of Conclusions
1	Fixed	Absolute; certain.	Personal beliefs that are self-evident. No justification or evidence given.
2	Fixed	Absolute; certain.	Recognized authorities. Direct observation of world.
3	Fixed	Temporarily uncertain.	Authorities or direct observation when knowledge is uncertain.
4	Changes	Permanently uncertain.	Idiosyncratic beliefs.
5	Changes	Permanently uncertain.	Rules of inquiry for a particular context (e.g., societal norms).
6	Changes	Certain in a context.	Evaluation objective evidence via personal criteria.
7	Changes	Certain in a context.	Formalized rules of inquiry (e.g., logic). Evaluation of empirical data.

Source: From *The Relationship Between Epistemological Beliefs, Causal Attributions, and Reflective Judgment* by M. F. Dunkle, G. Schraw, and L. Bendixen, 1993, April. Paper presented at the Annual Meeting of the American Educational Research Association, Atlanta, GA.

Stage 4 represents a dramatic change from the three earlier stages in that knowledge and beliefs now are viewed as fundamentally uncertain. Truth becomes relative within this framework because, as is often the case, different views can be supported or refuted by a variety of incompatible facts. One important advantage to this way of thinking is the recognition that what is true for one person will not necessarily be true for another. One main liability of this stage is that truth and knowledge must be justified on a person-to-person basis; hence, beliefs and assumptions may differ dramatically even between individuals who share otherwise similar worldviews.

Individuals in Stage 5 possess an even greater sense of epistemological uncertainty in that objective knowledge is assumed to be nonexistent. Knowledge within this framework becomes completely relative because the ultimate truth or falsity of an argument can be evaluated only within the context in which the information occurs; thus, conclusions regarding knowledge are always subject to change, given a different context to interpret the issues. According to Kitchener and King (1981), choosing between competing interpretations often is resisted during this stage, on the assumption that no single solution can ever be completely validated.

In contrast, Stage 6 reasoners recognize that some arguments are better than others and can be evaluated on their merit. A further assumption by individuals in this stage is that the basic process of evaluating arguments remains unchanged even if the context in which the argument is presented changes. Stage 6 reasoners appreciate the reciprocal relationship between the process and the product of justification; that is, the conclusions one reaches are determined, in part, by the kind of argumentation one uses to reach those conclusions. Individuals in Stage 6 also recognize that multiple "constructions" of a problem are possible and, indeed, desirable.

Stage 7 reasoning differs still further in that although interpretations of truth and knowledge change across different contexts, some interpretations are more justifiable than others on the basis of either evidence or the rigor of one's argumentation. Knowledge is constructed during this stage on the basis of personal inquiry into the nature of the problem and evidence that supports or refutes one's tentative conclusions. Beliefs are justified probabilistically on the basis of evidence available to the individual. In addition is the recognition that what is accepted currently as the most reasonable solution to a problem may be changed later to accommodate new information or arguments that were not considered previously.

Kitchener and King's model provides a useful framework for understanding the development of reasoning skills as they relate to changes in beliefs about the certainty and verifiability of knowledge. Individuals whose reasoning is typical of earlier stages (Stages 1, 2, and 3) view their world in a rather fixed and limited way on the assumption that knowledge is certain; individuals in later stages (Stages 6 and 7) see the world in a more flexible way on the assumption that knowledge is not fixed.

Reflective Judgment and Education

The work of Kitchener and King raises important questions about the nature of teaching and learning. One question is how the classroom environment affects a student's reasoning. Does greater student autonomy lead to better reflective judgment? How do dispositional characteristics, such as one's degree of efficacy, attributional style, or personal goal orientation, affect one's willingness to engage in or improve one's reflective thinking? How are age, educational background, and home environment related to the development of reflective judgment?

Kitchener and King (1981) investigated some of these issues and reported dramatic differences among individuals in each of the seven stages. One question concerned whether students reasoned about different problems in similar ways. Results of Kitchener and King's initial study with high school and college students revealed that given individuals tended to reason about different kinds of problems in a highly similar way. Style of reasoning typically was confined to the same or adjacent stages, suggesting that people's basic assumptions about knowledge lead to predictably similar conclusions.

A second question concerned the relationship among age, educational experience, and reflective judgment. As one might expect, high school students tended to reason at lower stages (the average stage was 2.77) compared with college undergraduates (the average stage was 3.65) or graduate students (the average stage was 5.67). The difference between high school and graduate students was especially strong (three full stages), suggesting that the amount of education that one receives is clearly linked with the sophistication of one's reflective reasoning.

Other relationships were tested as well. Although no differences were found between males and females in any of the seven stages, students' verbal ability was highly correlated with reasoning ability. Those with better verbal skills tended to reason at higher stages than those with lower scores. Several tests of formal-operational problem solving revealed that virtually all 60 students participating in the study had achieved some degree of formal reasoning. Apparently, however, the ability to engage in formal-operational reasoning was not a sufficient condition for advanced reflective judgment. Many students capable of such reasoning scored at Stage 3 or lower.

In a related study, Kitchener et al. (1989) conducted a 6-year analysis of change in reflective judgment. One important finding was that students progressed sequentially through adjacent stages rather than skipped one or more stages. Another finding was that some groups progressed faster than others, although differences in the rate of development were attributable, in part, to the fact that some groups started at a very high level to begin with. During the 6-year period, high school students progressed the most, moving roughly two full stages—from 2.83 to 4.99. During the same period, college undergraduate students improved slightly more than one full stage—from 3.72 to 4.89. College graduate students showed little improvement at all, moving from 6.15 to 6.27.

A comparison of these stage scores reveals several interesting points. First, high school students progressed two full stages during a 6-year period, reasoning at a level commensurate with college undergraduates. This finding indicates that differences in reflective judgment need not be viewed as permanent. Given adequate instruction and age-related maturation, most students can be expected to improve their reasoning abilities over time. In contrast, college undergraduates failed to bridge the gap between themselves and graduate students after a 6-year follow-up even though the latter group showed no statistically significant improvement. One reason may be that better reasoners go on to graduate school, whereas poorer reasoners do not. An alternative explanation is that graduate school improves one's reflective judgment substantially. Unfortunately, Kitchener and King's (1981) study does not allow us to answer this question with any degree of certainty because none of the original pool of college undergraduates continued on to graduate school.

A study by Dunkle, Schraw, and Bendixen (1993) provided some insights into this problem. Dunkle et al. first measured undergraduate and graduate students' epistemological beliefs by using the instrument designed by Schommer (1990). They next asked students to respond to an open-ended dilemma ("Is truth unchanging?") and scored these responses by using Kitchener and King's Reflective Judgment Scale. Results were that students who believed more strongly in innate ability, simple knowledge, and quick learning were more likely to score in the lower stages of Kitchener and King's Reflective Judgment Scale. Most students scoring in Stages 5 through 7 were graduate students, whereas none of those scoring in the three lowest stages were graduate students. These findings suggest that graduate students engage in more sophisticated reasoning partly because of differing epistemological beliefs. Thus, increased education may improve reasoning because it enables students to change their implicit (or even explicit) beliefs about knowledge.

Education and Thinking

One question left unanswered by Kitchener and King's research is the effect that formal education has on reflective judgment. Several studies have provided surprising insights into this question (see Pascarella & Terenzini, 1991, for a comprehensive review). In a follow-up study on her earlier research, Schommer (1991) found that college undergraduates hold different epistemological beliefs depending on their academic major. Education majors were far more likely than science majors to believe in certain knowledge and quick learning. In general, undergraduate science majors held more sophisticated beliefs about knowledge, which appeared to affect their everyday decision making. Unfortunately, Schommer's research does not allow us to determine whether students with less sophisticated beliefs chose an academic major that allows them to persist in those beliefs or whether simple beliefs are the consequence of one's academic major.

A study by Lehman, Lempert, and Nisbett (1988), however, suggests that one's academic major can shape one's way of thinking in very important ways. Lehman et al. tested graduate students in four disciplines (medicine, law, psychology, and chemistry) at the beginning of their first and third years. Participants were given four types of conceptual reasoning tests: (1) statistical reasoning applied to everyday life, (2) methodological reasoning that tested one's ability to detect flaws in an argument attributable to lack of a control group, (3) conditional reasoning that required students to establish necessary and sufficient conditions for an outcome to be true, and (4) verbal reasoning designed to evaluate students' ability to evaluate evidence. In one experiment, 1st-year graduate students were compared with 3rd-year graduate students in the same program. In a second experiment, another group of students was compared during their first year and again 2 years later.

Results were similar in both cases. An analysis of 1st-year students across the four disciplines revealed no differences on graduate school admission tests; that is, all were of roughly the same ability level. First-year students also performed similarly on the four reasoning tests, with the exception of chemistry students, who scored significantly lower on the statistical and verbal reasoning tests. A comparison of verbal reasoning scores between the 1st- and 3rd-year students revealed no important differences across the four groups. This outcome was expected because students in each of the disciplines were expected to be proficient in this skill prior to entering graduate school. The difference between beginning and advanced psychology students on the statistical reasoning test was that they improved roughly 70 percent—a rather startling gain. Medical students improved by roughly 25 percent, whereas law and chemistry students did not improve at all.

One might ask why the psychology students improved so dramatically compared with the other groups. The answer, at least for those who have completed such a program, is rather obvious: Graduate psychology programs typically require students to complete at least three advanced-level statistics classes, as well as several classes on basic research methodology. It should not be surprising that psychology students improved far more than students who were not required to take such courses.

A comparison of conditional reasoning scores led to somewhat different findings, however. In this case, the medical, law, and psychology students improved 30–40 percent during their first 2 years of graduate school, whereas the chemistry students did not improve. Again, the reason for such improvement can be traced to extensive use of conditional reasoning skills in these graduate programs. Students are required on a daily basis to establish the conditions under which legal, medical, or experimental evidence is necessary and/or sufficient to prove a particular hypothesis. Why chemistry students did not improve remains unclear. One likely explanation is that Lehman et al. (1988) did not include a test sensitive to the improvement made by chemists.

Results of the Lehman et al. study answer some of the important questions raised earlier. First, students' reasoning skills are affected by the intellectual training they receive. One example is that students trained in law improve conditional reasoning skills that are not improved by graduate training in chemistry. Second, students do not appear to choose an academic discipline solely on the basis of skills they already possess. None of the students differed initially on any of the reasoning tasks or on intellectual ability. In general, students seem to enter graduate programs with similar types of intellectual skills and develop greater proficiency with some of these skills only as a result of their academic training. Returning momentarily to Schommer's (1991) findings, it is probably the case that undergraduate education majors, compared with science majors, subscribe to different beliefs about knowledge for one of two reasons: Either they are never required to question these beliefs, and so they do not, or beliefs supporting simple knowledge and quick learning are reflected in the classes they take.

Summary of Beliefs About Knowledge

The research we have described indicates that people's beliefs about the certainty and complexity of knowledge profoundly affect their reasoning. The work of Perry (1970), Ryan (1984), and Schommer (1990) suggests that individuals hold many beliefs about knowledge and that these beliefs constrain information processing. Kitchener and King's (1981) research further indicates that different epistemological assumptions constrain the level of reflective judgment in which individuals engage. This conclusion is strengthened further by the research conducted by Dunkle et al. (1993). Last, the Lehman et al. (1988) study revealed that epistemological beliefs and reasoning skills are the result of one's intellectual environment rather than the determinants of what type of academic discipline one pursues.

Hope and Attitude Change

At this point, we shift our attention briefly to another kind of belief that has attracted researchers' attention—hope! Ongoing investigations by Snyder and colleagues (Babyak, Snyder, & Yoshinobu, 1993; Harney, 1989; Langelle, 1989; Snyder, 1995; Snyder et al., 1996) have reported an impressive number of statistically significant relationships between people's expressed hope and academic achievement. Hope consists of two important components that Snyder et al. (1991) refer to as **agency** and **pathways** or, more colloquially, as the "will" and the "ways." The former refers to an individual's sense of self-determination and perseverance when faced with challenges. The latter refers to how well an individual can generate workable solutions to those challenges.

To test the relationship between hope and other outcomes, Snyder et al. (1991) devised a 12-question inventory containing some questions that measure a person's sense of agency and pathways. One example of an agency question is "My past experiences have prepared me well for the future." An example of a typical pathways question is "There are lots of ways around any problem." Snyder and colleagues have used this instrument in a variety of studies that compared performance on the hope inventory with frequently used measures of life orientation, life experiences, self-esteem, hopelessness, depression, stress, optimism, and sense of control. In most cases, the hope inventory is correlated with these measures to a significant degree, although none of these instruments seem to be measuring quite the same dimension as hope.

As one might expect, the two dimensions measured by the hope inventory are highly correlated, suggesting that a greater sense of self-determination usually is associated with the corresponding belief that challenges can be met and overcome. Snyder and colleagues have conducted studies examining how responses to this inventory are related to specific academic and social outcomes. In a study by Yoshinobu (1989), people with high hope scores demonstrated significantly more self-determination in the light of failure. Those receiving high hope scores reported more potentially useful solutions to challenging circumstances than did those receiving low hope scores. Roedel et al. (1994) also reported that the pathways component was correlated strongly with learning goals and controllable attributions but was uncorrelated with performance goals.

Subsequent studies have shown that people high on hope have a greater preference for difficult tasks that cannot be explained by differences in intellectual ability. When confronted with obstacles, high-hope students showed greater self-determination and solution pathways than medium- or low-hope individuals. People scoring high on the hope inventory were more likely as well to have a greater number of specifiable goals across several domains, including job, personal relationships, health, and spiritual development. Hope also correlated with perceived academic goal attainment, indicating that those who score higher on hope expect to get higher grades in college classes. In fact, students with higher hope and academic expectations do receive higher grades even when their academic ability is taken into consideration!

Other important findings have been found in these studies as well. First, scores on the hope inventory appear to be independent of intellectual ability. Second, a person's tendency to score high or low on hope is unrelated to gender. Third, the degree of hope expressed by people appears to be stable over time, suggesting that some individuals seem predisposed to be more hopeful than others.

Changing Beliefs

One important question raised by Snyder et al.'s research, as well as by the research on goal orientations and epistemological beliefs, is how easily maladaptive beliefs can be changed. Most research suggests that changing beliefs may be far more complicated than people assume. One reason is that beliefs are formed on the basis of cognitive and affective information (Breckler & Wiggins, 1989). In this view, cognitive appraisal of information is objective and rational; affective appraisal is subjective and based on emotional reactions to an object. Whether beliefs are changeable may depend, in large part, on how beliefs were formed initially. Those formed on the basis of affective responses may be resistant to change by cognitive means; those formed on the basis of cognitive responses may be resistant to affective means of persuasion.

Several experiments by Edwards (1990) addressed this issue. Individuals in one experiment were asked to examine some fictitious consumer products, such as a high-energy drink and a portable copier. Participants received information about these products in two stages: During the first stage, people received affective information (e.g., tasting the drink), followed by cognitive information (e.g., reading an advertisement for the product), or they received cognitive information first, followed by affective information. In the second stage, Edwards provided participants with additional information designed to conflict with information provided in the first stage. Half of the people received cognitive information first, followed by affective information; half received information in the reverse order. The purpose of the study was to examine whether attitudes that develop through affective and cognitive means are more resistant to change when the conflicting information is presented by using the same or a different means of persuasion.

Edwards (1990) found that beliefs acquired through affective persuasion were easier to change through affective means and that beliefs acquired through cognitive persuasion were easier to change through cognitive means. Of special interest, however, was the magnitude of change. Beliefs acquired through cognitive persuasion were more resistant to change than beliefs acquired through affective means. In addition, neither affective nor cognitive persuasion appears to be very useful when one is attempting to change beliefs that were formed by using another mode of persuasion; that is, beliefs based on affective responses show little change when individuals are presented with contradictory cognitive information.

To further complicate matters, other studies suggest that affective information may alter our beliefs even when we have no conscious awareness of this information (Greenwald, Klinger, & Lui, 1989; Niedenthal, 1990). One study by Niedenthal (1990) asked college students to describe their impressions of cartoon faces after first viewing human faces that were presented below their perceptual threshold (below the level at which visual information can be consciously recognized). Some of these slides showed faces marked by disgust; others showed faces expressing joy. As expected, subjective evaluation of the cartoon faces was significantly more negative after viewing faces conveying disgust.

These studies all seem to suggest that attitudes and beliefs are acquired in complex ways and may be highly resistant to change (Bendixen, 2002; Dole & Sinatra, 1998; Kuhn & Loa, 1998). Appealing to students through use of well-reasoned cognitive arguments may be of little use if beliefs were formed initially by affective means. For example, consider the difficulty that educators or parents face trying, through cognitive means, to dissuade teenagers from drinking alcoholic beverages when these teens are exposed to affective appeals from television commercials showing happy, carefree young adults leading the good life on a sunny California beach, beer in hand.

From a teacher's or parent's perspective, changing beliefs about intelligence, knowledge, or any other complex phenomenon may be a slow process. Clearly, special emphasis should be placed on providing environments in which students are given opportunities to reflect on their own beliefs and shift gradually to new modes of thought (Baxter-Magolda, 1999; Reybold, 2001). As discussed in chapter 14, experts agree that some degree of cognitive disequilibrium is needed to fuel the conceptual change process (Baxter-Magolda, 2002; Dole & Sinatra, 1998; Patrick & Pintrich, 2001; Sinatra & Pintrich, 2002).

Teachers' Beliefs

Teachers hold many beliefs that affect their attitudes and behavior in the classroom. These beliefs, more often than not, involve tacit assumptions about students, learning, the material to be taught, and the organization of the class (Kagan, 1992) and are as diverse as perceptions of self-efficacy, subjective attitudes about content knowledge, and how it can be taught most effectively (Borko & Putnam, 1996; Borko, Mayfield, Marion, Flexer, & Cumbo, 1997; Calderhead, 1996). Teachers' beliefs frequently affect student-teacher interactions and instructional planning. For example, Gibson and Dembo (1984) found that high-self-efficacy teachers provided less criticism and persisted in helping struggling students more than low-self-efficacy teachers. Ashton and Webb (1986) reported similar findings. High-efficacy teachers used more student praise, engaged in more task-oriented instruction, and ran classrooms that led to higher achievement.

Teachers' beliefs about content material also shape in-class pedagogy (Cobb & Bowers, 1999; Hargreaves, Earl, Moore, & Manning, 2001; Hashweh, 1996; Hiebert, Gallimore, & Stigler, 2002). Freeman and Porter (1989) found that teachers' beliefs about mathematics led to noticeable differences in how the course textbook was used. Hollon, Anderson, and Roth (1991) reported similar findings in that teachers' beliefs led to instructional practices consistent with those beliefs. Teachers' beliefs about how learning occurs also affect how teachers teach course content (Holt-Reynolds, 2000; Johnston, Woodside-Jiron, & Day, 2001). In one study, Smith and Neale (1989) compared three teaching orientations and their effect on teacher planning and instruction. "Discovery" teachers provided interesting activities designed to invoke student curiosity and exploration. "Didactic" teachers (those who emphasize structured content, facts, and principles) were more likely to select and organize content material, give tests, and demonstrate key concepts. In contrast, "conceptual change" teachers focused on evaluation of student beliefs, restructuring of existing knowledge structures, and providing incongruent data to students.

Surprisingly, preservice teachers tend to leave teacher training programs with many of the beliefs and attitudes they held when they entered the programs (Borko & Putnam, 1996; Kagan, 1992). This alarming fact suggests that some teacher training programs may be ineffective at altering beliefs even though they expose students to different perspectives on pedagogy (see chapter 14). Overall, studies examining a wide range of teachers' beliefs suggest that these beliefs are quite stable and resistent to change, are associated with a congruent style of teaching, and are affected most directly by practice rather than by continuing education (see Calderhead, 1996; Howard, McGee, Schwartz, & Purcell, 2000).

Currently, it is unclear how to facilitate change in teachers' beliefs. Research does provide a three-pronged strategy for changing students' beliefs that may apply to older students (e.g., teachers in training) as well (Brownlee, Purdie, & Boulton-Lewis, 2001; Cobern, 2000; Joram & Gabriele, 1998; Posner, Strike, Hewson, & Gertzog, 1982). First, students in teacher training programs must experience a classroom environment in which implicit beliefs become explicit. One way is to encourage open discussion and reflection on beliefs about course content and approaches to learning. Second, students should be confronted with the inconsistency of their beliefs. Third, the teacher should provide opportunities for students to weigh conflicting evidence and to restructure their existing knowledge such that it can be accommodated to course content.

Generally, beliefs about three classroom factors affect teachers' behaviors the most (Schraw & Olafson, 2003). One factor is course content. Research indicates that teachers plan instruction in ways that are consistent with their assumptions about class material. Teachers who hold a belief in certain knowledge are more likely to focus on didactic instruction and essential course content while deemphasizing discovery in the classroom (Pallas, 2001; Rennie, 1989). A second factor is the type of student receiving the instruction. Most teachers form strong opinions about students. These beliefs are based on several factors, including physical characteristics, test scores, class performance, social skills, parental attitudes, and student self-efficacy (Kagan, 1992). A third factor is the teacher's own explicit beliefs about teaching. One of the most consistent findings in the teacher belief literature is that teachers plan and implement instruction in a way that is consistent with their personal epistemologies.

Little is known about how teachers view knowledge and intelligence (Levitt, 2001; White, 2000; Wilcox-Herzog, 2002). We believe that many such studies will be conducted throughout the first decade of the 21st century. One important question is whether instruction and learning are facilitated when teachers' and students' beliefs match. Dweck and Leggett's (1988) theory, for instance, suggests that learning-oriented students may find it quite difficult to adjust to a classroom run by a teacher with strong performance goals. Similarly, teachers' epistemological beliefs may interfere with learning or create excessive disequilibrium when they do not match students' beliefs. This is not to say that teachers must accommodate students' beliefs; rather, a mismatch in beliefs and assumptions is apt to create disequilibrium in the classroom. As Posner et al. (1982) suggest, disequilibrium may be used productively to promote conceptual change, or it may preclude successful student-teacher interactions if handled poorly.

Implications

1.　*Everyone holds beliefs about intelligence and knowledge.*　The beliefs we hold affect the choices we make inside and outside the classroom. Many of these beliefs are implicit. Generally speaking, explicit awareness of one's beliefs makes them easier to identify and change. Beliefs about intelligence affect classroom satisfaction and persistence. Beliefs about knowledge affect reasoning skills and reflective judgment.

We believe that teachers should help students develop an awareness of their beliefs. Many younger and even older students hold implicit beliefs that nevertheless exert a profound influence on their thinking and behavior. Developing reflective awareness of these beliefs through journals and peer-based discussions gives students the opportunity to change them as they see fit.

2.   *Beliefs about intelligence and knowledge affect our behaviors.*   Research has demonstrated convincingly that our attitudes about intelligence and knowledge affect our learning. Individuals who believe that intelligence is fixed or who believe in simple knowledge and quick learning are less likely to persist and use helpful learning strategies. Those who adopt an entity theory are more likely to explain their success and failure in terms of different attributional responses.

3.   *Beliefs about intelligence and knowledge affect the way we reason.*   Thinking does not occur in an intellectual vacuum. The kinds of assumptions we hold about how people think and learn determine, in part, the kinds of educational opportunities to which we expose ourselves and the kind of knowledge we accept as legitimate. Studies by Kitchener and King (1981), Kuhn (1991), and Lehman et al. (1988) all illustrate this important point. For this reason, beliefs about intelligence and knowledge should be an important topic of discussion in classrooms, especially those with older students.

4.   *Education affects the kinds of beliefs we hold.*   Our beliefs about knowledge and intelligence are shaped by our classroom experiences. Teachers model viewpoints that echo views held at home or perhaps conflict with them. The kinds of beliefs modeled in the classroom may change the way students think. This possibility places a special responsibility on educators to analyze carefully the viewpoints they express in their classes and to provide ample time to explore their implications.

5.   *Educational experiences affect reasoning skills.*   The study by Lehman et al. (1988) is notable in that it illustrates how environmental constraints affect the development of cognitive skills. Recall that even graduate students experienced substantial changes in reasoning skills that were linked with the specific experiences they had in graduate school. This finding suggests that the specific demands of a discipline (e.g., statistical reasoning in the social sciences) help develop certain skills. Whether the intellectual demands of different disciplines also affect the kinds of epistemological beliefs that students hold is uncertain (cf. Jehng, Johnson, & Anderson, 1993).

6.   *Beliefs are not strongly related to ability.*   This statement may seem surprising to you. We often think of "smart" people as those with the most sophisticated (or adaptive) beliefs. The research described in this chapter, however, generally points to the conclusion that beliefs about intelligence and knowledge are far more related to home (e.g., parental beliefs) and school (e.g., performance demands) variables than to one's measured ability. One implication of this conclusion is that adaptive beliefs (e.g., believing in incremental learning) may compensate for average or low ability (Schraw et al., 1994). We are committed to the view that high academic achievement

is attainable by virtually all students, provided they develop a belief system that encourages them to use their existing skills and to cultivate more advanced thinking skills, such as metacognition. We are equally committed to the belief that teachers must initiate and facilitate these changes for them to be truly successful. To see a dramatic portrayal of how this might be accomplished, we recommend that all readers view the movie *Stand and Deliver*.

Summary

This chapter examined the effect that beliefs about intelligence and knowledge have on academic performance. We introduced the topic of implicit theories—that is, tacit belief systems. Dweck and Leggett's theory described two kinds of theories: Entity theorists maintain a belief that intelligence is fixed; incremental theorists believe that intelligence is changeable.

Entity and incremental theories give rise to performance and learning goals, which in turn lead to maladaptive and adaptive behaviors, respectively. Individuals characterized by a performance orientation are less persistent, are less apt to use learning strategies, and attribute their failure to ability and teachers. Individuals characterized by a learning orientation, however, are more persistent, are more likely to use strategies, and attribute their success to strategy use and effort.

Some epistemological beliefs can affect reasoning. Individuals who can be characterized by a belief that knowledge is complex and relative, that learning is incremental, and that one's ability to learn is not innately determined engage in more sophisticated forms of thinking.

We examined teachers' beliefs as well. These beliefs tend to change slowly, yet they strongly affect the attitudes that teachers hold about their students. Teachers' beliefs determine what content the teachers cover and how they cover it (e.g., direct lecture vs. a discovery approach). Research suggests that some teacher trainees leave education programs with the same beliefs about teaching they had when they entered the programs. Identification and discussion of these beliefs were described as a possible belief-changing strategy.

Suggested Readings

Dweck, C. S., & Leggett, E. S. (1988). A social-cognitive approach to motivation and personality. *Psychological Review, 95,* 256–273.

This review article presents Dweck and Leggett's influential theory in a highly readable fashion.

Hofer, B., & Pintrich, P. R. (2002). *Personal epistemology: The psychology of beliefs about knowledge and knowing*. Mahwah, NJ: Erlbaum.

This edited volume provides an excellent overview of recent theory and research on epistemological beliefs.

Kuhn, D. (1991). *The skills of argument*. New York: Cambridge University Press.

This book describes a comprehensive study examining argumentative reasoning. Chapter 7 provides an excellent discussion of the relationship between epistemological beliefs and reasoning skills.

Sinatra, G. M., & Pintrich, P. R. (Eds.). (2002). *Intentional conceptual change*. Mahwah, NJ: Erlbaum.

This edited volume summarizes recent theory and practice in conceptual change.

Problem Solving and Critical Thinking

EVERY DAY, WE ENCOUNTER HUNDREDS OF PROBLEMS ranging in difficulty from deciding which breakfast cereal to eat to planning our long-term career goals. Because we face so many types of problems, it is often difficult to say with certainty
what a problem is or to know how to categorize them. In addition, the sheer range of
problems we encounter makes it very difficult to approach problem solving systematically. Word problems in algebra, for example, seem to have little in common with
the choices and decisions we face when buying a car.

Loosely, a problem exists when our current state differs from a desired state
(Bransford & Stein, 1984; Lovett, 2002). Thinking of problem solving in this way
can be helpful for several reasons. First, it emphasizes the continual process of
problem solving, in which we move from an initial state to a more clearly defined end state. Second, thinking about problem solving as a process of change
from one state to another helps us understand that virtually every problem we
encounter can be solved by using the same general strategy despite apparent
surface differences.

Even though most adults possess some form of general problem-solving strategy,
it is not the case that all problems are similar to one another. Rather, experts agree
that problems differ with respect to how much structure they provide the problem
solver (Hayes, 1988). An **ill-defined problem** has more than one acceptable solution and no universally agreed-on strategy for reaching it (Kitchener, 1983). World-
wide ecological problems, such as global warming and ozone layer destruction,
provide good examples of ill-defined problems because scientists disagree about the
causes of, and possible solutions to, these problems. A **well-defined problem** has
only one correct solution and a guaranteed method for finding it. Solving a quadratic
equation in algebra class by using the quadratic formula is a good example of a well-
defined problem because there is not only a unique solution but also a guaranteed
means of obtaining it.

Historical Perspectives on Problem Solving

Thorndike, Dewey, and the Gestalt Psychologists

Interest in problem solving among psychologists and educators developed early in the 20th century. One of the earliest views was proposed by E. L. Thorndike (1911), who conducted a series of experiments in which he observed cats as they attempted to escape from a carefully constructed wooden crate by pressing a lever. Noting that cats typically would try several random behaviors prior to pressing the escape lever successfully, Thorndike concluded that problem solving consists largely of trial-and-error behaviors that eventually lead to a solution. He argued that problem solving (at least in cats) was not intentional, but rather occurred one step at a time as unsuccessful attempts were eliminated from a cat's repertoire. Thorndike was to argue in subsequent work that human problem solving takes place in much the same way as it does with any other animal: Success occurs incrementally as a function of the trial-and-error attempts to solve the problem.

In contrast with Thorndike, John Dewey (1910) viewed problem solving as a conscious, deliberate process governed by a naturally occurring sequence of steps. Dewey's model included five basic steps that he considered to be teachable skills. In Step 1, *presentation of the problem,* students (or teachers) recognize the existence of a problem. In Step 2, *defining the problem,* the problem solver identifies the nature of the problem and identifies important constraints on its solution. In Step 3, *developing hypotheses,* one or more plausible solutions are proposed. In Step 4, *testing the hypotheses,* the most feasible solution is determined. In Step 5, *selecting the best hypothesis,* the best hypothesis is determined, given the relative strengths and weaknesses of each.

A third approach to problem solving was that of the Gestalt psychologists, a group of European psychologists whose views differed widely from those of American behaviorists. One foremost Gestalt theorist was Wolfgang Köhler (1929), who conducted a series of studies on problem solving using chimps. The most famous of Köhler's chimps was Sultan. In one experiment, Sultan was placed in a cage in which a banana was suspended from the ceiling just beyond his reach. Köhler also placed in various parts of the cage some wooden crates that could be used to build a platform to reach the banana, but only if Sultan correctly grasped the concept of *using the crates in a tool-like fashion.* After several unsuccessful attempts and some apparent deliberation on Sultan's part, he succeeded in stacking the crates and reached the banana. Köhler argued that Sultan's behavior provided evidence of insight in problem solving in several ways. First, Sultan did not make numerous trial-and-error attempts to reach the banana as Thorndike would predict. Second, the crates bore no ostensible relationship to solving the problem (at least from the chimp's perspective) yet were used without prompting in a purposeful way to achieve the primary goal of reaching the banana. Köhler's findings and interpretation were considered extremely controversial at the time and continue to be debated today, in part, because researchers differ as to the nature of insight and, in part, because they suggested skilled, reflective problem solving in an animal.

Another important phenomenon introduced by a Gestalt psychologist was **functional fixedness,** a condition that arises when we lose the ability to view familiar objects in a novel way (Duncker, 1945). In one experiment, Duncker provided people with a candle, a box of matches, and some tacks. The object of the study was to attach the candle to a wooden door; the problem could be solved only by first attaching the matchbox to the door with the tacks and then using the box as a platform for the candle.

Duncker added one other constraint as well: Some people received the matchbox with matches inside, whereas others received the matchbox and matches separately. Although apparently a trivial difference, individuals who received the empty matchbox solved the problem more quickly.

Duncker concluded from this study that individuals in the empty box condition solved the problem more efficiently because they were more likely to view the box as a potential platform rather than as a receptacle for matches. Including the matches in the box induced functional fixedness in that it activated preconceived notions (schemata) of what a matchbox is and what it can be used for. When the matchbox was perceived in a slightly different context (without matches), individuals were better able to imagine alternative uses for it. Duncker's experiment elegantly illustrated the profound impact of preexisting knowledge and how that knowledge inhibits novel solutions or uses of objects during problem solving.

Contemporary Approaches to Problem Solving

Research on problem solving has received a great deal of attention since Thorndike, Dewey, and the Gestalt psychologists. Since the 1950s, computer scientists and cognitive psychologists have attempted to develop a general problem-solving model that can be applied in domains as diverse as physics and medical diagnosis (J. R. Anderson, 1993; Hayes, 1988; Newell & Simon, 1972). These models generally emphasize two major components: (1) the use of a general problem-solving procedure and (2) a high degree of metacognitive monitoring by the problem solver. Although several models have appeared, most are quite similar to one another and can be summarized into a five-stage sequence (Bransford & Stein, 1984; Gick, 1986; Hayes, 1988): (1) identifying the problem, (2) representing the problem, (3) selecting an appropriate strategy, (4) implementing the strategy, and (5) evaluating solutions. One might note that these five stages are quite similar to the five steps described by Dewey. Within each of the five stages, component subskills have been identified as well. We consider each of these stages separately and then discuss the relative merits of a general problem-solving model at the end of this section.

Identifying the Problem   Identifying a problem is one of the most difficult and challenging aspects of problem solving because it requires creativity and persistence yet a willingness to ponder a problem for a long period of time without committing to a solution too early in the process (Hayes, 1988). Many problems (and their solutions) that seem obvious in retrospect are not so obvious to begin with. Consider that batting helmets were not used routinely in major league baseball until the early 1950s despite the fact that several players had been killed over the years by being struck in the head by wild pitches!

Obstacles to effective problem finding have been identified by researchers. One obstacle is that most people are not in the habit of actively searching for problems. Usually, we let the problem "come to us" rather than seek it out. A good argument could be made, however, that virtually all great discoveries are made only after a previously unrecognized problem has been "discovered." A good case in point is the germ theory of disease. Prior to the 19th century, many physicians believed that illnesses originated from such sources as evil spirits, bad air (e.g., malaria), and poisoned blood. These beliefs led to many nonproductive treatments, such as incantations, whipping, and bloodletting. Not until the advent of a germ theory of disease did physicians correctly identify the source of many treatable diseases.

A second obstacle to successful problem finding is the degree to which the problem solver possesses relevant background knowledge. Problems in the development of computer microchips, for instance, cannot be solved or even identified without a great deal of preexisting knowledge about computer circuitry. Similarly, consider how background knowledge affects "problem finding" in a highly familiar activity such as reading (see chapter 11). Research indicates that prior knowledge facilitates the perception and temporary elaboration of new information. More important, prior knowledge (the use of *content schemata*) enables readers to attend selectively to important information in the text and to encode new information into an existing schematic structure with less effort.

A third obstacle to problem finding is that people do not take as much time as they need to reflect carefully on either the nature of a problem or its solution. In a landmark study of artistic creativity, Getzels and Czikszentmihalyi (1976) found that the time spent investigating objects prior to drawing a still life was a significantly better predictor of originality than was time spent making the drawing! This relationship was found even when the artist's technical ability was taken into consideration. From extensive observations and interviews, Getzels and Czikszentmihalyi concluded that artists who considered more options during the initial stages of problem finding were more original in their solutions. Most surprising of all was the finding that time spent discovering problems during the initial stages of problem solving correlated highly with artistic success 7 years later!

Getzels and Czikszentmihalyi also described other interesting findings in their study. One was that the majority of successful art students listed "problem finding" as the primary goal of their work. These artists were more concerned with finding and coming to terms with a perceived problem than they were in solving it. Successful artists also tended to possess three dispositional characteristics that facilitated problem finding. First, they were more open to the problem; that is, they did not allow first impressions to interfere with discovering alternative approaches to artistic expression. Second, they engaged in more exploratory activities, such as handling objects in a still life or viewing those objects from different perspectives. Third, they permitted the problem and their initial solution to evolve as they worked with it.

Moore (1990) examined the problem-finding behaviors of experienced teachers and university students studying to be teachers. One difference found between these groups was that experienced teachers spent significantly more time planning when placed in a hypothetical classroom setting. In addition, experienced teachers spent more time than novices investigating and manipulating objects found in the classroom and also provided more solutions to potential classroom problems. In many respects, experienced teachers appear to behave in much the same way as successful artists in the Getzels and Czikszentmihalyi study.

Another aspect of time spent identifying problems is the persistence of problem solvers in the face of initial difficulties. Some individuals give up too easily after only a short period of time because they view problem solving as a time-limited activity (Gick, 1986). In this regard, Schoenfeld (1983) found that students solving mathematical word problems tended to give up after 5 minutes on the assumption that if the solution did not occur during this period, it would not occur at all. Research reviewed by Gick (1986) and Hayes (1988) clearly suggests that successful problem solving is related to the amount of time one spends during the initial stages of problem finding, as well as to the number of solutions that are considered. In many situations, expert problem solvers spend more time identifying problems than do novices.

Finally, effective problem finding is strongly related to divergent thinking. **Divergent thinking** occurs when a problem solver explores solutions that are novel or even inconsistent with the problem at hand. Hollowing out a brick so that it can be used as a mug is a good illustration of divergent thinking because it exemplifies one unusual way an object can be used when we see it in a new light. As you might expect, divergent thinking is related to creativity and problem finding, although problem-finding ability appears to be a better predictor of creativity than is divergent thinking (Csikszentmihalyi, 1996; Runco, 1991). The ability to find problems and to think divergently seems to enhance the evaluation of proposed solutions during problem solving. One reason is that problem solvers are better able to plan in advance, which enables them to eliminate poor potential solutions early on. Divergent thinking helps students think more broadly not only when they are generating ideas but also when they are testing them.

Representing the Problem   Representing a problem can occur in several ways. One form of representation is simply thinking about problems abstractly, without committing one's thoughts to paper. Another is expressing the problem in some tangible form, such as a graph, picture, story problem, or equation. Representing problems on paper has important advantages. One is that many problems are so complex that they impose severe demands on short-term memory unless we find a convenient way to summarize information. Think back to all of the information you needed to consider when applying to college. Some individuals find themselves trying to remember the cost of tuition and housing, distance from home, quality of institution, availability of desirable academic majors, and social opportunities. Perhaps you had to compare this information for 10–15 universities. Clearly, this is too much to consider at one time. Using some form of external representation can reduce greatly the amount of information that needs to be remembered in order to identify and solve a problem.

Using external representations of problems can be useful for another reason. Sometimes, problems are just too difficult to solve mentally because we consider so many possible solutions. Using a visual representation can help us keep track of these solutions or reason more clearly. Consider the Monk's Trip problem, in which a monk journeys all day on foot to the top of a mountain, meditates overnight, and then returns by foot again the following morning by way of the exact same path, making the return trip down the mountain in two thirds of the time. The problem is to determine whether there is a spot on the trail that the monk crosses at exactly the same time each day. Take a few moments now to think about this problem before you examine Figure 8-1, which provides a visual representation of this problem.

As Figure 8-1 illustrates, it is impossible for the monk to make the return trip without crossing one spot on the trail at exactly the same time of day. Solving this problem pictorially seems to make this point obvious, whereas solving the problem without the benefit of a picture can be rather difficult. One reason for this difficulty is that much of our limited cognitive capacity in short-term memory is exhausted just trying to remember relevant information. Few resources are left over to actually solve the problem!

Representing problems either internally or externally can be made easier when we analyze the component parts of a problem. Most theorists distinguish among four components that are known collectively as the *problem space:* goal state, initial state, operators, and constraints on operators. The **problem space** refers to all of the operators and constraints on operators involved in the problem. Some problem spaces are small, such as choosing a personal computer that meets your needs and your

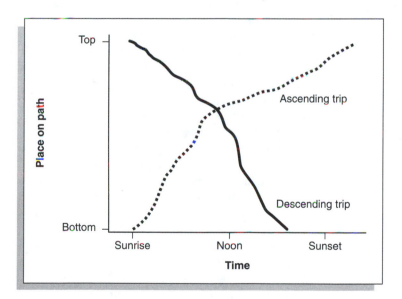

Figure 8-1
A Graphic Representation of the Monk's Trip Problem
Source: Adapted from Cognitive Psychology, *by J. R. Hayes, 1978, Homewood, IL: Dorsey. Adapted with permission.*

budget; others are extremely complex, such as finding a vaccine against HIV. Problems that include many possible solution paths (more paths from the initial state to the goal state) have larger problem spaces than those with few paths, although the size of a problem space may vary considerably between two people, depending on the way the problem is understood by each person (Hayes, 1988).

The **goal state** refers to what we want to accomplish once the problem is solved. Goals vary in their specificity and complexity, although the clearer the goal, the easier it will be to solve the problem, all things considered. The initial state refers to what is known about the problem before one attempts to solve it. How much information do you have about the problem? What information is most important? Is information missing that you will need to consider before proceeding? Can the problem be broken down into smaller subproblems? Have you ever solved a problem like this before? **Operators** refers to objects or concepts in the problem that can be manipulated to reach a solution. Pieces on a chessboard are operators as are variables (e.g., x and y) in an algebraic equation. When taking a test, time and knowledge about the content of the test are operators. **Constraints on operators** refers to restrictions that limit the use of one or more operators. In a game of chess, queens can move in horizontal, vertical, or diagonal directions on the board, whereas bishops can move only diagonally. Knights are restricted to an entirely different set of moves (two spaces in a horizontal or vertical direction, then one step at a 90° angle to the first). On a test, you are limited frequently to 1 hour or less, and you may not use books or notes.

A good deal of research has investigated the importance of operators and constraints on operators (see Hayes, 1988, for a summary). One consistent finding is that good problem solvers distinguish relevant from irrelevant constraints on a problem more efficiently than do poor problem solvers, and they use this information to facilitate problem solving (Kaplan & Simon, 1990; Ross & Kennedy, 1990). For example, good readers know when to slow down rather than skim a text; that is, they identify relevant information and allocate more attention to it.

Good and poor problem solvers also differ in their ability to categorize problems. Good problem solvers tend to group problems according to "deep structure" principles, such as what kind of solution strategy is required to solve the problem. In contrast, poor problem solvers rely on "surface structure" features, such as the objects that appear in the problem (Hardiman, Dufresne, & Mestre, 1989). When novice problem solvers are taught to categorize by using deep structure principles, their performance usually improves compared with that of other novices. These findings suggest two important conclusions. First, effective problem solving is attributable, in part, to experience; those with more practice solving a particular type of problem can categorize problems more efficiently because of their background knowledge and experience. Second, students can learn to categorize (represent) problems more efficiently by analyzing problems differently. Less attention should be given to surface features of the problem; more attention should be given to the underlying nature of the problem.

Selecting an Appropriate Strategy   People use many kinds of strategies to solve problems. Some of these are highly structured and are referred to as algorithms. An algorithm is really just another name for a rule. Using algorithms or rule-based strategies can be very effective because they are guaranteed to work. Finding the roots of a quadratic equation by using the quadratic formula is a good example of a rule-based strategy. But sometimes it is not possible to use a rule-based strategy because either a rule does not exist or the student lacks proficiency at using it. In this case, people rely on **heuristics,** or "rules of thumb," to help them solve problems. Heuristics are not as efficient as algorithms because they do not always guarantee a solution; in fact, they may even make problem solving more difficult if the student uses the wrong heuristic (Tversky & Kahneman, 1974).

Two of the more common heuristics are **trial and error** and **means-ends analysis.** Trial and error is clearly the least efficient of all the methods because learners have no strategic plan whatsoever. Trial and error may be our only alternative when we are faced unexpectedly with an unfamiliar problem. Often, however, most people will use a trial-and-error approach at the onset of the problem and then switch to a more efficient method after some preliminary information is gained about the problem.

Means–ends analysis differs from trial and error in that the problem solver tries to reduce the distance to the goal by taking a sequence of steps that can be evaluated individually. In essence, means–ends analysis requires the learner to do three things: (1) formulate a goal state, (2) break down the problem into smaller subproblems, and (3) evaluate the success of one's performance at each step before proceeding to the next. One example of means–ends analysis is writing a compare-and-contrast essay on a timed test. The first step is to identify the goal state (the position you want to defend), the second step is to break down the paper into smaller problems (e.g., introduction, comparison of evidence, conclusion), and the third step is to proceed through the paper one section at a time.

Not surprisingly, good and poor problem solvers differ in the kinds of strategies they use to solve problems. Experts tend to use some form of means–ends analysis in which they first categorize the problem on the basis of the kind of solution it requires, then break down the problem into smaller parts, and finally solve each part in a sequential manner. In contrast, inexperienced or poor problem solvers often resort to trial and error or use a crude form of means–ends analysis based on surface features of the problem. Novice problem solvers also are more likely to break down a problem into fewer meaningful parts and to solve those parts out of sequence.

Another difference between good and poor problem solvers is the ability to plan— a skill that depends on experience, background knowledge, and one's awareness of different kinds of problem-solving strategies. Good problem solvers plan farther in advance and coordinate the entire problem-solving sequence more efficiently. Research in the area of writing suggests that some writers plan "locally," whereas others plan "globally" (Berciter & Scardamalia, 1987). Global planning seems to contribute greatly to effective writing. As with other types of problem solving, good writing and good planning depend on declarative knowledge about how a text is structured, as well as procedural knowledge about how to compose a text.

Implementing the Strategy   The success one has when implementing a strategy depends, in large part, on how well one identifies and represents the problem and on the type of strategy one adopts. Clear differences exist at each of these levels between good and poor problem solvers. In addition, good problem solvers coordinate the solution phase of problem solving more efficiently. One consistent finding is that experts change strategies more often (strategy shifting), consider more solutions, evaluate solutions more carefully before discarding them, and reach conclusions that are more workable than do novices.

In one study that compared expert and novice teachers, Swanson, O'Connor, and Cooney (1990) found that expert teachers used more strategies while solving classroom management problems than did novices. Experts placed a high priority on defining and representing the problem before deciding on a solution; novices did not. Experts also tended to classify problems at a "deeper" level by carefully evaluating the type and severity of classroom misbehavior; novices tended to categorize problems on the basis of how they would respond to them. As a consequence, experts were more likely to consider different solutions, and to evaluate those solutions, given the larger context of the classroom environment. Novices were more likely to choose a single solution based on the apparent severity of the misbehavior. Another important difference between the two groups was that expert teachers were more likely to choose externally based interventions, such as physically separating children, whereas novices were more likely to select internally based interventions, such as counseling students.

One reason for different problem-solving strategies between expert and novice teachers is that the former possess a great deal of procedural knowledge gained from experience that allows them to focus more of their attention on defining the problem rather than on selecting a strategy to solve the problem. In contrast, novices feel a greater need to reach a solution early, often at the expense of analyzing the problem carefully. One implication of this research is that novice teachers may be poorer problem solvers because they focus too much attention on finding a solution even before they understand the problem. Presumably, novice teachers could benefit by considering problems more carefully or, if that were not possible in a busy classroom, by considering various solutions to problems before they enter the classroom.

Evaluating Solutions   One might think that evaluating solutions is unimportant because it typically occurs after the problem has been solved. This simply is not true. Those who fail to evaluate both the products and the process of problem solving miss an excellent opportunity to improve these skills. An abundance of research in the areas of metacognition (Baker, 1989), reflective practice (Schön, 1987), and self-regulation (Zimmerman, 1990) all strongly suggest that most of the improvement we experience in learning is the result of purposeful evaluation. Evaluation helps us better understand the usefulness and applicability of a particular strategy. Considering why a strategy did not work in one context may enable a learner to use it more efficiently in another. In addition, evaluating solutions permits us to reflect at a deeper level about the process of problem solving.

For these reasons, any complex problem-solving task such as reading, writing, studying, or learning new skills in the classroom, should be accompanied by two types of evaluation. The first is an analysis of *products*. Is the end result the best solution available? How does this solution compare with others? Are other solutions likely that were not considered? The second type of evaluation examines the *process*. How well did you do? What did you do right or wrong? How could you improve? Only by asking these types of questions can students be expected to improve significantly their problem-solving skills and their understanding of how to solve problems.

Expert Knowledge in Problem Solving

In the above section, we described a general model of problem solving that can be applied to any domain. Many researchers have noted that people's ability to solve a problem usually depends on two crucial factors: one is the amount of domain-specific knowledge at our disposal; another is the amount of experience we have in trying to solve a particular class of problems (Taconis, Ferguson-Hessler, & Broekkamp, 2001). Debate continues concerning the most useful way to improve problem solving in the classroom and the workplace, with some researchers emphasizing the development of domain-specific knowledge and others stressing the role of general problem-solving skills (cf. Perkins & Salomon, 1989). Before we attempt to compare the relative strengths and weaknesses of the two approaches, it may be helpful to consider the role of domain-specific and general knowledge in greater detail.

Domain Knowledge

The realm of knowledge that individuals have about a particular field of study is called domain-specific knowledge, or simply **domain knowledge** (Alexander, 1992). Knowledge domains typically are subject areas (e.g., mathematics and modern art) but also can represent areas of activity (e.g., bicycle mechanics, taxi driving, and gardening). They encompass declarative, procedural, and metacognitive knowledge and can operate at a tacit or an explicit level. For many tasks, including school-related ones, the amount of domain knowledge required to perform successfully is very large indeed. For instance, try to visualize the amount of knowledge needed to make sense out of novels such as *The Color Purple* or *Moby Dick,* a momentum problem in physics, or a description of gene-splicing techniques.

Examples of domain knowledge can be seen all about us every day. Each plays a role in an individual's functioning effectively. Examples of domain knowledge that is more declarative in nature are the knowledge needed to make sense of a road map, the information required to judge what kind of home loan might be best for a person's circumstances, and knowledge of the capitals of Eastern Europe. Examples of domain knowledge that is more procedural also abound—for instance, the knowledge that an office worker reveals as she or he duplicates a report or runs a spreadsheet program or that a mechanic exhibits in successfully diagnosing the cause of a poorly running automobile and the skills an athlete exercises, say, in the course of a volleyball match. Likewise, domain-related metacognitive knowledge is shown as students make the observation that they are "poor in math," find main ideas in a science text, and plan their parts in a class project on the Civil War.

One major goal of schooling is to build all three dimensions of students' domain knowledge (Taconis et al., 2001). By the time students finish formal schooling, we expect them to possess a large and usable body of information in each of several curricular fields, such as history, literature, mathematics, biology, and foreign languages. We also hope that students will have built their domain knowledge in several areas of everyday life, such as jobs, the environment, and community functioning.

An Example of Domain Knowledge in Cognition

The influence of domain knowledge is tremendous even though we often lose sight of it. Consider, for example, the role of domain knowledge in reading. Typically, we think of differences in what students comprehend and remember from reading as attributable to their basic abilities in reading, not to their domain knowledge. We do know, however, that good readers remember more of what they read and possess more knowledge about the world than poor readers (see Taft & Leslie, 1985). At the same time, good readers not only remember more about what they read but also read a great deal more than poor readers. This close relationship between reading ability and knowledge has made research in the area difficult. A study by Recht and Leslie (1988), however, was designed in a way that allowed them to see what effect domain knowledge had on students' memory for what they read.

Recht and Leslie searched for a topic that not only some good readers and some poor readers would know a great deal about but also some good and some poor readers would know very little about. They settled on baseball. After identifying some junior high school students who were very good readers and some who were poor readers, Recht and Leslie tested all of them about their knowledge of baseball. This procedure allowed the researchers to identify good readers who knew a great deal about baseball, good readers who knew very little about baseball, poor readers who knew a great deal about baseball, and poor readers who knew very little about baseball. Next, the students were asked to read a 625-word passage that described half an inning of a baseball game between a local team and a visiting rival. They then were tested in several ways for their ability to remember the passage: (1) reenacting the inning with a model field and miniature wooden players while verbally describing what happened, (2) summarizing the passage, and (3) sorting 22 sentences taken from the passage on the basis of how important the sentences were to the happenings of the inning.

Results of Recht and Leslie's (1988) study were striking. On each measure of memory, poor readers who knew a great deal about baseball greatly outperformed good readers who knew very little about baseball. In fact, they performed nearly as well as the good readers who knew a great deal about baseball. Poor readers who knew very little about baseball, however, remembered the least about the passage on all measures. Thus, knowledge in the domain of baseball had a very powerful influence on how much and what was remembered.

The influence of students' domain knowledge on new learning reaches far more broadly than baseball, of course. Remembering information in areas as diverse as chess, art, computer programming, electronics, and biology all have been shown to be related to previous knowledge. In general, the more students know about a specific topic, the easier it is for them to learn and remember new information about that topic.

Not surprisingly, domain knowledge is related closely to problem-solving abilities. Experts, be they artists, mechanics, or nuclear physicists, know that problems in their field are solved most easily when they can be related to other, similar problems. Experts typically think before they act. They also understand the importance of sketches and diagrams in problem solving. Novices, in contrast, may work very hard at problem solving—even harder than experts—but their strategies are less productive because of their limited domain knowledge and the inefficient ways they go about trying to make their knowledge relevant to problems.

General Knowledge

Although domain knowledge is fundamental for day-to-day problem solving, another kind of knowledge—general knowledge—also is needed. General knowledge is broad knowledge that is not linked with a specific domain (Buehl, Alexander, & Murphy, 2002). Think back to our example in chapter 1, where Kari grappled with the assignment of writing a report. To produce this report, she had to have information, skills, and strategies beyond the specific topic of the paper. For example, she needed a declarative network of concepts and a vocabulary to express her ideas, knowledge of punctuation and grammar to guide her writing, general information about reports and their functions, and procedural skills for operating a word processor. She also needed metacognitive knowledge to organize and carry out all of these activities. None of this general knowledge is related directly to the topic she chose to write about, but it nonetheless is essential for completing this and virtually all problem-solving tasks.

Because it is information that can be applied to almost any task, general knowledge can be thought of as complementary to domain knowledge. Of course, what constitutes general knowledge and what constitutes domain knowledge can shift as the task focus shifts. For students reading a novel by Willa Cather and trying to understand her use of certain literary devices, the relevant domain knowledge may be primarily in the realm of English literature. If her descriptions of the native prairie are being studied by a biology class for how they characterized prairie ecology nearly a century ago, however, and the task is to map changes that may be occurring in the prairie environment, the relevant domain knowledge now centers on the plants, animals, and environment, with literary knowledge becoming general knowledge.

Ordinarily, however, one can think of general knowledge as knowledge appropriate to a wide range of tasks but not tied to any one task. The declarative networks represented by our vocabulary, knowledge of current affairs, and historical knowledge; the procedural knowledge for speaking, for doing mathematics, and for carrying on a conversation; and the metacognitive skills we use across a variety of cognitive tasks are all examples of general knowledge that is useful for a very broad array of activities. Indeed, one can consider the almost infinite amount of general knowledge necessary for a

15-year-old such as Kari to function on a day-to-day basis at home, in her social world, and at school.

Domain Knowledge and Expertise

Let's turn our attention now to what it takes to become an expert. Researchers studying the development of expertise estimate that it takes about 5–10 years or on the order of 10,000 hours to develop true expertise in a domain regardless of intellectual aptitude (Ericsson, 1996; Ericsson & Smith, 1991; Hayes, 1988)! In many cases, it may take even longer. It may surprise (or alarm) you to know that beginning radiologists (X-ray specialists) perform far below experienced experts even after completing 4 years of medical school (Lesgold, 1988).

One reason why expertise develops so slowly is that much of the declarative and procedural knowledge needed to master a domain is acquired *tacitly* over a long period of time (Bereiter & Scardamalia, 1993; Wagner & Sternberg, 1985). For example, most college students possess a great deal of expert knowledge about their native languages. They read and write fluently, using syntactic (grammar) and semantic (meaning) knowledge to convey complex meanings. They also use language metaphorically to convey nonliteral meaning (e.g., *prisons are junkyards*). Yet, most of them find it very difficult to describe what it is they know about language or how they learned it. Indeed, we often can use what we know but cannot explain it.

Evidence suggests that much of our knowledge is acquired tacitly even when we receive a great deal of formal training in a domain (Buehl et al., 2002; Wagner, 1987). Because of this, even highly skilled experts often find it difficult to describe what it is they know about a body of knowledge and, as a consequence, may be poor decision makers when forced to reflect on their knowledge (Johnson, 1988). Typically, however, experts are better problem solvers than novices for a variety of reasons, including experience, background knowledge, and information processing advantages that are the consequence of expert knowledge (Glaser & Chi, 1988). Figure 8-2 lists seven key characteristics of experts.

Figure 8-2
Seven Characteristics of Experts

1. Experts excel only in their own domain.
2. Experts process information in large units.
3. Experts are faster than novices.
4. Experts hold more information in short-term and long-term memory.
5. Experts represent problems at a deeper level.
6. Experts spend more time analyzing a problem.
7. Experts are better monitors of their performance.

Source: From *Glaser and Chi* (1988).

Seven Characteristics of Expert Performance

Although our intuitions may suggest otherwise, the first characteristic of experts is that they usually are no better able to solve problems in unfamiliar domains than novices; that is, expertise is domain-specific. Consider a brilliant chemist whose car breaks down on a deserted highway. The chances are good that the stranded motorist will walk to the nearest gas station rather than solve the problem herself or himself *unless* she or he happens to have expert knowledge about auto repair as well. No evidence suggests, however, that expertise in one domain readily transfers to another. Rather, expertise develops slowly, is highly labor-intensive, and is confined to a particular body of knowledge.

A second characteristic of experts is that they organize information far more efficiently than do novices. Typically, this is accomplished by chunking information into larger recognizable units than a novice might use (see chapter 4). Chase and Simon (1973a, 1973b) found that one main difference between expert and novice chess players was not the absolute size of their working memories (about seven pieces of information), but rather how much information they could analyze and remember in a single brief exposure (their ability to categorize information). Chess experts were able to view complex chess configurations for as little as 5 seconds yet remember them in remarkable detail; novices remembered very little of what they saw. Surprisingly, when the same experiment was conducted using nonmeaningful chess patterns, no difference was found between the experts and the novices!

A third characteristic is that experts are faster than novices at processing meaningful information because they search and represent problems more efficiently (Charness, 1991). If you ever have had the experience of watching an expert mathematician solve word problems, you observed how easily the expert identified relevant information and selected an appropriate strategy. Although rather disconcerting to the novice, the expert's behavior may be less impressive than it appears because she or he probably has solved hundreds or perhaps thousands of similar problems in the past. The experience gained by solving these problems enables the expert to remember similar problems and solutions and to select appropriate strategies with little effort. These differences even have been observed when comparing expert and novice figure skaters (Deakin & Allard, 1991).

A fourth characteristic that makes experts better (and faster) problem solvers is that their thoughts and actions are highly automatized. Being automatic allows experts to use their short-term memory in a more efficient way compared with novices. Expert mathematicians, for instance, activate and implement appropriate solution strategies so efficiently that they place very few demands on their cognitive resources. These resources can be used to accomplish higher order cognitive tasks, such as monitoring one's progress and evaluating solutions.

As a fifth characteristic, experts represent problems differently from novices. Experts usually focus more of their attention on the underlying structure of the problem rather than on superficial surface features. Many studies show that expert physicists categorize physics problems on the basis of mechanical principles, whereas novices categorize them on the basis of objects mentioned in the problem (e.g., the angle of a shadow). Experts also are more likely to break problems into subgoals and to work forward toward the desired end state (use means-ends analysis).

A sixth characteristic is that the experts spend more time than novices analyzing the problem at the *beginning* of the problem-solving process. In studies reported by Voss and Post (1988), experts were found to spend a greater proportion of their time identifying and representing the problem, compared with novices, even though they spent considerably less time choosing an appropriate solution strategy once the problem had been clarified. Experts also were more apt to rely on complex conditional strategies for reducing a problem into smaller component problems (Clancey, 1988).

The seventh characteristic is that experts are better monitors than novices in most situations *within their domain of expertise*. Experts are more likely to generate alternative hypotheses before solving a problem and are quicker to reject inappropriate solutions during problem solving. Experts also judge the difficulty of problems more accurately than novices and ask more appropriate questions at all stages of the problem-solving process.

The characteristics described above all point to one simple conclusion about the nature of expertise: Experts are faster, more efficient, and more reflective *because of the depth and breadth of their knowledge*. We do not mean to imply by this statement that extensive knowledge guarantees expert performance. Most researchers agree that true expertise represents a complex interaction between general problem-solving strategies and extensive domain-specific knowledge. These two components can best be thought of as complementary processes: Expert knowledge facilitates strategy use, whereas knowledge about general problem-solving strategies enables learners to use their expert knowledge more efficiently (cf. Perkins & Salomon, 1989; Taconis et al., 2001).

Role of Deliberate Practice

Novices do not become experts overnight. As we have said, becoming truly expert typically is a 10-year process. But what is this process like? Is it the same for everyone? And how much does the development of expertise depend on "native talent"? Researchers have become increasingly interested in these questions during the past decade and have generated some rather surprising answers.

The development of expertise occurs in rather predictable stages. Bloom (1985), in a landmark study of the development of talent among children and adolescents, identified three stages that he referred to as the early, middle, and late years. Early years are characterized by playful engagement, typically in a highly supportive home environment in which parents stress motivation and effort rather than native ability. Middle years mark a turn in which the novice begins to develop the first true signs of expertise and becomes increasingly dependent on highly skilled mentors. These mentors typically are not parents but rather skilled professionals. The emphasis during this period is on developing a steady regimen of practice, competition, and feedback. Late years are characterized by finding a master teacher who can help the individual develop true expertise. Peer relationships also become increasingly important as developing experts encounter one another on a frequent basis. Total psychological commitment is expected of individuals at this stage.

The process of developing expertise appears to be remarkably consistent across all disciplines. For example, Bloom (1985) concluded that young athletes, musicians, and mathematicians develop in more or less the same way (three stages extending over a 10-year period or more). Research on skill acquisition suggests substages within stages. Ackerman (1988, 1992) proposed that skill acquisition is characterized by *knowledge acquisition, skill proceduralization,* and *automated application* stages. These stages may reoccur each time a developing expert enters a new level of skill acquisition (e.g., the transition from the early to middle years).

Ericsson and colleagues (Ericsson, 1996; Ericsson, Krampe, & Tesch-Romer, 1993) have conducted studies on the role of deliberate practice in the acquisition of expertise. The most important finding of these studies is that skill development and expertise are strongly related to the time and efficiency of deliberate practice. The more one practices, the better one gets *regardless of initial talent and ability*. A second finding is that initial differences attributable to talent and ability *decrease* over time as a function of practice. This means that highly talented individuals lose their edge over time if they do not practice, compared with less talented individuals. A third finding is that the *quality,* in addition to the *quantity,* of practice is extremely important. The highest quality practice takes place early in the morning before peak resources are allocated to other tasks. It generally is most efficient for 1 to 3 hours, with the ideal being about 2 hours. Practice is associated with informational feedback (knowledge about errors and how to improve performance). The best practice occurs under the watchful guidance of a skilled mentor who helps the developing expert set goals and monitor improvement.

Perhaps the most surprising (and inspirational) finding in this research is that deliberate, extended practice counts much more than native ability. Ericsson et al. are quite emphatic on this point, stating the following:

> In summary, our review has uncovered essentially no support for the fixed innate characteristics that would correspond to general or specific natural ability (in the development of expertise) [emphasis added], and, in fact, has uncovered findings inconsistent with such models.   (Ericsson et al., 1993, p. 399)

Bloom draws a similar conclusion based on extensive longitudinal data, as follows:

> No matter how precocious one is at age ten or eleven, if the individual doesn't stay with the talent development process over many years, he or she soon will be outdistanced by others who continue.   (Bloom, 1985, p. 538)

This is not to suggest that native talent and ability are unrelated to skill development and expertise (Ackerman, 1992; Ree, Carretta, & Teachout, 1995). Talent clearly helps skilled individuals develop faster, and some researchers continue to believe that native talent and the "rage to master" determines one's ultimate success (Winner, 1996, 2000). Nevertheless, talent alone is not sufficient, and it remains to be seem what level of initial talent is necessary to achieve high levels of expertise. Research reveals that less talented individuals reach higher levels of accomplishment than more talented peers by virtue of guided, deliberate practice. When students are denied the opportunity to develop expertise due to socioeconomic reasons, this may result in substantial talent loss in a society (Plank & Jordan, 2001). In short, there is no easy path to expertise, but there is no reason to believe that the road is blocked for some people more than others, provided all individuals have the temporal and financial resources to engage in extended, deliberate practice. Those who work the hardest for the longest period of time and have access to skilled mentors usually reach the highest level of skill attainment.

Problem-Solving Transfer

One important question is the degree to which problem-solving skills in one domain transfer to another. Some researchers believe that transfer occurs very rarely, if ever, because expertise (and expert problem-solving skills) are welded to specific domains (Detterman, 1993). In contrast, Cox (1997), Halpern (1998), and Mayer and Wittrock (1996) suggest that problem-solving skills may transfer provided educators help students use these skills in a variety of settings and promote the use of metacognitive self-regulation. Some instructional methods appear to work better than others in this regard. One of the most useful is to provide structured practice that promotes automated problem solving (Lovett, 2002; Sweller, 1999). Automated skills appear easier to transfer than unautomated skills. A second strategy is to relate problem-solving skills in one domain to those in a new domain by using analogies (see Pressley, 1995, for a further discussion). A third strategy is to provide students with detailed worked-out examples (Paas, 1992) and feedback (Bernardo, 2001). Other methods, such as unstructured discovery, appear to be less productive, although several recent studies indicate that structured discovery promotes deeper learning as well as spontaneous transfer between different types of problems (Chi, de Leeuw, Chiu, & La Vancher, 1994; Kuhn, Schauble, & Garcia-Mila, 1992).

Implications: Improving Problem Solving

Problem-solving skills can be improved in many ways, some of which require a long-term investment (e.g., accumulating extensive expert knowledge) and some of which lead to more rapid improvement (e.g., mimicking expert strategies). In general, we emphasize the fundamental role of expert knowledge in effective problem solving. Although it is possible to improve problem-solving skills by improving general knowledge about problem solving, there probably is no substitute for the expert knowledge acquired through the 10,000 or so hours of engagement in the domain. With this caveat, we suggest the following steps:

1. *Facilitate the acquisition of expert knowledge.* Years of research indicate that extensive domain knowledge is clearly the most important constraint on effective problem solving (Taconis et al., 2001). One instructional strategy is to help students acquire as much expert knowledge as quickly as possible. Educators should seriously consider what constitutes an "expert" body of knowledge in their discipline and attempt to convey this information to all students. This means that teachers must make

a special effort to select and organize the core body of knowledge one needs to learn to become an expert.

Another highly effective strategy, though one that is neglected too often, is for a novice to ask an expert for help when she or he does not understand a problem. One reason to do so is to acquire an expert's "way of knowing" the problem. Indeed, it could be argued that learning what kinds of strategies experts use is less important than understanding why they use them.

2.   *Develop an awareness of a general problem-solving strategy.* Everyone, to some extent, can become a better problem solver by understanding the basic process of problem solving (Bransford, Sherwood, Vye, & Rieser, 1986). The five-step sequence outlined earlier provides an excellent framework for developing component skills (e.g., representing problems externally), as well as for understanding the relationships among component skills. Teaching specific skills such as predicting outcomes (Hurst & Milkent, 1996) and inductive reasoning (Tomic, 1997) facilitates problem solving as well.

Studies investigating the value of teaching younger students a general problem-solving method have yielded fairly impressive findings. In one study, King (1991) compared groups of fifth-grade students in which the students solved problems by using or not using a problem-solving prompt card. Those using the prompts solved problems better. Delclos and Harrington (1991) compared three groups of fifth- and sixth-grade students; one group received problem-solving and monitoring training, another received problem-solving training, and a third received no training. Although the combined group (metacognitive and problem-solving training) outperformed all others, the problem-solving-only group outperformed the control group.

Together, these studies suggest that problem-solving training has a beneficial effect on younger students. Problem-solving training also is enhanced when it is coupled with other kinds of instruction, such as question answering (King, 1991) and metacognitive training (Delclos & Harrington, 1991). Readers interested in teaching general problem-solving skills may wish to consult Bransford and Stein (1984) and Gick (1986) for further information.

3.   *Focus on discovering and identifying problems.* Many studies reveal that problem discovery is the most crucial stage of the problem-solving sequence. Indeed, to be a good problem finder, one must be highly creative and motivated. Individuals should be encouraged to "linger" on a problem during this stage because of the direct relationship between time spent conceptualizing a problem and the quality of its solution. Those wishing to promote the creative aspect of problem finding may wish to consult Dacey (1989) and Weisberg (1993).

4.   *Use external representations whenever possible.* One limitation that most individuals face when trying to solve problems is overloading their cognitive resources. Sensory and short-term memory are limited to about seven pieces of information at a time. Many problems greatly exceed this limitation, which results in the inability to hold all relevant pieces of a problem in working memory. Representing problems in written or graphic form can reduce this cognitive overload greatly and, in turn, improve problem-solving effectiveness.

5.   *Mimic expert strategies.* Sometimes, it is possible to teach individuals without expert knowledge to act like experts. Using "expert" fingering techniques when playing the piano, for example, may hasten one's improvement. At other times, expert strategies are useless without the knowledge needed to use those strategies in a planful way. Consider a chess novice who is taught the Sicilian Defense but who gets into trouble quickly by trying to use it against a skilled opponent. When it comes to problem solving, the saying "A little bit of knowledge is a dangerous thing" often rings true. Using experts' strategies may be helpful in some situations but not others. Professional discretion is advised!

Critical Thinking

A long-standing debate in U.S. education is whether schools should direct their efforts to teaching students how to think rather than what to think. The fact that such questions continue to be asked (e.g., Ennis, 1987; Halpern, 1998; Kuhn, 1999; Perkins, Jay, & Tishman, 1993; Pithers & Soden, 2000) invites us to consider what it means to "think critically." Most of us would agree that critical thinking is important, that it is complex, and that it encompasses a host of lesser skills, such as identifying and evaluating information. But how does critical thinking differ from problem solving or creativity? In this section, we examine these issues and address three related questions as well: What skills are necessary to think critically? Is critical thinking constrained by intelligence? And how should one go about designing a critical thinking program?

Toward a Definition of Critical Thinking

For most experts, **critical thinking** differs from problem solving in two ways (Halpern, 1997; Marzano, 1992). One way is that problem solving usually requires an individual to solve specialized problems in a particular domain. These problems typically are well-defined and have one or perhaps two correct solutions. Solving word problems in algebra class and replicating a heat-exchange experiment in a science class provide good examples. Performance on such problems has been shown to correlate highly with the amount of domain-specific expertise that learners have.

In contrast, critical thinking usually requires us to consider general issues that cut across several domains. These "problems" frequently are ill-defined and have many possible solutions or even may be unsolvable. Consider some issues we must weigh when choosing a president: how to eliminate (or at least reduce) the national debt, the constitutionality of abortion and capital punishment, and whether financial aid should be offered to formerly hostile foreign nations.

A second way that problem solving differs from critical thinking is in the nature of what is being evaluated. Most problems are external states, whereas most critical thinking is directed toward internal states. Choosing a political affiliation, for instance, is part problem solving in that we must choose whom to vote for, but it is also part critical thinking in that we first need to clarify and evaluate our own beliefs and expectations about each of the candidates.

One definition of critical thinking is *reflective thinking focused on deciding what to believe or do* (Ennis, 1987). We believe that an analysis of some key terms in this definition are helpful for understanding what critical thinking entails. First, critical thinking is a *reflective* activity. Often, its goal is not to solve a problem but rather to better understand the nature of the problem. Critical thinking also is *focused* in that we are not just thinking, but thinking about something we wish to understand more thoroughly. The purpose of thinking critically is to weigh and evaluate information in a way that ultimately enables us to make informed *decisions*. Finally, unlike problem solving, the content of our critical thinking is often a *belief* or a motive we wish to examine more thoroughly.

A second definition of critical thinking is *better thinking* (Perkins, 1987, 2001). This view suggests that learning to think critically will improve our ability to gather, interpret, evaluate, and select information for the purpose of making informed choices. We suspect that this is the definition most teachers and parents have in mind when they say, "Students need to think more critically about their lives." Of course, statements such as these require us as parents and professional educators to think more critically about how to improve students' thinking!

A third definition of critical thinking is *distinguishing between thinking that is directed at adopting versus clarifying a goal* (Nickerson, 1987). Adopting is closer to problem solving because it emphasizes a "product" view of decision making, whereas clarifying emphasizes the "process" one uses to reach that decision. We view critical thinking as more than decision making and believe that the process of informed decision making is more important than the decision itself. Let's turn now to some skills involved in critical thinking.

Component Skills in Critical Thinking

Earlier, we described important skills used in problem solving. We now turn our attention to an analogous set of skills used in critical thinking. Ennis (1987) has proposed the most comprehensive set of skills thus far in which he distinguishes between two major classes of critical thinking activities: *dispositions* and *abilities*. The former refers to affective and dispositional traits that each person brings to a thinking task, such as open-mindedness; an attempt to be well-informed; and sensitivity to others' beliefs, feelings, and knowledge. The latter refers to the actual cognitive abilities necessary to think critically, including focusing, analyzing, and judging. A similar set of skills has been proposed by Halpern (1998).

Figure 8-3 lists 12 skills included in Ennis's taxonomy. An inspection of these skills (and selected subskills) suggests that some are appropriate for any type of thinking, whether critical or creative. Others, such as making value judgments, seem to be less important when solving physics problems than when voting for a presidential candidate. According to Ennis (1987), each subskill contributes to critical thinking in its own unique way, helping us clarify our goals and objectives, acquire

Figure 8-3
Twelve Critical Thinking Abilities Described by Ennis (1987)

1. Focusing on the question
2. Analyzing arguments
3. Asking and answering questions of clarification
4. Judging the credibility of a source
5. Observing and judging observational reports
6. Deducing and judging deductions
7. Inducing and judging inductions
8. Making value judgments
9. Defining terms and judging definitions
10. Identifying assumptions
11. Deciding on an action
12. Interaction with others

and analyze an adequate knowledge base, make inferences, and interact with others in a rational manner.

Analyzing critical thinking in terms of separate subskills can be somewhat risky because we are apt to lose sight of what critical thinking entails: critical examination of beliefs and courses of action. Instead, some authors suggest that a smaller set of general skills should be used to describe critical thinking (Halpern, 1997, 1998; Kurfiss, 1988; Quellmalz, 1987; Swartz & Perkins, 1990). These skills are knowledge, inference, evaluation, and metacognition.

Critical thinking of any kind is impossible without the first of these components—*knowledge*. Knowledge is something we use to think critically and also acquire as the result of critical thinking. As we have seen, expert knowledge enables individuals to solve problems faster, better, and differently from those without such knowledge. Knowledge provides the basis for judging the credibility of new information or points of view; it also helps us to critically scrutinize our goals and objectives. Knowledge in the form of strategies actively shapes the direction we take when trying to resolve a dilemma.

Inference refers to making some type of connection between two or more units of knowledge. Much of successful critical thinking draws on our ability to make simple, though insightful, inferences between otherwise unrelated facts. In chapter 6, for example, you learned that each of us makes attributional inferences concerning our success and failure in the classroom. Some of these inferences may be inappropriate under certain circumstances (e.g., beginning algebra students attributing their failure to low ability), whereas others are more appropriate (e.g., poor performance in algebra may be attributable to lack of prior knowledge, domain-specific strategies, and automaticity). Making inferences is an essential step in critical thinking because it enables individuals to understand their situations at a deeper, more meaningful level.

Several types of inference processes seem to be especially important. One is *deduction,* the process by which we reach specific conclusions from given information.

Logicians and mathematicians have identified a variety of deductive reasoning approaches that are useful when solving well-defined problems, such as syllogisms. No matter what the approach, all deductive inferences are similar in that conclusions are based only on the information provided by the problem. In the parlance of chapter 2, deduction is a data-limited reasoning process. Thus, if Josh borrows his mother's car and returns with a dented fender, we can deduce that Josh had an accident with the car. We cannot deduce that he was speeding, legally drunk, or watching a pedestrian while driving, which, in turn, caused the accident.

Another kind of inference process is *induction,* the process by which we reach general conclusions from given, or perhaps inferred, information. Induction is in many ways the opposite of deduction in that conclusions can be reached that go beyond the limits of the data. Inductive inferences tend to be broader and more sweeping than deductive inferences. One of the best examples of inductive reasoning is making up a theory to explain an event before it is investigated (or perhaps even happens). Darwin's theory of natural selection provides a stunning example of inductive Inference because it transcends the data described in *On the Origin of Species.*

The third component described above—*evaluation*—refers to related subskills, including analyzing, judging, weighing, and making value judgments (Perkins & Grotzer, 1997; Swartz & Perkins, 1990). These skills probably come closest to what we usually think of as critical thinking. *Analyzing* includes activities that enable us to identify and select relevant information. *Judging* requires us to assess the credibility of information or sources of information in an effort to eliminate bias. *Weighing* consists of comparing all information at our disposal, choosing the most appropriate information, and organizing it as logically as possible. *Making value judgments* assumes that we have some moral, ethical, or emotional response to the information that affects our decision making.

The final component of critical thinking is *metacognition* (Halpern, 1998; Kuhn, 1999; McGuinness, 1990; Swartz, 1989). As described in chapter 4, metacognition refers to "thinking about thinking." Clearly, an important aspect of critical thinking is our ability to analyze the adequacy of our decisions. Insufficient data or conflicting beliefs and attitudes may require us to postpone an important decision and may limit our ability to construct an informed opinion on a topic. Metacognition is essential to the critical thinking process because it allows us to monitor the adequacy of the information on which we base our opinions, as well as the reasonableness of our inferences.

Does Intelligence Constrain Critical Thinking?

In the previous section, we described skills necessary for critical thinking. One might ask whether these skills depend on intellectual aptitude. If they do, educators are faced with difficult decisions about grouping students on the basis of ability. Until recently, an ability groups model formed the backbone of the U.S. educational system. But what if thinking skills are not strongly linked with ability? How, then, should educators go about planning instruction?

Surprisingly, not a great deal of research has been done on the relationship between intellectual ability and critical thinking skills, although existing research does suggest that normatively high intellectual ability is neither a necessary nor sufficient condition for successful thinking (for further discussion see Baron, 1988; Halpern, 1997). Earlier, we reported that Kitchener and King (1981) found that verbal ability (a correlate of general intellectual ability) was not related to reflective judgment. Swanson (1990) found that metacognitive awareness among children was not constrained by intellectual ability.

Many contemporary researchers have adopted a broad view of what it means to be intelligent and how intellectual skills affect critical thinking (cf. Brody, 1992; Gardner, 1983; Sternberg, 1997). One view that we find particularly attractive is the model of critical thinking proposed by Perkins and colleagues (Perkins, 1987, 1995; Perkins & Grotzer, 1997). Perkins's model addresses three distinct aspects of intelligence: power, knowledge, and tactics. *Power* refers to the basic level of intellectual aptitude that each of us brings to a task. Clearly, this potential differs from person to person and, in many cases, differs within a single person across a variety of tasks (cf. Gardner, 1983). *Knowledge* refers to the domain-specific and general knowledge at our disposal. Every intellectual activity that we undertake is affected in some way by what we already know. One way in which knowledge helps us is in facilitating the organization of incoming information. Prior knowledge also enables us to construct meaning based on what we already know about a topic.

Unlike power and knowledge, *tactics* can be improved dramatically in only a short period of time (Perkins, Faraday, & Bushey, 1991). Tactics refers to the mental strategies we use to make a cognitive task easier to understand or perform. Perkins and many others (cf. Pressley et al., 1990) place a high premium on tactical knowledge for one important reason: Even a modest repertoire of tactics can compensate for lack of power or knowledge. The compensatory nature of tactics has been demonstrated in many studies (King, 1991; Swanson, 1990).

The fact that a compensatory relationship exists among power, knowledge, and tactics is of tremendous importance to educators (see Figure 8-4). When developing

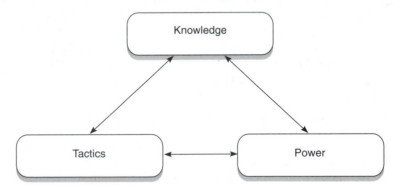

Figure 8-4
Components Involved in Learning, Problem Solving, and Critical Thinking
Source: Perkins, D. N. Thinking frames: An integrated perspective on teaching cognitive skills. From: Teaching Thinking Skills by Baron and Sternberg. Copyright © 1987 by W. H. Freeman and Company. Used with permission.

critical thinking skills, teachers and students alike should be encouraged to focus less attention on the role of power and more attention on knowledge and tactics. Teachers and students should also bear in mind that some tactics are "welded" to a particular body of knowledge, whereas others are not (Perkins, 1987). For example, factoring a quadratic equation to find its roots (a tactic) is difficult to separate from knowledge about quadratic equations because the two tend to be learned together. Other tactics, however, such as monitoring one's comprehension, are not specific to any particular body of knowledge. Monitoring is as useful when learning about American history as it is when assembling a sump pump or reading a road map. Some tactics need to be taught within a specific context for knowledge to be mastered; others are far more general and may be used successfully in many domains.

Tactics need not be limited to simple strategies such as skimming a text, factoring an equation, or carrying an umbrella when the weather looks like rain. Perkins (1987) has described a broader tactical approach to learning that he refers to as **thinking frames.** According to Perkins, a thinking frame is a guide or structure that organizes and supports thought processes. One example of a thinking frame is the "scientific method" commonly taught to beginning science students. Another example is the SQ3R (survey, question, read, recite, review) method of study. Other examples encountered in this text are levels of processing (a frame for understanding the depth of encoding), epistemological beliefs (a frame for explaining how individuals think about knowledge), and the general problem-solving method described above (a frame for attempting to solve any kind of well-defined problem).

One advantage to having thinking frames is that they provide an organizational structure for understanding new information and learning new skills. The Lehman et. al. (1988) study described in chapter 7 indicated that graduate students in different disciplines acquire expertise in reasoning skills that are especially important to their discipline (e.g., statistical reasoning). Acquiring these skills is one way that graduate students learn to "think like" experts. Another way is for graduate students to acquire the thinking frames a discipline holds about the phenomena it studies. For example, medical researchers assume that bacteria and viruses cause diseases; thus, the researchers search for cures for these diseases on the basis of external-agent models (they use a germ theory thinking frame).

Perkins (1987) has described three stages in frame development: acquisition, automaticity, and transfer. *Acquisition* refers to learning a thinking frame and, in turn, using a thinking frame to think and reason. Perkins is a strong proponent of teaching frames directly, including extensive modeling. *Automaticity* refers to being able to apply the frame automatically. As with other skills, using a thinking frame automatically is the result of extensive practice. the more practice one gets, the more automatic the frame becomes. *Transfer* refers to using the frame in a new context. Perkins (1987) and Perkins and Salomon (1989) have identified two kinds of transfer. The first kind of transfer, *high-road transfer,* occurs when students make a conscious, reflective effort to abstract the basic principles of the frame in a way that they can be applied in a different content area. High-road transfer requires students to be active, constructive, and reflective. In contrast, the second kind of transfer, *low-road transfer,* occurs spontaneously without awareness, given a narrow range of examples. As a consequence, students may not achieve a thorough (transferable) understanding of the frame. High-road transfer can be promoted by emphasizing reflection, self-monitoring, and extensive practice in a variety of settings (Mayer & Wittrock, 1996).

Perkins strongly advocates the direct teaching and modeling of tactics and thinking frames for several reasons. First, he believes that power (native ability) is extremely difficult to change. Second, he assumes that developing a body of expert knowledge is too time- and labor-intensive, taking perhaps thousands of hours. In contrast, strategy instruction can be accomplished in a much shorter period of time. Although strategies cannot substitute completely for power and knowledge, they often are able to compensate for lower levels of power and knowledge.

Planning a Critical-Thinking Skills Program

Programs designed to improve thinking, reasoning, and problem-solving skills fall into one of two categories: stand-alone and embedded programs. Stand-alone programs focus on the development of thinking skills independent of content area material. Embedded programs focus on improving thinking skills within the context of a particular content area, such as history or science.

Most experts suggest that thinking skills be embedded in specific content areas at least some of the time (Beyer, 1987; Swartz & Perkins, 1990). One reason is that content material may increase students' interest in learning in a way that is not possible with stand-alone programs. A second reason is that scant evidence suggests that learning thinking skills is made more difficult when students are asked to learn new content material as well.

This section provides guidelines for designing either a stand-alone or an embedded thinking-skills program. These programs should include the following three goals: (1) identifying appropriate skills, (2) implementing instruction, and (3) evaluating the program. We consider each of these steps separately.

Identifying Appropriate Skills   Program design should begin with questions about the kind of model that will guide instruction (Halpern, 1998). *Descriptive models* explain how good thinking actually happens. Often, good thinkers use sophisticated rules, strategies, and heuristics to evaluate information and reach decisions. This does not mean that such thinking is free of errors or is the best way to think in a particular setting. Rather, it describes what good thinkers actually do. *Prescriptive models* explain how good thinking ought to happen. They presume that some forms of thinking are better than others. Educators sometimes design instruction based on a prescriptive model that is too complicated or time-consuming to be used in most everyday settings. An alternative is to approach the teaching of thinking skills from a descriptive standpoint, emphasizing how good thinkers solve problems and reach decisions in everyday life even if their thinking is less than optimal.

Instructors also must decide what kinds of thinking skills they wish to include in their program. Table 8-1 presents a summary of some component skills and assumptions involved in four kinds of thinking programs: critical thinking, creative thinking,

Table 8-1
Characteristics of Four Thinking Skills

Type of Skill	Goals	Component Skills
Critical Thinking	To evaluate contrasting positions or the clarity of ideas	Identify position or idea, analyze competing views, weigh evidence, gather new information
Creative Thinking	To generate new ideas, develop new products	Establish need for idea, restructure existing view of problem, generate possibilities
Decision Making	To reach an informed decision	Consider available information, evaluate information, identify options, weigh options, make the decision
Problem Solving	To reach one or more adequate solutions to the problem	Identify, represent, select a strategy, implement the strategy, evaluate progress

Source: Adapted from *Teaching thinking: Issues and approaches*, by R. J. Swartz and D. N. Perkins, 1990, Pacific Grove, CA: Critical Thinking Press & Software.

decision making, and problem solving. It is important to recall that some of these skills may exceed students' developmental limitations. Some programs also may require more time or resources than others.

Last, instructors should consider whether *direct* or *indirect* instruction will be used. The former refers to teacher-directed instruction that focuses on clearly identified rules for good thinking. The latter refers to a student-directed approach to instruction that emphasizes the discovery of meaningful criteria for good thinking. Direct instruction appears to be most effective in situations in which an easy-to-identify strategy exists and problem solutions are limited. Indirect instruction may be most useful when attempting to develop guidelines for thinking about ill-defined problems, such as moral and ethical dilemmas faced in everyday life.

Implementing Instruction   To be effective, teachers must present thinking skills in a clear and meaningful sequence. Instructors should identify this sequence and model it for students. The first part of this chapter described a representative five-step problem-solving sequence. An analogous decision-making sequence might include (1) generating hypotheses about the causes of an event, (2) establishing rules for what constitutes acceptable evidence, (3) accumulating evidence from internal and external sources, (4) assessing the reliability of the evidence, and (5) evaluating the reasonableness of different causal claims.

Several general rules are helpful when considering sequencing. One rule is to start broadly, even in embedded programs. A second rule is to provide ample time to teach the thinking-skill sequence. In general, planning on a 6-month to 1-year time frame seems most reasonable. A third rule is to use what Swartz and Perkins (1990) refer to as bridging. **Bridging** involves grafting a skill previously used in a stand-alone program onto a regular content class, such as history or biology. In essence, bridging refers to embedding previously isolated thinking skills. Bridging is important because eventually students should be able to use general thinking skills in a variety of settings and in a variety of content areas.

Students also must be helped to increase their awareness of new skills. To increase awareness, students should be encouraged to reflect on the acquisition and use of new thinking skills (see chapter 4). One method is to include in-class discussion of these skills. Other methods are the use of small cooperative discussion groups, journals, and "think aloud" exercises in which one student explains the skill while he or she performs it.

Promoting awareness and discussion of thinking skills, including the component steps involved in each skill, is useful because students are not always as aware as we would like them to be. Along these lines, Swartz and Perkins (1990) have identified four levels of awareness. At the lower end of the scale is the *tacit use of a skill,* which is characterized by skilled performance without awareness. In comparison, *aware use of a skill* occurs when an individual is aware of using it even though the skill cannot be explained. Consider how easily we use grammatical rules and knowledge without explicit knowledge of these rules. *Strategic use* occurs when an individual possesses conscious awareness about the skill and uses this knowledge to regulate the use of the skill. *Reflective use* occurs when an individual reflects on the skill, understands how the skill works, knows how to use it strategically, and can explain it to others.

Effective instruction also must provide varied, extensive practice. The idea of practice as a means for developing automaticity is an important one. Researchers know that automaticity develops faster if a skill is practiced regularly, over a long period of time, and in a variety of settings.

Evaluating the Program   Most experts agree that thinking-skills programs are underevaluated rather than overevaluated (Barrel, 1991; Perkins et al., 1995; Swartz & Perkins, 1990). Unfortunately, common problems can undermine the evaluation process. One frequent problem is that teachers encounter resistance to teaching "thinking skills," as opposed to teaching "content." Some students, parents, and administrators may be suspicious of such programs. A second problem is that very few tests reliably measure improvements in thinking. A third problem is that successful thinking-skills programs may take years to achieve their aims.

Notwithstanding these concerns, instructors should evaluate three aspects of every program (Norris & Ennis, 1989; Swartz & Perkins, 1990). One aspect is the design adequacy of the program *before* it is implemented. Questions to ask at this stage include the following: (1) Does the program include the kind of skills you want to improve? (2) Is the program sustainable for long enough to achieve its goals? (3) Are support systems available? (4) Will the criterion skills transfer to new domains? and (5) Does it provide plenty of opportunities to practice the new skills?

A second aspect is the need to evaluate the program *during* implementation. Questions to ask at this stage include the following: (1) Are the criterion skills being mastered?

(2) Are the new skills being used inside and outside the classroom? (3) Do the new skills seem to make a difference in students' thinking? (4) Does the program provide sufficient feedback to students? and (5) Does the instructor have access to evaluative feedback?

A third aspect is the need for evaluation *after* the program has been implemented. Questions to ask at this stage include the following: (1) Has the program achieved its goals? (2) Did the program improve students' thinking? (3) Was this improvement seen in other areas of thinking or across the curriculum? (4) Are provisions made for maintaining the progress made in the program? and (5) Was the program the most effective use of the students' time?

Examples of Stand-Alone Programs

During the past 3 decades, many stand-alone programs designed to teach problem solving and critical thinking skills have appeared. Typical examples that have been studied are the Productive Thinking Program (Covington, Crutchfield, Davies, & Olton, 1974), the IDEAL Problem Solver (Bransford & Stein, 1984), the CoRT Thinking Materials (de Bono, 1973), and the Feuerstein Instrumental Enrichment (FIE) Program (Feuerstein, Rand, Hoffman, & Miller, 1980). We review each of these approaches briefly. For a discussion of other thinking-skills programs, see Pressley (1995) and Vye, Delclos, Burns, and Bransford (1988).

The Productive Thinking Program   This program includes a set of 15 lessons designed to teach general problem-solving skills to upper level elementary school children. Each lesson (see Covington et al., 1974, for a more complete description) consists of a booklet describing a basic lesson, accompanied by supplementary problems. The lessons describe two children who face "mystery" situations requiring detectivelike activities. Under the guidance of an uncle, the children attempt to solve the mystery (the problem). Presented in a gamelike way, the lessons are grounded in a model of problem solving similar to the 5-point sequence described above. Lessons deal with problem definition, getting the "facts" (knowledge), checking facts, making plans, and rerepresenting problems. The lessons are designed to be completed during a one-semester period. Evaluation suggests that students of differing abilities all show rather striking improvement on measures of problem-solving skill compared with comparable control groups (see Mansfield, Busse, & Krepelka, 1978; Olton & Crutchfield, 1969).

The IDEAL Problem Solver   The IDEAL Problem Solver describes five stages consistent with the IDEAL mnemonic (Bransford & Stein, 1984). The first, *identifying problems* (I), asks the solver to seek actively some problems requiring solution. The second step, *defining problems* (D), focuses on problem representation. Emphasis is placed on obtaining a clear picture of the problem prior to any solution attempts. The third step, *exploring alternatives* (E), involves generation and analysis of alternatives (operators) that might deal with the problem. The fourth step, *acting on a plan* (A), is closely linked with Step 5, *looking at the effects* (L).

Because it is a general stand-alone model, IDEAL can be adapted to a wide range of age and ability groups. It can also be embedded in many content domains, such as physics, history, and composition. Research on IDEAL and other similar programs has been quite positive, especially when the method is used to improve children's problem-solving skills (Delclos & Harrington, 1991; King, 1991; Vye et al., 1988).

The CoRT Thinking Materials   CoRT (Cognitive Research Trust) materials consist of a 2-year course for improving thinking skills (de Bono, 1973). The lessons include not only problem-solving skills but also the development of interpersonal skills and creative thinking. The lessons are presumed to be appropriate to children of a wide age range. The six units of materials include such topics as planning, generating alternatives, analyzing, comparing, selecting, and evaluating. A unit designed for a 10-week period consists of a series of leaflets, each discussing a single topic. Also included are examples, practice items, and ideas for further practice on the topic. The leaflets can be used easily in group settings. Games called Think Links are designed to facilitate practice with the topics. In the Gestalt tradition (see chapter 2), de Bono stresses the perceptual aspect of problem solving and tries to teach students effective techniques for breaking loose from ineffective patterns. He also believes that thinking skills are improved by practice; thus, following a brief description of each principle in a leaflet, the bulk of instructional time is spent practicing the principle.

The Feuerstein Instrumental Enrichment Program   Feuerstein's Instrumental Enrichment (FIE) system centers on what Feuerstein (Feuerstein et al., 1980) calls *mediated-learning experiences* (MLEs). Mediated-learning experiences provide activities that teach learners to interpret their experience. MLEs are deliberate interventions, by teachers, parents, or others, designed to help learners interpret and organize events. The basic task of the MLE is to teach the child to play an active role in critical thinking and, ultimately, to think and solve problems independently.

Instructionally, FIE provides a series of exercises (called "instruments" by Feuerstein) that provide the context for learning. At present, 14 or 15 instruments, arranged in order of increasing complexity, are available for 10- to 18-year-old students. The program is designed to be taught three to five times per week for 2 or 3 years. The exercises are paper-and-pencil activities designed to help the student identify problem-solving procedures and permit the teacher to "bridge" from the activities (problems) to subject matter of interest to student and teacher. Most FIE lessons provide "practice" exercises carried out under teacher supervision to provide feedback to students in their attempts to identify and evaluate the strategies used in solution attempts. FIE also provides a language for teaching problem-solving concepts such as *planning, strategy choice, evaluation,* and the like. Each instrument is designed to have wide generality. A special feature of this program is the deliberate focus on instruction of special populations. Thus, it has been used with youngsters who have mental retardation, learning disabilities, behavioral disorders, and hearing impairment.

Bransford, Arbitman-Smith, Stein, and Vye (1985) and Savalle, Twohig, and Rachford (1986) have evaluated the effectiveness of FIE. On the basis of a wide range of evaluation studies conducted in Israel, Venezuela, the United States, and Canada, students exposed to the FIE program performed better than control groups on tests such as the

Raven's Progressive Matrices and some achievement subtests, such as mathematics. The effects were found with a wide variety of student types. Studies have also shown, however, no significant difference as a result of FIE training. In general, features of successful studies were the presence of well-trained FIE teachers and student instruction that lasted 80 hours or more.

Teaching Wisdom

Many educators and researchers have become interested in the acquisition and development of wisdom (Baltes & Staudinger, 2000; Halpern, 2001; Perkins & Sternberg, 2001). **Wisdom,** as Sternberg (2001) defines it, is the willingness to use one's skills and knowledge to act in the soundest manner. Sternberg has developed what he refers to as a *balance theory of wisdom* that includes three main components: tacit knowledge, values, and goals. *Tacit knowledge* is procedural in nature and often acquired without direct help from others or through formal learning. *Values* are attitudes and dispositions that enable a person to shape and adapt to his or her environment. *Goals* are desired outcomes that reflect common good. Thus, wisdom is the process of using one's tacit knowledge to adapt to one's environment in a manner that promotes common good.

Sternberg (2001) and others have argued that wisdom is essential for adaptation and should be included in the school curriculum. One reason is that schools emphasize "book knowledge" that promotes narrow expertise without enhancing day-to-day wisdom. A second reason is that wisdom is an essential part of community involvement and responsible citizenship.

Sternberg (2001) has developed 16 principles for teaching wisdom. We summarize the main points of this program as follows: (a) demonstrate how wisdom is essential to a satisfying life, (b) emphasize the relationship between wisdom and practically intelligent action, (c) discuss and model day-to-day adaptive strategies, and (d) teach students to monitor the extent to which they and others make wise choices. Sternberg also has developed a 12-week curriculum suitable for middle school students that promotes wisdom. Several early studies suggest favorable results, although the jury will remain out for at least several years until the curriculum can be modified, implemented, and evaluated over time.

Research on wisdom and how to improve it in school settings is in its infancy. However, we view this research as promising because it acknowledges the central role of wisdom in our lives. Clearly some people are wiser than others. It behooves us to understand wisdom, how it develops, what aspects of schooling improve it, and how wisdom trickles down through our lives in helpful ways.

Summary

This chapter examined problem solving and critical thinking. Both types of thinking are constrained by two important factors: (1) expert knowledge within a domain and (2) knowledge about a general problem-solving (or critical thinking) strategy.

Expert knowledge improves problem solving for several reasons, including faster processing, better representation, more effective use of solution strategies, and better monitoring. Knowledge of a general problem-solving strategy also improves performance, even among children. Five stages in this strategy were described: problem finding, representing problems, selecting a strategy, implementing a strategy, and evaluating the solution.

We also provided several definitions of critical thinking, a cognitive activity that is assumed to overlap with problem solving but differs from it as well. Critical thinking is related more closely to ill-defined problems, whereas problem solving often relates to well-defined problems. We described four general skills known to influence it: knowledge, inference, evaluation, and metacognition.

We next considered whether intellectual ability constrains problem solving and critical thinking. We argued for a compensatory relationship among power, knowledge, and tactics, emphasizing that although native ability affects critical thinking, it can be compensated for through the selective use of knowledge and strategies.

A plan for identifying, implementing, and evaluating a critical thinking program was presented as well. Basic components of such programs include defining an instructional sequence, promoting higher order awareness of critical thinking skills through the development and use of metacognition, and providing ample time for students to engage in extensive and varied practice of newly acquired thinking skills.

We examined several stand-alone instructional programs to improve general problem solving and critical thinking: the Productive Thinking Program, the IDEAL Problem Solver, the CoRT Thinking Materials, and the Feuerstein Instrumental Enrichment Program. Research indicates that all of these programs enhance thinking skills, although each promotes a different set of skills.

We also summarized emerging research on wisdom. Wisdom was defined as the use of tacit knowledge and values to act in a reasonable manner for the common good. Researchers currently are developing and testing short-term learning programs designed to increase wisdom.

Suggested Readings

Baron, J. (1996). *Thinking and deciding* (2nd ed.). New York: Cambridge University Press.

This scholarly text considers problem solving, critical thinking, and reasoning from an in-depth perspective. Although it is highly technical and requires some knowledge of cognitive psychology, it is well-written and provides a sweeping view of the field.

Ericsson, K. A. (Ed.). (1996). *The road to excellence: The acquisition of expert performance in the arts, sciences, sports, and games*. Mahwah, NJ: Erlbaum.

This edited volume examines the role of deliberate practice and talent in considerable detail.

Sternberg, R. F. (1999). The theory of successful intelligence. *Review of General Psychology, 3,* 292–316.

This article summarizes Robert Sternberg's theory of practical intelligence. It describes the relationships among intelligence, expertise, critical thinking, and wisdom.

Swartz, R. J., & Perkins, D. N. (1990). *Teaching thinking: Issues and approaches*. Pacific Grove, CA: Midwest.

This book, by two highly regarded experts, is directed toward helping nonexperts design, implement, and evaluate a thinking-skills program.

Weisberg, R. W. (1993). *Creativity: Beyond the myth of genius*. San Francisco: Freeman.

This book combines a review of research with interesting case studies to dispel many myths about creativity. Easily accessible to readers with a limited knowledge of cognitive psychology.

Chapter 9

Classroom Contexts for Cognitive Growth

Constructivism: Role of the Learner in Building and Transforming Knowledge ■
Social Cognition: Social Factors in Knowledge Construction ■ *Implications for Teaching:*
A Portrait of the Reflective Classroom ■ *Summary* ■ *Suggested Readings* ■

THE EVOLUTION OF COGNITIVE PSYCHOLOGY away from "purely cognitive" variables of memory and thought to include learners' motivational and belief systems that we described in earlier chapters also has led to another important understanding— the role of social interaction and discourse in fostering cognitive development.

It seems obvious to anyone who has ever been a student or a teacher, a child or a parent, that teaching and learning are highly social activities. From the very earliest interactions between parent and child on up to a graduate student's relationship with a graduate advisor, much of our learning takes place through interactions with adults or peers who have greater knowledge and is influenced by the larger culture in which we live.

Despite this seemingly obvious importance of the social context in learning, cognitive development research did not begin to focus on social processes and their effect on cognition until the past 2 or 3 decades. The translation and publication in 1962 of *Thought and Language* by the Russian psychologist Lev Vygotsky, and in 1978 of his book *Mind in Society: The Development of Higher Mental Functions,* began a major shift of focus. Vygotsky's assertion that higher mental functions originate in our social life when children interact with adults or more capable peers (Vygotsky, 1978) resonated with researchers and educators who felt that the information processing approaches to cognitive development had a major weakness in lacking any account of the social context of learning.

Information processing approaches to theories of cognitive development, as described in chapters 2–5, have focused on describing mechanisms such as encoding, retrieval and strategy choice that operate internally when a learner is participating in a task. These are excellent descriptions of the internal processes occurring during learning, but they fail to describe the social processes often involved—Vygotsky's interaction with adults or more capable peers.

The social context of cognition and its applications to learning and instruction received increasing attention from theorists and researchers through the 1980s and

1990s (Lave, 1988; Moll & Whitmore, 1993; Moshman, 1982; Newman, Griffin, & Cole, 1989; Pressley & Wharton-McDonald, 1997; Rogoff, 1990; Rogoff et al., 1993). The idea of children as active learners, who construct their own knowledge and reflect on their learning with the help of more experienced partners, expanded the way we think about classroom teaching and our ideas of the teacher's role. Teachers became more than information givers, serving in new roles as coaches and guides and facilitating students' knowledge building. This increasing emphasis on the social context and the effects of the wider culture on cognition and learning has led researchers to consider new roles for teachers, such as guided participation (Rogoff, 1990) and Schön's reflective practitioner model (1987), and to look beyond the classroom to the cognitive effects of the provision and regulation of children's everyday activities (Gauvain, 1999). Our view of the centrality of these ideas to education is reflected in two of our cognitive themes, outlined in chapter 1: that learning is a constructive, not a receptive process, and that social interaction is fundamental to cognitive development.

Another of Vygotsky's important contributions to the thinking about cognitive development was the concept of language as one of the most important social and cognitive tools. As researchers have recognized the importance of the social context of cognition, interest has also grown in the role of classroom discussion, or discourse, in building knowledge. A classroom discussion can be seen as the everyday expression of the idea that students are active agents in their own learning, enabling students to construct new conceptions and acquire new ways of thinking. Yet research suggests that classroom discussion often fails to achieve these goals (Chinn et al., 2001). The ideas of Calfee (1994), Chinn and Waggoner (1992), Chinn et al. (2001), O'Flahavan and Stein (1992), and others help define ways that teachers can guide classroom discourse to create a more "reflective" classroom and foster cognitive growth.

The social contexts of cognition and learning have obvious applications to the classroom. As any teacher knows, the classroom is above all a social environment and teaching is a form of social interaction. The challenge to teachers is to provide classroom environments that support knowledge development in all its forms and that encourage students' self-awareness and self-direction. One of the most important perspectives directing how researchers and educators think about the social context of the classroom has its roots in Vygotsky's work: the perspective of *constructivism*.

Constructivism: Role of the Learner in Building and Transforming Knowledge

Constructivism is a broad term with philosophical, learning, and teaching dimensions, but it generally emphasizes the learner's contribution to meaning and learning through both individual and social activity (Biggs, 1996; Steffe & Gale, 1995). In the constructivist view, learners arrive at meaning by selecting information and constructing what they know. Scholars differ in the degree to which they ascribe knowledge construction solely to the learner (see, e.g., Moshman, 1982; Prawat, 1996; Steffe & Gale, 1995). Some constructivists view mental structures as reflective of external realities, while others see no independent reality outside the mental world of the individual.

Although there are many dimensions of constructivism, most constructivists share two main ideas: that learners are active in constructing their own knowledge and that social interactions are important to knowledge construction. In our discussion here, we concentrate most strongly on a form of constructivism—**dialectical constructivism** (Moshman, 1982)—that highlights the importance of social interactions in developing knowledge and thought. In our judgment, this view best helps us identify the elements most likely to create a reflective classroom—one in which teachers and students interact in ways that stimulate both knowledge construction and cognitive growth.

Many key concepts of cognitive psychology, such as *schema theory* and *levels of processing,* represent constructivist thinking. Constructivist perspectives also are shaping significant changes in curriculum and instructional practices in the United States. A constructivist view of learning has provided support for meaning-based approaches to reading instruction, such as those advocated in the *Standards for the English Language Arts* (NCTE, 1996), developed by the International Reading Association and the National Council of Teachers of English. The *Principles and Standards for School Mathematics* (NCTM, 2000) of the National Council of Teachers of Mathematics, though not explicitly constructivist, have a strongly constructivist flavor, as do the *Benchmarks for Science Literacy* (AAAS, 1993) of the American Association for the Advancement of Science and the *National Science Education Standards* (NRC, 1996) of the National Research Council.

The aim of teaching, from a constructivist perspective, is not so much to transmit information as to encourage *knowledge formation* and *metacognitive processes for judging, organizing, and acquiring new information.* A constructivist approach will manifest itself in the classroom in numerous ways, including the following:

- *selection of instructional materials: employing materials that children can manipulate or use to interact with their environments*
- *choice of activities: encouraging students to observe, gather data, test hypotheses, and participate in field trips*
- *nature of classroom processes: using cooperative learning and guided discussions*
- *integration of curricula, such as developing long-term thematic projects combining mathematics, science, reading, and writing*

In constructivist classrooms, students typically are taught to plan and direct their own learning to some extent. Students are encouraged to take an active role in their learning and teachers adopt new roles as coaches and facilitators rather than serving only as primary sources of information.

Types of Constructivism: A Closer Look

Although some discuss constructivism as if it were a unified philosophical, psychological, and educational perspective, a more differentiated understanding is useful for considering its implications for instruction. Moshman (1982; see also Pressley, Harris,

& Marks, 1992; Pressley & Wharton-McDonald, 1997) has distinguished among three types of constructivism: exogenous constructivism, endogenous constructivism, and dialectical constructivism. All involve knowledge construction but reflect different views of how knowledge construction occurs.

In **exogenous constructivism,** knowledge formation is basically a reconstruction of structures, such as cause–effect relationships, presented information, and observed behavior patterns, that already exist in external reality. In this view, our mental structures reflect the organization of the world outside—or *exogenous* to—ourselves. Although they cannot be classified exclusively as examples of exogenous constructivism, important concepts in cognitive psychology such as schemata, network models, and production systems (see chapter 3), clearly fit within this perspective. Exogenous constructivism emphasizes the strong external influence of physical reality, presented information, and social models on knowledge construction. Knowledge is "true" from this perspective to the extent that it accurately copies the external structures that it ideally represents (Moshman, 1982).

Contrasted with exogenous constructivism is **endogenous constructivism,** where cognitive structures are created from earlier structures, not directly from information provided by the environment. In endogenous constructivism, according to Moshman, the key process is coordination of cognitive actions; knowledge exists at a more abstract level and develops through cognitive activity within—*endogenous* to—ourselves. Cognitive structures are created from other, earlier structures and follow one another in predictable sequences. Piaget's stages of cognitive development are a prominent example of endogenous constructivism.

The third category of constructivism represents a point between the extremes of exogenous and endogenous constructivism. **Dialectical constructivism** places the source of knowledge in the *interactions* between learners and their environments. Knowledge is a "constructed synthesis" that grows out of contradictions that individuals experience during these interactions (Moshman, 1982, p. 375). Dialectical constructivism is linked with yet another philosophical point of view that has become increasingly influential in American psychology—*contextualism*—which holds that thought and experience are inextricably intertwined with the context in which they occur.

Although these types of constructivism represent divergent views, Moshman argues that each can be useful for understanding different ways in which individuals might construct knowledge. If, for instance, our primary interest is how accurately children perceive the organization of some body of information, such as concepts in biology, we likely would find an exogenous view of constructivism inviting. If our interest is children's cognitive growth from naive to sophisticated mathematical or scientific concepts (see chapters 14 and 15), an endogenous constructivism is more likely to be useful.

A dialectical perspective incorporates both elements and focuses our attention on the *interaction* between internal and external factors. For instance, if we are considering instruction aimed at children's *interpretations* of literature or at challenging children's naive conceptions in mathematics or science, we enter the realm of the dialectic.

Of the three, dialectical constructivism provides the most general perspective and has become increasingly important in cognitive psychology. To better understand dialectical constructivism we need to examine the views of its most distinguished proponent, the Russian psychologist Lev Vygotsky. Although Vygotsky did his pivotal research in the 1920s and died at the young age of 37 in 1934, it wasn't until translation and publication of his monograph *Thought and Language* that his work began to be known in the West. The publication of *Mind in Society* and subsequent translations of his work (e.g., Rieber & Carton, 1987) fueled the interest in Vygotsky's thinking and marked the beginning of an era in which his ideas have had great influence on psychology and education.

Vygotsky's Dialectical Constructivism

The core of Vygotsky's theory is that higher mental functions have their origin in social life as children interact with more experienced members of their community, such as parents, other adults, and more capable peers. Vygotsky emphasizes the integration of internal and external aspects of learning and the social environment for learning (Newman, Griffin, & Cole, 1989). In Vygotsky's view, cultures externalize individual cognition in their tools, by which he means not only the shared physical objects of a culture (e.g., a toothbrush, an automobile, and artwork) but also more abstract social-psychological tools, such as written language and social institutions. Physical tools are directed toward the external world, but social-psychological tools are "symbol systems used by individuals engaged in thinking" (John-Steiner, 1997). Cognitive change occurs as children use these mental tools in social interactions and internalize and transform these interactions.

Perhaps Vygotsky's most influential concept has been the **zone of proximal development.** The zone of proximal development can be defined as the difference between the difficulty level of a problem that a child can cope with independently and the level that can be accomplished with adult help. In the zone of proximal development, a child and an adult (or novice and expert) work together on problems that the child (or novice) alone could not work on successfully.

Cognitive change takes place in the zone of proximal development or, in the phrase of Newman et al. (1989), in the "construction zone." Children bring a developmental history to the zone of proximal development; adults bring a support structure. As children and adults interact, they share cultural tools. This culturally mediated interaction, in Vygotsky's view, is what yields cognitive change. The interaction is internalized and becomes a new function of the individual.

Vygotsky's colleague, Leont'ev (1981), suggested the term *appropriation* to describe how learners internalize cultural knowledge from this process of interaction. Children, Leont'ev suggested, need not, and in fact should not, reinvent the artifacts of a culture. The culture has built up these artifacts over thousands of years, and children can *appropriate* them to their own circumstances as they learn how to use them.

Internalization of knowledge in the zone of proximal development is not an automatic reflection of external events. Children bring their own understanding to social interactions and make whatever sense they can of exchanges with adults. They can participate in activities beyond their understanding, but still be affected by them; think of a 2-year-old "reading" a book with his or her parent. Likewise, adults may not fully understand children's perspectives but play an important role in their cognitive change. As children and adults interact, children are exposed to adults' advanced systems of understanding, and cognitive change—learning—becomes possible.

Part of the attractiveness of Vygotsky's thinking for cognitive and educational theorists has been his stress on the social influences in cognitive change. Cognitive development, in Vygotsky's view, is not simply a matter of individual change, but rather is the result of social interactions in cultural contexts.

Many educators find the emphasis on adult–child interactions in cognitive growth especially appealing. The concept of **instructional scaffolding,** for example, is closely aligned with Vygotsky's theory of the zone of proximal development. As we see in more detail later in our discussion of classroom discourse, in instructional scaffolding a teacher provides students with selective help, such as asking questions, directing attention, or giving hints about possible strategies, to enable them to do things they could not do on their own. Then, as students become more competent, the support is withdrawn gradually (for a discussion of scaffolding see Beed, Hawkins, & Roller, 1991).

Some researchers feel that this view of scaffolding tends to focus too much on the adult's contribution to the process and reduces the child to being only a recipient of adult help (Gauvain, 2001). A perspective that focuses more on the learner's contribution is that of *social cognitive theory*.

Social Cognition: Social Factors in Knowledge Construction

Early cognitive research and theory focused on individual memory and thought, with relatively little emphasis on the context in which individuals were functioning. The information processing model we presented in the earlier chapters largely follows this approach. Under the influence of theorists such as Vygotsky, however, cognitive theory now includes a much greater recognition of social influences on cognition. As a consequence, researchers increasingly are turning their attention to children's interactions with parents, peers, and teachers in their homes, neighborhoods, and schools.

The perspective guiding these investigations is *social cognitive theory*. Closely related to dialectical constructivism, social cognitive theory stresses how human skill, activity, and thought develop in the context of specific historical and cultural activities of the community (Sternberg & Wagner, 1994). Social exchanges between individuals are seen as the primary source of cognitive growth. In the next sections, we examine two influential social cognitive models: Rogoff's apprenticeships in thinking model (1990, 1995) and Schön's reflective practitioner model (1983, 1987).

Rogoff's Apprenticeships in Thinking Model

Barbara Rogoff (1990), following the lead of Vygotsky, has argued that cognitive development occurs when children are guided by adults in social activities that stretch their understanding of, and skill in using, the tools of the prevailing culture. When children are with their peers and adults, they are *apprentices in thinking*. In an apprenticeship, a novice works closely with an expert in joint problem-solving activity (J. S. Brown et al.,

1989). The apprentice also typically participates in skills beyond those that he or she is capable of handling independently. In the manner of an apprenticeship, Rogoff states, development builds on "the internalization by the novice of the shared cognitive processes, appropriating what was carried out in collaboration to extend existing knowledge and skills" (p. 141). Rogoff argues that cognitive development is inherently social in nature, requiring mutual engagement with one or more partners of greater skill.

Other children form one important pool of "skilled partners." For instance, children's play and their dialogues with each other help them think collaboratively and offer a host of possibilities for considering others' perspectives. Play also involves imagination and creativity and so helps children extend themselves into new roles, interactions, and settings. Peers are highly available and active, Rogoff (1990) points out, providing each other with "motivation, imagination, and opportunities for creative elaboration of the activities of their community."

For most children, however, adults are the most reliable and important skilled partners. Parents, relatives, and teachers routinely play many roles with important implications for cognitive development. These include (1) stimulating children's interest in cognitive tasks, (2) simplifying tasks so that children can manage them, (3) motivating children and providing direction to their activities, (4) giving feedback, (5) controlling their frustration and risk, and (6) demonstrating idealized versions of the acts to be performed (Rogoff, 1990).

Adults often engage in **guided participation** (Rogoff, 1995) with children, a process by which children's efforts are structured in a social context and the responsibility for problem solving is gradually transferred. In guided participation, children learn to solve problems in the context of social interactions. Guided participation always involves interpersonal communication and stage setting to build bridges between what children already know and the new information they encounter.

Rogoff argues that mental processes are enriched in guided participation because they occur in the context of *accomplishing something;* that is, cognitive processes direct intelligent, purposeful actions. Participants develop a sense of common purpose through extended dialogue and a shared focus of attention. Children are intrinsically motivated to come to a better understanding of their world and often initiate and guide interactions in which cognitive growth takes place.

Guided participation is not always formal or explicit, however. Events often are shared without participants being aware of efforts at guided participation or intending them to be instructional. A parent may help a child order at a restaurant or trim a tree branch, without thinking of it as teaching. Similarly, a preschool child may learn about what teachers and students do by playing school with an older brother or sister.

In sum, Rogoff views cognitive development as a process growing out of interactions with other children and adults. Individual cognition is constructed from the intellectual tools that a particular society has available. Although children's interactions with their peers provide support for building new knowledge, adults play a unique role in helping children move to new cognitive levels. Parents and teachers are reliable expert partners with children in guided participation. These interactions help children build bridges between what they know and what they don't and support children's efforts at acquiring new knowledge.

Schools provide a unique resource for cognitive development, especially for acquiring the more "formal" tools of language and thought. Schools offer structured opportunities for guided participation with adults and for appropriating adults' knowledge and strategies for problem solving—activities such as acquiring a technical vocabulary for understanding perspective in painting, learning ways to search for information, using cause–effect frameworks for understanding historical events, employing algorithms for solving word problems in mathematics, or applying formal research methods for gathering and categorizing data. Among the most basic challenges for teachers is learning how best to help students acquire effective mental tools. As is discussed later in the chapter, classroom dialogue guided by the teacher can provide important conditions to meet these challenges.

Schön's Reflective Practitioner Model

Like Rogoff, Schön (1987) also has taken a dialectic constructivist perspective on cognitive development. Schön draws less explicitly from Vygotsky, and his interests have been centered mainly on teaching and learning in the professions rather than with children. His perspective on cognitive development nonetheless shares several key elements with Vygotsky's theory and with Rogoff's approach: guided discovery, learning by doing, and the importance of social interactions in building knowledge and understanding. Schön developed his system around three key concepts: knowing-in-action, reflection-in-action, and reflection on reflection-in-action.

Knowing-in-Action   **Knowing-in-action** is tacit knowledge, the sort of knowledge that is unarticulated but revealed in our intelligent actions (Polanyi, 1967; see also our discussion of implicit memory in chapter 3). We show our tacit knowledge whenever we act in reasonable ways, such as driving a car, greeting a friend, or typing a letter, but are not explicitly aware of the thinking underlying our actions.

Much of what we know is knowing-in-action and is revealed only as we go about our daily lives. Although it is possible to describe the implicit knowing that underlies your actions, these descriptions will always be *constructions,* "attempts to put into explicit, symbolic form a kind of intelligence that begins by being tacit and spontaneous" (Schön, 1987, p. 25). By describing knowing-in-action, we convert it to **knowledge-in-action,** making it a part of our semantic memory.

Ordinarily, however, knowing-in-action is not verbalized; our actions consist largely of spontaneous, routinized responses. As long as the situation is normal and there are no surprises to our knowledge-in-action categories, our scripts flow smoothly into action. *Surprises*—outcomes that do not fit our scripts—are not necessarily negative events, however. In fact, they are the key to triggering reflection-in-action, a mechanism Schön argues is crucial for change and cognitive growth.

Reflection-in-Action   **Reflection-in-action** is conscious thought about our actions and about the thinking that accompanies them. Reflection-in-action is a form of metacognition in which we question both the unexpected event and the knowledge-in-action that brought it on. A child entering a new class may tug and pull at the teacher's clothing, an action that brought positive attention from a former teacher but brings a reprimand from the new teacher. A formerly successful routine now is not working, and the surprise forces the child to reflect both on his or her actions and on the reasons for the changed circumstances.

Schön's concept of *reflection-in-action* has a great deal in common with both dimensions of metacognition discussed in chapter 4: *knowledge of cognition* and *regulation of cognition*. Reflection-in-action stimulates a kind of on the spot thought experiment. Depending on the extent of prior knowledge, unexpected failures and successes may lead in various directions: to *exploration,* in which the learner makes no predictions; to *testing moves,* in which different paths are tested for their feasibility; or to *hypothesis testing,* in which competing hypotheses are tested to determine which is valid.

Under a skilled teacher's guidance, a similar process can lead to student learning. The potential for learning lies in the constructive nature of reflection-in-action. When students are placed in situations that are uncertain and where they are motivated to change, Schön contends, they begin a process of exploration, movement, and hypothesis testing.

Reflection on Reflection-in-Action   All of us construct and reconstruct our cognitive worlds as we experience the events of our lives and reflect on them. By assisting students in constructing new knowledge, skilled teachers can help learners do much more than they could do alone. Schön (1987) refers to this process as **reflection on reflection-in-action.** Skilled teachers can help learners to develop reflection-in-action, that is, to articulate the thoughts guiding their actions and to judge their adequacy. Consistent with Vygotsky's views of the zone of proximal development, the teacher's goal is to be literally "thought-provoking" (Schön, 1987, p. 92). Ideally, the teacher creates an interactive setting in which both the teacher and the students are colearners, but students' self-discovery has the highest priority.

According to Schön, students cannot be taught what they need to know, *but they can be coached toward self-understanding*—a form of dialectical, social constructivism. Schön advocates creating *practice situations*—relatively low-risk events in which students can learn by doing and receive rich feedback—that motivate learners toward understanding and contain at least some elements that the students themselves have created.

Because of its unfamiliarity, students may initially strongly resist this kind of coaching approach and become unsettled, even angry, when there seem to be "no right answers." They may become frustrated and demand to be told what is "correct." The teacher–coach must keep in mind that he or she is managing a transaction between learners and environment, not offering information. Uncertainty and conflict about values are inevitable. In Schön's view, this uncertainty is among the most powerful motivating forces teachers have available.

In summary, Schön reflects social-cognitive and constructivist points of view by portraying learning as a social-interactive process in which students are helped to create new understandings. The key goal is students' reflection-in-action—metacognitive reflection on unexpected events or variations in phenomena and the thinking that led to them. In Schön's view, students learn when they act and are helped to think about their actions. Learning by doing forces them to make judgments; reflection helps them recognize their assumptions and see what is important. Although students initially may perceive this kind of instruction as threatening, ambiguous, or confusing, clarification comes when students stay with problems and dialogue continues between the teacher–coach and the students.

Together, Rogoff's and Schön's models reflect a social-cognitive viewpoint consistent with Vygotsky's. The exchanges between teachers and students create a zone of proximal development in which students construct new knowledge and acquire habits of reflection and increased metacognitive knowledge. These exchanges with teachers and advanced peers are essential to cognitive change and growth and are vital to creating useful situated knowledge and thought. Dialogue between teachers and students is not the only mechanism for building students' understanding and revealing their misunderstandings, of course, but it is among the most potent tools that teachers have available. In the next section, we extend our examination of social cognitive theory by exploring the nature of the discussions that take place in the classroom. We consider the potential of different kinds of classroom dialogue for building knowledge and fostering reflection.

Role of Classroom Discourse in Knowledge Construction

Most people's prototypical images of the classroom involve language use: teachers asking questions and students answering, classes discussing works of literature, students poring over textbooks, and students struggling with writing satisfactory answers to test questions. Language is the medium by which concepts are presented and clarified and through which students' knowledge typically is expressed and judged.

Language, as we learned from Vygotsky (1978, 1981), also is one of the most important social and cognitive tools, yet it often is not used effectively in the classroom. Language can play a critically important role in the classroom when it becomes discourse and is used as a tool for fostering cognitive growth. One theoretical perspective on how students learn from discourse is based on Vygotsky's view that higher mental functions develop through a process by which the learner internalizes and transforms the content of social interaction (Fall et al., 2000).

Discourse is a general term referring to structured, coherent sequences of language. In discourse, propositions (see chapter 3) take on meaning in relationship to one another. Meaning is drawn from the context. Discourse has **coherence,** and references forward or backward give meaning to individual elements. A conversation is an example of discourse: as two people discuss an event, the structure builds, each new idea taking meaning from the ones that came before. Essays, short stories, novels, and classroom discussions also are examples of discourse. Here we are interested in **classroom discourse,** which refers to the verbal exchanges in the classroom.

Researchers increasingly consider the quality of classroom discourse to be one of the most critical elements in effective schooling (e.g., Calfee et al., 1994; Chinn et al., 2001; Kuhn, Shaw, & Felton, 1997; Nystrand & Gamoran, 1991; Wiencek & O'Flahavan, 1994). Classroom discourse, they argue, is a primary vehicle by which teachers guide, organize, and direct their students' activities. Like Rogoff and Schön, these researchers view learning as a constructive process in which social exchanges with others are fundamental to students' construction of meaning. As Hull and her associates (Hull, Rose, Fraser, & Castellano, 1991) have stated, "In the classroom, it is through talk that learning gets done, that knowledge gets made" (p. 318). This view is being translated into research aimed at finding the discourse structures and uses of classroom discourse that best promote learning (e.g., Calfee et al., 1994; Chinn & Waggoner, 1992; Kuhn et al., 1997; O'Flahavan & Stein, 1992; Wiencek & O'Flahavan, 1994).

Traditional classroom discourse has not been particularly supportive of student expression and reflection. Classroom discourse at all levels, from primary grades through college, is almost universally dominated by teacher talk. Students typically say little, and students' questions are rare. Most classroom talk centers on a single dominant discourse pattern: A teacher asks a question, a student responds, and the teacher gives feedback (Alvermann, O'Brien, & Dillon, 1990; Cazden, 1988; Mehan, 1979). Often simply called the **IRE pattern** (Initiate, Respond, Evaluate), the sequence in slightly more elaborated form is as follows:

1. *Teacher Initiates.* The teacher informs, directs, or asks students for information. For example:

   TEACHER: Jeni, can you tell me the name of the town where they were going?

2. *A Student Responds.* Students' responses to the teacher's prompt or question can be verbal or nonverbal.

   JENI: Uh . . . I think it was Peatwick.

3. *The Teacher Evaluates.* The teacher comments on the student's reply or reacts to it nonverbally.

   TEACHER: Right. Peatwick. Good. And where were they . . .

As Cazden and others have pointed out, the IRE is the "default pattern" for classroom exchanges between teacher and student; that is, IRE is what happens unless deliberate intervention is made to achieve some alternative. Although this pattern can support a discussion of sorts, it most often is used for *recitation* in which a teacher quizzes students about content they have just studied. It often is accompanied by minilectures—periods of teacher talk that the teacher uses to elaborate on information already being discussed or to present new information. Chinn and Waggoner (1992) and others (e.g., Alvermann & Hayes, 1989; Cazden, 1988) have pointed out that it is extraordinarily difficult for teachers to move away from these patterns and their variations. It may be, as Chinn and Waggoner speculate, that teacher control and authority are at stake, or it simply may be that teachers stick to this pattern because it is useful for probing student attention and comprehension.

Toward a More Reflective Classroom

We have been building the case in this chapter that cognitive growth is best fostered in a social environment in which students are active participants and where they are helped to reflect on their learning. For teachers to create a reflective classroom in which students build new knowledge and learn to manage their own learning, they almost certainly need to extend classroom discourse beyond the IRE recitations and the IRE-type discussions in which turn-taking rotates between teacher and students.

Calfee et al. (1994) have proposed the idea of **disciplined discussion** as an alternative to the IRE. Disciplined discussion draws on the best features of both *conversation,* which ordinarily is structured informally and student generated, and *instruction,* which typically refers to a more formal and teacher-directed interaction organized around a lesson. In disciplined discussion, a classroom discussion group approaches a text or other information source strategically with a particular goal in mind. The roles and responsibilities of the participants are defined: Students solve problems by using interactive processes they have learned through modeling, practice, and feedback; a teacher plays several important but not dominating roles, acting as an organizer and participant or simply as an observer.

But what kinds of interactions are most likely to help students build knowledge and reflect on their learning? Chinn and Waggoner (1992) suggest that teachers first need to ensure that students have sufficient knowledge to support the discussion topic, knowledge that may come from personal experience, reading, or other sources. Beyond this are two fundamental criteria, both reflecting a social-cognitive viewpoint: (1) that students share alternative perspectives and (2) that the discourse has an open participation structure.

When students share *alternative perspectives,* they give their personal reactions and interpretations and consider the viewpoints of other participants. A group of students reading a short story, for instance, are likely to interpret parts of it in different ways. A good discussion provides a forum for determining things they agree on and for building metacognitive awareness. Similarly, children examining a picture of a snail may disagree about whether particular protrusions on its head are antennae or eyes. Discussion can stimulate further inquiry, such as closer observation or consulting other text sources, which will lead to an answer or resolution of the disagreement.

Open participation structure, which refers to the ability of students to talk freely with each other as they would in ordinary conversations, also is vital to building knowledge and reflection. In an open participation structure, both students and the teacher can initiate topics and ask questions (Chinn & Waggoner, 1992), which helps involve students in the discussion. When classroom discourse incorporates both of these functions, it can become *authentic* (J. S. Brown et al., 1989; Calfee et al., 1994; Graesser, Long, & Horgan, 1988; Nystrand & Gamoran, 1991); that is, organized around genuine questions of interest to the students and eliciting their perspectives.

The CORE Model   What are some ways that discussions can affect the development of knowledge and reflective thought in participating students? Calfee et al. (1994) suggest four possibilities in their CORE (**c**onnecting, **o**rganizing, **r**eflecting, and **e**xtending) model of instruction (Calfee, Chambliss, & Beretz, 1991). First, discussions provide *connections* for learning. Useful knowledge is contextual, grounded in what students already know. Good discussions draw on students' prior domain and general knowledge and allow them to share what they know with their discourse partners. To take part effectively in discussions, students must recall information and use their metacognitive knowledge to link and sequence their ideas. Students learn that good discussions have coherence. By staying on topic and building on the ideas brought up by the participants, together they create a new body of shared information.

Second, discussions help *organize* knowledge. Knowledge construction is not simply a matter of accumulating particular facts or even of creating new units of information. It also involves organizing old information into new forms. Discussions are uniquely suited for these purposes. As participants strive to understand and contribute to discussions, they are forced to relate and organize what they know.

Third, good discussions can *foster reflective thought*. Discussions offer many opportunities for students to become aware of their thinking and to learn skills for regulating their thoughts and actions. Like all forms of discourse, discussions require participants to externalize thought. Presenting, organizing, clarifying, and defending ideas push students' cognitive processes into the open. Reactions of others in the discussion provide feedback on whether they have been persuasive and coherent. The act of explaining their reasoning promotes students' learning, particularly when reasons are elaborated with further evidence (Chinn et al., 2000). Teachers, by coaching before and after discussions and adopting roles that allow them to scaffold student thought during discussions, can significantly influence students' abilities to reflect on their interactions and on the substance of their thinking (O'Flahavan & Stein, 1992).

Guthrie (1993) gives an example of how discussion can stimulate reflection, describing how fifth graders in one of his project classrooms were engaged in a debate about whether life might exist on Mars. One student, John, insisted he had read that life did exist on Mars. He was challenged immediately by other students to identify the book that supported this belief. One student, Patty, proposed that the book in question most likely discussed what it *might be like* to live on Mars but that it did not say life *actually* existed on Mars. After further discussion, she volunteered to go to the school library to try to find more information that would resolve the question. This information did lead to more discussion and finally to resolution of the question (Patty was correct). Discussions like these, involving debate and reaching a conclusion, have a strong reflective component and stimulate students' use of strategic skills (Guthrie & McCann, 1997).

Finally, discussions help *extend* knowledge. As students work on long-term projects, their discourse can lead quite naturally into new domains. Guthrie (1993) observed that student discourse on one topic (the moon and its phases) quickly extended into several related topics. Students' declarative and procedural knowledge expanded rapidly as they searched for answers to questions they had posed; metacognitive knowledge increased as they discussed strategies for acquiring information with their peers and with the teacher and as they tried to explain their findings to their classmates.

Using Classroom Discourse to Build Knowledge

It is one thing to assert that high-quality discourse is at the heart of the reflective classroom; it is another actually to create classrooms in which knowledge construction and reflective thinking are the norm. On the one hand, when the teacher retains too much involvement in discussion, the result often is the IRE pattern, in which classroom discourse more nearly resembles recitation sequences than authentic exchanges. On the other hand, a laissez-faire approach to discussion that totally gives up social and interpretive authority to student groups is an invitation to chaos and deprives students of essential contributions by the teacher (Rogoff, 1995; Schön, 1987; Wiencek & O'Flahavan, 1994).

So what is the best way to engage students in authentic, extended discourse with each other and with their teacher? O'Flahavan (O'Flahavan & Stein, 1992; Wiencek & O'Flahavan, 1994) suggests that because discussions are highly complex, it is useful to consider them from a variety of perspectives, each involving a somewhat different form of knowledge construction. In O'Flahavan's view, the most effective classroom discussions are likely to be created when teacher and students work together from the outset to (1) develop the norms for participating in the discussions, (2) determine the interpretive agenda for a group's discussion, and (3) reflect after each discussion about the group's success in achieving both its social and interpretive goals.

O'Flahavan argues that teachers can play two especially important roles in these discussions: *coaching* and *scaffolding*. Although O'Flahavan favors decentralized, student-centered discussions, he considers teacher involvement essential for developing students' cognitive strategies, motivation, and expertise over the long term. In addition to managing some of the discussion, teachers are responsible for other features important to their success: creating the physical context for discussions, including determining group size and composition; devising seating arrangements; and making texts and other materials available.

The most basic strategy for creating productive discussion groups is to help students construct **group participation norms.** Most students understand basic social norms for interacting in classroom groups, such as raising their hands and not interrupting. But they may not know how to work well with other students or to listen to them, particularly in decentralized groups in which the teacher is not directing the interactions. One approach is to teach interactive skills directly (e.g., "These will be our rules. We should . . ."). A more effective approach is to allow students to help create their own rules for interaction. O'Flahavan and Stein (1992), for instance, had their students keep running lists of their group's participation norms, which typically included such rules as paying attention, not interrupting, and taking turns. Because these were the students' own norms, they were highly valued, probably more so than if the teacher had devised them. At the same time, the teacher plays an important role in helping the students reflect on whether their participation norms are effective. By serving as a *group process monitor* (O'Flahavan & Stein, 1992), the teacher can help the students periodically evaluate how well their group processes are working.

A second strategy is to help students develop **interpretive norms** for judging their progress. Students need to assume considerable responsibility for decentralized discussions to be effective. Assume, for instance, that a high school biology class is preparing a detailed report for local officials on the environmental threats to a nearby wetland. To meet this challenge, the class must make decisions on how it will proceed, such as what data it will gather, how it will be gathered, and the format of the document it eventually will produce. An effective teacher is likely to adopt a stance somewhere between authoritarian determination of the group's intellectual agenda (e.g., "OK, first I want you to study these maps of eastern Douglas County . . .") and laissez-faire inattention to students' attempts to grapple with this complex and metacognitively demanding task.

A third strategy in helping students develop a reflective stance is **coaching.** In O'Flahavan and Stein's (1992) judgment, students will be most productive when they are allowed to work together in their groups for significant blocks of time—say, 15 to 20 minutes—with the teacher coaching at the boundaries of discussion, before and after discussion blocks.

For O'Flahavan and Stein (1992), coaching takes two major forms: (1) providing students with guidance and direction and (2) helping students reflect on their interactions and achievements. For instance, think of a long-term science project for middle school students in describing the status of a wetlands habitat. Most students would need coaching in basic strategies for gathering information, such as determining what is important, drawing inferences from texts, and monitoring their understanding while reading about birds, plants, and insects. They also likely would need coaching in such procedural strategies as keeping reflective logs, identifying variables for observation, recording their observations, and planning simple experiments. The teacher also might want to remind students of supplies and resources they are likely to need to complete tasks and to discuss ways these might be obtained. Students who need information about marsh plants and water beetles could be coached in using indexes and tables of contents to search books in the library for relevant information. These kinds of guidance are all effective forms of coaching.

A fourth strategy for creating effective discourse is **scaffolding,** where the teacher enables students to do things they cannot do on their own by helping them articulate what they are thinking, reminding them of assumptions they are making, drawing their attention to information, and providing new perspectives. Scaffolding makes use of Vygotsky's idea of the zone of proximal development, described earlier in this chapter. The teacher, as the more expert person, provides frames of reference and modes of interpretation that students are capable of acquiring but do not yet have. In a discussion relating to sources of information about wetlands, for instance, one teacher became aware that her students did not know how to get information about land use and so posed an indirect question about where it might be found, suggesting "Maybe we should think about where we might find information about land use." Students, given this hint and occasional suggestions, soon began to debate the merits of such sources as surveying, aerial photography, satellite images, and landowner reports. Without the teacher's direction, the students likely would have been unable to continue their inquiry. With the scaffolding, they soon began to search library resources and initiated a series of productive contacts with landowners, agencies, and governmental units. The teacher's comment helped move them toward considering new information and frames of reference.

O'Flahavan defines several distinct roles that can be useful for scaffolding student thought. Among these are the role of the *framer,* in which the teacher draws attention to relevant background knowledge or helps students in interpretation; the *elicitor,* in which the teacher focuses the group's thinking on a point by bringing forth elaboration and extension from students; and the *interpretive peer,* in which the teacher is a participant in the group's inquiry.

Finally, *positive motivation* is critical to successful classroom discourse. Perhaps the most fundamental motivational requirement is that discussions be authentic, accessing the real culture of the students (J. S. Brown et al., 1989; Calfee et al., 1994; Nystrand et al., 1993). This can be ensured if the group communicates about goals and issues that are meaningful to them. For instance, upper level elementary students would find activities such as developing a class book about their neighborhoods, writing and directing a play for presentation at "Parents' Night," or creating a mural promoting school safety for younger students meaningful and motivating. In addition to rich topics, other factors important to motivation include the extent of teacher participation (not too much or too little), the teacher's ability to value and take up students' ideas and incorporate them into the ongoing discussion (Nystrand & Gamoran, 1991), and giving students greater control over interpretation, turn taking, and topic selection (Chinn et al., 2001).

Implications for Teaching: A Portrait of the Reflective Classroom

We return now to our starting point—the goal of building student knowledge and habits of reflection. Building knowledge is not a simple matter. As we know from earlier chapters, there are several kinds of knowledge, each important in its own right. Expertise in any domain requires large networks of declarative knowledge, as well as readily available arrays of procedural skills. It requires metacognitive awareness and the regulatory knowledge of knowing how and when to apply what is known. Because the amount of knowledge we need is very large and the relationships among the knowledge elements so complex, the process of acquiring significant domain knowledge requires motivated, long-term student effort. The challenge to teachers is considerable.

If we succeed in building an ideal reflective classroom, what might it look like? We could begin by imagining a classroom in which the teacher has placed student knowledge construction at its center. To help accomplish this goal, the teacher has organized class activities around long-term, thematic projects in which students can make choices and use knowledge in ways that help them achieve their goals (Corno & Randi, 1997; Guthrie & Wigfield, 1997). We see a hands-on teacher who makes little use of the IRE pattern and who lectures infrequently. Instead, in our reflective classroom, we see a teacher working as a partner with the students and organizing classroom activities around student information seeking and information exchange. One of this teacher's primary roles is guiding and supporting students in becoming self-directed, strategic learners.

A strong sense of purpose is evident in our ideal classroom. As teacher and students work together to reach project goals, activities alternate among whole-class instruction, in which students are coached on how to find and organize information; student reading and writing, in which students search for, find, and organize information and reflect on how they found it; and small-group discussions and collaboration, in which students report what they have learned, discuss their differing points of view, and judge their progress. We see our teacher helping students pick meaningful goals, coaching them on possible strategies for reaching their goals, and scaffolding their thinking as needed.

Over time, we see the students in our ideal classroom becoming more and more expert and self-directed. Their growing knowledge is not inert and isolated facts memorized from texts, but is organized and meaningful because it grows from authentic projects in which they have been allowed to choose topics and decide on the means of gathering and presenting information. Students have learned not only "what," but also "how," and "why." As a consequence, they can readily explain the strategies they use to find information, why that information is useful, and how it is organized.

Although our classrooms may fall short of this ideal, we still can draw on some of the basic principles presented below to help us move toward a reflective classroom.

1. *Take a broad perspective on knowledge.* Declarative knowledge is a good starting point, as is procedural knowledge—knowing how. Both, however, need to be contextualized by being linked with metacognitive awareness and self-regulation. In the long run, these metacognitive dimensions may be the most critical aspects of knowledge acquisition. Because what is known changes rapidly and the amount of information available far exceeds anyone's ability to acquire it, students must develop the capacity to direct their own learning and the motivation to acquire new information and skills.

2. *Develop students' information-seeking skills.* Modern communication technologies provide access to a wealth of information but also require that students learn to search for information, organize it, and judge its reliability. Teaching these skills in the context of long-term projects can be especially effective. Guthrie and his colleagues, for instance (e.g., Guthrie, 1993; Guthrie, Bennett, & McGough, 1994), helped fifth graders not only to learn multiple strategies for acquiring information from texts but also to judge the utility of the information they found.

3. *Organize instruction in ways that favor knowledge construction.* One of cognitive psychology's most valuable contributions has been to remind us that learners' activities affect what is learned and how functional it will be. We therefore must help students engage all of their learning capabilities. Rote rehearsal, in which meaning is ignored, tends to generate rote, listlike, fragile learning. Approaches aimed at student comprehension of the meaning of what is to be learned, in contrast, are much more likely to help students understand, organize, retain, and use the information they encounter.

4. *Create a "thinking classroom."* Effective knowledge construction and good thinking flourish in classroom cultures organized to support them (Tishman et al., 1995). Early cognitive theory tended to portray intellectual growth as a solitary pursuit, but social cognitive theory and research now emphasize family, school, community, and cultural influences on cognitive development (e.g., see Gauvain, 2001; Rogoff & Chavajay, 1995). Rogoff's ideas of guided participation and the child as cognitive apprentice and Schön's concept of reflection on reflection-in-action both emphasize the social nature of cognitive growth.

5. *Use discourse structures that promote reflection and knowledge construction.* Among the most important resources for knowledge construction and reflection are

classroom discussions in which students interact freely and grapple with authentic questions. As Rosenblatt argued many years ago in her classic book *Literature as Exploration* (1938), we need first to encourage students to express what works mean to them and then to use discussion to negotiate what they mean. In any subject area, students' initial understandings, though often immature and incomplete, are the only legitimate starting point for learning. As students continue their exchanges with each other and with the teacher about what they are learning, their understanding will deepen.

6. *Use coaching and scaffolding to build student understanding.* Like the guidance provided by the master craftsperson, teachers' coaching and scaffolding are vital to creating new levels of student understanding. As we saw earlier in the chapter, O'Flahavan and Stein (1992) argue for concentrating coaching at the boundaries of discussions. Before discussions, teachers can help students set the agenda for discussion; after discussions, teachers can assist students in reflecting on their successes and failures. Within discussions, scaffolding works effectively as teachers help students clarify their ideas and judge whether they're reaching their goals.

7. *Consider decentralizing discussions.* Although large-group discussions can be productive (Calfee et al., 1994), the opportunity for individual students to participate always will be limited by group size. Also, some students are reluctant to take part in a full-class setting because of perceived lack of knowledge or shyness. O'Flahavan and his colleagues (e.g., O'Flahavan & Stein, 1992) and Guthrie and his associates (e.g., Guthrie & McCann, 1997) have shown that groups of four to six upper level elementary students can carry on long-term inquiry relatively independent of the teacher if they are supported periodically by teacher coaching and scaffolding. Students in such groups can learn both to reflect on their interactions and to monitor progress toward their goals.

8. *Make tolerance a basic rule for classroom interaction.* Students do not necessarily come to our classrooms with highly refined social and cognitive skills. They often need to learn rules for classroom and small-group discussion. For instance, the prevailing norms governing whole-class discussions may specify what kinds of replies to questions are considered appropriate, points at which it is acceptable to interrupt, and preferred ways to get others' attention. For a variety of reasons, such as family history or ethnic background, however, some students' communication styles will not match those of the class. Students who interrupt frequently, for example, may have developed this style of communication in their families, have had success with it in other classes, or simply may be extraordinarily eager to do well (see Hull et al., 1991).

Variations in style and skill levels demand that both students and teachers practice basic principles of respect for others' ideas. For the long term, it seems to be useful for discussion groups to develop their own participation norms (see O'Flahavan & Stein, 1992; Wiencek & O'Flahavan, 1994). The rules that students themselves generate (e.g., "Take turns," "No putdowns," and "Don't hog the discussion") have been shown to be more effective and will be viewed as less coercive than any the teacher might impose. Also, students can periodically monitor whether their rules are creating effective working groups or need to be modified.

Summary

This chapter describes processes by which cognitive growth can be fostered in the classroom. Knowledge acquisition is viewed as a constructive process in which learners build and organize knowledge. Three types of constructivism were outlined: exogenous constructivism, endogenous constructivism, and dialectical constructivism. Of these, dialectical constructivism is the most generally applicable to student learning.

Stimulated by the work of the Russian psychologist Vygotsky and his concept of zone of proximal development, cognitive scientists now increasingly emphasize social processes in knowledge formation. Social interactions between a child and a peer or an adult providing guided participation help build bridges between what children already know and the new information they encounter. In effect, children are "apprentices in thinking" whose knowledge and ways of knowing grow out of interactions with others. The child's cognitive development is embedded in the social and cultural context.

Classroom discourse is a significant factor in building knowledge and shaping cognitive growth. If discourse is authentic, honors the students' points of view, and has continuity, it will engage students and become a basis for knowledge construction and reflective thinking. The tenor of classroom discourse also shapes students' perceptions of self and learning; it can be supportive or threatening, uplifting or demeaning.

The best discussions allow alternative perspectives and have open participation structures. By providing a forum for expression and feedback, they create opportunities to extend knowledge and to develop reflective thought. Strategies for creating productive discussion groups include having the groups develop and modify their own social and interpretive norms, teacher coaching before and after discussions, and teacher scaffolding during discussions. Such approaches enhance the possibility of knowledge construction and development of self-directed, strategic, reflective approaches to learning.

Because expertise requires organized, flexible knowledge, teachers need to help students learn ways to seek and judge information. Ideally, classrooms provide authentic contexts for developing expertise by providing learning that students find meaningful, that builds on prior knowledge, and that allows self-expression. The ideal outcome is for students not only to acquire knowledge but also to become independent, self-regulated learners.

Suggested Readings

Vygotsky, L. (1986). *Thought and language*. Cambridge, MA: The MIT Press.

This revised and enlarged edition of Vygotsky's important work includes an excellent overview of Vygotsky's thinking by Alex Kozulin that explains his influential ideas in easily understandable terms.

Rogoff, B. (1990). *Apprenticeship in thinking: Cognitive development in social context*. New York: Oxford University Press.

Rogoff's text provides a useful exposition of the perspective of social cognitive theory, especially as it applies to early child development.

Gauvain, M. (2001). *The social context of cognitive development*. New York: Guilford Press.

This scholarly but quite readable book examines cognitive development from a social vantage point, arguing that understanding children's learning requires us not only to understand information processing principles but also the social and cultural contexts for learning.

Chapter 10

Technological Contexts for Cognitive Growth

How Can Students Use Technologies? ■ *Cognitive Load Theory and Multimedia Design* ■
The Four Component Instructional Design (4C/ID) Model and Complex Skill Development ■
Social Cognitive Theory and Development of Classroom Communities ■ *Implications for
Teaching* ■ *Summary* ■ *Suggested Readings* ■

THIS CHAPTER IS ABOUT TECHNOLOGIES for learning and teaching. Simply put, a
technology is any device or system that we humans use to accomplish our goals.
The wheel, an oar, an abacus, a hammer, a toothpick, and a TV set are various
examples. In education, some technologies have been with us for hundreds and even
thousands of years—items to write with (e.g., a stylus, pen, pencil, and chalk), record
ideas (e.g., papyrus, paper, and chalkboards), and preserve and share information in
an organized way (e.g., scrolls and books).

When educators refer to technology, however, they almost always are referring to a
cluster of rapidly evolving electronic hardware [e.g., computers, laptops, personal digital assistants (PDAs), and CD and DVD players], communication networks linking these
devices (e.g., wireless networks, cable TV, and the Internet), and associated software
(e.g., word processing, presentation programs, simulations, games, Web browsers, and
e-mail programs). In this chapter, we focus on these electronic technologies and examine the implications of cognitive psychology for their design and use.

In an era that is placing a great emphasis on reform in education, educators increasingly are looking to technology as a way of changing how learning and teaching
take place. While education arguably has lagged behind other segments of society in
using technology (e.g., a relatively low level of classroom use compared to, say, technology's integral part of our daily lives as we talk to each other by phone, use e-mail,
bank, shop, and register for classes), there is considerable optimism (e.g., Gardner,
2000) that technology can help improve, even revolutionize, how students learn and
teachers teach.

Our modern era, however, is not the first in which there has been a high level of
optimism about technology's promise. When movies and television first appeared, for
example, there were predictions that they would replace most if not all classroom instruction. But today's versatile technologies do seem to warrant some optimism. With
technology an obvious feature in all of our lives and playing an increasing role in

schools (e.g., students using the Internet; communicating via e-mail; and having access to Web-based resources such as course syllabi, assignments, reading materials, and practice exams), there is growing interest in how it might be best used. Should students work alone or collaboratively on computers? Can technology facilitate classroom discussions? Can it promote educational equity? Can online education be effective? Should we spend scarce school resources on putting laptops or PDAs into students' hands or would well-equipped computer labs be a better investment?

The point of this chapter is not to recommend specific new instructional technologies shown by research to produce gains in learning outcomes. There are none. One of the most consistent findings when the research literature on technology is carefully reviewed is that there are few if any improvements in learning outcomes specifically attributable to the technology alone. That is, when new technologies (e.g., online presentation and discussion of teaching case studies by teacher education students) are compared with traditional approaches (e.g., the same students reading and discussing teaching case studies in the classroom), there seldom are learning benefits attributable to the technology itself (e.g., see Clark, 1983, 1994, 2001, 2003; Salomon, 1984).

What research on instructional technology *does* show is that learning is influenced primarily by good instructional methods that *take advantage of what technologies have to offer*. That is, it is not the technology *per se* that motivates learners and produces learning, but how that technology is used. Thus, we focus on technology in the hands of highly skilled teachers, teachers who understand cognitive and motivational principles and can turn those principles into effective instruction. When such teachers guide technology's use, what can it do for student learning and cognitive growth?

We begin by examining some of the many technology-based resources available to students. Which ones are best suited to different kinds of learning goals? Simultaneously we look at several key cognitive skills and strategies that students need for using technology effectively. Taking full advantage of technology's potential requires that students have a repertoire of knowledge, cognitive strategies, and beliefs. We highlight several of these that we see as especially important for students using technology effectively.

In the next three sections we turn to the theory and research guiding today's instructional technology development. What kinds of cognitive and motivational theories currently are informing choices about instructional technology design and use? The first of these three sections describes *cognitive load theory* and multimedia design. Cognitive load theory, which we introduced in chapter 2, has become one of the focal points for thinking about instructional multimedia. We present principles based on this theory that will help you make better informed judgments about whether media are well designed. The second of our theory sections summarizes the **Four Component Instructional Design (4C/ID) model,** which provides a blueprint for how technology can be used to develop complex skills. The last of the three sections on theory and research analyzes educational technology use from the standpoint of *social cognitive theory*. Our attention here moves away from individuals interacting with technology to ways of using technology to create and support communities of learners. We describe two examples of programs designed to make technology the hub of learning communities where students work together on authentic, engaging problems. We conclude our chapter by presenting implications for the educational use of technology. In light of the theories of technology-based learning and technology's growing capabilities, what can we do to help students benefit from the technologies available to them?

How Can Students Use Technologies?

Technology itself seldom is the driving force behind learning, but what it can do is amplify and extend students' educational experiences (Means & Olson, 1994). When we look at computer- and Internet-related technologies, we can see many ways they can be used in education and sense its growing educational potential. New software makes it easier to create Web-based resources, for example, whereas creation of wireless classrooms makes it feasible to link class members' laptops or PDAs and installation of high-speed modems allows students to share graphics and diagrams. Table 10-1 presents several ways that students can use educational technology to enhance their educational experience, while Table 10-2 presents some of the key cognitive skills needed to take advantage of them.

The category listed first in Table 10-1—students *receiving information* via technology—is not a new one. It has a history dating back to movies and television and even before. Many teachers now use software such as *PowerPoint,* for example, to present information to students. This software typically has a number of capabilities for enhancing presentations, such as the ability to use varied type fonts and backgrounds and to include features such as clipart, pictures, animations, and sound. These features can make information more attractive and interesting but, if used ineffectively, can distract learners and lead to loss of comprehension.

The second category of technology use, however, has developed quite recently. With widening Internet access in U.S. schools and classrooms, technology has opened a significant resource for student learning—*access to information and ways of searching for it*. Web browsers open the way to the Internet, and search engines allow students to find information easily and quickly. In contrast to the problem of lack of information, which many schools and students still face with shrinking libraries and scarce textbooks, technology is creating ironic new challenges—information overload coupled with access to information of dubious quality. As shown in Table 10-2, students need to learn systematic methods of searching for information and recognizing differences in its quality; without these skills, student searches can be dictated by momentary factors (e.g., unusual links turned up by search engines and a succession of interesting-looking links) and result in erroneous or biased information (e.g., from personal Web sites or Web sites run by unmonitored groups).

Increasingly, technology can help students *organize and present information*. Programs such as Inspiration allow students to compile information in a variety of formats ranging from semantic maps to outlines. These then can serve as multimedia storyboards or frameworks for essays or stories. To actually present information, many choices are available, including word processing (e.g., *Word*), desktop publishing

Table 10-1
Selected Student Uses of Technology

Use	Examples of Technologies Available	Examples of Student Use
1. Receive information	• Presentation packages (e.g., *PowerPoint*)	• Ninth-grade biology students view multimedia presentation that includes film clips on cell reproduction
2. Search for and find information	• Web browsers (e.g., *Netscape Navigator* and *Internet Explorer*) • Search engines (e.g., *Google* and *Yahoo*)	• Fourth graders identify keywords to search Web for information on habitats of foxes, coyotes, and dingos • Eleventh graders gather information about Lewis and Clark expedition by visiting National Geographic Web site
3. Organize and present information	• Organizing, outlining programs (e.g., *Inspiration*) • Presentation packages • HTML editors, authoring packages (e.g., *Dreamweaver*)	• A pair of sixth-grade students creates a semantic map to guide their writing on their paper "Life in the Rain Forest" • Teacher education students develop a several-part "philosophy of teaching" that is posted on their class Web site
4. Explore simulated environments	• Simulations, visualization tools (e.g., *Sim City, Geometer's Sketchpad*)	• Fifth graders make hypotheses about effects selected changes will have on Sim City and then change city features to see what will happen
5. Participate in authentic learning environments	• Communication software (e.g., *Eudora, Outlook*, and *Communicator*) • Databases (e.g., *Access, Filemaker Pro*) and Web sites • Statistical packages (e.g., *SAS* and *SPSS*)	• High school students in several states gather water quality and climate data from their area, send it via the Internet into a database, make hypotheses about trends in data, and compare findings with each other
6. Communicate and collaborate with other students	• Communications software and interaction-collaboration software (e.g., *Lotus Notes*)	• Graduate students located in several countries taking a school administration distance learning course participate in threaded discussions, work groups, and projects to complete course requirements
7. Practice skills and receive feedback on progress	• CD-ROM based programs aimed at skill development • Course management software (e.g., *Blackboard, WebCT,* and *e-Learn* testing program) for supporting online learning	• First graders practice matching letters to letter sounds using an animated computer program • College students in psychology take several practice quizzes sampling unit objectives, use results to gauge their progress and decide when to take unit mastery tests

(continued)

Table 10-1
(continued)

Use	Examples of Technologies Available	Examples of Student Use
8. Use technologies for cognitive support and extending abilities	• Screen readers (e.g., *JAWS*) that convert on-screen text into speech • Voice recognition systems (e.g., *Kurzweil Voice*) allowing computer users to dictate text directly • Word prediction programs (e.g., *Read & Write*) that "float" on open applications and offer likely words after only a few letters are typed	• Visually impaired graduate student explores Internet from a Windows environment • Eighth grader with poor writing skills dictates work into a word processing system • Learning disabled high school student uses word prediction program to reduce misspellings in an assigned paper

(e.g., *Pagemaker*), multimedia development (e.g., *Flash* and *Director*), and Web design programs (e.g., *Dreamweaver*). Of course, what students produce—papers, multimedia presentations, or Web pages—can range from relatively simple summaries to highly complex productions involving gathering, organizing, refining, and presenting information. The best of them can call on virtually all of a student's cognitive, self-regulatory, and motivational resources.

As students increasingly become involved in complex processes beginning with information gathering and leading to information transformation and presentation, teachers need to consider the many challenges students will face in such activities and to devise strategies to help them be successful. Self-regulation skills are critical, of course, as students need to monitor their progress and adjust their strategies in order to continue toward their goals. Many will need assistance not only with becoming skillful in using the technology (i.e., developing procedural skills) but also in developing a mastery orientation (see Table 10-2) toward both learning to use the technology itself expertly and completing complex projects utilizing several different kinds of technology (e.g., word processing, multimedia development, and Web authoring programs).

Many educators also recognize the growing potential of technology giving students opportunities to learn in new ways. Students can use *simulated environments* and visualization tools to create and visualize things as diverse as mathematical functions (e.g., using *Geometer's Sketchpad*) and a city's functioning (e.g., *Sim City*). Because they required powerful computing, technology-based simulations were largely confined to higher end applications until relatively recently (e.g., in film studios, architectural firms). This situation is rapidly changing, however, with PC-based simulations offering increasingly greater realism and responsiveness. Technology also offers a route to *authentic learning*—learning where students see learning activities as worthwhile in their own right (Means & Olson, 1994). A starting point is an authentic

Table 10-2
Some Key Cognitive Skills Students Need to Use Technologies Effectively

Key Student Skill	Potential Pitfalls for Students in Using Technology	Strategies Teachers Can Use
1. Locating and judging information	• Following links randomly • Attending to seductive details • Getting "lost" in information searches • Being overwhelmed by too much information • Selecting erroneous or low quality information	• Limit searches to few questions and limited number of sites (e.g., WebQuest) • Explicitly teach search and summarization strategies • Allow careful preparation for searching • Teach students to self-monitor search and summarizing success
2. Communicating effectively using technology	• Lack of effective writing skills • Lack of media design skills • Not understanding purposes of communication • Uncertainty about roles in learning communities • Receiving negative feedback on communication attempts	• Arrange "authentic" communication opportunities • Explicitly teach writing and media design strategies • Encourage students to use graphic and other organizers to prepare for communication • Create "safe" environment for online communication
3. Using self-monitoring and self-regulation skills when using technology	• Not understanding overall goals for learning • Failing to monitor progress toward goals • Producing low quality products (e.g., writing, multimedia presentations) • Participating erratically in activities, projects	• Help students select interesting, intrinsically motivating projects • Help students set goals and subgoals for projects • Teach self-regulation skills, including monitoring of progress toward goals • Create opportunities for students to share products and receive feedback • Provide frequent feedback to students on progress toward goals
4. Proceduralizing knowledge	• Not practicing skills sufficiently • Lack of just-in-time information • Lack of awareness of skills' role in larger tasks	• Give students repeated practice opportunities to proceduralize program knowledge • Engage students in discussions about skills needed to achieve goals • Help students link procedural skills to conceptual understanding
5. Contextualizing knowledge	• Failing to comprehend virtual structures (e.g., organization of word processing programs, browsers, operating systems) • Not applying already-learned	• Complement development of procedural skills with "conceptual" instruction • Provide graphic organizers to aid students in linking features

(continued)

Table 10-2
(continued)

Key Student Skill	Potential Pitfalls for Students in Using Technology	Strategies Teachers Can Use
	skills and knowledge to solving new problems	
6. Adopting a mastery orientation toward technology-based learning	• Not using alternative strategies when difficulties are encountered • Losing motivation to continue with projects	• Help students set and monitor progress toward intermediate, long-term goals • Remind students of utility of learning • Give frequent feedback on students' progress toward goals

problem that students are interested in working on; technology can provide an avenue for working on the problem with students in other schools or regions and also offer access to coaching and feedback from experts.

Mirroring our culture's everyday use of cell phones, faxes, and the Internet to communicate, educational *uses of technology for communication and collaboration* are growing. Students and teachers now routinely use e-mail to interact; class Web sites and listservs can provide class members with easy access to information, the ability to share it with class members, and chances to work together on projects. Success in communication does not happen accidentally, of course; it requires authentic issues to communicate about and hinges on students' writing and media skills. While such skills may develop to some extent as a part of simply working with communication technologies (e.g., sending e-mails and contributing to a discussion on a class listserv), more likely they will require coaching and feedback, plus extensive practice to develop the proceduralized knowledge needed for skilled performance.

Technologies can provide *opportunities for practice and feedback* that previously have not been easily available. Many elementary students now are using at least some computer-based technology for skill development. While they vary tremendously in quality, a host of instructional programs on CD-ROM or DVD have been produced, for instance, to help develop elementary students' literacy (e.g., a program for beginning readers includes practice in picking out rhyming words) and math skills (e.g., a program for third and fourth graders presents practice sets of addition or subtraction problems). Similarly, students in high school and college classrooms now can use the Web to take repeated practice quizzes sampling unit content. The feedback they receive allows them to judge how close they are to mastery.

Finally, a cluster of technology-related products and equipment, collectively called *assistive technology,* have been developed to aid and extend the abilities of learners with disabilities. Assistive technologies have multiplied since the early 1980s, stimulated by developments in fields as disparate as computer hardware and software, robotics, and speech recognition. Some assistive technologies, such as environmental control devices and robots, are primarily aimed at helping individuals who have physical disabilities. Others, more directly related to the cognitive focus of this text, provide significant assistance to individuals with disabilities that interfere with performance of school-related tasks, such as reading, writing, spelling, and math.

For example, intelligent word prediction programs for word processors, e-mail, or data entry programs can help learners with severe spelling problems. Individuals using the program need only to sound out the beginning of a word they cannot spell (a task much easier than correctly spelling the word itself) and type the first few letters of the word. The program then displays a list of likely words; the writer selects one to enter into the document being typed. Many other sophisticated programs also are available to aid and extend students' cognitive abilities, including reading systems that read scanned text aloud, Web browsers that translate Web content into speech, and voice recognition systems that allow users to dictate text directly into computers.

In summary, instructional technology has the potential to provide students with many learning opportunities and to extend their cognitive functioning. Some are not really new, for example, using technology to receive information from a presentation. Others, however, are opening up avenues to learning resources that have not been available previously and which seem to have potential for supporting active, meaningful learning. Technology uses range from gathering, organizing, and presenting information to interacting with others on group projects. Still other uses are targeted at learners with disabilities, providing a range of technological supports ranging from speech recognition to text-to-speech conversion. The active uses of technology, especially, require many different competencies (see Table 10-2) ranging from knowing how to search for information to having a mastery orientation that will carry students through the challenges of completing complex, long-term projects with technology. To help us think more specifically about productive uses of technology and how students can use it, we now turn to the theory and research on technology, cognition, and education, beginning with cognitive load theory.

Cognitive Load Theory and Multimedia Design

Cognitive load theory, proposed by John Sweller and his associates (Sweller, 1999; Sweller, van Merrienboer, & Paas, 1998), focuses on the role of working memory in instructional design. Cognitive load theory increasingly has been applied to the design of educational multimedia, such as computer-based instructional programs and multimedia (Clark, 2003; Kalyuga, Chandler, & Sweller, 2000; Mayer & Moreno, 2002). From a cognitive load perspective, meaningful learning depends on active cognitive processing in learners' working memory. The difficulty is that working memory can only process a few units of information at any given time (see chapter 2). If learners encounter too many elements in a multimedia presentation—for example, one combining animations, graphics, sounds, printed text, and narrated text—working memory can be overwhelmed. The result of too many pieces of information being juggled in working memory—excessive cognitive load—is decreased processing efficiency and, at worst, a collapse of the learning process.

Understanding two types of cognitive load, intrinsic cognitive load and extraneous cognitive load, can help us analyze whether given multimedia presentations are likely to create issues of cognitive load. **Intrinsic cognitive load,** according to Sweller, is a characteristic of the materials themselves. Any content being learned creates intrinsic cognitive load in working memory based on its difficulty and complexity. For example, a multimedia presentation for ninth graders on, say, biodiversity, will generate a certain amount of intrinsic cognitive load associated with the complexity of the topic of biodiversity and associated concepts. Because it relates to the content itself, intrinsic cognitive load therefore typically cannot be altered. **Extraneous cognitive load,** on the other hand, is related to the instructional design, such as how a multimedia presentation is organized and the kinds of information included (e.g., clipart, animations, and text). If a presentation contains multiple information sources such as diagrams and texts that need to be mentally integrated, for example, extraneous cognitive load will be generated. In contrast to intrinsic cognitive load, extraneous cognitive load is controllable—better instructional designs create less of it, less effective ones more.

Intrinsic and extraneous cognitive load are additive; if both are high, working memory capacity can be substantially exceeded. Because only extraneous cognitive load is under the control of instructional designers (i.e., *how* content is presented can be changed, but typically not the content), the challenge is designing instruction that reduces extraneous cognitive load. To meet this challenge, Sweller and his colleagues have focused especially on two resources: (1) LTM, with its nearly unlimited capacity and processes of schema formation and (2) the unique nature of working memory.

First, because LTM has great capacity and many learners possess domain-related knowledge schemas (e.g., a biology student with prior knowledge of cell division processes and a music history student with knowledge about Baroque and Classical composers), multiple elements of information often can be chunked into a single element (see chapter 3). Chunking reduces the burden on working memory for these learners (Kalyuga et al., 2000). Also, the more automated schemata are, the more working memory capacity learners will have for concentrating on cognitive goals such as comprehension and problem solving. Thus, a number of multimedia designers (see Sweller et al., 1998; Merrill, 2000; van Merrienboer, 1997) include features targeted at encouraging schema automation.

One approach has been to present *goal-free problems,* in which students practice repeatedly on problem subgoals to attain automaticity (e.g., in a geometry program, calculating many different angles until this skill is very well-learned) *before* they encounter the more complex overall problem-solving task (e.g., proving a geometry theorem). Expressed in the terms introduced in chapter 8, cognitive load is reduced when part of the instruction allows students to use a *goal-free* as opposed to a *mean–ends* strategy. Many times, in trying to solve problems, learners are asked to hold and process too much in working memory simultaneously—the current problem state, the goal state, operators to reduce differences—plus a set of subgoals. While Sweller and others (e.g., van Merrienboer, Clark, & de Croock, 2002) caution against overuse, a goal-free approach can be effective because it requires remembering only a specific subgoal and operators applying to it (Sweller et al., 1998), thereby reducing cognitive load.

A second major way of reducing working memory in multimedia designs is to take advantage of the unique nature of working memory. As discussed in chapter 2, working memory involves two separate channels (Baddeley, 2001; Paivio, 1986a): the visual channel (the *visuospatial sketchpad*) that takes input from the eyes and makes a pictorial representation and the auditory channel (the *phonological loop*), which has been produces an auditory representation. As shown, awareness of working memory's visual and auditory channels is important in designing multimedia that avoid cognitive overload problems.

In a series of studies in the early 1990s, Mayer and his associates (see Mayer & Moreno, 2002) compared learning outcomes for students receiving computer-presented materials consisting of narration alone to conditions in which narration was paired with an animation. As expected, students having both narration and animation learned better. In further studies, Mayer and his group compared narration and animation presented at the same time (*simultaneous group*) with successive presentation of the same information (*successive group*). In each of the studies Mayer conducted on this topic (see Mayer & Moreno, 2002), students learned better from simultaneous than from successive presentations. In Mayer and Moreno's view, these results occurred because simultaneous presentation aided learners in making connections between verbal and visual representations in working memory. In these studies, students showed little effects of excessive cognitive load.

In other studies, however, Mayer and his colleagues began to experiment with multimedia conditions calculated to test the capacity of verbal and visual working memory channels. In one set of studies, Mayer's group examined a common practice of multimedia designers—creating highly active screen designs in multimedia presentations by adding interesting explanations or sound effects. The view of many designers is that such features make learning more interesting and motivating. What Mayer et al. found, however, were negative effects on learning. In an instructional multimedia sequence about lightning, for instance, adding interesting facts (e.g., that people in swimming pools are sitting ducks!) and sounds to illustrate the steps in lightning formation (e.g., gentle wind, static, and thunder) actually reduced learners' problem-solving transfer, as did including instrumental background music. Mayer attributed these results to cognitive load issues. Consistent with predictions from cognitive load theory and contrary to common belief, students learned more deeply when multimedia did *not* include such words and sounds.

A further interesting test of cognitive load theory in multimedia design involved pairing either on-screen or narrated text presentations with animations to test the so-called *modality* (e.g., Mayer & Moreno, 1998; Moreno & Mayer, 1999) or *split-attention* effect (Mousavi, Low, & Sweller, 1995). Cognitive load theory predicts that when animations are used, adding on-screen text can overload working memory because both text and animation must be processed *in the visual channel*. In contrast, when animation is paired with *narrated* text, having the text presented in spoken form should reduce load in the visual channel and increase the chances of deeper cognitive processing. This, in fact, is what these researchers found.

Another common belief among many multimedia designers is that providing multiple sources of the same information (e.g., animation and on-screen text and plus narration of the on-screen text) creates useful *redundancy*. Redundancy should improve learning, from this perspective, because learners can choose to learn in their preferred style (e.g., some learners will learn better from animations, others from reading, and still others from listening). Generally, however, redundancy does not promote deeper learning, but actually diminishes it (e. g., Craig, 2002; Mayer, Heiser, & Lonn, 2001).

In summarizing this research, Mayer and Moreno (2002; Mayer & Moreno, 2003) have proposed several principles for guiding multimedia designs that take cognitive load demands into account. Among them is the principle of *contiguity,* which refers to presenting related information simultaneously rather than successively. For instance, when related verbal and visual information (e.g., a diagram and explanatory text) are encountered simultaneously in a multimedia presentation rather than successively, learning and problem-solving transfer will be improved. A second principle is *coherence,* based on research (e.g., Moreno & Mayer, 2000) showing better learning when learners don't have to process extra words, sounds, and pictures. Paralleling cognitively based work in Web design, where "cleaner" designs (e.g., small numbers of features, minimal words on a page) are seen to be better at guiding attention and memory (e.g., Czerwinski & Larson, 2003), the most effective presentations are those that are not embellished and where focus is kept on content directly relevant to learning goals.

A third principle, *modality,* refers to taking advantage of working memory's structure by providing information that can be processed through visual *and* verbal modes (such as presenting animations with narrated text, where one can be processed visually and the other verbally). Closely related are the potentially negative effects of *redundancy* in multimedia instruction. Adding redundant information to concise, but effective, explanations is usually unhelpful, especially when redundant information must be processed in the same channel as the primary information. For example, in multimedia materials using animations (processed *visually*), adding on-screen text (also processed *visually*) that duplicates narrated text (processed *auditorily*) is likely to create extraneous cognitive load by placing too many demands on visual working memory.

In summary, cognitive load theory provides much food for thought for those designing or selecting instructional multimedia. Instructional multimedia need to make effective use of working memory if students are to achieve deeper learning—such as comprehending scientific principles and transferring problem-solving skills. Learners need to actively process, organize, and link multimedia content in working memory, but we also need to insure that multimedia learning activities do not overload it. Two ways of avoiding this are drawing on learners' schemas from LTM and helping automate new ones. Others are connecting information so that it can be processed simultaneously and not presenting too much information in a single channel. These strategies will help decrease extraneous cognitive load and increase students' chances of success.

The Four Component Instructional Design (4C/ID) Model and Complex Skill Development

In the previous section, we discussed cognitive load theory and its implications for matching multimedia materials to the characteristics of working memory. Of course, multimedia designers often also must grapple with larger scale issues of organizing and sequencing whole instructional programs, particularly if they are designing systems for developing complex cognitive skills, such as those that experts perform (e.g., doctors making a medical diagnosis, architects designing a building, and pilots responding to emergencies).

Van Merrienboer's Four Component Instructional Design (4C/ID) Model (van Merrienboer, 1997; van Merrienboer et al., 2002), based on work in cognitive psychology and cognitive science, has been formulated to guide this kind of complex instructional design. The basic premise on which the 4C/ID Model rests is that complex skills are learned by performing them. Thus, instructional multimedia design based on the 4C/ID model focuses on giving *practice opportunities,* not the more common use of media to present information. The system therefore is aimed at learners acquiring skills through practice, with information made available as needed to support skill acquisition.

The first of the 4C/ID model's four components is the *learning task.* As van Merrienboer et al. (2002) point out, complex learning always involves achieving integrated sets of learning goals, not learning separate skills in isolation. The 4C/ID model thus promotes use of learning tasks that are whole, authentic, and concrete. A computer-based course for developing expertise in photography might be organized, say, around the task of creating a black-and-white photo essay (an authentic task); however, it also would consist of subprograms for developing required skills and associated knowledge needed to perform the task (e.g., skills and concepts related to composition, focus and depth of field, lighting, film developing, and making prints).

Learners participating in technology-based instruction based on the 4C/ID model typically would begin work on a cluster of relatively simple, but meaningful, tasks (called *task classes*). They then progress toward more complex ones. Complexity is determined by the number of skills involved in task classes, how they interact with each other, and the amount of knowledge needed to perform them. The lowest level task classes—where instruction of novices would begin—are the simplest versions of whole tasks that experts would encounter in the real world (e.g., for medical students, being asked to make a diagnosis where the symptoms are fairly obvious and the probability of correct diagnosis high). The top-level task classes correspond to the most complex problems that experts would encounter in the real world. High levels of support are given for learning tasks early in a task class; this support would include such techniques as *worked-out examples,* which have been shown to reduce cognitive load (Sweller et al., 1998), or an expert performing a task while simultaneously doing a thinkaloud explaining the problem-solving processes behind task performance. By the time learners reach the final learning task, support has been faded out. This pattern of scaffolding and fading support is repeated for each subsequent task class.

The second and third components of the 4C/ID Model are *supportive information* and *Just-In-Time (JIT) information.* These two types of information each play a different role in developing complex skills via technology. To understand these roles, we need to revisit a distinction made earlier in our text between controlled and automatic information processing (see chapter 2). As you recall, *controlled processes* are effortful, error-prone, easily overloaded, and require focused attention. They basically are equivalent to *schemata* (see chapter 3). In contrast, *automatic processes* correspond to *procedures* (see chapter 3); they occur with little or no effort, are data-driven, and require little or no conscious attention. In the 4C/ID model, the schemalike controlled processes are called **nonrecurrent skills** (van Merrienboer et al., 2002; see also chapter 3), whereas the procedurelike automatic processes are called **recurrent skills.**

Nonrecurrent and recurrent skills together comprise complex cognitive skills; that is, complex cognition consists of both controlled and automatic processes. From the standpoint of the 4C/ID model, the primary challenge in developing complex cognition is to refine and automate *nonrecurrent skills*. Learners need them because schemata represent the powerful generalized knowledge required to solve new, unfamiliar problems (van Merrienboer et al., 2002). But complex skills also depend on being able to automatically execute productionlike recurrent skills. The main instructional goal for these, in van Merrienboer's view, is to automate them as much and as rapidly as possible.

Returning to the second and third components of 4C/ID model, instructional technology systems need to provide *supportive information* to help learners master the *nonrecurrent* aspects of complex cognitive tasks. Supportive information provides a bridge between learners' prior knowledge and the learning tasks. In our example of a computer-based course intended to develop photography expertise, supportive information early in instruction might include analogies between the camera and the eye and between a photo essay and a story or computer-presented illustrations of high- and low-contrast scenes (e.g., showing changes in how clearly objects can be viewed against varying backgrounds). Similarly, in a computer-based system for developing novice physicians' diagnostic skills, supportive information might include a computer-presented "guided tour" highlighting key dimensions of a hypothetical patient's lab work and presenting symptoms or a video clip of an experienced physician talking her way through a diagnosis.

The goal of supportive information is to help learners acquire the kinds of flexible schemata needed to cope with the varied problems of real life. Because schemata are formed and refined through a process of induction, the best route to nonrecurrent skill development is experience with a series of authentic learning tasks. According to van Merrienboer, a series of progressively more complex problems, coupled with supportive information and learner reflection, are likely to achieve this goal.

In contrast to supportive information, *JIT information* is aimed at the *recurrent* aspects of complex skills. JIT information promotes recurrent skill automation. Recall that recurrent skills are performed almost identically in many different problem situations and also that automaticity depends heavily on consistent, repetitive practice. JIT gives learners the step-by-step information required to perform recurrent skills and, as the name implies, is provided as needed. It then is quickly faded. For our medical students, for example, JIT information might include specific prompts on how to use a stethoscope to listen for and recognize certain clinical symptoms (a recurrent skill) or to "read" basic clinical findings, such as heart rate, blood pressure, or blood test results (also recurrent skills). The goal is to make these basic, but critical, skills as automatic as possible as soon as possible, thereby freeing cognitive resources for the nonrecurrent, problem-solving dimensions of medical diagnosis.

The fourth and final component of the 4C/ID model is *part-task practice*. Although computer-based instructional systems can develop both nonrecurrent and recurrent skills, extra practice often is needed to achieve required levels of automaticity. Experienced photojournalists, for instance, can respond very rapidly to new situations and changing conditions without attending consciously to subskills (e.g., without thinking about framing shots, depth of field, and lighting). Similarly, we want to have medical personnel concentrating on diagnostic problem solving leading to treatment, not thinking about performing basic skills.

As described in chapter 8, expertise is ordinarily a very slow-developing process depending on practice to automatize the productions that directly control behavior. Part-task practice is a way to accomplish automatization of procedural knowledge more rapidly and circumvent some of the cognitive load problems resulting when learners try to develop skills while simultaneously trying to solve the overall problem. In our example of the online photography course, novices might take part in a simulation, say, of the steps involved in making a print, practicing them repeatedly. Their practicing would be supported by appropriate JIT information until automaticity had been achieved. Medical students might practice listening to sounds of heartbeats and respiration using a simulation where they could vary stethoscope placements until they were able to gather needed information very rapidly and without error.

Van Merrienboer and his associates do not recommend that instructional sequences contain a great deal of part-task practice but argue that part-task practice can help reduce task complexity. If part-task practice is used, they advise relatively short and spaced periods of it intermixed with work on complex, authentic tasks; this provides both the opportunity to practice subskills and relate them to the overall cognitive skill (van Merrienboer et al., 2002).

Summary of the 4C/ID Model

The 4C/ID model, which is based on research on cognitive learning and expertise, provides a framework for understanding important issues in designing technology systems for developing complex skills. According to the model, learners' primary experiences should be with realistic and increasingly more authentic tasks, such as projects, cases, and scenarios. Instruction should focus on practice, not information giving. The primary goal of the training is schema construction and refinement, which are developed by learners working with varied, authentic tasks. At the same time, the training system needs to develop the automated skills essential to any complex cognitive activity. Information provided to the learner must be tailored to the kind of learning taking place; supportive information (e.g., coaching and modeling) is designed to aid in schema development, whereas JIT information (e.g., online help and pop-up menus) is provided to support automaticity. Research based on the model and model features is promising, but further studies are needed to adequately test whether technology-based instruction based on the 4C/ID model produces superior transfer and problem solving (see Clark, 2003). In the meantime, research continues on such 4C/ID-related topics as the timing of information presentation, presentation modalities, and optimizing step sizes (see van Merrienboer et al., 2002).

Social Cognitive Theory and Development of Classroom Communities

The instructional theory and design issues discussed in the previous two sections are good examples of the relationship of cognitive principles to educational technology. How educational technology is designed has important effects on student learning and transfer. Whether students are watching a teacher's *PowerPoint* presentation, completing computer-based practice exercises, or working in Web-based distance learning courses, their cognitive systems are at work and being challenged by what they are doing and seeing. Good instructional technology design takes into account both the ways our cognitive systems work (e.g., attention, working memory, and long-term memory) and how complex cognitive skills develop (e.g., controlled and automatic processes, schema activation, and needs for supportive and JIT information) into account. Good instructional technology works with, rather than against, our cognitive systems. It promotes active processing, but does not overload working memory through redundancy or too much information presented through a single channel.

Understanding how technology affects individual cognition is important, but not all we need to know about the relationship between cognition and technology, however. While excellent research continues on technology-related factors affecting individual learning and cognitive growth, other researchers have focused in on technology's role in *classroom interactions and knowledge construction*. Some of their key questions are the following:

- How can technology be used to help students collaborate?
- Can technology aid in the creation of a classroom learning community?
- Can technology help community members actively engage in learning?
- How can technology make learning activities more meaningful?
- Can technology be used in ways that develop intrinsic motivation?
- How can technology help learners use diverse viewpoints as a resource for learning?

As you no doubt recognize, this perspective represented by these questions fits closely with one of the themes of our book—that social interaction is fundamental to cognitive growth. More generally, it represents a *social cognitive point of view*— where cognitive growth is seen as resulting from social and cultural processes (Barron, 2000; Cognition and Technology Group at Vanderbilt, 1997; Gauvain, 2001). As discussed in chapter 9, this view stresses the importance of social interactions in developing knowledge and thought. Exchanges between teachers and students and between students and their peers are among the most important of these.

During the past dozen or so years, social cognitive theory has been used as a basis for designing a number of large-scale classroom projects in which technology plays a central role. Two of the best known of these are the *Adventures of Jasper Woodbury,* a technology-based instructional series developed by members of the Cognition and Technology Group at Vanderbilt (CTGV), and *CSILE* (Computer Supported Intentional Learning Environment), developed by Bereiter and Scardamalia at the University of Toronto. Both are innovative uses of technology growing out of cognitive and social cognitive learning principles and both have been used and evaluated extensively across North America and beyond.

The Adventures of Jasper Woodbury Series

In the early 1990s, using findings from their earlier cognitive research and a growing awareness of social cognitive theory, the Cognition and Technology Group at Vanderbilt (CTGV) began to develop a set of problem-based curricula called the *Adventures of Jasper Woodbury* (the *Jasper* series). The *Jasper* series, which utilizes videodisk, CD-ROM, Internet, and other technologies, consists of 12 video-based adventures (plus supporting materials) aimed at improving the mathematical thinking of middle school students. Each *Jasper* adventure revolves around a complex problem requiring extended effort to solve (Barron et al., 1995; CTGV, 1997). The fact that the problems in the *Jasper* series are complex (some contain more than a dozen subproblems) also makes them difficult to solve alone; thus, students need to work together in problem solving.

The *Jasper* series uses technology in implementing what has been called the "thinking curriculum" (Bruer, 1993), in which the primary goals are ability to reason, think critically, reflect, argue, and learn independently. As mentioned in this section's introduction, *Jasper* embodies a social cognitive view (see chapter 9); the specific approach used is called *anchored instruction* (CTGV, 1997), where "anchors" are complex problems that become the focal point of student interactions. Video-based stories are used to make these complex problems engaging and accessible to students. Because the problems involve collaborative learning, individual student contributions become important. Students notice different aspects of problems, which pays off in higher levels of problem solving. The fact that anchors typically have more than one right answer means that students must evaluate and defend their ideas as they search for solutions.

For example, one of the early *Jasper* adventures, *Rescue at Boone's Meadow,* focuses on concepts of distance, rate, and time. *Rescue* begins with Jasper's friend Larry teaching another friend, Emily, how to fly an ultralight plane. Jasper and his friends also discuss a planned fishing and camping trip to a remote area, Boone's Meadow, which he will reach by hiking in. As the adventure unfolds, important *embedded data* are introduced—facts and numbers that will become critical in generating solutions to the challenge. Examples of embedded data in *Rescue* include information on who knows how to fly the ultralight, their weight, the plane's weight, its payload and gas consumption, the location and accessibility of Boone's Meadow, and so on. Having data like these means that, when students are trying to solve problems, they need to engage in reasoned decision making, not just exchange opinions.

The situation unfolds when Jasper, now on his camping trip, hears a gunshot, discovers a wounded eagle, and radios for help. In a complex scenario in which additional embedded data are revealed [e.g., speed limits on nearby highways and the weight of the bald eagle (around 15 pounds!)], learners come to the central problem: Emily needs to find the quickest feasible way to get the eagle to Dr. Ramirez, a veterinarian in Cumberland City. Many alternative solutions to this problem are possible (e.g., various people walking, driving, and using the ultralight). Obviously, students need to consider many different kinds of data, estimate such things as fuel consumption and travel time, and solve several subproblems in order to make the best choice about how to reach and transport the eagle.

Another of the Jasper adventures is *The Big Splash,* where Jasper's friend Chris wants to help his school raise money to buy a new camera for the school TV station. His idea is to have a dunking booth at his school's fun fair where teachers would be dunked when students hit a target. In order to get a loan from the school's principal to fund the idea, Chris needs a business plan that will convince the principal that he has thoroughly thought through his idea, including estimating total revenue, detailing expenses, and planning the logistics for making it all work. Students have to sort through pros and cons of such varied subproblems as deciding how to fill the pool, using survey data to set ticket prices, and estimating income. They also work on related analogous problems (e.g., Would Chris's plan work if ticket prices were raised from $1.00 to $1.50?) designed to deepen their understanding.

Anchors like the two we have described provide a forum for many kinds of communication and forms of problem solving. As the Vanderbilt group has experimented with *Jasper*'s design and implementation, it has been extended in a number of ways. A video-based SMART (Special Multimedia Arenas for Refining Thinking) Challenge series, for example, was developed to link teachers and students together across classrooms and schools to solve various *Jasper*-related challenges. Internet and telecommunications technology have been used to give students feedback on how other students are thinking about the problems. A related set of software, SMART tools, allows students to create their own mathematical tools for representing information, such as distance–time graphs and spreadsheets. Other tools provide just-in-time scaffolding to help students visualize problems better, such as one showing top views of playground equipment in a challenge requiring students to design a playground for their neighborhood.

As it has evolved over several years, the *Jasper* series has been extensively evaluated. Among consistent findings are that, while knowledge of basic mathematical concepts (e.g., figuring area and decimals) of *Jasper* students is about the same as matched non-*Jasper* students (which would be expected since *Jasper* does not focus on specific math skills), students in *Jasper* score better in word problems testing transfer of the kinds of knowledge taught in *Jasper*, in their ability to identify what needs to be considered in complex problems (e.g., answering questions like "Why does Casey need to think about in figuring how long her trip will take?"), in problem subgoal comprehension (e.g., answering a question like "Why did Casey divide the distance from Broken Bow to Ainsworth by the speed she'll be driving?"), and in their attitudes toward math and its utility (CTGV, 1997).

CSILE/Knowledge Forum: A Knowledge-Building Community Model

According to Hewitt and Scardamalia (1998), a **knowledge-building community** is a group of individuals dedicated to sharing and advancing the knowledge of the group. Scientific research teams are good examples of knowledge-building communities; others might be marketing teams in a company, a graduate research seminar, film societies, and even some families (Scardamalia & Bereiter, 1994). The common thread is that group members are committed to investing their resources in the collective upgrading of knowledge. *CSILE* attempts to create a knowledge-building community by supporting student work in a multimedia environment.

CSILE provides a computer-based multimedia setting for students and their teachers that allows students to generate "nodes" containing ideas or pieces of information about whatever topics are being studied and to interact with their classmates about these ideas. It basically consists of a multimedia database containing the ongoing research of the class on a particular topic. First developed in the late 1980s and deployed on small clusters of networked computers, *CSILE* creates a collaborative environment in which students can enter text and notes, including graphics, about the topic under study. All the students can read and comment on each other's notes and build on each other's ideas.

As the program of research and development to create and refine *CSILE* has developed over the years (e.g., see Hewitt & Scardamalia, 1998), several important **design principles**—rules guiding how programs such as *CSILE* are structured—have evolved. These include the following:

1. *Support educationally effective peer interactions.* In *CSILE,* computers serve as the medium for student discourse. One of the difficulties of face-to-face interactions is that shy or soft-spoken students may be closed out. *CSILE*'s computer-supported environment gives all students a voice and affords time for reflection and revision before an idea is submitted for public scrutiny. *CSILE* researchers have noted (e.g., see Hewitt et al., 1998) that students of all abilities contribute ideas to the knowledge community.

2. *Integrate different forms of discourse.* In using *CSILE,* teachers are coached to use both face-to-face (oral) and online (written) discourse or to combine the two. For instance, groups of students may gather around a common computer to construct notes together or visit with one another to share references, sources, illustrations, and ideas before they work on *CSILE* (Hewitt & Scardamalia, 1998). Thus students can get the best of both oral communication (i.e., spontaneity and immediate feedback) and online communication (i.e., a permanent record of thinking and time to reflect).

3. *Focus students on common problems.* According to Hewitt and Scardamalia (1998), the challenge of coming to a shared understanding places a demand on students to "clarify ideas, refine theories, answer each others' questions, and negotiate meaning with one another" (p. 88). In *CSILE*'s discussion facility, for instance, any student can start a discussion by making a note or posing a question in the "problem

area" of a discussion screen. The discussions themselves then take place in the second part of the screen; all discussions are public and everyone in the class or group can take part.

4. *Promote awareness of participants' contributions.* Hewitt and Scardamalia note that, in a typical classroom, it is relatively rare for students to have the chance to read each other's work. In contrast, *CSILE* teachers try to highlight interesting student work and encourage students to explore *CSILE*'s database. Two ways that interaction with other students' ideas are facilitated are by (1) the *Knowledge Map,* which provides a graphical overview of the class's notes, and (2) a search capability, where students can retrieve and organize their own or classmates' notes by naming the author of the notes, topic name, key words, or any one of several other possibilities in their search.

5. *Encourage students to build on each other's work as a community.* Again in contrast to many classrooms, students in *CSILE* classrooms can build on other students' work. The *Knowledge Map* provides a visual display that lets students see which notes are highly connected and which are not. Teachers also encourage students to respond to and build on each other's ideas and questions and extend them through online discussion. Because many students are used to a work mode in school where what individuals do is most important, students often initially see *CSILE* as a way of storing their individual work. They also tend to see writing as assessment (Hewitt & Scardamalia, 1998). What *CSILE* teachers instead try to instill in students is that the reason they are using *CSILE* is to contribute to a larger group mission of advancing the class's knowledge. They also remind students that, in order to make a real contribution to the group, they need to know what the group knows. Finding out what their peers know leads to deeper understanding of the content and also to a greater appreciation of their peers' knowledge.

In recent years, *CSILE* has been developed as an Internet-based commercial application called *Knowledge Forum*. *Knowledge Forum* retains the key features of *CSILE*—serving as a repository for student ideas and questions and providing a forum for exchanging ideas. As in earlier versions, students build on ideas and questions of their classmates, reference each other's work, and reorganize information in the knowledge base. The system has graphics capabilities addressing the structural dimensions of knowledge building; for example, a "views" capability provides graphical organizers for notes. Notes can be added in one or more views, clustered together, and moved around to represent different organizing frameworks. *Knowledge Forum* also provides scaffolds, supports for analysis of texts, theory building, and debating.

Summary of Tools for Building Learning Communities

Programs such as *Jasper* and *CSILE/Knowledge Forum* have been designed using cognitive and social cognitive principles. They aim at developing deep understanding and start with the assumption that having students interact on issues important to them will produce deep understanding. *Jasper* uses "anchors" as its focal point—challenging, complex, multidimensional problems that generate a multitude of problem solving and communication activities. *CSILE/Knowledge Forum* begins with an empty knowledge base, which is seeded with an issue or set of related issues that become the focal point of information gathering, inquiry, and discussion. A key feature for both of these systems is their emphasis on learner contributions—the information they have gathered, learners' perspectives on that information, and their reactions to others' viewpoints. Each is a complex technology-based system for stimulating individual cognitive growth through the participation and growing sophistication of a community of learners.

Implications for Teaching

We began this chapter by describing technology's uses in education and by outlining key cognitive skills students need to take advantage of. Cognitive theory proves essential for helping judge whether specific uses of technology by either individuals or groups are likely to facilitate learning and cognitive growth. The following implications draw on this discussion, with special emphasis on work of Clark (2003), the Cognition and Technology Group at Vanderbilt (CTGV, 1997), Means and Olson (1994), and Merrill (2000):

1. *Use cognitive principles as criteria for judging technology-based instruction.* As the technology-based applications for education rapidly multiply, educators increasingly will need to make informed decisions about their purchase and use. With advancements in software development and graphics, virtually all applications marketed to educators will be attractively designed and function well. The key questions for educators, however, should focus on whether an application is likely to produce student learning and motivation. Does, say, a DVD-based program targeted at beginning readers represent a solid literacy curriculum and are its activities likely to produce meaningful learning? Are its demonstrations clear (Merrill, 2000) and screens designed in such a way as to avoid excessive cognitive load? Does the application connect appropriately to children's prior knowledge? Questions like these are essential for distinguishing between computer-based instruction that merely entertains and has dubious educational value and instruction likely to develop important knowledge and skills.

2. *Emphasize technology's sense-making uses.* From a cognitive perspective, technology's best uses are those producing meaningful learning. One way to reach this goal is to have students use technology *as a resource* for achieving such goals as finding and organizing information, discussing and refining concepts, and presenting ideas and creating new products. For example, working on a group project with other students in an 11th-grade environmental studies class, a student might use a search engine such as *Google* to look for the latest information from the Center for Disease Control for a project focusing on the SARS virus, put country-by-country data into a spreadsheet, and graph the growth of cases by region since 2002 to share with other members of her or his working group to get their reactions, and use an HTML editor

to create pages for the school Web site, perhaps even including some animation on the pages with *Flash*. Booklets might also be created using a word processor, along with an automated *PowerPoint* presentation for parents' night. Activities like these— each involving significant technology use—are likely to be productive of deeper learning because, in each of them, students don't just look at information, but must make sense out of it to do something with it.

3.   *Support authentic, challenging tasks with technology.* Well-chosen projects in which students use technology to accomplish project subtasks and overall goals are examples of the authentic, challenging tasks Means and Olson (1994) describe as supporting extended, motivated intellectual activity. Such authentic, real-world problems (Merrill, 2000) are linked to the learner's world. Tasks focusing on learning by doing, with information supporting skilled performance, are most likely to produce complex cognitive skills (van Merrienboer et al., 2002). As students work with such tasks, teachers move from information presenter to roles such as arranging learning resources and serving as a coach. These kinds of tasks also lend themselves to developing habits of self-assessment and reflection, processes that lead to cognitive growth.

4.   *Use technology to create and support collaborative learning communities.* In projects such as the CTGV's *Jasper* series and *CSILE*, technology provides the hub for learner interactions—planning collaboratively, sharing ideas across workgroups and classrooms, building on each other's ideas, getting feedback from classmates, and presenting ideas. These interactions, which focus on important content and data and take place over extended periods, are the building blocks for learning communities and create a context for cognitive growth.

5.   *Use technology as appropriate to provide practice and feedback.* Many current commercial instructional programs—especially those designed for students with learning, language, and reading difficulties—focus on skill development through practice. Although there is a legitimate worry about "drill and kill," where students endlessly practice skills of dubious value, the computer can be an ideal partner for some kinds of practice. Technology can present information, prompt responses, and give feedback to learners—all without tiring. For example, students can practice literacy-related skills such as letter or word identification, which may be valuable in helping them move toward automaticity in these areas. They do need to understand, however, how such skills relate to their ultimate goals of understanding what they are reading and getting pleasure from it.

6.   *Help disabled students access and make use of assistive technologies.* Assistive technology can provide the critical support many disabled students need to achieve success. While assistive technologies cannot remove the difficulties that come with having a disability, they can assist students in meeting the challenges of the classroom. Assistive technologies are becoming increasingly versatile and powerful. A rapidly growing number of them also are available, ranging from tools for organizing information to speech recognition and text-to-speech conversion programs that increase opportunities for literacy-related disabilities to achieve classroom success.

Summary

This chapter is about the new technologies, cognition's relationship to them, and their utility for learning and teaching. The chapter begins by exploring ways students can use technology and outlines key cognitive skills they need to take advantage of it. Several cognitive theories and the research they support are discussed in relation to technology design and use. Among them are cognitive load theory, which focuses on working memory; the 4C/ID model, which is a cognitively based design framework for developing complex cognitive skills; and social cognitive theory, which has informed the design of large-scale interventions based on technology. Whereas cognitive load theory and the 4C/ID model apply most directly to individual learning, social cognitive theory focuses on interactions among learners and provides a framework for creating technology-based learning communities. The chapter concludes with implications aimed at helping teachers and students use technology most effectively.

Suggested Readings

Clark, R. (2003). Research on web-based learning: A half-full glass. In R. Bruning, C. Horn, & L. PytlikZillig (Eds.), *Web-based learning: What do we know? Where do we go?* Greenwich, CN: Information Age.

Richard Clark, a leading authority on learning outcomes and multimedia, analyzes a number of claims about Web-based learning in light of what research actually shows.

Mayer, R., & Moreno, R. (2002). Aids to computer-based multimedia learning. *Learning and Instruction, 12,* 107–119.

Mayer and Moreno summarize findings from more than 10 years of research based on their cognitive theory of multimedia learning. In their discussion, they draw on dual coding theory, cognitive load theory, and constructivist learning theory to offer several important principles for designing instructional multimedia.

van Merrienboer, J. J. G., Clark, R. E., & de Croock, M. B. M. (2002). Blueprints for complex learning: The 4C/ID model. *Educational Technology Research and Development, 54 (1),* 39–64.

This technical article provides a fine overview of how complex skills can be analyzed and how instructional technology systems should be designed for developing complex skills.

Learning to Read

A T FIRST GLANCE, learning to read seems straightforward. Words have meanings; becoming a reader, therefore, means learning to make straightforward translations from symbols to thought or to speech. When explored more deeply, however, reading reveals itself to be a very complex domain resting on an understanding of language and the world in which linguistic and cognitive factors interact.

Through reading, we can make contact with the thoughts and imaginations of people removed in time and space, learn from them, and share their feelings. These functional qualities are the reason that reading is so important. Because it gives children entry into the literate world, learning to read marks an important transition point. We begin early by teaching first graders to read, and reading soon becomes instrumental for achievement in other areas of study. Without the ability to read, a child's likelihood of success in virtually any area of the school curriculum is seriously diminished. Reading's importance extends well beyond school, of course; reading is crucial to most jobs and a significant source of information and pleasure for many adults. In this chapter, the first of three on literacy, we describe the basic linguistic and cognitive processes involved in reading and how these processes interact in beginning reading.

We begin the chapter with an examination of the linguistic and cognitive prerequisites of reading. As is shown, although reading is complex, its complexity does not make it incomprehensible. We then explore the relatively brief period during which children make the transition to becoming readers. In this section, we describe how children consolidate their growing knowledge about language sounds and print, moving from prereaders to "experts" with the skills to decode unfamiliar words accurately and to understand what they have read. Finally, we end with a discussion of beginning literacy instruction, highlighting literacy teaching methods and materials and summarizing key issues in the sometimes-heated debates over how best to teach beginning reading.

Literacy's Foundations in Language Development

More than a quarter-century of research on language development has shown it to be an extraordinarily interesting and fertile research area. This research has not only given us a fascinating account of children's language acquisition (e.g., see Crystal, 1997) but also revealed how closely language development and literacy are intertwined. As a consequence, to understand literacy development better, literacy researchers now regularly study language-related phenomena as diverse as children's classroom discussions and their awareness of print and its uses. This research has shown that literacy is closely linked with children's uses of language in their homes and communities (Purcell-Gates, 1996; Sulzby, 1991).

By first grade, children's ability to perceive and use language is very impressive indeed. Their language skills have been developing rapidly since the second year of their lives; for example, many first graders will have extensive vocabularies of 5,000 or more words (Chall, Jacobs, & Baldwin, 1990). They also have a solid command of the mechanics of their native language and can use it to communicate effectively. Literacy, however, requires them to become explicitly aware of their own language use and of language in general. Acquiring metacognitive knowledge (see chapter 4) about language—called **metalinguistic awareness**—is a key to children's transition into literacy.

Although virtually every student has the basic linguistic capacity to learn to read and write, students in most classrooms typically will vary in their language backgrounds and metalinguistic awareness in ways that affect their progress toward literacy. Mixed in with differences in competence and rapid developmental changes also are significant variations in the ways children of different social and cultural backgrounds use language. Furthermore, for a growing number of children in the United States, learning to read may take place in a language other than their first one. The diversity in students' language backgrounds presents a significant challenge to teachers teaching children to read. To help in better understanding the nature of language-related factors and how they affect learning to read, we begin with an overview of the major dimensions of language. As children acquire knowledge about each of these, they not only are becoming a part of a language community but also are setting out on the road to literacy.

Dimensions of Language

Human languages are immensely complex systems of conventions for linking symbols with meanings for the purpose of communication. In virtually all of them, the primary symbols are speech sounds. Human languages also are structured; they don't just randomly or idiosyncratically collect sounds into words, words into sentences, and sentences into larger units. Instead, at each level of structure, units combine meaningfully according to general organizational principles.

The starting point for most discussions of language is its meanings and messages—the ways humans use it. These uses of language, which linguists refer to as **pragmatics,** are its most important feature. Because of their central role in human evolution and behavior, language pragmatics are of great interest not only to linguists but also to a host of other scholars as diverse as geneticists and archeologists. The other major aspect of language is its *structure,* and we describe three important structural levels: (1) **words,** including word meanings (semantics) and how speech sounds are formed into words; (2) **syntax,** the combining of words into phrases, clauses, and sentences; and (3) **discourse,** the organizing of sentences into higher order units, such as paragraphs, stories, reports, and conversations (see Figure 11-1; see also chapter 9 for details on classroom discussions as an example of discourse).

Pragmatics   Language is very important to humans. It must be; we have had it for a very long time—100,000 years or more is a common estimate—and every 1 of the more than 5,000 human cultures has developed a highly complex language system. In contrast, no other species, including the great apes, seems to have more than rudimentary language capabilities. Having language gives us a tremendous evolutionary advantage; it allows us to refer to things not directly observable by others, to describe the past, and to imagine and plan for the future. Also, the fact that language can be separated or *displaced* from events actually observed or experienced gives us the potential for abstract thinking and problem solving. Simply put, language is pragmatic in that it fulfills vital human needs and affects every aspect of our lives.

When we think about language, we often think about using it to communicate information. Indeed, virtually everything we know has been transmitted to us by language or interpreted through language, from our family stories to the scientific principles we read in our texts. Some (e.g., Locke, 1994) have argued, however, that language's social and emotional pragmatic uses may be even more important

Figure 11-1
Language Uses and Structures

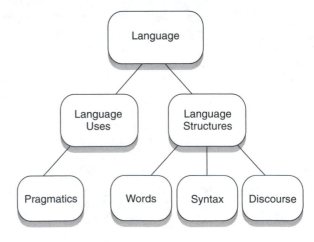

than its cognitive ones of communicating information. The content of the language accompanying our daily interactions with others may be far from profound, but it is vital for creating and maintaining our connections with our families, neighborhoods, and society. Talk not only supports ongoing work and play but also conveys our feelings and values.

Words: The Building Blocks of a Language   Words are the building blocks of every language. We use a vast number to label, describe, and signal our intentions—as many as 40,000 a day, by one estimate (Locke, 1994). As you can imagine, the study of words and their meanings, called **semantics,** is of great interest to many scholars. For most of us, however, the most familiar area of semantics is vocabulary. Children seem to come by semantic knowledge very naturally; once they start speaking, they acquire new vocabulary words at a remarkable rate: 60 or more words a month. As we have seen earlier, the result is that most children enter school with vocabularies numbering in the thousands of words, which provide a tremendous resource for their literacy development.

Spoken words are formed from speech sounds. We humans can vocalize an extraordinary variety of them, ranging from clicks, chirps, and babbling to our familiar vowels and consonants. These vocalizations, called **phones,** are the raw material of language. Among the huge number of possible sounds, however, only a very small subset—the **phonemes** of a language—are perceived as meaningful by speakers and listeners in that language. Each phoneme forms a kind of perceptual category that carries meaning (Crystal, 1997). English, for instance, has approximately 44 phonemes, and comprehending English speech depends on an individual distinguishing them from one another (e.g., distinguishing between /1/ and /r/ lets us tell the difference between *load* and *road*) in order to access the meanings the sounds carry.

Each of the world's languages has its own distinct set of phonemes. Thus, although phonemes in different languages do overlap, one language's phonemes may not be phonemes in another. For instance, the sound /v/, which is a phoneme (has meaning) in English (e.g., *viper* and *wiper* are distinctly different words), is not a phoneme in the Thai language. As a consequence, native Thai speakers attempting to learn English words containing the sound /v/ (e.g., *divide*) may hear the English /v/ as the familiar phoneme /w/ (/w/ is a phoneme in Thai) and perceive and pronounce such words incorrectly (e.g., as *dewide*). They also would experience considerable difficulty distinguishing between two words differing only in these consonants. The tables are turned, of course, when English speakers encounter other languages. For instance, English speakers often experience difficulty perceiving phonemes that are meaningful in, say, Spanish, Chinese, or Russian—differences obvious to native speakers of those languages but initially very difficult or impossible for nonnative speakers to perceive.

By the time children enter school, most have a sophisticated knowledge of their language's sound system. Recognizing sound patterns and meanings has been essential to their becoming members of a language and social community. Although their abilities to perceive and pronounce sounds are not fully mature, most children can accurately recognize and produce their language's sound segments. Their pronunciation and intonation patterns also conform closely to those of adults. As we previously have stated, however, learning to read depends on *metalinguistic* capabilities, many of which are only in their beginning developmental stages when children start school.

One of the most important metalinguistic capabilities—**phonemic awareness**—is the awareness that phonemes are individual and separable speech sounds and being able to manipulate them. At age 4, few children know that words can be broken down into phonemic segments; by age 6, however, most are beginning to show some degree of phonemic awareness (Nation & Hulme, 1997). In alphabetic languages, such as English and Spanish, wherein letters represent sounds, phonemic awareness is crucial to learning how to read and write. For instance, phonemic awareness is involved in understanding how sounds are combined to form words (e.g., "*Cub-ab-tub . . . CAT*") and how specific words are similar or different in sound structure (e.g., *How are MAT and SAT alike? How are they different?*).

Learning to read requires connecting this metalinguistic understanding about oral language to written symbols—letters, words, and sentences. Making this connection requires that students also acquire an understanding of the **alphabetic principle**—phonemes. In learning to read, students need to not only identify and label letters and the phonemes they represent, knowing that printed letters and letter combinations represent sounds, but also segment, rearrange, and substitute phonemes for each other (Adams, 1990; Bryne & Fielding-Barnsley, 1991, 1993, 1995; Ehri, 1994; Moats & Foorman, 1997; Stanovich, 2000; Vellutino, 1991).

Although learning English letter–sound relationships is a significant challenge for most children, it is not impossible. The relationship of spelling to sound in English is complex but not arbitrary. Especially for words of Anglo-Saxon origin, which are some of the oldest and most common words in the English language (e.g., *eat, drink, sleep, work, play, nose, mouth, mother,* and *father* all have Anglo-Saxon roots), pronunciations are mostly predictable. For this reason, beginning reading instruction often focuses on this group of words.

Another language concept important for beginning reading is the **morpheme.** Whereas phonemes are the minimal meaningful distinctions in language sounds, morphemes are sounds or combinations of sounds that are the minimal units of meaning (Crystal, 1997). English words are made up of one or more morphemes. For example, the word *cat* is a single morpheme. The word *joyfully,* in contrast, is a combination of three morphemes, joy + ful + ly (of course, the word *joyfully* contains multiple phonemes corresponding to the basic sounds making up the word). Each of the three morphemes in *joyfully* conveys a dimension of meaning of the word. The root word *joy* has a meaning of itself; adding *-ful* to the noun joy converts it to its adjectival form; and adding *-ly* to *joyful* transforms it to its adverbial form. Only certain combinations of morphemes are possible in a given language; for instance, native speakers know immediately that utterances such as *fuljoy, joylyful,* and *joyly* are not English. English morphology allows only a few of a near-infinite number of possibilities.

Like metalinguistic knowledge about language sounds, metalinguistic knowledge about English morphology is vital to literacy, which requires that children break words into syllables and other meaningful parts in order to comprehend and write them. For example, children have acquired important morphological knowledge when they learn that many English words are made up of chunks that can be combined (RAIN + COAT = RAINCOAT), divided (UNCOVER = UN + COVER), and even redivided (UNCOVER = UN + COV + ER). As is true for each area of language, children already have morphological capabilities on which to build a metalinguistic understanding of morphology. They have been using morphological rules from the time they were toddlers—adding markers such as *-s* and *-ed* for pluralization and tense soon after their speech moved beyond the single-word level. In their speech, young children first tend to overapply their growing morphological knowledge (e.g., two *sheepses* and she *goed* home) but gradually move to more mature forms. In literacy, developing morphological awareness is likewise complex and contextual; learning its basics begins early, but mastering its subtleties continues throughout the entire period of formal schooling and beyond.

Words Combined: The Syntax of a Language   At the next higher level of language structure is **syntax**—the organization of words into larger units, such as phrases, clauses, and sentences. The study of syntax (and the related topic of grammar) has long been a major emphasis in linguistics, but especially so after the publication of Noam Chomsky's landmark *Syntactic Structures* in 1957 and *Aspects of the Theory of Syntax* in 1965. These books transformed the way linguists looked at language learning, especially at how syntactical knowledge is acquired and used. Chomsky took a strongly nativist position, arguing that much syntactical knowledge is "hardwired" in human beings and that children don't completely acquire syntactic structures through learning processes such as modeling and feedback.

In most languages, syntactic information is vital to comprehension. Syntactic speech is closely linked with propositional thought (see chapter 3); propositions ordinarily cannot be understood except through their expression in the syntax of language. For instance, the information contained in the syntax of the sentence *The horse kicked Eddie* is essential to knowing what the sentence is saying; that is, to the encoding of the proposition underlying the sentence. Obviously, the sentences *Eddie kicked the horse* and *The horse kicked Eddie* carry very different meanings!

Syntactic regularity appears very early in children's speech, even earlier than morphology; children use consistent word order as soon as they begin to use two-word sequences (Anisfeld, 1984; R. Brown, 1973). The ability to reflect on and manipulate the internal structure of sentences, however, does not develop until middle childhood, with syntactic development continuing well beyond the middle elementary grades. Because of this and the fact that primary-level students have difficulty comprehending sentences with complex syntax (e.g., *The cat that chased the butterfly around the yard of my Aunt Nellie's sister was orange and black*), most materials used in beginning reading instruction have simple grammatical structures.

Discourse Structure: Frameworks for Comprehension   Children's knowledge about the highest level of language structure—**discourse**—also is vital to their learning to read. In discourse, propositions take on a meaning in relation to one another, with references forward or backward affecting the meaning of individual elements. Even for children just learning to talk, word meanings are shaped by prior and subsequent utterances. Most everyday language is discourse. Writing and reading almost always involve extended discourse sequences; comprehension and building semantic knowledge depend on readers' abilities to tie discourse elements together. To do so, they must recognize, at least implicitly, the structure of stories and texts.

Two **discourse structures** of particular importance for literacy development are narratives and exposition. **Narratives** are "stories" structured by a temporal sequence of events. Most children begin to recognize narrative structure not long after they begin to use language (Applebee, 1983; McNamee, 1987) and use this knowledge to understand stories being read or told to them. Most first graders already know quite a bit about narrative structure. Here, for instance, is a story by a first grader that reflects her understanding of a narrative sequence.

> And then she got some ice cream.
>
> And then she put it in the cone.
>
> And then he . . . she went outside.
>
> And a . . . the kitty-cat scared her.
>
> And she dropped the cone.
>
> And she looked real mad.

Many narratives, of course, are much more complex than this child's; they can range from very simple recountings like this one to complex plays, novels, and historical accounts. The essential feature of all narratives is a structure based on the temporal sequence of events. Narratives are episodic.

Exposition, in contrast with narratives, reflects the organization of abstract thought about a topic or a body of information. Although expository texts may contain narrative elements (and vice versa), the basic structure of exposition is logical and informational, not temporal. Textbooks, essays, and persuasive arguments typically use expository structure. Because expository structure is based more on logical relations than on directly observed temporal associations, the belief that children's ability to comprehend exposition lags well behind their understanding of narratives has been widely shared. Perhaps for this reason, the vast majority of children's early reading instruction continues to be organized around narratives, not expository texts. Recent research has shown, however, that even young children have considerable knowledge about what expository texts are like and respond positively to teaching about that genre (e.g., Donovan, 1996; Duke & Kays, 1998; Pappas, 1993). Duke (2000), for example, has argued that development of knowledge about exposition in the early grades lags primarily because children are not exposed to it. In a sample of first-grade classrooms she studied, Duke found less than 3 percent of print displayed in classrooms and 10 percent of books in classroom libraries were informational, with even lower percentages in lower social economic status classrooms. Total time per day spent in written activities with informational texts averaged only 3.6 minutes per day, a very small proportion of the time students spend in school, in class, and with written language.

Summary of Linguistic Prerequisites for Reading

Becoming literate represents a significant challenge. In reading and writing, children must link their oral language with a new, visual system of symbols. Children's language capabilities are a tremendous resource for literacy. Becoming literate, however, requires them also to develop their metalinguistic capabilities—knowledge about the uses of print, how print represents sounds, how words are formed, how sentences are put together, and how sentences become stories or reports. Literacy both requires and enhances readers' knowledge about the abstract properties of language. For literate individuals, language itself becomes an object of awareness and analysis (Olson, 1994). Literacy changes the character of discourse, thought, and problem solving and gives us new ways of representing the world.

Table 11-1 presents a summary of several key metalinguistic abilities related to beginning reading. Most teachers of beginning reading see developing these abilities in their students as essential. Direct "skills" instruction on these and other aspects of reading, however, without connecting them with each other and embedding them in a meaningful literacy context, does not seem to be a particularly good idea. If children are unable to connect the skills they are learning with the larger context of becoming literate, they can come to view reading as an incomprehensible set of fragmented tasks (Norris, 1988). A better approach is to teach skills systematically but always to relate them to the central purpose of reading: understanding and enjoying what is being read.

Becoming literate draws on many kinds of metalinguistic knowledge, but in alphabetic languages like English none is more important to beginning readers than *phonemic awareness,* the ability to recognize and manipulate sounds in oral language. Thus, developing students' phonemic awareness is an important goal in most early literacy instruction. A second goal for beginning reading instruction connects this knowledge with print—that students acquire the *alphabetic principle,* learning that individual letters and letter combinations represent speech sounds.

If instruction is poor or incomplete, the challenge of learning to read can be daunting. If all goes well, however, in the space of a few months children will reliably recognize the unfamiliar and highly abstract representations provided by printed letters and words and map them onto the oral language system they already possess. Researchers may differ on specific instructional methods on this topic (e.g., see discussion by Stahl, Duffy-Hester, & Stahl, 1998), but most generally agree that explicit teaching of decoding skills (generally called **phonics instruction**) makes a great deal of sense.

Even though phonemic awareness can develop without instruction and some students will discover the alphabetic principle on their own—through immersion in literacy activities involving books, writing, storytelling, and the like—simple exposure is not enough for most children. Without teaching, acquiring the metalinguistic ability to analyze language sounds and to link them with an abstract symbol system is not a certainty, no matter how rich the linguistic environment. For most students, the process of becoming literate, while having many parallels to first language learning, requires instructional support. In particular, most children need explicit instruction in letter–sound relationships to move them as rapidly as possible to the meaning-making purpose of reading.

Table 11-1
Some Metalinguistic Abilities Underlying Early Reading

Pragmatic Abilities	
Print awareness	Understanding that print carries meaning; that reading is directional, can represent objects or speech, has special words (e.g., *word, letter,* and *pronounce*) to describe literacy's features and activities
Word-Level Abilities	
Graphic awareness	Recognition of letter details (e.g., difference between *d* and *b*) and that words are composed of letters
Phonemic awareness	Ability to hear the separate sounds in words; recognition of words' similarities and differences; knowledge that spoken units can be analyzed and compared (e.g., *sh* and *ch*)
Awareness of grapheme/phoneme correspondence	Knowledge of the alphabetic principle that letters and sounds "go together"; ability to apply that knowledge to decoding unknown words
Morphological awareness	Capability of breaking words into their constituent parts; pronouncing syllables in words; combining word parts to form new words
Syntactic-Level Abilities	
Syntactic awareness	Recognition and use of clauses and sentence-level patterns; using within-sentence context of words (e.g., correctly pronouncing *read* in the sentence *The girl read the book*)
Discourse-Level Abilities	
Text-structure awareness	Comprehension of relationships between parts of text, including recognition of cohesive elements in text, general knowledge of text structures (e.g., narratives and exposition)

Cognitive Prerequisites of Learning to Read

Reading is a language-based activity that also involves constructing meaning from text. As Mason and Au (1990) point out, reading is not word calling or "sounding out" but rather a special form of reasoning in which both the reader and the writer contribute perspective, inference, and logic. In this section, we highlight three cognitive factors on which children's success in learning to read depends: (1) world knowledge, (2) working and long-term memory capabilities, and (3) the ability to focus attention. These are not discrete, separable factors, of course; when readers read successfully, all of these dimensions operate at once and interact with linguistic knowledge. In discussing beginning reading, however, it is useful to separate them. Just as is true with children's language experience, some children may be better prepared on some dimensions than others. A beginning reader who has reasonably good skills overall may perform well on certain reading tasks but not on others requiring different knowledge or skills.

World Knowledge

We read to understand. This search for meaning—the process of comprehension—depends on both the writer and the reader. As we have stressed throughout this text, schema theory has had an especially important role in helping us better understand the nature of comprehension processes, including those in reading (Pressley, 1994). To illustrate, let's turn again to a "piggy bank" passage, this one considerably simpler than the one presented in chapter 3:

> Toby wanted to get a birthday present for Chris. He went to his piggy bank. He shook it. There was no sound.

As you now recognize, the knowledge a young reader needs in order to comprehend even a brief passage like this can be very extensive. For instance, the reader must know that getting a birthday present means buying one, that Toby went to his piggy bank to get some money (the passage does not say so), that piggy banks contain money (the passage does not say so), that this money typically is in coin form, that coins in shaken piggy banks make noise, and that no rattling meant no money. For adults, comprehension comes without any special effort; we recognize all of these things automatically (and mostly without consciousness of their recognition). Many primary-level students, however, have not had experience with piggy banks; with buying and giving presents; or, for that matter, with birthday parties. With any part of this knowledge missing, the whole sequence of events in the passage can become incomprehensible. The main point of reading—getting meaning—would not be achieved by these students.

Our knowledge directs attention in reading, guides interpretations, and makes comprehension possible (R. C. Anderson, 1984; Ruddell, 1994). The meaning that an active reader constructs, therefore, is not exactly what the author had in mind as he or she wrote the passage. Neither is it simply the reader's own mental constructions and inferences. As children read, they necessarily interpret words and events in terms of what they know. Children who have helped care for a garden by watering, cultivating, and feeding the plants and who have gathered produce from the garden, for example, would be much more likely to make sense of a story about, say, a young

Chippewa girl who works with her father harvesting wild rice than children who have not had these kinds of experiences.

It is useful for teachers and parents to remind themselves that reading is a constructive process aimed at comprehension. As we see below, even when children mispronounce and misidentify words, teachers should continue to direct considerable attention to the meaning of what is being read. Although beginning readers undeniably need decoding skills, such as letter, sound, and word identification, these skills in themselves do not add up to reading. To focus solely on "skills" with beginning readers misses the main point of learning to read—getting meaning from what is read. Indeed, children even can be misled about the purposes of reading and can come to believe that "reading" consists of figuring out pronunciations, doing exercises with words, and completing worksheets (Cairney, 1988).

Working and Long-Term Memory Capabilities

Because it depends on world and linguistic knowledge, reading is an act of memory. A child fixating on a particular word, for instance, must keep that word in mind long enough to build up the more complex meaning of phrases, sentences, and whole passages. New meaning requires the continuing availability of earlier information; comprehension processes depend on linking the meanings of words currently being processed and those processed earlier (Ruddell, 1994; Stanovich, 2000; Swanson, 1992).

As shown in chapter 2, many studies have shown that human working memory is limited and often quite fragile. Young children's working memory capacity is especially restricted, most likely because they lack well-developed skills for encoding and rehearsal (e.g., Pressley & Schneider, 1997). For example, the number of digits a 5-year-old can recall from a single presentation is only four or so (Dempster, 1981) compared with seven for an adult. If the number of digits presented exceeds this amount, the immediate memory span is exceeded and all or most of the information will be lost.

Reading consists of sequential encounters with related, not isolated, elements, however. Letters are clustered into meaningful words, words into phrases and sentences, and sentences into text. Thus, although it might appear that information encountered while reading would almost immediately exceed the immediate memory span (e.g., after a child has read five or six words), it ordinarily does not. When words and sentences make sense, readers can use their semantic and syntactic knowledge to "chunk" information or, perhaps more accurately, to convert it into *propositions* (see chapter 3). In reading, words are part of meaningful patterns, not discrete, isolated units.

Obviously, both working and long-term memory processes are needed to make reading meaningful. Constructing meaning depends on their interaction. New information must be "kept alive" in working memory while previously encountered information is drawn from long-term memory. With this interaction in mind, some researchers who have examined reading from a memory perspective (e.g., Breznitz &

Share, 1992; Swanson, 1992) have argued that slower-than-normal speeds of word decoding may place higher-than-normal demands on working memory and interfere with meaningful reading. When words are decoded slowly, each one's meaning must be held in memory longer in order for the reader to comprehend the meaning of a sentence or paragraph. Some evidence has been presented in support of this position, although conflicting demands on attention for the poor decoder (poor decoders do not comprehend as well because they must concentrate more on decoding, whereas good decoders decode more automatically, allowing more attention to meaning) also appears strongly involved in poor decoders' inability to comprehend and recall what they have read (Samuels, 1994). That is, because poor readers' word-level decoding often is not automatic, they need to devote additional attention to it. This puts further stresses on their ability to comprehend (Stanovich, 2000)

Attention

Reading requires attention. For example, children obviously must have a book out, be oriented toward it, and be looking at it in order to read. Reaching even this point with some children is not a trivial accomplishment. However, teachers can take advantage of a large array of behavioral management systems (e.g., see Kazdin, 1994) developed to help foster attentional skills.

Subtler forms of attention within the act of reading also are critical. Readers must learn to direct their attention to the relevant elements of text in an organized, systematic way (e.g., "Sean, when you look at those two words—*lane* and *cane*—how can you tell that they rhyme?"). Attention is needed to control their eye movements, focus on specific words, and at least in English, move their eyes in left-to-right sweeps. Their attention must move successively from word to word and be directed to important ideas in the text. It must shift appropriately between text and illustrations. During formal instructional periods, the problem of focusing attention becomes even more complex as attention must be allocated, in turn, to the text, to classmates' responses, and to the teacher's directions and feedback. As discussed in the next chapter, acquiring metacognitive strategies for guiding these and related processes is vital to reading comprehension.

Summary of Cognitive Prerequisites for Reading

At first glance, reading seems simply to be a matching task in which children learn to link visual cues with their vocabulary. In fact, reading is a highly complex interaction with text, requiring orchestration of a stream of complex graphic input with several levels of linguistic and world knowledge. Reading places demands on working memory and requires children to draw on their long-term memory to understand what they are reading. It also necessitates involvement with books and other reading materials and learning to attend to details of letters, words, and text.

From Reading Readiness to Emergent Literacy

Almost everyone would agree that there are developmental limits on how early children can profitably be taught to read. Today, most children in the United States learn to read during their 1st year in school, when they are about 6 or 7 years old. Only a small minority of students know how to read when they enter school. For many years, our thoughts about when to begin to teach reading were shaped by the concept of **reading readiness,** the idea that a certain level of mental maturity is necessary to begin reading instruction. The notion of reading readiness was given considerable impetus by an early study by Morphett and Washburne (1931), who examined the relationship between general intellectual functioning and reading success. Their data led them to conclude that reading success was considerably greater for children who had a mental age of at least 6 years and 6 months when they started school. From their analysis, Morphett and Washburne recommended that it was prudent to postpone reading instruction until children reached this mental age, which usually occurs during the first grade.

Whereas the tradition of beginning reading instruction in first grade has continued, the idea of reading readiness began to be defined more specifically, as time passed, as subskills thought to underlie reading—such as letter name knowledge and visual, auditory, and perceptual readiness. A major influence in this transformation was the development of so-called reading readiness tests, which were attempts to measure critical factors underlying the ability to read (see Sulzby, 1991). This view of reading readiness fit well with a conception of reading instruction as development of a carefully sequenced hierarchy of "prereading" and reading skills and with the task-analysis approach to learning and teaching that was prominent in the 1960s and 1970s (e.g., Gagne, 1965, 1970; see also chapter 1). Hierarchical sequences of reading skills soon provided the framework for many **basal reader series**—the comprehensive packages of texts, teacher guides, and student activities around which reading instruction still is organized.

A major difficulty with the reading readiness concept is that it categorizes children into two discrete groups: those who are ready to read and those who aren't. Also, reading is artificially isolated from writing and other language skills as the "real" dimension of literacy. The concept of **emergent literacy,** however, has provided an alternative point of view. From the perspective of emergent literacy, a position we strongly endorse, literacy development is based in language and cognitive development and begins well before children actually begin to read (Heath, 1986; Purcell-Gates, 1996; Ruddell & Ruddell, 1994; Sulzby, 1991). A child who is not yet reading is neither "ready to read" nor "not ready to read." Instead, literacy development, like general language development, is seen as a process that has begun far in advance of formal instruction and continues far beyond the point when a child has "learned how to read." Table 11-2 is a summary of some points of comparison between the reading-readiness and emergent-literacy perspectives.

Children's movement into reading does, in fact, seem more continuous than discontinuous. Although they cannot yet read, many prereaders already have discovered

Table 11-2
Contrastive Views: Reading Readiness and Emergent Literacy

Reading Readiness	Emergent Literacy
General Focus	
Reading as a critical skill in literacy	Broad literacy development, including reading, writing, listening, and speaking
Prototypical View of Reading	
Reading as hierarchy of skills	Reading as a functional activity
Function of Preschool Language Activity	
Preparation for reading	Multifaceted language development experience, including all forms of language
Focus In Learning to Read	
Formal instruction in reading	Engagement with literate adults; adult modeling, self-exposition; peer interaction; formal instruction in reading, writing, speaking, and listening
Sequencing of Instruction	
Read first, write later	Simultaneous use of all language forms—writing, reading, speaking, and listening
Nature of Curriculum	
Sequenced reading instruction and hierarchical array of reading skills	Variable language sources, language-based activities that include reading

much about the processes of reading and writing. They know that literacy's purposes are to get and convey meaning, that the print context often provides cues for meaning, and that reading and writing have many functional uses (Clay, 1991; Purcell-Gates, 1996; Sulzby, 1991). Also, as we saw earlier in this chapter, the kinds of metalinguistic knowledge so vital to reading—what literacy's uses are, phonemic awareness, analysis of syntactic structure, knowledge of story structure—continue to develop throughout the preschool and primary school years.

From the standpoint of emergent literacy, reading is not the only important language skill learned in school, but rather is one among a complementary array of critical language-based skills: reading, writing, speaking, and listening. Learning to read occurs best when the student is actively engaged in a variety of meaningful communication activities, such as purposeful writing assignments and group projects. Beginning literacy instruction needs to be planned and organized carefully so that important aspects of literacy are not overlooked, but we need to remember that literacy is a natural expansion of children's linguistic knowledge to the medium of print. The emergent literacy perspective reminds us also that the goal of "learning to read" should be broadened considerably. Learning to read is the foundation of literacy but is not all there is to it. Competent use of all forms of language for thinking and expression should be our goal, not simply functional literacy (Calfee, 1994).

Transition to Reading

As we have seen, the ability to read rests on many linguistic and cognitive skills, each necessary but not sufficient for learning to read. Young children display a wide array of reading and writing behaviors (e.g., looking at picture books and scribbling) that precede and develop into conventional literacy (Sulzby, 1991). From this standpoint, it seems inappropriate to label children as "readers" or "nonreaders" because literacy-related behaviors are developing on multiple dimensions. Nonetheless, it is useful to map the changes that young readers go through in the crucial period when they move from having little or no facility in decoding words to a point where they can do so easily. Making this transition is at the heart of learning to read and is one of its primary accomplishments.

Linnea Ehri (1991, 1994, 1998; Ehri & Wilce, 1985) has conducted a series of elegant research studies that has provided a window on how children's decoding skills develop as they first begin reading. Initially, children have little or no skill in decoding words. Then, her work has shown, children typically move into what she calls visual-cue reading, on to phonetic-cue reading, and finally to "expert" status, in which they use systematic phonemic decoding. We describe each of these levels in the following sections.

Prereaders

Our starting point is children who are unable to read any primer or preprimer words in isolation. They are in a *prealphabetic* phase (Ehri & Soffer, 1999), in which alphabetic knowledge is not used at all to read words. Given a list containing such words as *bat, hit, go,* and *is,* for instance, these children would be unable to read any of them. Many of them already know quite a bit about literacy, however, such as the fact that newspapers, coupons, and magazines tell people something (Purcell-Gates, 1996). They even may be able to "read" in the sense of identifying the names of products or businesses from signs. What these children are reading is more context than print, however. They cannot read any print materials removed from context and pay little attention to the graphic (letter) cues.

A good example of this phenomenon can be seen in a study by Masonheimer, Drum, and Ehri (1984). Masonheimer et al. located some 3- to 5-year-olds who could identify "environmental words" (e.g., *Pepsi* and *Wendy's*) in their familiar context (as part of a logo). Most of these children, however, could not read these same words when they appeared in contexts other than the original ones (simply as printed words). They also were unable to detect alterations in the graphic cues (e.g., *xepsi*). Children at this stage are primarily responding to their environment and not to the print (Mason, Herman, & Au, 1991). To become a "real" reader, skills other than those acquired from simple exposure to the environment are needed (Ehri, 1994; Stanovich, 2000).

Visual-Cue Reading

In Ehri's view, **visual-cue reading** is the first "real" reading. In this stage, also called the *partial alphabetic phase* (Ehri & Soffer, 1999), children begin to rely less on the context in which words are embedded and more on the characteristics of words themselves. The word features to which many children first pay attention seem to be visually distinctive ones. Examples of these cues are the "tail" at the end of the word *dog* and the "look" of a word. For children attempting to read with a visual-cue strategy, reading is a kind of paired-associate task (see chapter 3) of linking a word's look with its pronunciation and meaning (Ehri, 1994). Unfortunately, because words' distinctive visual features are exhausted quickly and because of the arbitrary nature of these associations, visual-cue readers are unable to read consistently over time. The memory demands of reading in this way soon become overwhelming. In Ehri's judgment, this associative strategy soon is abandoned by most readers in favor of one relying more on generalizations based on phonetic information.

Phonetic-Cue Reading

Ehri contends that a major step occurs when children begin to process letter–sound relations and to use phonetic cues. In **phonetic-cue reading** (also called *novice alphabetic reading*) words are read by forming and storing associations between some (but not all) of the letters in words' spellings and some of their sounds in pronunciation. For instance, a child may learn to read the word *fix* by associating the letter names *f* and *x* with the word's sounds or write the word *giraffe* as *jrf.* These associations, though incomplete, are not arbitrary and therefore are much easier to remember and more effective in reading than the visual cues of word and letter shape.

Systematic Phonemic Decoding

In Ehri's judgment, children have unlocked an important key to reading when they use phonemic information to distinguish among similarly spelled words and read them with reasonably high accuracy. They are using **systematic phonemic decoding.** They understand the alphabetic principle, where they have learned the alphabet, can identify the separate sounds in words, and understand that spellings more or less systematically correspond to pronunciations (Ehri, 1991, 1994, 1998). In an alphabetic language, such as English, this means they are mastering a cognitive mapping system linking the 40 or so English phonemes with letters and letter combinations. Of course, these children are not yet "expert readers" in the more general sense, but they do show considerable phonemic awareness and the ability to use it in decoding. As we have pointed out, however, reading is a complex, interactive process focused on comprehension, not just decoding. Decoding is important to learning to read but is not the only factor and not necessarily even the first thing that should be taught (Calfee & Patrick, 1995). Reading places demands on the full range of a child's linguistic and world knowledge, and reading instruction needs to draw on all of these dimensions.

Decoding and Beginning Reading

Virtually all authorities agree that decoding skills are vital to learning to read. Rapid and eventually automatic decoding underlies the ability to read effectively; context is useful but cannot substitute for the ability to identify words rapidly and accurately (Adams & Bruck, 1995; Perfetti, 1992; Stanovich, 2000). Agreement is less certain, however, about what to emphasize in beginning reading instruction-decoding or the more global dimensions of literacy. What should be the focus of beginning reading instruction? Following the lead of many reading experts (e.g., Adams, 1990; Calfee & Patrick, 1995; Hiebert & Raphael, 1998; Juel, 1996), we would argue that the answer to this question may be analogous to the advice for a healthy diet: varied and balanced fare combining the acquisition of decoding skills with contextual analyses in a meaningful reading activity (McIntyre & Pressley, 1996; Pressley, 2000).

Consider, for example, the passage in Figure 11-2. Take a moment to try to make sense of it. Although the parallel to beginning reading is not exact because of your superior knowledge as an adult, we believe that it is highly instructive. Think especially about the kinds of knowledge you use in reading it. If you are like most readers, reading a text like this forces you to draw on a variety of information. Letter- and word-level decoding obviously is important. Like beginning readers, you probably made a rough correspondence between many of the letters and sounds but not all of them. You also used your knowledge of syntax and your pragmatic knowledge that this passage probably has meaning. As soon as you were able to decode your first word or two, your knowledge about the world—in this case, your knowledge about real estate sales—could be brought into play.

Just as it was for you in this "bungalow" passage, beginning readers' word decoding is not just mapping symbols on phonemes and words, although this is very important. Reading is a meaning-making activity in which all kinds of knowledge are used. Sentence and passage meaning facilitate decoding, whereas decoding is the route to sentence

dɪlʌks bʌŋəloz̧. ɛksepš̌ʌnlǫ prɛstɪž lʌkšurǫ lokešʌn. ɪmidiʌt akypʌnciz̧ θri larǰ bɛdrumzz̧, lɔts ʌv specz̧, atǐčt gʌrɔǰ'. əplyʌnsʌz stez̧. hy θrietiz. kal čïd at ʌfɔrdəbl riʌltiz. 555-1234

Figure 11-2
A Short Passage from the Chronicle

and passage meaning. Thus, instructional methods stressing only a single approach to learning to read may handicap children who need multiple keys to unlock the meanings of words, sentences, and stories.

Skilled teachers draw on children's knowledge to help them read, interweaving information from the text and its illustrations and from a child's own memory to develop the ability to read. A demonstration from Norris (1988) shows this very well. It uses an illustrated text from Wagner (1971) that describes how Tony, a friendly lion that lives in a zoo, is approached by a bird needing some of his hair for a nest.

The teacher begins by pointing back and forth between a picture of Tony and the lion's name in print and says, "This is Tony." The teacher then explains what the author wants the child to know about Tony. For example, in pointing to the first sentence, which tells that Tony lived in a zoo, the teacher might say, "This tells you where Tony lived." If the child is able to use the context cues available in the picture and the teacher's facilitation, the sentence is very predictable without specific knowledge of any of the words. The teacher points to the words as the child provides the information. If the child is unable to make use of the context cues, more information can be provided to direct the child's attention to them. Each line of text is treated as an extension of the idea communicated in the first sentence so that the child views reading as a series of integrated thoughts rather than as a series of disconnected ideas or words. For instance:

> FACILITATOR: Now it tells you what kind of zoo animal Tony was.
> CHILD: Tony was a lion.
> FACILITATOR: Oh, a lion! A lion who lives in a zoo [pointing to relevant words in the text].

New or unpredictable words, such as friendly, are introduced by using them in context. Cohesive terms that tie segments of discourse together (e.g., the pronoun *he* referring to Tony) are introduced. Similarly, the child's attention can be drawn to specific features of words, such as suffixes, that modify their meanings. For example:

> CHILD: He was a friend lion.
> FACILITATOR: It's not telling you that Tony was a friend. It's telling you how he acted. He acted friendly [pointing to the word]. He was nice and did not bite or growl. Tell me about Tony.
> CHILD: He was a friend . . . a friendly lion!
> FACILITATOR: I'm glad he was friendly and not mean!

Similarly, children's misreadings are pointed out by repeating previous information and providing new cues.

> CHILD: He saw a friendly lion.
> FACILITATOR: No, I don't think he saw a friendly lion. This is telling you about Tony: He's the one who was friendly.
> CHILD: He was a friendly lion.

After the child has finished "reading" the ideas on the page and understood their meaning, the child can be asked to tell the story by using the words on the page—that is, by reading the words from the print. Context cues still can be provided as necessary, but the emphasis shifts strongly to using print to decode. For instance:

> FACILITATOR: Remember, this [pointing to the appropriate line in the text] tells you where Tony lived.
>
> CHILD: Tony lived in the . . . zoo.
>
> FACILITATOR: And this tells you what kind of animal Tony was.
>
> CHILD: Tony was a lion.
>
> FACILITATOR: And this tells you that he was nice.
>
> CHILD: Tony was a friendly lion.
>
> FACILITATOR: When we know it is Tony, this [pointing to the word he] is the other word we can use to talk about him.
>
> CHILD: He was a friendly lion.

Ideas in unpredictable and difficult sentences can be developed within the sentence one at a time, in a logical order.

> FACILITATOR: The bird needs to build something to keep her eggs in. I wonder what that is.
>
> CHILD: A nest?
>
> FACILITATOR: Oh, a nest [pointing to those words in the sentence]. And she needs something from Tony [pointing to his hair in the picture] that she can use to build her nest.
>
> CHILD: Hair?
>
> FACILITATOR: Oh, I see, hair . . . [rising intonation, pointing to a nest].
>
> CHILD: Hair for a nest!
>
> FACILITATOR: Right! But she doesn't tell him that she wants all of it, just . . . [pointing to the word some].
>
> CHILD: Some of it.
>
> FACILITATOR: So tell me [pointing to the sentence within quotes] what the bird said she needed.
>
> CHILD: She needs some hair for a nest.
>
> FACILITATOR: Right, but it is the bird who is talking, so she doesn't say, "She needs some," she says. . . .
>
> CHILD: I need some hair for a nest. (Norris, 1988, p. 671)

The principal skills this teacher demonstrates are drawing out the child's considerable knowledge about language while maintaining a clear focus on meaning. Although some information is provided for the child, the teacher mainly *focuses the child's attention on the text and elicits text-relevant information from the child*. In the preceding example, that information is as diverse as knowledge about zoos and zoo animals and information about how language is used. Included in the latter are the child's experience with sequencing of ideas, cohesiveness of text, and communication purposes, plus specific aspects of sentence structure and vocabulary use. At the same time, the child is not allowed simply to continue to use the context. From the outset, attention is directed to the words and the need to decode their specific features (e.g., *friend/friendly, was/saw,* and *a/the*).

Reading instruction reflects a balance between meaning and decoding. Each aspect is used to create a source of information for the other. Reading is not just a "guessing game" in which text features can be ignored, nor should it involve abstract, out-of-context drill and practice activities in which children cannot use their prior knowledge or connect the activities to actual reading tasks. The strategy is to help the children construct the meaning expressed in print and see how letters and words represent meaning. The goal of increasingly rapid and automatic decoding—translating the printed word into speech and meaning—is embedded in a meaningful context. When we help children draw on all of their available cognitive and linguistic resources, their decoding, sentence analysis, and text comprehension abilities will develop simultaneously.

Methods of Teaching Reading

In the example above, a skillful literacy teacher draws on several categories of children's knowledge in teaching reading. In the same way, teachers' overall objectives need to be broadly based, focusing on all the important dimensions of reading. Calfee and Henry (1986), for instance, have identified mastery of four general dimensions as vital to successful reading. As you can see, these dimensions correspond closely to the categories of language structure—words, syntax, and discourse—that were discussed earlier.

Decoding. Printed words must be translated into their pronounceable equivalents.

Vocabulary. Meaning must be assigned to words and a network of associations activated.

Sentence and paragraph comprehension. Text units need to be "fit" to their functional roles (e.g., as the subject or predicate of a sentence or as topic sentences).

Text comprehension. Complete texts need to be understood as entities—as "stories" (narratives), as information (expository) texts, or as dialogues, for instance.

A sensible curriculum for teaching children to read must address each of these dimensions, as well as help them see the uses and benefits of literacy. The history of reading instruction, unfortunately, often has not been one of balanced attention to all factors important to literacy development. Instead, proponents of one approach or another often have advocated, sometimes with near-religious zeal, methods such as "systematic phonics" or "patterning." Others have favored their interpretations of "meaning-based," "literature-based," or "whole language" approaches with equal fervor. Over the years, numerous controversies have raged about how best to teach children to read.

A landmark event in the debate about beginning reading instruction was Jeanne Chall's 1967 book *Learning to Read: The Great Debate.* As part of a comprehensive analysis, she divided reading methods into two broad categories: **code-emphasis methods** and **meaning-emphasis methods.** The former referred to approaches that initially emphasized decoding, learning the correspondence between letters and sounds. Prominent among code-emphasis methods was **phonics,** which stressed acquisition of basic letter/sound relationships and the rules for sounding out words.

Contrasted with these code-emphasis methods were meaning-emphasis approaches, which Chall judged to favor meaning over decoding in beginning reading. Included in the meaning-emphasis category were the **sight word methods** (sometimes called "*look-say*"), which stressed the need for children to acquire at least a limited stock of familiar words they could recognize on sight. Another meaning-emphasis approach was **language experience,** a general method in which children's oral language, such as their narratives about their experiences and observations, is dictated and written down; what is written then becomes the basis for reading. Thus, skills are taught in the context of the child's own direct experience with language and the world.

Chall's analysis showed that code-emphasis approaches to beginning reading instruction generally produced superior achievement as measured by standardized tests. Many others (e.g., Goodman, 1989, 1996; Goodman & Goodman, 1979; F. Smith, 1982; Weaver, 1994), however, have disagreed with her and have continued to advocate meaning-based instruction for beginning readers. Most current models of reading (e.g., Adams, 1994; Kintsch, 1988, 1998; Stanovich, 2000) and authorities on reading instruction (e.g., Adams, 1990; Calfee, 1994; Clay, 1991; Pressley, 2000) stake out a middle ground between code and meaning emphases, arguing that both are essential in learning to read. They suggest that reading is not best construed as "either–or," that is, neither as an exclusively bottom-up, data-driven process nor as a top-down process dominated by higher level cognitive and language activity.

Despite the seeming reasonableness of a balanced approach, beginning literacy instruction has been and continues to be an area of conflict between those strongly emphasizing either code- or meaning-emphasis approaches (see, for example, discussion in Pressley, 2002). In an era that conceptualized learning to read as acquiring a hierarchy of reading skills, meaning-based approaches languished in the 1970s. In some instances, beginning reading instruction followed a pattern dominated by seatwork and skill-development worksheets prescribed by the basal readers. Also, to simplify basal reading materials, the strategies of restricting vocabulary choices and employing readability formulas (which provide a quantitative estimate of text difficulty typically derived from sentence length and word frequency) were often used. Unfortunately, these attempts to control a text's predictability and readability often ignored other critical aspects of text that make it comprehensible and interesting. For instance, a good story line, coherence, conflict, and surprise all contribute to comprehension and interest but are not captured by readability measures (Brennan, Bridge, & Winograd, 1986). The result of modifying text by using readability measures was often text that, though theoretically carefully matched with the student's grade level, was disjointed, poorly formed, and not very readable.

By the early 1980s, analyses of classroom instruction and the contents of basal reading materials began to reveal the extent to which reading comprehension and the literary value of reading materials were being neglected (e.g., see Durkin, 1978–1979, 1981). Also, the development of more clearly articulated theories of comprehension from cognitive psychology (e.g., R. C. Anderson & P. D. Pearson, 1984) provided curriculum developers and writers with a theoretical basis for emphasizing comprehension. Again, however, what began as a sensible antidote to decontextualized skill-based instruction was misinterpreted by some as a call to abandon virtually all teaching of strategies and skills, including instruction in decoding. A few individuals purporting to represent whole-language approaches to literacy seemed to be proposing that children would learn to read simply through exposure to good literature, much like they earlier learned to speak in the language-rich environment of home and community (for interesting discussions of these issues, see Pressley, 1994; Weaver, 1994).

Although some still prefer to push toward extremes and "reading wars" sometimes seem more prevalent than reasoned discussion, there seems to be a more widespread understanding of the need for balance in beginning reading instruction. A greatly expanded pool of excellent children's literature now is available, both in trade books and in basal reading series themselves. Widely used **basal reading series**—the packages of materials for literacy instruction that include coordinated texts, teachers' manuals, and student activities—emphasize comprehension, analysis, and extension as well as decoding. Consistent with the strong scientific evidence of the role that automatic word recognition processes play in skilled reading (see, for example, Stanovich, 2000), primary teachers recognized for their excellence make teaching decoding a fundamental part of their literacy instruction (Pressley, Allington, Wharton-McDonald, Block, & Morrow, 2001; Pressley, Rankin, & Yokoi, 1996). Other positive developments are review processes that have broadened the range of racial and cultural backgrounds represented in the trade book and basal literature and eliminated most sexist portrayals of characters. To us, these changes generally represent the desired "balanced diet" of meaningful reading instruction and the development of a more coherent view of literacy as an interactive, multifaceted process.

Summary of Beginning Literacy Instruction

Beginning literacy instruction is a highly variable and often emotion-laden enterprise representing many viewpoints on how best to teach reading. Some methods strongly emphasize decoding; others place greater stress on text meaning and using general and linguistic knowledge. In most schools, however, literacy instruction reflects an eclectic perspective represented by basal reading series. In the past, basal reading series were appropriately criticized for providing a less-than-coherent view of reading; poorly structured, uninteresting, and stereotypical reading materials; and boring worksheet-based practice activities that meant little to children. Most basal readers now have moved toward improved literary quality, greater emphasis on comprehension, and systematic skill development in a literate context of writing, speaking, and listening.

Implications for Beginning Reading Instruction

For most children, a skilled teacher's assistance is essential in learning to read. Becoming literate depends on children's ability to link written symbols with their spoken language and draws heavily on their linguistic and world knowledge. In alphabetic languages such as English, children must learn a system that maps *graphemes* (letters and combinations of letters) to *phonemes* (the sounds of the language). As we have seen, however, reading depends on decoding words but is much more than decoding; linguistic and cognitive processes ranging from basic perception of letter shapes to the highest levels of thinking and problem solving are involved. Thus, beginning literacy instruction cannot be a simpleminded, drill and practice activity. Success requires teachers to orchestrate the many components of literacy into a meaningful whole. The scaffolding techniques discussed in chapters 4 and 9 are particularly useful, with teachers helping students use their linguistic knowledge to meet the challenges of literacy. Without a skilled teacher's help, many will not succeed. Following are themes that we believe are vital to helping students make the successful transition to literacy.

1. *Approach reading as a meaningful activity.* Reading is a meaning-making act. This fact may be lost in some kinds of literacy instruction. Although acquiring decoding skills is essential to learning to read, decoding needs to be connected to reading's purpose—meaning making. When learning to read is defined as skill development, children can lose track of the overall purposes of literacy and come to perceive literacy instruction as a kind of training. We need to remind ourselves of the basic reasons for literacy—learning, communicating, and enjoyment—and demonstrate them for our students.

2. *Take a broad perspective on literacy.* We believe that "critical literacy" (Calfee, 1994), which refers to the ability to read, write, listen, and speak effectively, is a better goal for literacy instruction than "learning to read." Critical literacy is achieved by having children use their developing language skills in meaningful tasks and by helping develop students' overall linguistic and cognitive competence. Although learning to read is an essential goal for the primary grades, the broader purpose is to help students use language in all its forms to think, reason, and communicate effectively.

3. *Help beginning readers move toward automatic decoding.* One of the themes of this text is the importance of automatic cognitive processes in complex cognitive skills. Skilled reading is no exception in depending on a set of automatic cognitive processes—rapid, fluent word decoding. Although beginning readers can and should use context to help them decode words, they need to develop highly automatic word recognition to become skilled readers.

Good readers eventually rely little on context for their decoding, although they can use it very effectively if they need to (Adams & Bruck, 1995; Perfetti, 1992). In contrast, poor readers typically have difficulty in automatic word decoding (Stanovich, 2000). Early, explicit decoding instruction is essential, but it does not follow that children therefore should be drilled endlessly on decoding exercises, word analysis, phonics rules, and the like. Students can move toward more rapid, automatic decoding in a number of ways, not the least of which is through guided meaningful reading, in which the teacher directs students' attention to relevant graphic and phonemic characteristics of words. Rereading passages to improve fluency and attain automaticity also may be very helpful (Samuels, 1994).

4. *Draw on children's domain and general knowledge.* Knowledge underlies virtually all effective cognitive functioning (see chapters 8 and 9). The cognitive processes of reading are no exception. Unless reading connects to children's experiences, it can become a meaningless exercise in word calling. All children have knowledge about their worlds that teachers can use in beginning reading instruction. Evoking their frames of reference allows them to understand what they are reading and better regulate their own learning.

5. *Encourage children to develop their metalinguistic knowledge.* A central idea of this chapter, echoing the self-regulation theme of this book, is that becoming literate depends heavily on children learning about language—their metalinguistic awareness. Virtually all children have the basic linguistic capabilities they need to become readers, but most need to develop the metalinguistic abilities that will enable them to understand the role letters, words, sounds, and text structure play in literacy. Children coming from language traditions other than English face special challenges in American schools. No matter what level of language skill the children bring, however, a teacher can build students' metalinguistic awareness by building on their current capabilities with language and drawing their attention to its many dimensions. Becoming an independent, self-regulated reader and moving to more advanced levels of literacy both depend on increasing metalinguistic awareness.

6. *Expect children to vary widely in their progress toward fluent reading.* Most children move into literacy relatively uneventfully, but some will struggle with learning to read. In any given group of readers, as many as 10 to 15 percent will fall one or two years behind their peer group in reading level by third or fourth grade. From 3 to 5 percent will have more serious problems and will lag two or more grade levels behind their peers.

A Comment on Reading Difficulties

The origins of reading difficulties vary and are a matter of debate. Some students simply are not developmentally ready for reading instruction in the first grade and find it difficult to grasp the abstract linguistic tasks of learning to read. Others come from cultural or language backgrounds that poorly match their experiences in reading instruction. All of these groups of children likely would have performed well if reading instruction had been improved or delayed; a significant challenge is avoiding these kinds of problems in the first place and, for those who have not yet succeeded, undoing the false concept of themselves as "poor readers."

A few students will have considerable difficulty in learning to read even with excellent instruction. Some of these students have low general ability; their difficulty is less with reading than with the cognitive demands of comprehension. Others, however, will have normal or above-normal intelligence but have a specific handicap or learning disability in the area of reading. These children differ from children who are simply poor readers. Many have notable speech and language deficits, often coupled with difficulty in spelling and writing. In fact, the root problem for many disabled readers may well be one of language. A genetic basis seems probable for some reading disabilities (Berninger, 1994; Rayner & Pollatsek, 1989): They tend to occur more among males than females and among left-handers than right-handers and to run in families.

Poor reading skills, of course, make school achievement difficult. Yet, many children with severe reading disabilities do go on to high levels of accomplishment, both by using their own knowledge and strategies to compensate for lack of reading skill and by drawing on the talents of teachers specially trained in methods designed to help disabled readers learn to read. As teachers, we need to recognize the difficulties that disabled readers face and to help them obtain the specialized assistance they need.

Reading Recovery: One Approach to Reading Difficulties

Reading Recovery, an intervention for first-grade children in the lowest 10 to 20 percent of their classes, was started in New Zealand in the 1970s by Marie Clay, who also gave us the term *emergent literacy.* Brought to the United States in the mid-1980s, it has become increasingly popular across the country as an intervention for first-grade children experiencing significant problems in learning to read. Reading Recovery is designed around a comprehensive model of literacy development that includes the following:

1. A diagnostic process in which children are assessed on a variety of literacy tasks, such as their ability to identify letters, read words, write, and do oral reading, as well as on their literacy knowledge and strategies.
2. A series of daily tutorials, 30 minutes in length, in which a Reading Recovery teacher works one-on-one with an individual student.
3. "Standardized" sessions that provide a systematic set of activities, including having the child practice letters and words, read from short books, and produce short compositions that are cut up and reread.
4. A systematic process of staff development in which teachers are trained by Reading Recovery trainers.

The goal of the tutoring is to have the child make faster than average progress (Lyons, Pinnell, & DeFord, 1993) in order to reach the school average for reading ability, whereupon the tutoring program is discontinued. For a typical student, Reading Recovery sessions will span some 12 to 16 weeks and include up to 60 half-hour sessions.

Reading Recovery embodies characteristics of successful beginning reading instruction, including phonemic awareness, systematic observation and teaching, high expectations for achievement, student goal setting and regular review of goals, repeated readings of text, and experimentation with language through writing (Hiebert & Raphael, 1996). Although not explicitly developed from Vygotsky's theory (see chapter 9), the emphasis is on teacher–student collaboration and on teacher scaffolding, with teachers giving hints and otherwise helping students develop a system or organized strategies that improve their reading. It also affords students considerable instructional time and teachers many opportunities to directly assess students' literacy skills. Less clear, however, is whether Reading Recovery is the best and most cost-effective approach for children who have difficulties learning to read. Although Reading Recovery almost certainly produces some positive results and proponents firmly back Reading Recovery's approach, data are not entirely clear on whether it produces its desired outcomes and whether gains are maintained over time (Hiebert, 1994; Snow, Burns, & Griffin, 1998). One important practical concern is cost. With each Reading Recovery teacher serving 16 or fewer students in a school year and with an intensive training period for each teacher, the per-pupil costs are very high (Hiebert, 1994; Juel, 1996). Reading Recovery proponents counter that the program, though admittedly costly in the short term, is less expensive in the long run than special education or other remedial programs. In general, it would seem that, although Reading Recovery is a promising instructional approach based on a solid conception of literacy, more research is needed to fully evaluate its short- and long-term effectiveness and to determine whether other, lower cost interventions might prove equally effective.

Summary

Learning to read is a significant linguistic and cognitive achievement that most children accomplish early in their primary school years. Superficially viewed, reading seems to be simply word-by-word decoding, but it is in fact a multifaceted process orchestrating all aspects of language and cognition. Beginning readers' success hinges on metalinguistic abilities and on knowledge activation, memory, and attention. Metalinguistic awareness makes it possible for children to map the visual symbols of written language onto oral language and to create meaning. World knowledge underlies comprehension, as readers use their working and long-term memory to process information sequentially, hold it in memory, and relate it to existing knowledge and language structures. Managing attention also is essential; readers must focus strategically on key features of letters, words, sentences, and texts in order to read effectively.

Learning to read was once seen as depending on reading readiness. A more current view, emergent literacy, is that reading develops out of children's early language experiences. Well before they begin to read, most children already know something about reading's purposes and conventions. They often can "read" environmental cues, such as signs and logos. True reading, however, requires attention to word and text features. In their earliest attempts to read, children often rely on visual cues in text, such as word shapes. Children who know the alphabet and are aware of language sounds, however, can use partial phonetic cues supplied by letter names. Expert decoders can use the entire range of phonemic cues supplied by letters and letter combinations.

Decoding is necessary but not sufficient for learning to read. Literacy also depends on understanding the pragmatic uses of literacy and on knowing vocabulary, syntax, and text structures. Beginning literacy instruction generally includes each of these areas, but different instructional methods vary in their emphasis. Some emphasize bottom-up processing, counting on fluent word decoding to lead to meaning. Others stress meaning, with the expectation that comprehension and context will assist in decoding. Because reading is an interactive process involving simultaneous processing at multiple levels of language and cognition, it is unlikely that any narrow approach will be effective. Each of reading's dimensions contributes to reading success. Successful reading instruction needs to emphasize reading as a meaningful process, no matter what feature of reading is being developed.

Suggested Readings

Adams, M. J. (1990). *Learning to read: Thinking and learning about print.* Cambridge, MA: MIT Press.

Marilyn Adams brings together a large body of research on reading and learning to read in this now-classic volume, arguing that effective instruction must combine an emphasis on meaning with an emphasis on developing decoding skills.

Pressley, M. (2002). *Reading instruction that works: The case for balanced teaching* (2nd ed.). New York: Guilford Press.

As the title implies, Michael Pressley makes the case in this volume for a balanced approach to teaching reading that includes not only components of both whole-language and skills instruction, but also motivation.

Stanovich, K. E. (2000). *Progress in understanding reading: Scientific foundations and new frontiers.* New York: Guilford Press.

Written by a leading reading researcher, this volume summarizes his fine work and the progress of research on reading and reading disabilities over the past quarter-century.

Reading to Learn

A T ABOUT THE THIRD GRADE, when most students have acquired basic literacy skills, the emphasis in many classrooms shifts from learning to read to "reading to learn." Elementary school students may read about pioneer life, for example, about the moon, or about animals and their homes. As they move toward middle school and high school, the emphasis on reading as a primary avenue to learning becomes more pronounced. Eighth graders may be expected to learn basic principles of ecology from a general science textbook; 12th graders routinely are assigned readings in texts or anthologies in preparations for discussions. Many college teachers rely heavily on reading assignments in textbooks as part of their instructional approach. You may, in fact, be reading this chapter as part of an assignment. The assumption, of course, is that at least part of what is important for you to learn can be acquired by reading this text.

Although reading to learn is generally regarded as very important, recent assessments [e.g., National Center for Educational Statistics (NCES), 1999, 2001] show that many elementary, middle, and high school students have difficulty in reading to gain information. In the 1998 administration of the National Assessment of Educational Progress (NAEP) to 4th, 8th, and 12th graders, on a scale that included Basic, Proficient, and Advanced levels, only 31 percent of 4th graders, 33 percent of 8th graders, and 40 percent of 12th graders scored at or above the Proficient level. Less than 10 percent scored at the Advanced level. In 2000, when the NAEP was administered only to 4th graders, 32 percent of the 4th graders scored at or above the Proficient level. Given the importance of reading to learn for many school and vocational goals, this relatively low reading performance continues to concern many authorities.

Educational psychologists always have been intensely interested in learning from reading, and their research on this topic has generated a massive literature (e.g., see Hiebert & Raphael, 1996). Early research tended to focus on acquiring information; more recent work (e.g., see Alexander & Jetton, 2000; Block & Pressley, 2002; Trabasso & Bouchard, 2000) has emphasized reading comprehension, factors affecting it, and strategies for improving it. In this chapter, we examine several dimensions of "getting meaning" from texts. To provide an overall context for our discussion, we begin by describing three types of reading comprehension models. Then we explore several aspects of text comprehension. First, we focus on a basic but important outcome of reading—learning new vocabulary. We examine factors that influence vocabulary acquisition during reading and their implications. Second, we shift to a more general outlook emphasizing how organized knowledge is acquired. Here, we take a schema theory perspective on comprehension processes and illustrate how readers construct and remember representations of text material. We also discuss the effect of readers' world knowledge and reading strategies on comprehension. Third, in the last section of the chapter, we outline an elaborative processing model that suggests how readers give their attention to important aspects of text materials. Using this model, we describe a series of aids to reading comprehension.

Models of Reading Comprehension

Reading comprehension models can be clustered into three general groups: data-driven, conceptually driven, and interactive (Rayner & Pollatsek, 1989). **Data-driven processing** (also called *bottom-up processing*) refers to processing guided primarily by external stimuli; data flow quickly and mostly automatically through the information processing system. **Conceptually driven** (or *top-down*) **processing,** in contrast, refers to processing guided heavily by conceptual frameworks stored in memory. **Interactive processing** refers to processing guided by an interaction between automated processes generated by the data a text provides, on the one hand, and by the reader's knowledge and strategies, on the other.

In the following sections we first examine models by Philip Gough and Kenneth Goodman that are early examples of data-driven and conceptually driven models of reading, respectively. Most current models (e.g., Goldman & Rakestraw, 2000; Goldman, Varma, & Cote, 1996; Just & Carpenter, 1987, 1992; Kintsch, 1988, 1998) are interactive, incorporating both data-driven and conceptually driven processes. The Gough and Goodman models are instructive, however, because they highlight different processes critical to comprehension. Our descriptions of them also will aid you in understanding features of current interactive models. We turn first to Gough as an example of a data-driven model of reading.

Gough's Data-Driven Model

Data-driven models of reading emphasize decoding and word meanings (Andre, 1987b; Rumelhart & McClelland, 1981). In portraying the comprehension of a passage, for instance, such models identify a starting point, such as word identification. Higher order structures, such as sentences, then are built up word by word as the reader moves through the text (Rayner & Pollatsek, 1989). In this perspective, information flows from words (or even letters) to syntactic structures to discourse and semantic structures.

One early but particularly well-developed data-driven model was formulated by Gough (1972). To understand Gough's model, it is necessary to review some issues from basic research on reading. Many researchers, Gough among them, have used eye-tracking equipment to follow the movements of readers' eyes as they move across a page of printed text. Typically, readers' eye movements consist of a series of stops and starts. The eyes focus briefly on one point of text (called a **fixation**) and then move rapidly to another point. The movement is referred to as a **saccade.** Vision is limited, during fixations, to a visual span of only a few letters (McConkie, 1997; Rayner, 1997).

Gough used the results of eye-tracking research as a starting point for his model. According to his model, readers proceed through a sentence "letter by letter, word by word" (p. 354). Reading processes begin with an eye fixation at the first segment of text, followed by a saccade, a second fixation, and so on through the text. Gough posited that each fixation places about 15–20 letters into iconic memory. Once that information is in the iconic store (in raw, unprocessed form), pattern-matching processes begin, moving one letter at a time from left to right. Gough estimated that it would take about 10–20 milliseconds for the identification of each letter. Gough further assumed that the information would last about 0.25 seconds in the iconic store and that readers could perform about 3 fixations per second. On the basis of these assumptions (which were based on data about readers' eye movements), Gough estimated that reading rates of about 300 words per minute were possible.

Gough envisioned that once pattern-matching processes on each letter were complete, a mapping response occurs as representations of letters' sounds are recalled and blended together to form the representation of the sound of the word. When the representation of a word's sound is complete, the word meaning is retrieved from memory and the process repeats with the next word. The decoded words are held in short-term memory, and the meaning of sentences is determined there. If a clear understanding has been gained, the gist of the meaning passes on to long-term memory.

Although no data-driven models of reading totally exclude the role of long-term memory or presume meaning to be determined completely by stimulus input, Gough's model is one of the clearest examples of a data-driven approach. It portrays each letter of each word as being processed in serial fashion; meaning is assigned automatically on the basis of stored meanings in memory. Gough himself, however, saw some serious shortcomings with such strict data-driven models (see Andre, 1987b, for a detailed analysis of data-driven models). Among them are the fact that information does not necessarily come from the iconic store serially (i.e., reading off the iconic store from left to right), that strict translations of letters into their sound representations would not allow readers to comprehend homonyms (or words in which spelling–sound correspondences are irregular, such as *through, enough,* and *cough*), and that the context of words in sentences often determines their meaning (e.g., Bob admitted to the judge that he *stole* the fur *stole*).

Goodman's Conceptually Driven Model

In contrast to data-driven models, **conceptually driven models of reading** comprehension emphasize the guiding role of knowledge. Instead of describing reading as a sequential, letter-by-letter, word-by-word analysis of text to gain meaning, conceptually driven models are based on the premise that readers' expectations about a text and their prior knowledge determine the comprehension process. In this view, readers use their knowledge and the printed symbols on a page to construct meaning.

Perhaps the best known model emphasizing conceptually driven processing is Kenneth Goodman's. Unlike Gough's model, which was based on analyses of eye movements during reading, Goodman's model grew out of his observations of children's oral reading errors. In Goodman's research (see Goodman, 1982b, 1982c) children were asked to read stories aloud that were somewhat difficult for them. Goodman's analysis of the kinds of mistakes children made indicated to him that they constantly were predicting the contents of upcoming text. Further, Goodman believed that readers used the text as a means of confirming or disconfirming their predictions about what the text was going to say, describing reading as a "psychological guessing game."

Unlike Gough's model of reading, Goodman's does not require a sequence of invariant steps. Instead, Goodman's model posits four cycles of processing occurring simultaneously and interactively: *visual* (picking up the visual input), *perceptual* (identifying letters and words), *syntactic* (identifying the structure of the text), and *semantic* (constructing meaning for the input) (Goodman, 1994). Once a reader starts reading, an initial meaning is constructed for the text. This meaning then is a prediction against which future input is judged. If the reader's prediction is confirmed, reading continues and the constructed meaning is enriched with new information. If the reader's prediction is incorrect, however, the reader will slow down, reread, or seek additional information to construct a more accurate meaning.

Goodman's model suggests that errors, or *miscues,* as he prefers to call them, should be fairly common. They are not necessarily the result of poor reading, but instead stem from the same processes as good reading. In fact, the strongest support for Goodman's idea that constructed meanings govern reading comes from his research on reading errors (Goodman, 1982a; Goodman & Goodman, 1982). When the children Goodman observed made errors in oral reading, they spontaneously corrected errors that interfered with meaning—typically by rereading and correcting themselves. When children made errors that did not affect meaning, however, these errors seldom were noticed or corrected (e.g., reading *headlights* for *headlamps*). Generally, if words that children called out fit the meaning they had constructed for the story, they seldom saw them as errors, regardless of whether they were read correctly.

The strength of Goodman's model lies in its highlighting conceptually driven processes, and its base in the analysis of children's reading errors makes it appealing. Andre (1987b) has contended, however, that the model overemphasizes conceptually driven processes; he also notes that Goodman's model has not been particularly helpful in guiding reading research or applications. The model does remind us of the importance of readers' knowledge, however, and the necessity of their understanding what they read.

Kintsch's Construction-Integration Model

A purely data-driven model of reading comprehension, on the one hand, has problems accounting for the effects of readers' knowledge and the influence of context.

Conceptually driven models, on the other hand, focus on the role of knowledge but tend to be vague and to overlook the importance of data-driven processes such as phonemic knowledge and word decoding in reading comprehension. Because of these apparent limitations of data-driven and conceptually driven models, several interactive models were proposed beginning in the 1970s (e.g., Adams & Collins, 1977; Kintsch & Van Dijk, 1978; Rumelhart & McClelland, 1981). In interactive models of reading, both data-driven and conceptually driven processes are present. Reading comprehension is a product of their interaction. One interactive model that has been especially influential in guiding researchers' thinking about how readers process text information was proposed originally by Kintsch and Van Dijk (1978; Kintsch, 1986). In its current form, the model is referred to as the **Construction-Integration (CI) Model** (Kintsch, 1988, 1998).

The CI model is a simulation that models how text is represented and integrated with readers' knowledge. It focuses on discourse processing (the comprehension of main ideas or themes included in a text) and on how meaning is constructed as readers move through texts. In the CI model, the basic meaning of sentences is represented by propositions (see discussion of "Building Blocks of Cognition" in chapter 3) and the meanings of texts as hierarchical semantic networks of propositions. As you recall, a single sentence can contain several simple propositions. In early versions of the model (e.g., Kintsch & Van Dijk, 1978), these simple propositions were used as input to the model. The CI version uses complex propositions as its input; each consists of several simple propositions related to a core meaning. Complex propositions include such features as category (whether the proposition represents an action, event, or state), modifiers, and circumstance (time and place).

One key distinction in the CI model is between a text's microstructure and its macrostructure (Kintsch, 1998). The **microstructure** of a text consists of the propositions generated from the sentence-by-sentence information in the text, plus some information from readers' long-term memories. The microstructure consists of all of the propositions in a text, linked to each other to the extent that they share common elements, or nodes. In Kintsch's conception, readers automatically link propositions that are embedded in one another or share common elements. Through short cycles of processing words, phrases, and sentences, a microstructure is built up from the basic propositions of the text. Repetition of vocabulary, inferences, and limitations on working memory all play important roles in determining the microstructure that a reader constructs.

At the same time readers are building a microstructure, they also are creating a **macrostructure** corresponding to the gist, or overall meaning, of the text. Whereas the microstructure consists simply of the propositions in text, the macrostructure is hierarchical and represents a text's global structure. The macrostructure can be signaled by the text (e.g., by headings or sections), but often it needs to be inferred by the reader (Kintsch, 1998). The macrostructure thus combines the knowledge and inferences of the individual with the text's microstructure. In essence, macrostructure elements are main ideas, propositions abstracted from the microstructure.

Out of this process, readers form two distinctive types of representations. The first, called the **textbase,** is the text ". . . as the author of the text intended it" (Kintsch,

1998, p. 50). Textbase representations generally are relatively faithful to the presented passage, consisting of propositions derived from the input sentences plus a small set of basic inferences (Goldman et al., 1996). The more complete representation of how readers understand texts, however, is the **situation model,** which is composed *both* of text-derived propositions (the textbase) and propositions contributed from long-term memory. The situation model integrates readers' prior knowledge with text information. Situation models are not simply what the text *states,* but reflect both the information in the text and what readers know. Understanding a text, therefore, almost never consists of a pure textbase; instead, it is the personal interpretation of readers combining information in the text with information from their long-term memory (Kintsch, 1998).

Early versions of Kintsch's model (e.g., Kintsch & Van Dijk, 1978) included strong assumptions about top-down, schema-driven processes for forming situation models. As the model has evolved (e.g., Kintsch, 1988, 1998), however, greater emphasis has been given to automatic processes. The current CI model, while still interactive, represents a more data-driven view of comprehension than previously, highlighting automatized processes of constructing and integrating information within a connectionist framework (see chapter 3). Sequential cycles of processing first generate networks of propositions and their associations that then are, in effect, shaped through an integration process that settles on the meaning.

As represented by the CI model, the process of comprehension consists of two stages, a construction phase and an integration phase. In the **construction phase,** readers' propositions and concepts automatically activate a network of associations and simple inferences. Elements in the network (e.g., words and propositions) are connected at varying levels of strength. Assume, for example that readers encounter the sentence we mentioned earlier, "The pilot put the plane into a steep bank" in a passage about near-misses in commercial aviation. A number of relevant associations will be generated (e.g., *flying, turn, danger,* and *wings*) but so will a number of associations to *bank* that are valid, but off-target for the passage's meaning (e.g., *money, tellers,* and *vault*). In this construction phase, however, all associations—relevant and irrelevant—simply are created by automatic, context-free associative processes. The result is a connection net consisting of elements having varying *association strengths* with one another.

In the **integration phase** a kind of pruning occurs as for associations that do not fit the text's overall discourse structure. As the reader encounters new phrases and sentences and the propositional network is activated and reactivated, it begins to stabilize. Propositional nodes related to the meaning of what is being read (e.g., *flying, turn, danger,* and *wings*) continue to be activated and become stronger, whereas others unrelated to the meaning of the passage (e.g., *money* and *tellers*) are not activated and drop out. In the end, therefore, what a text means to a reader is represented by a network of highly activated nodes that have been formed through multiple cycles.

The CI model and its earlier versions have generated many predictions and much empirical research (e.g., see Britton & Graesser, 1996). The Kintsch models predict, for example, that propositionally complex texts will take longer to read than texts with fewer propositions, even with length held constant. They do. Another prediction of such models, based on assumptions about propositions and their importance, is that memory for higher level propositions in microstructure and for gist will be better than memory for lower level information. These predictions also have been supported. Some recent work with the CI model has focused on the match of learners with texts, based on the assumption that there is a "zone of learnability" (see Kintsch, 1998) when the text is at the right level of difficulty. Too-difficult texts do not provide the necessary overlap between the text information and student knowledge to provide necessary activation; too-easy texts fail to stimulate learning because they don't activate anything new.

Overall, the CI model and related models of reading give researchers important theoretical tools for advancing understanding of how comprehension occurs. The features of the CI model, for instance, in which overall text representation (its meaning) results from multiple memory traces for successive sentences being connected with the prior knowledge structures of the individual, plausibly describe a process in which meaning is built up out of the basic structure of the text, the structure of what a person knows, and inferences connecting the two.

Common Assumptions of Current Reading Models

Kintsch's CI model is arguably the most influential of the current models of reading, but by no means is the only one. Among many others are those of Britton (e.g., Turner, Britton, Andraessen, & McCutchen, 1996), Goldman (e.g., Goldman & Varma, 1995; Goldman, Varma, & Cote, 1996), Gernsbacher (1996), Just and Carpenter (1987, 1992), van den Broek (e.g., van den Broek, Risden, Fletcher, & Thurlow, 1996), and Zwaan (1996). Most of these share a number of common features in the ways that they represent the process of reading comprehension. The following list is derived from Graesser and Britton (1996), Goldman et al. (1996), and others:

1. *Comprehension involves processing at multiple levels.* In order to comprehend text, readers need to interact with word meanings, syntax, and discourse structures, to name only a few dimensions of language (see chapter 11). When they read, readers generate associations to words; convert sentences into propositions; link those propositions to information already in their long-term memory; and, if they understand the big picture, get a sense of the overall structure of a text.

2. *Comprehension involves the management of working memory.* One of the assumptions of the CI model is that active processing focuses on the current sentence, plus relevant information from memory. Kintsch (1998) describes the role of working memory in text comprehension as being like a spotlight moving across a text, sentence by sentence, with a mental representation being constructed and integrated in the process. In short, comprehension has to be accomplished within the constraints of a limited capacity working memory (Goldman et al., 1996). Just and Carpenter (1992) have shown, for instance, that if the demands on working memory during reading exceed its limitations, comprehension performance will deteriorate, sometimes dramatically.

3. *Comprehension involves inference generation.* As Goldman and Rakestraw (2000) point out, understanding involves more than interpreting what is explicitly stated in a text. To comprehend, readers must access relevant world knowledge and generate interferences that make a text coherent. Some inferences are generated quickly—for instance, those that address readers' goals ("I don't really need to know this!") and those explaining why actions and events occur in stories ("He wouldn't have acted that way unless he was embarrassed or hurt!"). Other inferences are less automatic, such as inferences about what information is relevant and what isn't relevant in a math word problem.

4. *Comprehension requires a dynamically developing system.* Reading comprehension involves taking in information sequentially, while simultaneously building up a text representation. As each new segment of text is encountered, it immediately needs to be integrated with the text information currently being held in working memory. Thus, comprehension cannot be a static representation. That is, it is not a collection of pieces corresponding to sentence meanings, but a mental model that is continuously being developed and revised.

Summary of Models of Reading

Although reading models continue to evolve, our judgment is that modern interactive models strike an appropriate balance between data-driven and conceptually driven processes. Models such as Kintsch's CI model and a number of other current models propose an extensive foundation of relatively automatic processes for reading, such as the reader's fixations on words in text or converting sentences to propositions. At the same time, these automatized processes are seen as guided by the reader's general knowledge and as interacting with the meaning the reader is constructing. In common with a top-down view and in contrast with a completely bottom-up model, they take into account the role of context (e.g., making inferences based on memory for what stories are like, interpreting word meanings based on what the text is about). No current models, however, neglect the text itself; all strongly emphasize how contact with the text is the basis for meaning construction, with the reader's prior knowledge shaping the meaning that finally results.

This brief description of models of reading comprehension is intended to focus our thinking on several levels of processes almost certainly involved in reading comprehension. At a basic level, we see how reading comprehension builds on automatic or near-automatic processes, such as letter perception, word recognition, and sentence understanding. At the same time, models of reading must account for readers' knowledge and reading strategies. Models of reading such as Kintsch's help us see more clearly how readers might construct unique representations of meaning from what they already know, the strategies they select, and the texts they encounter. The models also remind us that the knowledge constructed can take a variety of forms, depending on readers' goals for reading. We now turn to a basic, but vital, kind of knowledge constructed extensively through reading—knowledge about words.

Building Vocabulary Through Reading

"Words embody power, words embrace action, and words enable us to speak, read, and write with clarity, confidence, and charm" (Duin & Graves, 1987, p. 33). This statement rings true to most educators, who observe firsthand that in many areas vocabulary knowledge is linked closely with competence. Understanding words and knowing how to use them—vocabulary knowledge—is an important index of domain and general knowledge. Vocabulary knowledge also influences learning efficiency; larger vocabularies aid cognitive processing in ways as diverse as more rapid listening and reading comprehension and more precise expression of ideas in speaking and writing.

The link between vocabulary knowledge and important educational outcomes has been known for many years. In an early but representative study, for instance, Conry and Plant (1965) found correlations of .65 and .46 between vocabulary scores and high school rank and college grades, respectively. Correlations between vocabulary scores and intelligence test scores typically are very high, often +.80 or above. Important language-based skills, such as reading comprehension (e.g., Stahl & Fairbanks, 1986; Sternberg, 1987) and writing quality (e.g., Duin & Graves, 1987), also are linked closely with vocabulary.

Because knowing words is so important, educators concentrate a great deal of energy on helping students acquire them. Direct instruction has been the most common approach, with teachers often having students memorize words and their definitions. The limitations of direct vocabulary instruction, however, have been pointed out by Nagy and his associates (R. C. Anderson, 1996; Nagy, Anderson, & Herman, 1987; Nagy & Herman, 1987). They contend that, for most students, reading is the more likely route to vocabulary growth.

Their argument for reading as the main source of vocabulary growth is as follows. First, vocabulary growth during the years children are in school is extraordinary. Nagy et al. (1987) have estimated, for instance, that children add as many as *3,000* words per year to their vocabularies between the 3rd and 12th grades; students may accumulate a reading vocabulary of something like 25,000 words by 8th grade and as many as 50,000 words by the end of high school (Graves, 2000).

Second, learning word meanings to a level where they can be accessed quickly and usefully takes considerable time. Because the time that can be devoted to direct vocabulary instruction is limited, only a small portion of vocabulary growth during the school years, perhaps 200 to 300 words per year, actually can be attributed to direct instruction (Mason et al., 1991; Nagy & Herman, 1987).

Nagy and his associates contend that reading is a much more compelling explanation for students' rapidly growing vocabularies, even though acquiring meanings through reading is a slow, incremental process. A single contact with a word, for instance, typically produces only partial learning, and full comprehension of a new word requires multiple encounters.

Reading does, in fact, provide ample opportunities for vocabulary learning. In a series of carefully designed studies examining how words might be learned from context, Nagy and his coworkers showed that incidental learning of word meanings does occur during normal reading and that the absolute amount of learning is quite small.

The probability of acquiring significant word knowledge from reading a word once in text is not more than 10 percent or so (Nagy et al., 1987; Nagy & Herman, 1987).

This small increment in word knowledge becomes very important, however, when the amount of reading children do in and out of school is considered. R. C. Anderson, Wilson, and Fielding (1988), for instance, showed that a typical fifth-grade student reads about 300,000 words from books outside school per year; other print materials, such as newspapers and comic books, increase the total to about 600,000 words. When a conservative estimate of 15 minutes per day of reading in school is added, the number of words read by the typical fifth grader is upward of a million a year; avid readers read many times this amount. The strong inference from data like these is that reading is indispensable to vocabulary growth; the words that students learn through reading likely represent a third or more of the words most acquire annually.

This argument that reading is a primary avenue of vocabulary growth has been strengthened further by research relating amount of **print exposure** to vocabulary size. Stanovich and his colleagues (Cunningham & Stanovich, 1991; Stanovich, 2000; Stanovich & Cunningham, 1993; Stanovich, West, & Harrison, 1995) measured print exposure through checklists in which respondents indicated whether they were familiar with particular authors, book titles, magazines, and newspapers. The assumption was that the more items respondents checked, the more reading they had done. Real items on the checklists were mixed with foils so that guessing could be controlled; for instance, a list of children's book titles included titles of real books (e.g., *A Light in the Attic* and *Polar Express*), as well as plausible-sounding but nonexistent book titles (e.g., *The Lost Shoe* and *Curious Jim*).

Print exposure as measured by these scales turned out to be a potent predictor of vocabulary knowledge for fourth- and fifth-grade children (Cunningham & Stanovich, 1991), college students (Stanovich & Cunningham, 1993), residents of a retirement community (Stanovich et al., 1995), and even a sample of adults who completed the scales in an airport waiting room (West, Stanovich, & Mitchell, 1993). Moreover, the relationship of print exposure to vocabulary holds even when the influence of general ability (e.g., high school grade point average, mathematics ability test scores, and reading ability scores) is removed statistically, suggesting that differential exposure to information through reading is the key factor in vocabulary size no matter what the individual's ability level. Print exposure is not only a unique predictor of vocabulary size but also a better one than ability measures (e.g., see Stanovich, 2000), which as shown earlier, almost always relates significantly to vocabulary.

Word Knowledge: What It Means to Know a Word

It might seem from our discussion that vocabulary knowledge is an either-or thing—either you know a word or you don't. Picture for a moment, however, the answers you might get if you asked a group of college students the meaning of a relatively rare word, say, *ascetic*. Some would have no idea at all; some might venture a guess (e.g., "Is it something like 'clean'?"). Others would be more confident (e.g., "I think it means 'austere, self-denying'") and perhaps even add an instance of its use (e.g., "The monk lived an *ascetic* life, denying himself all but the most basic necessities"). Still others might ask for clues before they ventured a guess (e.g., "Could you use it in a sentence for me?"). Given the example "He looked like a student, thin and *ascetic,*" some of them might propose, "Well, it has something to do with a student and how he or she looks. It's either 'pale' or 'poor,' . . . could be either!" Still others simply would be confused: "Isn't it something like 'art appreciation'?" "Knowing a word" obviously is not an all-or-none phenomenon!

Graves (1992) has pointed out that learning a word's meaning varies markedly, depending on the learner's current knowledge and the depth of understanding required. For instance, first graders often are asked to read words they already have in their oral vocabularies (e.g., *house, car,* and *mother*). It is a different challenge to learn a new meaning for a known word, however. Many words are *polysemous;* that is, they have multiple meanings (e.g., *run* and *set*). Still another demand arises when the student must learn a new word for a known meaning (e.g., a child understands the idea of "being on time" but does not understand the word *punctual* when she reads it). Finally, in some instances, a student may have neither the concept nor the word, as in reading research or text materials that contain unfamiliar concepts (e.g., *paradigm* and *dysfunctional*). Initially, our goal is for students to understand the words they are reading. Our ultimate goal, however, is much more ambitious: We hope they learn to use the words fluently in writing and speaking.

Definitional Versus Contextual Word Knowledge

In thinking about goals for learning new vocabulary, vocabulary researchers have found it useful to distinguish between definitional and contextual word knowledge. **Definitional knowledge** refers to the relationship between a word and other known words, as in a dictionary definition (e.g., an *octroi* is a tax paid on certain goods entering a city). When asked about vocabulary, most people envision definitional knowledge first. A definition places a word within a semantic network of words the learner presumably already knows and can be a way for students to acquire useful knowledge about a word.

The knowledge developed from seeing or hearing words in context is often more useful, however. For example, a native speaker of English immediately recognizes the oddity of certain vocabulary choices in sentences like *"She drove her plane to Austin, Texas;" "I hope I have a capable application to your program;" "He initiated his car's engine;"* and *"She despaired her hope of ever meeting him again."* When we consider words individually, we are tempted to think of their meanings as unrelated to their context. With rare exceptions, however, word use in natural language is highly contextual: what words mean often depends on how they are combined with others. Thus, student vocabulary knowledge needs to extend well beyond words' dictionary definitions to **contextual knowledge,** understanding how they are actually used in writing and speaking.

The contextual nature of word meanings has led some authorities (e.g., Nagy, 1988; Nagy & Scott, 2000) to propose that vocabulary knowledge be viewed as organized in schemalike structures containing not only the meaning of the word but also a host of temporal, spatial, and grammatical cues. Look, for instance, at their following sentence:

> As the mechanic tried to tighten the bolt one last turn, the bolt _____, and his wrench clattered to the concrete.

If we are asked to supply a word for the blank, we immediately draw on our linguistic, metalinguistic, and world knowledge. Choices such as *cried, sensitive,* and *happily* are discarded as either "unboltlike" or grammatically nonsensical, and we quickly move on to more acceptable possibilities.

In even a very short passage, suitable word choices typically are surprisingly constrained by the syntactic and discourse context in which the word needs to be embedded. Many clues to the meaning of the word come from outside the word itself. Thus, in our example, we quickly surmise from the context that the missing word must be a verb, something that might happen to a bolt when a mechanic tightened it one last time, and that, if it happened to a bolt, would result in the wrench's flying off and clattering to the floor. In this example, a word was missing, but the process is very similar when readers encounter any unknown word while reading.

With the word present, however, even an unknown one, within-word **morphological cues** also become available to the reader. Consider the following example:

> To his dismay, the inventor found that his automatic bed-maker was *unmarketable.*

A reader unfamiliar with, say, the word *unmarketable* also has, in addition to the external cues, several within-word cues available. From earlier instruction or from other experiences with prefixes and suffixes, many students are able to analyze the parts of the word and recognize *un-* as a prefix, *market* as the stem or root word, and *-able* as a suffix indicating an adjectival form of a word. From contact with an array of more frequent words beginning with *un-*, such as *unsafe, unhappy,* and *unclear,* these students should have a sense of *un-* as indicating negation. Knowledge of the root word *market* may enable them to recognize that the word *unmarketable* has to do with buying and selling.

This assortment of internal cues, coupled with those from the external context, make it possible for students to approximate word meanings as they read. Having both within-word and external context cues by no means ensures that students will be able to use or even recognize them as potential clues to figuring out words, however. The less sophisticated the readers, the fewer linguistic and metalinguistic cues they will recognize. Also, some contexts in which new words are encountered are relatively rich, whereas others are not (Graves, 1992; Nagy et al., 1987).

Understanding words in context does not necessarily mean consciously "figuring them out." In ordinary reading and as portrayed in current models of reading such as Kintsch's, fixations on a word simply trigger automatized knowledge related to word recognition and use. For example, we automatically comprehend the different meanings of the word *left* as we read the following sentences: "He is *left*-handed" and "He was *left* at the altar". Similarly, when we speak, we almost never pay attention to words' dictionary definitions. We just use them, making statements without hesitation like "I think I've broken my *foot!*," "That pitch was outside by a *foot!*," *or* "My kitten Crouton wants to sleep at the *foot* of my bed."

In summary, word knowledge is not a simple either/or matter; "knowing a word" goes far beyond dictionary definitions to subtle knowledge about words' meanings and how they are used. Thus, vocabulary knowledge is an excellent example of this book's theme that knowledge is contextual. While vocabulary knowledge can seem to be quite explicit, much of what we know about vocabulary is tacit and unrecognized—knowing what words go with others, for instance. Vocabulary knowledge also is highly automatized and arguably more procedural than declarative (e.g., as in the correct recognition and use of the polysemous words *left* and *foot* in our examples; see Nagy & Scott, 2000). Reading is an ideal way of acquiring this contextualized knowledge about words, their meanings, and their uses.

Helping Students Use Reading to Build Vocabulary

How best do we help students increase their vocabularies? An obvious starting point is simply to encourage reading in any way possible. From the work by Nagy and his associates, we know that vocabulary growth is strongly related to how much students read. Over their lifetimes, students will acquire most of their vocabulary as they read, on their own, without having been taught (Graves, 2000). Thus, reading is one of the most important gateways to this vital category of learning (R. C. Anderson, 1996).

Beyond encouraging reading, however, there are several strategies teachers can use to stimulate vocabulary growth. Reading provides a rich context for learning vocabulary, but only if students are prepared to use this context. Learning how to use context may be even more important than learning specific words; students can be helped to acquire reading strategies for using context to figure out word meanings. Morphological, syntactical, and discourse clues are potentially available for students to use, but students often need encouragement and practice in using their linguistic and world knowledge effectively.

The vocabulary knowledge that students acquire through reading should be supplemented by at least some direct vocabulary instruction (Graves, 2000). Functional vocabulary knowledge is built on a solid foundation of declarative knowledge about word meanings and their relationships to one another. Especially when words are presented around a theme or topic, knowledge structures develop that make new vocabulary acquisition and reading comprehension more likely.

Direct instruction can be used also to encourage students to notice and learn new words as they read. In an intensive vocabulary instruction condition in Duin and Graves's (1987) study, for instance, students were asked to keep track of the times they read, spoke, or heard selected words in outside activities. Because students were encouraged actively to notice the new words (which they did), Duin and Graves found that they also were more inclined to learn them and to use them on their own.

Building Organized Knowledge Through Reading

Recall from chapter 3 that schemata are organized knowledge structures in memory. Schema theory holds that meaning is constructed by readers on the basis of the information they encounter, what they already know, and the way they interact with new information. Consider the following paragraph drawn from a well-known study by R. C. Anderson, Reynolds, Schallert, and Goetz (1977). As you read the paragraph, form some preliminary thoughts about Tony.

> Tony got up slowly from the mat, planning his escape. He hesitated a moment and thought. Things were not going well. What bothered him most was being held, especially because the charge against him had been weak. He considered his present situation. The lock that held him was strong, but he thought he could break it. He knew, however, that his timing would have to be perfect. Tony was aware that it was because of his early roughness that he had been penalized so severely—much too severely, from his point of view. The situation was becoming frustrating; the pressure had been grinding on him for too long. He was being ridden unmercifully. Tony was getting angry now. He felt he was ready to make his move. He knew that his success or failure would depend on what he did in the next few seconds. (R. C. Anderson et al., 1977, p. 372)

If you are like many readers, you may have decided that Tony is a prisoner in a jail cell. Enough segments in this paragraph match up with people's "prisoner" schemata so that this decision is reasonable. On the other hand, you may be like readers who decide that Tony is a wrestler because several elements of the passage fit "wrestler" schemata. As in the examples we gave in chapter 3, the meanings that readers construct for passages depend on the particular schemata they activate during reading. These constructed meanings, of course, affect what individuals will remember. Indeed, we know that if we were to test people's memory for the Tony passage by giving them a free-recall test, we would find qualitative differences in recall between those people who decided Tony was a prisoner and those who decided Tony was a wrestler.

Because schema theory was discussed in depth in chapter 3, we do not recapitulate it here. In understanding learning from reading, however, it is important to note that schemata play key roles in reading comprehension (Andre, 1987b) in keeping with our book's general theme that mental structures organize memory and guide thought. Among these roles are the following:

- Providing the knowledge base for assimilating new text information
- Guiding the ways readers allocate their attention to different parts of reading passages
- Allowing readers to make inferences about text material
- Facilitating organized searches of memory
- Enhancing editing and summarizing of content
- Permitting the reconstruction of content

How knowledge affects understanding should be clear from your recent reading of the Tony passage. Your understanding was created within the knowledge framework you activated. The ways schemata guide readers' attention during reading are somewhat more difficult to demonstrate, but if we overtly activate certain schemata prior to reading, readers' selective allocation of attention can be seen. For instance, if we gave some people the Tony passage with the title "The Wrestler" but gave other people the same passage with the title "The Prisoner," we almost certainly would see differences in the ways readers in these two groups attended to specific elements of the passage. Those people reading from the wrestler perspective likely would focus on elements of the passage related to wrestling, and those individuals reading from the prisoner perspective would most closely examine materials congruent with a "prisoner" schema.

Another reason why schema theory is important for understanding reading is that text comprehension depends heavily on learner inferences. No text exhaustively lists the information required for understanding. From our Piggo example in chapter 3, you recall our presenting a brief passage about a girl breaking open a piggy bank. Not stated in that passage were such things as what Piggo was made of, what Piggo looked like, and what size Piggo was. Your knowledge of piggy banks, however, let you infer these things almost instantly and construct the passage's meaning. The schemata readers activate and how elaborate they are guide which inferences they will make.

Schemata also facilitate organized searches of memory. To use R. C. Anderson and Pearson's (1984) example, if you were reading a passage about a ship's christening, your schema for "ship christening" likely represents a cluster of related instances of knowledge. Thus, if you encountered questions related to the passage such as "What kind of bottle was broken on the ship?" or "Where was the bottle broken on the ship?", your search of memory would be guided by this schema.

Schemata make it possible for readers to summarize content. New information constantly is being assimilated to readers' schemata, which allows readers to edit input in an efficient manner (e.g., "That fits what I know about schema theory; I know this stuff. I'll speed up until I see something new"). To summarize a passage, readers need to select some parts of the passage as more important than others, condense materials and substitute higher level superordinate concepts, and integrate what is being read into a coherent, accurate representation (Goldman & Rakestraw, 2000; Pressley & Schneider, 1997). Without knowledge structures, none of these are possible.

Finally, as shown in chapter 5, human memory is more reconstructive than a copy of experience; schemata guide how content is reconstructed. When we read to learn, we seldom are required to recall passages in verbatim form. More often, our goal is to remember a passage's *gist* and reconstruct it as needed. So, if you were asked to recall the Piggo passage from chapter 3, the probability is high that you could do a very fine job of describing a girl's destruction of a piggy bank. It also is very likely, though, that you would reconstruct the passage based on your knowledge of piggy banks—your "piggy bank" schema—rather than recite it verbatim.

The Importance of Linking New Information with Old

An important prediction from schema theory is that, to the extent to-be-learned information can be linked with what readers already know, their memory for the to-be-learned information should increase. This view has led to some very useful lines of inquiry and a widespread set of applications. In this section, we introduce the topic of *advance organizers,* which predated schema theory but has many similarities to it, and then return to schema theory to extend the discussion of *schema activation* that we began in chapter 4.

Advance Organizers   **Advance organizers** are "appropriately relevant and inclusive introductory materials . . . introduced in advance of learning . . . and presented at a higher level of abstraction, generality, and inclusiveness" than subsequent to-be-learned reading materials (Ausubel, 1968, p. 148). Advance organizers are designed to provide "ideational scaffolding" that assist in the retention of the more detailed and differentiated material that follows. In short, they provide frameworks for materials to be learned.

The idea of advance organizers has been one of the most intuitively appealing and long-lived concepts in research on reading comprehension. Anything that can help learners relate new information to what they already know ought to be valuable. Early research on advance organizers was, in fact, quite promising. For example, Ausubel and Fitzgerald (1961) had students read a passage about Buddhism and tested them for their mastery of the content in three conditions: (1) a condition in which subjects first read a historical introduction, (2) a condition in which the principles of Buddhism were first set forth in abstract and general terms, and (3) a condition that first used a review of Christianity as an organizer designed to relate what the students already knew about religions to the material they were being asked to learn on Buddhism. Results were clear: On the posttest, students who read the advance organizer relating Christianity to Buddhism outperformed students in the two other conditions.

Although Ausubel and his associates obtained positive results on the utility of advance organizers, other researchers soon encountered difficulties, and by the mid-1970s, the research on advance organizers had become quite confused. Whereas some studies showed effects, others did not. Careful reviews of the advance organizer literature by Barnes and Clawson (1975) and Faw and Waller (1976), however, began to clarify the area by pointing out problems in the research. Perhaps the most serious problem was that the definition of advance organizers was so vague that standardization was impossible. Text features as diverse as outlines, questions, pictures, graphs, and paragraphs were being defined in one study or another as advance organizers. Coupled with the methodological problems often seen in early research (e.g., not keeping track of how long students studied material, not employing true control groups, and poor development of posttests), the vagueness of what made for an effective advance organizer limited research progress.

By the 1980s, researchers began to clear up the methodological problems and to tie their work into schema theory, which then was becoming more widely known (Derry, 1984; Mayer & Bromage, 1980). In these studies, advance organizers in the form of a paragraph or two of material prefacing the to-be-learned content showed consistent, if somewhat small, beneficial effects on readers' memory for materials. Still, the problem with defining organizers remained.

A series of studies by Glover and his colleagues suggested that good written organizers have common characteristics. In general, organizers that give readers an analogy for upcoming content, that are concrete and use concrete examples, and that are well-learned by readers are more beneficial than abstract, general, or poorly learned organizers (Corkill, 1992; Corkill, Glover, & Bruning, 1988; Dinnel & Glover, 1985). Thus, if properly developed, advance organizers can be effective for enhancing readers' comprehension of text. The same is true for a set of procedures grouped under the label *schema activation*.

Schema Activation   **Schema activation** refers to an array of activities designed to activate relevant knowledge in students' memory prior to encountering new, to-be-learned information (e.g., Derry, 1996; Schallert, 1991). These activities typically involve having students answer questions germane to an upcoming topic, review previous learning, or develop a "schema map" of related knowledge already in memory.

In many ways, schema activation procedures attempt to accomplish the same goal as advance organizers (tying new information with what is already known) but rely more heavily on readers' generation of information from their own knowledge and experiences. The emphasis is on helping students remember and use things they already know that are relevant to a new topic. Consider, for example, a study conducted by Peeck, Van Den Bosch, and Kruepeling (1982), who had a group of Dutch fifth graders read a brief (125 words) passage about a fictional fox. Prior to reading, half of the children activated relevant prior knowledge by generating ideas from memory about foxes. The remaining half of the children generated ideas about a topic not relevant to the fox passage—American farms. Immediately after reading, the children were tested through free recall. Results indicated that the children who had activated their knowledge about foxes remembered significantly more passage content than the other children. Not all schemata are created equal, however, at least insofar as their activation assists learning a particular set of information. As Schallert (1991) has cautioned, background knowledge needs to be relevant and well-learned for its activation to be useful in new learning. Thus, a general exhortation to "teach the prior knowledge required," purportedly a schema activation technique, may make little or no sense in a given instructional setting (e.g., if children have little or no experience with a topic). Activated knowledge, to be useful in anchoring new learning, must itself be stable and well-organized.

Both advance organizers and schema activation techniques are consistent with the idea that learning is a constructive process (see chapter 1). Both approaches emphasize how reading comprehension and recall can be improved by finding ways to help students relate new information to what they already know. The research on both topics suggests that these procedures can be effective and useful additions to one's teaching strategies. In general, the more ways teachers can help students relate new information to what they already know, the better their comprehension and the more they will learn and retain.

The Importance of Reading Comprehension Strategies

As discussed in chapter 4, a cognitive view of learning emphasizes teaching students a set of adaptable strategies they can use to construct meaning and comprehend text (Block & Pressley, 2002; Dole, 2000; Pressley, 2000a; Pressley & Wharton-McDonald,

1997). The goal is to help students acquire metacognitive awareness and gain conscious control over their learning. Awareness of the need to teach students reading strategies came from research identifying metacognitive reading skills associated with reading comprehension (see Baker, 2002). In the next few pages, we examine five strategies that research has shown to be among the most effective in helping students comprehend what they read.

Determining Importance   To comprehend what they are reading, readers must locate the most important ideas in reading passages. Many readers, even if they can fluently decode the words in a passage, have difficulty determining what is important and what is not. As a consequence, the metacognitive activity of determining importance has received a great deal of research attention over the years.

Palincsar and Brown have provided a broad and flexible program—**reciprocal teaching**—that includes teaching students to judge the importance of ideas in texts (e.g., A. L. Brown & Palincsar, 1989; Palincsar & Brown, 1984; see also Rosenshine, Meister, & Chapman, 1996). In Palincsar and Brown's approach, a teacher models reading comprehension strategies aloud and guides students in performing them. At the start of a lesson, the teacher engages the students in a short discussion designed to activate relevant prior knowledge (see our earlier discussion of schema activation). Both the teacher and the students then silently read a brief passage, and the teacher models summarizing the passage, developing a question about the main point, clarifying difficult ideas, and predicting what will happen next. Everyone then reads another passage, with the teacher now asking the students questions that give him or her clues about what the students are thinking and what kind of instruction they need. As the students respond, often haltingly at first, the teacher provides guidance and support, helping them ask questions, summarize, comprehend, and predict.

Gradually, across sessions, the teacher shifts responsibility to the students so that they are the ones asking questions, summarizing, clearing up misunderstandings, and predicting future happenings. Highlighted in the process is how the teacher and the students think as they try to comprehend (Hart & Speece, 1998). Teacher scaffolding may be fairly direct when the teacher guides the process (e.g., a teacher comments, "Try putting yourself in Juan's place for a moment") or rather informal (e.g., a comment to a student, "I like to check after each section to see if I can say what it's all about—the main idea, you know"). Reciprocal teaching also includes direct instruction on how to perform comprehension activities, as well as tips for reading more effectively.

The outcomes of research on teaching strategies for determining the importance of ideas in passages generally have been very positive (see Dole, Duffy, Roehler, & Pearson, 1991; Pressley, El-Dinary, et al., 1992; Pressley & Schneider, 1997; Pressley & Wharton-McDonald, 1997). Students' ability to determine importance improves with practice and feedback, especially when the instruction focuses on developing the self-awareness and understanding students need to regulate their own metacognitive strategies.

Summarizing Information   Summarizing requires not only determining the most important ideas in a passage but also creating a new text that represents the original one. As we indicated at the beginning of the chapter, recent assessments (e.g.,

NCES, 1999, 2001) show that students continue to have difficulty in summarizing information. Research on teaching students to summarize, however, suggests the utility of focusing on this skill. In their extension of the reciprocal teaching approach to at-risk college students, Hart and Speece (1998) had students practice summarizing passages. At first, the teacher modeled summarization with a think-aloud procedure, but leadership soon was transferred to the students, who practiced summarization in groups and modeled it for each other. As students developed their summarization skills, the teacher's role shifted to providing feedback, prompts, and praise for good work.

Hart and Speece used the following rules, derived from the work of Hidi and Anderson (1986) and Kintsch and Van Dijk (1978) for teaching summarization: (1) delete minor and unimportant information, (2) combine similar ideas into categories and label them if needed, (3) state the main idea when the author does not provide it, and (4) invent the main idea when the author does not provide it. Overall, summarizing means integrating materials into a coherent, accurate representation. For shorter passages, these may be two or three sentences in length, but for longer passages may be a paragraph or more. In producing summaries, readers essentially are creating new compositions representing the longer original text (Hidi & Anderson, 1986).

Whether summarization training has emphasized a tutoring approach (e.g., Palincsar et al., 1987) or a more didactic approach in which rules for summarizing are taught directly, results of research on teaching summarization skills have been positive. When students learn to summarize text as they read and to use their summarization skills in studying, significant improvements in learning occur (Dole et al., 1991; Hart & Speece, 1998; Pressley & Wharton-McDonald, 1997).

Drawing Inferences Every text leaves many things unsaid. Text comprehension depends on readers inferring information (e.g., when a character's age is not mentioned but his or her traits suggest immaturity). Drawing inferences from reading materials also includes the ability to infer ideas beyond the realm of a reading passage (e.g., your thinking as you read these materials about how you could enhance the reading comprehension of your own students). As you might expect, making inferences about reading materials is a skill good readers have that tends to be absent in less-skilled readers (Dewitz, Carr, & Patberg, 1987).

Several studies have shown that learning to make inferences enhances reading comprehension. Groundbreaking studies on teaching inference skills were conducted by Raphael and her colleagues (e.g., Raphael & McKinney, 1983; Raphael & Pearson, 1982; Raphael & Wonnacott, 1985). Raphael and Wonnacott (1985), for example, contrasted fourth graders in a control condition with students of similar ability levels who received training in finding the answers to questions about reading materials. Three types of questions were used: (1) those for which the answers were *explicit* in the text, (2) those for which the answers were *implicit* in the text (inferences were needed, much as the inference used in determining someone's age from her or his description), and (3) those for which an *integration* of the reader's background knowledge and text information was required (inferences required were similar to those you might make in using the content of this chapter to devise methods for improving your students' reading comprehension). Students in the experimental condition received 4 days of training and practice in answering the three types of questions. Considerable attention was given to showing students how to answer the questions. Results indicated that the training greatly facilitated students' ability to draw inferences about text materials and significantly improved their comprehension.

In a second experiment, Raphael and Wonnacott (1985) taught teachers in an in-service program how to train students to answer the three types of questions. Results again were highly positive. Instruction in how to answer the different kinds of questions, coupled with practice and feedback, resulted in students' significant improvements in reading comprehension.

Another technique, called **elaborative interrogation,** also has been used as a device for generating inferences about texts (e.g., Woloshyn, Paivio, & Pressley, 1994; Wood, Pressley, & Winne, 1990). In its simplest form, learners are asked to read target sentences and then to answer a "why" question to clarify the relationship between the subject and the predicate of the sentence. For instance, if children read the sentence "Cats like to lie in the sun," they would be asked *why*—that is, to generate a reason why this fact might be true (e.g., because the sun makes them warm). Recall of facts processed in this way is increased substantially, with a similar effect present when elaborative interrogation is used with expository paragraphs (see Seifert, 1993, for a summary of elaborative interrogation studies). In general, elaborative interrogation seems to enhance readers' comprehension by stimulating their inferences about what they are reading.

Generating Questions   Good readers frequently ask themselves questions about their comprehension, think about how the information might be used, and decide whether ideas are important. As you recall, self-questioning and clarification of content are integral parts of Palincsar et al.'s reciprocal teaching. Because self-questioning is embedded in their overall program, however, it is difficult to determine how this skill alone contributes to reading comprehension. King et al. (1984), however, reported results of a self-questioning condition contrasted with the control and summarizing conditions we described earlier. Students in one condition were asked to form "higher level" questions based on the text (students first were taught what "higher level" meant on the basis of a taxonomy of learning), to record them as notes, and then to read the passage to gain the answers. Results showed that the students who used self-questioning during reading did not recall as much content as the students who summarized, but they did recall nearly 20 percent more of the passage's ideas than the control group. More recent work by King, in which children have been systematically taught *how* to construct inferential questions that prompt deeper thinking, has shown better discussions of texts by students trained to construct such questions along with significantly improved performance on several kinds of comprehension tests (e.g., King, 1994). As a general comprehension strategy, self-questioning also can easily be extended to thinking aloud and to creating classroom exchanges organized around asking and answering student-generated questions about text (see chapter 9; see also King et al., 1998).

Monitoring Comprehension   One difference between good and poor readers is that good readers know when they are comprehending and when they are not (Afflerbach, 2002). They also are better at controlling and adapting their strategic processes accordingly. These two parts—*monitoring* the quality and degree of comprehension and *knowing what to do about it*—describe comprehension monitoring (Dole, 2000; Hacker, 1997). As you can see, these two components parallel the two dimensions of metacognition—knowledge of cognition and regulation of cognition.

One approach used frequently to study comprehension monitoring is the **error detection task,** in which readers are asked to detect inconsistencies or anomalies in text as they are reading. The assumption is that if readers are monitoring their comprehension, they will readily detect anomalies. Researchers document the accuracy and speed of error detection.

Although readers seem to develop a nonverbal awareness of anomalies before they actually can report them, even fairly sophisticated readers often have trouble reading critically and can struggle when they are asked to identify errors and inconsistencies in reading materials (Hacker, 1997). Research suggests, however, that students can be taught to be more critical and to do a better job of detecting errors. Grabe and Mann (1984), for instance, taught fourth graders to detect inconsistencies through an activity they called the Master Detective game. In this approach, the children read a series of 10 statements displayed on a computer screen. The statements supposedly were made by 10 different crime suspects. Five of the statements were consistent; five contained inconsistencies. The point of the game was for the children to find the inconsistencies, such as in the sample below taken from Grabe and Mann:

> All the people that work on this ship get along very well. The people that make a lot of money and the people that don't make much are still friends. *The officers treat us like dirt.* [Emphasis added.] We often eat our meals together. I guess we are just one big happy family. (Grabe and Mann, 1984, p. 136)

The children in Grabe and Mann's experimental condition played the game once as a pretest, four times for practice (with different sets of statements each time), and once as a posttest. The children in the control condition merely played the game twice, as a pretest and a posttest. Results showed that the children who completed the four practice sessions far outperformed the children in the control condition on the posttest. Practice with feedback in identifying inconsistent statements (in a motivating game situation) brought about significant improvement in the identification of inconsistencies, suggesting that fairly simple procedures may improve students' monitoring whether texts are making sense.

Closely related to the ability to identify errors or inconsistencies in reading materials is how well students can estimate how much they have learned from reading. The correlation between what students believe they have learned from reading passages and their actual test performance is referred to as their **calibration of comprehension** (Schraw, Wise, & Roos, 1998).

When students set out to learn text materials, it seems reasonable that they read and study until they believe that they have mastered the material and then stop. If they are studying for an exam, for example, studying too little is risky. Studying more than is needed to master the material, however, may be seen as a waste of time. Students have many responsibilities and must divide their time among tasks wisely.

Our day-to-day experiences as educators suggest that most students have a reasonably good sense of how well they have mastered the material they study—an accurate calibration of comprehension. After all, many students regularly succeed on tests. In contrast with this intuitively appealing belief, however, are the findings of Glenberg and his associates (e.g., Epstein, Glenberg, & Bradley, 1984; Glenberg & Epstein, 1985; Glenberg, Smith, & Green, 1977; Glenberg, Wilkinson, & Epstein, 1982) that showed that many students were quite poor at monitoring their performance. Other research (e.g., Weaver, 1990) has shown that methodological problems account for some of the discrepancy between judgments and actual performance, but that many students still need to improve their ability to monitor their comprehension.

Fortunately, relatively simple procedures can be used to improve students' estimates of learning from text. For example, Pressley, Snyder, Levin, Murray, and Ghatala (1987) found that when readers have the opportunity to test their learning during reading, their performance estimates improve substantially. Activities such as self-questioning and summarizing and aids such as checklists can aid students in estimating how well they understand what they have read (e.g., Afflerbach, 2002; Butler & Winne, 1995). In general, we believe that any program designed to improve reading comprehension should include a component focused on having students learn to make more accurate judgments about their learning.

Building Organized Knowledge Through Reading: Summary and Applications

Cognitive theory holds that readers construct meaning on the basis of the information they encounter, what they already know, and the ways they interact with new information. Advance organizers and schema activation are approaches designed to facilitate meaning construction by bringing about a more complete interaction of readers' general knowledge with passage information. Extensive research supports the use of such techniques for helping readers relate what they already know to what they are learning. Teachers also may want to highlight the value of linking already acquired knowledge to what is being learned.

Another large body of research (see Block & Pressley, 2002; Pressley & Schneider, 1997; Trabasso & Bouchard, 2000, 2002) supports the wisdom of teaching key comprehension strategies and metacognitive skills to allow readers to use them appropriately and flexibly. Strategies we have discussed include determining the importance of information, summarizing what has been read, drawing inferences, generating questions, and monitoring comprehension. Others include learning to use mental imagery (e.g., forming mental pictures of what has been described) and using story grammars (e.g., drawing a story map to represent the plot of a story). Reciprocal teaching is one well-documented approach for teaching a constellation of strategies. The research indicates, however, that strategies can be taught usefully either alone or in combination (Pressley, 2002; Pressley, Woloshyn, & Associates, 1995). In general, as students master strategies, their reading comprehension improves. Most are reasonably straightforward. They can be taught to any reader beginning to use reading for learning, but should need to be taught systematically.

Some basic reading comprehension strategies can be acquired implicitly, but more flexible and strategic reading is likely when strategies are taught explicitly (Dole, 2000; Duffy, 2002; Pressley, 2002). By describing the purposes of strategies, modeling their use, and explaining how each can be implemented, teachers can gradually shift more and more responsibility to the students. Students can model strategy use for each other, for instance. Teachers soon can assume the position of coach, encouraging strategy use, prompting students to self-evaluate their strategies, and giving them feedback. Because developing high-level cognitive skills requires a great deal of practice, strategy instruction is a long-term process (Pressley, et al., 1995) that often needs to be continued throughout the school year and even across years. Although teaching reading strategies is time-consuming, almost all authorities feel it is time well spent.

Remembering What Has Been Read: Memory for Text Materials

Thus far, we have focused on two important outcomes of reading to learn: acquiring vocabulary and the strategies leading to comprehension and building organized knowledge. Research in these areas has been influenced heavily by schema theory and by the research on metacognition.

Another very large body of research in educational psychology has focused on *what is retained* as a result of reading. This research, which has come to be known as "memory for text" or "memory for prose" research, represents a wide variety of theoretical frameworks. Because of this theoretical diversity, we limit our discussions primarily to studies linked to the concepts of *schema theory* and *elaboration of processing* (see chapters 3 and 4).

Text Signals

Text signals are devices designed to improve the cohesion of reading materials or to indicate that certain elements of the text are more important than others (Lorch & Lorch, 1995). The assumption behind using signaling in text is that signals help readers discern a text's topic structure, inducing them to change their text processing strategies. As signals direct attention to a text's topics and its relations, recall of text structure and content should be improved.

Several kinds of text signals are used by writers, including the following:

- Number signals (e.g., The three most important points are [1] . . . , [2] . . . , and [3] . . .)
- Headings (e.g., See the heading at the top of this section)
- Underlined, italicized, or bold text
- Preview sentences (e.g., As we will see in chapter 15, . . .)
- Recall sentences (e.g., Recall from chapter 4, where we . . .)

The literature on text signals has implications for structuring handouts, worksheets, and reading assignments.

One of the most common forms of text signal is the *number signal* (Lorch, 1989). Number signals are exactly what they sound like—numbers used to enumerate a set of points, a set of steps in a process, a list of names, or other reading content. Number signals are useful for identifying important elements of a text that students are to remember (e.g., four causes of the War of the Roses and five steps in readying a lathe for operation). When students read a brief passage, such as on a handout sheet, they tend to give more of their attention to the signaled content than to the unsignaled content and better remember the signaled material (Lorch & Chen, 1986).

Similar to number signals is the use of *italic or bold print.* When either of these techniques is used sparingly, students pay more attention to the highlighted material and remember it better (e.g., Glynn & DiVesta, 1979). *Headings* have a somewhat different effect in that they serve to improve the cohesion and readability of text (Wilhite, 1986).

Number signals, underlining, bold print, and headings all are useful devices in constructing study materials for students. When specific elements of reading materials are crucial, they should be italicized or bold. Students pay more attention to such signaled content and are more likely to remember it. When a set or series of ideas, names, or steps is to be remembered, number signals are useful. Headings break up longer text into segments of thematically related content and reduce the amount of cognitive effort required to comprehend the material.

Two other types of text signals are *preview sentences* and *recall sentences.* Preview sentences signal upcoming contents; recall sentences signal back to previously learned material. Preview sentences placed early in a reading passage tend to focus readers' attention on the upcoming material that they signal and help students better remember it (Lorch, 1989). Students also tend to cluster the signaled content and the information in which the signal was embedded when they recall it (Glover, Dinnel, et al., 1988).

Recall sentences, on the other hand, signal back to previously learned material. They often are used by textbook writers, but they also have uses in shorter assignments by helping students remember information relevant to the content in which the signal is embedded. They also help students cluster information in memory and to assimilate new information with knowledge they already possess (Glover, Dinnel, et al., 1988).

Adjunct Questions

More than 35 years ago, Ernst Rothkopf began an influential research program exploring how inserted questions affected readers' memory for expository text. In one of his initial studies (1966), participants read material taken from an expository text and were tested on their ability to remember the content. Some participants answered questions (called **adjunct questions**) every so often while they read; others did not. The positioning of the questions was varied across the conditions in which participants answered questions. In addition, the adjunct questions were relevant to only some parts of the reading materials. Much of the content was not surveyed through the adjunct questions.

After Rothkopf's participants finished reading, they took a test on the material. Some test items were repeated versions of the adjunct questions; others covered content not related to the adjunct questions. We may think of the repeated questions as tapping *intentional learning*—learning required to answer the adjunct questions. The posttest questions not assessing content relevant to the adjunct questions tap *incidental learning*—learning not required by the adjunct questions.

Four major findings came from Rothkopf's pioneering study. First, adjunct questions had a powerful effect on intentional learning; that is, students' performance on the posttest questions that assessed their knowledge of content required for the adjunct questions was far superior to students' performance on questions assessing incidental learning. Second, when adjunct questions were placed *after* reading materials, they facilitated both intentional and incidental learning, although the impact on incidental learning was not large. Third, when adjunct questions prefaced reading materials, they enhanced intentional learning but did not facilitate incidental learning. Indeed, on measures of incidental learning, a control group that received no adjunct questions but that was asked to study hard and to remember the details of the passage outperformed the group that received prefatory adjunct questions. Fourth, reading times (including the answering of adjunct questions during reading) seemed to vary directly with participants' performance on the posttest.

Rothkopf's study had an important influence, both methodologically and conceptually, on subsequent research. After his seminal article came an explosion of research on adjunct questions inserted in expository texts. Results of these studies generally have painted a consistent picture. Below, we review the findings and highlight the practical applications of adjunct question research. Before proceeding, however, it is important to note that, for all practical purposes, the findings on adjunct questions are identical to those on the use of instructional objectives given to students; that is, studies that have contrasted how instructional objectives (or learning objectives) and adjunct questions influence readers have indicated little or no difference between them (e.g., Petersen, Glover, & Ronning, 1980).

Level of Questions   Although many ways to classify questions used in reading materials have been proposed over the years, none has been more influential than the hierarchy of instructional objectives created by Bloom, Englehart, Furst, Hill, and Krathwohl (1956). It also has been widely used in development of test items. The Bloom et al. **Taxonomy of Educational Objectives** posits six levels of learning that vary based on the sophistication and complexity of the learning required. The levels of learning described in the taxonomy, moving from simple to complex, are knowledge, comprehension, application, analysis, synthesis, and evaluation. We briefly describe the kind of learning required by questions at each level of the Bloom et al. taxonomy.

Knowledge-level learning merely requires the retention of facts, such as names or dates. It is akin to rote learning and is the learning tapped by the level of question employed by Rothkopf in his 1966 study. *Comprehension-level* questions require more sophisticated knowledge, as they require students at least be able to paraphrase the to-be-learned material in their own words. *Application-level* learning requires the use of information in some concrete form. It differs from comprehension-level learning in requiring the implementation of knowledge, such as the distinction between when a student is able to explain the concept of *irony* (comprehension) and actually use *irony* in a segment of writing (applications). *Analysis-level* learning is more complex yet in that learners must be able to break down information into its component parts so that the relationship among all components is clear. For example, the request "Compare and contrast levels of processing with schema theory" requires that students break down both schema theory and levels of processing into their component parts (e.g., encoding and storage) and relate them one to another. *Synthesis-level* learning demands that students put together old knowledge in new ways. For example, the request "Using your knowledge of encoding specificity, construct a test over content you are teaching that will enhance students' test performance" requires the use of knowledge you already have (both how to construct tests and the concept of encoding specificity) in a new way. At the highest level of Bloom's taxonomy is *evaluation-level* learning, which involves students making judgments about the value of methods or materials, based on their knowledge. For example, if you were shown three videotapes of teachers presenting a lesson and were asked to rate how well each teacher employed the principles of cognitive psychology and justify your choices, you would be engaging in evaluation-level learning.

When we review results of research on adjunct questions in terms of the level of learning required by the questions, some interesting findings emerge. Knowledge-level questions tend to facilitate only knowledge-level learning, and their effects are focused primarily on intentional learning (Andre, 1987a). Comprehension-level questions also have a strong effect on intentional learning and a limited but consistent effect on incidental learning. Higher order questions (at the application level or above) tend to enhance both intentional and incidental learning. Further, higher order questions have their facilitative effect regardless of whether they preface or follow reading materials, although their greatest effect occurs when they preface text. Higher order questions also seem to enhance both lower order (knowledge and comprehension) and higher order learning (see Andre, 1987a).

Considering level of questions in terms of applications, two lines of reasoning are possible. In the first line, if teachers want students to learn specific facts from expository passages, they should employ lower order questions prefacing text. The problem with such an approach, however, is that it tends to result in a "post hole" effect; that is, students tend to learn in depth only those segments of text specifically indicated by the questions. The remainder of the text and perhaps even the main point of the passage may receive very little elaboration and, consequently, be poorly remembered.

The second line of reasoning emerges if teachers are more interested in overall comprehension. In this case, teachers should use higher order questions. Higher order questions cannot be answered by locating a specific term or phrase in a passage. Instead, they require that large segments of a passage be attended to. Consequently, students remember the gist of passages better after answering higher order questions than after answering lower order questions (Benton, Glover, & Bruning, 1983).

The kinds of thinking required by higher order questions are not restricted to high school or even middle school students (e.g., see King, 1994, for a description of approaches used to teach children "thinking" questions). Application, analysis, synthesis, and evaluation learning activities are well within the abilities of elementary school children if the activities are structured in ways that are meaningful to them. Elementary school children do require systematic practice to reliably develop and answer higher order questions, but it seems to us that the time taken to model higher order thinking systematically and to give children practice with feedback for application, analysis, synthesis, and evaluation is likely to be rewarded.

Questions Requiring Decisions   Adjunct questions can have positive effects on students' memory for expository text. It turns out, however, that questions requiring students to make decisions are more effective than questions at the same level of the Bloom et al. (1956) taxonomy that do not require decisions. The act of making a decision (e.g., yes/no) about some content, in addition to answering the question, appears to result in considerably more elaborated processing (see our earlier discussion of elaborative interrogation and also chapter 4), leading to better memory for the content (Benton, Glover, & Bruning, 1983). If student decision making is a part of a teacher's instructional goals, adjunct questions should be written so that students go beyond simply writing an answer to recording a decision.

Location of Questions   In general, research suggests that students' overall recall of content will be best if higher order questions precede text and lower order questions follow it (Hamaker, 1986; Hamilton, 1985). Because higher order questions require more extensive and elaborated processing, they result in better learning when they preface materials. In this arrangement, students must carefully search and evaluate large segments of text to determine their relevance to the questions. When higher order questions follow reading, however, students must rely on their memories to answer the questions. Consequently, although the effect of higher order questions following sections of expository text is still greater than that of lower order questions in any configuration, their impact is considerably less than if they preface text.

Number of Questions   Only a handful of studies have examined how different numbers of questions influence readers' memory for content (see Andre, 1987a). In general, it seems that only a few higher order questions need to be employed to enhance optimally students' memory for text. Perhaps one higher order question for every 1,000 words of text is sufficient to ensure elaborated processing of the text materials. When lower order questions are considered, the number of questions is less critical and should be determined on the basis of specific instructional goals.

Implications for Teaching

This chapter focused on the processes of reading to learn—"getting meaning" from text materials. The importance of reading to learn is difficult to overestimate; it is a key to school learning, a significant part of effective living, and an unparalleled source of enjoyment. As a consequence, most educators would endorse readily the goal of what Guthrie and his associates (Baker, Dreher, & Guthrie, 2000; Guthrie & Ozgungor, 2002) call **engaged reading**—students choosing to read frequently for a variety of reasons and having the requisite cognitive skills for comprehending what they read. This chapter has highlighted key dimensions of reading that are important in this quest. The following implications for teaching draw on these dimensions.

1. *Help students become active readers.* Current models of reading show with increasing certainty that comprehension involves an array of processes. Some are highly automatized processes of perception and association, while others are more top-down and directed consciously by readers. None can be ignored if reading comprehension is the goal. The more active readers are—asking questions about what is read, relating what is read to what they already know, thinking of implications, putting ideas into their own words—the more likely comprehension and learning become. Both result from active readers interacting with text materials.

2. *Build on what readers already know.* Virtually all reading theorists view learning from reading as resulting from an interaction between the reader and the materials being read. When information to be learned is linked with what the reader already knows, understanding will be heightened. Two prominent methods for accomplishing this linking are *advance organizers* and *schema activation.* Advance organizers are materials given to readers to serve scaffolding for what is to be learned; they provide a known framework for new, unfamiliar material. Schema activation has similar functions but relies more on the readers themselves to generate frames of reference and knowledge. Because both methods tend to make reading materials more meaningful, their effect is to increase both comprehension and recall.

3. *Teach comprehension strategies explicitly.* Nearly a generation of research has shown us the utility of reading strategies for promoting comprehension. Students need, for example, to tell the difference between important and unimportant information and to summarize extended chunks of information into more manageable ones. They need to make appropriate inferences from what they read and to monitor whether they are understanding. We know that students who generate imagery and questions as they read are likely to comprehend better and learn more. Each of these strategies has been shown to help students read more effectively and adaptively. If they are taught these strategies systematically with modeling, coaching, and extended practice in their use, almost all children can become expert strategy users.

4. *Encourage students to become active vocabulary learners.* We all know about the importance of words. Having a large, flexible vocabulary is a major part of what it means to be educated. Reading is the primary avenue to vocabulary growth. The more readers read, the larger their vocabularies and the richer the networks of knowledge underlying these words will be. Voracious readers tend to have very large vocabularies; moderate readers, moderate vocabularies; and infrequent readers, small ones. Although vocabulary growth from reading can occur without intervention, teachers can assist students in acquiring vocabulary from reading by teaching them strategies for using context effectively. Direct instruction also can supplement vocab-

ulary growth, but its effects are augmented when students are encouraged to notice new words and have strategies for learning them (Graves, 2000).

5.   *Encourage wide reading.*   Read, read, read! Teachers need to take the lead in encouraging students to read. Reading is linked strongly with success in school and in the workplace. Even with the current emphasis on a variety of media, reading remains the primary source of the information underlying deep understanding in almost every field of endeavor. A growing body of evidence shows that students today are not reading effectively, however; for too many of them at all levels, comprehension is literal and at a basic level (Guthrie & Wigfield, 1997; NCES, 1998). Thus, we need to work hard at developing engaged readers—readers who not only are motivated to read for a variety of purposes but also have the skills to comprehend the materials they select to read.

Although this is far from a trivial challenge, it is not an impossible one. For instance, teachers and schools can establish school–home reading programs that encourage reading at home and library use. Being read to by parents and reading to parents and siblings can form values and habits that last a lifetime. In school, teachers can make reading more rewarding by selecting interesting reading materials and by using reading in ways that students find meaningful and functional. Teachers can also help students develop comprehension skills. By modeling comprehension skill use and by systematically teaching these skills, teachers can help students read more effectively. As students' abilities to comprehend improve, reading becomes a more positive and productive experience.

Summary

We began this chapter by describing examples of three types of reading comprehension models: data-driven, conceptually driven, and interactive. Data-driven models primarily emphasize automatized processes of perception and association in explaining reading. Conceptually driven models, in contrast, emphasize meaning construction based on readers' background knowledge. Interactive models envision both data-driven and conceptually driven processes interacting in the construction of meaning. A prominent example of such interactive models—Kintsch's CI model—portrays reading comprehension as based on automatic processes generating multiple associations, which are linked to one another at varying levels of strength in an associative network. What a passage means to the reader is represented by the associations remaining after the network stabilizes. One important outcome of reading is vocabulary acquisition, a process that occurs naturally as students read. Although acquisition of word meanings during reading occurs in small increments, the knowledge acquired is particularly useful because it includes information about word context. Contact with words during reading appears to be a major source of vocabulary growth, which proceeds at a phenomenal rate during the school years. In general, the more students read, the larger their vocabularies. Students' effectiveness as vocabulary learners, however, can be enhanced by encouraging them to notice new words and by teaching them strategies for using context to figure out what words mean.

Wide reading is a primary means for acquiring organized knowledge, with schema theory providing a general backdrop for understanding reading comprehension. In a schema theory view, readers construct meaning from the text material, their knowledge, and their purposes for reading. Research on advance organizers, schema activation, and metacognitive reading strategies all emphasize the importance of active, strategic approaches to reading.

Advance organizers preface to-be-learned reading materials and are designed to help students tie new material to what they already know. Schema activation is a process whereby students activate relevant knowledge prior to reading. Both facilitate readers' comprehension of text. Readers also can acquire strategies that improve reading comprehension. These strategies can be taught individually or together in comprehensive training programs, such as the reciprocal teaching approach of Palincsar et al. (1987). Finally, a large body of research has concentrated on recall of content from expository texts. Two aspects of this literature have concentrated on the influence of signals in text and the effects of adjunct questions. In general, text signals focus readers' attention on specific segments of text and help make reading materials more coherent. The effect of adjunct questions (questions inserted in text) depends on the level of the questions and where they are placed. Comprehension is best aided by a few higher order questions prefacing text.

Suggested Readings

Block, C., & Pressley, M. (Eds.). (2002). *Comprehension instruction: Research-based best practices.* New York: Guilford Press.

This edited volume contains more than 20 very readable chapters by authorities on reading comprehension.

Kamil, M. L., Mosenthal, P. B., Pearson, P. D., & Barr, R. (Eds.). (2000). *Handbook of reading research:* Volume III. Mahwah, NJ: Lawrence Erlbaum Associates.

This scholarly volume, which includes chapters on reading research methods and instructional approaches, contains authoritative reviews on such topics as decoding processes, vocabulary learning, comprehension instruction, and models of reading.

Pressley, M., & Wharton-McDonald, R. (1997). Skilled comprehension and its development through instruction. *School Psychology Review, 26,* 448–466.

This review presents the argument that young readers benefit from explicit teaching of comprehension strategies, either by direct explanation or by modeling. The review also addresses and attempts to debunk several "myths" about comprehension strategies instruction, including claims that strategies already are widely used, unnatural, and not constructivist.

Ruddell, R. B., Ruddell, M. R., & Singer, H. (Eds.). (1994). *Theoretical models and processes of reading* (4th ed.). Newark, DE: International Reading Association.

This outstanding book is a classic collection of chapters by many leading authorities in reading. Sections on comprehension processes, reader response, metacognition, and theoretical models of reading relate particularly closely to the topics of reading comprehension and learning from text materials.

Writing

Many students find it difficult to use writing to state their ideas, express their feelings, and persuade others (Applebee, Langer, Jenkins, Mullis, & Foertsch, 1990; Graham & Harris, 1993, 1996) and their confidence as writers is low. Although they judge writing to be very important for such things as success in school and on the job, many plainly do not see themselves as good writers (Shell, Colvin, & Bruning, 1995; Shell, Murphy, & Bruning, 1989).

This difficulty with writing is not surprising, because writing is one of the most complex tasks that students face. Writing a text requires a student to coordinate and implement a large set of mental activities (Alamargot & Chanquoy, 2001) and exerts a heavy cognitive load. Writing is such a complex cognitive task that it involves almost all of the processes and concepts we have discussed in earlier chapters, including working and long-term memory, procedural and declarative knowledge, motivation, self-regulation, and beliefs and attitudes. No wonder students can find writing assignments intimidating.

One reason for students' lack of skill and confidence in writing may be that, until the early 1990s, students were getting very little, if any, writing practice. Surveys and other research done in the 1980s (e.g., Applebee, 1984, 1988; Applebee, Langer, & Mullis, 1986a, 1986b) showed that most students were doing very little writing in school and that the quality of writing had declined steadily.

The small amount of writing students were doing was mostly low-level activity, such as making lists, copying instructions, and taking notes. Even on those occasions when significant writing, such as a term paper, was required, it too often involved an arbitrary topic, inadequate preparation in how to approach the writing task, and grading based mainly on errors in grammar and usage. These conditions hardly could be called ideal for developing writing skill, confidence, and pleasure.

Since the early 1980s positive developments have occurred as both researchers and educators have begun to heed concerns about the amount and quality of writing instruction. Much more writing is occurring in our schools now, especially at the elementary levels. Writing is integrated with reading and incorporated into language arts instruction, and is appearing across the curriculum in science, social studies, and even mathematics.

Research on writing and cognitive models of writing also has become more sophisticated (e.g., Bereiter & Scardamalia, 1987; Hayes, 1996; Hayes & Flower, 1986; Levy & Ransdell, 1996; Olive & Levy, 2001), and as a consequence, we now understand much more about the writing process. Researchers have applied cognitive principles to writing instruction with good effect, showing that such techniques as modeling writing strategies, encouraging students to plan and revise, giving students a schema for revision, and creating a supportive writing environment can significantly improve student writing and their attitudes about writing (e.g., Atwell, 1987; Bereiter & Scardamalia, 1987; Boscolo & Mason, 2001; Calkins, 1986; Freedman, 1992; Graham & Harris, 1993, 1996; Harris & Graham, 1992; Tynjala, Mason, & Lonka, 2001).

In this chapter we present a cognitive model of the writing process and applications based on cognitive research. We begin by examining a model that has had great influence in guiding research on writing—the model of Flower and Hayes. We then explore the issue of individual differences in writing, comparing the qualities of more sophisticated writers with those of writers who are less developed. In the final major section of the chapter, we describe the implications of cognitive research for writing instruction in the classroom. We end with some thoughts on the topic of creative writing.

As you read this chapter, you will see the close relationship between our cognitive themes for education and the writing process. The writing process vividly illustrates several of our themes in action. Learning as a constructive process, mental structures for organizing memory and guiding thought, motivation and beliefs as integral parts of cognition, and social interaction as a fundamental part of cognitive development all play major roles in the writing process.

A Cognitive Model of Writing

Writing can take many forms. Novels, letters to the editor, poetry, and grocery lists all are forms of writing. Writing tasks also can differ dramatically in intent, length, and the amount of creativity expected. Writing also varies in complexity and quality according to topic, the writer's goals and the student's age—just compare a third grader's narrative about Christmas vacation with a college student's essay on the Middle East peace process.

One feature of a good theoretical model is that it can take variations such as these into account, highlighting components and processes that remain stable regardless of the type of activity under consideration. A good model also helps researchers think productively about a phenomenon and guides the design of research. Probably more than any other model of writing, the model proposed by Linda Flower and John Hayes (e.g., Carey & Flower, 1989; Flower & Hayes, 1984; Hayes, 1996) has served these important purposes.

The Flower and Hayes model (see Figure 13-1) portrays writing as a problem-solving activity with three major components: the task environment, long-term memory, and working memory. Each major component contains subcomponents representing specific writing processes.

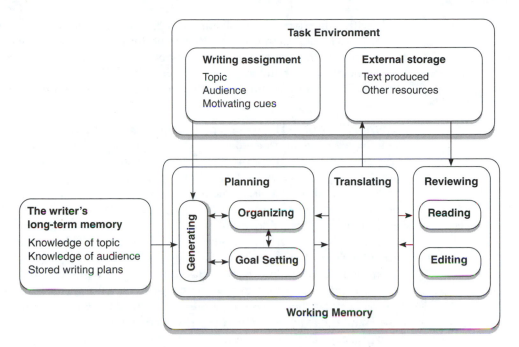

Figure 13-1
The Flower and Hayes Model of Writing
Source: From Cognitive Processes in Writing *(p. 11), by L. W. Gregg and E. R. Steinberg, 1980, Mahwah, NJ: Erlbaum. Copyright 1980 by Erlbaum. Adapted with permission.*

The Task Environment

The task environment, for Flower and Hayes, essentially "defines the writer's problem." It consists of two major components: the writing assignment (the writing task faced by the writer) and external storage (the writing a writer produces and the external aids she or he may use).

The Writing Assignment   In Flower and Hayes's model, *writing assignment* is a generic label referring to the external conditions that provide a framework for a writer's initial representation of the writing task. School writing assignments, for instance, often furnish such a framework. They usually describe a topic and its scope, imply an intended audience, and often contain motivating cues. Take, for instance, an assignment that asks students to write a two-page essay on the political issues involved in curtailing global warming. Such an assignment clearly specifies the topic and scope of the essay. Although audience is not mentioned, students typically would know whether it is for the teacher's consumption, or for judges in an essay contest. Motivating cues, such as grades (e.g., "This essay is worth one hundred points") or other outcomes (e.g., "Five winners will receive scholarships to the university's Summer Institute of Environmental Sciences") also often are significant aspects of a writing assignment.

As with other forms of problem solving, how the writing task is initially represented has a great deal to do with ultimate performance. Assignments vary in how effective they are in helping students represent their writing goals. Unclear assignments can produce poor or incomplete representations of writers' goals, with likely outcomes of low-quality writing or writing that is mismatched with its audience.

External Storage   The second part of the task environment in Flower and Hayes's model is *external storage*—the text the writer is creating and other materials that serve as resources to the writer. For example, a student working on an essay has the partially completed essay itself to look back on. She also may have notes she has written to herself about the assignment (e.g., "Be sure to mention how auto emissions contribute to global warming"). For longer assignments, such as term papers, students often have several forms of external storage to consult as they write, including note cards, drafts of the paper, summaries of sources they have read, and their own evaluations of different parts of what they have written.

External storage of information drastically reduces memory load as the writer creates new information. Compared with speakers, who typically have no external records of what they have said, writers can consult their work multiple times. The Flower and Hayes model shows the writer drawing on external storage as she rereads, evaluates, and revises her writing.

Long-Term Memory

The second major component in Flower and Hayes's model is **long-term memory,** which affects all the processes of writing (Hayes, 1996). Bereiter and Scardamalia (1987) divide the knowledge that writers can access in long-term memory into two major groupings: *knowledge about content* (knowledge about the topic itself) and *knowledge about discourse processes* (e.g., knowledge about audiences and metalinguistic knowledge about the structures of different writing genres). This knowledge continually changes as the writer reads and writes. In fact, it is useful to think of an ongoing interaction between the external environment and long-term memory; reading materials, notes, and the writing itself constitute external resources for writing, and memory provides internal resources.

Cognitive processes interact continually in working memory and long-term memory as writers think about their goals, search for ideas and vocabulary, and evaluate and review text they have written. Writers do not simply check with long-term memory at the outset of their writing; rather, long-term memory is a continuing resource throughout the writing process.

No matter how well-developed a writer's composing abilities are, the ultimate quality of writing produced depends on the writer's ability to apply both content and discourse knowledge to a particular writing task (Bereiter & Scardamalia, 1987; Hayes, 1996). Lacking content knowledge, even Shakespeare might have written poorly had he been assigned an essay on a subject like nuclear physics. Conversely, only a very few nuclear physicists could produce a literary work of the highest quality, at least partly because most would lack substantive knowledge about the more subtle features of literary discourse.

Working Memory

Information from the environment and from long-term memory are combined in the third major component of the Flower and Hayes model, **working memory.** Working memory is where the major cognitive activity of writing takes place. Flower and Hayes envision three major processes occurring there: *planning, translating,* and *reviewing.* Writers do not necessarily go from planning to translating to reviewing, however. Instead, most move back and forth between processes as the need arises. For instance, a writer may shift from reviewing back to planning and then to translating. More complex arrangements, in which a writer accesses the external task environment and long-term memory, also are likely. We begin our discussion of working memory processes with planning.

Planning   The planning process includes three subprocesses: goal setting, generating, and organizing. These subprocesses interact vigorously and may be initiated at any time during writing. *Goal setting* refers to establishing objectives for writing. Goals may be long-term (e.g., "I'll write an A+ paper," and "This chapter has to fit into the rest of the book") or short-term (e.g., "Here I need to give a few examples" and "I probably should do a summary that will lead into the next section"). Goals are a part of the writer's preparation for writing but also may be set after an initial writing session has been completed (e.g., "I think I'd better add something about the Adirondacks"). As you can see, goal setting is not a one-time activity, but rather occurs many times during the course of writing.

Goal-setting is particularly critical in certain kinds of writing, such as the persuasive compositions often included in assessment tests. In this type of writing, setting specific subgoals is necessary but is often a very difficult task for students. Ferretti et al. (2000) found that giving students an elaborated goal that included explicit subgoals helped students produce much more persuasive, well-reasoned essays.

The *generating* subprocess refers to the development of the ideas and content used in writing. Ideas may be generated from long-term memory (e.g., "Let's see, didn't we talk about that in class?") or from the external environment ("I know it's in my notes here somewhere. Oh, great, here it is!"). Generation is an ongoing process influencing all other parts of the writing model. For example, suppose you are responding to an essay question about presidential elections. At first, you may plan to analyze the choice of the last three vice presidents. Soon, however, you discover that you cannot remember all their names. To continue, either you will need to consult some source for this information or your goals must be altered. Goals may also change as a result of generating unanticipated ideas, as when you hit on a good example or unexpectedly recall facts about an event.

The *organizing* subprocess of planning is closely related to both generating and setting goals. In organizing, writers create sensible, coherent structures out of their goals and ideas. Although organizing also typically is seen as happening early in writing, writers return to it again and again as writing proceeds. Each new paragraph and sentence requires attention to organization, as do any changes in goals or in the ideas available to a writer.

Translating   In Flower and Hayes's model, *translating* is a second process in working memory. Translating involves transforming one's ideas into written text. Translating requires accessing semantic memory, finding vocabulary to express ideas, putting words into sentences, and reading off words as they are written. Like planning, translating can put a strain on the capacity of writers' working memories (McCutchen, 1996). As many translating activities become automatic or nearly so in good writers, however, the load is reduced greatly (Hayes & Flower, 1986). The automaticity of experienced writers is a good example of how automaticity can decrease cognitive load on working memory, as discussed in chapter 2.

Reviewing   The reviewing process in working memory involves reexamining what has been written and comparing this product with the writer's internal standards for acceptable writing. Although we think of reviewing occurring when writing is finished, it happens at any time during writing, even when the initial plans for a passage are being created (Hull, 1987).

Reviewing consists of two subprocesses: evaluating and revising. *Evaluating* is basically rereading the text and judging its quality. Obviously, evaluating what has been written depends not only on the writer's general content knowledge but also on the writer's sophistication with the particular form of writing he or she was attempting to produce (Hull, 1987; Smagorinsky & Smith, 1992).

Good and poor writers differ dramatically in how well they evaluate their writing. For example, given samples of poor writing, good writers are apt to point to flaws in the writer's construction, coherence, and choice of words. Poor writers, in contrast, tend to blame their own inability to decode the text as the source of the problem. In other words, good writers understand what good and poor samples of text are like. They further understand that good writing involves a writer's need to blend both content and discourse knowledge. Poor writers do not readily identify these features; instead, they tend to believe that their reading is at fault. This general pattern also is seen when writers critique their own products. Good writers often identify problems in their own work, but poor or immature writers are less likely to see shortcomings and often miss potential comprehension problems for readers (Beal, 1996).

Revising, the second subprocess involved in reviewing, refers to the rewriting and restructuring of text. Again, depending on the sophistication of the writer, revising can vary tremendously. Less-skilled writers often have great difficulty even seeing that a first draft might benefit from additional editing (Graham & Harris, 1993). When less-skilled writers do edit, editing often is limited to minor changes of wording or just adding content. More accomplished writers are much more likely to revise materials they have written, viewing almost any sample of their work as preliminary and subject to editing (Bereiter & Scardamalia, 1987; Britton, 1996).

Struggling writers often have difficulty regulating the planning and revising processes when writing. Directly teaching these processes to older elementary students can improve how much and how well they write (Graham & Harris, 2000b). This is an example of how self-regulation is critical to cognitive development and learning—one of our cognitive themes outlined at the beginning of the book.

An Example of the Writing Model

Perhaps the best way to capture the flavor of the Flower and Hayes model is to follow a hypothetical individual through the task of completing a writing assignment. Let's try to keep up with Evelyn. She is enrolled in a high school journalism class and has been assigned the task of writing an article for the school newspaper.

"Hmmm," reflects Evelyn, "I need to write a 250- to 275- word article describing the three candidates for senior class president. Well, I do have a file of the candidates' descriptions of themselves. It'd make sense to look at those first."

Evelyn pulls out a folder and begins flipping through it until she comes to the set of candidate descriptions. She examines them carefully, tapping her pencil on her desk. "Some of these are pretty fancy and use big words. But everybody in school has to be able to read the article. I won't try to impress anybody with my vocabulary. Also, when Mr. Barker says, 'Keep it brief,' he means 'keep it brief.'"

Evelyn turns on her computer and glances at a handout Mr. Barker gave out that day. On a yellow pad, she begins to scratch together an outline and thinks, "I'll just start by putting down their names and listing the honors and awards they've won so far in high school. That should be pretty easy to do. Next, I'll take their responses to the candidate survey they filled out and try to summarize how each person feels about the 'issues,' using his or her own words, of course. I also need to find one special thing to say about each person. Mr. Barker will like that."

Evelyn's reaction to the assignment is not especially unusual or striking, but it does allow us to see some elements of the model in action. The initial *task environment* (the assignment, the questionnaire, and Mr. Barker himself) seemed quite clear to Evelyn. She immediately began using her long-term memory in planning at least a rough framework for the whole writing task. Note that, in her planning, Evelyn used both *content knowledge* (her knowledge of the candidates) and *discourse knowledge* (e.g., knowledge that her audience was both Mr. Barker and the students at her school, that she was writing a journalistic-style article, and that her writing could be guided by the handout describing the candidates' responses to the issues). Evelyn's brief thoughts also allow us to see that she was busy organizing the material she was going to write as she began to form, at least loosely, her goals for writing.

Later, as we look back in on Evelyn, we see that she has begun actually writing and is working in short bursts, stopping now and again to stare at the computer screen. "Oh, what a horrible sentence!" she mutters. She deletes the line and starts again. "I don't want to make it sound like Susan doesn't like sports at all," she muses, "just because she thinks sports shouldn't be so important. Instead, I'll try this: 'Susan Smith believes that sports are . . . .'"

Evelyn writes several more lines and then stops, leaning closer to the computer screen: ". . . believe . . . ," she mutters to herself. "No, it's 'The group *believes,*' because group is one thing—singular."

This little segment of Evelyn's thinking lets us in on the *translating process,* in which she turns her ideas into words. In addition, we can see that she is reviewing her work as she goes along. She evaluated a sentence, found that it did not convey the meaning she wanted, deleted it, and revised it. She then made another attempt at translating, this time producing an appropriate sentence.

Looking back at Evelyn one last time, we find that she finally has completed her article and is rereading it, making changes as she moves along. "OK. That sounds pretty decent. But this doesn't. Wow, not so good, Evy—can do better! Gotta fix that pronto. . . . Mmm. I think a comma goes there and, well, I'd better cut out that *which* . . . capitalize *Kappa.* . . . Hey, this is pretty good, if I say so myself."

In this final observation of Evelyn, we see that her reviewing was typical of most better writers' reactions to their work: She carefully evaluated the material and made revisions where needed, some of them fairly substantial. Further, she made a last check of the mechanics of writing (punctuation, capitalization) after the task was complete.

Even a small sample of a writer's work, such as Evelyn's, tells a great deal about the dynamics of the writing process. *What is written is linear, but the processes of writing are not.* Writers do not move from planning to translating to reviewing in a neat, orderly progression. Instead, they cycle back and forth among the subprocesses involved in writing. In fact, some of the most important individual differences among writers seem to be based in their abilities to shift rapidly from operation to operation.

Individual Differences in Writing

Over the years, much research has focused on how individual writers differ in ways other than the obvious differences in ability to write (e.g., see Benton, Glover, Kraft, & Plake, 1984; Dickinson & Snow, 1986; Graham & Harris, 1996; Sanders & Van Wijk, 1996). Some surprising and not so surprising differences have been documented. In terms of traditional measures, good and poor writers at the same grade level do not differ widely in measures of intelligence or academic achievement (Benton et al., 1984). They do differ, however, in reading ability (Benton et al., 1984; S. Brown, 1986) and in the amount of writing they have been required to produce (Mazzie, 1987).

Generally, good readers are better writers than poor readers. Correlational studies have indicated that measures of reading comprehension are positively related to writing ability (+.50 or above) and to students' beliefs about their ability as writers (Shell et al., 1995). These relationships are not surprising when we consider that frequent reading exposes students to many more samples of writing, most of which, we would assume, are of reasonably good quality. At least indirectly, reading can teach students about good writing. It likely also helps develop students' abilities to detect errors in text and monitor comprehension, which relate to revision and writing quality (Beal, 1996; McCutchen, Francis, & Kerr, 1997).

Better writers also have done more writing. This fact also should not be surprising because writing is a complex cognitive skill and, like any other skill, improves with practice and feedback. In general, we would expect that as students are asked to write more and more, their ability to write will improve. As an editor put it to one of the authors several years ago: "If you want to write, you have to write, write, write. No person ever mastered writing by talking about it."

Beyond reading ability and amount of practice in writing, however, writers differ in several other dimensions. One of these is how individual writers process information.

Information Processing Differences

Several early studies examined differences in how more and less effective writers process information (e.g., Benton et al., 1984; Daiute, 1986; Kellogg, 1984). Benton et al., (1984), for instance, contrasted better and poorer college student writers (defined on the basis of how samples of their writing were scored by a panel of judges) on a series of information processing tasks. They found no significant differences in the students' grade point averages or achievement test scores, which confirmed earlier work. They also found no differences between the groups in short-term memory, but they did find differences in how individuals in the two groups manipulated information.

In one task, Benton et al., exposed subjects to a series of letters randomly generated by computer. After the last letter was presented, subjects were instructed to reorder the letters they were holding in working memory into alphabetical order. All subjects completed several trials to allow reliable estimates of their abilities to reorder the letters. The results indicated that better writers were both faster and more accurate on this task than poorer writers.

Although letter reordering might be seen as a rather trivial task not closely related to writing skills, other information-manipulation tasks closer to those required in actual writing activities showed comparable results. On a word-reordering task (presumed to be similar to actually forming a sentence from memory), subjects were given sets of words with 9 to 14 words in random order. Their task was to reorder the words into the one order that made a sentence for each string of words. Across several trials, the better writers again proved to be faster and more accurate than the poorer ones. They also were better on a task that required them to put sets of randomized sentences into a well-formed paragraph (presumed to be similar to assembling a paragraph during actual writing) and on a task that required organizing sets of 12 sentences into three different paragraphs (presumed to be similar to organizing information for writing).

Benton et al.'s first experiment then was replicated with a sample of high school students. On each of the information-manipulation tasks, better writers again were significantly more rapid and accurate than poorer writers. This finding supports the conclusion that better writers are superior at manipulating information; they can reorder letters, words, sentences, and paragraphs more efficiently than less skilled writers.

Directly related to the information processing differences just described are the ways different writers allocate their attention. Young writers, for instance, often need to focus on the mechanics of writing, such as manipulating a pencil and forming letters. For very young writers, especially, the motor skill demands of writing often can be such that they mouth each letter and word as they write it. With practice, children begin to gain automatic control over the motor aspects of writing and no longer need to devote as much of their attention to making letters. In work with beginning writers with and without a handwriting disability, Graham et al. (2000) found that handwriting is causally related to learning to write. They theorized that handwriting instruction improved the quality of students' writing because difficulty with handwriting is such a drain on the student's attentional capacity that it limits their use of other writing processes.

Even older writers will show wide differences in attention. Less skilled writers and writers with learning problems continue to focus on mechanical features of writing, such as grammar, punctuation, capitalization, and spelling, but good writers seem better able to concentrate on the meaning they intend to impart (Bereiter & Scardamalia, 1987; Graham & Harris, 1993, 1996; Robbins, 1986). Writers with more advanced skills perform mechanical functions, such as punctuation and spelling, automatically or put off worrying about mechanical issues until a first draft of the ideas has been put onto paper. It seems likely that many information processing differences observed by Benton et al. (1984) and others may be the result of better writers having developed their skills to a more automatic level. As these skills become more automatic, writers can concentrate their attention more fully on the meaning they are trying to express—an example of the function of automaticity in cognitive development described in our cognitive themes for education.

Idea Generation

As one might suspect, considerable differences are found in the number and quality of ideas for writing assignments generated by students of different ages and abilities (Graham & Harris, 1996; Harris & Graham, 1992; Robbins, 1986). Older children generally will have more ideas than younger ones, and adults more than either. One of the most persistent problems for young writers is finding enough to say. Development is only one of several factors affecting idea generation, however. Other factors are knowledge about the topic (Carey & Flower, 1989), knowledge of audience (Bates, 1984), knowledge about what makes for a good story (Root, 1985), and acquisition of metacognitive writing strategies (Englert et al., 1991). The extent to which writers have acquired tools for idea generation seems to be at least as important as development per se.

One of the more interesting studies examining the idea-generation phenomenon in writing was conducted by Root (1985), who surveyed the idea-generation techniques of professional expository writers. The writers in his sample were professionals who wrote magazine and newspaper articles. Most focused their efforts on developing a wide range of marketable stories similar to those seen in general-interest magazines (e.g., "The Great Northern Line," a story about railroading; and "Three-Mile Island Revisited," a story about the aftermath of an accident at a nuclear power plant); a few emphasized book-length projects. Because these people made their living from writing, idea generation was critical.

Results of Root's survey were at once commonsensical and interesting. These professional writers spent a great deal of their time reading. Although they read about specific topics primarily while working on particular stories (e.g., reading about nuclear power when preparing a story on the dangers of nuclear reactors), their general tendency was to read widely and to look for ideas in varied places. These professional writers also typically kept newspaper and magazine clippings along with their own notes about ideas for later use, even when they had no idea that the notes would ever be helpful.

Root's study results parallel one major thesis of this volume: *Knowledge plays a key role in effective cognitive functioning.* Knowledge has no substitute if idea generation is the goal. For most young children and even for many older ones, this knowledge comes from their own experiences, but having strategies for finding and comprehending text materials can greatly expand their knowledge base for writing (Bruning & Schweiger, 1997; Pressley, 2002).

Our students typically are novices at writing and will not have the broad range of knowledge possessed by professional writers. We can, however, increase the number of ideas on which students can draw by simple techniques in which they brainstorm vocabulary and writing topics either prior to or during writing. These kinds of strategies can be learned by students of almost any age and ability level (see Englert et al., 1991; Graham & Harris, 1993, 1996; Harris & Graham, 1992) and have significant effects on the amount and quality of writing that students produce. Encouraging students to generate ideas and inferences even before they know a subject well helps them to elaborate and reflect on their ideas, producing better writing and more meaningful learning (Tynjala et al., 2001). With careful attention from the teacher, students can learn strategies for idea generation and will realize that it is a critical part of writing effectively.

Planning Differences

Writers exhibit important differences in what they attempt to accomplish with their writing. Effective writers will concentrate on *expressing meaning* as their primary goal. This is not to say that they ignore grammar, spelling, punctuation, and other related dimensions, but most are concerned about such writing mechanics only because they see errors as interfering with communicating their meaning.

In contrast, concern with mechanics and avoiding errors tends to dominate the writing and editing processes of less effective and less experienced writers. Where better writers will focus more globally on large blocks of text (e.g., an entire essay), with the emphasis on meaning, less capable writers concentrate their attention on individual words and sentences. Less capable writers often limit revision to checking for mechanical errors, such as spelling, and recopying a document to make it look neater (Bates, 1984; Graham & Harris, 1993, 1996). Wallace et al. (1996) found that prompting student writers to revise globally produced positive effects on their writing.

Writers with less developed skills also tend to write associatively, with one idea simply prompting the next; that is, they perform mostly as *knowledge tellers* (Bereiter &

Scardamalia, 1987). Faced with a writing task, these writers often will stick very literally to their text sources (e.g., Sanders & van Wijk, 1996) and may write down what they know about a topic with little apparent monitoring of the structure or coherence of what they are writing.

Some forms of associative writing, such as free writing, can be useful, especially when employed as an antidote to students' obsession with mechanics and fear of making mistakes. In *free writing,* students can be encouraged to quickly produce as many ideas as possible without worrying about organization, correctness, or precision. Later, on the "voyage home," students can be helped to select, organize, and revise what they have written (Elbow, 1981).

Differences in Organization

Good writing is organized. Organization in writing has a variety of dimensions, including well-formed sentences, paragraphs that express ideas clearly, and arguments that flow logically, and differs by the type of text being created—narratives have one form, expository texts another. One dimension of organization that appears in all texts and that varies considerably across writers is a property of texts called cohesion.

Cohesion refers to writers' and speakers' use of linguistic devices to link ideas (Crystal, 1997; Halliday & Hasan, 1974; Norris & Bruning, 1988). These linguistic devices, called **cohesive ties,** come in many forms. Among the most common are referential ties, conjunctive ties, and lexical ties (for a more complete discussion, consult Butterfield, 1986, or Halliday & Hasan, 1974). *Referential ties* may employ pronouns (e.g., Enrique fell asleep. *He* was tired.) and definite articles (e.g., Three writers were there: a hack, a poet, and a playwright. *The* hack made the most money.). *Conjunctive ties* employ conjunctions to connect ideas (e.g., Kesia ate the pizza *and* Quinn's french fries), to show causation (e.g., Felicia tossed and turned all night *because* she ate too much pizza), and to show the obverse of ideas (e.g., Hiroshi had heard about pineapple pizza *but* couldn't believe anyone actually would eat such a concoction). *Lexical cohesion* binds together ideas through word choice. A simple form of lexical cohesion employs the same word or phrase on more than one occasion (e.g., Royce found himself a *sunny* spot in the bleachers. He thought that two hours of *sun* would be perfect.).

Good writers use both more and more varied cohesive ties. Consider the following sample of a child's writing lacking these connections:

> Lynette and Marissa went to town. She saw a store with glasses and marbles in the window. She bought some from the woman. She was happy.

The reader of this paragraph has no idea whether Lynette or Marissa saw the store or which item was purchased. Also, beyond not knowing who made the purchase, the reader does not know who went away happy—the buyer or the seller.

As writers develop, they become more sensitive to the need for cohesion in texts and begin to make their writing more "considerate." For instance, more experienced writers often use transition sentences between paragraphs (notice how the first sentence in this paragraph tied back to previous material) and occasionally preface paragraphs with sentences that tie the upcoming content back to things discussed on previous pages (e.g., "As you recall, . . ."). Experienced writers also use text signals (see chapter 12) to alert readers to coming content (e.g., "As you will see in the next chapter, . . .") and insert summaries of information at reasonable intervals. Teachers can improve students' writing by helping them learn to use cohesive devices to guide readers' attention and ensure comprehension and teaching them to monitor their writing to see whether it hangs together.

Improving Students' Writing

In the first two major sections of this chapter, we examined the Flower and Hayes model of the writing process and reviewed factors that underlie individual differences in writers. In this section, we turn to applied research on writing. Like other areas of cognitive research, writing research increasingly has drawn on a social cognitive perspective (see chapter 1, also see chapter 10) in designing and testing ways to help young writers improve their skills. In this section, we review methods for developing writing ability that research has shown to be effective. The foundation for most of these methods is creating an atmosphere of collaborative problem solving and social support for writing. We begin there.

Creating a Context for Writing: The Literacy Community

Writing content and quality vary tremendously, depending on the context in which writing is embedded and how it is used. As we saw in the beginning of this chapter, writing has largely been used ineffectively as a learning tool in our schools until recently. On those occasions when students were asked to do extended writing, the goal often was only to test their knowledge of specific content (e.g., "Describe three factors that shaped the search for a new world order in the years immediately following World War I"). This type of writing does little to help students acquire new writing skills (Applebee, 1984).

When writing is used to test content knowledge, students often need only provide information that a teacher or textbook has previously organized and presented. It emphasizes **knowledge telling,** or simply repeating what is known. A better goal for students' writing is **knowledge transforming,** a much richer cognitive activity where writers construct new knowledge by combining what they know about the topic with their knowledge about discourse processes and goals (Bereiter & Scardamalia, 1987). Another drawback to using writing solely for assessment is that prewriting activities typically are minimal, often consisting of little more than instructions about topic, length, and desired writing form. As we know from the research of Graham and Harris (1993, 1996), such prewriting activities as brainstorming, goal setting, and planning can have a substantial impact on writing quality. When knowledge is simply written down and not transformed, as in content testing exercises, it is likely to remain isolated and detached. Testing content knowledge typically gives students little opportunity to bring in their own ideas, try out new thoughts on their classmates, or even organize what they know about a particular subject area.

Consider a different kind of context for writing. Here, the teacher conceives of writing as a tool for learning rather than as a way of displaying what the student already has learned. Writing is a knowledge-transforming process, where students actively construct new knowledge. In this setting, writing is motivated by a student's desire to communicate and is valued as an expression of what he or she wants to say. Social interactions are not only desirable in this context, they are fundamental; the scope of writing activities widens from individual composing operations to social and collaborative knowledge building (Tynjala et al., 2001). Students are members of a literacy community consisting of their peers and the teacher. Reading, writing, speaking, and listening are the main activities of this community.

Students in the Literacy Community   Students are full-fledged members of the literacy community, discussing writing plans, writing, reading their own and others' writing, and reflecting on their own writing. The social interactions occurring in the literacy community can create a powerful context for students to write effectively and pleasurably (Dyson, 1993; Dyson & Freedman, 1991; Englert et al., 1991; Freedman, 1992). Two important dimensions of these interactions are students (1) engaging in dialogue with one another and (2) using each other as editors.

With the increased recognition that social interaction is fundamental to cognitive development (see chapter 1) has come increased recognition of the importance of *student dialogue* to writing. Talking with peers helps students consider different perspectives, more clearly formulate their ideas, and consider audiences for their writing. In peer groups, students can give and receive advice, ask and answer questions, and learn and teach (Cazden, 1988; Freedman, 1992). Such activities are highly consistent with assumptions of a social constructivist perspective that thought is the internalization of social interactions and that social exchanges in family, school, and culture are sources of cognitive growth (see chapters 1 and 9).

The second dimension of social interaction increasingly used to support the teaching and learning of writing is *peer editing*. In its simplest form, students are paired with writing partners. Each student in a pair edits the other's writing, giving feedback on what he or she likes about the writing and talking about ways the writing might be improved. Peer editing in a classroom need not be limited to pairs of students; larger groups of up to four or five students can work together effectively.

Peer editing may be varied in many ways. It often includes editing prewriting activities, such as plans for writing or oral versions of a story or expository text. It may also involve reading each other's paper aloud to one another, collaborating on revisions, trading papers and revising each other's work, and so on.

Peer editing has been used successfully with writers of all ages, ranging from primary level to college age. Research on peer editing has shown positive outcomes as diverse as enhanced quality of writing and improved student attitudes toward writing (Englert et al., 1991; Harris & Graham, 1992; Hilgers, 1986; Olson, Torrance, & Hildyard, 1985).

What makes peer tutoring successful? Our analysis of the technique suggests several reasons. One reason is that students are writing for a specific audience. Unlike traditional writing assignments, peer editing puts a very real premium on audience awareness, which you will recall was an important element in the Flower and Hayes model. In Englert et al.'s (1991) words, peers "silently but effectively represent the needs of the audience and make the concept of audience visible" (p. 340). In reading other students' drafts, students also begin to adopt the perspective of readers. They learn quite directly how writing communicates or fails to communicate meaning to another person.

A second reason is the immediate or near-immediate feedback that students receive on their planning and writing. While a teacher may need several days to get through 100 or more essays, students can readily share plans for writing with their partners, write brief segments of prose, trade with their partners, and react to their partners' materials within a class period or two. It also seems that students may be more willing to share their ideas with peers (Lacasa et al., 2001) and to accept the judgments of their peers more readily than those of adults.

A third reason for the success of peer editing is that the skills generalize to the planning, evaluation, and revision of one's own writing. Improved editing leads directly to establishing and using personal standards for writing, especially when read aloud techniques are stressed.

Our judgment is that, with appropriate preparation of the students and teacher guidance of the interactions, peer editing can be used successfully in almost every writing program. Beyond the instructional emphasis we described above, the technique also has the advantage of freeing the teacher for teacher–student writing conferences in which teachers can help students develop their ideas and motivate them to acquire the specific skills they need.

The Teacher in the Literacy Community   Teachers play a vital leadership role in the literacy community, orchestrating an environment in which all dimensions of literacy—speaking and listening, as well as writing and reading—occur productively. As we have seen, some environments and teacher activities do little to support writing growth and may even be counterproductive. Other activities can contribute greatly to students' development as writers and to their positive attitudes toward writing (Borkowski, 1992; Tynjala, 1998).

An initial challenge for teachers is finding stimulating writing tasks that will challenge students to be thoughtful and inventive as they plan, write, and revise. Often, these kinds of writing tasks are found in in-depth student projects, in which students work on a topic or theme over several days or weeks.

Another challenge for teachers is the need for flexibility in adopting new teaching roles that may be quite different from traditional ones. In the environment of the literacy community, the teacher is much more likely to function as a coach and facilitator than as an authority and information source, making use of the "zone of proximal development" described by Vygotsky (1978) and discussed in chapter 9. This instruction is varied and often individualized, with teachers providing collaborative support to students as they move ahead in their writing. Often, this support includes teacher–student dialogue aimed at helping the student better define the writing task, think of alternative ways to express ideas, and make decisions about revision.

Although generally underused as a technique for developing students' writing (Sperling, 1990), the teacher–student conference can be an extremely useful mechanism for stimulating productive dialogue between teachers and students.

In some teacher–student conferences, interactions are dominated by the teacher, with students seeking and receiving input from the teacher. In others, however, dialogue is much more like conversation than instruction, with active negotiations between teacher and writer aimed at developing ideas and strategies for writing. Overall, teacher–student conferences are occasions for a good deal of negotiation and meaning making, where students gradually acquire the cultural knowledge about what it means to be a good writer (Sperling, 1990).

In teacher–student writing conferences, the emphasis should be on the quality of the students' writing, the process by which the students arrived at their product, and the relationship between writing processes and the quality of writing (Olson et al., 1985). During such conferences, which are held with individual students, the teacher poses questions about the quality of the writing, the meaning the student wants to convey, and the cognitive processes the student is using during writing. This interaction can help the teacher single out important aspects of the writing for discussion.

Teacher–student conferences also can provide time for students to write while talking about the process. Having students write while the teacher observes and interacts can be an effective way to teach skills in a personalized manner. Consider, for example, the following exchange drawn from a 10th-grade composition class:

TEACHER: I like how you described Fiver, but let me read the sentence about Hazel aloud. You listen critically.

STUDENT: OK.

TEACHER: "Hazel was leader material but he didn't know yet."

STUDENT: It doesn't sound so good, does it?

TEACHER: No, but I think you can do much better. Here [points at note pad], write another sentence and share your thinking as you do.

STUDENT: OK. Let's see . . . "Hazel had" . . . I mean a word that says he didn't know about . . . "undiscovered"?

TEACHER: That'd work.

STUDENT: "Hazel had undiscovered leadership."

TEACHER: OK, but not just leadership.

STUDENT: I see. It doesn't fit just . . . Mmmm. "Hazel had undiscovered leadership abilities."

TEACHER: That's a good sentence!

STUDENT: Yeah. You don't just have it. It's like a skill or something, so you have to say "abilities."

As you can see, the teacher was acting like an editor and gently nudging the student along as he constructed a clear sentence. The teacher also was careful to praise the student's efforts when positive change occurred. Modeling can be seen in an excerpt drawn from a conference the teacher had with another student.

STUDENT: "Sir Holger fought the followers of the evil mage."

TEACHER: That's a pretty good sentence. The meaning you want to share is very clear. I don't like the structure as well as I could, though. I prefer to avoid the way you've used *of*. I like possessives instead. They save words. For example, "Sir Holger fought the evil mage's followers." It flows a little better.

STUDENT: It does sound better that way.

TEACHER: Some teachers might disagree, but I've always thought that if you can eliminate unnecessary words, you've helped your writing. Look here [points to an assigned reading]. I thought of this last night. Instead of "Bring me the swords that are sharpest," I'd say, "Bring me the sharpest swords."

Given both positive and negative examples of writing samples, students are better able to discriminate between them and begin to internalize standards for their own writing. "Internalizing standards," of course, is a shorthand way of describing writers' growing metalinguistic awareness about writing and their increasing ability to use that knowledge to regulate their writing activities.

Implications for Teaching: Encouraging the Writing Process and Building Writing Skills

Once neglected by both researchers and educators, writing now is recognized as a window to cognitive activity and important to cognitive growth. Studies of writing have given researchers many insights into human cognitive processes and their development. Writing has been shown to be a multifaceted process with many important cognitive elements, including those of problem solving. Writers use their goals, sense of audience, and knowledge about discourse to transform content knowledge into new forms.

Educators also have an interest in writing as a tool for cognitive growth. When students plan their writing, try to express themselves, and examine their own and other students' writing, they are engaging in constructive processes that research has shown lead to cognitive growth.

Beginning in the late 1970s, programs such as Writing Across the Curriculum began to focus on writing-to-learn, or using writing as a way to build knowledge in a specific domain or subject area. Since then, the results from writing research and the emphasis on writing in the National Science Education Standards of the National Research Council (1996) and the Principles and Standards for School Mathematics of the National Council of Teachers of Mathematics (2000) have led to increasing use of writing in all subjects.

What does this mean for the classroom teacher? Writing can be an effective and useful learning tool in math, science, social studies, and other classrooms, but its effectiveness varies according to how writing assignments are structured. Tynjala et al. (2001) suggest that teachers structure writing assignments to meet certain conditions.

They suggest that writing tasks should make use of students' previous knowledge and existing conceptions and beliefs, encourage students to reflect on their own experiences and theorize about them, involve students in applying theories to practical situations and solving practical problems, and be integrated with classroom discourse and other schoolwork.

Incorporating writing into the classroom does not have to be complicated. The following implications, drawn from both the basic cognitive literature on writing and the work of applied writing researchers (Calkins, 1986; Englert et al., 1991; Graham & Harris, 1993, 1996; Graves, 1993; Tynjala et al., 2001) suggest some straightforward strategies for effective classroom writing.

1. *Have students write frequently.* More than 40 years ago, McQueen, Murray, and Evans (1963) performed an impressive study of factors leading to proficient writing performance of entering college freshmen. Their findings pointed to one factor as the most important determinant of writing skill—how much the students had written in high school.

Many teachers still do not use writing extensively, possibly because frequent student writing requires both an extensive commitment of time and a change of teaching style. Yet few school activities are more productive of cognitive growth than having students write often and receive thoughtful feedback on their writing. One way to include more writing without drastically increasing the teacher's workload is to use peer editing, where students read and edit one another's work. This also offers the benefit of social interaction among students, which, as you will recall from our themes in chapter 1, is vital to cognitive development.

2. *Create an informal, supportive climate for writing.* Traditional writing instruction, particularly at the secondary level and above, has tended to follow a teacher-centered course in which student writing is a response to teacher assignments and instructions. Until recently, most writing instruction also was based on the view that writing is a solitary activity, with writing evaluated primarily by grades and comments from the teacher.

Newer conceptions of writing, however, are based on the social constructivist assumption, as outlined in chapter 9, that learning to write, like all language acquisition tasks, is primarily a social activity. If this assumption is correct, and we believe that it is, then productive writing environments will involve students and teachers interacting with each other about writing. In these settings, students will generate a great deal of written language and talk about it; social interactions will be organized around students thinking about writing, writing, and revising; and students will receive positive confirmation for their writing efforts. Creating these kinds of environments is within the reach of every teacher and every school, but to establish them teachers may need to adopt new, possibly unfamiliar roles as a coach, conversation partner, and facilitator of discussions.

3. *Emphasize prewriting strategies.* Of all the strategies for helping writers develop their skills, few are more important than those taking place prior to writing. Determining goals for writing, for instance, motivates writing, gives students a basis for making decisions about content and writing strategy, and allows them to determine

whether they have been successful. Brainstorming to generate ideas improves the quality of students' writing. Thinking about their audience also shapes students' writing and helps them improve it. As Bereiter and Scardamalia (1987) recognized, the time spent in advance of writing is not only evidence of the writer's level of sophistication, but also is very important to writing quality.

4. *Stress knowledge transforming, not knowledge telling.* One of the most useful distinctions made by writing researchers is Bereiter and Scardamalia's (1987) contrast between knowledge telling and knowledge transforming approaches to writing. As we have seen, in knowledge telling, planning and goal setting are minimal; writers generate ideas on a topic and basically write them down until their supply is exhausted. Knowledge transforming, however, is a generative, problem-solving process involving active reworking of thoughts. In knowledge transforming, thinking is affected by the composing activity itself. Instead of writing being a process of individuals telling what they know, the act of writing transforms and develops writers' knowledge—knowledge is actively constructed, one of our major cognitive themes in education. Viewed in this way, writing clearly is closely linked with higher level cognitive processes—elaboration of ideas, problem solving, and reflective thought—and can become a tool for learning in any subject area.

Students of all ages can become knowledge-transforming writers. Several teaching approaches have been shown to be effective in helping students use writing to transform knowledge. One approach is to teach planning, writing, and revision strategies directly (Beal, 1996; Englert et al., 1991; Graham & Harris, 1993, 1996). Bereiter and Scardamalia (1987) noted that knowledge-transforming writers spend considerably more time planning before they begin writing than do knowledge-telling writers. During this time, they are engaged in such activities as making notes, thinking about their audience, and mentally "trying out" various discourse structures. Even very young writers can be helped to acquire variations on these skills.

Interacting with peers is an equally important approach for developing knowledge-transforming writers. Writing-to-learn tasks should not be purely writing activities; they should be integrated with social interaction and classroom discussion (Tynjala, 1998). When they talk with others about their writing, read others' work, or even just write with others around, students learn to envision the content, form, and creation of a text and to think about its audience (Dyson, 1993; Schultz, 1997). The external dialogue of the novice gradually becomes the metalinguistic awareness and self-regulation of the mature writer.

Teachers are a final important key in the third teaching approach to the development of knowledge-transforming writers. By the writing tasks they choose and through their interactions with students, teachers can set expectations for high-quality writing. One way of doing this is to provide students with excellent models of specific kinds of writing (L. M. Phillips, 1986; Smagorinsky & Smith, 1992). An obvious way of learning to write short stories is by reading and discussing short stories. Similarly, an important part of students' learning to write essays may be asking them to read essays and to use good ones as models for their own.

Teachers provide the vital support that bridges the gap between the novice writer's ability and the level of performance required to solve the problems of writing. Teachers' scaffolded instruction helps students think of strategies for attaining their goals and supports the development of fragile new skills and abilities (Englert et al., 1991).

5. *Encourage students to develop productive revision strategies.* One of the surest signs of novice writers is their belief that once something has been written, no change can or should be made. When these writers do make revisions, they tend to be "cosmetic," focused on such things as neatness and spelling. More expert writers, however, have learned that revision greatly improves their writing; they make editing and revising an integral part of the writing process.

Several avenues lead to improved revision strategies. First, students need an appropriate schema for the task of revision. Many student writers will have defined revision to themselves as involving only changes in words or sentences and will limit their revision efforts accordingly. When they are prompted to think more globally about revision, such as reorganizing text or adding or deleting whole sentences while considering audience needs, their revisions can improve significantly (Wallace et al., 1996).

Second, dialogue with peers can lead to improved revision strategies. As Englert et al. (1991) have pointed out, peers represent an important audience for student writing and make the concept of audience real. Talking with peers helps provide the foundation for the internal dialogue of the accomplished writer.

Third, revision strategies can be taught directly and can produce positive effects on writing quality. Graham and Harris (1993, 1996) developed a multistep approach to teaching strategies that increases students use of given strategies and their understanding of how and when to apply them. A fourth way of improving revision strategies is to have students set aside things they have written for a period of time before rereading and revising. Imposing a delay between the time when something is written and when it is reread allows some forgetting to occur and facilitates the possibility of fully processing the material as if it had been written by someone else (see Dellarosa & Bourne, 1985, for a discussion of this phenomenon).

A fifth avenue is to have students read their writing aloud to peers, parents, or siblings. Tell the students to trust their ears and to revise sentences that sound awkward. Our experience has been that students often overlook mistakes when reading silently to themselves (e.g., adding missing words, deleting unneeded words, and fixing tenses) but that reading their writing aloud often makes errors obvious. Children quickly find that some writing "sounds wrong" and that good writing is pleasing to the ear. Reading aloud to others also provides students with immediate feedback on the quality of their writing. Merely reading aloud is not enough, of course; students need to rewrite the awkward places until they "sound right."

6. *Take advantage of computer-based technology.* As access to computer technology in our schools grows, more and more student writing is being done on the computer. Some of this writing plainly can be impressive. Consider the following essay written by a first grader near the end of the school year:

The Little Bear Goes Camping

Once there was a little bear. She had a mom and a dad. It was summer and little bear had nothing to do. Then her mother and father desited maybe to let little bear go camping with her big cousen. So they asked little bear if she wanted to. So they asked little bear and she said yes she thoaght that was a great idia. So little bear got all packed. Then her cousen came. So they went to the woods and started to camp. They had a wunderful time. They went fishing and they did a hole bunch of stoff When they got home they started to talk all about what they did when they went camping. They had a wunderful time. Little bear broaght back flowers for her faimly pretty ones i mean it!!!! THE! END!!!

There really is no doubt that a story of the quality and length of "The Little Bear Goes Camping" would have been less likely for this first grader to write with paper and pencil rather than with a computer. For young children just learning to write— transcription processes, such as handwriting—can generate significant demands on cognitive resources (Berninger et al., 1997; Graham, Berninger, Abbott, Abbott, & Whitaker, 1997), demands that may be reduced when transcription difficulties are eased by technology.

As students gain facility in keyboarding and word processing, the ease with which they can rearrange and save segments of text reduces the logistic efforts involved in editing and revising. When students can easily add and delete words, insert sentences, and rearrange a text, much less effort is required than when the entire product must be rewritten by hand or retyped. Energy that once had to be devoted to transcribing and recopying can now be focused on the content, quality (Daiute, 1986), and creative design (Sharples, 1996) of the writing. Computers, however, are not a miracle cure for problems in writing instruction. Students still need to write often and receive good feedback on their writing. Also, because student access to computers in U. S. schools remains very uneven, writing instruction that relies heavily on computers will not reach many children.

7. *Keep grammar and language mechanics in perspective.* Must a writer know that a gerund is not a small, white-and-brown furry animal related to hamsters in order to compose a good sentence? Is the skill of diagramming a sentence into its constituent parts important for the budding young novelist? Research designed to shed light on such questions has been done since at least 1904 (De Boer, 1959), with consistent results. Apparently, no relationship exists between knowledge of grammar and the ability to write. What? That's right; research dating back to the beginning of the 20th century shows no relationship between grammatical knowledge on the one hand and an ability to write on the other (see Olson, Torrance, & Hildyard, 1985). The situation seems analogous to that of carpentry and structural engineering. One does not need to know the formal discipline of structural engineering in order to frame in a window.

Also, no evidence has been found that teaching students grammar improves their ability to write (De Boer, 1959; Frogner, 1939; Kraus, 1957). In fact, the literature abounds with one failure after another of teaching grammar as a means of improving writing (see Olson et al., 1985). As long ago as 1939, Frogner contrasted teaching students grammar with teaching them a "thought" method (an approach based on analyzing meaning) as a means of improving their writing. Whereas teaching grammar made no difference, an emphasis on meaning brought about a very clear change in writers' abilities. Nonetheless, many teachers continue to emphasize grammar at the expense of meaning, perhaps unaware of the evidence showing that writers' knowledge of grammar is not critical to writing skill.

We are not suggesting that students should not be helped to acquire the morphological and syntactic skills fundamental to writing (punctuation, capitalization, and spelling) or that a shared classroom vocabulary about grammar is not very helpful (e.g., student and teacher both understanding what adjectives and adverbs are). We believe, instead, that encouraging and developing writing is a matter of "first things first." Students need to understand that the basic reason for writing is the making of meaning—stating ideas, expressing feelings, and persuading others. Communicating meaning, not acquiring grammar facts, is the better focus of writing instruction.

Acquiring basic language skills, nonetheless, is very important. Writing needs to communicate effectively. Poor writing can distract, confuse, and frustrate readers, and misspelled words, misplaced commas, and poor sentence structure detract from communication. For writing teachers, the challenge is to develop students' mechanical skills with language within the framework of the meaning they are trying to convey.

A Final Note: Creative Writing

Thus far, we have emphasized using writing for expressing ideas and developing thinking and have avoided the issue of creative writing. The literature on creative writing is large and of great interest to many (see Carey & Flower, 1989, for a brief overview). Not much of this literature has dealt with the cognitive processes that might be involved in creative writing, and little has examined instructional procedures designed to make writing more creative. Still, some important issues are worth reviewing.

Creativity and the Evaluation of Writing   One debate about creative writing has focused on evaluation. Some have argued that creativity in writing and evaluation of writing are antithetical; that is, writers cannot be creative if they are constrained by the possible evaluation of their work. The arguments supporting this position are based on reasoning that writers will not be willing to take risks and to explore new paths if they are worrying about evaluation. From this perspective, the way to foster creative writing is to withhold all forms of evaluation from writing and to form a safe environment in which writers feel free to express themselves.

The argument that creative writing requires an evaluation-free, judgment-free environment has led to the belief among some teachers that creative writing should not be graded. Many teachers gave up correcting spelling, punctuation, and grammar because they believed that this would limit creativity. But a careful analysis of this approach to teaching writing, suggests that it not only fails to enhance creativity but also keeps students from improving the mechanics of their writing (Applebee et al., 1986b).

Encouraging creativity and evaluating writing need not be mutually exclusive. Most published work, requires an expression of creativity, yet most editors would be unlikely to bother to read a manuscript unless it is mechanically correct. To write creatively in the world of editors and publishers, one must first be able to write correctly. Just as in expressing creativity in playing a musical instrument, a certain level of technical competence is necessary for creative writing.

Although teacher evaluation has not been shown to restrict creativity, care should be taken to avoid quashing new ideas or attempts to be creative. Your feedback should make it very clear that you are not trying to discourage students from being creative, but rather are helping them express their ideas more effectively. We advise that teachers always provide students with feedback designed to improve the quality of their writing without being needlessly critical. Teachers' expectations are important. Students are far more likely to strive for creativity if teachers expect it.

Carey and Flower (1989) point out that creative writing cannot occur without a great deal of knowledge about both the topic and the processes of writing. Building students' knowledge about the writing topic and teaching them about writing will increase their chances of writing creatively. Our argument is similar to what writers and editors long have said to beginning writers: "To write well, you need to write about what you know."

One highly successful writer who followed the dictum of writing about things he knew is James Michener. Michener, author of *Caravans, Tales of the South Pacific, Centennial, Space,* and many other novels, spent years of his life acquiring the knowledge he needed to write. Michener took months and even years to learn about the areas and cultures he wanted to write about. In fact, as he became more successful, he hired an entire staff of researchers to travel with him and help him learn enough to write knowledgeably. Although one can argue over how creative Michener was, an examination of his habits and the results of research on other writers (e.g., Root, 1985) sheds light on a seldom-mentioned issue related to creativity: Gathering information, an important part of planning for writing, is an integral part of creative writing.

Summary

Long neglected in the United States by both researchers and educators, writing now is increasingly important in both cognitive research and educational curriculum design. An especially useful model describing how thought and language are linked in writing is that developed by Linda Flower and John Hayes. This model describes writing as a problem-solving activity involving three interacting components: task environment, long-term memory, and working memory. The major cognitive processes of writing—planning, translating, and reviewing—occur in working memory.

More and less effective writers show some differences. Among these are the ability to manipulate information, generate ideas, plan, and organize.

Creating a supportive environment for writing is a key to effective writing instruction. Procedures such as peer editing and teacher–student conferences can be used to create a literacy community that will enhance the quality of students' writing and their enjoyment of writing activities. Teaching grammar directly seems to have little effect on writing quality; a better approach appears to be to provide feedback on writing mechanics as students engage in meaningful writing activities. Creativity also can be facilitated by a supportive, nonthreatening environment that gives students many opportunities to write and helps them learn firsthand about the processes of writing.

Suggested Readings

Bereiter, C., & Scardamalia, M. (1987). *The psychology of written composition.* Mahwah, NJ: Erlbaum.

This classic work by Carl Bereiter and Marlene Scardamalia significantly expanded the understanding of the writing process. Their research concentrated on the distinction between knowledge telling and knowledge transforming in writing. Results of that research, summarized in this book, have helped us understand the nature of writing and how it develops, and have pointed the way to strategies that educators use widely for developing writing ability.

Harris, K. R., & Graham, S. (1992). *Helping young writers master the craft: Strategy instruction and self-regulation in the writing process.* Cambridge, MA: Brookline.

Karen Harris and Steve Graham have led an outstanding program of research aimed at helping students with learning difficulties acquire writing strategies and learn to use them at the appropriate times. This volume provides a useful structure that educators can use in teaching students of all ability levels to improve their writing.

Levy, C. M., & Ransdell, S. (Eds.). (1996). *The science of writing: Theories, methods, individual differences, and applications.* Mahwah, NJ: Erlbaum.

This edited scholarly volume by Levy and Ransdell contains chapters by John Hayes and others that update the earlier Flower and Hayes model and illustrate current approaches to cognitively based writing research.

Chapter 14

Cognitive Approaches to Mathematics

Knowledge Acquisition ▪ *Arithmetic Problem Solving* ▪ *Problem Solving in Algebra* ▪ *Cognitive Psychology and Mathematics Instruction* ▪ *Implications for Instruction* ▪ *Summary* ▪ *Suggested Readings* ▪

Teaching mathematics is a complex task involving many factors. Students need to acquire procedural skills for solving mathematics problems and, more important, to understand the concepts and principles to which the skills relate. For too long, mathematics was viewed and taught in the United States as a set of isolated skills to be learned mostly through repetitive practice. An unfortunate result is that many students today lack understanding of what they are doing; they can do mathematics problems but have little comprehension of the underlying principles. Students often are unable to use knowledge about mathematics in their lives or even to use their skills on mathematics problems that are even slightly different from those they have studied.

The beliefs that many students in the United States hold about mathematics also have tended to be negative and unproductive. Many regard the mathematics learned in school as having little or nothing to do with the real world. One particularly damaging and widely held belief of American students is that mathematics skill is innate (see chapter 7) and that ordinary students cannot be expected to understand what they are being asked to learn. At least partly as a consequence of such negative beliefs, many students take only the minimum sequence in math. Approximately four fifths of the students in the United States take a first algebra course, but fewer than one half take a second, and fewer than one tenth of all students enroll in calculus, a key to entry in many occupational fields. Dropping out is disproportional by gender and ethnicity: significantly fewer girls than boys go on to advanced classes, and significantly fewer African American and Hispanic students than White students take classes beyond beginning algebra. Although recent data show trends toward improvement for all students, the gap in achievement between White students and African American and Hispanic students continues to exist, and obvious difficulties remain in the area of mathematics instruction and learning (NAEP, 2000).

Like many other subject areas, mathematics has been "reinvented" within a cognitive and social contructivist framework. National statements of goals, such as the *Curriculum and Evaluation Standards for School Mathematics* (NCTM, 1989), *Reshaping School Mathematics* (NRC, 1990), and *Principles and Standards for School Mathematics* (NCTM, 2000) offer a dramatically different perspective on the learning and teaching of mathematics. These statements stress goals that help students make sense of mathematics. The overall aim could be called "quantitative literacy," in which students are able to interpret data and use mathematics in their everyday lives. Mathematics is envisioned as a subject of ideas and mental processes, not one of learning facts. In this new, cognitive conception of mathematics learning, students are encouraged to construct mathematical knowledge by formulating conjectures, exploring patterns, and seeking solutions rather than merely practicing repetitive exercises and memorizing procedures and formulas (Carpenter et al., 1994; Fennema, Franke, Carpenter, & Carey, 1993).

The knowledge base supporting this new conception of mathematics is expanding constantly, as both researchers and practitioners use the theory and methods of cognitive science to study mathematics learning and teaching (e.g., see Greeno & The Middle School Mathematics Through Applications Project Group, 1998; Hiebert & Carpenter, 1992; Romberg, 1992; Schoenfeld, 1992; Sternberg & Ben-Zeev, 1996). The growing body of cognitive research in mathematics, though strongly domain specific, is built on the basic model of cognition we outlined in the early chapters of this book.

As described in chapter 8, a major characteristic of problem solving in any domain is acquiring specialized and organized knowledge. Mathematics is no different. Students must acquire a body of conceptual and procedural knowledge in mathematics to support an array of problem-solving strategies. They need to know how to understand and represent problems in mathematical terms (Mayer & Hegarty, 1996). They need to acquire positive beliefs and attitudes about themselves and their mathematical knowledge and the self-regulatory skills to use their knowledge in flexible and adaptive ways (Schoenfeld, 1992). For students' mathematical problem solving to be useful, they need to generalize their conceptual knowledge and procedural skills across school subjects and beyond the school setting.

This expectation requires a conceptual understanding of mathematics that has sufficient flexibility to permit students to analyze informal problems that occur outside the boundaries of the conventional tasks presented in mathematics curricula. Along with their mathematical understanding, students must acquire a set of procedures for the operations of mathematics. Evidence from studies of simple addition and subtraction (e.g., Blote, van der Burg, & Klein, 2001; Carpenter et al., 1994; Fuson, 1992; Fuson & Fuson, 1992; Riley, Greeno, & Heller, 1983) suggests, however, that even these apparently simple procedures are much more complex and rooted in conceptual understandings than most teachers and other adults believe.

As you have seen throughout this text, cognitive research on instruction emphasizes the value of comprehension-based approaches to learning. In this chapter, we pursue in considerable depth the learning and teaching of two important and illustrative components of the mathematics curriculum: addition/subtraction and algebra. Each topic is examined in some detail to demonstrate its complexity, as well as the usefulness of cognitive approaches for understanding the mathematical processes that students acquire. In contrast with the judgments of many that arithmetic is a rote skill and algebra more "conceptual," we portray both addition/subtraction and algebra as problem-solving processes.

The thrust of much cognitive research in both areas has been to search for clearer understanding of the mental processes students use to solve mathematics problems. For instance, Riley et al. (1983) and Kintsch and Greeno (1985) proposed that representing mathematics problem solving as schemata provides a vehicle for such an understanding. A *set schema,* for instance, represents the idea of parts and a whole. To illustrate, the concept of *addition* can be understood as the presentation of two or more sets (parts) mathematically combined to form a whole (the superset). In addition to a set schema, addition also requires a *change schema* to show how parts may be combined. Much of arithmetic, and potentially much of other mathematics, can be described by using these two schemata. In general, we argue that mathematics operations are not rote learning but rather require the acquisition of networks of mental representations. Understanding grows as networks become larger and more organized. The class of operations we collectively call mathematics is built on the understanding these networks represent.

For mathematics knowledge to be functional, networks of schemata must be linked with a set of procedures. These procedures, more commonly called **algorithms,** guide the actions necessary to solve problems. As you may remember from the discussion in chapter 8, algorithms are procedures (rules) that apply to a particular type of problem and that, if followed correctly, guarantee the correct answer. In arithmetic, for example, children use various counting algorithms, whereas in algebra, students learn various algorithmic routines. Algorithms are important to mathematics, but sometimes teachers and students have confused algorithmic skills with problem solving itself. Carrying out an algorithm is not problem solving, but when a student creates an algorithm and applies it to a set of problems, he or she has engaged in problem solving (Mayer & Hegarty, 1996; Wilson, Fernandez, & Hadaway, 1993).

For algorithms to be flexible enough to be used in problem solving, they need to be initiated and guided by conceptual knowledge. If they are run off in a rote manner on the basis of the surface features of problems, results can be extremely poor (e.g., see Bransford et al., 1996). Allowing students to create their own algorithms helps them link conceptual knowledge with the procedures they select. Also, as they try out various algorithms, the consequences (success or failure) of using certain procedures often will result in changes in the conceptual framework (Schoenfeld, 1992). This iterative process or interactive feedback between conceptual and procedural knowledge leads to improved representation of problems and increasingly sophisticated mathematics proficiency (Rittle-Johnson, Siegler, & Alibali, 2001).

Knowledge Acquisition

As students acquire a larger conceptual and procedural base in mathematics and a greater linkage among these conceptual and procedural elements, they become more efficient and flexible problem solvers (Carpenter et al., 1994; Hiebert & Carpenter, 1992; Schoenfeld, 1992). Expert mathematicians use the semantic (meaning) aspects of a problem to encode its relevant features. Many students in mathematics, however, appear to lack semantic information and therefore often rely on problem form—the syntactic, or surface, features of problem presentations (see Bransford et al., 1996; Mayer & Hegarty, 1996). Schoenfeld (1985) observed that many textbooks in arithmetic have taught a kind of "keyword" problem-solving method based heavily on syntactic structure. With this method children may learn a set of rote operations based on the keywords without necessarily understanding the semantic structure of the problem and being able to specify the relationships among the variables (Carpenter et al., 1994; Fennema, Franke, Carpenter, & Kelly, 1993; Kieran, 1992). Consider the following arithmetic word problem:

> Bill has six marbles and gives two to Joe. How many marbles does Bill have left?

If a student is reacting only to keywords, he or she would identify the two numbers in the problem and a keyword—in this case, *left*—that elicits the schemata for subtraction. Focusing on keywords will give the correct response for this problem. Schoenfeld (1985) observed that, in one major textbook series, the "keyword method" gave the "right" answer for virtually all problems (97 percent). But what if the problem were stated in the following "inconsistent" manner?

> Bill gave two marbles to Joe. He has four left. How many marbles did Bill have to begin with?

Many students will find this version more difficult, both for language-related and problem-representation reasons. Real-life mathematical problems are much less neatly packaged. In general, any teaching strategy permitting students to solve problems without requiring them to form meaningful (semantic) problem representations seems unlikely to help them develop flexible and sophisticated problem-solving strategies. Students need to extend the conceptual web of their mathematics knowledge by linking it with new information they understand. Only if this information is meaningful will students develop algorithms appropriate to a wide variety of mathematical tasks.

Since the early 1980s, empirical research in mathematics carried out from an information processing perspective has burgeoned. As Mayer and Hegarty (1996) have pointed out, in many ways mathematics is an ideal area in which to study cognition. The structure of mathematics provides a clear base from which to examine the development of problem solving in elementary and secondary school students. Mathematics also is very well-suited for modeling cognitive processes (see chapter 3) and illustrating our cognitive themes in education, particularly those of learning as a constructive process; the use of mental structures to organize memory and guide thought; and the contextual nature of knowledge, strategies, and expertise. We examine this body of research by focusing on problem solving first in arithmetic and then in algebra.

Arithmetic Problem Solving

At one time, mathematics educators distinguished between *computational* aspects of mathematics, which in most cases focused on learning rules such as the algorithms for addition and division, and *conceptual* aspects of mathematics, which involved problem solving and understanding. The general assumption was that basic skills were the foundation on which conceptual understandings are built. One outcome of this assumption was that beginning mathematics instruction traditionally has been aimed at mastery of arithmetic facts and computational procedures. Only after these basics were acquired and as students progressed through the grades could the emphasis gradually shift to the conceptual content and the methods of inquiry of mathematics. With the basic skills mastered, students were ready to learn and understand the content of more advanced subjects, such as algebra, probability, and calculus.

This traditional approach of "skills first, concepts later" persists in many elementary schools. Although elementary teachers now increasingly are using conceptual-based hands on approaches to teaching mathematics, arithmetic continues to be taught in many classrooms as a drill-and-practice activity in which mathematics facts and computations are discrete items to be practiced and learned. As a consequence, competence in arithmetic often is weighted toward rapid, accurate performance. This view has a long history in American education. We vividly recall, for instance, "arithmetic races" from our own elementary school experiences in which expertise was demonstrated by racing to the chalkboard and solving problems (e.g., summing several three-digit numbers) before a classmate could do the same. Even today, accurate and rapid access to basic arithmetic facts is admired.

More and more, however, researchers and educators have argued that the fundamental nature of mathematics is conceptual, not procedural (Baroody & Standifer, 1993; Bransford et al., 1996; Carpenter et al., 1994; Hiebert & Carpenter, 1992; Schoenfeld, 1992). A wealth of recent theory-driven research with young children has shown that children's knowledge about addition and subtraction (e.g., their strategies for adding or subtracting two numbers), far from being algorithmic, consists of a succession of increasingly complex and efficient conceptual structures that they invent and revise (e.g., Fuson, 1992; Fuson & Fuson, 1992; Ginsburg, 1996; Siegler, 1996). Although the computational operations for addition and subtraction are habitual for most adults and superficially seem to represent what arithmetic "is," our near-automatic performance obscures their basic problem-solving nature. The addition and subtraction algorithms that most adults employ with such ease and competence were once, for all of us, problems in the sense of our definition of problem solving in chapter 8.

Whether adult or child, we need a set of highly flexible ways of representing problems in order to employ algorithms effectively in the varied situations that require mathematical competence. If this conceptual understanding is rigid or lacking, algorithms will be applied in a rote manner and transfer of learning will be poor. Conceptually based instruction in mathematics, particularly in addition and subtraction, can be more successful in teaching students a flexible way of thinking (Blote et al., 2001). Consequently, we take the perspective that all mathematics, perhaps most especially the early stages of children's acquiring knowledge about arithmetic, should be viewed as a problem-solving activity.

What "Bugs" Can Teach Us

Studying the errors that children make in addition and subtraction has contributed greatly to our understanding of the nature of arithmetic problem solving. In their early examination of the subtraction errors of a large number of children, for instance, J. S. Brown and Burton (1978) discovered that a sizable number were consistently using one or more incorrect versions of the general subtraction algorithm. Many of the incorrect algorithms gave correct solutions part of the time and incorrect solutions in other applications. For example, some children consistently applied a subtraction algorithm, "Take the smaller number from the larger in each column", that led them to subtract smaller numbers from larger ones regardless of which number was on top:

$$
\begin{array}{rrrr}
8 & 23 & 47 & 52 \\
-3 & -16 & -35 & -17 \\
\hline
5 & 13 & 12 & 45
\end{array}
$$

Note that this incorrect, or "buggy", algorithm as Brown and Burton (1978) called them, does give the correct answer in the first and third problems; in those problems the child's subtraction algorithm seems correct. Yet, the algorithm used throughout these four problems yields the wrong answer in the second and fourth problems.

A teacher seeing all of the problems in sequence might well dismiss the mistake in the second problem as carelessness and the one in the fourth as a difficulty with borrowing, not recognizing that the child is using the same defective subtraction algorithm for all of the problems. Failure to diagnose a consistent error like this may well prevent the teacher from isolating conceptual difficulties the child is having.

By analyzing the performance of thousands of schoolchildren, (Brown and Burton, 1978; Burton, 1981) identified and classified more than 300 different subtraction bugs. This impressive array of bugs in subtraction alone led to a closer examination of the processes children use in both addition and subtraction. A first step in this examination has been to classify the different types of addition and subtraction problems so that meaningful analyses of algorithm errors could be pursued.

Problem Typologies

Finding the best way of organizing the many kinds of addition and subtraction situations that exist in the real world has been the subject of much research (Fuson, 1992). One organization possibility is to treat addition and subtraction problems as open "sentences." By varying the unknown, six addition and six subtraction sentences (e.g., $a + b = ?$ or $a - ? = c$) can be created (Carpenter & Moser, 1983). These deceptively simple tasks, in fact, do provide the content for much of early elementary school arithmetic. For elementary school students, the numbers used in these sentences yield whole-number solutions drawn from the basic arithmetic facts. These sentence types are not of equal difficulty to early elementary school children, however. In general, subtraction sentences are more difficult than addition sentences (but see Fuson & Fuson, 1992). Sentences of the form $a + b = ?$ or $a - b = ?$ are easier than sentences of the form $a + ? = c$ or $a - ? = c$, and sentences with the operation to the right of the equal sign (e.g., $c = ? - b$) are more difficult than parallel problems with the operation to the left of the equal sign. Exactly why differences like these exist has not been determined with certainty; one plausible hypothesis is that teachers and textbooks present problems in one form much more frequently than in the others. This means that students get much more practice with $a + b = ?$ structures than those with operations on the right of the equal sign. Another possibility is that some structures map better than others on the addition and subtraction strategies that children are constructing (Fuson, 1992).

Drawing on earlier work by Carpenter and Moser (1982), Riley et al. (1983), and Fuson (1992), Baroody and Standifer (1993) have classified addition and subtraction into five basic situations: change-add-to, change-take-from, part-part-whole, equalize, and compare. Both change-add-to and change-take-from involve beginning with a single collection and changing it by adding to or removing something from it. This results in a larger or smaller collection. For instance:

CHANGE-ADD-TO: Heather had six apples. Chris gave her five more apples. How many apples does Heather have altogether?

CHANGE-TAKE-FROM: Chris has five apples. He gave away two apples. How many apples does he now have?

Part-part-whole, equalize, and compare all begin with two quantities, which are either added or subtracted to find the whole of one of the parts. Two numbers are operated on to produce a unique third number. For example:

PART-PART-WHOLE: Heather had six red apples and five green apples. How many apples does she have?

EQUALIZE: Heather has six apples. Chris has three apples. How many more apples does Chris have to buy to have as many as Heather?

COMPARE: Heather has twelve apples. Chris has five apples. How many more apples does Heather have than Chris?

Each of these problem types also can be presented in different ways; for instance, the compare problem above has an unknown *difference* but also could be stated as having an unknown second part (e.g., Heather has twelve apples. She has seven more than Chris. How many apples does Chris have?) or unknown first part (e.g., Heather has some apples. She has seven more than Chris, who has five. How many apples does Heather have?).

Because primary-grade children use counting as a main means of adding and subtracting, determining how children solve these problems and their various forms requires an examination of counting strategies. Most children come to kindergarten with some counting skills, and many can count sets up to 10 objects (Van de Walle & Watkins, 1993) because 4-year-olds often are taught by parents, older siblings, or others to count to 10. In the beginning, however, children may have learned only a sequence of words and do not yet understand the critical idea of a one-to-one correspondence between a collection of objects and a particular number. But they soon begin to integrate counting to cardinal meanings of number words (e.g., that the word *three* corresponds to three things) and can use counting strategies for solving problems.

Examination of protocols of young children solving addition problems such as those outlined previously reveals three levels of counting strategies for solving problems. A description of these situations follows.

Counting All with Model   Carpenter and Moser (1982) have shown that, in carrying out the simplest addition strategy, children use physical objects or their fingers to represent each number or set to be combined, after which the combination of the two sets is counted. So, to add 4 and 7, a child represents each addend (set to be added) with a model of blocks or other objects (4 and 7, respectively) and then counts the combination of the two [in this case, 1, 2, 3, 4 (pause), 5, 6, 7, 8, 9, 10, 11].

Counting On from First   As children gain experience with numbers, their strategies change. In this more efficient addition strategy, the child recognizes that it is not necessary always to begin from 1, but begins with the first addend and then counts forward the number of the second addend. So, the child counts as follows: 4 (pause), 5, 6, 7, 8, 9, 10, 11.

Counting On from Larger   Later, an even more efficient strategy appears: The child begins with the larger addend. In our example, the child counts as follows: 7 (pause), 8, 9, 10, 11. This strategy often is used when children are asked to add numbers greater than 10, which are difficult to represent with their fingers.

During their first 4 years in school, children invent a series of increasingly abbreviated and abstract strategies to solve addition and subtraction problems (Carpenter & Moser, 1984; Fuson, 1992; Fuson & Fuson, 1992). Instruction can help students learn specific strategies in the developmental sequence. Fuson and Fuson (1992), for instance, examined students' acquisition and use of *counting on* and *counting up* strategies in a long-term project aimed at giving first and second graders opportunities to solve a wide range of addition and subtraction word problems. Children were taught to use a *counting up* strategy for subtraction. This strategy involves beginning with the first addend and then keeping track of the *number of words* said after the first addend word. For instance, to solve 10 – 7, a child would say, "7 (pause), 8, 9, 10," while keeping track of the number of words after the pause. Fuson and Fuson showed that children learned to both count on and count up very accurately. Moreover, they were as accurate and fast at counting up for subtraction as they were at counting on for addition. An important benefit of using counting up for subtraction, Fuson and Fuson argued, is that counting up uses ordinary forward counting and avoids the much more difficult backward counting that is part of the usual take away meaning of subtraction. Thus, children acquired a reliable method for subtracting, an important developmental achievement in becoming competent in solving such problems. Perhaps even more important, children in the study acquired a broader conceptual understanding of different meanings of subtraction and the minus sign.

As Fuson and Fuson point out, counting on and counting up do eventually drop out, and children move on to other strategies. The majority of first graders use some form of counting strategy. In second grade, about one third of such responses appear to be based on number facts, and by the third grade, almost two thirds of the responses are based on number facts (Carpenter & Moser, 1983). Fuson and Fuson observed, however, that many children continued using these strategies for a long time because these strategies yield reliable results. Counting methods do not appear to be crutches that interfere with more complex problem solving. In Fuson and Fuson's study, children were observed to use them productively in addition and subtraction as complex as four-digit problems with regrouping.

An early study by Lankford (1972) suggests that more than one-third of seventh graders still may be using counting strategies, rather than stored arithmetic facts, in solving addition and subtraction problems. Careful observation of adult addition and subtraction behavior also suggests that counting strategies are not limited to children! Studying the seemingly simple operations of single-digit addition and subtraction reveals their true complexity; we can easily imagine the extent of conceptual knowledge and associated algorithms needed to add and subtract two-, three-, and four-digit numbers. Although most children do acquire the necessary algorithms for solving these more complex problems, research in this area provides persuasive evidence that children will need a great deal of both conceptual and procedural knowledge to use their problem-solving skills flexibly. What specifically do children need to know in order to solve addition and subtraction problems?

Arithmetic Knowledge

Riley et al. (1983) analyzed arithmetic tasks, such as those we have described, and developed a theoretical model of the solution process. Their model takes the form of a computer simulation that solves problems of the change: It combines (part-part-whole), compares, and equalizes form. In their model, the problem text (the statement of the problem) provides the basis for task comprehension, which in turn leads to a problem representation. This representation is drawn from a network of problem schemata stored in long-term memory.

When particular problem schemata are activated, an action schema (a production) then is represented in working memory and is carried out as a solution attempt. Riley et al. propose that strategic knowledge (see chapter 3) is required to generate a sequence among the production rules that permits top-down planning for efficient and accurate problem solving. In Riley et al.'s view, every arithmetic problem requires knowledge of three sorts: (1) problem schemata (derived from the semantic structure of the problem statement), (2) action schemata (stored actions for solving problems), and (3) strategic knowledge for sequencing (planning) solutions to problems.

Problem Schemata   Riley et al. (1983) suggest that one or more problem schemata (mental representations of a problem) can be applied to every problem. Consider the following change-take-from problem:

> Joe had eight marbles. Then he gave five marbles to Tom. How many marbles does Joe have now?

Riley et al. propose that the problem representation for this task consists of three components. The first component is the *start set,* or initial quantity—eight marbles. The second component, a change, must be recognized; this is called the *take-out set*—five marbles. Finally, the fact that the remaining marbles form the third component must be recognized; this is the *result set*—three marbles.

Action Schemata   Once a problem has been represented, its solution requires knowledge of action schemata. In the marble problem above, beginning with an empty set, the problem statement instantiates a schema (put-in) such that the start set equals eight marbles (representing the sentence "Joe had eight marbles"). Then the action schema (take-out) indicates the change, the removal of five marbles from the initial set. Finally, another action schema (count-all) counts the objects remaining— giving the result set, represented by the sentence "How many marbles does Joe have now?"

Strategic Knowledge   Note that because even simple addition and subtraction problems require differing action schemata, learners need *strategic knowledge* to choose schemata appropriate to different types of problems. In addition to problem and action schemata, a top-down (strategic) approach must be acquired that matches existing schemata stored in memory with problem representations and, in turn, with action schemata. For children learning addition and subtraction, a continuing difficulty is to acquire enough flexibility in the choice of schemata so that the right schema is applied to a particular problem at the right time. Blote et al. (2001) found that teaching conceptual understanding along with procedural skills helped second graders acquire this flexibility in choosing schemata and procedures. Learning to apply schemata appropriately also involves regulation of cognition, a form of metacognitive knowledge discussed in chapter 4.

Language: Another Factor

Simple problems in arithmetic can be made more or less difficult, depending on the language used in the problem statement. In an early study, Hudson (1980) gave children problems similar to the one shown in Figure 14-1 and asked them one of the following questions: (1) How many more dogs than cats are there? (2) Suppose the dogs all race over and each one tries to chase a cat! Will every dog have a cat to chase? How many dogs won't have a cat to chase? Kindergarten children answered 25 percent of such problems correctly in response to the first question, but they answered 96 percent correctly in response to the second type. Clearly, the form of the question affects the problem representation and, consequently, the application of an appropriate solution schema. Question 1, cast in a more abstract manner, seems to lead to more problem-representation errors.

The question of level of abstraction of problem statement leads naturally to an issue of long-time concern in mathematics—word problems. Most of us can remember having difficulty with so-called story problems in algebra. Comprehending the text (an aspect of

Figure 14-1
Dogs and Cats. Hudson (1980) used problems such as this one to determine children's
difficulty with "How many more_____than_____are there?" problems.

which Hudson's study touches on), as well as comprehending the appropriate mathematical schema, apparently makes such problems difficult. Text comprehension as it
relates to arithmetic problem solving has been the topic of careful study.

Text Comprehension and Arithmetic Problem Solving

Building on work in text-processing theory by Kintsch and Van Dijk (1978; Van Dijk &
Kintsch, 1983), which proposes that readers comprehend text by segmenting sentences into propositions and by relating these propositions to one another within the
text structure (see discussion in chapter 12), Kintsch and Greeno (1985) posed this

general question: How does text processing (reading a word problem) interact with understanding the semantic information in the problem and the generation of appropriate mathematical schemata for problem solution? In other words, how are text comprehension and problem solving in mathematics related? They proposed that solving word problems is a two-step process. In the first step, the reader creates schemata for comprehending the text of the word problem. In the second step, these text schemata activate mathematics schemata. In other words, when students encounter a word problem, they first need to make sense of the problem's text. The schemata for text comprehension generate a second set of schemata for mathematics problems that lead to problem solution.

In Kintsch and Greeno's view, comprehending a word problem means constructing a conceptual representation from the text that problem-solving processes can be applied to. For example, consider a part-part-whole arithmetic problem of the sort we described earlier:

Jill has three marbles. Jack has five marbles. How many marbles do they have altogether?

This problem provides information about two sets of marbles (Jill's and Jack's). It has an unknown—the superset, or sum, of the two given sets. Kintsch and Greeno (1985) suggested that one useful representation of this task involves the creation of a set schema.

Table 14-1 represents a general set schema suitable for problems such as these. In the table, the *object slot* refers to a common noun labeling the sort of objects in the set. The *quantity slot* provides either the number of objects or a place holder (SOME and HOW MANY) denoting an indefinite statement or question. The *specification slot* distinguishes one set from the others either by name of owner or by other description. Finally, the *role slot* provides a relational term that puts a particular set in the context or structure of the entire problem.

The slots and values given in Table 14-1 describe a set schema. For the three propositions contained in the first sentence in this problem ("Jill has three marbles"), the

Table 14-1
A Schema for Representing Sets

Slot	Value
Object	(noun)
Quantity	(number), SOME, HOW MANY
Specification	(owner), (location), (time)
Role	Start, transfer, result; superset, subset; largest, smallest, difference

Source: From "Understanding and Solving Arithmetic Word Problems," by W. Kintsch and J. G. Greeno, 1985, *Psychological Review, 92*, p. 114. Copyright 1984 by the American Psychological Association. Adapted by permission.

schema slots and values (in the same order as in Table 13-1) are as follows: *object* (marbles), *quantity* (three), and *specification* (Jill). Similarly, the three propositions in the second sentence ("Jack has five marbles") take the following form: *object* (marbles), *quantity* (five), and *specification* (Jack). The last item in the schema (role) is unknown for these two sentences until the last sentence of the problem is read. To this point, the problem solver has formed two sets: a set of three for Jill and a set of five for Jack. For the third sentence ("How many marbles do they have altogether?"), the propositions are as follows: *object* (how many marbles) and *specification* (Jill and Jack together). At this point, the *role* is determined (find the superset). This leads to an action strategy—making a superset for Jill and Jack combined.

The assignment of subset roles to both Jill's and Jack's marbles is not in the text statement but rather is an inference the reader must make from the text; that is, the need to form these sets is not mentioned specifically in the problem. The necessity for such inferences intuitively suggests a potential source of error—incorrect inferences—in correctly representing word problems. Finally, the solution to the problem is computed by a procedure such as a count-all strategy that counts the total of the two subsets taken together. The superset is formed.

This elongated description of simple processes—addition and subtraction—once more illustrates the underlying cognitive complexity of mathematical learning and problem solving. The language of cognitive psychology—*knowledge acquisition, problem representation, schemata*—provides a way to picture the task of mathematical problem representation. It seems clear that helping children achieve the schema of a set is vital to success in understanding problems such as those given in the examples above. Note, however, that understanding and carrying out such an activity does not mean children must acquire the *formal* language of sets and supersets, although at some point this may well be important in mathematics instruction.

The schema-formation process we have described is especially useful for analyzing the problem solving of children having difficulty. A careful analysis of a child's schematic representations for each part of a problem may well provide a diagnosis of a "bug" in the way the schema is formed. The specificity of this process can lead to error determination and specific corrective action.

Kintsch and Greeno (1985) proposed that propositions of the type we have discussed are created as children read or hear a problem. Whenever a proposition triggers a set-building strategy, the set is formed and stored in working memory. Kintsch and Greeno also described how this intricate process relates to working-memory capacity and the use of long-term memory. They concluded that models of text processing, coupled with the hypotheses Riley et al. (1983) suggested about understanding word problems, provide plausible descriptions of arithmetic word-problem solving.

Much elaboration of these ideas is needed to provide a comprehensive description of addition and subtraction. Kintsch and Greeno point out, however, that it is not enough simply to have knowledge (say, of the meaning of a superset). Problem solvers must have strategies for building such structures as they read a problem. In some cases, teachers may find that arithmetic problems actually are reading problems. For example, Hanich et al. (2001) found that second graders with both mathematical and reading difficulties had a greater disadvantage in solving story problems than children with only a math difficulty. Teachers may need to provide support (e.g., reading a problem to a child) so that the child's attention may be focused on the arithmetic schemata activated by reading rather than on the mechanics of reading.

Developmental Issues in Arithmetic Problem Solving

Before we conclude our discussion of arithmetic problem solving in elementary school children, a significant developmental issue must be addressed. The well-known work of Piaget describes a series of developmental stages through which all children pass. These stages are age-related, with most children of kindergarten age in the preoperational stage, and children of elementary age (Grades 1 through 5) reaching the concrete-operations stage. It is in the concrete operations period that children can begin to understand concepts such as conservation of number that are necessary to mathematics learning.

One general strategy used by educators has been to look at mathematics curriculum in terms of the cognitive demands it places on children. The traditional curriculum tends to hone children's mechanical counting skills and then move almost immediately to addition and subtraction. The abstractness of arithmetic and the need for time for children to construct a variety of number relationships suggests that formal mathematics instruction might profitably be delayed in favor of informal problem-centered approaches that help children construct their own mathematical concepts (e.g., see Carpenter et al., 1994; Van de Walle & Watkins, 1993).

The reasons why children might or might not be ready for formal mathematics are not completely clear, but one possibility is that mathematical skills require dealing with a variety of bits of information and make large demands on the short-term memory capabilities of young children. Case (1978, 1985) systematically examined the short-term memory capacity of young children, defining what he called **M-space** (memory space or memory capacity, in chunks). Short-term memory capacity in adults has long been estimated to be approximately seven plus or minus two chunks of information (see chapter 3). Case's work suggests that young children are far below this adult level of performance.

Romberg and Collis (1987) carried out a systematic evaluation of short-term memory capacity in young children as a part of a larger study of mathematics competence. They proposed situations such as the following, in which a child of age 6 or 7 was asked to find a sum as follows:

TEACHER: What number equals 2 + 4 + 3?
CHILD: 2 + 4 = 6, now what was the other number?
TEACHER: What number equals 2 + 4 + 3?
CHILD: Now, 2 plus, uh, what are the numbers?

According to Romberg and Collis (1987), this conversation reveals a short-term memory difficulty. They suggested the following explanation: the request for the other number in the first response of the child does not imply an operational failure but rather a memory failure. The second response of the child suggests that the child's effort to remember the third number has resulted in a capacity overload that prompts the request to repeat the numbers. Using a series of memory tests, Romberg and Collis demonstrated that average M-space directly increases with grade level, although, as might be expected, with rather large within-grade variability. On their best measure of M-space, Romberg and Collis discovered that kindergarten children had M-space scores of almost exactly 1, whereas first grader M-spaces equaled about 1.23, and the M-spaces of second graders averaged just over 3. These data suggest a considerable difficulty with memory for younger children that might inhibit even simple abstract arithmetic problem solving.

A direct implication of these findings is that kindergarten and first-grade children are likely to face storage and processing problems in working memory when dealing with arithmetic involving abstract symbols. For the present, it seems reasonable to conclude that some apparent lack of "readiness" that primary school children exhibit may be seen more precisely as a lack of short-term memory capacity. New approaches to teaching arithmetic concepts increasingly rely on manipulables (physical objects such as dice, dominos, blocks) and on children's own invented strategies for visualizing number concepts (e.g., using fingers to count), both to build comprehension and to avoid short-term memory failures (Baroody & Standifer, 1993). Most elementary school children, of course, even without formal instruction, develop and use a variety of techniques to make arithmetic tasks visual and hence reduce memory demands.

Different aspects of mathematics also involve different cognitive abilities (Geary, Hamson, & Hoard, 2000), which may cause children to have difficulties in different areas of mathematics. Some children might have weaknesses in fact retrieval but understand counting principles and mathematical concepts; others might have strong computational skills but a weak understanding of concepts (Jordan & Hanich, 2000).

How younger children build conceptual and procedural knowledge in mathematics has dominated much of our discussion thus far. To examine these processes at a different level, we now turn to an examination of mathematical knowledge and problem solving in algebra. Understanding the cognitive processes involved in algebra also is important from a very practical standpoint: Ensuring student success in algebra is crucial because it often functions as a dividing point beyond which many students do not venture. Again we focus on word problems because of the challenge they present to many students.

Problem Solving in Algebra

Most of us recall, perhaps painfully, our experiences with algebra word or story problems (e.g., "A river steamer was going upstream . . ."). Word problems in algebra typically are encountered after a brief initial period of algebra instruction that provides basic information dealing with equations, unknowns, and so forth, and in most cases follows 7 or 8 years of instruction in various aspects of arithmetic. Thus, word problems would appear to be built on a substantial knowledge base of prior instruction in mathematics. It is unfortunate that the knowledge base is such that, in many cases, algebra word problems are perceived as something entirely new rather than as growing out of and extending prior knowledge.

The need for students to construct a problem representation while reading the problem likely is what makes algebra word problems new and difficult. The propositions in the text must be understood and converted into a mathematical representation. Student performance with algebra word problems, coupled with students' expressed dislike for such tasks, suggests that the issues raised by Kintsch and Greeno (1985) in the previous section are real. The dual tasks of reading and comprehending the text of an algebra problem and at the same time constructing the appropriate mathematics representation for problem solution pose a difficult challenge to many students. An adequate representation of a problem is critical because only a good representation will lead to a solution (Brenner et al., 1997; Mayer & Hegarty, 1996; Rittle-Johnson et al., 2001). In many mathematics curricula, however, students have little experience with comprehension processes and problem representation. Story problem solving is likely to be difficult unless algebra students are given extensive guided practice in both comprehending and representing mathematics problems stated in story form.

In an important early study, Mayer (1981) analyzed algebra word problems in high school algebra textbooks. He found more than 100 problem types, including 12 kinds of distance/rate/time problems. He also discovered that problems differed in frequency of appearance in the textbooks and that when he asked students to read and then recall a series of 8 story problems, they remembered high-frequency problems more successfully (Mayer, 1982). This finding suggests that students store their story schemata for common types of algebra problems in long-term memory.

Silver (1981), in an interesting example of studies of schema development for algebra word problems, asked seventh graders to sort 16 story problems into piles and then compared the sorting performance of good and poor problem solvers. Good problem solvers tended to sort the stories on the basis of an underlying algebra schema. Poor problem solvers, however, tended to group stories on the basis of the problems' *surface structure*. One may conclude from studies like these that successful problem solving is related to the formation of a wide variety of problem schemata types. However, Mayer's (1981) finding of a variety of problem types (as many as 12) within a problem category suggests that rather than needing to learn and store perhaps 16 to 18 clusters of schemata, algebra problem solvers must develop and store as many schemata as there are varieties of problems within a cluster—as many as 100 subtypes. To represent them all, students are likely to need systematic instruction in representing problems in a wide variety of ways, including diagrams, pictures, concrete objects, equations, number sentences, and verbal summaries in the students' own words (Brenner et al., 1997).

Explaining Algebra Errors

The implication that students need to store a very large number of schemata seems disconcerting. If algebra problems demand a new schema for each subtype, then sheer numbers make it likely that not all will be learned. Furthermore, as the size of the pool of schemata increases, the chances of learning and storing faulty schemata also must increase. Reed's work on algebra errors suggests that this may indeed be the case.

Using Inappropriate Schemata   Just as appropriate schemata can help a problem solver represent and solve word problems, so too can inappropriate schemata hinder correct problem representation and solution. Reed and his colleagues (Reed, 1984, 1987; Reed, Dempster, & Ettinger, 1985) carried out several studies of students' ability to estimate answers to algebra word problems. Consider the following problem from Reed (1984, p. 781):

> Flying east between two cities that are 300 miles apart, a plane's speed is 150 mph. On the return trip, it flies 300 mph. Find the average speed for the round trip. (Answer: 200 mph)

Working with college students, Reed (1984) found that 84 percent estimated 225 mph as the average speed. Only 9 percent gave the correct response. Why the high failure rate? Students' responses clearly showed that the problem elicited an "average speed" schema, but the overwhelming majority of students saw the problem as one of a *simple* average (find the sum of the two speeds and compute the mean; 450/2 = 225 mph) rather than as a *weighted* average. In other words, for many students the problem elicited a schema ("find the average") that yielded an incorrect response. Note that implied in the problem is the fact that the plane flew twice as long at the slower speed, taking 3 hr to fly 600 miles, giving an average speed of 200 mph. Many students, unfortunately, apparently failed to make that inference.

As the work of Kintsch and Greeno (1985) and Riley et al. (1983) suggests, the need to make inferences from the written text of the word problem may activate inappropriate schemata. To test that hypothesis, Reed (1984, p. 781) gave the following version of the same problem to a group of students:

> A plane flies 150 mph for 2 hours and 300 mph for 1 hour. Find its average speed.

Note that, in this version, the fact that the plane flew slowly for 2 hours is made explicit. This time, 40 percent of students gave the correct response, and only 19 percent chose the incorrect 225-mph response. Although a substantial number still did not solve the problem correctly, making the problem more explicit apparently evoked the appropriate schema for "estimating a weighted average" in a much larger number of students.

Making Faulty Estimates   A major question growing from Reed's (1984) research was students' ability to evaluate the reasonableness of answers. For mathematics teachers and tutors, evaluating whether an answer makes sense is almost axiomatic. Yet, Reed's data suggest that few students had adequate schemata for making useful estimates of whether an answer is correct. This is illustrated more clearly with an example of a "work schema" problem, such as the following:

> It takes Bill twelve hours to cut a large lawn. Bob can cut the same lawn in eight hours. How long does it take them to cut the lawn when they both work together?

Thirty percent of students estimated the simple average—10 hours. This answer, of course, contains a serious inconsistency, implying that it takes longer for Bill and Bob to mow the lawn together than for Bob to do it alone! These students apparently lacked not only an intuitive schema for when and how to compute weighted averages, they also lacked an "estimation" schema for evaluating the reasonableness of their answers. Reed pointed out the value of estimation as a tool for detecting a student's intuitive "problem-solving" schema. He further argued that students develop schemata for a particular type of algebra problem that translate into an algorithm for solution. If a student does not estimate well and lacks number sense (e.g., Van de Walle & Watkins, 1993), then this is partial evidence that an algorithm is being applied by rote and is not based on understanding.

Failure to Use Analogies Effectively   New learning occurs more readily if it is seen as analogous to previously mastered concepts. For instance, Gick and Holyoak (1980, 1983) used analogies to help problem solvers represent tasks. They gave general problems and solutions to students who then were asked to solve related problems. Although the procedure generally was helpful, many students did not use the first problem to solve the second until they were given an explicit hint that it was valuable for solving the second problem.

Reed et al. (1985) hypothesized that, in an area such as algebra word problem solution with a limited number of problem types, analogies might prove more directly useful. They predicted that solvers given a practice problem from a particular cluster of problems would use that information to solve similar problems from the same cluster. Reed et al. carried out an elaborate set of experiments to test this hypothesis, but the results were, in the main, disappointing. Students were able to use a practice problem as an analogy for solving subsequent equivalent problems *only when the practice problem was carefully analyzed and summarized for them*. When given problems similar, but not equivalent, to the practice problems, they failed to see them as analogous and could not solve them. Instead, most students attempted to match exactly the solution of the practice problem with the new problem. This resulted in failure, of course, because the problems were not identical.

Careful research efforts like these suggest that reducing errors in algebra word problem solving is difficult. Apparently, students' schemata often are incompletely understood or stored so specifically that they are not perceived as useful for solving other problems. Further, if a match is made with their stored schemata, solvers often appear to use it almost by rote, so problems not identical to stored schemata often are not solved.

To summarize, a schema-based approach to mathematics may be useful both to explain learning and as a means for diagnosing errors, but learners may or may not use schemata effectively. Schema-based approaches seem to work well in arithmetic, but the research in algebra suggests that although students do form schemata, the schemata by themselves often are not sufficient for problem success. One crucial difference between the two subject areas may be the number of schemata that must be learned. Another difference may be the extent to which the schemata are learned meaningfully and grounded in students' informal knowledge (Ginsburg & Baron,

1993). The evidence supplied by Reed and his colleagues suggests that, in too many cases, algebra instruction produces rote acquisition of schemata that cannot be applied to problems even slightly different from those on which the schemata were based. These kinds of findings have broad implications for the need for basic changes in the teaching of mathematics.

Cognitive Psychology and Mathematics Instruction

As we indicated at the beginning of this chapter, new conceptions of mathematics teaching and learning and their expression in the standards of the National Council of Teachers of Mathematics (2000, 1991) emphasize the goals of building understanding and positive attitudes. Procedural skills in mathematics are not neglected—without reliable algorithms, problems cannot be solved—but they need to be grounded in a strong, flexible knowledge base containing linked conceptual, procedural, and strategic knowledge.

Our view of mathematics learning and teaching is fully in keeping with this perspective. We contend that, in both arithmetic and algebra, a cognitive perspective provides useful insights into their problem-solving nature. We take the position that all of mathematics instruction might be treated as a predominantly cognitive enterprise and, in particular, as a problem-solving activity. This has not led us to include a chapter on problem solving in mathematics, but rather to recommend problem solving as the instructional orientation for all topics in the mathematics curriculum. Is this approach viable? Is it necessary?

Carpenter (1985) and others (e.g., Fuson, 1992; van de Walle & Watkins, 1993) have asserted that, prior to formal instruction in arithmetic, almost all children exhibit reasonably sophisticated and appropriate mathematics problem-solving skills, including attending, counting, modeling problems, and inventing more and more efficient procedures. Unfortunately, children's performance several years later is too often characterized by their trying to solve problems by arithmetic operations based on surface details. The traditional push toward computational skill mastery seems to cause many children to abandon earlier, more flexible problem-solving approaches in favor of more compartmentalized numeric thinking and application of rote skills. Traditional, computation-oriented instruction can have the result of teaching children that mathematics is merely an exercise in symbol manipulation unrelated to problem solving. Unfortunately, acquiring that belief can create tremendous obstacles in learning mathematics. Once students divorce mathematics from problem solving, difficulties in later course work seem inevitable.

Are these scholars correct? By the eighth or ninth grade, many students do appear to apply algebra schemata in highly specific, inflexible ways, suggestive of a rote process. At the same time, the research in arithmetic problem solving provides reasonable evidence that possession of more powerful and flexible strategies grounded in conceptual knowledge leads to improved problem solving. This knowledge, not computational skills, permits problem solving. Versatile mathematics performance requires combining conceptual, procedural, and strategic knowledge. In a study of highly effective Korean mathematics classrooms, Grow-Maienza, Hahn, and Joo (2001) found that Korean teachers' focus on the systematic conceptual development of procedures and operations was a major difference from mathematics teaching in Japan and the United States.

Procedures can be taught essentially by rote, of course. The challenge for all teachers and, in the context of this chapter, the challenge to mathematics teachers especially is to help students develop the conceptual web of information and metacognitive knowledge underlying the procedures and strategies for using them flexibly. The problem-solving approaches that young children bring to the learning of mathematics must be nurtured and built on, not extinguished (see Bransford et al., 1996; Hiebert & Carpenter, 1992; van de Walle & Watkins, 1993).

In the late 1970s, the National Council of Teachers of Mathematics first proposed that problem solving be the focus of mathematics instruction. The growing body of research and the many changes in curriculum since then indicate that this proposal has had considerable impact on mathematics research and practice. The view of simple addition and subtraction as problem solving, rather than algorithm memorization, is a case in point. The limited success that many algebra students have in using their knowledge flexibly, however, suggests that the view of mathematics learning as involving student reasoning, problem solving, and creative thinking has not yet been fully translated into instruction.

Many mathematics instructors continue to emphasize the development of procedures and too many students' mathematics knowledge still is being acquired by rote. Although emphasizing procedures may seem to make sense, a too-frequent outcome is the development of highly specific schemata that students can apply only to a limited number of problems (Maher, 1991). From this perspective, students faced with algebra problems requiring procedures even slightly different from their rote-memorized ones quickly display the inadequacy of their problem-solving skills. Such inadequate problem solving is not inevitable. Work by Bransford and his associates using technology to create meaningful contexts for mathematical problem solving (see chapter 10) and by Mayer and his associates on developing students' abilities to represent problems in multiple ways (Brenner et al., 1997; Mayer & Hegarty, 1996) has shown that students can learn effective mathematics problem-solving strategies. Further studies, such as those of Chipman (1988) and Jones, Krouse, Feorene, and Saferstein (1985), provide evidence that instructional sequences dealing with different types of problems within clusters, coupled with emphasis on the relevant semantic features that show the similarities and differences among problems, significantly improve student problem solving.

Accurate and flexible performance in algebra, like performance in arithmetic, comes only from acquiring a web of conceptual understandings. This conceptual structure includes declarative, procedural, and conditional knowledge from which solutions can be derived. As is true for younger children's performance with arithmetic word problems, instruction in algebra word problems must help students develop a semantic understanding and ability to represent problems in mathematical terms. Only when problem representation is based on understanding will students be able to apply their knowledge to a wide variety of problems. Highly specific approaches aimed at identifying keywords or memorizing solution algorithms will yield predictable results—a focus on surface features of problems and, most particularly, a failure to solve even slightly different problems.

Implications for Instruction

Cognitive approaches to learning mathematics imply a thoughtful approach to instruction (Maher, 1991), one that promotes learning with understanding. In learning with understanding, knowledge is constructed and mental representations are built as new information is connected with old and as new relationships are constructed (Hiebert & Carpenter, 1992). The following suggestions summarize current thinking about mathematics instruction from a cognitive perspective.

1.   *All mathematics should be taught from a comprehension-based, problem-solving perspective.*   Specific facts and concepts, procedures, algorithms, and schemata should be learned in the framework of meaningful problem solving, not as isolated items. Just as readers construct an understanding of what they read, mathematics students need to construct their knowledge about mathematics. They are most likely to do so when they are allowed to use mathematical knowledge in solving problems that are interesting and meaningful to them (Bransford et al., 1996). The process of constructing meaning in mathematics is not smooth or predictable, but over time, students can construct relationships and build understanding (Hiebert & Carpenter, 1992).

Group processes are very useful for developing flexible mathematics thinking and positive attitudes toward mathematics. For example, the *Jasper* series embeds problem-solving activities in classroom contexts that require extensive communication among students, along with applying math concepts in real-world settings and long-term projects. Students may need explicit instruction in how to work together in mathematics problem solving. While many students can interact effectively in exploring and representing problems, others will benefit from interventions stressing effective collaborative communication (Vye et al., 1997).

2.   *Mathematics instruction should focus on processes, structures, and decisions, not on answers.*   Students need to be encouraged to reflect on their own thinking and activities (see chapter 9). Problems should be structured so that students are not simply searching for right answers, but for *reasons* why a procedure might or might not be useful in a particular situation. Flexible mathematics knowledge includes not only conceptual and procedural knowledge but also metacognitive knowledge related to using it appropriately and effectively (Mevarech & Kramarski, 1997; Schoenfeld, 1992).

3.   *Build on students' informal knowledge.*   In any domain, students construct meaning from their experience. J. S. Brown et al. (1989), in their discussion of situated cognition, argue that mathematics instruction should not immediately attempt to abstract mathematics concepts and procedures from the contexts that initially gave them meaning. The implication is that, at least initially, learning should be linked with authentic problem situations that students understand well. Because procedures are built on comprehension, students will be able to apply their knowledge more flexibly.

Appropriate materials and tasks also are essential. Those most likely to develop the processes of mathematical understanding have some common features: (1) build on students' prior knowledge, (2) involve scaffolding by the teacher and peer interaction, (3) require high-level performance by the students, (4) sustain pressure for explanation and meaning, and (5) necessitate self-monitoring (Mevarech & Kramarski, 1997; Stein, Grover, & Henningsen, 1996).

4. *Teachers need to spend time verbally modeling mathematics problem-solving behavior.* Students can benefit greatly from hearing teachers think out loud while solving exemplar problems "cold." Talking through solution strategies details the procedural and strategic processes that can be used to solve problems and shows their importance. Also made explicit in teacher think alouds is the sequence of thinking, as well as the relationships between the information contained in the problem and the strategies the teacher is considering. Incorrect solutions also should be demonstrated; they show not only that errors are a natural part of mathematics reasoning but also where and how such errors can occur.

5. *Assist students in verbalizing and, if possible, visualizing processes used in solution attempts.* When mistakes occur and students get stuck, teachers can enhance student problem solving by asking them to examine what they are doing and to look for errors or new approaches. Rather than providing the correct answer when students get stuck, teachers should be coaches and facilitators.

6. *Use students' errors as a source of information on students' understanding.* How students think about mathematics problems is a source of valuable information for teachers. Errors provide especially rich information that teachers can use to search for specific misunderstandings (e.g., see Woodward & Howard, 1994). Close examination of student problem-solving processes may reveal errors attributable to a student's lack of conceptual, procedural, or metacognitive knowledge. Errors should not be taken lightly; superficial examination of error patterns may lead teachers to inappropriate conclusions about the nature of student problem-solving performance.

7. *Provide a mixture of problem types.* The common practice of grouping together all problems solvable with a particular approach seems ill-advised. A better practice is to provide a variety of problems or, even better, settings in which students can apply various kinds of mathematics knowledge as they attempt to solve a complex problem (Bransford et al., 1996; Brenner et al., 1997). Students need practice in recognizing different problem types; exposure to a variety of problems leads to both discrimination among problem types and better generalization of mathematical knowledge.

8. *Teachers themselves need appropriate levels of mathematics skill.* Implicit in the preceding suggestions is the requirement for teachers who are well prepared in mathematics and comfortable with the topic. Children enter elementary school with well-developed problem-solving skills that should be enhanced by a skilled teacher, not extinguished. Many current teachers, however, especially at the elementary level, do not have adequate levels of preparation in mathematics or understanding of new mathematics teaching methods. The National Assessment of Educational Progress (2000) found that eighth graders whose teachers majored in mathematics or mathematics education scored higher, on average, than did students whose teachers

did not major in these fields. In recognition of this situation, teacher education institutions are increasing the level of mathematics preparation required of their teachers. Also, agencies such as the National Science Foundation (NSF) increasingly are providing in-service teachers with the opportunity to learn new teaching strategies based on cognitive approaches. This increased emphasis should produce teachers who are not only more competent and confident in their own mathematics abilities but also able to use cognitively based approaches in their teaching.

Summary

A major purpose of this chapter was to demonstrate the value of a cognitive perspective for understanding how students learn mathematics. An extensive body of research on arithmetic operations, such as counting, addition, and subtraction, has shown that success in arithmetic seems to depend on the acquisition of an increasingly organized body of conceptual knowledge. Procedures (algorithms) for solving problems need to be linked closely with this conceptual knowledge. Students also need metacognitive or strategic knowledge for knowing when and how to apply their mathematical knowledge. Treating the content of addition and subtraction and other arithmetic operations as problems to be solved, rather than as sets of facts to be stored in memory, appears to be a productive approach to the learning of arithmetic content.

An examination of how students solve algebra word problems suggests that difficulties stem from students' failures to learn flexible and powerful strategies based in conceptual knowledge. Students often develop procedures applicable to only a very narrow range of problems. Consequently, faced with problems beyond that range, they have no basis for understanding the task. Some authorities have argued that traditional mathematics instruction (which is focused on content acquisition rather than on problem solving) turns productive, problem-solving primary-grade children into rigid, unproductive middle school and secondary school students. Although this position may be somewhat overstated, there is little doubt that instruction focusing on developing mathematical understanding and problem solving is an integral component of mathematics instruction.

Suggested Readings

Kilpatrick, J., Swafford, J., Findell, B. (Eds.) (2001). *Adding it up: Helping children learn mathematics*. Washington DC: National Academy Press.

This accessible volume explores how students in pre-K through eighth grades learn mathematics and recommends how teaching, curricula, and teacher education should change to improve mathematics learning during these critical years.

Grouws, D. A. (Ed.). (1992). *Handbook of research on mathematics teaching and learning*. New York: Macmillan.

Another productive undertaking of the National Council of Teachers of Mathematics, this handbook contains chapters by noted authorities reviewing research on mathematics teaching and learning in their areas of specialization.

Sternberg, R. J., & Ben-Zeev, T. (Eds.). (1996). *The nature of mathematical thinking*. Mahwah, NJ: Erlbaum.

This edited scholarly volume contains both basic and applied research about the nature of children's mathematical knowledge and how to develop students' mathematical understanding.

Chapter 15

Cognitive Approaches to Science

Naive Science Conceptions ■ *Expert-Novice Differences in Science* ■ *A Model for Teaching Science* ■ *A Model of Science Achievement* ■ *Implications for Instruction* ■ *Summary* ■ *Suggested Readings* ■

As our world grows increasingly technological and complex, a knowledge and understanding of science becomes a necessity for all students. Although only an estimated 2 percent of students actually will become scientists, the need to be able to analyze scientific information and understand scientific concepts will pervade all students' lives. *Before It's Too Late: A Report to the Nation from the National Commission on Mathematics and Science Teaching for the 21st Century* (2000) outlined four key reasons for increased science and mathematics competency: the rapid pace of change in the global economy and the workplace, the role of math and science in everyday decision making, its close ties to our national security, and its intrinsic role in shaping and defining our common life, history, and culture.

These are compelling reasons but they are not new. As science knowledge and discovery has accelerated since the early 1970s, the concern over science education also has grown—more than 400 science education reform documents have been published since 1970. Publications outlining the national science standards, including the *National Science Education Standards* (National Research Council, 1996), *Benchmarks for Science Literacy* (American Association for Advancement of Science, 1993), and *Inquiry and the National Science Education Standards* (National Research Council, 2000), all advance the perspective that the goal of science teaching should be *scientific literacy* for all children.

Scientific literacy extends far beyond the rote memorization of facts and definitions, emphasizing that students develop an understanding of the scientific method and scientific concepts. To fully appreciate the scientific method (the development and testing of hypotheses), students must learn science as a problem-solving process—it must be inquiry-based and constructivist in nature (Tobin, Tippins & Gallard, 1994). Unfortunately, many science curricula and science textbooks place a premium on vocabulary rather than on problem-solving. Carey (1986) found that middle school and high school science texts introduce more new vocabulary per page than foreign language texts! For students to become scientifically literate, they must move beyond learning vocabulary and learn to use scientific concepts to solve problems, not only in the classroom and laboratory but also in real life.

How can we foster scientific literacy? Much of what we have discussed in previous chapters comes into play when we think about the cognitive basis for developing scientific literacy: memory, declarative and procedural knowledge, encoding and retrieval processes, and other cognitive factors all play a part. But certain factors that have been recognized to play pivotal roles in all learning are especially relevant to the learning and teaching of science. In *How People Learn* (2000), Bransford et al. distill a broad review of learning research down to three key findings, all of which relate to our discussions in this text:

- Students come to the classroom with preconceptions about how the world works, and if their initial understanding is not engaged, they may fail to grasp new concepts and information, or they may not retain them once they leave the classroom.
- To develop competence in an area of inquiry, students must: (a) have a deep foundation of factual knowledge, (b) understand facts and ideas in a contextual framework, and (c) organize knowledge in ways that facilitate retrieval and application.
- A metacognitive approach to instruction can help students learn to take control of their own learning by helping them to define learning goals and to monitor their progress in achieving goals.

These three findings are especially applicable to developing science literacy and will structure some of our thinking about how to foster science learning in the classroom.

Perhaps more than in any other discipline, students bring many tenacious preconceptions to the science classroom that strongly effect how they learn science. We begin this chapter by examining how these preconceptions evolve and what educators can do to change them. Much of this research draws on seminal studies of naive theories conducted during the 1980s and on later studies of conceptual change. The first section of this chapter deals with the effects of such preconceptions and how they can be confronted and changed.

Many of the important ways that students can develop competence in science can be illustrated through research contrasting the ways that experts and novices learn. One key assumption is that expertise differences are related to differences in problem-solving processes (Anzai, 1991). Much research on effective problem solving, which is possibly the core competency of science learning, has compared the performance of experts (e.g., college physics instructors) and novices (e.g., undergraduate physics majors). These studies reveal that it is the *way* experts learn and use their knowledge, not simply their general abilities in memory or intelligence, that makes them expert (Bransford et al., 2000). Experts differ from novices in the depth of their knowledge and the ways that they organize and transform their knowledge. They also tend to have well-developed metacognitive strategies. The discussion in this chapter of the differences between science experts and novices parallels the discussion in chapter 8.

The third part of this chapter describes a model for science instruction based on current research and practice that focuses on inquiry and scaffolded instruction and the development of scientific thinking and metacognitive skills—applying to the science classroom many of the techniques for fostering cognitive growth that were discussed in chapter 9. In the last part of this chapter, we overview a model of science achievement that considers the effects of family, prior learning, instructional time, and instructional quality on students' science achievement.

Naive Science Conceptions

Young children are intuitive scientists who from an early age constantly observe and question their world, developing hypotheses and concepts about how the world works. By the time children enter school they already have many well-formed, strongly held, yet often scientifically incorrect, scientific conceptions. Children and many adults hold these **naive beliefs** that are often remarkably well-articulated theories of scientific phenomena developed on the basis of their everyday experiences. These theories provide people with causal explanations for how the world operates McCloskey (1983).

In a now-classic experiment, McCloskey, Caramazza, and Green (1980) asked college students to respond to situations like that shown in Figure 15-1. They then used students' reactions to these situations to determine the extent to which they understood Newtonian (classic) physics. Students encountered the two drawings of a coiled tube shown in the figure. Each drawing shows a marble leaving the exit of a coiled tube. The students' task was to determine which line (straight or curved) better depicted what would happen if someone rolled a marble through the tube. One solution (the straight line) represents both what the laws of physics say will happen and what actually happens when this experiment is conducted.

Surprisingly, McCloskey et al. found that even students who had taken a course in high school physics gave answers that showed naive conceptions of physical laws. One-third of the students indicated that the ball would continue in a curved line, an outcome that violates Newton's first law (inertia), which states that any object continues either in a state of rest or in uniform, straight-line motion unless acted on by another force.

The errors observed by McCloskey et al. and those reported in a similar study that used gravity problems (Champagne, Klopfer, & Anderson, 1980) reveal that incorrect responses represent people's naive, intuitive conceptions of physics. The ordinary experiences of everyday life, and even prior schooling, are a source of data that seem to support naive

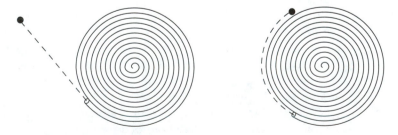

Figure 15-1
Balls Leaving Coiled Tubes. McCloskey, Caramazza, and Green (1980) used figures like this one to determine students' understanding of Newtonian physics.

theories. Consequently, the presence of well-developed, but incorrect, theories, coupled with everyday experiences that seem consistent with these theories, leads to beliefs about how the world operates that are very difficult to change. In fact, many students find their naive concepts superior to the abstract and, in many cases, seemingly counterintuitive principles of Newtonian physics.

To illustrate, Clement (1983) presented data on naive beliefs about motion. In this problem, an object, such as the block in Figure 15-2, is tossed into the air and is caught by the tosser. The problem solver is asked to draw a diagram and to use arrows to show the direction of the force acting on the block at any particular point. The left side of Figure 15-2 shows an expert's response; the right side shows a typical incorrect response.

The "simple" expert drawing (see Figure 15-2) appears to ignore (and contradict) the intuitive, and incorrect, "upward motion" illustrated in the right part of the figure—what students call the "force of the throw." Clement (1983) reported that only 12 percent of engineering students responded correctly to this question prior to taking a college physics course. He then gave the same problem to two more experienced groups of students. Only 28 percent of a group who had completed the introductory course in mechanics (in which motion is a prominent topic) responded correctly. And only 30 percent of a second group, who had completed two semesters of physics (including mechanics), solved the problem correctly. Although these data suggest that instruction improves class performance somewhat, a remarkably high percentage (more than 70 percent) continued to display naive responses. Teaching effectiveness aside, these data suggest the difficulty that teachers may have in overcoming naive beliefs (Clement, 1991, 1992).

Another example of the naive concepts that students have about the workings of the world can be seen in Osborne and Freyberg's (1985) study in which, among other questions related to biology, children were asked whether certain objects were plants. Amazingly, only 60 percent of 12- and 13-year-olds in the study identified carrots as plants, and only 80 percent of 14- and 15-year-olds agreed that oak trees were plants. In

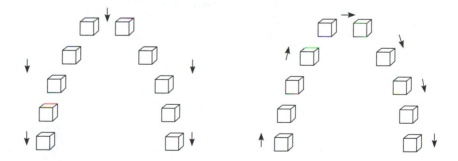

Figure 15-2
Conception of the Force Acting on a Block Tossed into the Air (arrows indicate direction of force). An expert's conception of the force acting on a block tossed into the air is presented on the left. The right side is a novice's response. This task is similar to that used by Clement (1983).

fact, 10 percent of 12- and 13-year-olds thought that grass was not a plant. It was not clear from the study what the dissenting children thought carrots, oaks, and grass were, but there is no question that their conceptual systems related to plants were rudimentary.

Still another instance of poorly developed conceptual systems can be seen in an experiment reported by Osborne and Freyberg (1985) that focused on a typical elementary school science problem—electrical flow. In this case, Osborne and Freyberg presented children with a simple electrical circuit problem (see Figure 15-3) in which a battery was used to light a bulb. When the students were asked to show how the electric current flows in the circuit, about 35 percent of 10- to 14-year-old participants reported that current in both wires flowed from the battery to the bulb. In fact, only 80 percent of 17- to 18-year-old participants were able to make the correct response and indicate that current flows through the wire in one direction, with the same current level in both wires. The overwhelming evidence indicates that students not only lack scientific information but also bring misinformation that affects the way they try to understand problems (Clement, 1991, 1992; Linn, Songer, & Eylon, 1996; Pintrich, Marx, & Boyle, 1993). Students' misconceptions tend to be very powerful—in some areas, negating direct evidence they observe in experimental and classroom settings. Some researchers (see Kuhn, 1989, for a review) argue that this misinformation is more than a simple set of false beliefs. Instead, they argue that most students lack a coordinated and consistent conceptual system for understanding the world. They appear to have a set of incomplete and uncoordinated schemata that arise primarily from unguided experience—that is, uncontrolled observation.

Other researchers have taken an even stronger position, arguing that many students possess well-organized but incorrect conceptual systems. For example, Carey (1985) and Carey and Smith (1993) have argued that elementary school children have very rich conceptual frameworks. These frameworks are not simply fragmentary, unconnected false beliefs; instead, they are coherent conceptual systems, albeit incorrect, that are consistent with many real-life observations.

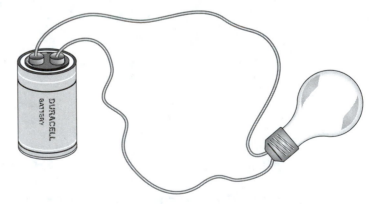

Figure 15-3
A Simple Electrical Circuit. A figure such as this one was shown to children in Osborne and Freyberg's (1985) study.

Regardless of which view of children's misinformation is correct, students bring considerable erroneous information to science classes. This information must be unlearned before appropriate conceptual systems can be acquired. Unfortunately, because students' incorrect conceptual systems are the result of a life's worth of personal, unguided observations of the world, these systems may be strongly held and difficult to change. Teachers must expect children to have incorrect conceptions and, indeed, seek them out. Because children's beliefs have developed out of their life experiences, children are not likely to abandon them unless they are presented with instruction that shows new ideas are "more intelligible, more plausible, and more fruitful" than old, incorrect beliefs (Osborne & Freyberg, 1985, p. 48).

To summarize, as a consequence of long periods of informal knowledge accumulation, many, perhaps most, students have misconceptions about science that may be difficult to change through classroom instruction. Before students can learn new and more appropriate scientific concepts they often need to reconceptualize these deeply held misconceptions—a process that is likely to be slow and will require more than simply correcting errors (Bransford, Brown, & Cocking, 2000). Many naive scientists appear to trust their intuitions more than they do laboratory experiments that appear to contradict those intuitions. Teachers must be aware of students' intuitive (and often incorrect) science knowledge, draw out and work with existing misconceptions, and use this as a starting point for new learning (Bransford et al., 2000). Substantial instructional time must be used to present students with situations that expose their naive beliefs so that they may be confronted.

Confronting Naive Beliefs

Unlike mathematics, where much of the content is taught first in school settings, children accumulate science knowledge based on observations they make in daily life. Children learn physical "laws" as they throw a ball, do a sit-up, play on a slide, or turn on a lamp. These experiences permit the development of inadequate, incomplete, and often incorrect conceptions of how the world operates. Much of this knowledge is tacit, unarticulated information embedded in the actions of the child (Kuhn, 1989). These conceptions are stored in memory and, quite naturally, provide the basis for explanations when children are faced with science problems. Teachers not only should expect to find these naive beliefs but also must find ways of seeking them out before systematic science instruction can begin.

The best way to eliminate naive, incorrect beliefs is to expose them and confront them directly (Pintrich et al., 1993). Such confrontation requires more than the mere teaching of basic science facts, or *cold* conceptual change, as Pintrich et al., refer to it. Instead, instruction in science must be experience-based within the context of the classroom and must provide a motivational incentive to change.

In summarizing a comprehensive review of studies in conceptual change, Pintrich et al., identified four necessary conditions for meaningful conceptual change to occur. One condition is *dissatisfaction* with current conceptions. Unless students (and teachers) have sufficient reason to abandon naive beliefs, it is unlikely that a radical change will occur. A second condition is that new conceptions must be *intelligible*. Clearly, students will feel little need to replace existing beliefs with new beliefs that have even less explanatory power. A third condition is that new conceptions must be *plausible*. In essence, plausibility increases the chances that new beliefs will be related meaningfully to existing knowledge structures and be used during scientific problem solving. The final condition is that new frameworks must appear *fruitful* in order to facilitate further investigation.

Other researchers have investigated the extent to which conceptual restructuring is necessary (Chinn & Brewer, 1993; Vosniadou & Brewer, 1987). Special emphasis has been put on two kinds of conceptual change. The first is *weak restructuring,* in which existing knowledge in a specific domain, such as physics, is reorganized but not added to. This kind of conceptual change may be appropriate when students possess relevant expert knowledge that nevertheless leads to erroneous conclusions. The second kind of conceptual change is *radical restructuring,* which is appropriate when students possess naive theories that are deficient, compared with those of experts. In this case, students "do not simply have an impoverished knowledge base compared to that of an expert; the novice has a different theory, different in terms of its structure, in the domain of the phenomenon it explains, and in its individual concepts" (Vosniadou & Brewer, 1987, p. 54). Radical restructuring may be necessary when students possess relevant knowledge but lack relevant conceptual structure to that knowledge. Only by redefining what they already know (and perhaps adding new knowledge) can these students hope to understand important scientific concepts adequately.

A Model for Changing Naive Beliefs

Nussbaum and Novick (1982) proposed a threefold strategy for changing naive beliefs: (1) reveal and understand student preconceptions, (2) create conceptual conflict with those preconceptions, and (3) encourage the development of revised or new schemata about the phenomena in question. We examine each step below.

Revealing Student Preconceptions   Teachers must first engage students in activities that reveal their naive beliefs (Demastes, Good, & Peebles, 1996; White, 1993). Figure 15-4, based on the work of Nussbaum and Novick (1982), presents the responses of

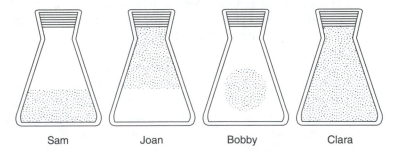

Sam   Joan   Bobby   Clara

Figure 15-4
Children's Depictions of a Science Problem. These depictions are representative of those made by elementary students at a university laboratory school when they were told half the air in the flasks had been pumped out.

some elementary students at a laboratory school to an exposing event dealing with the particle theory of gases. In this event, students were shown a flask and a vacuum pump. They were told that half of the air in the flask had been drawn out with the pump. The children then were asked to imagine that they possessed magic spectacles that permitted them to see the air remaining in the flask. Finally, they were asked to draw a picture on the chalkboard of the air remaining in the flask. On completing the drawings, students were asked to describe and explain them. This class activity thus generated both verbal and pictorial accounts of student preconceptions.

Figure 15-4 shows that students hold a wide range of conceptions about the nature of gases. Obviously, all members of the class do not share the same view of the properties! During this first stage of instruction, the teacher's major role is to help students express their ideas clearly and concisely. The teacher also encourages students to confront each other's ideas but does not judge the adequacy of students' responses. Students' exchange of views not only is interesting to them but also serves to clarify each student's own thinking. These activities serve to move the students to the next phase.

Creating Conceptual Conflict   The drawings and explanations generated by the class are posed as alternatives to whatever view each child holds. If it happens that the "correct" or "scientific" view is not posed by the children, the teacher may wish to supply it as one given by a student in another class. The teacher resists students' appeals for "which is the right one?"

Student-to-student discussion in itself may change some students' conceptions. After allowing substantial time for discussion, the teacher leads the students to see the need for an empirical test to determine the merits of the alternatives. Teacher questions such as "How can we decide which is better?" or "What can we do to decide?" may help students see the need to gather evidence for decision making.

The test must be selected so that, after careful examination, it will eliminate all but the scientifically correct alternative. In the example from Nussbaum and Novick, the teacher diverted the children to a different task altogether. She took a syringe, closed the opening at the end, and then drove the plunger halfway into the barrel. She asked the class to describe the nature of the contents of the apparently empty syringe, to which they responded, "air." She then asked what happened to the air when she pushed the syringe halfway home. Students readily generated answers that included some version of "squeezing" or "compressing" the air. As a technique for generalizing the meaning of the concept of *compression,* the teacher reminded the children of earlier work with liquids and solids that had demonstrated their relative lack of compressibility and asked them to speculate about the special characteristics of air that permitted it to be compressed.

Following discussion of this question, the teacher returned the children's attention to the "exposing event" (the partially evacuated flask) and asked them to think about the air in the flask and the syringe. According to Nussbaum and Novick, in several replications of this experience, some child always made a comment such as "Maybe the air is made up of little pieces with empty space between." The class then reviewed the drawings made during the exposing event and began to make inferences and to eliminate various alternatives. In this process, students raise questions that lead to the final phase.

Encouraging Cognitive Accommodation   After the empirical test has been completed and discussed, the teacher needs to give students support, new information, and elaboration of existing information that will help them restructure their ideas about the situation in question. In the gas example, students frequently asked such questions as "What holds the particles apart?" This question brought up another property of gases—the inherent motion of the particles. To complete the teaching example, the teacher drove the plunger still farther into the syringe and asked the students to comment. Finally, she asked whether she could compress the air to zero volume, reminding the students that a limit of compressibility is reached when no space is left between the particles.

The air example provides you with some sense of the complexity of obtaining student explanations of physical phenomena and how those naive explanations can, by use of the students' own questions and comments, be used to lead them toward more scientific conceptual structures. When students' discussions are followed by empirical tests that permit students to discover a more nearly scientific explanation, many students acquire more accurate science schemata.

Expert-Novice Differences in Science

It goes without saying that few elementary or secondary school students will achieve the expertise of professional physicists, chemists, or biologists. Nor is it reasonable to think that they should. Researchers study experts and the ways they solve problems not in the belief that every student should become an expert, but because the study of expertise shows what successful learning looks like (Bransford et al., 2000). But just what are the characteristics of expert problem solvers in science?

Differences in Problem Solving

Studies of experts show that they possess substantially more information than novices (Ericsson, 1996; Glaser & Chi, 1988). Experts also solve problems much more quickly than novices. This finding suggests that experts, even though they have far more relevant knowledge to search in memory, are much more efficient at searching a particular solution space. Their retrieval of information is more fluent. This fluency of retrieval is important because it places fewer demands on the problem solver's conscious attention and frees up more attention for other parts of the task (L. Anderson, 1981; Schnieder & Shiffrin, 1985), as discussed in chapter 3.

Studies of solution time also reveal that experts' superior recall can be explained in terms of how they *chunk* information. You may recall from chapter 3 that chunks are schemalike structures for storing declarative knowledge. For example, in solving a problem an expert may recall a number of equations all linked with a particular physics principle as a single configuration, or "bundle"; this is followed by a pause, and then the recall of another bundle of equations appropriate to another relevant principle. Novices, in contrast, show no such chunking patterns. The presence of bursts of recall among experts suggests, consistent with our discussion of mathematics problem solving, the presence of meaningfully linked schemata elicited as bundles when appropriate problem demands are encountered.

This ability to chunk information and to organize it into schemas underlies another trait of experts—the ability to recognize meaningful patterns of information. Studies of chess masters (DeGroot, 1965; Chi, 1978) and expert mathematicians (Hinsley, Hayes, & Simon, 1977) show that experts can quickly recognize patterns of information, such as successful chess moves and particular problem types, and realize the implications of the patterns.

A major difference between experts and novices is that experts organize their knowledge around the big ideas or core concepts in their domain. Novices tend to organize their problems around the surface structure of the problems (equations to use and how to use them), whereas an expert tends to begin with the fundamental science principles (Newton's laws) that often only are implied by problem statements (Anzai, 1991).

Research contrasting experts and novices in science also has revealed some differences that are more difficult to describe. One important difference between novices and experts is experts' use of what Larkin (1977) referred to as "qualitative analysis" and what Simon and Simon (1978) called "physical intuition." In both cases, the authors were referring to the development of rather elaborate problem representations, often representations that include the construction of a sketch or other physical version of the problem. Such elaborate problem representations, whether visual or verbal or both, typically are constructed as a first (or early) step in problem solving. They apparently serve to locate ambiguity in problem descriptions and to clarify or make specific aspects of the problems that must be deduced or inferred. Once constructed, these sophisticated task representations serve to generate succeeding solution steps, such as particular solution equations.

Still another difference between experts and novices is in their choice of strategies. As described in chapter 8, experts consistently use a *working-forward* (or means–ends) strategy, whereas novices use a *working-backward* approach (Anzai, 1991). Experts appear to identify problem variables and then move forward to generate and solve equations that use existing information. Novices, in contrast, seem to begin the solution process with an equation that contains the problem unknown (the desired end product). If the equation contains a variable that was not given, novices work backward from that equation, searching for one that yields (they hope) the variable they need.

For example, suppose the solution to a physics problem required solving the equation $V = mgh$, where the several values in the equation are unknown but h is the unknown asked for by the question. The novice, on the one hand, typically works backward from that equation, seeking to generate other equations that will give the values of m, g, and V so that ultimately the equation can be solved for h. The expert, on the other hand, apparently understanding the problem in a more fundamental way, works forward from a set of equations generated from the problem statement, concluding the solution sequence with the equation $V = mgh$ in a fashion so that all relevant values are known and are placed in the equation, and the solution to h is calculated. It seems the rich network of information that experts possess is organized into schemata that use key concepts from problem statements and from their own knowledge base to instantiate forward-moving solution procedures. These science schemata seem very similar to the algebra schemata described in chapter 14.

Once schemata related to the fundamental principles are activated, experts use stored procedural knowledge to generate solution attempts that then are tested against the requirements of the problem statement. Experts possess substantially more procedural knowledge than novices. This difference in procedural knowledge may account for the differences in problem-solving strategies chosen by experts (working forward) and novices (working backward).

Differences in Understanding Theories

Profound differences exist between experts and novices in their understanding of science (diSessa, 1993; Linn et al., 1996; White, 1993). Kuhn, Amsel, and O'Loughlin (1988) and Kuhn (1989) examined some of these differences among children, lay adults, and practicing scientists. Kuhn and colleagues proposed that children experience more difficulty with science for two reasons. One is that they lack domain-specific knowledge and strategies used by adult experts. These differences were described above. Another reason is that children fail to understand the structure and scientific uses of a theory.

Formal scientific theories have at least two distinguishable parts: a *formal aspect* (postulates about how a phenomenon occurs) and an *empirical aspect* (a test of those postulates, usually in the form of data or mathematical proofs). Kuhn (1989) found that most children and many lay adults (e.g., young adults who did not attend college) failed to distinguish between these two aspects of a theory. As a consequence, they either adjusted experimental data to fit the theory or changed the theory to fit the data even when the data were ambiguous or unreliable. Both of these adjustment strategies were faulty for one important reason: They prevented children from coordinating data and theory. In contrast, educated adults and especially practicing scientists, were quite skilled at coordinating data and theory.

Kuhn (1989) identified three essential skills in scientific reasoning: (1) having explicit awareness of what a theory says, (2) distinguishing between evidence that supports or refutes the theory, and (3) justifying why the data support one theory but not another. It turns out that many children and lay adults often fail to understand the theories they are expected to work with and therefore find the two remaining steps impossible to complete (Carey & Smith, 1993; Linn et al., 1996). In addition, ample evidence suggests that children and many adults fail to distinguish between different kinds of evidence (Kuhn, 1991). For example, Kitchener and King (1981) found that many college undergraduates could not provide a detailed justification for why data support one viewpoint but not another.

Kuhn has proposed some strategies for improving scientific reasoning. One strategy is to help students recognize and compare alternative theories, a second is to provide practice coordinating a given set of data with competing theories, and a third is to increase metacognitive awareness of the scientific reasoning process itself. Studies have reported that teacher modeling coupled with guided discovery improves each of these dimensions significantly (Kuhn et al., 1992; Schauble, 1990).

Carey and Smith (1993) have suggested a fourth strategy for improving scientific reasoning that addresses the relative sophistication of students' epistemological beliefs (see chapter 7). In this view, some children fail to distinguish between theories and to coordinate evidence within a theory because they adopt a *commonsense,* rather than a *critical,* epistemological worldview. The former assumes (often tacitly) that a theory is a collection of facts based on unequivocal data. The latter assumes that a theory is a constructed approximation to reality that may or may not be supported by the data (or rational analysis). As a consequence, students adopting a critical epistemology place a great deal more emphasis on evaluating the quality of data and coordinating it with the formal postulates of the theory.

Carey and Smith designed a scientific thinking curriculum that focused on two important skills: theory building and explicit reflection on the theory-building process (see chapter 9). Carey, Evans, Honda, Jay, and Unger (1989) tested this approach by asking junior high students to conduct a research program aimed at discovering why yeast, sugar, and water produced a gas when combined. Results were mixed in that awareness of scientific reasoning improved but not enough to suggest that genuine conceptual change had occurred. A similar study by Kuhn et al. (1992), however, indicated that guided discovery significantly improved scientific reasoning skills.

A Model for Teaching Science

The major goal of science education today is for all students to achieve scientific literacy, which encompasses much more than the big ideas curriculum (Linn et al., 1996) that educators promoted during the first half of the 20th century. Scientific literacy is not only knowing the big ideas and major principles of science, but also being able to use science-related knowledge in our everyday lives, being able to analyze scientific issues by asking relevant questions and proposing explanations based on evidence, and having a sufficient understanding of science to be informed citizens (AAAS, 1993; National Commission on Mathematics and Science Teaching for the 21st Century, 2000).

How students can best learn science has been the focus of much research in the past 2 decades (National Research Council, 1996, 2000; Bransford et al., 2000; Bybee, 1997; Collins, Brown, & Newman, 1989; Tobin, 1993). As we discussed in the introduction and early parts of this chapter, science classrooms should emphasize the development of understanding through inquiry-based instruction and scaffolded, cooperative learning environments. But the first challenge to teachers is to draw out students' existing misconceptions about science and engage students in tasks that reveal their thinking. These tasks must be chosen carefully, first to confront the naive beliefs, and to then cause conceptual change by giving students multiple examples of the same concept at work, leading them to develop and store schemata related to fundamental scientific laws (Kuhn, 1989; Linn et al., 1996).

To develop competence in science, students must be taught to think more like experts than novices. In addition to a good foundation of factual knowledge, they must understand those facts in a contextual framework and organize their knowledge in ways that lead to more fluent retrieval and application (Bransford et al., 2000).

Teachers need to help students acquire both declarative and procedural science knowledge and, to an even greater extent, understand the role of theories in scientific reasoning. Instruction should help students think about science problems in terms of the underlying scientific laws of the discipline. Research indicates that novices need a great deal of support in acquiring these skills and in making inferences from problem statements. For experts, such inferences lead to the activation of schemata that trigger solutions. Knowledge, independent of well-organized conceptual schemata, is not sufficient to generate procedures for successful problem solving.

Science instruction, according to this view, should be directed at building knowledge structures (schemata) that allow learners to react to problems with appropriate solution procedures. The trick is to help students organize their knowledge into schemata that are productive and related to fundamental scientific concepts. Such organization is critical.

Research shows that it is important that subject matter be taught in depth; fewer topics should be covered in more detail, allowing better understanding of key concepts (Bransford et al., 2000). One way to achieve this is to extend science instruction over many years rather than to devote 1 year to chemistry and another to physics. Aldridge (1992) has argued that using a "layer cake" approach in which students study a topic, such as chemistry, and then move on to other topics without ever returning to chemistry fails to provide sufficient depth within the topic area. Another approach is to adopt a "spiral" approach to instruction, in which students return to important issues in chemistry or physics on a yearly basis. Achieving this goal will require much better coordination of the curricula across school years.

Using a metacognitive approach to instruction helps students define their learning goals and monitor their own progress in achieving goals—leading to much greater self-regulation and learning. Direct instruction in the skills of reflective thinking and self-assessment, combined with formative assessment strategies that provide feedback to guide students, have been shown to increase the degree to which students will transfer learning to new situations (Palincsar & Brown, 1984).

Inquiry-Based Instruction

If there is any sort of consensus in the research about science teaching and learning, it centers on the importance of inquiry. The documents outlining national standards for science education, supported by much of the educational research, stress the need for inquiry-based instruction to develop the broad understanding and critical-thinking and problem-solving skills necessary for science literacy.

What is inquiry? The inquiry-based classroom grows from the constructivist viewpoint and has many of the characteristics we outlined in chapter 9. In these classrooms the teacher supports students who are active learners. Students participate in varied hands-on activities, posing scientifically oriented questions, collecting and using evidence to answer questions, evaluating their explanations, and communicating results to others. Inquiry is not only a hands-on process; reading, writing, and discussion play key roles in helping students construct new knowledge.

In addition to these activities, the National Research Council in *Inquiry and the National Education Standards* (2000) emphasizes the need for students to use scientific thinking. Students with scientific-thinking skills go beyond learning facts or doing a hands-on activity and become able to use logic and reasoning skills to develop scientific knowledge and an understanding of scientific processes. Inquiry-based learning can help students develop these skills.

Before we define in more detail how teachers can effectively put this model into action, we discuss the learning strategies—both dysfunctional and functional—that students bring to the science classroom.

Learning Strategies

Students come to instructional settings with learning strategies acquired from other school experiences, as well as from unstructured settings. One goal of science education is to teach students new learning strategies that help them acquire and organize information. Evidence suggests that this goal is not always met. Some students actually acquire learning strategies that interfere with learning new science material.

In one study, Roth (1985) asked middle school students to read science materials (written at their grade level) and examined how they thought about it. She identified five learning strategies used by the children, only one of which, unfortunately, resulted in restructuring and refining naive schemata. The five strategies are described briefly in the following paragraphs.

Overreliance on the Sufficiency of Prior Knowledge   Students who exhibited the strategy of overreliance on prior knowledge read the assignment and then reported that they understood the text; in fact, many reported that they had "known this stuff" before they even read the material. One student, after reading a passage that used milk as an example of how all food ultimately can be traced back to green plants (the food producers), reported the passage was "about milk." The point of the reading—that plants make food that cows convert to milk—was missed entirely. In this student's view, he already knew the content. Instead of using the knowledge just acquired from the text to answer questions, students using this type of strategy tended to associate the new material with their prior knowledge and report that the text simply was repetitious.

Overreliance on Text Vocabulary   In this strategy, students isolated new words or phrases in the assignment, often out of context, but felt they comprehended the text if they could state that it was about a specific word—for example, "photo-something" (photosynthesis). According to Roth, the children reported feeling confused about the text only if they could not decode the new words. For these children, answering questions about the text simply required recall of new or big terms and a phrase or sentence around them. Unfortunately, this strategy often pays off when the teacher's questions about text materials are requests for definitions or identifications of new words, but do not represent the construction of new knowledge.

Overreliance on Factual Information   Many students have adopted a view of science as the accumulation of facts (e.g., air expands when heated and water boils at 212° Fahrenheit). Such students see science learning as demanding recall of facts and other natural phenomena. In Roth's study, such students displayed quite accurate recall of these bits of information, but the ideas were not linked into meaningful schemata, nor were major points differentiated from trivial points. These students did best with teachers who employed a vocabulary-oriented view of science.

Overreliance on Existing Beliefs   Many students in Roth's studies relied on naive beliefs (Burbules & Linn, 1991; Pintrich et al., 1993), as discussed in the beginning of the chapter. For these students, new topics were understood in terms of their naive beliefs based on prior knowledge. These well-motivated students sought to link text knowledge with existing prior knowledge. But the goal of these students was not to modify the structure of existing knowledge (their naive theory) but rather to confirm its correctness. In many cases, students distorted or even ignored information inconsistent with existing knowledge. In contrast with the overreliance on the sufficiency of prior knowledge learning strategy, these students realized that the information was new but they did not appear to understand that it might challenge their existing beliefs.

Conceptual-Change Strategy   Conceptual-change students see text materials as a vehicle for changing existing schemata. In Roth's study, they worked to reconcile old ideas with new material. As a result, they not only identified and learned the main ideas in the text but also were able to state where the text or other materials conflicted with their existing schemata. They also saw the text as a source of new knowledge and were willing to revise their old schemata in the light of new information. Interestingly, but not surprisingly, this group of students was most often likely to admit to being confused or puzzled by the text.

The reason for such differences in learning strategies is unclear. Nonetheless, teachers need to anticipate them. If students report new material as "old stuff," the teacher must provide a teaching situation that shows how the new material challenges old beliefs, making it clear that the material is, in fact, new and must be accommodated by students into revised schemata. Similarly, students who see science as vocabulary or fact acquisition may be presented with situations (e.g., experiments, demonstrations, and field studies) that require the linking of words and facts into schemata that help them better understand and explain the world. The teaching strategies discussed below provide methods for addressing these different learning strategies and moving students toward scientific literacy.

Teaching Strategies

According to the National Science Education Standards, the most direct way to improve science achievement for all students is through better science teaching. The general model for teaching science outlined at the beginning of this section can be put into action through two general teaching strategies: (1) confronting and changing naive beliefs and (2) promoting constructive learning in the classroom through inquiry-based teaching and instruction in metacognitive and scientific-thinking skills.

Confronting and Changing Naive Beliefs   As described earlier in this chapter, teachers need to draw out students' naive beliefs and misconceptions and then move them toward conceptual change. One way to uncover students' misconceptions is through discussion of their beliefs about the nature of science itself (Linn et al., 1996) and to engage students in tasks that reveal their thinking. Determining students' initial beliefs about science—their prior knowledge—and using this knowledge as a starting point for new instruction is the most effective way to enhance the learning of science (Bransford et al., 2000).

Having exposed naive beliefs and preconceptions, teachers then must show students many examples of a concept at work and provide clearly understandable scientific explanations of the concept. This step requires that teachers have a good understanding of scientific inquiry and fundamental scientific facts and concepts. Unfortunately, many science instructors are not as knowledgeable as they should be regarding all aspects of the science curriculum. Low-knowledge teachers provide less cohesive explanations, ask fewer questions, and provide fewer opportunities for students to test their scientific wings by theorizing and testing their theories in laboratory settings (Tobin et al., 1994).

Once students have a firm factual basis for a concept, they can be moved toward conceptual change by comparing and contrasting a variety of competing viewpoints. One effective way to accomplish this goal is to use cooperative learning environments in the classroom. Research reviewed by Tobin et al. (1994) suggests that cooperative learning may be an effective way to increase elaboration and evaluation of scientific ideas.

Promoting Constructive Learning   The second general teaching strategy is to provide inquiry-based learning, cooperative learning environments (Pea, 1993; Tobin et al., 1994), and instruction in scientific thinking and metacognitive skills.

The teacher plays a crucial role in an *inquiry-based classroom,* especially in promoting learning via guided, scaffolded participation in activities (Collins, Brown, & Newman, 1989). Because good science inquiry provides many ways for students to approach a new topic and a wide variety of student activities (Kluger, 1999), the teacher's direction is vital for launching an inquiry, focusing students' attention on methods and topics and modeling the skills of scientific inquiry. The teacher also plays a major role in structuring the classroom discourse (see chapter 9). Much of scientific inquiry centers on the asking and answering of questions, a special form of discourse. Effective science teachers have been found to ask more and better questions, pose questions with higher cognitive demand, and ask more follow-up questions. They begin lessons with thought-provoking questions and focus on student understanding rather than looking for a right or wrong answer. In effective classrooms, large and small group discussions are common, questioning is encouraged, and feedback is frequent.

Cooperative learning environments are a common and effective feature of inquiry-based classrooms. Small cooperative groups in which each student develops a particular area of expertise have been found to promote learning via "distributed cognition," as students learn from one another (Campione, Brown, & Jay, 1992). Linking students to mentors and learning centers that promote self-efficacy and utilizing computer learning environments (Demastes, Good, & Peebles, 1996) can expand the inquiry-based classroom environment.

Inquiry-based teaching is closely tied to the teaching of *scientific-thinking skills*. It can be used to engage students in asking scientific questions and give them hands-on opportunities to explore such questions and collect meaningful data. Through inquiry, teachers can help students to interpret data, develop explanations and evaluate and communicate what they have learned. This active engagement in the scientific process is necessary for students to develop a true understanding of science and become scientifically literate.

In recent years there has been a growing evidence of the importance of metacognitive skills to learning and student achievement (see chapter 4). This is also true in science learning. Teachers should stress development of the skills of reflective thinking and self-assessment. Directly teaching students metacognitive strategies such as predicting outcomes, thinking about why an approach doesn't work, self-assessment, and planning ahead have been shown to increase science learning. Writing tasks are one method of encouraging students to think about their own learning (Scardamalia, Bereiter, & Steinbach, 1984). Writing assignments that communicate results of experiments and projects are not only excellent vehicles for teaching metacognitive strategies, they can also increase understanding of the subject. Journals are another method for helping students to reflect on knowledge and beliefs and can be a means of creating a dialogue between the teacher and the student.

Developing formative assessments that give feedback to students can be valuable in helping them reflect on their learning and guiding their learning processes. Tobin et al. (1994) reported that alternative assessment strategies, such as creating and maintaining portfolios of personal work, encourage metacognitive skills of reflection and self-assessment. Classroom portfolios also give students more control over their own learning and build self-awareness.

Supporting Teacher Development

The expectations outlined for teachers in the preceding sections are considerable. Because the depth of a teacher's science and pedagogical knowledge are the greatest indicators of effective science teaching, teachers must be lifelong learners in both of these areas. Teacher training and professional development for teachers are paramount concerns in creating learning environments that foster scientific literacy. We recommend three changes involving teacher-training institutions, the public schools, and the schools' relationships with the public.

First and foremost, the requirements of students studying to become elementary school teachers must be revised to increase teacher knowledge. Many colleges and universities still allow elementary education students to complete their undergraduate degrees with no more than one "real" science course. Science requirements must be increased. Elementary school teachers must attain a basic level of literacy in biological, physical, and earth sciences that will allow them to model the kind of expert conceptions science instruction requires. In many cases, this also will require new college-level science curricula.

Lack of adequate teacher preparation presents serious obstacles to effective science instruction (R. D. Anderson & Mitchener, 1994). One obstacle is the lack of consensus about how to train science teachers. Contemporary science education appears to be divided between teacher-oriented "learn and practice" and student-centered "construct and understand" methods. A second obstacle is the inadequate subject matter preparation that all science educators, but especially those at the elementary school level, receive; it restricts what they teach and how effectively they teach it. All too frequently, elementary teachers complete two or three science methods classes without taking a laboratory-based science class. A third obstacle is the fact that up to 40 percent of science educators leave teaching after their first 2 years, greatly limiting the extent to which students receive science instruction from a well-seasoned expert. Another consequence of high turnover is that skilled science mentors are unavailable to many students.

A second direction for change focuses on the schools and their relationships with their communities. Essentially, the schools, including the faculty, administration, and school boards, will have to educate their communities on science instruction matters. Such educational efforts will have to be as rigorous as the changes we prescribe for higher education. The reason is economic. Inquiry- and laboratory-based educational experiences are expensive. The monies needed to provide laboratory experiences must come from taxpayers. The schools and those who support the schools must begin an education campaign to provide a solid base of intellectual and economic support in the community; even the best prepared teachers will come up short if they do not have the laboratory facilities and materials needed for instruction.

A third direction for change also has a clear school orientation: Science instruction must be given time. The most excellent teachers employing the finest methods and materials will not succeed if science is not a regular part of each child's school day. Time on task has been found to be one of the major determinants of science and mathematics achievement.

Benefits of Effective Instruction

There is little doubt that high-quality science instruction improves student learning, and one of the critical factors in high-quality instruction is the teacher's knowledge of science. For example, Tobin and Fraser (1990) reported that teachers' knowledge was related to the quality of teacher-student interactions. Less knowledgeable teachers interacted less often and less successfully with students. Teacher knowledge also was related to the amount and quality of teacher questions. High-knowledge teachers asked deeper level questions that were more likely to promote constructive thinking among students.

High quality instruction also changes students' cognitive structures (R. D. Anderson & Mitchener, 1994). In a study of 10 fifth- and sixth-grade students, Kuhn et al. (1992)

asked the group to investigate why using some balls led to better tennis serves than using others, and a similar group of 10 students to investigate what led to better performance among three cars. Both groups participated in seven 30-min discussions over a 2-month period. Students were asked to generate a theory about either the balls or the cars and to support that theory by using available evidence.

The longitudinal nature of this study allowed Kuhn et al. (1992) to draw inferences about several critical behaviors. One conclusion was that scientific reasoning improved over time in similar ways even though the two groups solved different problems. This finding suggested that guided discovery improves scientific thinking at a level beyond the specific domain of the problem. A second conclusion was that strategies used to solve the problem were revised and improved over time. This finding suggested that students discover, revise, and delete solution strategies on a continuous basis, given extended experimentation on a single problem (see Siegler & Jenkins, 1989, for a similar finding).

As discussed earlier in this chapter, students need several examples of a single concept and more depth of coverage of topics for effective learning. Last, but certainly not least, high-quality instruction increases student motivation, which increases learning. Bruning and Schweiger (1997) identified several ways that quality learning environments motivate students to learn more science. These settings typically include scaffolded instruction, along with the opportunity to experience science on a first-hand, participatory basis. One benefit of authentic participation is that it increases observation of natural phenomena. Participation also increases student interest, which in turn is closely linked with student engagement and learning (Deci, 1992). Students who are given the chance to participate also experience greater autonomy, which is strongly linked with higher achievement (Deci & Ryan, 1987) and mastery of goals (Dweck & Leggett, 1988) (see chapters 6 and 7). In addition, active participation increases the level of classroom discourse among students, which has been linked with knowledge restructuring and metacognitive awareness (see chapter 9).

Instructional sequences such as those described above take a lot of classroom time. Teachers may well argue that because time available for science already is limited, it is not feasible to use these approaches except occasionally for demonstration purposes. Clement (1983), in discussing the difficulties of tackling naive physics beliefs of college students, takes issue with this point of view and has argued that much more instructional time at the college level should be devoted to examining such preconceptions, a sentiment that is only now becoming the rule rather than the exception. He asserts that attempts to cover many physics topics, especially while using formal scientific or mathematical language, may make it impossible for students to gain an intuitive understanding of Newtonian concepts of physics.

Researchers generally have found that science instruction leads to important changes in the way students represent and think about science concepts when the emphasis is on *coordinating knowledge* and on *how* one thinks about science problems rather than on *what* one thinks about (Kuhn et al., 1992; Linn et al., 1996). Thoughtful teachers will find many ways to increase science learning that meet the basic goals the model described earlier: expose naive beliefs, create conceptual conflict, and encourage cognitive accommodation to more mature views of science.

A Model of Science Achievement

What factors above and beyond expert knowledge and problem-solving strategies lead to science achievement? Reynolds and Walberg (1991, 1992) conducted several studies involving more than 5,000 students across the nation to answer this question. Their research considered potential influences among middle school and high school students, including home environment, prior science achievement, motivation, instructional time, and instructional quality. The relative contribution of each variable was considered by using a complex statistical modeling procedure called LISREL. Analyses such as LISREL allow researchers to investigate the interrelationships among many variables simultaneously.

One advantage of this approach is that the direct and indirect effects of a variable can be separated. A direct effect occurs when one variable directly causes a change in another variable. For example, Reynolds and Walberg (1991) found that instructional time was related directly to science achievement in eighth grade; that is, more instructional time led to higher achievement regardless of other variables. In contrast, an indirect effect occurs when the relationship between two variables is mediated by another. In the Reynolds and Walberg studies, home environment affected prior science achievement (in seventh grade), which in turn affected eighth-grade science achievement. Thus, home environment did not have a direct effect on eighth-grade science achievement even though it had a substantial indirect effect.

The Reynolds and Walberg studies of middle school and high school science achievement reported similar findings; for this reason, results of these studies are summarized in a single model shown in Figure 15-5. The model shown in this figure is

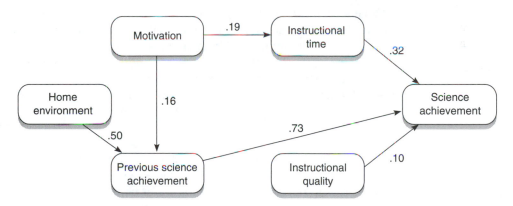

Figure 15-5
A Model of Science Achievement
Source: Adapted from "A Structural Model of Science Achievement and Attitude: An Extension to High School," by A. J. Reynolds and H. J. Walberg, 1991, Journal of Educational Psychology, *84, 371–382. Copyright 1991 by the American Psychological Association. Adapted by permission.*

referred to as a path diagram. Measured variables are represented as boxes; the relationships among these variables are shown by arrows. The number beside each arrow is the correlation between variables. The absence of an arrow indicates that a meaningful statistical relationship was not found between variables.

Figure 15-5 suggests some important conclusions. The most important conclusion is that prior science achievement is strongly related to current science achievement. This finding highlights the vital role of prior knowledge and distributed practice in learning and scientific problem solving (see chapter 5 and the beginning of this chapter). Another conclusion is that the amount of instructional time is related to current science achievement. This finding indicates that the amount of science instruction makes an important contribution to learning. One possible reason is that students are given a greater diversity of training. An alternative may be that students spend more time delving into a small number of problems but do so in detail. A third conclusion is that home environment plays an important role in current science achievement by facilitating prior achievement. One interpretation of this outcome is that the beliefs and attitudes that parents and siblings have about science affect a student's involvement in science throughout her or his early school career.

The model shown in Figure 15-5 also is noteworthy in that several intuitively obvious relationships were not found. For example, no relationship was found between instructional time and instructional quality, nor was a strong relationship found between instructional quality and current science achievement. At face value, these findings suggest that the amount of instruction is far more important than the quality of instruction. Caution is needed when interpreting these results, however, because it is quite possible that instructional quality was uniformly high (or low) across this sample—a condition that would tend to reduce the observed magnitude of the correlation.

Results of these studies are consistent with the main themes of this book— namely that prior knowledge and time on task lead to higher levels of academic achievement, whether in reading, mathematics, or science. Home environment and motivation also were found to be important determinants of science achievement, a finding that strengthens the argument for a global approach (one involving parents and siblings) to improving science education. This does not mean that other variables included in the Reynolds and Walberg studies were unimportant, only that they affected current achievement far less than prior knowledge, instructional time, and home environment.

In summary, even though science achievement ends with expert conceptual knowledge, a flexible repertoire of problem-solving strategies, and an understanding of the distinction between theory and data, it begins with a home environment that motivates students and a school environment that provides equal access for all students. The acquisition of knowledge and skills necessary to excel at science is a very complex process that clearly transcends the schoolroom. A very broad approach to science instruction will be needed in the future if American students are to compete in our global, technological economy and workforce.

Implications for Instruction

1.   *Teach science as a problem-solving process.* The ambitious goal of creating scientific literacy provides great challenges to teachers. Cognitive approaches to learning science recommend that science be presented to students as a problem-solving process rather than simply as a knowledge (vocabulary or facts) acquisition process. Inquiry-based approaches to science teaching have been shown to be a highly effective way of teaching problem-solving and scientific-thinking skills.

2.   *Identify naive beliefs.* Students bring to science a wealth of preconceptions, many of which are incomplete or incorrect. These preconceptions must be identified before effective instruction can occur. The identification process often is slow and uncertain and requires considerable teaching time. The process is enhanced by a careful choice of instructional materials that elicit the student's own thinking, not just verbalization of information the student thinks a teacher desires.

3.   *Confront naive beliefs immediately.* Most science educators believe that science curricula should begin with a focus on ideas that students bring with them and then provide students with a set of experiences that ask them to confront their preconceptions in ways that lead to more informed conceptions. The magnitude of this task should not be underestimated. Historically, science curricula have been written from the perspective of the expert, not the novice. Writing materials that challenge the naive beliefs of children in productive ways and that ultimately lead them to more expertlike knowledge structures requires careful attention.

Techniques that effectively confront children's naive beliefs include introduction of exposing events, introduction of discrepant events, generation of a range of conceptual responses to an exposing event, and practice extending new conceptual responses to a broad range of situations. These activities are most valuable when accompanied by direct student involvement with science materials and with other students.

4.   *Use hands-on demonstrations.* Because scientific schemata often appear to be in conflict with experience-based schemata (naive beliefs), experiments or demonstrations usually are necessary to challenge the preconceptions. These demonstrations must be chosen thoughtfully so that they require children to examine their own preconceptions about concepts in ways that lead them to consider and adopt more scientific views. Hands-on activities should also promote more opportunities for students to engage in metacognitive self-questioning of their learning strategies and conclusions. Substantial teacher patience and openness are necessary so that students feel free to verbalize their own thinking and to use their own language to come to grips with inconsistencies or inadequacies in their thinking. Although students can memorize correct explanations, observations of explanatory behavior following such memorization suggest that students frequently return to explanations consistent with earlier preconceptions. As pointed out previously, knowledge alone is insufficient to change habits of thought. Students must have experience-based activities that encourage them to construct new understandings (accommodations) consistent with more mature, expert views of science.

5. *Give students adequate time to restructure knowledge.* Conceptual change in science is a slow, long-term process. Students need opportunities to see for themselves why their scientific views of the world are inadequate. Progress in science teaching should be assessed over relatively lengthy periods of time rather than at the close of each class period. This is not to say that teachers should not evaluate the effectiveness of their instruction frequently, but rather that expecting rapid changes in students is unrealistic. If expectations are too high, both student and teacher may become discouraged.

Some studies also suggest that restructuring and strategy development are most effective when students work through a complex problem repeatedly over time. Doing so may help students generate, test, and discard problem-solving strategies as newer, more efficient strategies are constructed to match their developing conceptions of the problem. Jumping from unit to unit may be counterproductive even though it exposes students to a wider range of materials and problems. Covering fewer topics in more depth will produce greater understanding of scientific concepts.

6. *Monitor the use of dysfunctional strategies.* Even older students often rely on dysfunctional strategies when reading science texts (Roth, 1985). The most common of these are overreliance on prior knowledge, vocabulary, and factual information rather than reliance on relational knowledge. Interviewing and questioning are good techniques for sounding out students' beliefs and strategies.

7. *Help students understand the nature of scientific theories.* Research indicates that few students prior to high school have a thorough understanding of the distinction between theory and data. Learning about the process of scientific inquiry, however, is almost impossible without this distinction. Students must be helped to understand the properties of a theory, how a theory differs from data, and how the two are coordinated.

8. *Involve parents and siblings.* Research by Reynolds and Walberg (1991) suggests that effective long-term science instruction needs to involve parents and siblings. No doubt, views expressed about science at home are crucial. In addition, the kind of epistemological worldview (commonsense vs. critical) modeled at home may play an important role in a student's understanding of the scientific process. Teachers may need to address problems that arise between older students' views of science and opposing parental views.

Summary

Scientific literacy has become the major goal of science education. Students who are scientifically literate develop an understanding of the scientific method and scientific concepts and can apply them not just in the laboratory and classroom but also in their daily lives. The first step in effective science instruction is helping students reveal their preconceptions or naive beliefs about that domain. Students need exposure to carefully chosen empirical and scientific events that lead them to examine their preconceptions and to revise these preconceptions in the direction of more scientific (expertlike) conceptions. The process of confronting naive beliefs and moving students toward conceptual change is lengthy. Teachers should not only present challenging experiences to students but also allow them sufficient time to examine their naive beliefs. Carefully scaffolded instruction is one strategy for accommodating students' naive beliefs in the direction of more scientific views.

Studying the differences in problem-solving behavior between novices (beginning students in a science) and experts (usually Ph.D.-level practitioners) has revealed effective strategies in science learning. Experts not only have deeper factual knowledge, they have different strategies and conceptual frameworks than novices. Their ability to recognize meaningful patterns, chunk information into schemalike packages and retrieve it fluently, and organize their knowledge around the big ideas or core concepts in their domain all contribute to successful learning. Experts' schemata include procedural, as well as declarative, information, whereas most novices appear to lack useful procedural components. Experts and novices also differ in very important ways with respect to distinguishing formal and empirical aspects of theories. Novices often "adjust" either the theory itself or the data in a way that obscures genuine scientific understanding.

Teachers must confront students' naive beliefs about science and their dysfunctional learning strategies before new material can be learned effectively. Middle school students' dysfunctional learning strategies include overreliance on vocabulary and prior knowledge, and learning factual information in isolation. The use of demonstrations, followed by carefully guided and constructed discussions and questions, appears to help students confront misconceptions and change poor learning strategies.

Science classrooms should emphasize the development of understanding through inquiry-based instruction and the teaching of scientific thinking and metacognitive skills. The teacher plays a critical role in inquiry learning, especially in promoting learning via guided, scaffolded participation in hands-on activities and the structuring of classroom discourse through effective questioning. Direct instruction in metacognitive skills, such as reflective thinking and self-assessment, has been shown to improve learning. Alternative methods of assessment, such as having students create personal portfolios, have been shown to increase reflective thinking.

Research suggests that the factors having the greatest effect on promoting science achievement include prior science achievement, amount of instructional time, and the home environment. This reinforces other research suggesting that more time spent studying science and including parents and siblings in science activities can contribute to greater science achievement.

Suggested Readings

Bransford, J. D., Brown, A. L., & Cocking, R. R. (Eds.). (2000). *How people learn: Brain, mind, experience, and school*. Washington, DC: National Academy Press.

This easy to understand, comprehensive overview of educational research and practice is one of the most significant recent publications on learning and teaching and gives excellent insight into the current views on science teaching.

Ericsson, K. A., & Smith, J. (1991). *Toward a general theory of expertise: Prospects and limits*. New York: Cambridge University Press.

This edited volume includes science-relevant articles (e.g., Y. Anzai), as well as a more general approach to understanding expertise.

Kuhn, D. (1989). Children and adults as intuitive scientists. *Psychological Review, 96,* 674–689.

This article reviews important differences among children's, lay adults', and scientists' thinking about theories and the process of coordinating theory with data.

Glossary

4C/ID Model: An instructional design model formulated by van Merrienboer focusing on complex cognitive skills (chapter 10)

Action Control: Ability to control actions (e.g., motivation and concentration) that help an individual self-regulate (chapter 4)

Adjunct Questions: Questions inserted in text materials that readers answer as they read (chapter 12)

Advance Organizer: Brief prefatory material written at a high level of abstraction that serves as a framework for materials to be learned (chapters 4 and 12)

Agency: An individual's sense of self-determination and perseverance when faced with challenges (chapter 7)

Algorithm: Procedure in computer science or mathematics that applies to a particular kind of problem and that, if followed correctly, guarantees the correct answer (chapters 8 and 14)

Assignment of Meaning: Stage of perception in which meaning is given to a stimulus (chapter 2)

Attention: Mental energy used in perception and thought; the focused allocation of resources to a stimulus (chapters 2 and 11)

Attenuated Processing Model: Model of attention that postulates that most attention is allocated to one channel, whereas a small portion is allocated to the unshadowed channel (chapter 2)

Attribute: Feature shared across the examples of a concept (e.g., water is an attribute of the concept of ocean); attributes essential to defining the concept and shared across all examples of a concept are called defining attributes (chapter 3)

Attribution: Causal interpretation of an event or outcome (e.g., that academic success is attributable to ability) (chapter 6)

Attributional Retraining: Programs designed to change the attributional responses that individuals make in specific settings (chapter 6)

Attribution Theory: Theory proposed by Weiner to explain the attributional process (chapter 6)

Automaticity: Performing of any cognitive skill automatically; automated procedures require very few resources (chapter 2)

Bottom-Up Processing: See Data-Driven Processing (chapter 12)

Bridging: Activities designed to promote transfer of knowledge from one domain to another (chapter 8)

Calibration of Comprehension: Relationship between what students believe they have learned and what they actually have learned; this metacognitive ability is important for gauging amount of effort required for successful performance (chapter 12)

Chunk: Stimulus, such as a letter, number, or word, that becomes unitized; the concept of chunk was proposed by Miller as a unit against which short-term memory capacity could be calibrated (chapter 3)

Classroom Discourse: The verbal exchanges in the classroom (chapter 9)

Code-Emphasis Methods: As used by Chall, beginning reading instruction methods that emphasize learning the correspondence between letters and sounds (chapter 11)

Cognitive (Informational) Feedback: Specific information that links information about performance with the nature of the task (chapter 6)

Cognitive Load Theory: A theory proposed by John Sweller and his associates focusing on working memory's role in instructional design (chapter 10)

Cognitive Modeling: Procedure for developing students' performance that involves giving a rationale for the performance, demonstrating the performance, and providing opportunity for practice (chapter 6)

Cognitive Unit: In network models, a concept or schema that is a node in the network (chapter 3)

Coherence: Property of discourse in which individual elements derive their meaning from earlier or later elements (chapter 9)

Cohesion: Relations of meaning that exist within a text and that define it as a text (chapter 13)

Cohesive Ties: Instances of cohesion, such as repetition of words and anaphoric reference, that link a pair of cohesively related items in a text (chapter 13)

Concept: One of the fundamental building blocks of cognition, a concept is a mental structure that represents a meaningful category and enables us to group objects or events together on the basis of perceived similarities (chapter 3)

Conceptually Driven Model: Model of reading comprehension that stresses the guiding role of the reader's knowledge and expectations (chapter 12)

Conceptually Driven (Top-Down) Processing: Cognitive processing guided, in large part, by prior knowledge and predictions, rather than external data (chapter 12)

Conditional Knowledge: Knowledge about when and why to use strategies (chapter 4)

Conjunctive Rules: In concept identification, rules for identifying concepts that require two or more attributes to be present (chapter 3)

Connectionist Model of Memory: Memory model that represents memory as the strength of connections between units (chapter 3)

Conservative Focusing Strategy: In concept acquisition, an approach in which learners concentrate on selecting new examples of a concept that differ in only one attribute from the first (chapter 3)

Constraints on Operators: Restrictions that limit the use of objects or variables used to solve a problem (chapter 8)

Construction-Integration Model: A model developed by Kintsch and his associates that represents the reading comprehension process (chapter 12)

Constructivism: Point of view that holds that what individuals learn and understand is constructed through their mental processes and social interactions (chapter 9)

Constructive Memory: The memory that is created by learners interacting with new information and situations (chapter 1)

Contextual Knowledge: In vocabulary knowledge, understanding how words actually are used in written and spoken language; see also Definitional Knowledge (chapter 12)

Controllability: In attribution theory, causal dimension that defines the degree to which the cause of an outcome can be controlled (chapter 6)

Controlled Processes: Cognitive processes (e.g., allocation of attention) that are under the conscious control of the learner (chapter 2)

Controlling Action: Action that individuals engage in for extrinsic reasons, such as expectation, reward, or punishment (chapter 6)

Controlling Rewards: Rewards used to control students' behavior or performance (chapter 6)

Criterion-Referenced Evaluation: Evaluation in which an individual's performance is evaluated with respect to preestablished criteria that are unaffected by other students' performance (chapter 6)

Data-Driven Model: Model of comprehension that emphasizes "bottom-up" processes, such as those involved in decoding and understanding word meanings (chapter 12)

Data-Driven (Bottom-Up) Processing: Cognitive processing guided, in large part, by external information versus prior knowledge (chapter 12)

Data-Limited Task: Cognitive activity that is limited because of insufficient or degraded stimuli or information (chapter 2)

Declarative Knowledge: Systematically organized factual knowledge; "knowing what" (chapters 3 and 4)

Defining Attribute: Attribute of a concept that is essential to defining it (chapter 3)

Definitional Knowledge: In vocabulary knowledge, understanding of the relationship between a word and other words, as in a dictionary definition; see also Contextual Knowledge (chapter 12)

Design Principles: Rules guiding how instructional programs are structured (chapter 10)

Dialectical Constructivism: Form of constructivism that places the source of knowledge in the interactions between learners and their environments; dialectical constructivism represents a midpoint between the extremes of endogenous and exogenous constructivism (chapter 9)

Dichotic Listening Task: Task in which a person listens to different messages in the right and left ears, usually paying special attention to only one message (chapter 2)

Disciplined Discussion: Calfee's term for classroom discourse that combines the features of informal conversation and formal instruction; in disciplined discussion, students use interactive processes they have learned to reach goals they have set (chapter 9)

Discourse: Structured, coherent sequences of language in which sentences are combined into higher order units, such as paragraphs, narratives, and expository texts; conversations and extended sequences of writing are examples of discourse (chapters 9 and 11)

Discourse Structure: Form into which discourse is organized; common discourse structures include narratives (stories) and exposition (expository text) (chapter 11)

Disjunctive Rules: In concept identification, rules for identifying concepts that are "either/or" in nature; that is, an object would be an example of a disjunctive concept with two defining attributes if it contained either of the two attributes (chapter 3)

Distal Goal: Long-term goal (chapter 6)

Distinctiveness of Encoding: View that information is memorable to the extent that it is made distinctive (chapter 4)

Distributed Practice: Practice completed at regular intervals (chapter 5)

Distributed Representation: Feature of connectionist models of memory in which information is stored in the connections among a very large number of simple processing units, not in the units themselves (chapter 3)

Divergent Thinking: Thinking characterized by the generation and testing of multiple and diverse solutions (chapter 8)

Domain Knowledge: Knowledge that individuals have about particular fields of study, such as subject areas and areas of activity (chapter 8)

Dual Coding Theory: Paivio's theory of memory that proposes that information is encoded within one or both of two distinct memory systems, one specialized for verbal information and the other for images (chapter 3)

Dual Process Model of Recall: View that recall requires two steps—generation and test—whereas recognition requires only the latter (chapter 5)

Elaborative Interrogation: Instructional method in which, in its simplest form, learners are asked to read sentences and to answer "why" questions to clarify the relationship between the subject and the predicate of the sentence (chapters 5 and 12)

Elaborative Rehearsal: Techniques, such as mnemonics, used to elaborate information in short-term memory (chapter 4)

Embedded Program: Program that teaches critical thinking skills as part of a regular content class, such as history (chapter 8)

Emergent Literacy: Concept that reading is only one dimension of an array of language-related skills and a natural extension of children's knowledge about language to the print medium (chapter 11)

Enactive Learning: Learning that occurs by performing a task (chapter 6)

Encoding: Process of transferring information from short-term to long-term memory (chapter 4)

Encoding Specificity: Assumption that one's ability to retrieve information depends on the degree to which conditions at encoding are reinstated at retrieval (chapters 5 and 12)

Endogenous Constructivism: Form of constructivism that portrays cognitive structures as developing out of other, earlier cognitive structures, not created directly from information provided by the environment; see also Dialectical Constructivism and Exogenous Constructivism (chapter 9)

Engaged Reading: Reading where the reader is deeply involved cognitively and motivationally (chapter 12)

Entity Theory: Assumption that one's intellectual ability is fixed (chapter 7)

Episodic Memory: Memory individuals have for events in their lives; the storage and retrieval of personal, autobiographical experiences (chapters 3 and 5)

Epistemological Belief: Belief about the nature and acquisition of knowledge (chapter 7)

Error Detection Task: Experimental method, used to determine whether readers are monitoring their comprehension, in which individuals are asked to detect inconsistencies or anomalies in text materials (chapter 12)

Exogenous Constructivism: Form of constructivism in which knowledge formation is considered a reconstruction of structures that exist in external reality and is seen as reflecting the inherent organization of the world. See also Endogenous Constructivism and Dialectical Constructivism (chapter 9)

Explicit Memory: Memory that we recognize as corresponding to some past event; explicit memory involves conscious recall or recognition of previous experiences (chapter 3)

Expository Text: Written discourse organized around abstractions about a topic or body of information; textbooks, essays, and persuasive arguments are common examples of expository text (chapter 11)

Extraneous Cognitive Load: Cognitive load that is related to features of instructional design (chapter 10)

Extrinsic Motivation: Motivation in which behaviors are motivated by an external reward (chapter 6)

Feedback: See Cognitive Feedback and Performance Feedback (chapters 6 and 10)

First-Letter Method: Mnemonic in which the first letters of to-be-learned words are used to generate an acronym, such as FACE (for the spaces on the treble clef) (chapter 4)

Fixation: In the eye movements of reading, the brief period during which eyes focus on a point in the text (chapter 12)

Flashbulb Memory: Graphic memory about a specific, important event (chapter 5)

Focus Gambling: Concept acquisition strategy in which learners vary more than one attribute of a stimulus at once (chapter 3)

Focus Unit: Starting point for activation in network models (chapter 3)

Free Writing: Method of writing instruction in which students are encouraged to write as many ideas as possible without worrying about organization or precise expression (chapter 13)

Full Processing Model: Model of attention that postulates that full, parallel processing is allocated to two channels simultaneously (chapter 2)

Functional Dissociation: Instance in which implicit and explicit memory performances are unrelated; to some memory theorists, functional dissociations imply separate memory systems; others propose differences in information processing (chapter 3)

Functional Fixedness: Inability to use familiar objects in a novel way (chapter 8)

Functional Significance: Subjective impression of why an action or event takes place (chapter 6)

General Knowledge: Knowledge appropriate to a wide range of tasks but not linked with a specific domain (chapter 8)

Generation Effect: Finding that verbal material that people generate at encoding is better remembered than material merely read (chapter 5)

Goal State: Terminal objective when solving a problem (chapter 8)

Group Participation Norms: In classroom discussions, rules that students follow as they participate in the discussion; see also Interpretive Norms (chapter 9)

Guided Participation: Process of structuring children's efforts in a social context and gradually releasing responsibility to them; see also Instructional Scaffolding and Zone of Proximal Development (chapter 9)

Hedge: Statement that qualifies rules for identifying concepts, required because most natural concepts are ambiguous or "fuzzy" (chapter 3)

Heuristic: General problem-solving strategy or "rule of thumb" that often is helpful when solving a problem, but does not guarantee a solution (chapters 8 and 14)

Icon: Another name for the visual sensory register (chapter 2)

Ill-Defined Problem: Problem with more than one acceptable solution and no guaranteed method for finding the solution (chapter 8)

Implicit Beliefs: Beliefs that affect one's behavior without any explicit awareness of the beliefs themselves (chapter 7)

Implicit Memory: Nonconscious, tacit form of retention in which we do not recognize the operation of memory but behave in ways that clearly show that our earlier experiences are affecting current ones (chapter 3)

Implicit Theory: Theory about some phenomenon or set of events that has not been formalized explicitly (chapter 7)

Incremental Theory: Assumption that one's intellectual ability is changeable (chapter 7)

Inert Knowledge: Domain-specific knowledge that does not transfer to other domains (chapter 4)

Informational Rewards: Rewards that provide useful feedback to students (chapter 6)

Information-Oriented Feedback: Specific information that emphasizes how one's performance can be improved (chapter 6)

Information Processing Model: Computerlike model of memory that portrays humans as acquiring, storing, and retrieving information (chapter 2)

Initial State: What is known about a problem at the beginning of the problem-solving process (chapter 8)

Instantiation: Linkage of a particular configuration of values with the representation of the variables of a schema; a schema, which is a mental structure, is instantiated by particular patterns of experience that fit the schema (chapter 3)

Instructional Scaffolding: Selective help provided by a teacher and gradually withdrawn that enables students to do things they could not do by themselves; see also Zone of Proximal Development (chapter 9)

Interactive Model: Model of comprehension that blends conceptual and data-driven elements and that portrays comprehension as a product of their interaction (chapter 12)

Interactive Processing: Processing guided both by external stimuli and by conceptual frameworks and strategies stored in memory (chapter 12)

Interpretive Norms: In classroom discussions, judgments that students make about whether they have achieved their intellectual purposes for the discussion (chapter 9)

Intrinsic Cognitive Load: Cognitive load that is due to the materials themselves (chapter 11)

Intrinsic Motivation: Motivation in which behaviors are performed solely for personal satisfaction (chapter 6)

IRE Pattern: Pattern of classroom discourse in which a teacher initiates a discourse segment by asking a question, the student responds to the questions, and the teacher evaluates the student's response; the IRE pattern is the "default pattern" for most classroom exchanges (chapter 9)

Keyword Method: Mnemonic in which a distinctive sound is identified from a to-be-learned word and then that sound is associated with a distinctive image (chapter 4)

Knowledge-Building Community: A group of individuals dedicated to advancing knowledge of the group (chapter 10)

Knowing-in-Action: In Schön's theory, implicit knowledge that is unarticulated but is revealed in our intelligent actions (chapter 9)

Knowledge-in-Action: Knowing-in-action that has been described and put into explicit, symbolic form (chapter 9)

Knowledge Telling: Bereiter and Scardamalia's term for writers simply writing what someone else has said or written with little transformation (chapter 13)

Knowledge Transforming: Bereiter and Scardamalia's term for writers constructing new knowledge by combining their topical knowledge with

knowledge about discourse processes and goals (chapter 13)

Knowledge of Cognition: Knowledge about cognitive processes and how they can be controlled (chapter 4)

Language Experience: As used by Chall, method of reading instruction in which children's own oral language, written down, becomes the basis for their initial reading instruction (chapter 11)

Learned Helplessness: State in which individuals have learned that any behavior they try will fail; thus, they refuse to engage in a task because they assume they cannot succeed (chapter 7)

Learning Goal: Strong desire to improve one's performance and achieve mastery in a domain; also called mastery goal (chapter 7)

Levels of Processing: View that information is processed at increasingly deeper levels of sophistication (chapter 4)

Lexical Network: Memory network in which the names of concepts are stored (chapter 3)

Link: In network models of memory, relations between cognitive units (chapter 3)

Link Method: Mnemonic in which elaborative links are generated among unrelated items that one must remember (chapter 4)

Locus of Control: In attribution theory, causal dimension that defines whether the cause of an outcome is under internal or external control (chapter 6)

Long-Term Memory (LTM): Memory over long periods of time, ranging from hours to days and years; long-term memory is the permanent repository for the information we have acquired (chapters 3 and 12)

Macrostructure: In Kintsch and Van Dijk's discourse processing model, the reader's representation of the main idea or gist of the text; the macrostructure combines the prior knowledge of the individual with the microstructure of the text (chapter 12)

Maintenance Rehearsal: Techniques, such as repetition, used to hold information in short-term memory without elaborating it (chapter 4)

Massed Practice: Practice completed at irregular intervals, but especially in short, concentrated bursts (chapter 5)

Meaning-Emphasis Methods: As used by Chall, beginning reading instruction methods that favor meaning over decoding (chapter 11)

Means-Ends Analysis: Method of learning and problem solving in which a large problem is broken into subgoals that are solved sequentially (chapter 8)

Mediated Response: Subjective, internalized interpretation of an event prior to a response (chapter 6)

Mediation: Encoding strategy in which to-be-learned information is related to knowledge in memory (chapter 4)

Metacognition: Knowledge about cognition; knowledge used to regulate thinking and learning (chapters 4 and 8)

Metamemory: Knowledge about the contents and functioning of one's memory (chapter 4)

Method of Loci: Mnemonic in which to-be-learned information is associated with points in a familiar location (chapter 4)

Microstructure: In Kintsch and Van Dijk's discourse processing model, knowledge structure that readers build by linking common elements in the text's propositions; the microstructure directly represents the propositions in the text (chapter 12)

Mnemonics: Techniques (e.g., mental images) used to elaborate factual information to make it more memorable (chapter 4)

Modal Model: Model of memory that combines the common features of information processing models (chapters 2 and 3)

Modeling: Demonstrating and describing the component parts of a skill to a novice (chapter 6)

Morpheme: Sound or combination of sounds that is a minimal unit of meaning in a language; words may be made up of one or more morphemes (chapter 11)

Morphological Cues: Within-word cues, such as prefixes, root words, and suffixes, that provide information on a word's meaning (chapter 12)

Morphology: Set of principles that describe how sounds are combined into words in a given language (chapter 11)

M-space: Case's concept of memory space or memory capacity, in chunks (chapter 14)

Naive Beliefs: Inaccurate beliefs about a phenomenon, acquired through uncontrolled observation (chapter 15)

Narrative: Form of discourse that is structured by a temporal sequence of events; a "story" (chapter 11)

Network Models: Models of memory, such as J. R. Anderson's ACT, that represent memory as large networks of knowledge (chapter 3)

Node: Cognitive unit, usually a proposition or schema, in network models of memory (chapter 3)

Norm-Referenced Evaluation: Evaluation in which an individual's performance is evaluated with respect to the group average (chapters 6 and 7)

Nonrecurrent Skills: Schemalike controlled processes in complex cognitive skills (chapter 10)

Operators: Objects or variables that can be manipulated to solve a problem (chapter 8)

Outcome (Performance) Feedback: Feedback that provides specific information about performance (chapter 6)

Parallel Distributed Processing Model: Cognitive model that has no central processor, only simple processing units dedicated to specific processing tasks; stored in memory are connection strengths among these simple processing units (chapter 3)

Parallel Processing: Simultaneous, rather than sequential, processing of information in a cognitive system (chapter 3)

Pattern Recognition: Identifying a perceptual stimulus (chapter 2)

Pathways: How well an individual can generate workable solutions to challenges (chapter 7)

Peg Method: Mnemonic in which to-be-learned objects are associated with familiar "mental pegs," such as numbers or a rhyme (chapter 4)

Perception: Process of sensing, holding, recognizing, and making meaning of sensory information (chapter 2)

Performance Goal: Strong desire to demonstrate one's performance and to achieve normatively high success in a domain (chapter 7)

Performance-Oriented Feedback: Specific information about the correctness of one's performance (chapter 6)

Personal Teaching Efficacy: Belief that a teacher can produce significant positive change in students (chapter 6)

Phonemes: Small subset of speech sounds (phones) that are perceived as meaningful by speakers and listeners in a particular language (chapter 11)

Phonemic Awareness: Ability to recognize phonemes as individual, separable speech sounds; this type of metalinguistic knowledge is critical to learning how to read (chapter 11)

Phones: Range of vocalizations of which humans are capable; the "raw material" of spoken languages (chapter 11)

Phonics: Form of reading instruction in which letter/sound relationships are taught explicitly (chapter 11)

Pragmatics: The meanings, messages, and uses 'of language (chapter 11)

Problem Space: All of the operators and constraints on operators involved in a problem (chapter 8)

Proceduralize: Transforming declarative knowledge into condition-action relationships that can be applied across a variety of situations; proceduralization is a function of practice (chapter 3)

Procedural Knowledge: Knowledge that enables an individual to perform certain activities; "knowing how" (chapters 3 and 4)

Productions: Condition-action rules in an "if/then" form that represent procedural knowledge; they state actions to be performed and the conditions under which the action should be taken (chapter 3)

Production Systems: Networks of productions; in production systems, multiple productions can be active at the same time (chapter 3)

Proposition: Smallest unit of knowledge that can stand as a separate assertion and be judged as true or false; propositions are fundamental units in many network theories of memory (chapter 3)

Propositional Networks: Arrays of propositions in which propositions sharing one or more elements are linked with one another, often in hierarchical fashion (chapter 3)

Prototype: "Most typical" instance of a concept that best exemplifies the concept (chapters 2 and 3)

Proximal Goal: Short-term goal (chapter 6)

Reading Readiness: Idea that a given level of mental maturity is required before reading instruction can begin. Contrasted with the concept of emergent literacy (chapter 11)

Recall Threshold: Minimal level of cuing needed to recall information (chapter 5)

Reciprocal Determinism: Term used by Bandura to highlight the causal relationships among self-beliefs, experience, and external feedback (chapter 6)

Reciprocal Teaching: Method of sequenced instruction, developed by Palincsar and Brown, in which teachers model comprehension strategies and guide students in their use; reciprocal teaching initially relies on scaffolding students' responses; responsibility then is shifted gradually to the students (chapters 6 and 12)

Recognition Threshold: Minimal level of cuing needed to recognize information (chapter 5)

Reconstructive Memory: Assumption that information is reconstructed at recall on the basis of an incomplete record rather than remembered verbatim (chapter 5)

Reflection-in-Action: In Schön's system, conscious thought about our actions and about the thinking that accompanies our actions (chapter 9)

Reflection on Reflection-in-Action: According to Schön, what skilled teachers do to stimulate students' reflective thinking about their actions and the thought processes accompanying those actions (chapter 9)

Reflective Judgment: Degree to which one evokes epistemological assumptions and reasoning skills that lead to informed conclusions (chapter 7)

Regulation of Cognition: Knowledge that enables one to control and regulate cognitive activities (chapter 4)

Rehearsal: See Elaborative Rehearsal and Maintenance Rehearsal (chapter 4)

Relational Links: In network models of memory, the connections between cognitive units (chapter 3)

Resource-Limited Task: Cognitive activity that is limited because of insufficient attentional resources (chapter 2)

Retrieval: Process of transferring information from long-term to short-term memory (chapters 4 and 5)

Saccade: In reading, rapid movement of the eyes from one fixation to the next (chapter 12)

Scanning Strategy: Strategy for concept acquisition in which learners attempt to test several hypotheses at once, which can overload their ability to remember the information they are processing (chapter 3)

Schema (pl. Schemata): Hypothesized mental framework that helps us organize knowledge, directs perception and attention, and guides recall; schemata serve as scaffolding for organizing experience (chapters 2 and 3)

Schema Activation: Instructional techniques designed to bring to mind students' relevant knowledge prior to their encountering new information (chapters 4 and 12)

Scripts: Schema representations that provide mental frameworks for proceduralized knowledge (chapter 3)

Self-Determined Action: Action that individuals choose to engage in for intrinsic reasons (chapter 6)

Self-Efficacy: Degree to which an individual feels confident that he or she can perform a task successfully (chapter 6)

Self-Regulated Learning: Ability to control and explicitly understand all aspects of one's learning (chapter 6)

Semantic Memory: Individuals' memories for general concepts and principles and for the relationships among them; unlike episodic memory, semantic memory is not linked with a particular time and place (chapters 3 and 5)

Sensory Memory: Holding systems in memory that maintain stimuli briefly so that perceptual analysis can occur; most is known about visual and auditory sensory memory (chapter 2)

Sensory Register: Buffer where perceptual information is momentarily stored until it is recognized or forgotten (chapter 2)

Serial Processing: Information processing in which activation proceeds from one step to the next in a fixed, sequential order (chapter 3)

Short-Term Memory (STM): Memory over short periods of time, ranging from seconds to minutes (chapter 2)

Sight Word Methods: As used by Chall, beginning reading instructional methods that stress the need for children to acquire a stock of familiar words they can recognize on sight (chapter 11)

Slot: Informal term in schema theory referring to a variable in a schema; if slots in a schema match data in the environment (e.g., a particular word problem is recognized as a subtraction problem), specific data values are assigned to appropriate slots in the schema (chapter 3)

Solution Paths: Set of potential solutions to a specific problem (chapter 8)

Spreading Activation: In network models such as ACT-R, input units causing other units to be activated via their connections, with activation eventually spreading to response units (chapter 3)

Stability: In attribution theory, causal dimension that defines whether the cause of an outcome is temporary or enduring (chapter 6)

Stand-Alone Program: Program that teaches critical thinking skills in isolation (chapter 8)

State-Dependent Learning: Ability to remember information only in the state (e.g., in a drug-induced condition) one learned it in (chapter 5)

Storage: Process of holding information in long-term memory in some organized fashion (chapters 2 and 4)

Story: Mnemonic in which a meaningful story is generated from unrelated words that one must learn in order to aid recall (chapter 4)

Syntax: Ways words in a language are grouped into larger units, such as phrases, clauses, and sentences (chapter 11)

Taxonomy of Educational Objectives: A framework proposed by Bloom and his associates for classifying learning objectives into a six-level hierarchy

Teachable Language Comprehender (TLC): Collins and Quillian's early network model of semantic memory (chapter 3)

Teaching Efficacy: Belief that the process of education affects students in positive ways (chapter 6)

Text Base: Ordered list of propositions created by analyzing the propositional structure of an expository text (chapters 3 and 12)

Text Signals: Words, phrases, and other devices used in reading materials to indicate that certain elements of a text are more important than others or to improve the text's cohesion (chapter 12)

Thinking Frame: Framework for organizing knowledge and guiding thought processes; see also Schema (chapter 8)

Top-Down Processing: See also Conceptually Driven Processing (chapter 12)

Trial and Error: Method of learning and problem solving in which one attempts different solutions randomly (chapter 8)

Vicarious Learning: Learning that occurs through observation of a skilled model (chapter 6)

Vocabulary Knowledge: Understanding words and knowing how to use them (chapter 12)

Well-Defined Problem: Problem with only one acceptable solution and a guaranteed method for finding it (chapter 8)

Wisdom: Willingness to use one's skills and knowledge to act in the soundest manner (chapter 8)

Working Memory: Portion of memory containing the "current contents" of consciousness; as models of memory have shifted from a storage to a processing emphasis, the concept of short-term memory has been largely replaced by the concept of working memory (chapters 2, 3, and 12)

Zone of Proximal Development: In Vygotsky's theory, difference between the difficulty level of a problem a child can cope with independently and the level that can be accomplished with the help of older or more expert individuals; interactions of children and adults in the zone of proximal development are the source of children's cognitive growth (chapter 9)

References

Ackerman, P. L. (1988). Determinants of individual differences during skill acquisition: Cognitive abilities and information processing. *Journal of Experimental Psychology: General, 117,* 288-318.

Ackerman, P. L. (1992). Predicting individual differences in complex skill acquisition: Dynamics of ability determinants. *Journal of Applied Psychology, 77,* 598-614.

Adams, M. J. (1990). *Beginning to read: Thinking and learning about print.* Cambridge, MA: MIT Press.

Adams, M. J. (1994). Modeling the connections between word recognition and reading. In R. B. Ruddell, M. R. Ruddell, & H. Singer (Eds.), *Theoretical models and processes of reading* (4th ed., pp. 838-863). Newark, DE: International Reading Association.

Adams, M. J., & Bruck, M. (1995). Resolving the "Great Debate." *American Educator, 20*(7), 9-20.

Adams, M. J., & Collins, A. (1977). A schema-theoretic view of reading (Tech. Report No. 32). Urbana: University of Illinois, Center for the Study of Reading.

Afflerbach, P. (2002). Teaching reading self-assessment strategies. In C. Block & M. Pressley (Eds.), *Comprehension instruction: Research-based best practices* (pp. 96-111). New York: Guilford Press.

Ahsen, A. (1987). The new structuralism [Special issue]. *Journal of Mental Imagery, 11.*

Alamargot, D., & Chanquoy, L. (Eds.). (2001). *Through the models of writing.* Dordrecht, The Netherlands: Kluwer Academic.

Alba, J. W., & Hasher, L. (1983). Is memory schematic? *Psychological Bulletin, 93,* 203-231.

Alderman, M. K. (1999). *Motivation for achievement: Possibilities of teaching and learning.* Mahwah, NJ: Erlbaum.

Aldridge, B. G. (1992). Project on scope, sequence, and coordination: A new synthesis for improving science education. *Journal of Science Education and Technology, 1,* 13-21.

Alexander, J. M., Carr, M., & Schwanenflugel, P. J. (1995). Development of metacognition in gifted children: Directions for future research. *Developmental Review, 15,* 1-37.

Alexander, P. A. (1992). Domain knowledge: Evolving themes and emerging concerns. *Educational Psychologist, 27*(1), 33-51.

Alexander, P. A., & Jetton, T. L. (2000). Learning from text: A multidimensional and developmental perspectives. In M. L. Kamil, P. B. Mosenthal, P. D. Pearson, & R. Barr (Eds.), *Handbook of reading research* (Vol. 3, pp. 285-310). Mahwah, NJ: Erlbaum.

Alvermann, D. E., & Hayes, D. A. (1989). Classroom discussion of content area reading assignments: An intervention study. *Reading Research Quarterly, 24,* 305-335.

Alvermann, D. E., O'Brien, D. G., & Dillon, D. R. (1990). What teachers do when they say they're having discussions of content area reading assignments: A qualitative analysis. *Reading Research Quarterly, 25,* 296-322.

American Association for the Advancement of Science (AAAS). (1993). *Benchmarks for science literacy.* New York: Oxford University Press.

Ames, C. (1992). Classrooms: Goals, structures, and student motivation. *Journal of Educational Psychology, 84,* 261-271.

Ames, C., & Archer, J. (1988). Achievement in the classroom: Student learning strategies and motivational processes. *Journal of Educational Psychology, 80,* 260-267.

Anderson, J. R. (1976). *Language, memory, and thought.* Mahwah, NJ: Erlbaum.

Anderson, J. R. (1981). *Cognitive skills and their acquisition.* Hillsdale, NJ: Erlbaum.

Anderson, J. R. (1983a). *The architecture of cognition.* Cambridge, MA: Harvard University Press.

Anderson, J. R. (1983b). A spreading activation theory of memory. *Journal of Verbal Learning and Verbal Behavior, 22,* 261-295.

Anderson, J. R. (1993). Problem solving and learning. *American Psychologist, 48,* 35–44.

Anderson, J. R. (1996). ACT: A simple theory of complex cognition. *American Psychologist, 51,* 355–365.

Anderson, J. R. (2000). *Cognitive psychology and its implications* (5th ed.). New York: Worth.

Anderson, J. R., & Bower, G. H. (1973). *Human associative memory.* Washington, DC: Winston.

Anderson, J. R., & Matessa, M. (1997). A production system theory of serial memory. *Psychological Review, 104,* 728–748.

Anderson, J. R., & Reder, L. M. (1979). An elaborative processing explanation of depth of processing. In L. S. Cermak & F. I. M. Craik (Eds.), *Levels of processing in human memory* (pp. 385–404). Mahwah, NJ: Erlbaum.

Anderson, L. (1981). Short-term students' responses to classroom instruction. *Elementary School Journal, 82,* 97–108.

Anderson, R. C. (1984). Role of the reader's schema in comprehension, learning, and memory. In R. C. Anderson, J. Osborn, & R. J. Tierney (Eds.), *Learning to read in American schools: Basal readers and content texts* (pp. 243–258). Mahwah, NJ: Erlbaum.

Anderson, R. C. (1996). Research foundations to support wide reading. In V. Greaney (Ed.), *Promoting reading in developing countries* (pp. 55–77). New York: International Reading Association.

Anderson, R. C., & Biddle, W. B. (1975). On asking people questions about what they are reading. In G. H. Bower (Ed.), *The psychology of learning and motivation* (Vol. 9, pp. 175–199). San Diego: Academic Press.

Anderson, R. C., & Pearson, P. D. (1984). A schema-theoretic view of basic processes in reading comprehension. In P. D. Pearson (Ed.), *Handbook of reading research* (pp. 255–291). New York: Longman.

Anderson, R. C., Reynolds, R. E., Schallert, D. L., & Goetz, E. T. (1977). Frameworks for comprehending discourse. *American Educational Research Journal, 14,* 376–382.

Anderson, R. C., Spiro, R., & Anderson, M. C. (1978). Schemata as scaffolding for the representation of information in connected discourse. *American Educational Research Journal, 15,* 433–440.

Anderson, R. C., Wilson, P. T., & Fielding, L. G. (1988). Growth in reading and how children spend their time outside of school. *Reading Research Quarterly, 23,* 285–303.

Anderson, R. D., & Mitchener, C. P. (1994). Research on science teacher education. In G. L. Gabel (Ed.), *Handbook of research on science teaching and learning* (pp. 3–44). New York: Macmillan.

Andre, T. (1987a). Processes in reading comprehension and the teaching of reading comprehension. In J. A. Glover & R. R. Ronning (Eds.), *Historical foundations of educational psychology* (pp. 259–296). New York: Plenum.

Andre, T. (1987b). Questions and learning from reading. *Questioning Exchange, 1,* 47–86.

Anisfeld, M. (1984). *Language development from birth to three.* Mahwah, NJ: Erlbaum.

Anzai, Y. (1991). Learning and use of representations for physics expertise. In K. A. Anders & J. Smith (Eds.), *Toward a general theory of expertise* (pp. 64–92). New York: Cambridge University Press.

Applebee, A. N. (1983). *The child's concept of story.* Chicago: University of Chicago Press.

Applebee, A. N. (1984). Writing and reasoning. *Review of Educational Research, 54,* 577–596.

Applebee, A. N. (1988, April). *The national assessment.* Paper presented to the Annual Meeting of the American Educational Research Association, New Orleans.

Applebee, A. N., Langer, J., Jenkins, L., Mullis, I., & Foertsch, M. (1990). *Learning to write in our nation's schools.* Princeton, NJ: Educational Testing Service.

Applebee, A. N., Langer, J. A., & Mullis, I. V. S. (1986a). *Writing report cards.* Princeton, NJ: Nation's Report Card, National Assessment of Educational Progress.

Applebee, A. N., Langer, J. A., & Mullis, I. V. S. (1986b). *Writing: Trends across the decade, 1974–1984.* Princeton, NJ: National Assessment of Educational Progress. (ERIC Document Reproduction Service No. ED 273 680)

Archer, J. (1994). Achievement goals as a measure of motivation in university students. *Contemporary Educational Psychology, 19,* 430–446.

Ashcraft, M. H. (1994). *Human memory and cognition* (2nd ed.). New York: HarperCollins.

Ashton, P. T., & Webb, R. B. (1986). *Making a difference: Teachers' sense of efficacy and student achievement.* New York: Longman.

Atkinson, R. C. (1975). Mnemotechnics in second-language learning. *American Psychologist, 30,* 821–828.

Atkinson, R. C., & Raugh, M. R. (1975). An application of the mnemonic keyword method to the acquisition of a Russian vocabulary. *Journal of Experimental Psychology: Human Learning and Memory, 104,* 126–133.

Atkinson, R. C., & Shiffrin, R. M. (1968). Human memory: A proposed system and its control processes. In K. W. Spence & J. T. Spence (Eds.), *The psychology of learning and motivation: Advances in research and theory* (Vol. 2, pp. 89–195). San Diego: Academic Press.

Atwell, N. (1987). *In the middle: Writing, reading, and learning with adolescents.* Montclair, NJ: Boynton/Cook.

Ausubel, D. P. (1960). The use of advance organizers in the learning and retention of meaningful verbal material. *Journal of Educational Psychology, 51,* 267–272.

Ausubel, D. P. (1968). *Educational psychology: A cognitive view.* New York: Holt, Rinehart & Winston.

Ausubel, D. P., & Fitzgerald, D. (1961). The role of discriminability in meaningful verbal learning and retention. *Journal of Educational Psychology, 52,* 266–274.

Ausubel, D. P., & Youssef, M. (1963). Role of discriminability in meaningful parallel learning. *Journal of Educational Psychology, 54,* 331–336.

Baars, B. J. (1986). *The cognitive revolution in psychology.* New York: Guilford.

Babyak, M. A., Synder, C. R., & Yoshinobu, L. (1993). Psychometric properties of the hope scale: A confirmatory factor analysis. *Journal of Research in Personality, 27,* 154–169.

Baddeley, A. D. (1978). The trouble with levels: A reexamination of Craik and Lockhart's framework for memory research. *Psychology Review, 85,* 139–152.

Baddeley, A. D. (1986). *Working memory: Theory and practice.* London, UK: Oxford University Press.

Baddeley, A. D. (1998). *Human memory: Theory and practice.* Boston: Allyn & Bacon.

Baddeley, A. (2001). Is working memory still working? *American Psychologist, 56,* 851–864.

Baddeley, A. D., & Hitch, G. (1974). Working memory. In G. H. Bower (Ed.), *The psychology of learning and motivation* (Vol. 8, pp. 47–90). San Diego: Academic Press.

Baer, D. M., Wolf, M. M., & Risley, T. R. (1968). Some current dimensions of applied behavior analysis. *Journal of Applied Behavior Analysis, 1,* 91–97.

Baker, L. (1989). Metacognition, comprehension monitoring, and the adult reader. *Educational Psychology Review, 1,* 338.

Baker, L. (2002). Metacognition in comprehension instruction. In C. Block & M. Pressley (Eds.). *Comprehension instruction: Research-based best practices* (pp. 77–95). New York: Guilford Press.

Baker, L., Dreher, M. J., & Guthrie, J. T. (2000). *Engaging young readers: Promoting achievement and motivation.* New York: Guilford.

Baker, L., & Wagner, J. L. (1987). Evaluating information for truthfulness: The effects of logical subordination. *Memory & Cognition, 15,* 279–284.

Baltes, P. B., & Staudinger, U. M. (2000). Wisdom: A metaheuristic (pragmatic) to orchestrate mind and virtue toward excellence. *American Psychologist, 55,* 122–136.

Balzer, W. K., Doherty, M. E., & O'Connor, R. (1989). Effects of cognitive feedback on performance. *Psychological Bulletin, 106,* 410–433.

Bandura, A. (1969). *Principles of behavior modification.* New York: Holt, Rinehart & Winston.

Bandura, A. (1986). *Social foundations of thought and action: A social cognitive theory.* Upper Saddle River, NJ: Prentice Hall.

Bandura, A. (1993). Perceived self-efficacy in cognitive development and functioning. *Educational Psychologist, 28,* 117–148.

Bandura, A. (1997). *Self-efficacy: The exercise of control.* New York: Freeman.

Bandura, A., & Wood, R. (1989). Effect of perceived controllability and performance standards on self-regulation of complex decision making. *Journal of Personality and Social Psychology, 56,* 805–814.

Barker, G. P., & Graham, S. (1987). Developmental study of praise and blame as attributional causes. *Journal of Educational Psychology, 79,* 62–66.

Barnes, B. R., & Clawson, E. U. (1975). Do advance organizers facilitate learning? *Review of Educational Research, 45,* 637–660.

Baron, J. (1988). *Thinking and deciding.* New York: Cambridge University Press.

Baroody, A. J., & Standifer, D. J. (1993). Addition and subtraction in the primary grades. In R. J. Jensen (Ed.), *Research ideas for the classroom: Early childhood mathematics* (pp. 72–102). New York: Macmillan.

Barrel, J. (1991). *Teaching for thoughtfulness.* New York: Longman.

Barron, B. (2000). Problem solving in video-based microworlds: Collaborative and individual outcomes of high-achieving sixth-grade students. *Journal of Educational Psychology, 92,* 391–398.

Barron, B., Vye, N., Zech, L., Schwartz, D., Bransford, J., Goldman, S. et al. (1995). Creating contexts for community based problem solving: The Jasper challenge series. In C. Hedley, P. Antonacci, & M. Rabinowitz (Eds.), *Thinking and literacy: The mind at work*. Hillsdale, NJ: Erlbaum.

Bartlett, F. C. (1932). *Remembering: A study in experimental and social psychology*. Cambridge, UK: Cambridge University Press.

Baker, L. (2002). Metacognition in comprehension instruction. In C. Block & M. Pressley (Eds.), *Comprehension instruction: Research-based best practices* (pp. 77-95). New York: Guilford Press.

Bates, P. T. (1984). Writing performance and its relationship to the writing attitudes, topic knowledge, and writing goals of college freshmen. *Dissertation Abstracts International, 56*, 02A.

Baxter-Magolda, M. B. (1999). The evolution of epistemology: Refining contextual knowing at twentysomething. *Journal of College Student Development, 36*, 205-216.

Baxter-Magolda, M. B. (2002). Epistemological reflection: The evolution of epistemological assumptions from age 18 to 30. In B. Hofer & P. R. Pintrich (Eds.), *Personal epistemology: The psychology of beliefs about knowledge and knowing* (pp. 89-102). Mahwah, NJ: Erlbaum.

Beal, C. (1996). The role of comprehension monitoring in children's revision. *Educational Psychology Review, 8*, 219-238.

Beed, P. L., Hawkins, E. M., & Roller, C. M. (1991). Moving learners toward independence: The power of scaffolded instruction. *Reading Teacher, 44*(9), 648-655.

Bendixen, L. D. (2002). A process model of epistemic belief change. In B. K. Hofer & P. R. Pintrich (Eds.), *Personal epistemology: The psychology of beliefs about knowledge and knowing* (pp. 191-208). Mahwah, NJ: Erlbaum.

Bendixen, L. D., Schraw, G., & Dunkle, M. E. (1998). Epistemic beliefs and moral reasoning. *Journal of Psychology, 132*, 187-200.

Benton, S. L., Glover, J. A., & Bruning, R. H. (1983). The effect of number of decisions on prose recall. *Journal of Educational Psychology, 75*, 382-390.

Benton, S. L., Glover, J. A., Kraft, R. G., & Plake, B. S. (1984). Cognitive capacity differences among writers. *Journal of Educational Psychology, 76*, 820-834.

Benton, S. L., Glover, J. A., Monkowski, P. G., & Shaughnessy, M. (1983). Decision difficulty and recall of prose. *Journal of Educational Psychology, 75*, 727-742.

Bereiter, C., & Scardamalia, M. (1987). *The psychology of written composition*. Mahwah, NJ: Erlbaum.

Bereiter, C., & Scardamalia, M. (1993). *Surpassing ourselves: An inquiry into the nature and implications of expertise*. Chicago: Open Court.

Bernardo, A. B. I. (2001) Principle explanation and strategic schema abstraction in problem solving. *Memory & Cognition, 29*, 627-633.

Berninger, V. W. (1994). *Reading and writing acquisition: A developmental neuropsychological perspective*. Dubuque, IA: Brown & Benchmark.

Berninger, V. W., Vaughan, K. B., Abbott, R. D., Abbott, S. P., Rogan, L. W., Brooks, A. et al. (1997). Treatment of handwriting problems in beginning writers: Transfer from handwriting to composition. *Journal of Educational Psychology, 89*, 652-666.

Berry, D., & Dienes, Z. (1993). Toward a working characterization of implicit learning. In D. Berry & Z. Dienes (Eds.), *Implicit learning: Theoretical and empirical issues* (pp. 1-18). Mahwah, NJ: Erlbaum.

Beyer, B. (1987). *Practical strategies for the teaching of thinking*. Boston: Allyn & Bacon.

Biggs, J. (1996). Enhancing teaching through constructive alignment. *Higher Education, 32*, 347-364.

Blachowicz, C. L. Z., & Fisher, P. (2000). Vocabulary instruction. In M. L. Kamil, P. B. Mosenthal, P. D. Pearson, & R. Barr (Eds.), *Handbook of reading research* (Vol. 3, pp. 503-523). Mahwah, NJ: Erlbaum.

Black, A. E., & Deci, E. L. (2000). The effects of instructors' autonomy support and students' autonomous motivation on learning organic chemistry: A self-determination perspective. *Science Education, 84*, 740-756.

Block, C., & Pressley, M. (2002). *Comprehension instruction: Research-based best practices*. New York: Guilford Press.

Bloom, B. S. (1985). *Developing talent in young people*. New York: Ballantine Books.

Bloom, B. S., Englehart, M. D., Furst, E. J., Hill, W. H., & Krathwohl, D. R. (1956). *Taxonomy of educational objectives: The classification of educational goals: Handbook I. Cognitive domain*. New York: McKay.

Blote, A., van der Burg, E., & Klein, A. (2001). Students' flexibility in solving two-digit addition and subtraction problems: Instruction effects. *Journal of Educational Psychology, 93,* 627–638.

Blumenfeld, P. C. (1992). Classroom learning and motivation: Clarifying and expanding goal theory. *Journal of Educational Psychology, 84,* 272–281.

Bobrow, D. G., & Norman, D. A. (1975). Some principles of memory schemata. In D. G. Bobrow & A. M. Collins (Eds.), *Representation and understanding: Studies in cognitive science.* San Diego: Academic Press.

Boekaerts, M., Pintrich, P. R., & Zeidner, M. (Eds.). (2000). *Handbook of self-regulation.* San Diego: Academic Press.

Boggiano, A. K., Main, D. S., & Katz, P. A. (1988). Children's preference for challenge: The role of perceived competence and control. *Journal of Personality and Social Psychology, 54,* 134–141.

Boltwood, C. R., & Blick, K. A. (1978). The delineation and application of three mnemonic techniques. *Psychonomic Science, 20,* 339–341.

Bonk, C. J., Daytner, K., Daytner, G, Dennen, V., & Malikowski, S. (2001). Using web-based cases to enhance, extend, and transform pre-service teacher training: Two years in review. *Computers in the Schools, 18,* 189–211.

Borko, H., Mayfield, V., Marion, S., Flexer, R., & Cumbo, K. (1997). Teachers' developing ideas and practices about mathematics performance assessment: Successes, stumbling blocks, and implications for professional development. *Teaching & Teacher Education, 13,* 259–278.

Borko, H., & Putnam, R. T. (1996). Learning to teach. In D. C. Berliner & R. C. Calfee (Eds.), *The handbook of educational psychology* (pp. 673–708). New York: Macmillan.

Borkowski, J. G. (1992). Metacognitive theory: A framework for teaching literacy, writing, and math skills. *Journal of Learning Disabilities, 25,* 253–257.

Boscolo, P., & Mason, L. (2001). Writing to learn, writing to transfer. In G. Rijlaarsdam (Series Ed.) & P. Tynjala, L. Mason, & K. Lonka (Vol. Eds.), *Studies in writing: Vol. 7. Writing as a learning tool. Integrating theory and practice,* (pp. 83–104). Dordrecht, The Netherlands: Kluwer Academic.

Bouffard, T., Boisvert, J., Vezeau, C., & Larouche, C. (1995). The impact of goal orientation on self-regulation and performance among college students. *British Journal of Educational Psychology, 65,* 317–329.

Bourne, L. E. (1982). Typicality effects in logically defined categories. *Memory & Cognition, 10,* 3–9.

Bower, G. H. (1970). Organizational factors in memory. *Cognitive Psychology, 1,* 18–46.

Bower, G. H. (1981). Mood and memory. *American Psychologist, 36,* 129–148.

Bower, G. H. & Clark, M. C. (1969). Narrative stories as mediators for serial learning. *Psychonomic Science, 14,* 181–182.

Brandt, R. S. (Ed.). (2000). *Education in a new era.* Alexandria, VA: Association for Supervision and Curriculum Development.

Bransford, J., Sherwood, R., Vye, N., & Rieser, J. (1986). Teaching thinking and problem solving. *American Psychologist, 41,* 1078–1089.

Bransford, J. D., Arbitman-Smith, R., Stein, B. S., & Vye, N. J. (1985). Improving thinking and learning skills: An analysis of three approaches. In J. W. Segal, S. F. Chipman, & R. Glaser (Eds.), *Thinking and learning skills: Relating instruction to basic research* (Vol. 1, pp. 133–206). Mahwah, NJ: Erlbaum.

Bransford, J. D., Barclay, J. R., & Franks, J. J. (1972). Sentence memory: A constructive versus interpretive approach. *Cognitive Psychology, 3,* 193–209.

Bransford, J. D., Brown, A. L., & Cocking, R. R. (Eds.) (2000). *How people learn: Brain, mind, experience, and school.* Washington, DC: National Academy Press.

Bransford, J. D., & Franks, J. J. (1971). The abstraction of linguistic ideas. *Cognitive Psychology, 2,* 331–350.

Bransford, J. D., & Johnson, M. K. (1972). Contextual prerequisites for understanding: Some investigations of comprehension and recall. *Journal of Verbal Learning and Verbal Behavior, 11,* 717–726.

Bransford, J. D., & Johnson, M. K. (1973). Considerations of some problems of comprehension. In W. G. Chase (Ed.), *Visual information processing.* San Diego: Academic Press.

Bransford, J. D., & Stein, B. S. (1984). *The IDEAL problem solver.* New York: Freeman.

Bransford, J. D., Stein, B. S., Vye, N. J., Franks, J. J., Auble, P. M., Mezynski, K. J., & Perfetti, C. A. (1982). Differences in approaches to learning: An overview. *Journal of Experimental Psychology: General, 111,* 390–398.

Bransford, J. D., Zech, L., Schwartz, D., Barron, B., Vye, N., & the Cognition and Technology Group at Vanderbilt. (1996). Fostering mathematical thinking in middle school students: Lessons from research. In R. J. Sternberg & T. Ben-Zeev (Eds.), *The nature of mathematical thinking* (pp. 203–250). Mahwah, NJ: Erlbaum.

Braswell, J., Lutkus, A., Grigg, W., Santapau, S., Tay-Lim, B., & Johnson, M. (2001). *The Nation's Report Card: Mathematics 2000.* Washington, DC: National Center for Educational Statistics.

Breckler, S. J., & Wiggins, E. C. (1989). Affect versus evaluation in the structure of attitudes. *Journal of Experimental Social Psychology, 25,* 253–271.

Brennan, A. D., Bridge, C. A., & Winograd, R. N. (1986). The effects of structural variation on children's recall of basal reader stories. *Reading Research Quarterly, 21,* 91–104.

Brenner, M. E., Mayer, R. E., Moseley, B., Brar, T., Duran, R., Reed, B. S., & Webb, D. (1997). Learning by understanding: The role of multiple representations in learning algebra. *American Educational Research Journal, 34,* 663–689.

Breznitz, Z., & Share, D. L. (1992). Effects of accelerated reading rate on memory for text. *Journal of Educational Psychology, 84,* 193–199.

Britton, B. K. (1996). Rewriting: The arts and sciences of improving expository instructional text. In C. M. Levy & S. Ransdell (Eds.), *The science of writing: Theories, methods, individual differences, and applications* (pp. 323–345). Mahwah, NJ: Erlbaum.

Britton, B. K., & Graesser, A. C. (Eds.). (1996). *Models of understanding.* Mahwah, NJ: Erlbaum.

Brody, N. (1992). *Intelligence* (2nd ed.). San Diego: Academic Press.

Brousseau, B. A., Book, C., & Byers, J. L. (1988). Teacher beliefs and the cultures of teaching. *Journal of Teacher Education, 39,* 33–39.

Brouwers, A., & Tomic, W. (2001). The factorial validity on the of the Teacher Interpersonal Self-Efficacy Scale. *Educational and Psychological Measurement, 61,* 433–445.

Brown, A. L. (1980). Metacognitive development and reading. In R. J. Spiro, B. C. Bruce, & W. F. Brewer (Eds.), *Theoretical issues in reading comprehension* (pp. 458–482). Mahwah, NJ: Erlbaum.

Brown, A. L. (1987). Metacognition, executive control, self-regulation, and other more mysterious mechanisms. In F. Weinert & R. Kluwe (Eds.), *Metacognition, motivation, and understanding* (pp. 65–116). Mahwah, NJ: Erlbaum.

Brown, A. L., Day, J. D., & Jones, R. S. (1983). The development of plans for summarizing texts. *Child Development, 54,* 968–979.

Brown, A. L., & Palincsar, A. S. (1982). Inducing strategic learning from texts by means of informed, self-control training. *Topics in Learning and Learning Disabilities, 2,* 1–18.

Brown, A. L., & Palincsar, A. S. (1989). Guided, cooperative learning and individual knowledge acquisition. In L. Resnick (Ed.), *Cognition and instruction: Issues and agendas* (pp. 117–161). Mahwah, NJ: Erlbaum.

Brown, J. S., & Burton, R. B. (1978). Diagnostic models for procedural bugs in basic mathematical skills. *Cognitive Science, 2,* 155–192.

Brown, J. S., Collins, A., & Duguid, P. (1989). Situated cognition and the culture of learning. *Educational Researcher, 18,* 32–42.

Brown, R. (1973). *A first language: The early stages.* Cambridge, MA: Harvard University Press.

Brown, R., Cazden, C., & Bellugi, U. (1968). The child's grammar from 1 to 3. In J. P. Hill (Ed.), *Minnesota symposia on child psychology* (Vol. 2, pp. 70–126). Minneapolis: University of Minnesota Press.

Brown, R., & Kulik, J. (1977). Flashbulb memories. *Cognition, 5,* 73–99.

Brown, R., Pressley, M., Van Meter, P., & Schuder, T. (1996). A quasi-experimental validation of transactional strategies instruction with low-achieving second-grade readers. *Journal of Educational Psychology, 88,* 18–37.

Brown, S. (1986). *Reading–writing connections: College freshman basic writers' apprehension and achievement.* (ERIC Document Reproduction Service No. ED 274 965)

Brownlee, J., Purdie, N., & Boulton-Lewis, G. (2001). Changing epistemological beliefs in pre-service teaching education students. *Teaching in Higher Education, 6,* 247–268.

Bruer, J. T. (1993). *Schools for thought: A science of learning in the classroom.* Cambridge; MA: MIT Press.

Bruner, J. S., Goodnow, J. J., & Austin, G. A. (1956). *A study of thinking.* New York: Wiley.

Bruning, R., & Schweiger, B. (1997). Integrating science and literacy experiences to motivate student learning. In J. T. Guthrie & A. Wigfield (Eds.), *Reading engagement: Motivating readers through integrated instruction* (pp. 149–167). Newark, DE: International Reading Association.

Bryne, B., & Fielding-Barnsley, R. (1991). Evaluation of a program to teach phonemic awareness to young children. *Journal of Educational Psychology, 83,* 451–455.

Bugelski, B. R., Kidd, E., & Segmen, J. (1968). Image as a mediator in one-trial paired-associate learning. *Journal of Experimental Psychology, 76,* 69–73.

Buehl, M. M., Alexander, P. A., & Murphy, P. K. (2002). Beliefs about schooled knowledge: Domain specific or domain general? *Contemporary Educational Psychology, 27,* 415–449.

Burbules, N. C., & Linn, M. C. (1991). Science education and the philosophy of science: Congruence or contradiction? *International Journal of Science Education, 13,* 227–241.

Burger, J. M. (1985). Desire for control and achievement-related behaviors. *Journal of Personality and Social Psychology, 48,* 1520–1533.

Burton, R. B. (1981). Debuggy: Diagnosis of errors in basic mathematical skills. In D. H. Sleeman & J. S. Brown (Eds.), *Intelligent tutoring systems* (pp. 62–81). San Diego: Academic Press.

Butler, D. L., & Winne, P. H. (1995). Feedback and self-regulated learning: A theoretical synthesis. *Review of Educational Research, 65,* 245–281.

Butler, R. (1987). Task-involving and ego-involving properties of evaluation: Effects of different feedback conditions on motivational perceptions, interest, and performance. *Journal of Educational Psychology, 79,* 474–482.

Butterfield, J. (Ed.). (1986). *Language, mind, and logic.* New York: Cambridge University Press.

Bybee, R. W. (1997). *Achieving scientific literacy: From purposes to practices.* Portsmouth NH: Hienemann.

Byrne, B., & Fielding-Barnsley, R. (1991). Evaluation of a program to teach phonemic awareness to young children. *Journal of Educational Psychology, 83,* 451–455.

Byrne, B., & Fielding-Barnsley, R. (1993). Evaluation of a program to teach phonemic awareness to young children: A one-year follow-up. *Journal of Educational Psychology, 85,* 104–111.

Byrne, B., & Fielding-Barnsley, R. (1995). Evaluation of a program to teach phonemic awareness to young children: A two- and three-year follow-up and a new preschool trial. *Journal of Educational Psychology, 87,* 488–503

Cain, K. M., & Dweck, C. S. (1989). The development of children's conceptions of intelligence: A theoretical framework. In R. Sternberg (Ed.), *Advances in the psychology of human intelligence* (Vol. 5, pp. 47–82). Mahwah, NJ: Erlbaum.

Cairney, T. H. (1988). The purpose of basals: What children think. *Reading Teacher, 41,* 420–428.

Calderhead, J. (1996). Teachers: Beliefs and knowledge. In D. C. Berliner & R. C. Calfee (Eds.), *The handbook of educational psychology* (pp. 709–725). New York: Macmillan.

Calfee, R., & Bruning, R. (1996, April). *Beyond phonics: Teaching English orthography through the metaphonic principle.* Paper presented at the meeting of the Society for Scientific Study of Reading, New York.

Calfee, R., Chambliss, M., & Beretz, M. (1991). Organizing for comprehension and composition. In R. Bowler & W. Ellis (Eds.), *All language and the creation of literacy* (pp. 79–93). Baltimore: Orton Dyslexia Society.

Calfee, R., Dunlap, K., & Wat, A. (1994). Authentic discussion of texts in middle grade schooling: An analytic-narrative approach. *Journal of Reading, 37,* 546–556.

Calfee, R. C. (1994). Critical literacy: Reading and writing for a new millennium. In N. J. Ellsworth, C. N. Hedley, & A. N. Baratta (Eds.), *Literacy: A redefinition* (pp. 19–38). Mahwah, NJ: Erlbaum.

Calfee, R. C., & Henry, M. K. (1986). Project READ: An inservice model for training classroom teachers in effective reading instruction. In J. V. Hoffman (Ed.), *Effective teaching of reading: Research and practice* (pp. 199–299). Newark, DE: International Reading Association.

Calfee, R. C., & Patrick, C. L. (1995). *Teach our children well.* Stanford, CA: Stanford Alumni Association.

Calkins, L. M. (1986). *The act of teaching writing.* Portsmouth, NH: Heinemann.

Cameron, J., & Pierce, W. D. (1994). Reinforcement, reward, and intrinsic motivation: A meta-analysis. *Review of Educational Research, 64,* 363–423.

Campbell, D., & Stanley, J. (1963). *Experimental and quasi-experimental designs for research.* Chicago: Rand McNally.

Campione, J. C., Brown, A. L., & Jay, M. (1992). Computers in a community of learners. In E. DeCorte, M. C. Linn, H. Mandl, & L. Verschaffel (Eds.), *Computer-based learning environments and problem solving.* Berlin: Springer–Verlag.

Carey, L., & Flower, L. (1989). Cognition and writing: The idea generation process. In J. A. Glover, R. R.

Ronning, & C. R. Reynolds (Eds.), *Handbook of creativity* (pp. 305-321). New York: Plenum.

Carey, S. (1985). *Conceptual change in childhood*. Cambridge; MA: MIT Press.

Carey, S. (1986). Cognitive science and science education. *American Psychologist, 41,* 1123-1130.

Carey, S., Evans, R., Honda, M., Jay, E., & Unger, C. M. (1989). "An experiment is when you try it and see if it works": A study of grade 7 students' understanding of the construction of scientific knowledge. *International Journal of Science Education, 11,* 514-529.

Carey, S., & Smith, C. (1993). On understanding the nature of scientific knowledge. *Educational Psychologist, 28,* 235-251.

Carlson, L., Zimmer, J. W., & Glover, J. A. (1981). First-letter mnemonics: DAM (don't aid memory). *Journal of Genetic Psychology, 104,* 287-292.

Carmichael, L., Hogan, H. P., & Walter, A. A. (1932). An experimental study of the effect of language on the reproduction of visually perceived forms. *Journal of Experimental Psychology, 15,* 73-86.

Carney, R. H., & Levin, J. R. (2000). Mnemonic instruction, with a focus on transfer. *Journal of Educational Psychology, 92,* 783-790.

Carpenter, T. P., Fennema, E., Fuson, K., Hiebert, J., Human, P., Murray, H. et al. (1994, April). *Teaching mathematics for learning with understanding in the primary grades*. Paper presented at the Annual Meeting of the American Educational Research Association, New Orleans.

Carpenter, T. P., & Moser, J. M. (1982). The development of addition and subtraction problem-solving skills. In T. R. Carpenter, J. M. Moser, & T. A. Romberg (Eds.), *Addition and subtraction: A cognitive perspective* (pp. 42-68). Mahwah, NJ: Erlbaum.

Carpenter, T. P., & Moser, J. M. (1983). Acquisition of addition and subtraction concepts. In R. Lesh & M. Landau (Eds.), *Acquisition of mathematical concepts and processes* (pp. 106-113). San Diego: Academic Press.

Carpenter, T. P., & Moser, J. M. (1984). The acquisition of addition and subtraction concepts in grades one through three. *Journal for Research in Mathematics Education, 15,* 179-202.

Case, R. (1978). A developmentally based theory and technology of instruction. *Review of Educational Research, 48,* 439-463.

Case, R. (1985). *Intellectual development, birth to adulthood*. San Diego: Academic Press.

Cazden, C. (1988). *Classroom discourse: The language of teaching and learning*. Portsmouth, NH: Heinemann.

Ceci, S. J., & Bruck, M. (1993). Suggestibility of the child witness: A historical review and synthesis. *Psychological Bulletin, 113,* 403-439.

Chall, J. S. (1967). *Learning to read: The great debate*. New York: McGraw-Hill.

Chall, J. S., Jacobs, V. A., & Baldwin, L. E. (1990). *The reading crisis: Why poor children fall behind*. Cambridge, MA: Harvard University Press.

Champagne, A. B., Klopfer, L. E., & Anderson, J. H. (1980). Factors influencing the learning of classical mechanics. *American Journal of Physics, 48,* 1074-1079.

Champagne, A. B., Klopfer, L. E., Desena, A. T., & Squires, D. A. (1981). Structural representation of students' knowledge before and after science instruction. *Journal of Research in Science Teaching, 18,* 97-111.

Chandler, M., Boyes, M., & Ball, L. (1990). Relativism and stations of epistemic doubt. *Journal of Experimental Child Psychology, 50,* 370-395.

Chandler, P., & Sweller, J. (1990). Cognitive load theory and the format of instruction. *Cognition and Instruction, 8,* 293-332.

Charness, N. (1991). Expertise in chess: The balance between knowledge and search. In K. A. Ericsson & J. Smith (Eds.), *Toward a general theory of expertise*. Cambridge, UK: Cambridge University Press.

Chase, W. G. (1987). Visual information processing. In K. R. Boff, L. Kaufman, & J. P. Thomas (Eds.), *Handbook of perception and human performance: Vol. 2. Information processing* (pp. 28-1 to 28-60). New York: Wiley.

Chase, W. G., & Simon, H. A. (1973a). The mind's eye in chess. In W. G. Chase (Ed.), *Visual information processing* (pp. 215-281). San Diego: Academic Press.

Chase, W. G., & Simon, H. A. (1973b). Perception in chess. *Cognitive Psychology, 4,* 55-81.

Chi, M. T. H. (1978). Knowledge structures and memory development. In R. Siegler (Ed.), *Children's thinking: What develops* (pp. 73-96). Hillsdale, NJ: Erlbaum.

Chi, M. T. H., de Leeuw, N., Chiu, M., & La Vancher, C. (1994). Eliciting self-explanations improves understanding. *Cognitive Science, 18,* 439-477.

Chi, M. T. H., Slotta, J. D., & de Leeuw, N. (1994). From things to processes: A theory of conceptual change for learning science concepts. *Learning and Instruction, 4,* 27–43.

Chinn, C. A., Anderson, R. C., & Waggoner, M. A. (2001). Patterns of discourse in two kinds of literature discussion. *Reading Research Quarterly, 36,* 378-411.

Chinn, C. A., & Brewer, W. F. (1993). The role of anomalous data in knowledge acquisition: A theoretical framework and implications for science instruction. *Review of Educational Research, 63,* 1–49.

Chinn, C. A., O'Donnell, A. M., & Jinks, T. S. (2000). The structure of discourse in collaborative learning. *The Journal of Experimental Education, 69,* 77–97.

Chinn, C. A., & Waggoner, M. A. (1992, April). *Dynamics of classroom discussion: An analysis of what causes segments of open discourse to begin, continue, and end.* Paper presented at the Annual Meeting of the American Educational Research Association, San Francisco.

Chipman, S. (1988, April). *Cognitive processes in mathematics.* Paper presented at the Annual Meeting of the American Educational Research Association, New Orleans.

Chomsky, N. (1957). *Syntactic structures.* The Hague, The Netherlands: Mouton.

Chomsky, N. (1965). *Aspects of the theory of syntax.* Cambridge, MA: MIT Press.

Church, M. A., Elliot, A. J., & Gable, S. (2000). Perceptions of classroom context, achievement goals, and achievement outcomes. *Journal of Educational Psychology, 93,* 43-54.

Clancey, W. J. (1988). Acquiring, representing, and evaluating a competence model of diagnostic strategy. In M. Chi, R. Glaser, & M. Farr (Eds.), *The nature of expertise* (pp. 261–287). Mahwah, NJ: Erlbaum.

Clark, J. M., & Paivio, A. (1991). Dual coding theory and education. *Educational Psychology Review, 3,* 149–210.

Clark, R. E. (1983). Reconsidering research on learning from media. *Review of Educational Research, 53,* 445–459.

Clark, R. E. (1994). Media will never influence learning. *Educational Technology Research and Development, 42,* 21–29.

Clark, R. E. (2001). *Learning from media: Arguments, analysis and evidence.* Greenwich, CT: Information Age.

Clark, R. E. (2003). Research on Web-based learning: A half-full glass. In R. Bruning, C. Horn, & L. PytlikZillig (Eds.), *Web-based learning: What do we know? Where do we go?* (pp. 1-22). Greenwich, CN: Information Age.

Clay, M.M. (1991). Child development. In J. Flood, J. M. Jensen, D. Lapp, & J. R. Squire (Eds.), *Handbook of research on teaching the English language arts* (pp. 40-45). New York: Macmillan.

Clement, J. (1983). A conceptual model discussed by Galileo and used intuitively by physics students. In D. Gentner & A. L. Stevens (Eds.), *Mental models* (pp. 206-251). Mahwah, NJ: Erlbaum.

Clement, J. (1991). Nonformal reasoning in experts and in science students: The use of analogies, extreme cases, and physical intuition. In J. F. Voss, D. N. Perkins, & J. W. Segal (Eds.), *Informal reasoning and education* (pp. 345-362). Mahwah, NJ: Erlbaum.

Clement, J. (1992). Students' preconceptions in introductory physics. *American Journal of Physics, 50,* 66-71.

Cobb, P., & Bowers, J. (1999). Cognitive and situated learning perspectives in theory and practice. *Educational Researcher, 28,* 4-15.

Cobern, W. W. (2000). The nature of science and the role of knowledge and belief. *Science & Education, 9,* 219-246.

Cognition and Technology Group at Vanderbilt (1997). *The Jasper Project: Lessons in curriculum, instruction, assessment, and professional development.* Mahwah, NJ: Erlbaum.

Coladarci, T., & Breton, W. (1997). Teacher efficacy supervision and the special education resource-room teacher. *Journal of Educational Research, 90,* 230-239.

Collins, A. F., Brown J. S., & Newman, S. E. (1989). Cognitive apprenticeship: Teaching the craft of reading, writing, and mathematics. In L. B. Resnick (Ed.), *Cognition and instruction: Issues and agendas* (pp. 453-494). Mahwah, NJ: Erlbaum.

Collins, A. F., Gathercole, S. E., Conway, M. A., & Morris, P. E. (1993). *Theories of memory.* Hove, UK: Erlbaum.

Collins, A. M., & Loftus, E. F. (1975). A spreading-activation theory of semantic processing. *Psychological Review, 82,* 407-428.

Collins, A. M., & Quillian, M. R. (1969). Retrieval time from semantic memory. *Journal of Verbal Learning and Verbal Behavior, 8,* 240-248.

Collyer, S. C., Jonides, J., & Bevan, W. (1972). Images as memory aids: Is bizarreness helpful? *American Journal of Psychology, 85,* 31–38.

Conry, R., & Plant, W. T. (1965). WAIS and group test prediction of an academic success criterion: High school and college. *Educational and Psychological Measurement, 25,* 493–500.

Corkill, A. J. (1992). Advance organizers: Facilitators of recall. *Educational Psychology Review, 4,* 33–68.

Corkill, A. J., Glover, J. A., & Bruning, R. H. (1988). Advance organizers: Concrete vs. abstract. *Journal of Educational Research, 82,* 76–81.

Corno, L., & Randi, J. (1997). Motivation, volition, and collaborative innovation in classroom literacy. In J. T. Guthrie & A. Wigfield (Eds.), *Reading engagement: Motivating readers through integrated instruction.* Newark, DE: International Reading Association.

Covington, M., & Omelich, C. (1984). Task-oriented versus competitive learning structures: Motivational and performance consequences. *Journal of Educational Psychology, 77,* 1038–1050.

Covington, M. C., Crutchfield, R. S., Davies, L. B., & Olton, R. M. (1974). *The Productive Thinking program: A course in learning to think.* New York: Merrill/Macmillan.

Cowie, H., & van der Aalsvoort, G. (Eds.). (2000). *Social interaction in learning and instruction: The meaning of discourse for the construction of knowledge.* Amsterdam: Pergamon.

Cox, B. D. (1997). The rediscovery of the active learner in adaptive contexts: A developmental-historical analysis of transfer of training. *Educational Psychologist, 32,* 41–45.

Craik, F. I. M. (1979). Human memory. *Annual Review of Psychology, 30,* 63–102.

Craik, F. I. M. (2000, August). Human memory and aging. Paper presented at the Proceedings of the 27th International Congress of Pychology, Stockholm.

Craik, F. I. M., & Lockhart, R. S. (1972). Levels of processing: A framework for memory research. *Journal of Verbal Learning and Verbal Behavior, 11,* 671–684.

Craik, F. I. M., & Lockhart, R. S. (1986). CHARM is not enough: Comments on Eich's model of cued recall. *Psychological Review, 93,* 360–364.

Craik, F. I. M., & Tulving, E. (1975). Depth of processing and the retention of words in episodic memory. *Journal of Experimental Psychology: General, 104,* 268–294.

Cross, D. R., & Paris, S. G. (1988). Developmental and instructional analyses of children's metacognition and reading comprehension. *Journal of Educational Psychology, 80,* 131–142.

Crossman, E. R. F. (1959). A theory of the acquisition of a speed-skill. *Ergonomics, 2,* 153–166.

Crystal, D. (1997). *The encyclopedia of language* (2nd ed.). Cambridge, UK: Cambridge University Press.

Csikszentmihalyi, M. (1996). *Creativity: Flow and the psychology of discovery and invention.* New York, NY: HarperCollins.

Cunningham, A. E., & Stanovich, K. E. (1991). Tracking the unique effects of print exposure in children: Associations with vocabulary, general knowledge, and spelling. *Journal of Educational Psychology, 83,* 264–274.

Cunningham, J. W., & Fitzgerald, J. (1996). Epistemology and reading. *Reading Research Quarterly, 31,* 36–60.

Curren, M. T., & Harich, K. R. (1993). Performance attributions: Effects of mood and involvement. *Journal of Educational Psychology, 85,* 605–609.

Dacey, J. S. (1989). *Fundamentals of creative thinking.* Lexington, MA: D. C. Heath.

Daiute, C. (1986). Physical and cognitive factors in revising: Insights from studies with computers. *Research in the Teaching of English, 20,* 141–159.

Daneman, M., & Merikle, P. M. (1996). Working memory and language comprehension: A meta-analysis. *Psychonomic Bulletin & Review, 3,* 422–433.

Darwin, G. J., Turvey, M. T., & Crowder, R. G. (1972). An auditory analogue of the Sperling partial report procedure: Evidence for brief auditory storage. *Cognitive Psychology, 3,* 255–267.

Das, J. P. (1995). Some thoughts on two aspects of Vygotsky's work. *Educational Psychologist, 30,* 93–97.

Das, J. P., & Gindis, B. (1995). Lev S. Vygotsky and contemporary educational psychology [Special issue]. *Educational Psychologist, 30.*

Deakin, J. M., & Allard, F. (1991). Skilled memory in expert figure skating. *Memory & Cognition, 19,* 79–86.

De Boer, J. J. (1959). *Grammar in language teaching.* Elementary English, 36, 413–421.

de Bono, E. (1973). *CoRT thinking materials.* London: Direct Education Services.

Deci, E. L. (1992). The relation of interest to the motivation of behavior: A self-determination theory perspective. In K. A. Renniger, S. Hidi, & A. Krapp (Eds.),

The role of interest in learning and development (pp. 43–70). Mahwah, NJ: Erlbaum.

Deci, E. L., & Ryan, R. M. (1985). *Intrinsic motivation and self-determination in human behavior*. New York: Plenum.

Deci, E. L., & Ryan, R. M. (1987). The support of autonomy and control of behavior. *Journal of Personality and Social Psychology, 53,* 1024–1037.

Deci, E. L., Vallerand, R. J., Pelletier, L. G., & Ryan, R. M. (1991). Motivation and education: The self-determination perspective. *Educational Psychologist, 26,* 325–346.

deGroot, A. D. (1965). *Thought and choice in chess.* The Hague, The Netherlands: Mouton.

De Jong, T., & Ferguson-Hessler, M. G. M. (1996). Types and qualities of knowledge. *Educational Psychologist, 31,* 105–113.

Delclos, V. R., & Harrington, C. (1991). Effects of strategy monitoring and proactive instruction on children's problem-solving performance. *Journal of Educational Psychology, 83,* 35–42.

Dellarosa, D. (1988). A history of thinking. In R. J. Sternberg & E. F. Smith (Eds.), *The psychology of human thought* (pp. 1–18). New York: Cambridge University Press.

Dellarosa, D., & Bourne, L. E. (1985). Surface form and the spacing effect. *Memory & Cognition, 13,* 529–537.

Demastes, S. S., Good, R. G., & Peebles, P. (1996). Patterns of conceptual change in evolution. *Journal of Research in Science Teaching, 33,* 407–431.

Dempster, F. N. (1981). Memory span: Sources of individual and developmental differences. *Psychological Bulletin, 89,* 63–100.

Dempster, F. N., & Corkill, A. (1999). Interference and inhibition in cognition and behavior: Unifying themes for educational psychology. *Educational Psychology Review, 11*(1).

Derry, S. J. (1984). Effects of an organizer on memory for prose. *Journal of Educational Psychology, 76,* 98–107.

Derry, S. J. (1996). Cognitive schema theory in the constructivist debate. *Educational Psychologist, 31,* 151–162.

Detterman, D. K. (1993). The case for the prosecution: Transfer as an epiphenomenon. In D. K. Detterman & R. J. Sternberg (Eds.), *Transfer on trial: Intelligence, cognition, and instruction* (pp. 1–24). Norwood, NJ: Ablex.

Deutsch, D. (1987). Auditory pattern recognition. In K. R. Boff, L. Kaufman, & J. P. Thomas (Eds.), *Handbook of perception and human performance: Vol. 2. Information processing* (pp. 32-1 to 32-55). New York: Wiley.

Dewey, J. (1910). *How we think.* Boston: D. C. Heath.

Dewitz, R., Carr, E. M., & Patberg, J. P. (1987). Effects of inference training on comprehension and comprehension monitoring. *Reading Research Quarterly, 22,* 99–119.

Dickinson, D. K., & Snow, C. E. (1986). *Interrelationships among pre-reading and oral language skills in kindergartners from two social classes.* (ERIC Document Reproduction Services No. ED 272 860)

Diener, C. I., & Dweck, C. S. (1978). An analysis of learned helplessness: Continuous changes in performance, strategy, and achievement cognitions after failure. *Journal of Personality and Social Psychology, 36,* 451–462.

DiLollo, U., & Dixon, P. (1988). Two forms of persistence in visual information processing. *Journal of Experimental Psychology: Human Perception and Performance, 14,* 601–609.

Dinnel, D., & Glover, J. A. (1985). Advance organizers: Encoding manipulations. *Journal of Educational Psychology, 77,* 514–521.

diSessa, A. A. (1993). Toward an epistemology of physics. *Cognition and Instruction, 10,* 105–225.

Dole, J. (2000). Explicit and implicit instruction in comprehension. In B. M. Taylor, M. F. Graves, & van den Broek (Eds.), *Reading for meaning: Fostering comprehension in the middle grades* (pp. 52–69). New York: Teachers College Press.

Dole, J. A., Duffy, G. G., Roehler, L. R., & Pearson, P. D. (1991). Moving from the old to the new: Research on reading comprehension instruction. *Review of Educational Research, 61,* 239–264.

Dole, J. A., & Sinatra, G. A. (1998). Reconceptualizing change in the cognitive construction of knowledge. *Educational Psychologist, 33,* 109–128.

Donovan, C. A. (1996). First graders' impressions of genre-specific elements in writing narrative and expository texts. In D. Leu, K. Hinchman, & C. Kinzer (Eds.), *Literacies for the 21st century: Forty-fifth yearbook of the National Reading Conference* (pp. 183–194). Chicago: National Reading Conference.

Dooling, D. J., & Lachman, R. (1971). Effects of comprehension on retention of prose. *Journal of Experimental Psychology, 88,* 216–222.

Drummey, A. B., & Newcombe, N. (1995). Remembering versus knowing the past: Children's explicit and implicit memories for pictures. *Journal of Experimental Child Psychology, 59,* 549-565.

Duell, O. K., & Schommer-Aikins, M. (2001). Measures of people's beliefs about knowledge and learning. *Educational Psychology Review, 13,* 419-449.

Duffy, G. (2002). The case for direct explanation of strategies. In C. Block & M. Pressley (Eds.) *Comprehension instruction: Research-based best practices* (pp. 28-41). New York: Guilford Press.

Duin, A. H., & Graves, M. F. (1987). Intensive vocabulary instruction as a prewriting technique. *Reading Research Quarterly, 22,* 311-330.

Duke, N. (2000). 3.6 minutes per day: The scarcity of informational texts in first grade. *Reading Research Quarterly, 25,* 202-224.

Duke, N., & Kays, J. (1998). "Can I say 'once upon a time'?" Kindergarten children developing knowledge of information book language. *Early Childhood Research Quarterly, 13,* 295-318.

Duncker, K. (1945). On problem solving (L. S. Lees, Trans.) [Special issue]. *Psychological Monographs, 58*(270).

Dunkle, M. F., Schraw, G., & Bendixen, L. (1993, April). *The relationship between epistemological beliefs, causal attributions, and reflective judgment.* Paper presented at the Annual Meeting of the American Educational Research Association, Atlanta, GA.

Durkin, D. (1978-1979). What classroom observations reveal about reading comprehension instruction. *Reading Research Quarterly, 14,* 481-533.

Durkin, D. (1981). Reading comprehension instruction in five basal reading series. *Reading Research Quarterly, 16,* 515-544.

Dweck, C. S. (2000). *Self-theories: Their role in motivation, personality, and development.* Philadelphia: Psychology Press.

Dweck, C. S. (1975). The role of expectations and attributions in the alleviation of learned helplessness. *Journal of Personality and Social Psychology, 31,* 674-685.

Dweck, C. S. (1986). Motivational processes affecting learning. *American Psychologist, 41,* 1040-1048.

Dweck, C. S. (1999). *Self theories: Their role in motivation, personality, and development.* Philadelphia: Psychology Press.

Dweck, C. S., Chiu, C., & Hong, Y. (1995). Implicit theories and their role in judgments and reactions: A world from two perspectives. *Psychological Inquiry, 6,* 267-285.

Dweck, C. S., & Leggett, E. S. (1988). A social-cognitive approach to motivation and personality. *Psychological Review, 95,* 256-273.

Dyson, A. H. (1993). *Social worlds of children learning to write in an urban primary school.* New York: Teachers College Press.

Dyson, A. H., & Freedman, S. W. (1991). Writing. In J. Flood, J. M. Jensen, D. Lapp, & J. R. Squire (Eds.), *Handbook of research on teaching the English language arts* (pp. 754-774). New York: Macmillan.

Ebbinghaus, H. (1885). *Uber das Gedachtnis [Memory].* Leipzig, Germany: Duncker & Humbolt.

Eccles, J. S., & Wigfield, A. (2002). Motivational beliefs, values, and goals. *Annual Review of Psychology, 53,* 109-132.

Edwards, K. (1990). The interplay of affect and cognition in attitude formation and change. *Journal of Personality and Social Psychology, 59,* 202-216.

Ehri, L. (1991). Development of the ability to read words. In P. D. Pearson (Ed.), *Handbook of reading research* (2nd ed., pp. 395-419). New York: Longman.

Ehri, L. (1994). Development of the ability to read words: Update. (1994). In R. B. Ruddell, M. R. Ruddell, & H. Singer (Eds.), *Theoretical models and processes of reading* (4th ed., pp. 323-358). Newark, DE: International Reading Association.

Ehri, L. (1998). Research on learning to read and spell: A personal-historical perspective. *Scientific Studies of Reading, 2,* 97-114.

Ehri, L., & Robbins, C. (1992). Beginners need some decoding skill to read words by analogy. *Reading Research Quarterly, 27,* 12-26.

Ehri, L., & Soffer, A. (1999). Graphophonemic awareness: Development in elementary students. *Scientific Studies of Reading, 3,* 1-30.

Ehri, L. C., & Wilce, L. S. (1985). Movement into reading: Is the first stage of printed word learning visual or phonetic? *Reading Research Quarterly, 20,* 163-179.

Eichenbaum, H. (1997). How does the brain organize memories? *Science, 277,* 330-332.

Eisenberg, N., Martin, C. L., & Fabes, R. A. (1996). Gender development and gender effects. In D. C. Berliner & R. C. Calfee (Eds.), *The handbook of educational psychology* (pp. 358-396). New York: Macmillan.

Eisenberger, R., & Cameron, J. (1996). Detrimental effects of rewards: Reality or myth? *American Psychologist, 51,* 1153–1166.

Elbow, P. (1981). *Writing with power: Techniques for mastering the writing process*. New York: Oxford University Press.

Elliott, E. S., & Dweck, C. S. (1988). An approach to motivation and achievement. *Journal of Personality and Social Psychology, 54,* 5–12.

Elmes, D. G., & Bjork, R. A. (1975). The interaction of encoding and rehearsal processes in the recall of repeated and nonrepeated items. *Journal of Verbal Learning and Verbal Behavior, 14,* 30–42.

Engle, R. W., Kane, M. J., & Tuholski, S. W. (1999). Individual differences in working memory capacity and what they tell us about controlled attention, general fluid intelligence, and functions of the prefrontal cortex. In A. Miyake & P. Shah (Eds.), *Models of working memory: Mechanisms of active maintenance and executive control* (pp. 102–134). Cambridge, UK: Cambridge University Press.

Englert, C. S., Raphael, T. E., Anderson, L. M., Anthony, H. M., & Stevens, D. D. (1991). Making strategies and self-talk visible: Writing instruction in regular and special education classrooms. *American Educational Research Journal, 28,* 337–372.

Ennis, R. H. (1987). A taxonomy of critical thinking dispositions and abilities. In J. Baron & R. Sternberg (Eds.), *Teaching thinking skills: Theory and practice* (pp. 9–26). New York: Freeman.

Epstein, W., Glenberg, A. M., & Bradley, M. M. (1984). Coactivation and comprehension: Contribution of text variables to the illusion of knowing. *Memory & Cognition, 12,* 355–360.

Ericsson, K. A. (1996). The acquisition of expert performance. In K. A. Ericsson (Ed.), *The road to excellence: The acquisition of expert performance in the arts, sciences, sports, and games* (pp. 1–50). Mahwah, NJ: Erlbaum.

Ericsson, K. A., Chase, W. G., & Faloon, S. (1980). Acquisition of a memory skill. *Science, 208,* 1181–1182.

Ericsson, K. A., & Kintsch, W. (1995). Long-term working memory. *Psychological Review, 102,* 211–245.

Ericsson, K. A., Krampe, R. T., & Tesch-Romer, C. (1993). The role of deliberate practice in the acquisition of expert performance. *Psychological Review, 100,* 363–406.

Ericsson, K. A., & Smith, J. (1991). *Toward a general theory of expertise: Prospects and limits*. New York: Cambridge University Press.

Ervin, S. M. (1964). Imitation and structural change in children's language. In E. H. Lenneberg (Ed.), *New directions in the study of language* (pp. 163–189). Cambridge: MIT Press.

Fall, R., Webb, N. M., & Chudowsky, N. (2000). Group discussion and large-scale language arts assessment: Effects on students' comprehension. *American Education Research Journal, 37,* 911–941.

Farnham-Diggory, S. (1994). Paradigms of knowledge and instruction. *Review of Educational Research, 64,* 463–477.

Faw, H. W., & Waller, T. G. (1976). Mathemagenic behaviors and efficiency in learning from prose materials: Review, critique, and recommendations. *Review of Educational Research, 46,* 691–720.

Fennema, E., Franke, M. L., Carpenter, T. P., & Carey, D. A. (1993). Using children's mathematical knowledge in instruction. *American Educational Research Journal, 30,* 555–583.

Ferretti, R. P., MacArthur, C. A., & Dowdy, N. S. (2000). The effects of an elaborated goal on the persuasive writing of students with learning disabilities and their normally achieving peers. *Journal of Educational Psychology, 92,* 694–702.

Ferster, C. B., & Skinner, B. F. (1957). *Schedules of reinforcement*. New York: Appleton–Century–Crofts.

Feuerstein, R., Rand, Y., Hoffman, M. B., & Miller, R. (1980). *Instrumental enrichment: An intervention program for cognitive modifiability*. Baltimore: University Park Press.

Fishbein, H. D., Eckart, T., Lauver, E., Van Leeuwen, R., & Langmeyer, D. (1990). Learners' questions and comprehension in a tutoring setting. *Journal of Educational Psychology, 82,* 163–170.

Fisher, D. L., Duffy, S. A., Young, C., & Pollatsek, A. (1988). Understanding the central processing limit in consistent-mapping visual search tasks. *Journal of Experimental Psychology: Human Perception and Performance, 14,* 253–266.

Flavell, J. H. (1992). Perspectives on perspective taking. In H. Beilin & P. Pufall (Eds.), *Piaget's theory: Prospects and possibilities* (pp. 107–139). Mahwah, NJ: Erlbaum.

Flink, C., Boggiano, A. K., & Barrett, M. (1990). Controlling teaching strategies: Undermining children's self-determination and performance. *Journal of Personality and Social Psychology, 59,* 916–924.

Flower, L., & Hayes, J. R. (1984). The representation of meaning in writing. *Written Communication, 1,* 120–160.

Flowerday, T., & Schraw, G. (2000). Teacher beliefs about instructional choice: A phenomenological study. *Journal of Educational Psychology, 92,* 634–645.

Försterling, F. (1985). Attributional retraining: A review. *Psychological Bulletin, 98,* 495–512.

Freedman, S. W. (1992). Outside-in and inside-out: Peer response groups in two ninth-grade classes. *Research in the Teaching of English, 26,* 71–107.

Freeman, D. J., & Porter, A. C. (1989). Do textbooks dictate the content of mathematics instruction in elementary schools? *American Educational Research Journal, 6,* 207–226.

Friedman, A., Polson, M. C., & Dafoe, C. G. (1988). Dividing attention between the hands and the head: Performance trade-offs between rapid finger tapping and verbal memory. *Journal of Experimental Psychology: Human Perception and Performance, 14,* 60–68.

Frogner, E. (1939). Grammar approach vs. thought approach in teaching sentence structure. *English Journal, 28,* 518–526.

Fuchs, L. S., & Fuchs, D. (2000). Building student capacity to work productively in peer-assisted learning activities. In B. M. Taylor, M. F. Graves, & van den Broek (Eds.), *Reading for meaning: Fostering comprehension in the middle grades* (pp. 95–115). New York: Teachers College Press.

Furst, B. (1954). *Stop forgetting.* New York: Garden City Press.

Fuson, K. C. (1992). Research on whole number addition and subtraction. In D. A. Grouws (Ed.), *Handbook of research on mathematics teaching and learning* (pp. 243–275). New York: Macmillan.

Fuson, K. C., & Fuson, A. M. (1992). Instruction supporting children's counting on for addition and counting up for subtraction. *Journal for Research in Mathematics Education, 23,* 72–78.

Gagne, R. M. (1965). The analysis of instructional objectives for the design of instruction. In R. Glaser (Ed.), *Teaching machines and programmed learning: Vol. 2. Data and direction* (pp. 32–41). Washington, DC: National Education Association.

Gagne, R. M. (1970). *The conditions of learning* (2nd ed.). New York: Holt, Rinehart & Winston.

Gambrell, L., Morrow, L. M., Neuman, S., & Pressley, M. (Eds.) (1999). *Best practices in literacy instruction.* New York: Guilford Press.

Gardner, H. (1983). *Frames of mind: The theory of multiple intelligences.* New York: Basic Books.

Gardner, H. (2000). Technology remakes the schools. *The Futurist, 34*(2), 30–32.

Garner, R., & Alexander, P. A. (1989). Metacognition: Answered and unanswered questions. *Educational Psychologist, 24,* 143–158.

Garner, R., Gillingham, M. G., & White, C. S. (1989). Effects of "seductive details" on macroprocessing and microprocessing in adults and children. *Cognition and Instruction, 6,* 41–57.

Gauvain, M. (2001). *The social context of cognitive development.* New York: Guilford Press.

Geary, D. C., Hamson, C. O., & Hoard, M. K. (2000). Numerical and arithmetical cognition: A longitudinal study of process and concept deficits in children with learning disability. *Journal of Experimental Child Psychology, 77,* 236–263.

Gernsbacher, M. A. (1996). The structure-building framework: What is it, what it might also be, and why. In B. K. Britton & A. C. Graesser (Eds.), *Models of understanding text* (pp. 289–311). Mahwah, NJ: Erlbaum.

Getzels, J., & Czikszentmihalyi, M. (1976). *The creative vision: A longitudinal study of problem finding in art.* New York: Wiley.

Ghaith, G., & Yaghi, H. (1997). Relationships among experience, teacher efficacy, and attitudes toward the implementation of instructional innovation. *Teaching and Teacher Education, 13,* 451–458.

Gibson, S., & Dembo, M. H. (1984). Teacher efficacy: A construct validation. *Journal of Educational Psychology, 76,* 569–582.

Gick, M. L. (1986). Problem-solving strategies. *Educational Psychologist, 21,* 99–120.

Gick, M. L., & Holyoak, K. J. (1980). Analogical problem solving. *Cognitive Psychology, 12,* 306–355.

Gick, M. L., & Holyoak, K. J. (1983). Schema induction and analogical transfer. *Cognitive Psychology, 15,* 1–38.

Gillespie, D. (1992). *The mind's we: Contextualism in cognitive psychology.* Carbondale: Southern Illinois University Press.

Ginsburg, H. P. (1996). Toby's math. In R. J. Sternberg & T. Ben-Zeev (Eds.), *The nature of mathematical thinking* (pp. 175–202). Mahwah, NJ: Erlbaum.

Ginsburg, H. P., & Baron, J. (1993). Cognition: Young children's construction of mathematics. In R. J. Jensen (Ed.), *Research ideas for the classroom: Early childhood mathematics* (pp. 3–21). New York: Macmillan.

Glaser, R., & Chi, M. T. (1988). Overview. In M. Chi, R. Glaser, & M. Farr (Eds.), *The nature of expertise* (pp. 15–28). Mahwah, NJ: Erlbaum.

Glenberg, A. M., & Epstein, W. (1985). Calibration of comprehension. *Journal of Experimental Psychology: Learning, Memory, and Cognition, 11,* 702–718.

Glenberg, A. M., & Epstein, W. (1987). Inexpert calibration of comprehension. *Memory & Cognition, 15,* 84–93.

Glenberg, A. M., Smith, S. M., & Green, C. (1977). Type I rehearsal: Maintenance and more. *Journal of Verbal Learning and Verbal Behavior, 16,* 339–352.

Glenberg, A. M., Wilkinson, A. C., & Epstein, W. (1982). The illusion of knowing: Failure in the self-assessment of comprehension. *Memory & Cognition, 10,* 597–602.

Glover, J. A., Bruning, R. H., & Plake, B. S. (1982). Distinctiveness of encoding and recall of text materials. *Journal of Educational Psychology, 74,* 522–534.

Glover, J. A., & Corkill, A. (1987). The spacing effect in memory for prose. *Journal of Educational Psychology, 79,* 198–200.

Glover, J. A., Dinnel, D. L., Halpain, D., McKee, T., Corkill A. J., & Wise, S. (1988). Effects of across-chapter signals on recall of text. *Journal of Educational Psychology, 80,* 3–15.

Glover, J. A., Harvey, A. L., & Corkill, A. J. (1988). Remembering written instructions: Tab A goes into Slot C, or does it? *British Journal of Educational Psychology, 58,* 191–200.

Glover, J. A., Plake, B. S., & Zimmer, J. W. (1982). Distinctiveness of encoding and memory for learning tasks. *Journal of Educational Psychology, 74,* 189–198.

Glover, J. A., Rankin, J., Langner, N., Todero, C., & Dinnel, D. (1985). Memory for sentences and prose: Levels-of-processing or transfer-appropriate processing? *Journal of Reading Behavior, 17,* 215–234.

Glover, J. A., & Ronning, R. R. (Eds.). (1987). *Historical foundations of educational psychology.* New York: Plenum.

Glover, J. A., Timme, V., Deyloff, D., Rogers, M., & Dinnel, D. (1987). Oral directions: Remembering what to do when. *Journal of Educational Research, 81,* 33–53.

Glover, J. A., & Zimmer, J. W. (1982). Procedures to influence levels of questions asked by students. *Journal of General Psychology, 107,* 267–276.

Glover, J. A., Zimmer, J. W., Filbeck, R. W., & Plake, B. S. (1980). Effects of training students to identify the semantic base of prose material. *Journal of Applied Behavior Analysis, 13,* 655–667.

Glynn, S. M., & DiVesta, E. J. (1979). Control of prose processing via instructional and typographical cues. *Journal of Educational Psychology, 71,* 595–603.

Goddard, R. D., Hoy, W. K., & Hoy, A. W. (2000). Collective teacher efficacy: Its meaning, measure and impact on student achievement. *American Educational Research Journal, 37,* 479–507.

Godden, D. R., & Baddeley, A. D. (1975). Context-dependent memory in two natural environments: On land and underwater. *British Journal of Psychology, 66,* 325–332.

Goetz, E. T., Sadoski, M., Fatemi, Z., & Bush, R. (1994). That's news to me: Readers' responses to brief newspaper articles. *Journal of Reading Behavior, 26,* 125–138.

Goldman, S. R., & Rakestraw, J. A., Jr. (2000). Structural aspects of constructing meaning from text. In M. L. Kamil, P. B. Mosenthal, P. D. Pearson, & R. Barr (Eds.), *Handbook of reading research* (Vol. 3, pp. 311–335). Mahwah, NJ: Erlbaum.

Goldman, S. R., & Varma, S. (1995). CAPping the construction integration model of discourse comprehension. In C. Weaver, S. Mannes, & C. Fletcher (Eds.), *Discourse comprehension: Models of processing revisited* (pp. 337–358). Hillsdale, NJ: Erlbaum.

Goldman, S. R., Varma, S., & Cote, N. (1996). Extending capacity-constrained construction integration: Toward "smarter" and flexible models of text comprehension. In B. K. Britton & A. C. Graesser (Eds.), *Models of understanding text* (pp. 73–113). Mahwah, NJ: Erlbaum.

Goldman, S. R., & Varnhagen, C. K. (1986). Improving comprehension: Causal relations instruction for learning among handicapped learners. *Reading Teacher, 39,* 898–904.

Good, T., & Brophy, J. (1986). *Educational psychology* (3rd ed.). New York: Longman.

Goodman, K. S. (1982a). Miscues: Windows on the reading process. In F. V. Gollasch (Ed.), *Language and literacy* (Vol. 1, pp. 64–79). Boston: Routledge Kegan Paul.

Goodman, K. S. (1982b). Reading: A psycholinguistic guessing game. In E. V. Gollasch (Ed.), *Language and literacy* (Vol. 1, pp. 19-31). Boston: Routledge Kegan Paul.

Goodman, K. S. (1982c). The reading process: Theory and practice. In F. V. Gollasch (Ed.), *Language and literacy* (Vol. 1, pp. 33-43). Boston: Routledge Kegan Paul.

Goodman, K. S. (1989). Whole language research: Foundations of development. *Elementary School Journal, 90,* 207-220.

Goodman, K. S. (1994). Reading, writing, and written texts: A transactional sociopsycholinguistic view. In R. B. Ruddell, M. R. Ruddell, & H. Singer (Eds.), *Theoretical models and processes of reading* (4th ed., pp. 1093-1130). Newark, DE: International Reading Association.

Goodman, K. S. (1996). *On reading*. Portsmouth, NH: Heinemann.

Goodman, K. S., & Goodman, Y. M. (1979). Learning to read is natural. In L. B. Resnick & R. A. Weaver (Eds.), *Theory and practice of early reading* (pp. 51-94). Mahwah, NJ: Erlbaum.

Goodman, K. S., & Goodman, Y. M. (1982). Learning about psycholinguistic processes by analyzing oral reading. In F. V. Gollasch (Ed.), *Language and literacy* (Vol. 1, pp. 149-168). Boston: Routledge Kegan Paul.

Goswarmi, U. (2000). Phonological and lexical processes. In M. L. Kamil, P. B. Mosenthal, P. D. Pearson, & R. Barr (Eds.), *Handbook of reading research* (Vol. 3, pp. 251-267). Mahwah, NJ: Erlbaum.

Gottardo, A., Stanovich, K. E., & Siegel, L. S. (1996). The relationships between phonological sensitivity, syntactic processing, and verbal working memory in the reading performance of third-grade children. *Journal of Experimental Child Psychology, 63,* 563-582.

Gottfried, A. (1990). Academic intrinsic motivation in young elementary school children. *Journal of Educational Psychology, 82,* 525-538.

Gough, P. B. (1972). One second of reading. In E. Kavanagh & I. G. Mattingly (Eds.), *Language by ear and by eye* (pp. 331-358). Cambridge, MA: MIT Press.

Grabe, M., & Mann, S. (1984). A technique for the assessment and training of comprehension monitoring skills. *Journal of Reading Behavior, 16,* 131-144.

Graesser, A. C., & Britton, B. K. (1996). Five metaphors for text understanding. In B. K. Britton & A. C. Graesser (Eds.), *Models of understanding text* (pp. 341-351). Mahwah, NJ: Erlbaum.

Graesser, A. C., Long, K., & Horgan, D. (1988). A taxonomy for question generation. *Questioning Exchange, 2,* 3-16.

Graf, P., & Schacter, D. A. (1985). Implicit and explicit memory for new associations in normal and amnesic subjects. *Journal of Experimental Psychology: Learning, Memory, and Cognition, 11,* 501-518.

Graham, S. (1991). A review of attribution theory in achievement contexts. *Educational Psychology Review, 3,* 5-39.

Graham, S., & Barker, G. P. (1990). The down side of help: An attributional-developmental analysis of helping behavior as a low-ability cue. *Journal of Educational Psychology, 82,* 7-14.

Graham, S., Berninger, V. W., Abbott, R. D., Abbott, S. P., & Whitaker, D. (1997). The role of mechanics in composing of elementary school students: A new methodological approach. *Journal of Educational Psychology, 89,* 170-182.

Graham, S., & Harris, K. R. (1989). Components analysis of cognitive strategy instruction: Effects on learning disabled students' compositions and self-efficacy. *Journal of Educational Psychology, 81,* 353-361.

Graham, S., & Harris, K. R. (1993). Self-regulated strategy development: Helping students with learning problems develop as writers. *Elementary School Journal, 94,* 160-181.

Graham, S., & Harris, K. R. (1996). Self-regulation and strategy instruction for students who find writing and learning challenging. In C. M. Levy & S. Ransdell (Eds.), *The science of writing: Theories, methods, individual differences, and applications* (pp. 347-360). Mahwah, NJ: Erlbaum.

Graham, S., & Harris, K. (2000b). The role of self-regulation and transcription skills in writing and writing development. *Educational Psychologist, 35,* 3-12.

Graham, S., Harris, K., & Fink, B. (2000). Is handwriting causally related to learning to write? Treatment of handwriting problems in beginning writers. *Journal of Educational Psychology, 92,* 620-633.

Graham, S., & Weiner, B. (1996). Theories and principles of motivation. In D. C. Berliner & R. C. Calfee (Eds.), *The handbook of educational psychology* (pp. 63-84). New York: Macmillan.

Graves, D. H. (1983). *Writing: Teachers and children at work*. Portsmouth, NH: Heinemann.

Graves, M. F. (1992). The elementary vocabulary curriculum: What should it be? In M. J. Dreher & W. H. Slater (Eds.), *Elementary school literacy: Critical issues* (pp. 101–131). Norwood, MA: Christopher-Gordon.

Graves, M. F. (2000). A vocabulary program to complement and bolster a middle-grade comprehension program. In B. M. Taylor, M. F. Graves, & van den Broek (Eds.), *Reading for meaning: Fostering comprehension in the middle grades*. New York: Teachers College Press

Gredler, M. E. (1992). *Learning and instruction: Theory into practice* (2nd ed.). New York: Macmillan.

Greene, B. A., & Miller, R. B. (1996). Influences of achievement: Goals, perceived ability, and cognitive engagement. *Contemporary Educational Psychology, 21,* 181–192.

Greene, R. L. (1992). *Human memory: Paradigms and paradoxes*. Mahwah, NJ: Erlbaum.

Greeno, J. G., & The Middle School Mathematics Through Applications Project Group. (1998). The situativity of knowing, learning, and research. *American Psychologist, 53,* 5–26.

Greenwald, A. G., Klinger, M. R., & Lui, T. J. (1989). Unconscious processing of dichoptically masked words. *Memory & Cognition, 17,* 35–47.

Gregg, L. W., & Steinberg, E. R. (1980). *Cognitive processes in writing*. Mahwah, NJ: Erlbaum.

Grolnick, W. S., & Ryan, R. M. (1987). Autonomy in children's learning: An experimental and individual difference investigation. *Journal of Personality and Social Psychology, 52,* 890–898.

Grow-Maienza, J., Hahn, D., & Joo, C-A. (2001). Mathematics instruction in Korean primary schools: structures, processes, and a linguistic analysis of questioning. *Journal of Educational Psychology, 93,* 363–376.

Guskey, T. R., & Passaro, P. D. (1994). Teacher efficacy: A study of construct dimensions. *American Educational Research Journal, 31,* 627–643.

Guthrie, J. T. (1993, August). *An instructional framework for developing motivational and cognitive aspects of reading*. Division 15 Invited Address at the Annual Convention of the American Psychological Association, Toronto.

Guthrie, J. T. (in press). Classroom contexts for engaged reading. In J. T. Guthrie, A. Wigfield, & K. C. Perencevich (Eds.), *Concept-oriented reading instruction: Theory and implementation*. New York: Teachers College Press.

Guthrie, J. T., Bennett, L., & McGough, K. (1994). *Concept-oriented reading instruction: An integrated curriculum to develop motivations and strategies for reading* (Reading Research Rep. No. 10). College Park, MD: National Reading Research Center.

Guthrie, J. T., & McCann, A. D. (1997). Characteristics of classrooms that promote motivations and strategies for learning. In J. T. Guthrie & A. Wigfield (Eds.), *Reading engagement: Motivating readers through integrated instruction* (pp. 128–148). Newark, DE: International Reading Association.

Guthrie, J. T., Van Meter, P., McCann, A. D., Wigfield, A., Bennett, L., Poundstone, C. C. et al. (1996). Growth of literacy engagement: Changes in motivations and strategies during concept-oriented reading instruction. *Reading Research Quarterly, 31,* 306–332.

Guthrie, J. T., & Wigfield, A. (Eds.). (1997). *Reading engagement: Motivating readers through integrated instruction*. Newark, DE: International Reading Association.

Guthrie, J. T., Wigfield, A., & Perencevich, K. C. (in press). *Reading comprehension and engagement: Concept-oriented reading instruction*. Mahwah, NJ: Eribaum.

Hacker, D. J. (1997). Comprehension monitoring of written discourse across early-to-middle adolescence. *Reading and Writing: An Interdisciplinary Journal, 9,* 207–240.

Halliday, M., & Hasan, R. (1974). *Cohesion in English*. London: Longman.

Halpern, D. F. (1997). *Thought and knowledge: An introduction to critical thinking* (3rd ed.). Mahwah, NJ: Erlbaum.

Halpern, D. F. (1998). Teaching critical thinking for transfer across domains. *American Psychologist, 53,* 449–455.

Halpern, D. F. (2001). Why wisdom? *Educational Psychologist, 36,* 253–256.

Hamaker, C. (1986). The effects of adjunct questions on prose learning. *Review of Educational Research, 56,* 212–242.

Hamilton, R. (1985). A framework for the evaluation of the effectiveness of adjunct questions and objectives. *Review of Educational Research, 55,* 47–85.

Hamilton, R., & Ghatala, E. (1994). *Learning and instruction*. New York: McGraw-Hill.

Handel, S. (1988). Space is to time as vision is to audition: Seductive but misleading. *Journal of Experimental Psychology: Human Perception and Performance, 14,* 315-317.

Hanich, L. B., Jordan, N. C., Kaplan, D., & Dick, J. (2001). Performance across different areas of mathematical cognition in children with learning disabilities. *Journal of Educational Psychology, 93,* 615-626.

Harackiewicz, J. M., Barron, K. E., Tauer, J. M., Carter, S. M., & Elliot, A. J. (2000). Short-term and long-term consequences of achievement goals: Predicting interest and performance over time. *Journal of Educational Psychology, 92,* 316-330.

Hardiman, P. T., Dufresne, R., & Mestre, J. P. (1989). The relation between problem categorization and problem solving among experts and novices. *Memory & Cognition, 17,* 627-638.

Hargreaves, A., Earl, L., Moore, S., & Manning. S. (2001). *Learning to change: Teaching beyond subjects and standards.* San Francisco: Jossey-Bass.

Harney, P. (1989). *The Hope Scale: Exploration of construct validity and its influence on health.* Unpublished master's thesis, University of Kansas, Lawrence.

Harris, K. R., & Alexander, P. A. (1998). Integrated, constructivist education: Challenges and reality. *Educational Psychology Review, 10,* 115-128.

Harris, K. R., & Graham, S. (1992). *Helping young writers master the craft: Strategy instruction and self-regulation in the writing process.* Cambridge, MA: Brookline.

Harris, K., & Graham, S. (1996). *Making the writing process work: Strategies for composition and self-regulation.* Cambridge, MA: Brookline Books.

Harris, K., Graham, S., & Deshler, D. (Eds.). (1998). *Teaching every child every day: Learning in diverse schools and classrooms.* Cambridge, MA: Brookline Books.

Hart, E. R., & Speece, D. L. (1998). Reciprocal teaching goes to college: Effects for postsecondary students at risk for academic failure. *Journal of Educational Psychology, 90,* 670-681.

Hashweh, M. Z. (1996). Effects of science teachers' epistemological beliefs in teaching. *Journal of Research in Science Teaching, 33,* 47-63.

Hattie, J., Biggs, J., & Purdie, N. (1996). Effects of learning skills interventions on student learning: A meta-analysis. *Review of Educational Research, 66,* 99-136.

Hawkins, H. L., & Presson, J. C. (1987). Auditory information processing. In K. R. Boff, L. Kaufman & J. P. Thomas (Eds.), *Handbook of perception and human performance: Vol. 2. Information processing* (pp. 26-1 to 26-48). New York: Wiley.

Hayes, B. K., & Hennessy, R. (1996). The nature and development of nonverbal implicit memory. *Journal of Experimental Child Psychology, 63,* 22-43.

Hayes, J. R. (1978). *Cognitive psychology.* Homewood, IL: Dorsey.

Hayes, J. R. (1988). *The complete problem solver* (2nd ed.). Mahwah, NJ: Erlbaum.

Hayes, J. R. (1996). A new framework for understanding cognition and affect in writing. In C. M. Levy & S. Ransdell (Eds.), *The science of writing: Theories, methods, individual differences, and applications* (pp. 1-27). Mahwah, NJ: Erlbaum.

Hayes, J. R., & Flower, L. S. (1986). Writing research and the writer. *American Psychologist, 41,* 1106-1113.

Haygood, R. C., & Bourne, L. E., Jr. (1965). Attribute- and rule-learning aspects of conceptual behavior. *Psychological Review, 72,* 175-196.

Healy, A. F., & McNamara, D. S. (1996). Verbal learning and memory: Does the modal model still work? *Annual Review of Psychology, 47,* 143-172.

Heath, S. B. (1986). Separating "things of the imagination" from life: Learning to read and write. In W. H. Teale & E. Sulzby (Eds.), *Emergent literacy* (pp. 156-172). Norwood, NJ: Ablex.

Hennessey, B. A., & Amabile, T. M. (1988). The role of the environment in creativity. In R. Sternberg (Ed.), *The nature of creativity: Contemporary psychological perspectives* (pp. 11-38). New York: Cambridge University Press.

Henson, R. K., Kogan, L. R., & Vacha-Haase, T. (2001). A reliability generalization study of the Teacher Efficacy Scale and related instruments. *Educational and Psychological Measurement, 61,* 404-420.

Herbert, E., Lee, A., & Williamson, L. (1998). Teachers' and teacher education students' sense of self-efficacy: Quantitative and qualitative comparisons. *Journal of Research and Development in Education, 31,* 214-225.

Hewitt, J., & Scardamalia, M. (1998). Design principles for distributed knowledge building processes. *Educational Psychology Review, 10*(1), 75-96.

Hidi, S., & Anderson, V. (1986). Producing written summaries: Task demands, cognitive operations, and implications for instruction. *Review of Educational Research, 56,* 473-493.

Hiebert, E. H. (1994). Becoming literate through authentic tasks: Evidence and adaptations. In R. B. Ruddell, M. R. Ruddell, & H. Singer (Eds.), *Theoretical models and processes of reading* (4th ed., pp. 391-413). Newark, DE: International Reading Association.

Hiebert, J., Gallimore, R., & Stigler, J. W. (2002). A knowledge base for the teaching profession: What would it look like and how can we get one? *Educational Researcher, 31,* 3-15.

Hiebert, E. H., & Raphael, T. E. (1996). Psychological perspectives on literacy and extensions to educational practice. In D. C. Berliner & R. C. Calfee (Eds.), *Handbook of educational psychology* (pp. 550-602). New York: Macmillan.

Hiebert, E. H., & Raphael, T. E. (1998). *Early literacy instruction.* Orlando, FL: Harcourt Brace.

Hiebert, J., & Carpenter, T. P. (1992). Learning and teaching with understanding. In D. A. Grouws (Ed.), *Handbook of research on mathematics teaching and learning* (pp. 65-97). New York: Macmillan.

Higbee, K. L., & Kunihira, S. (1985). Cross-cultural applications of yodai mnemonics in education. *Educational Psychologist, 20,* 57-64.

Hilgers, T. C. (1986). How children change as critical evaluators of writing. Four three-year care studies. *Research in the Teaching of English, 20,* 36-55.

Hinsley, D. A., Hayes, J. R., & Simon, H. A. (1977). From words to equations: Meaning and representation in algebra word problems. In M. A. Just & P. A. Carpenter (Eds.), *Cognitive Processes in Comprehension* (pp. 89-106). Hillsdale, NJ: Erlbaum.

Hofer, B. K. (2000). Dimensionality and disciplinary differences in personal epistemology. *Contemporary Educational Psychology, 25,* 378-405.

Hofer, B. (2001). Personal epistemology research: Implications for learning and teaching. *Educational Psychology Review, 13,* 353-384.

Hofer, B. K., & Pintrich, P. R. (1997). The development of epistemological theories: Beliefs about knowledge and knowing and their relation to learning. *Review of Educational Research, 67,* 88-140.

Hofer, B. K., & Pintrich, P. R. (2002). *Personal epistemology: The psychology of beliefs about knowledge and knowing.* Mahwah, NJ: Erlbaum.

Hogarth, R. M., Gibbs, B. J., McKenzie, C. R. M., & Marquis, M. A. (1991). Learning from feedback: Exactingness and incentives. *Journal of Experimental Psychology: Learning, Memory, and Cognition, 17,* 734-752.

Holland, J., & Skinner, B. F. (1961). *The analysis of behavior.* New York: McGraw-Hill.

Hollon, R. E., Anderson, C. W., & Roth, K. J. (1991). Science teachers' conceptions of teaching and learning. In J. Brophy (Ed.), *Advances in research on teaching* (Vol. 2, pp. 145-186). Greenwich, CT: JAI Press.

Holt-Reynolds, D. (2000). What does the teacher do? Constructivist pedagogies and prospective teachers' beliefs about the role of the teacher. *Teaching and Teacher Education, 16,* 21-32.

Howard, B. C., McGee, S., Schwartz, N., & Purcell, S. (2000). The experience of constructivism: Transforming teacher epistemology. *Journal of Research on Computing in Education, 32,* 455-465.

Howe, M. L. (2000). *The fate of early memories.* Washington, DC: American Psychological Association.

Hudson, T. (1980, July). Young children's difficulty with "How many more than are there?" questions (Doctoral dissertation, Indiana University, 1980). *Dissertation Abstracts International, 41.*

Hull, C. L. (1934). The concept of the habit-family hierarchy and maze learning: Part 1. *Psychological Review, 34,* 33-54.

Hull, C. L. (1952). *A behavior system: An introduction to behavior theory concerning the individual organism.* New Haven, CT: Yale University Press.

Hull, G. (1987). The editing process in writing: A performance study of more skilled and less skilled college writers. *Research in the Teaching of English, 21,* 829.

Hull, G., Rose, M., Fraser, K. L., & Castellano, M. (1991). Remediation as social construct: Perspectives from an analysis of classroom discourse. *College Composition and Communication, 42,* 299-329.

Hulme, C., & Mackenzie, S. (1992). *Working memory and severe learning difficulties.* Mahwah, NJ: Erlbaum.

Hunt, E. (1987). Science, technology, and intelligence. In R. R. Ronning, J. A. Glover, & J. Conoley (Eds.), *The impact of cognitive psychology on measurement* (pp. 156-178). Mahwah, NJ: Erlbaum.

Hurst, R. W., & Milkent, M. M. (1996). Facilitating successful prediction problem solving in biology through application of skill theory. *Journal of Research in Science Teaching, 33,* 541-552.

Hyde, T. S., & Jenkins, J. J. (1969). Recall for words as a function of semantic, graphic, and syntactic orienting tasks. *Journal of Verbal Learning and Verbal Behavior, 12,* 471–480.

Intons-Peterson, M. J. (1993). Imagery and classification. In A. F. Collins, S. E. Gathercole, M. A. Conway, & P. E. Morris (Eds.), *Theories of memory* (pp. 211–240). Hove, UK: Erlbaum.

Jacobs, J. E., & Paris, S. G. (1987). Children's metacognition about reading: Issues in definition, measurement, and instruction. *Educational Psychologist, 22,* 255–278.

Jacoby, L. L. (1978). On interpreting the effects of repetition: Solving a problem versus remembering a solution. *Journal of Verbal Learning and Verbal Behavior, 17,* 649–667.

Jacoby, L. L. (1983). Remembering the date: Analyzing interactive processes in reading. *Journal of Verbal Learning and Verbal Behavior, 22,* 485–508.

Jacoby, L. L., & Craik, F. I. M. (1979). Effects of elaboration of processing at encoding and retrieval: Trace distinctiveness and recovery of initial context. In L. S. Cermak & F. I. M. Craik (Eds.), *Levels of processing in human memory* (pp. 1–22). Mahwah, NJ: Erlbaum.

Jacoby, L. L., Craik, F. I. M., & Begg, I. (1979). Effects of decision difficulty on recognition and recall. *Journal of Verbal Learning and Verbal Behavior, 18,* 585–600.

Jacoby, L. L., & Witherspoon, D. (1982). Remembering without awareness. *Canadian Journal of Psychology, 36,* 300–324.

Jehng, J. J., Johnson, S. D., & Anderson, R. C. (1993). Schooling and students' epistemological beliefs about learning. *Contemporary Educational Psychology, 18,* 23–35.

Jenkins, J. J. (1974). Remember that old theory of memory? Well, forget it! *American Psychologist, 25,* 785–795.

Jensen, A. R. (1992). Understanding g in terms of information processing. *Educational Psychology Review, 4,* 271–308.

Johnson, E. J. (1988). Expertise and decision under uncertainty: Performance and process. In M. Chi, R. Glaser, & M. Farr (Eds.), *The nature of expertise* (pp. 209–228). Mahwah, NJ: Erlbaum.

Johnson, M. K., Hashtroudi, S., & Lindsay, D. S. (1993). Source monitoring. *Psychological Bulletin, 114,* 3–28.

John-Steiner, V. (1997). *Notebooks of the mind: Explorations of thinking* (rev. ed.). New York: Oxford University Press.

John-Steiner, V., & Mahn, H. (1996). Sociocultural approaches to learning and development: A Vygotskian framework. *Educational Psychologist, 31,* 191–206.

Johnston, P., Woodside-Jiron, H. & Day, J. (2001). Teaching and learning literate epistemologies. *Journal of Educational Psychology, 93* (1), 223–233.

Jonassen, D. H., & Land, S. M. (Eds.) (2000). *Theoretical foundations of learning environments.* Mahwah, NJ: Erlbaum.

Jones, E. D., Krouse, J. P., Feorene, D., & Saferstein, C. A. (1985). A comparison of concurrent and sequential instruction of four types of verbal math problems. *Remedial and Special Education, 6,* 25–31.

Joram, E., & Gabriele, A. J. (1998). Preservice teachers' prior beliefs: Transforming obstacles into opportunities. *Teaching and Teacher Education, 14,* 175–191.

Jordan, N. C., & Hanich, L. B. (2000). Mathematical thinking in second-grade children with different types of learning difficulties. *Journal of Learning Disabilities, 33,* 567–578.

Juel, C. (1996). What makes literacy tutoring effective? *Reading Research Quarterly, 31,* 268–289.

Jussim, L. (1989). Teacher expectations: Self-fulfilling prophecies, perceptual biases, and accuracy. *Journal of Personality and Social Psychology, 57,* 469–480.

Jussim, L., & Eccles, J. S. (1992). Teacher expectations II: Construction and reflection of student achievement. *Journal of Personality and Social Psychology, 63,* 947–961.

Just, M. A., & Carpenter, P. A. (1987). *The psychology of reading and language comprehension.* Boston: Allyn & Bacon.

Just, M. A., & Carpenter, P. A. (1992). A capacity theory of comprehension: Individual differences in working memory. *Psychological Review, 99,* 122–149.

Kagan, D. M. (1992). Implications of research on teacher belief. *Educational Psychologist, 27,* 65–90.

Kahle, J. B., Parker, L. H., Rennie, L. J., & Riley, D. (1993). Gender differences in science education: Building a model. *Educational Psychologist, 28,* 379–404.

Kalyuga, S., Chandler, P., Tuovinen, J., & Sweller, J. (2001). When problem solving is superior to studying worked examples. *Journal of Educational Psychology, 93,* 579–588.

Kalyuga, S., Chandler, P., & Sweller, J. (2000). Incorporating learning experience into the design of multimedia instruction. *Journal of Educational Psychology, 92* (1), 126–136.

Kaplan, A., & Maehr, M. L. (1999). Achievement goals and student well-being. *Contemporary Educational Psychology, 24,* 330–358.

Kaplan, C. A., & Simon, H. A. (1990). In search of insight. *Cognitive Psychology, 22,* 374–419.

Karabenick, S. A., & Knapp, J. R. (1991). Relationship of academic help seeking to the use of learning strategies and other instrumental achievement behavior in college students. *Journal of Educational Psychology, 83,* 221–230.

Kardash, C. M., & Scholes, R. J. (1996). Effects of preexisting beliefs, epistemological beliefs, and need for cognition on interpretation of controversial issues. *Journal of Educational Psychology, 88,* 260–271.

Kazdin, A. E. (1994). *Behavior modification in applied settings.* Belmont, CA: Brooks/Cole.

Kellas, G., Ferraro, E. R., & Simpson, G. B. (1988). Lexical ambiguity and the timecourse of attentional allocation in word recognition. *Journal of Experimental Psychology: Human Perception and Performance, 14,* 601–609.

Kellogg, R. T. (1984). *Cognitive strategies in writing.* (ERIC Document Reproduction Service No. ED 262 425)

Kieran, C. (1992). The learning and teaching of school algebra. In D. A. Grouws (Ed.), *Handbook of research on mathematics teaching and learning* (pp. 390–419). New York: Macmillan.

Kilpatrick, J. (1985). Doing mathematics without understanding it: A commentary on Higbee and Kunihira. *Educational Psychologist, 20,* 65–68.

Kimball, M. M. (1989). A new perspective on women's math achievement. *Psychological Bulletin, 105,* 198–214.

King, A. (1991). Effects of training in strategic questioning on children's problem-solving performance. *Journal of Educational Psychology, 83,* 307–317.

King, A. (1992). Facilitating elaborative learning through guided student-generated questioning. *Educational Psychologist, 27,* 111–126.

King, A. (1994). Guiding knowledge construction in the classroom: Effects of teaching children how to question and how to explain. *American Educational Research Journal, 31,* 338–368.

King, A., & Rosenshine, B. (1993). Effects of guided cooperative questioning on children's knowledge construction. *Journal of Experimental Education, 61,* 127–148.

King, A., Staffieri, A., & Adelgeis, A. (1998). Mutual peer tutoring: Effects of structuring tutorial interaction to scaffold peer learning. *Journal of Educational Psychology, 90,* 134–152.

King, P. M., & Kitchener, K. S. (1994). *Developing reflective judgment.* San Francisco: Jossey-Bass.

King, P. M., & Kitchener, K. S. (2002). The reflective judgment model: Twenty years of research on epistemic cognition. In B. K. Hofer & P. R. Pintrich (Eds.), *Personal epistemology: The psychology of beliefs about knowledge and knowing* (pp. 37–62). Mahwah, NJ: Erlbaum.

King, P. M., Wood, P. K., & Mines, R. A. (1990). Critical thinking among college and graduate students. *Review of Higher Education, 13,* 167–186.

Kintsch, W. (1974). *The representation of meaning in memory.* Mahwah, NJ: Erlbaum.

Kintsch, W. (1986). *Learning from text. Cognition and Instruction, 3,* 87–108.

Kintsch, W. (1988). The role of knowledge in discourse comprehension: A construction-integration model. *Psychology Review, 95,* 163–182.

Kintsch, W. (1998). *Comprehension: A paradigm for cognition.* Cambridge, UK: Cambridge University Press.

Kintsch, W., & Greeno, J. G. (1985). Understanding and solving arithmetic word problems. *Psychological Review, 92,* 109–129.

Kintsch, W., & Van Dijk, T. A. (1978). Toward a model of text comprehension and production. *Psychological Review, 85,* 363–394.

Kirschner, P. A. (2002). Cognitive load theory: Implications of cognitive load theory on the design of learning. *Learning and Instruction, 12,* 1–10.

Kitchener, K. S. (1983). Cognition, metacognition, and epistemic cognition: A three-level model of cognitive processing. *Human Development, 4,* 222–232.

Kitchener, K. S., & Fischer, K. W. (1990). A skill approach to the development of reflective thinking. In D. Kuhn (Ed.), *Developmental perspectives on teaching and learning thinking skills* (pp. 48–62). Basel: Karger.

Kitchener, K. S., & King, P. A. (1981). Reflective judgment: Concepts of justification and their relationship to age and education. *Journal of Applied Developmental Psychology, 2,* 89–116.

Kitchener, K. S., King, P. A., Wood, P. A., & Davidson, M. L. (1989). Sequentiality and consistency in development of reflective judgment: A six-year longitudinal study. *Journal of Applied Developmental Psychology, 10,* 73–95.

Klein, S. B., Cosmides, L., Tooby, J., and Chance, S. (2002). Decisions and the evolution of memory: Multiple systems, multiple functions. *Psychological Review, 109,* 306–329.

Kluger, B. B. (1999). Recognizing inquiry: Comparing three hands-on teaching techniques. In *Foundations series: Vol. 2. Inquiry thoughts, views, and strategies for the K-5 classroom: A monograph for professionals in science, mathematics and technology education* (NSF Publication No. 99–148, pp. 39–50). Arlington, VA: National Science Foundation.

Kluwe, R. H. (1987). Executive decisions and regulation of problem solving. In F. Weinert & R. Kluwe (Eds.), *Metacognition, motivation, and understanding* (pp. 31–64). Mahwah, NJ: Erlbaum.

Köhler, W. (1929). *Gestalt psychology*. New York: Liveright.

Kohn, A. (1996). By all available means: Cameron and Pierce's defense of extrinsic motivators. *Review of Educational Research, 66,* 1–4.

Kolers, P. A. (1975). Memorial consequences of automatized encoding. *Journal of Experimental Psychology: Human Learning and Memory, 1,* 689–701.

Kosslyn, S. M. (1994). *Image and brain: The resolution of the imagery debate*. Cambridge: MIT Press.

Kraus, S. (1957). A comparison of three methods of teaching sentence structure. *English Journal, 46,* 275–281.

Kuhn, D. (1989). Children and adults as intuitive scientists. *Psychological Review, 96,* 674–689.

Kuhn, D. (1991). *The skills of argument*. New York: Cambridge University Press.

Kuhn, D. (1992). Thinking as argument. *Harvard Educational Review, 62,* 155–178.

Kuhn, D. (1999). A developmental model of critical thinking. *Educational Researcher, 28,* 16–26.

Kuhn, D., Amsel, E., & O'Loughlin, M. (1988). *The development of scientific reasoning skills*. San Diego: Academic Press.

Kuhn, D., Cheney, R., & Weinstock, M. (2000). The developmental of epistemological understanding. *Cognitive Development, 15,* 309–328.

Kuhn, D., & Loa, J. (1998). Contemplation and conceptual change: Integrating perspectives from social and cognitive psychology. *Developmental Review, 18,* 125–154.

Kuhn, D., Schauble, L., & Garcia-Mila, M. (1992). Cross-domain development of scientific reasoning. *Cognition and Instruction, 9,* 285–327.

Kuhn, D., Shaw, V., & Felton, M. (1997). Effects of dyadic interaction on argumentative reasoning. *Cognition and Instruction, 15,* 287–315.

Kuhn, D., & Weinstock, M. (2002). What is epistemological thinking and why does it matter? In B. K. Hofer & P. R. Pintrich (Eds.), *Personal epistemology: The psychology of beliefs about knowledge and knowing* (pp. 121–144). Mahwah, NJ: Erlbaum.

Kurfiss, J. G. (1988). *Critical thinking: Theory, research, practice, and possibilities* (Rep. No. 2). Washington, DC: Association for the Study of Higher Education.

Kyllonen, P. C., & Christal, R. E. (1990). Reasoning ability is (little more than) working memory capacity! *Intelligence, 14,* 389–433.

LaBerge, D., & Samuels, S. J. (1974). Toward a theory of automatic information processing in reading. *Cognitive Psychology, 6,* 283–323.

Langelle, C. (1989). *An assessment of hope in a community sample*. Unpublished master's thesis, University of Kansas, Lawrence.

Lankford, F. G., Jr. (1972). *Some computational strategies of seventh-grade pupils* (Rep. No. OEG-3-72-0035). Charlottesville: Virginia University. (ERIC Document Reproduction Service No. ED069496)

Larkin, J. H. (1977). *Skilled problem solving in experts* (Tech. Rep.). Berkeley: University of California, Group in Science and Mathematics Education.

Lave, J. (1988). *Cognition in practice: Mind, mathematics and culture in everyday life*. Cambridge, MA: Cambridge University Press.

Lave, J., & Wenger, E. (1991). *Situated learning: Le gitimate peripheral participation*. New York: Cambridge University Press.

Lehman, D. R., Lempert, R. O., & Nisbett, R. E. (1988). The effects of graduate training on reasoning. *American Psychologist, 43,* 431–442.

Leont'ev, A. N. (1981). *Problems in the development of mind*. Moscow: Progress.

Lepper, M. R. (1988). Motivational considerations in the study of instruction. *Cognition and Instruction, 5,* 289–309.

Lepper, M. R., Keavney, M., & Drake, M. (1996). Intrinsic motivation and extrinsic rewards: A commentary on Cameron and Pierce's meta-analysis. *Review of Educational Research, 66,* 5–32.

Lesgold, A. (1988). Problem solving. In R. Sternberg & E. Smith (Eds.), *The psychology of human thought* (pp. 188-213). New York: Cambridge University Press.

Levin, J. R. (1981). The mnemonic '80s: Keywords in the classroom. *Educational Psychologist, 16,* 65-82.

Levin, J. R. (1993). Mnemonic strategies and classroom learning: A 20-year report card. *Elementary School Journal, 94,* 235-244.

Levitt, K. E. (2001). An analysis of elementary teachers' beliefs regarding the teaching and learning of science. *Science Education, 86,* 1-22.

Levy, C. M., & Ramsdell, S. (Eds.). (1996). *The science of writing: Theories, methods, individual differences, and applications.* Mahwah, NJ: Erlbaum.

Lhyle, K. G., & Kulhavy, R. W. (1987). Feedback processing and error correction. *Journal of Educational Psychology, 79,* 320-322.

Linn, M. C., Songer, N. B., & Eylon, B. (1996). Shifts and convergences in science learning and instruction. In D. C. Berliner & R. C. Calfee (Eds.), *The handbook of educational psychology* (pp. 438-490). New York: Macmillan.

Locke, J. L. (1994). Phases in the child's development of language. *American Scientist, 82,* 436-445.

Loftus, E. R., & Loftus, G. R. (1980). On the permanence of stored information in the human brain. *American Psychologist, 35,* 409-420.

Loftus, E. T., Green, E. E., & Smith, R. H. (1980). How deep is the meaning of life? *Bulletin of the Psychonomic Society, 15,* 282-284.

Lohman, D. F. (1993). Teaching and testing to develop fluid abilities. *Educational Researcher, 22,* 12-23.

Lomax, R. G., & McGee, L. M. (1987). Young children's concepts about print and reading: Toward a model of word reading acquisition. *Reading Research Quarterly, 22,* 237-256.

Lorch, R. F., Jr. (1989). Text-signaling devices and their effects on reading and memory processes. *Educational Psychology Review, 1,* 209-234.

Lorch, R. F., Jr., & Chen, A. H. (1986). Effect of number signals on reading and recall. *Journal of Educational Psychology, 78,* 263-270.

Lorch, R. F., Jr., & Lorch, E. P. (1995). Effects of organizational signals on text-processing strategies. *Journal of Educational Psychology, 87,* 537-544.

Lovett, M. C. (2002). Problem solving. In D. Medin (Ed.), *Stevens' handbook of experimental psychology: Vol. 2. Memory and cognitive processes* (3rd ed., pp. 317-362). New York: Wiley.

Lyons, C., Pinnell, G., & DeFord, D. (1993). *Partners in learning: Teachers and children in reading recovery.* New York: Teachers College Press.

MacDonald, M. C., & Christiansen, M. H. (2002). Reassessing working memory: Comment on Just and Carpenter (1992) and Waters and Caplan (1996). *Psychological Review, 109,* 35-54.

MacLeod, C. M. (1988). Forgotten but not gone: Savings for pictures and words in long-term memory. *Journal of Experimental Psychology: Learning, Memory, and Cognition, 14,* 195-212.

Maddux, S. (2002). Self-efficacy: The power of believing you can. In C. R. Synder & S. J. Lopez (Eds.), *Handbook of positive psychology* (pp. 277-287). London: Oxford University Press.

Maher, C. A. (1991). Is dealing with mathematics as a thought subject compatible with maintaining satisfactory test scores?: A nine-year study. *Journal of Mathematical Behavior, 10,* 225-248.

Mandler, J. M. (1984). *Stories, scripts, and scenes: Aspects of schema theory.* Mahwah, NJ: Erlbaum.

Mansfield, R. S., Busse, T. V., & Krepelka, E. J. (1978). The effectiveness of creativity training. *Review of Educational Research, 48,* 517-536.

Markman, E. M. (1979). Realizing that you don't understand: Elementary school children's awareness of inconsistencies. *Child Development, 50,* 643-655.

Marshall, H. H. (1996). Recent and emerging theoretical frameworks for research on classroom learning: Contributions and limitations [Special issue]. *Educational Psychologist, 31.*

Marshall, S. P. (1995). *Schemas in problem solving.* Cambridge, UK: Cambridge University Press.

Martin, V., & Pressley, M. (1991). Elaborative integration effects depend on the nature of the question. *Journal of Educational Psychology, 83,* 253-263.

Marzano, R. J. (1992). *A different kind of classroom: Teaching with dimensions of learning.* Alexandria, VA: Association for Supervision and Curriculum Development.

Mason, J. M., & Au, K. H. (1990). *Reading instruction for today* (2nd ed.). Glenview, IL: Scott, Foresman.

Mason, J. M., Herman, P. A., & Au, K. H. (1991). Children's developing knowledge of words. In J. Flood, J. M. Jensen, D. Lapp, & J. R. Squire (Eds.), *Handbook of research on teaching the English language arts* (pp. 721-731). New York: Macmillan.

Masonheimer, R. E., Drum, P. A., & Ehri, L. C. (1984). Does environmental print identification lead children into word reading? *Journal of Reading Behavior, 16,* 257–271.

Mastropieri, M., & Scruggs, T. (1989). Constructing more meaningful relationships: Mnemonic instruction for special populations. *Educational Psychology Review, 1,* 83–111.

Mayer, R. (2001). *Multi-media learning.* Cambridge, UK: Cambridge University Press.

Mayer, R. E. (1981). Frequency norms and structural analysis of algebra word problems into families, categories, and templates. *Instructional Science, 10,* 135–175.

Mayer, R. E. (1982). Memory for algebra story problems. *Journal of Educational Psychology, 74,* 199–216.

Mayer, R. E., & Bromage, B. K. (1980). Different recall protocols for technical texts due to advance organizers. *Journal of Educational Psychology, 72,* 209–225.

Mayer, R., & Chandler, P. (2001). When learning is just a click away: Does simple user interaction foster deeper understanding of multimedia messages? *Journal of Educational Psychology, 93,* 390–397.

Mayer, R. E., & Hegarty, M. (1996). The process of understanding mathematical problems. In R. J. Sternberg & T. Ben-Zeev (Eds.), *The nature of mathematical thinking* (pp. 29–53). Mahwah, NJ: Erlbaum.

Mayer, R. E., Heiser, J., & Lonn, S. (2001). Cognitive constraints on multimedia learning: When presenting more materials results in less understanding. *Journal of Educational Psychology, 92,* 312–320.

Mayer, R. E., & Moreno, R. (2002). Aids to computer-based multimedia learning. *Learning and Instruction, 12,* 107–119.

Mayer, R. E., & Moreno, R. (2003). Nine ways to reduce cognitive load in multimedia learning. In R. Bruning, C. Horn, & L. Pytlikzillig (Eds.), *Web-based learning: What do we know? Where do we go?* (pp. 23–44). Greenwich, CN: Information Age.

Mayer, R. E., & Wittrock, M. C. (1996). Problem-solving transfer. In D. C. Berliner & R. C. Calfee (Eds.), *The handbook of educational psychology* (pp. 47–62). New York: Macmillan.

Means, B., & Olson, K. (1994). The link between technology and authentic learning. *Educational Leadership, 51*(7), 15–18.

Mazzie, C. A. (1987). An experimental investigation of the determinants of implicitness in spoken and written discourse. *Discourse Processes, 10,* 31–42.

McCann, R. S., Besner, D., & Davelaar, E. (1988). Word recognition and identification: Do word-frequency effects reflect lexical access? *Journal of Experimental Psychology: Human Perception and Performance, 14,* 693–706.

McClelland, J. L. (1988). Connectionist models and psychological evidence. *Journal of Memory and Language, 27,* 107–123.

McClelland, J. L., & Seidenberg, M. S. (2000). Why do kids say *goed* and *brang? Science, 287,* 47–48.

McClelland, J. L., McNaughton, B. L., & O'Reilly, R. C. (1995). Why there are complementary learning systems in the hippocampus and neocortex: Insight from the successes and failures of connectionist models of learning and memory. *Psychological Review, 102,* 419–457.

McClelland, J. L., Rumelhart, D. E., & Hinton, G. E. (1986). The appeal of parallel distributed processing. In D. E. Rumelhart, J. L. McClelland, & PDP Research Group (Eds.), *Parallel distributed processing: Explorations in the microstructures of cognition: Vol. 1. Foundations* (pp. 3–44). Cambridge: MIT Press.

McCloskey, M. (1983). Naive theories of motion. In D. Gentner & A. L. Stevens (Eds.), *Mental models* (pp. 71–94). Mahwah, NJ: Erlbaum.

McCloskey, M., Caramazza, A., & Green, B. (1980). Curvilinear motion in the absence of external forces: Naive beliefs about the motion of objects. *Science, 210,* 1139–1141.

McCloskey, M., Wible, C. G., & Cohen, N. J. (1988). Is there a special flashbulb-memory mechanism? *Journal of Experimental Psychology: General, 117,* 171–181.

McConkie, G. (1997). Eye movement contingent display control: Personal reflections and comments. *Scientific Studies of Reading, 1,* 303–316.

McCormick, C. B., & Levin, J. R. (1984). A comparison of different prose learning variations of the mnemonic keyword method. *American Educational Research Journal, 21,* 379–398.

McCutchen, D. (1996). A capacity theory of writing: Working memory in composition. *Educational Psychology Review, 8,* 299–325.

McCutchen, D., Francis, M., & Kerr, S. (1997). Revising for meaning: Effects of knowledge and strategy. *Journal of Educational Psychology, 89,* 667–676.

McDaniel, M. A., & Einstein, G. O. (1989). Material appropriate processing. *Educational Psychology Review, 1,* 113–145.

McDougall, R. (1904). Recognition and recall. *Journal of Philosophical and Scientific Methods, 1,* 229-233.

McElroy, L. A., & Slamecka, N. J. (1982). Memorial consequences of generating nonwords: Implications for semantic memory interpretations of the generation effect. *Journal of Verbal Learning and Verbal Behavior, 21,* 249-259.

McGuinness, C. (1990). Talking about thinking: The role of metacognition in teaching thinking. In K. Gilhooly, M. Keane, & G. Erdos (Eds.), *Lines of thinking* (Vol. 2, pp. 301-312). San Diego: Academic Press.

McInerney, D. M. (2000). Helping kids achieve their best: Understanding and using motivation in the classroom. St. Leonards, New South Wales, Australia: Allen & Unwin.

McIntyre, E., & Pressley, M. (Eds.). (1996). *Balanced instruction: Strategies and skills in whole language.* Norwood, MA: Christopher-Gordon.

McKeown, M. G., & Curtis, M. E. (1987). *The nature of vocabulary acquisition.* Mahwah, NJ: Erlbaum.

McKoon, G., & Ratcliff, R. (1986). Inferences about predictable events. *Journal of Experimental Psychology: Learning, Memory, and Cognition, 12,* 82-91.

McNamee, G. D. (1987). The social origins of narrative skills. In M. Hickmann (Ed.), *Social and functional approaches to language and thought* (pp. 287-304). San Diego: Academic Press.

McQueen, R., Murray, A. K., & Evans, E. (1963). Relationships between writing required in high school and English proficiency in college. *Journal of Experimental Education, 31,* 419-423.

McRobbie, C., & Tobin, K. (1995). Restraints on reform: The congruence of teacher and student actions in a chemistry class. *Journal of Research in Science Teaching, 32,* 373-385.

Means, B., & Olson, K. (1994). The link between technology and authentic learning. *Educational Leadership, 51*(7), 15-18.

Medin, D. L., Wattenmaker, W. D., & Hampson, S. E. (1987). Family resemblance, conceptual cohesiveness, and category construction. *Cognitive Psychology, 19,* 242-278.

Mehan, H. (1979). Learning lessons: *Social organization in the classroom.* Cambridge, MA: Harvard University Press.

Meichenbaum, D. (1977). *Cognitive behavior modification: An integrative approach.* New York: Plenum.

Merrill, D. M. (2000). *First principles of instruction* [online]. Paper presented at the annual convention of the Association for Educational Communications and Technology, Denver, CO. Available at: http://www.id2.usu.edu/Papers/5FirstPrinciples.PDF

Mevarech, Z. R., & Kramarski, B. (1997). IMPROVE: A multidimensional method for teaching mathematics in heterogeneous classrooms. *American Educational Research Journal, 34,* 365-394.

Meyer, B. J. F, & Rice, G. E. (1984). The structure of text. In P. D. Pearson (Ed.), *Handbook of reading research* (pp. 316-342). New York: Longman.

Midgley, C., Anderman, E. M., & Hicks, L. (1995). Differences between elementary and middle school teachers and students: A goal theory approach. *Journal of Early Adolescence, 15,* 90-113.

Midgley, C., Kaplan, A., & Middleton, M. (2001). Performance-approach goals: Good for what, for whom, under what circumstances, and at what cost? *Journal of Educational Psychology, 93,* 77-86.

Miller, G. A. (1956). The magical number seven, plus-or-minus two: Some limits on our capacity for processing information. *Psychological Review, 63,* 81-97.

Miller, R. B., Behrens, J. T., Greene, B. A., & Newman, D. (1993). Goals and perceived ability: Impact on student valuing, self-regulation, and persistence. *Contemporary Educational Psychology, 18,* 2-14.

Minsky, M. (1975). A framework for representing knowledge. In P. H. Winston (Ed.), *The psychology of computer vision* (pp. 211-277). New York: McGraw-Hill.

Mitchell, D. B., & Brown, A. S. (1988). Persistent repetition priming in picture naming and its disassociation from recognition memory. *Journal of Experimental Psychology: Learning, Memory, and Cognition, 14,* 213-222.

Miyake, A. (2001). Individual differences in working memory: Introduction to the special section. *Journal of Experimental Psychology: General, 130,* 163-168.

Miyake, A., & Shah, P. (1999). Toward unified theories of working memory: Emerging general consensus, unresolved theoretical issues, and future research directions. In A. Miyake & P. Shah (Eds.), *Models of working memory: Mechanisms of active maintenance and executive control* (pp. 442-481). Cambridge, UK: Cambridge University Press.

Moats, L. C., & Foorman, B. R. (1997). Introduction to the special issue of SSR: Components of effective reading instruction. *Scientific Studies of Reading, 1,* 187-189.

Moeser, S. D. (1983). Levels-of-processing: Qualitative differences or task-demand hypotheses? *Memory & Cognition, 11,* 316–323.

Moll, L. C., & Whitmore, K. (1993). Vygotsky in classroom practice: Moving from individual transmission to social transaction. In E. A. Forman, N. Minick, & C. A. Stone (Eds.), *Contexts for learning* (pp. 19–42). New York: Oxford University Press.

Montague, W. E., Adams, J. A., & Kiess, H. D. (1966). Forgetting and natural language mediation. *Journal of Experimental Psychology, 72,* 829–833.

Moore, M. T. (1990). Problem finding and teacher experience. *Journal of Creative Behavior, 24,* 39–58.

Moreno, R., & Mayer, R. E. (1999). Cognitive principles of multimedia learning: The role of modality and contiguity. *Journal of Educational Psychology, 91,* 358–368.

Moreno, R., & Mayer, R. (2002). Verbal redundancy in multimedia learning. *Journal of Educational Psychology, 94*(1), 156–163.

Moreno, R., & Mayer, R. E. (2000). A coherence effect in multimedia learning: The case for minimizing irrelevant sounds in the design of multimedia instructional messages. *Journal of Educational Psychology, 92*(1), 117–125.

Morphett, M. V., & Washburne, C. (1931). When should children begin to read? *Elementary School Journal, 31,* 496–503.

Morris, C. C. (1990). Retrieval processes underlying confidence in comprehension judgments. *Journal of Experimental Psychology: Learning, Memory, and Cognition, 16,* 223–232.

Morris, C. D., Bransford, J. D., & Franks, J. J. (1977). Levels of processing versus transfer appropriate processing. *Journal of Verbal Learning and Verbal Behavior, 16,* 519–533.

Moshman, D. (1981). Jean Piaget meets Jerry Falwell: Genetic epistemology and the anti-humanist movement in education. *Genetic Epistemologist, 10,* 10–13.

Moshman, D. (1982). Exogenous, endogenous, and dialectical constructivism. *Developmental Review, 2,* 371–384.

Mousavi, S. Y., Low, R., & Sweller, J. (1995). Reducing cognitive load by mixing auditory and visual presentation modes. *Journal of Educational Psychology, 87,* 319–334.

Mumford, M. D., Costanza, D. P., Baughman, W. A, Threlfall, K. V., & Fleischman, E. A. (1994). Influence of abilities on performance during practice: Effects of massed and distributed practice. *Journal of Educational Psychology, 86,* 134–144.

Nagy, W. E. (1988, April). *Some components of a model of word-learning ability.* Paper presented at the Annual Meeting of the American Educational Research Association, New Orleans.

Nagy, W. E., Anderson, R. C., & Herman, P. A. (1987). Learning word meanings from context during normal reading. *American Educational Research Journal, 24,* 237–270.

Nagy, W. E., & Herman, P. A. (1987). Breadth and depth of vocabulary knowledge: Implications for acquisition and instruction. In M. G. McKeown & M. E. Curtis (Eds.), *The nature of vocabulary acquisition* (pp. 19–35). Mahwah, NJ: Erlbaum.

Nagy, W. E., & Scott, J. A. (2000). Vocabulary processes. In M. L. Kamil, P. B. Mosenthal, P. D. Pearson, & R. Barr (Eds.), *Handbook of reading research* (Vol. 3, pp. 269–284). Mahwah, NJ: Erlbaum.

Nation, K., & Hulme, C. (1997). Phonemic segmentation, not onset-rime segmentation, predicts early reading and spelling skills. *Reading Research Quarterly, 32,* 154–167.

National Assessment of Educational Progress. (2000). *The Nation's Report Card: Mathematics.* Washington, DC: National Center for Education Statistics, U. S. Department of Education.

National Center for Educational Statistics (NCES). (1999). NAEP 1998 reading report card for the nation and states. Washington, DC: National Center for Educational Statistics.

National Center for Educational Statistics (NCES). (2001). The nation's report card: Fourth-grade reading 2000. Washington, DC: National Center for Educational Statistics.

National Commission on Mathematics and Science Teaching for the 21st Century. (2000). *Before it's too late: A report to the nation from the national commission on mathematics and science teaching for the 21st century.* Washington, DC: U. S. Department of Education.

National Council of Teachers of English (NCTE). (1996). *Standards for the English language arts.* Urbana, IL: National Council of Teachers of English.

National Council of Teachers of Mathematics (NCTM). (1989). *Curriculum and evaluation standards for school mathematics.* Reston, VA: Author.

National Council of Teachers of Mathematics (NCTM). (1991). *Professional standards for teaching mathematics.* Reston, VA: Author.

National Council of Teachers of Mathematics. (2000). *Principles and standards for school mathematics*. Reston, VA: Author.

National Institute of Child Health and Human Development. (2000). *Teaching children to read: An evidence-based assessment of the scientific research literature on reading and its implications for reading instruction* (National Reading Panel Rep., NIH Publication No. 00-4769). Washington, DC: U. S. Government Printing Office.

National Research Council (NRC). (1990). *Reshaping school mathematics*. Washington, DC: National Academy of Sciences.

National Research Council (NRC). (1996). *National science education standards*. Washington, DC: National Academy Press.

National Research Council. (2000). *Inquiry and the national science education standards: A guide for teaching and learning*. Washington, DC: National Academy Press.

Neath, I. (1998). *Human memory: An introduction to research, data, and theory*. Pacific Grove, CA: Brooks/Cole.

Neisser, U. (1967). *Cognitive psychology*. New York: Appleton–Century–Crofts.

Neisser, U. (1982). *Memory observed*. New York: Freeman.

Neisser, U., & Weene, P. (1962). Hierarchies in concept attainment. *Journal of Experimental Psychology, 64,* 640-645.

Nelson, T. O. (1977). Repetition and depth of processing. *Journal of Verbal Learning and Verbal Behavior, 16,* 151-171.

Nelson, T. O. (1985). Ebbinghaus's contribution to the measurement of retention: Savings during relearning. *Journal of Experimental Psychology: Learning, Memory, and Cognition, 11,* 472-479.

Neves, D. M., & Anderson, J. R. (1981). Knowledge compilation: Mechanisms for the automatization of cognitive skills. In J. R. Anderson (Ed.), *Cognitive skills and their acquisition* (pp. 86-102). Mahwah, NJ: Erlbaum.

Newby, T. J. (1991). Classroom motivation: Strategies for first-year teachers. *Journal of Educational Psychology, 83,* 195-200.

Newell, A., & Simon, H. A. (1972). *Human problem solving*. Upper Saddle River, NJ: Prentice Hall.

Newman, D., Griffin, P., & Cole, M. (1989). *The construction zone: Working for cognitive change in school*. Cambridge, UK: Cambridge University Press.

Newman, R. S., & Goldin, L. (1990). Children's reluctance to seek help with schoolwork. *Journal of Educational Psychology, 82,* 92-100.

Newman, R. S., & Schwager, M. T. (1995). Students' help seeking during problem solving: Effects of grade, goal, and prior achievement. *American Educational Research Journal, 32,* 352-376.

Nickerson, R. S. (1987). Why teach thinking? In J. Baron & R. Sternberg (Eds.), *Teaching thinking skills: Theory and practice* (pp. 27-38). New York: Freeman.

Niedenthal, P. M. (1990). Implicit perception of affective information. *Journal of Experimental Social Psychology, 26,* 505-527.

Nilsson, L., Law, J., & Tulving, E. (1988). Recognition failure of recallable unique names: Evidence for an empirical law of memory and learning. *Journal of Experimental Psychology: Learning, Memory, and Cognition, 14,* 266-277.

Noble, C. E. (1952). An analysis of meaning. *Psychological Review, 59,* 421-430.

Norman, D. A., & Bobrow, D. G. (1976). On the role of active memory processes in perception and cognition. In C. N. Cofer (Ed.), *The structure of human memory* (pp. 123-156). New York: Freeman.

Norris, J. A. (1988). Using communication strategies to enhance reading acquisition. *Reading Teacher, 41,* 668-673.

Norris, J. A., & Bruning, R. H. (1988). Cohesion in the narratives of good and poor readers. *Journal of Speech and Hearing Disorders, 53,* 416-424.

Norris, S., & Ennis, R. (1989). *Evaluating critical thinking*. Pacific Grove, CA: Midwest.

Nusbaum, H. C., & Schwab, E. C. (1986). The role of attention and active processing in speech perception. In E. C. Schwab & H. C. Nusbaum (Eds.), *Pattern recognition by humans and machines* (pp. 113-157). San Diego: Academic Press.

Nussbaum, J., & Novick, N. (1982). Alternative frameworks, conceptual conflict, and accommodation: Toward a principled teaching strategy. *Instructional Science, 11,* 183-200.

Nystrand, M., & Gamoran, A. (1991). Instructional discourse, student engagement, and literature achievement. *Research in the Teaching of English, 25,* 261-290.

Oakes, J. (1990). *Multiplying inequalities: The effects of race, social class, and tracking on opportunities to learn math and science*. Chicago: Rand McNally.

Oaksford, M., Morris, F., Grainger, B., & Williams, J. M. G. (1996). Mood, reasoning, and central executive processes. *Journal of Experimental Psychology: Learning, Memory, and Cognition, 22,* 476–492.

O'Flahavan, J. F., & Stein, C. (1992). In search of the teacher's role in peer discussions about literature. *Reading in Virginia, 17,* 34–42.

Olive, T., & Levy, C. M. (2001). Real time studies in writing research: progress and prospects. In G. Rijlaarsdam (Series Ed.) & T. Olive & C. M. Levy (Vol. Eds.), *Studies in writing: Volume 10. Contemporary tools and techniques for studying writing* (pp. 1–8). Dordrecht, The Netherlands: Kluwer Academic.

Olson, D. R. (1994). *The world on paper: The conceptual and cognitive implications of writing and reading.* Cambridge, UK: Cambridge University Press.

Olson, D. R., Torrance, N., & Hildyard, A. (1985). *Literacy, language, and learning.* New York: Cambridge University Press.

Olton, R. M., & Crutchfield, R. S. (1969). Developing the skills of productive thinking. In P. Mussen, J. Langer, & M. Covington (Eds.), *Trends and issues in developmental psychology.* New York: Holt, Rinehart & Winston.

Osborne, R., & Freyberg, R. (1985). *Learning science.* Portsmouth, NH: Heinemann.

Overton, D. A. (1985). Contextual stimulus effects of drugs and internal states. In P. D. Balsam & A. Tomie (Eds.), *Context and learning* (pp. 357–384). Mahwah, NJ: Erlbaum.

Paas, F. G. W. (1992). Training strategies for attaining transfer of problem-solving skill in statistics: A cognitive load approach. *Journal of Educational Psychology, 84,* 429–434.

Paivio, A. (1971). *Imagery and verbal processes.* New York: Holt, Rinehart & Winston.

Paivio, A. (1986a). Dual coding and episodic memory: Subjective and objective sources of memory trace components. In F. Klix & H. Hafgendorf (Eds.), *Human memory and cognitive capabilities: Mechanisms and performances* (Part A, pp. 225–236). Amsterdam: North-Holland.

Paivio, A. (1986b). *Mental representations: A dual coding approach.* New York: Oxford University Press.

Paivio, A., Clark, J. M., & Lambert, W. E. (1988). Bilingual dual-coding theory and semantic repetition effect on recall. *Journal of Experimental Psychology: Learning, Memory, and Cognition, 14,* 163–172.

Paivio, A., & Csapo, K. (1975). Picture superiority in free recall: Imagery or dual coding? *Cognitive Psychology, 5,* 176–206.

Paivio, A., Yuille, J. D., & Madigan, S. A. (1968). Concreteness, imagery, and meaningfulness values for 925 nouns. *Journal of Experimental Psychology, 76* (Suppl.), 1–25.

Pajares, F. (1996). Self-efficacy beliefs in academic settings. *Review of Educational Research, 66,* 543–578.

Pajares, F. (1997). Current directions in self-efficacy research. In M. Maehr & P. R. Pintrich (Eds.), *Advances in motivation and achievement* (Vol. 10, pp. 1–49). Greenwich, CT: JAI Press.

Palincsar, A. S., & Brown, A. L. (1984). Reciprocal teaching of comprehension monitoring activities. *Cognition and Instruction, 1,* 117–175.

Palincsar, A. S., Brown, A. L., & Martin, S. (1987). Peer interaction in reading comprehension instruction. *Educational Psychologist, 22,* 231–254.

Pallas, A. M. (2001). Preparing educational doctoral students for epistemological diversity. *Educational Researcher, 30,* 6–11.

Pappas, C. C. (1993). Is narrative "primary"? Some insights from kindergartners' pretend readings of stories and information books. *Journal of Reading Behavior, 24,* 97–129.

Paris, S. G., Cross, D. R., & Lipon, M. Y. (1984). Informal strategies for learning: A program to improve children's reading awareness and comprehension. *Journal of Educational Psychology, 76,* 1239–1252.

Paris, S. G., & Jacobs, J. E. (1984). The benefits of informed instruction for children's reading and comprehension. *Child Development, 55,* 2083–2093.

Pascarella, E. T., & Terenzini, P. T. (1991). *How college affects students.* San Francisco: Jossey-Bass.

Patrick, H., & Pintrich, P. R. (2001). Conceptual change in teachers' intuitive conceptions of learning, motivation, and instructions: The role of motivational and epistemological beliefs. In B. Torf & R. Sternberg (Eds.), *Understanding and teaching the intuitive mind* (pp. 117–143). Mahwah, NJ: Erlbaum.

Pea, R. D. (1993). Learning scientific concepts through material and social activities: Conversational analysis meets conceptual change. *Educational Psychologist, 28,* 265–277.

Pearson, P. D. (1984). Guided reading: A response to Isabel Beck. In R. C. Anderson, J. Osborn, & R. J.

Tierney (Eds.), *Learning to read in American schools* (pp. 21–28). Mahwah, NJ: Erlbaum.

Peeck, J. (1982). Effects of mobilization of knowledge on free recall. *Journal of Experimental Psychology: Learning, Memory, and Cognition, 8,* 608–612.

Peeck, J., Van Den Bosch, A. B., & Kruepeling, W. (1982). The effect of mobilizing prior knowledge on learning from text. *Journal of Educational Psychology, 74,* 771–777.

Pepper, S. C. (1961). *World hypotheses: A study in evidence*. Berkeley: University of California Press. (Original work published in 1942)

Perfetti, C. A. (1992). The representation problem in reading acquisition. In P. B. Gough, L. C. Ehri, & R. Treiman (Eds.), *Reading acquisition* (pp. 145–174). Mahwah, NJ: Erlbaum.

Perkins, D. N. (1987). Thinking frames: An integrated perspective on teaching cognitive skills. In J. Baron & R. Sternberg (Eds.), *Teaching thinking skills: Theory and practice* (pp. 41–61). New York: Freeman.

Perkins, D. N. (1995). *Outsmarting IQ: The emerging science of learnable intelligence*. New York: Free Press.

Perkins, D. N. (2001). Wisdom in the wild. *Educational Psychologist, 36,* 265–268.

Perkins, D. N., Faraday, M., & Bushey, B. (1991). Everyday reasoning and the roots of intelligence. In J. F. Voss, D. N. Perkins, & J. W. Segal (Eds.), *Informal reasoning and education* (pp. 83–106). Mahwah, NJ: Erlbaum.

Perkins, D. N., & Grotzer, T. A. (1997). Teaching intelligence. *American Psychologist, S2,* 1125–1133.

Perkins, D. N., Jay, E., & Tishman, S. (1993). Introduction: New conceptions of thinking. *Educational Psychologist, 28,* 1–5.

Perkins, D. N., & Salomon, G. (1989). Are cognitive skills context bound? *Educational Researcher, 18,* 16–25.

Perry, R. P., & Penner, K. S. (1990). Enhancing academic achievement in college students through attributional retraining and instruction. *Journal of Educational Psychology, 82,* 262–271.

Perry, W. G., Jr. (1970). *Forms of intellectual and ethical development in the college years*. San Diego, CA: Academic Press.

Peterson, C. (1990). Explanatory style in the classroom and on the playing field. In S. Graham & V. Folkes (Eds.), *Attribution theory: Applications to achievement, mental health, and interpersonal conflict* (pp. 53–75). Mahwah, NJ: Erlbaum.

Petersen, C. H., Glover, J. A., & Ronning, R. R. (1980). An examination of three prose learning strategies on reading comprehension. *Journal of General Psychology, 102,* 39–52.

Peterson, L. R., & Peterson, M. J. (1959). Short-term retention of individual verbal items. *Journal of Experimental Psychology, 58,* 193–198.

Phillips, D. C. (2000). An opinionated account of the constructivist landscape. In D. C. Phillips (Ed.), *Constructivism in education: Opinions and second opinions on controversial issues. Ninety-ninth Yearbook of the National Society of the Study of Education (Part I)*. Chicago, IL: University of Chicago Press.

Phillips, L. M. (1986). *Using children's literature to foster written language development*. (ERIC Document Reproduction Service No. ED 276 027)

Pichert, J. W., & Anderson, R. C. (1977). Taking different perspectives on a story. *Journal of Educational Psychology, 69,* 309–315.

Pintrich, P. (2000a). The role of goal orientation in self-regulated learning. In M. Boekaerts, P. Pintrich, & M. Zeidner (Eds.), *Handbook of self-regulation* (pp. 452–501). San Diego, CA: Academic Press.

Pintrich, P. R. (2000b). Multiple goals, multiple pathways: The role of goal orientation in learning and achievement. *Journal of Educational Psychology, 92,* 544–555.

Pintrich, P. R., & DeGroot, E. V. (1990). Motivational and self-regulated learning components of classroom academic performance. *Journal of Educational Psychology, 82,* 33–40.

Pintrich, P. R., Marx, R. W., & Boyle, R. A. (1993). Beyond cold conceptual change: The role of motivational beliefs and classroom contextual factors in the process of conceptual change. *Review of Educational Research, 63,* 167–199.

Pintrich, P. R., & Schunk, D. H. (2002). *Motivation in education: theory, research, and applications* (2nd ed.). Upper Saddle River, NJ: Merrill Prentice Hall.

Pithers, R. T., & Soden, R. (2000). Critical thinking in education: A review. *Educational Research, 42,* 237–249.

Plank, S. B., & Jordan, W. B. (2001). Effects of information, guidance, and actions on postsecondary destinations: A study of talent loss. *American Educational Research Association, 38,* 947–979.

Polanyi, M. (1967). *The tacit dimension*. Boston: Routledge Kegan Paul.

Polya, G. (1973). *How to solve it* (2nd ed.). Garden City, NY: Doubleday.

Pomerantz, J. R. (1985). Perceptual organization in information processing. In A. M. Aitkenhead & J. M. Slack (Eds.), *Issues in cognitive modeling* (pp. 157–188). Mahwah, NJ: Erlbaum.

Poole, M. B. G., Okeafor, K., & Sloan, E. C. (1989, April). *Teachers' interactions, personal efficacy, and change implementation*. Paper presented at the Annual Meeting of the American Educational Research Association, San Francisco.

Poplin, M. S. (1988). Holistic/constructivist principles of the teaching/learning process: Implications for the field of learning disabilities. *Journal of Learning Disabilities, 21,* 401–416.

Posner, G. J., Strike, K. A., Hewson, P. W., & Gertzog, W. A. (1982). Accommodation of a scientific conception: Toward a theory of conceptual change. *Scientific Education, 66,* 211–228.

Postman, L., Thompkins, B. S., & Gray, W. D. (1978). The interpretation of encoding effects in retention. *Journal of Verbal Learning and Verbal Behavior, 17,* 681–706.

Powell, J. S. (1988, April). *Defining words from context: Is helpfulness in the eyes of the beholder?* Paper presented at the Annual Meeting of the American Educational Research Association, New Orleans.

Prawat, R. S. (1996). Constructivisms, modern and postmodern. *Educational Psychologist, 31,* 215–225.

Pressley, M. (1977). Children's use of the keyword method to learn simple Spanish vocabulary words. *Journal of Educational Psychology, 69,* 465–472.

Pressley, M. (1994). Commentary on the ERIC whole language debate. In C. B. Smith (Moderator), *Whole language: The debate* (pp. 187–217). Bloomington, IN: ERIC/REC.

Pressley, M. (1995). *Advanced educational psychology for educators, researchers, and policymakers*. New York: HarperCollins.

Pressley, M. (2000a). Comprehension instruction in elementary school: A quarter-century of research progress. In B. M. Taylor, M. F. Graves, & van den Broek (Eds.), *Reading for meaning: Fostering comprehension in the middle grades*. New York: Teachers College Press.

Pressley, M. (2000b). What should comprehension instruction be the instruction of? In M. L. Kamil, P. B. Mosenthal, P. D. Pearson, & R. Barr (Eds.), *Handbook of reading research* (Vol. 3, pp. 545–561). Mahwah, NJ: Erlbaum.

Pressley, M. (2002). Comprehension strategies instruction: A turn-of-the-century status report. In C. Block & M. Pressley (Eds). *Comprehension instruction: Research-based best practices* (pp. 11–27). New York: Guilford Press.

Pressley, M. (2002). *Reading instruction that works* (2nd ed.). New York: Guilford Press.

Pressley, M., Allington, R., Wharton-McDonald, R., Block, C. C., & Morrow, L. M. (2001). *Learning to read: Lessons from exemplary first-grade classrooms*. New York: Guilford Press.

Pressley, M., Borkowski, J. G., & Schneider, W. (1987). Cognitive strategies: Good strategies users coordinate metacognition and knowledge. In R. Vasta & G. Whitehurst (Eds.), *Annals of child development* (Vol. 5, pp. 89–129). Greenwich, CT: JAI.

Pressley, M., El-Dinary, P. B., Gaskins, I., Schuder, T., Bergman, J. L., Almasi, J., & Brown, R. (1992). Beyond direct explanation: Transactional instruction of reading comprehension strategies. *Elementary School Journal, 92,* 511–554.

Pressley, M., & Ghatala, E. S. (1988). Delusions about performance on multiple-choice comprehension tests items. *Reading Research Quarterly, 23,* 454–464.

Pressley, M., Harris, K. R., & Marks, M. B. (1992). But good strategy instructors are constructivists! *Educational Psychology Review, 4,* 3–31.

Pressley, M., Levin, J. R., & Delaney, H. D. (1982). The mnemonic keyword method. *Review of Educational Research, 52,* 61–92.

Pressley, M., Rankin, J., & Yokoi, L. (1996). A survey of instructional practices of primary teachers nominated as effective in promoting literacy. *Elementary School Journal, 96,* 363–384.

Pressley, M., & Schneider, W. (1997). *Introduction to memory development during childhood and adolescence*. Mahwah, NJ: Erlbaum.

Pressley, M., Snyder, B. L., Levin, J. R., Murray, H. G., & Ghatala, E. S. (1987). Perceived readiness for examination performance (PREP) produced by initial reading of text and text containing adjunct questions. *Reading Research Quarterly, 22,* 219–235.

Pressley, M., Symons, S., McDaniel, M. A., Snyder, B. L., & Turnure, J. E. (1988). Elaborative integration facilitates acquisition of confusing facts. *Journal of Educational Psychology, 80,* 268–278.

Pressley, M., & Wharton-McDonald, R. (1997). Skilled comprehension and its development through instruction. *School Psychology Review, 26,* 448–466.

Pressley, M., Woloshyn, V., & Associates. (1995). *Cognition strategy instruction that really improves children's academic performance*. Cambridge, MA: Brookline Books.

Pressley, M., Woloshyn, V., Lysynchuk, L., Martin, V., Wood, E., & Willoughby, T. (1990). Cognitive strategy instruction: The important issues and how to address them. *Educational Psychology Review, 2*, 1–58.

Purcell-Gates, V. (1996). Stories, coupons, and TV Guide: Relationships between home literacy experiences and emergent literacy knowledge. *Reading Research Quarterly, 31*, 406–428.

Pylyshyn, Z. W. (1981). The imagery debate: Analogue media versus tacit knowledge. *Psychological Review, 88*, 16–45.

Quellmalz, E. S. (1987). Developing reasoning skills. In J. Baron & R. Sternberg (Eds.), *Teaching thinking skills: Theory and practice* (pp. 86–105). New York: Freeman.

Quillian, M. R. (1968). Semantic memory. In M. Minsky (Ed.), *Semantic information processing* (pp. 21–56). Cambridge, MA: MIT Press.

Rabinowitz, J. C., & Craik, F. I. M. (1986). Specific enhancement effects associated with word generation. *Journal of Memory and Language, 25*, 226–237.

Randi, J., & Corno, L. (2000). Teacher innovations in self-regulated learning. In M. Boekaerts, P. R. Pintrich, & M. Zeidner, (Eds.) *Handbook of self-regulation*. San Diego, CA: Academic Press

Raphael, T. E., & McKinney, J. (1983). An examination of fifth- and eighth-grade children's question answering behavior: An instruction study in metacognition. *Journal of Reading Behavior, 15*, 67–86.

Raphael, T. E., & Pearson, P. D. (1982). *The effects of metacognitive strategy awareness training on students' question answering behavior* (Tech. Rep. No. 238). Urbana: University of Illinois, Center for the Study of Reading.

Raphael, T. E., & Wonnacott, C. A. (1985). Heightening fourth-grade students' sensitivity to sources of information for answering comprehension questions. *Reading Research Quarterly, 16*, 301–321.

Ratcliff, R., & McKoon, G. (1996). Bias effects in implicit memory tasks. *Journal of Experimental Psychology: General, 125*, 403–421.

Rayner, K. (1997). Understanding eye movements in reading. *Scientific Studies of Reading, 1*, 317–339.

Rayner, K., & Pollatsek, A. (1989). *The psychology of reading*. Upper Saddle River, NJ: Prentice Hall.

Recht, D. R., & Leslie, L. (1988). Effect of prior knowledge on good and poor readers' memory of text. *Journal of Educational Psychology, 80*, 16–20.

Ree, J. M., Carretta, T. R., & Teachout, M. S. (1995). Role of ability and prior job knowledge complex training performance. *Journal of Applied Psychology, 80*, 721–730.

Reed, S. K. (1984). Estimating answers to algebra word problems. *Journal of Experimental Psychology: Learning, Memory, and Cognition, 10*, 778–790.

Reed, S. K. (1987). A structure-mapping model for word problems. *Journal of Experimental Psychology: Learning, Memory, and Cognition, 13*, 124–139.

Reed, S. K., Dempster, A., & Ettinger, M. (1985). Usefulness of analogous solutions for solving algebra word problems. *Journal of Experimental Psychology: Learning, Memory, and Cognition, 11*, 106–125.

Reeve, J. (2002). Self-determination theory applied to educational settings. In E. L. Deci & R. M. Ryan (Eds.), *Handbook of self-determination research* (pp. 183–203). Rochester, NY: University of Rochester Press.

Reeve, J., Bolt, E., & Cai, Y. (1999). Autonomy supportive teachers: How they teach and motivate students. *Journal of Educational Psychology, 91*, 537–548.

Rennie, L. J. (1989, April). *The relationship between teacher beliefs, management and organizational processes, and student participation in individualized classrooms*. Paper presented at the Annual Meeting of the American Educational Research Association, San Francisco.

Reybold, L. E. (2001). Encouraging the transformation of personal epistemology. *Qualitative Studies in Education, 14*, 413–428.

Reynolds, A. J., & Walberg, H. J. (1991). A structural model of science achievement. *Journal of Educational Psychology, 83*, 97–107.

Reynolds, A. J., & Walberg, H. J. (1992). A structural model of science achievement and attitude: An extension to high school. *Journal of Educational Psychology, 84*, 371–382.

Reynolds, R. E. (1992). Selective attention and prose learning: Theoretical and empirical research. *Educational Psychology Review, 4*, 345–391.

Reynolds, R. E. (1993). Selective attention and prose learning: Theoretical and empirical research. *Educational Psychology Review, 4*, 345–391.

Rhodewalt, F. (1994). Conceptions of ability, achievement goals, and individual differences in self-handicapping behavior: On the application of implicit theories. *Journal of Personality, 62,* 67–76.

Rich, Y., Smadar, L., & Fischer, S. (1996). Extending the concept and assessment of teacher efficacy. *Educational and Psychological Measurement, 56,* 1015–1025

Rickards, J. (1979). Adjunct postquestions in text: A critical review of methods and processes. *Review of Educational Research, 49,* 181–196.

Rieber, R. W., & Carton, A. S. (Eds.). (1987). *The collected works of L. S. Vygotsky* (N. Minick, Trans.). New York: Plenum.

Riley, M. S., Greeno, J. G., & Heller, J. I. (1983). Development of children's problem-solving ability in arithmetic. In H. P. Ginsburg (Ed.), *The development of mathematical thinking* (pp. 62–71). San Diego: Academic Press.

Rittle-Johnson, B., Siegler, S., & Alibali, M. (2001). Developing conceptual understanding and procedural skill in mathematics: An iterative process. *Journal of Educational Psychology, 93,* 345–362.

Robbins, J. T. (1986). *A study of the effect of the writing process on the development of verbal skills among elementary school children.* Dissertation Abstracts International, 47, 08A. (University Microfilms No. 86-87, 505)

Roedel, T. D., Schraw, G., & Plake, B. S. (1994). Validation of a measure of learning and performance goal orientations. *Educational and Psychological Measurement, 54,* 1013–1021.

Roediger H. L., III. (1990). Implicit memory: Retention without remembering. *American Psychologist, 45,* 1043–1056.

Roeser, R. W., Midgley, C., & Urdan, T. C. (1996). Perceptions of school psychological environment and early adolescents' psychological and behavioral functioning in school: The mediating role of goals and belonging. *Journal of Educational Psychology, 88,* 408–422.

Rogoff, B. (1990). *Apprenticeship in thinking: Cognitive development in social context.* New York: Oxford University Press.

Rogoff, B. (1995). Observing sociocultural activity on three planes: Participatory appropriation, guided participation, and apprenticeship. In J. V. Wertsch, P. D. Rio, & A. Alvarez (Eds.), *Sociocultural studies of mind* (pp. 129–164). Cambridge, UK: Cambridge University Press.

Rogoff, B. (1998). Cognition as a collaborative process. In W. Damon (Series Ed.) & D. Kuhn & R. S. Siegler (Vol. Eds.), *Handbook of child psychology: Cognition, perception, and language* (pp. 679–744). New York: Wiley.

Rogoff, B., Bartlett, L., & Turkanis, C. G. (2001). Lessons about learning as a community. In B. Rogoff, C. G. Turkanis, & L. Bartlett (Eds.), *Learning together: Children and adults in a school community.* Oxford, UK: Oxford University Press.

Rogoff, B., & Chavajay, P. (1995). What's become of research on the cultural basis of cognitive development? *American Psychologist, 50,* 859–877.

Romberg, T. A. (1992). Perspectives on scholarship and research methods. In D. A. Grouws (Ed.), *Handbook of research on mathematics teaching and learning* (pp. 49–64). New York: Macmillan.

Romberg, T. A., & Collis, K. E. (1987). Different ways children learn to add and subtract. *Journal for Research in Mathematics Education Monograph, 2.*

Root, R. L. (1985). *Assiduous string-savers: The idea generating strategies of professional expository writers.* Paper presented at the Annual Meeting of the Conference of College Composition and Communication. (ERIC Document Reproduction Service No. ED 258 205)

Rosch, E. (1978). Principles of categorization. In E. Rosch & B. B. Lloyd (Eds.), *Cognition and categorization* (pp. 28–48). Mahwah, NJ: Erlbaum.

Rosch, E., & Mervis, C. B. (1975). Family resemblance: Studies in the internal structure of categories. *Cognitive Psychology, 7,* 573–605.

Rose, S. (1992). *The making of memory: From molecules to mind.* New York: Anchor Books.

Rosenblatt, L. (1938). *Literature as exploration.* New York: Noble & Noble.

Rosenshine, B., Meister, C., & Chapman, S. (1996). Teaching students to generate questions: A review of the intervention studies. *Review of Educational Research, 66,* 181–221.

Rosenthal, R., & Jacobson, L. (1968). *Pygmalion in the classroom: Teacher expectation and pupils' intellectual development.* New York: Holt, Rinehart & Winston.

Ross, B. H., & Kennedy, P. T. (1990). Generalizing from the use of earlier examples in problem solving. *Journal of Experimental Psychology: Learning, Memory, and Cognition, 16,* 42–55.

Roth, K. J. (1985, April). *Conceptual change learning and student processing of science texts*. Paper presented at the Annual Meeting of the American Educational Research Association, Chicago.

Rothkopf, E. Z. (1966). Learning from written instructional materials: An exploration of the control of inspectional behaviors by test-like events. *American Educational Research Journal, 3,* 241–249.

Ruddell, M. R. (1994). Vocabulary knowledge and comprehension: A comprehension-process view of complex literacy relationships. In R. B. Ruddell, M. R. Ruddell, & H. Singer (Eds.), *Theoretical models and processes of reading* (4th ed., pp. 414–447). Newark, DE: International Reading Association.

Ruddell, R. B., & Ruddell, M. R. (1994). Language acquisition and literacy processes. In R. B. Ruddell, M. R. Ruddell, & H. Singer (Eds.), *Theoretical models and processes of reading* (4th ed., pp. 83–103). Newark, DE: International Reading Association.

Ruddell, R. B., & Unrau, N. J. (1994). Reading as a meaning-construction process: The reader, the text, and the teacher. In R. B. Ruddell, M. R. Ruddell, & H. Singer (Eds.), *Theoretical models and processes of reading* (4th ed., pp. 996–1056). Newark, DE: International Reading Association.

Rumelhart, D. E. (1975). Notes on a schema for stories. In D. C. Bobrow & A. M. Collins (Eds.), *Representation and understanding: Studies in cognitive science* (pp. 268–281). San Diego: Academic Press.

Rumelhart, D. E. (1980). *An introduction to human information processing*. New York: Wiley.

Rumelhart, D. E. (1981). Schemata: The building blocks of cognition. In J. T. Guthrie (Ed.), *Comprehension and teaching: Research reviews* (pp. 3–26). Newark, DE: International Reading Association.

Rumelhart, D. E. (1984). Schemata and the cognitive system. In R. S. Wyer & T. K. Srull (Eds.), *Handbook of social cognition* (Vol. 1, pp. 161–188). Mahwah, NJ: Erlbaum.

Rumelhart, D. E. (1990). Brain style computation: Learning and generalization. In S. F. Zornetzer, J. L. Davis, & C. Lau (Eds.), *An introduction to neural and electronic networks* (pp. 405–420). San Diego, CA: Academic Press.

Rumelhart, D. E., & McClelland, J. L. (1981). Interactive processing through spreading activation. In A. M. Lesgold & C. A. Perfetti (Eds.), *Interactive processes in reading* (pp. 37–60). Mahwah, NJ: Erlbaum.

Rumelhart, D. E., & McClelland, J. L. (1986). PDP models and general issues in cognitive science.

In D. E. Rumelhart, J. L. McClelland, & PDP Research Group (Eds.), *Parallel distributed processing: Explorations in the microstructures of cognition: Vol. 1. Foundations* (pp. 110–149). Cambridge, MA: MIT Press.

Rumelhart, D. E., & Norman, D. A. (1978). Accretion, tuning, and restructuring: Three modes of learning. In J. W. Cotton & R. Klatzky (Eds.), *Semantic factors in cognition* (pp. 161–184). Mahwah, NJ: Erlbaum.

Rumelhart, D. E., & Ortony, A. (1977). The representation of knowledge in memory. In R. C. Anderson, R. J. Spiro, & W. E. Montague (Eds.), *Schooling and the acquisition of knowledge* (pp. 99–135). Mahwah, NJ: Erlbaum.

Rumelhart, D. E., & Todd, P. M. (1993). Learning and connectionist representations. In D. E. Meyer & S. Kornblum (Eds.), *Attention and performance XIV: Synergies in experimental psychology, artificial intelligence, and cognitive neuroscience* (pp. 3–30). Cambridge, MA: MIT Press.

Runco, M. (1991). Creativity and the finding and solving of real-world problems. *Journal of Psychoeducational Assessment, 9,* 45–53.

Ryan, M. P. (1984). Monitoring test comprehension: Individual differences in epistemological standards. *Journal of Educational Psychology, 76,* 248–258.

Ryan, R. M., & Deci, E. L. (1996). When paradigms clash: Comments on Cameron and Pierce's claim that rewards do not undermine extrinsic motivation. *Review of Educational Research, 66,* 33–38.

Ryan, R. L., & Deci, E. M. (2000). Self-determination theory and the facilitation of intrinsic motivation, social development, and well being. *American Psychologist, 55,* 68–78.

Ryan, R. L., & Deci, E. M. (2002). Overview of self-determination theory: An organismic-dialectical perspective. In E. L. Deci & R. M. Ryan (Eds.), *Handbook of self-determination research* (pp. 3–33). Rochester, NY: University of Rochester Press.

Sadoski, M., Goetz, E. T., & Rodriguez, M. (2000). Engaging texts: Effects of concreteness on comprehensibility, interest, and recall in four text types. *Journal of Educational Psychology, 92,* 85–95.

Salomon, G. (1984). Television is "easy" and print is "tough": The differential investment of mental effort in learning as a function of perceptions and attributions. *Journal of Educational Psychology, 76,* 774–786.

Samuels, S. J. (1988). Decoding and automaticity: Helping poor readers become automatic at word recognition. *Reading Teacher, 41,* 756–760.

Samuels, S. J. (1994). Toward a theory of automatic information processing in reading, revisited. In R. B. Ruddell, M. R. Ruddell, & H. Singer (Eds.), *Theoretical models and processes of reading* (4th ed., pp. 816–837). Newark, DE: International Reading Association.

Sanders, T., & van Wijk, C. (1996). Text analysis as a research tool: How hierarchical text structure contributes to the understanding of conceptual processes in writing. In C. M. Levy & S. Ransdell (Eds.), *The science of writing: Theories, methods, individual differences, and applications* (pp. 251–269). Mahwah, NJ: Erlbaum.

Sansone, C., Sachau, D. A., & Weir, C. (1989). Effects of instruction on intrinsic interest: An examination of process and context. *Journal of Personality and Social Psychology, 57,* 819–829.

Sansone, C., Weir, C., Harpster, L., & Morgan, C. (1992). Once a boring task, always a boring task? Interest as a self-regulatory mechanism. *Journal of Personality and Social Psychology, 63,* 379–390.

Savalle, J. M., Twohig, P. T., & Rachford, D. L. (1986). Empirical status of Feuerstein's "instrumental enrichments" (FIE) technique as a method of teaching thinking skills. *Review of Educational Research, 56,* 381–409.

Scardamalia, M., & Bereiter, C. (1994). Computer support for knowledge-building communities. *Journal of the Learning Sciences, 3,* 265–283.

Scardamalia, M., Bereiter, C., & Steinbach, R. (1984). Teachability of reflective processes in written composition. *Cognitive Science, 8,* 173–190.

Schacter, D. L. (1993). Understanding implicit memory: A cognitive neuroscience approach. In A. F. Collins, S. E. Gathercole, M. A. Conway, & P. E. Morris (Eds.), *Theories of memory* (pp. 387–412). Hove, UK: Erlbaum.

Schacter, D. L. (1996a). *Searching for memory: The brain, the mind, and the past.* New York: Basic Books.

Schacter, D. L. (1996b). *The seven sins of memory.* Boston: Houghton Mifflin.

Schacter, D. L. (2001). *The seven sins of memory: How the mind forgets and remembers.* Boston, MA: Houghton Mifflin.

Schacter, D. L., & Cooper, L. A. (1993). Implicit and explicit memory for novel visual objects: Structure and function. *Journal of Experimental Psychology: Learning, Memory, and Cognition, 19,* 995–1009.

Schallert, D. L. (1991). The contribution of psychology to teaching the language arts. In J. Flood, J. M. Jensen, D. Lapp, & J. R. Squire (Eds.), *Handbook of research on teaching the English language arts* (pp. 30–39). New York: Macmillan.

Schank, R. C., & Abelson, R. (1977). *Scripts, plans, goals, and understanding.* Mahwah, NJ: Erlbaum.

Scharf, B., & Buss, S. (1986). Audition I: Stimulus, physiology, thresholds. In K. R. Boff, L. Kaufman, & J. P. Thomas (Eds.), *Handbook of perception and human performance: Vol. 1. Sensory perception and human performance* (pp. 14–1 to 14–71). New York: Wiley.

Scharf, B., & Houtsma, A. J. M. (1986). Audition II: Loudness, pitch, localization, aural distortion, and pathology. In K. R. Boff, L. Kaufman, & J. P. Thomas (Eds.), *Handbook of perception and human performance: Vol. 2. Sensory processes and perception* (pp. 15–1 to 15–60). New York: Wiley.

Schauble, L. (1990). Belief revision in children: The role of prior knowledge and strategies for generating evidence. *Journal of Experimental Child Psychology, 49,* 31–57.

Schiefele, U. (1991). Interest, learning, and motivation. *Educational Psychologist, 26,* 299–324.

Schmuck, R. A., & Schmuck, P. A. (1992). *Group processes in the classroom* (6th ed.). Dubuque, IA: William C. Brown.

Schneider, W., & Pressley, M. (1997). *Memory development between two and twenty* (2nd ed.). Mahwah, NJ: Erlbaum.

Schneider, W., & Shiffrin, R. M. (1985). Categorization (restructuring) and automatization: Two separable factors. *Psychological Review, 92,* 424–428.

Schoenfeld, A. (1983). Beyond the purely cognitive: Belief systems, social cognitions, and metacognitions as driving forces in intellectual performance. *Cognitive Science, 7,* 329–363.

Schoenfeld, A. H. (1985). *Mathematical problem solving.* San Diego, CA: Academic Press.

Schoenfeld, A. H. (1987). *Cognitive science and mathematics education.* Mahwah, NJ: Erlbaum.

Schoenfeld, A. H. (1992). Learning to think mathematically: Problem solving, metacognition, and sense making in mathematics. In D. A. Grouws (Ed.), *Handbook of research on mathematics teaching and learning* (pp. 334–370). New York: Macmillan.

Schommer, M. (1990). Effects of beliefs about the nature of knowledge on comprehension. *Journal of Educational Psychology, 82,* 498–504.

Schommer, M. (1991, April). *The relationship between students' beliefs about the nature of knowledge and academic experiences*. Paper presented at the Annual Meeting of the Midwestern Educational Research Association, Chicago.

Schommer, M. (1993). Epistemological development and academic performance among secondary students. *Journal of Educational Psychology, 85,* 406–411.

Schommer, M. (1994). Synthesizing epistemological belief research: Tentative understandings and provocative confusions. *Educational Psychology Review, 6,* 293–320.

Schommer-Aikins, M. (2002). An evolving theoretical framework for an epistemological belief system. In B. K. Hofer & P. R. Pintrich (Eds.), *Personal epistemology: The psychology of beliefs about knowledge and knowing* (pp. 103–118). Mahwah, NJ: Erlbaum.

Schommer, M., Crouse, A., & Rhodes, N. (1992). Epistemological beliefs and mathematical text comprehension: Believing it is simple does not make it so. *Journal of Educational Psychology, 84,* 435–443.

Schön, D. A. (1983). *The reflective practitioner: How professionals think in action*. New York: Basic Books.

Schön, D. A. (1987). *Educating the reflective practitioner.* San Francisco: Jossey-Bass.

Schoon, K. J., & Boone, W. J. (1998). Self-efficacy and alternative conceptions of science preservice elementary teachers. *Science Education, 82,* 553–568.

Schramke, C. J., & Bauer, R. M (1997). State-dependent learning in older and younger adults. *Psychology and Aging, 12,* 255–263.

Schraw, G. (1998). Promoting general metacognitive awareness. *Instructional Science, 26,* 113–125.

Schraw, G. (2000). Reader beliefs and meaning construction in narrative text. *Journal of Educational Psychology, 92,* 96–106.

Schraw, G. (2001). Current themes and future directions in epistemological research: A commentary. *Educational Psychology Review, 13,* 451–464.

Schraw, G., Bendixen, L. D., & Dunkle, M. E. (2002). Development and validation of the Epistemic Belief Inventory (EBI). In B. K. Hofer & P. R. Pintrich (Eds.), *Personal epistemology: The psychology of beliefs about knowledge and knowing* (pp. 261–275). Mahwah, NJ: Erlbaum.

Schraw, G., & Bruning, R. (1996). Readers' implicit models of reading. *Reading Research Quarterly, 31,* 290–305.

Schraw, G., & Dennison, R. S. (1994). The effect of reader purpose on interest and recall. *Journal of Reading Behavior: A Journal of Literacy, 26,* 1–18.

Schraw, G. & Flowerday, T., & Reisetter, M. F. (1998). The role of choice in reading engagement. *Journal of Educational Psychology, 90,* 705–715.

Schraw, G., Horn, C., Thorndike-Christ, T., & Bruning, R. H. (1994, April). *An investigation of academic goal orientations and course achievement*. Paper presented at the American Educational Research Association, New Orleans.

Schraw, G., & Moshman, D. (1995). Metacognitive theories. *Educational Psychology Review, 7,* 351–371.

Schraw, G., Olafson, L. J., & Klockow, J. (2003, April). Teachers' epistemological beliefs and teaching practices. Paper presented at the American Educational Research Association, Chicago.

Schraw, G., Potenza, M., & Nebelsick-Gullet, L. (1993). Constraints on the calibration of performance. *Contemporary Educational Psychology, 18,* 455–463.

Schraw, G., & Roedel, T. D. (1994). Test difficulty and judgment bias. *Memory & Cognition, 22,* 63–69.

Schraw, G., Wise, S., & Roos, L. (1998). Metacognition and computer-based testing. In G. Schraw & J. Impara (Eds.), *Issues in the measurement of metacognition*. Lincoln, NE: Buros-Nebraska.

Shuell, T. J. (1996). Teaching and learning in a classroom context. In D. C. Berliner & R. C. Calfee (Eds.), *Handbook of educational psychology* (pp. 726–764). New York: Macmillan.

Schultz, K. (1997). "Do you want to be in my story?": Collaborative writing in an urban elementary classroom. *Journal of Literacy Research, 29,* 253–287.

Schunk, D. H. (1983). Ability versus effort attributional feedback: Differential effects on self-efficacy and achievement. *Journal of Educational Psychology, 75,* 848–856.

Schunk, D. H. (1984). Sequential attributional feedback and children's achievement behaviors. *Journal of Educational Psychology, 76,* 1156–1169.

Schunk, D. H. (1987). Peer models and children's behavioral change. *Review of Educational Research, 57,* 149–174.

Schunk, D. H. (1989). Self-efficacy and achievement behaviors. *Educational Psychology Review, 1,* 173–208.

Schunk, D. H. (1991). *Learning theories: An educational perspective*. New York: Macmillan.

Schunk, D. H. (1996). Goal and self-evaluative influences during children's cognitive skill learning.

American Educational Research Journal, 33, 359-382.

Schunk, D. H., & Cox, P. D. (1986). Strategy training and attributional feedback with learning-disabled students. *Journal of Educational Psychology, 78,* 201-209.

Schunk, D. H., & Zimmerman, B. J. (1994). *Self-regulation of learning and performance: Issues and educational applications.* Mahwah, NJ: Erlbaum.

Schwab, E. C., & Nusbaum, H. C. (1986). *Pattern recognition by humans and machines: Vol. 1. Speech perception.* San Diego: Academic Press.

Schwanenflugel, P. J., & Rey, M. (1986). Interlingual semantic facilitation: Evidence for a common representational system in the bilingual lexicon. *Journal of Memory and Language, 26,* 505-518.

Schwartz, B., & Reisberg, D. (1991). *Learning and memory.* New York: Norton.

Schweikert, R., & Boruff, B. (1986). Short-term memory capacity: Magic number or magic spell? *Journal of Experimental Psychology: Learning, Memory, and Cognition, 12,* 419-425.

Scruggs, T. E., Mastropieri, M. A., McLoone, B. B., Levin, J. R., & Morrison, C. R. (1987). Mnemonic facilitation of learning disabled students' memory for expository prose. *Journal of Educational Psychology, 79,* 27-34.

Segar, C. A. (1994). Implicit learning. *Psychological Bulletin, 115,* 163-196.

Seifert, C. M., McKoon, G., Abelson, R. P., & Ratcliff, R. (1986). Memory connections between thematically similar episodes. *Journal of Experimental Psychology: Learning, Memory, and Cognition, 12,* 220-231.

Seifert, T. L. (1993). Effects of elaborative interrogation with prose passages. *Journal of Educational Psychology, 85,* 642-651.

Sharples, M. (1996). An account of writing as creative design. In C. M. Levy & S. Ransdell (Eds.), *The science of writing: Theories, methods, individual differences, and applications* (pp. 127-148). Mahwah, NJ: Erlbaum.

Shell, D., Colvin, C., & Bruning, R. (1995). Developmental and ability differences in self-efficacy, causal attribution, and outcome expectancy mechanisms in reading and writing achievement. *Journal of Educational Psychology, 87,* 386-398.

Shell, D., Murphy, C. C., & Bruning, R. (1989). Self-efficacy and outcome expectancy mechanisms in reading and writing performance. *Journal of Educational Psychology, 81,* 91-100.

Shiffrin, R. M., & Schneider, W. (1977). Controlled and automatic information processing, II: Perceptual learning, automatic attending, and a general theory. *Psychological Review, 84,* 127-190.

Shimojo, S., & Richards, W. (1986). "Seeing" shapes that are almost totally occluded: A new look at Park's canal. *Perception & Psychophysics, 39,* 418-426.

Siegler, R. S. (1996). *Emerging minds: The process of change in children's thinking.* New York: Oxford University Press.

Siegler, R. S., & Jenkins, E. (1989). *How children discover new strategies.* Mahwah, NJ: Erlbaum.

Silver, E. A. (1981). Recall of mathematical problem information: Solving related problems. *Journal for Research in Mathematics Education, 12,* 55-64.

Simon, D. P., & Simon, H. A. (1978). Individual differences in solving physics problems. In R. R. Siegler (Ed.), *Children's thinking: What develops?* (pp. 40-74). Mahwah, NJ: Erlbaum.

Sinatra, G. M. (2001). Knowledge, beliefs, and learning. *Educational Psychology Review, 13,* 321-324.

Sinatra, G. M., & Pintrich, P. R. (Eds.). (2002). *Intentional conceptual change.* Mahwah, NJ: Erlbaum.

Skinner, B. F. (1938). *The behavior of organisms.* New York: Appleton-Century-Crofts.

Skinner, B. F. (1953). *Science and human behavior.* New York: Macmillan.

Skinner, B. F. (1957). *Verbal behavior.* New York: Appleton-Century-Crofts.

Skinner, B. F. (1968). *The technology of teaching.* New York: Appleton-Century-Crofts.

Skinner, E. A., Wellborn, J. G., & Connell, J. P. (1990). What it takes to do well in school and whether I've got it: A process model of perceived control and children's engagement and achievement in school. *Journal of Educational Psychology, 82,* 22-32.

Slamecka, N. J., & Graf, P. (1978). The generation effect: Delineation of a phenomenon. *Journal of Experimental Psychology: Human Learning and Memory, 4,* 592-604.

Slamecka, N. J., & Katsaiti, L. T. (1987). The generation effect as an artifact of selective displaced rehearsal. *Journal of Memory and Language, 26,* 589-602.

Sloman, S. A., Hayman, C. A. G., Ohta, N., Law, J., & Tulving, E. (1988). Forgetting in primed fragment completion. *Journal of Experimental Psychology: Learning, Memory, and Cognition, 14,* 223-239.

Smagorinsky, P., & Smith, M. W. (1992). The nature of knowledge in composition and literary understanding: The question of specificity. *Review of Educational Research, 62,* 279–305.

Smith, D., & Neale, D. C. (1989). The construction of subject matter knowledge in primary science teaching. *Teachers and Teacher Education, 5,* 1–20.

Smith, F. (1982). *Understanding reading: A psycholinguistic analysis of reading and learning to read* (3rd ed.). New York: Holt, Rinehart & Winston.

Smith, S. M. (1986). Environmental context-dependent recognition memory using a short-term memory task for input. *Memory & Cognition, 14,* 347–354.

Smith, S. M., Vela, E., & Williamson, S. E. (1988). Shallow input processing does not induce environmental context dependent recognition. *Bulletin of the Psychonomic Society, 26,* 537–540.

Smylie, M. A. (1988). The enhancement function of staff development: Organizational and psychological antecedents to individual teacher change. *American Educational Research Journal, 25,* 1–30.

Snyder, C. R. (1995). Conceptualizing, measuring, and nurturing hope. *Journal of Counseling & Development, 73,* 355–360.

Snyder, C. R., Harris, C., Anderson, J. R., Holleran, S. A., Irving, L. M., Sigmon, S. T. et al. (1991). The will and the ways: Development and validation of an individual differences measure of hope. *Journal of Personality and Social Psychology, 60,* 570–585.

Snyder, C. R., Sympson, S. C., Ybasco, F. C., Borders, T. F., Babyak, M. A., & Higgins, R. L. (1996). Development and validation of the State Hope Scale. *Journal of Personality and Social Psychology, 70,* 321–335.

Solmon, M. A. (1996). Impact of motivational climate on students' behaviors and perceptions in a physical education setting. *Journal of Educational Psychology, 88,* 731–738.

Spear, N. E., & Riccio, D. C. (1994). *Memory: Phenomena and Principles*. Boston: Allyn & Bacon.

Spence, K. W. (1936). The nature of discrimination learning in animals. *Psychological Review, 43,* 427–449.

Spence, K. W. (1956). *Behavior theory and conditioning*. New Haven, CT: Yale University Press.

Sperling, G. (1960). The information available in brief visual presentations [Special issue]. *Psychological Monographs, 74*(498).

Sperling, G. (1983). *Unified theory of attention and signal detection. Mathematical studies in perception and cognition* (Rep. No. 83–3). New York: New York University, Department of Psychology.

Sperling, M. (1990). I want to talk to each of you: Collaboration and the teacher–student writing conference. *Research in the Teaching of English, 24,* 279–321.

Spiro, R. J. (1980). Constructive processes in prose comprehension and recall. In R. J. Spiro, B. C. Bruce, & W. E. Brewer (Eds.), *Theoretical issues in reading comprehension* (pp. 245–278). Mahwah, NJ: Erlbaum.

Squire, L. R. (1987). *Memory and brain*. New York: Oxford University Press.

Stahl, S., Duffy-Hester, A., & Stahl, K. (1998). Everything you wanted to know about phonics (but were afraid to ask). *Reading Research Quarterly, 33,* 338–355.

Stahl, S. A., & Fairbanks, M. M. (1986). The effects of vocabulary instruction: A model-based meta-analysis. *Review of Reading Research, 56,* 72–110.

Standing, L. (1973). Learning 10,000 pictures. *Quarterly Journal of Experimental Psychology, 25,* 207–222.

Standing, L., Conezio, J., & Haber, R. N. (1970). Perception and memory for pictures: Single trial learning of 2,500 visual stimuli. *Psychonomic Science, 19,* 73–74.

Stanovich, K. E. (1990). Concepts in developmental theories of reading skill: Cognitive resources, automaticity, and modularity. *Developmental Review, 10,* 72–100.

Stanovich, K. E. (2000). *Progress in understanding reading: Scientific foundations and new frontiers.* New York: Guilford Press.

Stanovich, K. E., & Cunningham, A. E. (1993). Where does knowledge come from? Specific associations between print exposure and information acquisition. *Journal of Educational Psychology, 85,* 211–229.

Stanovich, K. E., West, R. F., & Harrison, M. R. (1995). Knowledge growth and maintenance across the life span: The role of print exposure. *Developmental Psychology, 31,* 811–826.

Steffe, L., & Gale, J. (Eds.). (1995). *Constructivism in education*. Mahwah, NJ: Erlbaum.

Stein, M. K., Grover, B. W., & Henningsen, J. (1996). Building student capacity for mathematical thinking and reasoning: An analysis of mathematical tasks used in reform classrooms. *American Educational Research Journal, 33,* 455–488.

Sternberg, R. J. (1986). *The triarchic mind: A new theory of human intelligence*. New York: Penguin.

Sternberg, R. J. (1987). Most vocabulary is learned from context. In M. G. McKeown & M. E. Curtis (Eds.), *The nature of vocabulary acquisition* (pp. 89–105). Mahwah, NJ: Erlbaum.

Sternberg. R. J. (1999a). The theory of successful intelligence. *Review of General Psychology, 3*, 292–316.

Sternberg, R. J. (Ed.) (1999b). *The nature of cognition*. Cambridge, MA: MIT Press.

Sternberg, R. J. (2001). Why schools should teach for wisdom: The balance theory of wisdom in educational settings. *Educational Psychologist, 36*, 227–246.

Sternberg, R. J., & Ben-Zeev, T. (Eds.). (1996). *The nature of mathematical thinking*. Mahwah, NJ: Erlbaum.

Sternberg, R. J., & Ben-Zeev, T. (2001). *Complex cognition: The psychology of human thought*. New York: Oxford University Press.

Sternberg, R. J., & Wagner, R. K. (Eds.). (1994). *Mind in context: Interactionist perspectives on human intelligence*. Cambridge, UK: Cambridge University Press.

Sternberg, S. (1975). Memory scanning: New findings and current controversies. *Quarterly Journal of Experimental Psychology, 27*, 1–32.

Stevenson, H. H., & Stigler, J. W. (1992). *The learning gap*. New York: Touchstone Books.

Stipek, D. J. (1993). *Motivation to learn* (2nd ed.). Boston: Allyn & Bacon.

Stipek, D. J. (1996). Motivation and instruction. In D. C. Berliner & R. C. Calfee (Eds.), *The handbook of educational psychology* (pp. 85–113). New York: Macmillan.

Stipek, D., & Gralinski, J. H. (1996). Children's beliefs about intelligence and school performance. *Journal of Educational Psychology, 88*, 397–407.

Sulzby, E. (1991). The development of the young child and the emergence of literacy. In J. Flood, J. M. Jensen, D. Lapp, & J. R. Squire (Eds.), *Handbook of research on teaching the English language arts* (pp. 273–285). New York: Macmillan.

Svengas, A. G., & Johnson, M. K. (1988). Qualitative effects of rehearsal on memories for perceived and imagined complex events. *Journal of Experimental Psychology: Educational Psychologist, 24*, 113–142.

Swanson, H. L. (1990). Influence of metacognitive knowledge and aptitude on problem solving. *Journal of Educational Psychology, 82*, 306–314.

Swanson, H. L. (1992). Generality and modifiability of working memory among skilled and less skilled readers. *Journal of Educational Psychology, 84*, 473–488.

Swanson, H. L., O'Connor, J. E., & Cooney, J. B. (1990). An information processing analysis of expert and novice teachers' problem solving. *American Educational Research Journal, 27*, 533–556.

Swartz, R. J. (1989). Making good thinking stick: The role of metacognition, extended practice, and teacher modeling in the teaching of thinking. In D. Topping, D. Crowell, & V. Kobayashi (Eds.), *Thinking across cultures: The Third International Conference on Thinking* (pp. 417–436). Mahwah, NJ: Erlbaum.

Swartz, R. J., & Perkins, D. N. (1990). *Teaching thinking: Issues and approaches*. Pacific Grove, CA: Midwest.

Sweller, J. (1994). Cognitive load theory, learning difficulty, and instructional design. *Learning and Instruction, 4*, 295–312.

Sweller, J. (1999). Instructional design in technical areas. *Australian Education Review, 43*.

Sweller, J., van Merrienboer, J., & Paas, F. (1998). Cognitive architecture and instructional design. *Educational Psychology Review, 10*, 251–296.

Taconis, R., Ferguson-Hessler, M. G. M., & Broekkamp, H. (2002). Teaching science problem solving: An overview of experimental work. *Journal of Research in Science Teaching, 38*, 442–468.

Taft, M. L., & Leslie, L. (1985). The effects of prior knowledge and oral reading accuracy on miscues and comprehension. *Journal of Reading Behavior, 17*, 163–179.

Tal, Z., & Babad, E. (1990). The teacher's pet phenomenon: Rate of occurrence, correlates, and psychological costs. *Journal of Educational Psychology, 82*, 637–645.

Taylor, B. M., Graves, M. F., & van den Broek, P. (Eds.). (2000). *Reading for meaning: Fostering comprehension in the middle grades*. New York: Teachers College Press.

Thorndike, E. L. (1911). *Animal intelligence: Experimental studies*. New York: Macmillan.

Tishman, S., Perkins, D. N., & Jay, E. (1995). *The thinking classroom: Learning and teaching in a culture of thinking*. Boston: Allyn & Bacon.

Tobin, K. (Ed.) (1993). *The practice of constructivism in science education*. Washington, DC: AAAS Press.

Tobin, K., & Fraser, B. J. (1990). What does it mean to be an exemplary teacher in science? *Journal of Research in Science Teaching, 27*, 3–25.

Tobin, K., Tippins, D. J., & Gallrad, A. J. (1994). Research on instructional strategies for teaching science. In G. L. Gabel (Ed.), *Handbook of research on science teaching and learning* (pp. 45-93). New York: Macmillan.

Tollefson, N. (2000). Classroom applications of cognitive theories of motivation. *Educational Psychology Review, 12,* 62-83.

Tomic, W. (1997). Training in inductive reasoning and problem solving. *Contemporary Educational Psychology, 20,* 483-490.

Toth, J. P., Reingold, E. M., & Jacoby, L. L. (1994). Toward a redefinition of implicit memory: Process dissociations following elaborative processing and self-generation. *Journal of Experimental Psychology: Learning, Memory, and Cognition, 20,* 290-303.

Tuovinen, J. E., & Sweller, J. (1999). A comparison of cognitive load associated with discovery learning and worked examples. *Journal of Educational Psychology, 91*(2), 334-341.

Trabasso, T., & Bouchard, E. (2000). Text comprehension instruction. *In Report of the National Reading Panel: Teaching children to read. Reports of the subgroups* (Ch. 4, Pt. 2, pp. 39-69). Bethesda, MD: NICHD Clearinghouse.

Tschannen-Moran, M., Woolfolk Hoy, A., & Hoy, W. K. (1998). Teacher efficacy: Its meaning and measure. *Review of Educational Research, 68,* 202-248.

Tulving, E. (1972). Episodic and semantic memory. In E. Tulving & W. Donaldson (Eds.), *Organization of memory* (pp. 381-403). San Diego: Academic Press.

Tulving, E. (1983). *Elements of episodic memory*. Oxford, UK: Oxford University Press.

Tulving, E. (1985). On the classification problem in learning and memory. In I. Nilsson & T. Archer (Eds.), *Perspectives on learning and memory* (pp. 73-101). Mahwah, NJ: Erlbaum.

Tulving, E. (2002). Episodic memory: From mind to brain. *Annual Review of Psychology, 53,* 1-25.

Tulving, E., & Osler, S. (1968). Effectiveness of retrieval cues in memory for words. *Journal of Experimental Psychology, 77,* 593-601.

Tulving, E., & Thompson, D. M. (1973). Encoding specificity and retrieval processes in episodic memory. *Psychological Review, 80,* 352-373.

Tuovinen, J. E., & Sweller, J. (1999). A comparison of cognitive load associated with discovery learning and worked examples. *Journal of Educational Psychology, 91*(2), 334-341.

Turner, A., Britton, B. K., Andraessen, P., & McCutchen, D. (1996). A prediction sematics model of text comprehension. In B. K. Britton & A. C. Graesser (Eds.), *Models of understanding text* (pp. 33-71). Mahwah, NJ: Erlbaum.

Tversky, A. (1977). Features of similarity. *Psychological Review, 84,* 327-352.

Tversky, A., & Kahneman, D. (1974). Judgments under uncertainty: Heuristics and biases. *Science, 185,* 1124-1131.

Tynjala, P. (1998). Writing as a tool for constructive learning: Students' learning experiences during an experiment. *Higher Education, 36,* 209-230.

Tynjala, P., Mason, L., & Lonka, K. (2001). Writing as a learning tool: an introduction. In G. Rijlaarsdam (Series ed.) & Tynjala, P., Mason, L., & Lonka, K. (Vol. Eds.), *Studies in writing: Vol. 7. Writing as a learning tool: Integrating theory and practice*. Dordrecht, The Netherlands: Kluwer Academic.

Underwood, B. J., & Schultz, R. W. (1960). *Meaningfulness and verbal learning*. Philadelphia: Lippincott.

Urdan, T. C. (1997). Examining the relations among early adolescent students' goals and friends' orientation toward effort and achievement in school. *Contemporary Educational Psychology, 22,* 165-191.

Urdan, T., Midgley, C., & Anderman, E. M. (1998). The role of classroom goal structure in students' use of self-handicapping strategies. *American Educational Research Journal, 35,* 101-122.

Vallerand, R. J., Blais, M. R., Briere, N. M., & Pelletier, L. G. (1989). Construction et validation de l'Echelle de Motivation en Education [Construction and validation of the Motivation in Education Scale]. *Canadian Journal of Behavioral Sciences, 21,* 323-349.

van de Walle, J. A., & Watkins, K. B. (1993). Early development of number sense. In R. J. Jensen (Ed.), *Research ideas for the classroom: Early childhood mathematics* (pp. 127-150). New York: Macmillan.

van den Broek, P., & Kremer, K. E., (2000). The mind in action: What it means to comprehend during reading. In B. M. Taylor, M. F. Graves, & van den Broek (Eds.), *Reading for meaning: Fostering comprehension in the middle grades*. New York: Teachers College Press.

van den Broek, P., Risden, K., Fletcher, C. R., & Thurlow, R. (1996). A "landscape" view of reading: Fluctuating patterns of activation and the construction of a stable memory representation. In B. K. Britton &

A. C. Graesser (Eds.), *Models of understanding text* (pp. 165–187). Mahwah, NJ: Erlbaum.

Van Dijk, T. A., & Kintsch, W. (1983). *Strategies of discourse comprehension*. San Diego: Academic Press.

van Merrienboer, J. J. G. (1997). *Training complex cognitive skills: A four-component instructional design model for technical training*. Englewood Cliffs, NJ: Educational Technology Publications.

van Merrienboer, J. J. G., Clark, R. E., & de Croock, M. B. M. (2002). Blueprints for complex learning: The 4C/ID model. *Educational Technology Research and Development, 54*(1), 39–64.

Vellutino, F. R. (1991). Introduction to three studies on reading acquisition: Convergent findings on theoretical foundations of code-oriented versus whole-language approaches to reading instruction. *Journal of Educational Psychology, 83,* 437–443.

Von Wright, J. M. (1972). On the problem of selection in iconic memory. *Scandinavian Journal of Psychology, 13,* 159–171.

Vosniadou, S., & Brewer, W. F. (1987). Theories of knowledge restructuring in development. *Review of Educational Research, 57,* 51–67.

Voss, J. E., & Post, T. A. (1988). On the solving of ill-structured problems. In M. Chi, R. Glaser, & M. Farr (Eds.), *The nature of expertise* (pp. 261–287). Mahwah, NJ: Erlbaum.

Vye, N. J., Delclos, V. R., Burns, M. S., & Bransford, J. D. (1988). Teaching thinking and problem solving: Illustrations and issues. In R. Sternberg & E. Smith (Eds.), *The psychology of human thought* (pp. 337–365). New York: Cambridge University Press.

Vye, N. J., Goldman, S. R., Voss, J. F., Hmelo, C., Williams, S., & Cognition and Technology Group at Vanderbilt. (1997). Complex mathematical problem solving by individuals and dyads. *Cognition and Instruction, 15,* 435–484.

Vygotsky, L. (1962). *Thought and language*. New York: Wiley.

Vygotsky, L. (1978). *Mind in society: The development of higher psychological processes*. Cambridge, MA: Harvard University Press.

Vygotsky, L. (1986). *Thought and language* (rev. ed.). Cambridge, MA: MIT Press.

Wade, S. E., Schraw, G., Buxton, W. M., & Hayes, M. T. (1993). Seduction of the strategic reader: Effects of interest on strategies and recall. *Reading Research Quarterly, 28,* 3–24.

Wade, S. E., Trathen, W., & Schraw, G. (1990). An analysis of spontaneous study strategies. *Reading Research Quarterly, 25,* 147–166.

Wagner, K. (1971). Tony and his friends. In L. B. Jacobs (Ed.), *The read-it yourself storybook*. New York: Western.

Wagner, R. K. (1987). Tacit knowledge in everyday intelligent behavior. *Journal of Personality and Social Psychology, 52,* 1236–1247.

Wagner, R. K., & Sternberg, R. J. (1985). Practical intelligence in real-world pursuits: The role of tacit knowledge. *Journal of Personality and Social Psychology, 52,* 1236–1247.

Walker, N. (1986). Direct retrieval from elaborated memory traces. *Memory & Cognition, 74,* 321–328.

Wallace, D. L., Hayes, J. R., Hatch, J. A., Miller, W., Moser, G., & Silk, C. M. (1996). Better revision in eight minutes? Prompting first-year college writers to revise globally. *Journal of Educational Psychology, 88,* 682–688.

Watson, J. B. (1913). Psychology as the behaviorist views it. *Psychological Review, 20,* 158–177.

Watson, J. B. (1924). *Behaviorism*. New York: Norton.

Wattenmaker, W. D., Dewey, G. I., Murphy, T. D., & Medin, D. L. (1986). Linear separability and concept learning: Context, relational properties, and concept naturalness. *Cognitive Psychology, 18,* 158–194.

Waugh, N. C., & Norman, D. A. (1965). Primary memory. *Psychological Review, 72,* 89–104.

Weaver, C. (1994). *Reading process and practice* (2nd ed.). Portsmouth, NH: Heinemann.

Weaver, C. A. (1990). Constraining factors in calibration of comprehension. *Journal of Experimental Psychology: Learning, Memory, and Cognition, 16,* 214–222.

Weiner, B. (1986). *An attributional theory of motivation and emotion*. New York: Springer-Verlag.

Weiner, B. (1995). *Judgments of responsibility: A foundation for a theory of social conduct*. New York: Guilford Press.

Weiner, B. (2000). Intrapersonal and interpersonal theories of motivation from an attributional perspective. *Educational Psychology Review, 12,* 1–14.

Weisberg, R. W. (1993). *Creativity: Beyond the myth of genius*. New York: Freeman.

Welch, D. C., & West, R. L. (1995). Self-efficacy and mastery: Its application to issues of environmental control, cognition, and aging. *Developmental Review, 15,* 150–171.

Welch-Ross, M. K. (1995). An integrative model of the development of autobiographical memory. *Developmental Review, 15,* 338-365.

Weldon, M. S., & Roediger, H. L. (1987). Altering retrieval demands reverses the picture superiority effect. *Memory & Cognition, 15,* 269-280.

Wertsch, J. (1998). *Mind as action.* New York: Oxford University Press.

West, R. F., Stanovich, K. E., & Mitchell, H. (1993). Reading in the real world and its correlates. *Reading Research Quarterly, 28,* 34-50.

White, B. C. (2000). Pre-service teachers' epistemology viewed through perspectives on problematic classroom situations. *Journal of Education for Teaching, 26,* 279-05.

White, B. Y. (1993). ThinkerTools: Causal models, conceptual change, and science education. *Cognition and Instruction, 10,* 1-100.

Wiencek, J., & O'Flahavan, J. F. (1994). From teacher-led to peer discussions about literature: Suggestions for making the shift. *Language Arts, 71,* 488-498.

Wilcox-Herzog, A. (2002). Is there a link between teachers' beliefs and behaviors? *Early Education and Development, 13,* 79-106.

Wilhite, S. C. (1986, April). *Multiple-choice test performance: Effects of headings, questions, motivation, and type of retention test question.* Paper presented at the Annual Meeting of the American Educational Research Association, San Francisco.

Williams, G. C., & Deci, E. L. (1996). Internalization of biopsychosocial values by medical students: A test of self-determination theory. *Journal of Personality and Social Psychology, 70,* 767-779.

Willoughby, T., Waller, T. G., Wood, E., & McKinnon, G. E. (1993). The effect of prior knowledge on an immediate and delayed associative learning task following elaborative integration. *Contemporary Educational Psychology, 18,* 36-46.

Wilson, J. W., Fernandez, M. L., & Hadaway, N. (1993). Mathematical problem solving. In P. S. Wilson (Ed.), *Research ideas for the classroom: High school mathematics.* New York: Macmillan.

Wilson, P. S. (1993). Introduction: Becoming involved with research. In P. S. Wilson (Ed.), *Research ideas for the classroom: High school mathematics.* New York: Macmillan.

Winne, P. H. (1995). Inherent details in self-regulated learning. *Educational Psychologist, 30,* 173-187.

Winne, P., & Perry, N. (2000). Measuring self-regulated learning. In M. Boekaerts, P. Pintrich, & M. Zeidner (Eds.), *Handbook of self-regulation* (pp. 531-566). San Diego, CA: Academic Press.

Winner, E. (1996). The rage to master: The decisive role of talent in the visual arts. In K. A. Ericsson (Ed.), *The road to excellence: The acquisition of expert performance in the arts and sciences, sports and games* (pp. 271-302). Mahwah, NJ: Erlbaum.

Winner, E. (2000). The origins and ends of giftedness. *American Psychologist, 55,* 159-169.

Winograd, R. N. (1984). Strategic difficulties in summarizing texts. *Reading Research Quarterly, 14,* 404-424.

Winograd, T. (1975). Frame representations and the declarative-procedural controversy. In D. G. Bobrow & A. M. Collins (Eds.), *Representation and understanding: Studies in cognitive science* (pp. 185-210). San Diego: Academic Press.

Woloshyn, V. E., Paivio, A., & Pressley, M. (1994). Use of elaborative interrogation to help students acquire information consistent with prior knowledge and information inconsistent with prior knowledge. *Journal of Educational Psychology, 86,* 79-89.

Woltz, D. J. (1988). An investigation of the role of working memory in procedural skill acquisition. *Journal of Experimental Psychology: General, 117,* 319-331.

Wood, E., Pressley, M., & Winne, P. H. (1990). Elaborative interrogation effects on children's learning of factual content. *Journal of Educational Psychology, 82,* 741-748.

Woodward, J., & Howard, L. (1994). The misconceptions of youth: Errors and their mathematical meaning. *Exceptional Children, 61,* 126-136.

Woolfolk, A. E., & Hoy, W. K. (1990). Prospective teachers' sense of efficacy and beliefs about control. *Journal of Educational Psychology, 82,* 81-91.

Wortham, S. (2001). Interactionally situated cognition: A classroom example. *Cognitive Science, 25,* 37-66.

Yoshinobu, L. R. (1989). *Construct validation of the Hope Scale: Agency and pathways components.* Unpublished master's thesis, University of Kansas, Lawrence.

Zimmerman, B. J. (1990). Self-regulated academic learning and achievement: The emergence of a social cognitive perspective. *Educational Psychology Review, 2,* 173-201.

Zimmerman, B. J. (1995). Self-regulation involves more than metacognition: A social cognitive perspective. *Educational Psychologist, 30,* 217-221.

Zimmerman, B. J. (2000). Attaining self-regulation: A social cognitive perspective. In M. Boekaerts, P. R. Pintrich, & M. Zeidner (Eds.), *Handbook of self-regulation* (pp. 13–39). San Diego: Academic Press.

Zimmerman, B. J., & Bandura, A. (1994). Impact of self-regulatory influences on writing course attainment. *American Educational Research Journal, 31,* 845–862.

Zimmerman, B. J., & Martinez-Pons, M. (1990). Student differences in self-regulated learning: Relating grade, sex, and giftedness to self-efficacy and strategy use. *Journal of Educational Psychology, 82,* 51–59.

Zwann, R. A. (1996). Toward a model of literary comprehension. In B. K. Britton & A. C. Graesser (Eds.), *Models of understanding text* (pp. 241–255). Mahwah, NJ: Erlbaum.

Name Index

Subject Index